Microsoft® VISUAL BASIC® 2017 for Windows® Applications

INTRODUCTORY

Microsoft® VISUAL BASIC® 2017 for Windows® Applications

INTRODUCTORY

CORINNE HOISINGTON

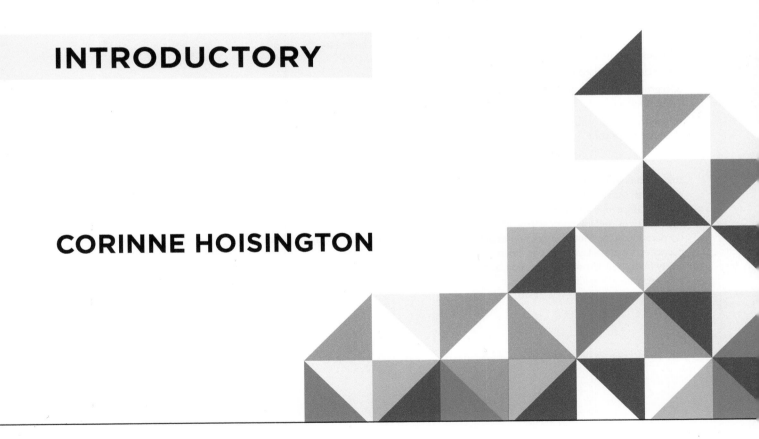

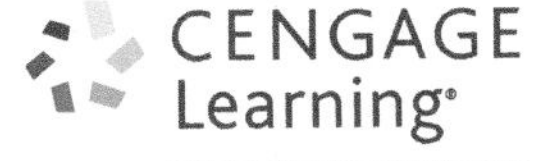

SHELLY CASHMAN SERIES®

Australia • Brazil • Mexico • Singapore • United Kingdom • United States

Microsoft® Visual Basic® 2017 for Windows® Applications Introductory
Corinne Hoisington

SVP, GM Science, Technology & Math: Balraj S. Kalsi

Product Director: Kathleen McMahon

Product Team Manager: Kristin McNary

Associate Content Developer: Brianna Vorce

Marketing Manager: Stephanie Albracht

Senior Content Project Manager: Jennifer K. Feltri-George

Art Director: Diana Graham

Project Manager: Hemalatha Velayutham, Lumina Datamatics Inc.

Manufacturing Planner: Julio Esperas

Development Editor: Lisa Ruffolo

QA Manuscript Reviewer: John Freitas

IP Analyst: Amber Hill

Senior IP Project Manager: Kathryn Kucharek

Production Service: Lumina Datamatics, Inc.

Text Designer: Joel Sadagursky

Cover Designer: Diana Graham

Background Cover Image: Piotr Zajc/ Shutterstock.com

Geometric image: Mrs. Opossum/ Shutterstock.com

WCN: 01-100-101

Library of Congress Control Number: 2017938498

Student Edition:

ISBN: 978-1-337-27920-8

Cengage Learning
20 Channel Center Street
Boston, MA 02210
USA

Cengage Learning is a leading provider of customized learning solutions with employees residing in nearly 40 different countries and sales in more than 125 countries around the world. Find your local representative at **www.cengage.com.**

Cengage Learning products are represented in Canada by Nelson Education, Ltd.

To learn more about Cengage Learning Solutions, visit **www.cengage.com.**

Purchase any of our products at your local college store or at our preferred online store **www.cengagebrain.com.**

Printed in the United States of America
Print Number: 01 Print Year: 2017

CONTENTS

PREFACE

The Shelly Cashman Series® offers the finest textbooks in computer education. This *Microsoft Visual Basic 2017* book utilizes an innovative step-by-step pedagogy, which integrates demonstrations of professional-quality programs with in-depth discussions of programming concepts and techniques and opportunities for hands-on practice and reinforcement. The new volume retains popular features and pedagogy from past editions, while emphasizing the changing development process in an increasingly mobile-oriented world. The popular Guided Program Development section supports students as they work independently to create useful, realistic, and appealing applications, building their confidence and skills while guiding them to select appropriate Visual Basic 2017 programming methods. Marginal elements, such as In the Real World boxes, provide expert tips to add interest and depth to topics. A robust and varied collection of exercises, including a series of practical case-based programming projects, ensures students gain the knowledge and expertise they need to succeed when developing professional programs.

Visual Basic 2017 builds on the features of Visual Basic 2015, which emphasized coding once and deploying on multiple devices. Some of the major enhancements to Visual Basic 2017 include cross-platform coding, including the ability to develop apps for Android, iOS, Windows, Linux, web, and cloud platforms. Visual Studio 2017 also allows you to extend and customize its environment by building your own extensions. Using Visual Basic 2017, you can design, create, and deploy Windows, Mobile, Web, Database, and cloud applications. Visual Studio 2017 includes several productivity enhancements such as debugging tools, mobile templates for both smartphones and tablet design, more powerful searching tools, a built-in suite of Azure tools for creating cloud-first apps, and more.

Objectives of This Textbook

Microsoft Visual Basic 2017 for Windows Applications Introductory is intended for a year-long course that introduces students to the correct ways to design and write programs using Visual Basic 2017. The goal of this text is to provide a rigorous and comprehensive course in computer programming for students with little or no previous programming experience. The objectives of this book are as follows:

- To teach the fundamentals of the Microsoft Visual Basic 2017 programming language
- To understand and apply graphical user interface design principles
- To emphasize the development cycle when creating applications, which mirrors the same approach that professional developers use
- To illustrate well-written and readable programs using a disciplined coding style, including documentation and indentation standards
- To demonstrate how to implement logic involving sequence, selection, and repetition using Visual Basic 2017
- To encourage the use of critical thinking skills in the application development process

- To write useful, well-designed programs for personal computers and mobile computers that solve practical business problems
- To encourage independent study and help those who are working on their own in a distance education environment

The Shelly Cashman Approach

Features of this *Microsoft Visual Basic 2017* book include the following:

- **Realistic, Up-to-Date Applications** Each programming chapter focuses on building a sample project, a complete, useful application that showcases Visual Basic 2017 features and the latest technology.
- **Guided Steps to Encourage Independence** After observing how a professional developer would build the chapter project and exploring related programming concepts and Visual Basic 2017 techniques, students create the sample application on their own in the Guided Program Development section. This step-by-step section provides enough guidance for students to work independently, with Hint Screens that verify students are performing the tasks correctly.
- **More Than Step-by-Step** Each chapter offers clear, thorough discussions of the programming concepts students need to understand to build the sample application. Important Visual Basic 2017 design and programming features are also highlighted, including time-saving techniques such as using IntelliSense, code snippets, and the Toolbox. As appropriate, students design and prepare for applications the way professional developers do — by creating or analyzing requirements documents, use case definitions, and event-planning documents.
- **Heads Up Boxes** Heads Up boxes appear in the margin to give advice for following best programming practices and tips about alternative ways of completing the same task.
- **In the Real World Boxes** This marginal feature provides insight into how developers use Visual Basic tools or programming techniques to save time or enhance professional development projects.
- **Watch Out For Boxes** These boxes explain how to avoid common pitfalls when using a particular command, programming structure, or technique.
- **Consider This Boxes** This element encourages independent problem solving by posing thought-provoking questions and providing answers related to programming and Visual Basic.
- **Critical Thinking Boxes** Critical thinking is an essential part of the programming process; developers need to be able to reason strategically and justify their decisions to craft an effective program. The Critical Thinking boxes encourage students to further explore the ideas in the chapters.

HEADS UP

Visual Basic 2017 can run on Windows 7, Windows 8, or Windows 10. In this book, the default operating system is Windows 10 with a screen resolution of 1366 × 768, but Windows applications such as the programs in these chapters work in all operating systems.

Organization of This Textbook

Microsoft Visual Basic 2017 for Windows Applications Introductory provides detailed instructions on how to use Visual Basic 2017 to build authentic, effective, and appealing applications for Microsoft Windows personal computers and mobile devices. The material is divided into six chapters and two appendices as follows:

Chapter 1 — Introduction to Visual Basic 2017 Programming Chapter 1 provides an overview of programming with Visual Basic 2017. The chapter defines a computer program, describes the role of a developer in creating computer programs, and discusses event-driven programs that have a graphical user interface (GUI). The chapter also explains the roles of input, processing, output, and data when running a program on a computer; examines the basic arithmetic and logical operations a program can perform; and explores the use of databases and computer programming languages in general. Finally, the chapter introduces Visual Studio 2017 and the .NET 4.6.2 Framework, including the .NET class libraries and related features, and surveys the types of Visual Basic 2017 applications.

Chapter 2 — Program and Graphical User Interface Design Chapter 2 introduces students to the major elements of the Visual Studio 2017 integrated development environment (IDE) while designing a graphical user interface mock-up. Topics include opening Visual Studio 2017, creating a Windows Forms App project, adding objects to a Windows form, assigning properties to objects, aligning objects on the Windows form, and saving Visual Basic projects. The chapter also discusses how to apply GUI design principles and examines the first two phases of the program development life cycle (PDLC).

Chapter 3 — Program Design and Coding Chapter 3 provides students with the skills and knowledge necessary to complete phases 2, 3, and 4 of the PDLC by enhancing a GUI mock-up, designing program processing objects, and coding a program. Topics include using IntelliSense when writing code and enhancing a Visual Basic 2017 form by changing the BackColor property of an object and displaying images. This chapter also explains how to enter Visual Basic 2017 code, correct errors, and run a completed program. Finally, the chapter discusses the value of creating an event-planning document.

Chapter 4 — Variables and Arithmetic Operations Chapter 4 introduces variables and arithmetic operations used in the coding of a Visual Basic application. The chapter provides in-depth coverage of declaring variables, gathering input for an application, differentiating data types, performing mathematical calculations, and understanding the proper scope of variables. The chapter also shows how to use various types of TextBox objects.

Chapter 5 — Decision Structures Chapter 5 explains how to create a Visual Basic 2017 Windows application that uses decision structures to take different actions depending on the user's input. Topics include using If...Then statements, If... Then...Else statements, nested If statements, logical operators, and Case statements. The chapter also explores how to use the GroupBox object, place RadioButton objects, display a message box, insert code snippets, and test input to ensure it is valid.

Chapter 6 — Loop Structures Chapter 6 presents another type of fundamental programming structure — the repetition structure, including Do While, Do Until, For...Next, For Each...Next, and While...End While loops. Topics include repeating a process using the For...Next and Do loops; priming a loop; creating a nested loop; selecting the best type of loop; avoiding infinite loops; validating data; and understanding compound operators, counters, and accumulators. The chapter also shows how to insert a MenuStrip object, use the InputBox function, display data using the ListBox object, debug programs using DataTips at breakpoints, and publish a finished application using ClickOnce technology.

Appendices This book concludes with two appendices. Appendix A explains the purpose of Unicode and provides a table two Unicode characters and their equivalents. Appendix B lists the common data types used in Visual Basic 2017, including the recommended naming convention for the three-character prefix preceding variable names.

End-of-Chapter Activities

A notable strength of this *Microsoft Visual Basic* 2017 book is the extensive student activities at the end of each chapter. Well-structured student activities can make the difference between students merely participating in a class and retaining the information they learn. These end-of-chapter activities include the following:

- **Knowledge Check** The Knowledge Check section includes short exercises and review questions that reinforce concepts and provide opportunities to practice skills.
- **Debugging Exercises** In these exercises, students examine short code samples to identify errors and solve programming problems.
- **Program Analysis** The Program Analysis exercises let students apply their knowledge of Visual Basic 2017 and programming techniques. In some exercises, students write programming statements that meet a practical goal or solve a problem. In other exercises, students analyze code samples and identify the output.
- **Case Programming Assignments** Six programming assignments for each chapter challenge students to create applications using the skills learned in the chapter. Each assignment presents a realistic business scenario and requires students to create programs of varying difficulty.
  - ● Easiest: The first two assignments provide most of the program design information, such as a requirements document and use case definition, for a business application. Students design an application, create an event-planning document, and write the code for the application.
  - ●● Intermediate: The next two assignments provide some of the program design information, such as a requirements document. Students create other design documents, such as a use case definition and event-planning document and then build the user interface and code the application.
  - ●●● Challenging: The final two assignments provide only a description of a business problem, and students create all the design documents, design the user interface, and code the application.

To the Instructor

Each chapter in this book focuses on a realistic, appealing Visual Basic 2017 application. A chapter begins with a completed application, which you can run to demonstrate how it works, the tasks it performs, and the problems it solves. The chapter introduction also identifies the application's users and their requirements, such as running the program on a mobile computer or validating input data.

The steps in the next section of a chapter show how to create the user interface for the application. You can perform these steps in class — each step clearly explains an action, describes the results, and includes a figure showing the results, with callouts directing your attention to key elements on the screen. Some marginal features, such as the Heads Up boxes, provide additional tips for completing the steps.

This section also explains the Visual Basic 2017 tools and properties needed to understand and create the user interface. For example, while placing a text box in an application, the chapter describes the purpose of a text box and why you should set its maximum and minimum size. You can discuss these ideas and strategies and then continue your demonstration to show students how to apply them to the chapter application.

After completing the user interface, the chapter explores the programming concepts students should understand to create the application, such as proper syntax, variables, data types, conditional statements, and loops. This section uses the same types of steps, figures, and marginal features to demonstrate how to enter code to complete and test the application.

To prepare students for building the application on their own, the chapter next considers the program design and logic by examining planning documents:

- *Requirements document* — The requirements document identifies the purpose, procedures, and calculations of the program and specifies details such as the application title, restrictions, and comments that help to explain the program.
- *Use case definition* — The use case definition describes what the user does and how the program responds to each action.
- *Event-planning document* — The event-planning document lists each object in the user interface that causes an event, the action the user takes to trigger the event, and the event processing that must occur.

You can discuss these documents in class and encourage students to review them as they create a program, reinforcing how professional developers create applications in the modern workplace.

In the innovative Guided Program Development section, students work on their own to create the chapter application. They complete the tasks within each numbered step, referring to Hint Screens when they need a reminder about how to perform a step or which method to use. Many tasks reference figures are shown earlier in the chapter. Students can refer to these figures for further help — they show exactly how to use a particular technique for completing a task. Steps end with a results figure, which illustrates how the application should look if students performed the tasks correctly. To reinforce how students learned the chapter material, the Guided Program Development section also focuses first on designing the user interface and then on coding the application. A complete program listing appears at the end of this section, which students can use to check their work.

At the end of each chapter, you'll find plenty of activities that provide review, practice, and challenge for your students, including exercises ranging from short, focused review questions to assignments requiring complete programs and related planning documents. You can assign the Knowledge Check, Debugging Exercises, and Program Analysis activities as necessary to reinforce and assess learning. Depending on the expertise of your class, you can assign the Case Programming assignments as independent projects, selecting one from each level of difficulty (easiest, intermediate, and challenging) or concentrating on the level that is most appropriate for your class.

INSTRUCTOR RESOURCES

The following resources are available through www.cengage.com to instructors who have adopted this book. Search for this title by ISBN, title, author, or keyword. From the Product Overview page, select the Instructor's Companion Site to access your complementary resources.

- **Instructor's Manual** The Instructor's Manual consists of Microsoft Word files, which include chapter objectives, lecture notes, teaching tips, classroom activities, lab activities, quick quizzes, figures and boxed elements summarized in the chapters, and a glossary page.
- **Syllabus** Sample syllabi, which can be customized easily to a course, cover policies, assignments, exams, and procedural information.
- **Figure Files** Illustrations for every figure in the textbook are available in electronic form. Figures are provided both with and without callouts.
- **PowerPoint Presentation** PowerPoint is a multimedia lecture presentation system that provides slides for each chapter. Presentations are based on chapter objectives. Use this presentation system to present well-organized lectures that are both interesting and knowledge based. PowerPoint presentations provide consistent coverage at schools that use multiple lecturers.
- **Solutions to Exercises** Solutions are included for all end-of-chapter and chapter reinforcement exercises.
- **Test Bank and Test Engine** Test Banks include a wide range of questions for every chapter, featuring objective-based and critical-thinking question types, and include page number references and figure references, when appropriate. The test engine, Cognero, is a flexible, online system that allows you to author, edit, and manage test bank content from multiple Cengage Learning solutions; create multiple test versions in an instant; and deliver tests from your LMS, your classroom, or wherever you want.
- **Printed Test Bank** A printable Rich Text File (.rtf) version of the test bank is also included.

- **Data Files for Students** Includes all the files that are required by students to complete the exercises.
- **Additional Activities for Students** These additional activities consist of Chapter Reinforcement Exercises, which are true/false, multiple-choice, and short answer questions that help students gain confidence in the material learned.

To the Student

Getting the Most Out of Your Book

Welcome to *Microsoft Visual Basic 2017 for Windows Applications Introductory*. To save yourself time and gain a better understanding of the elements in this text, spend a few minutes reviewing the descriptions and figures in this section.

Introduction and Initial Chapter Figures Each chapter presents a programming project and shows the solution in the first figure of the chapter. The introduction and initial chapter figure let you see firsthand how your finished product will look and illustrate your programming goals.

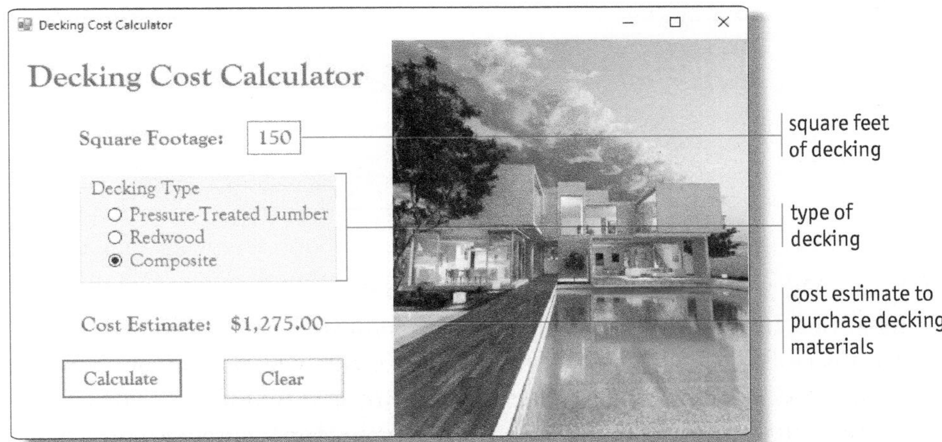

Franck Boston/Shutterstock.com

Guided Program Development After reading through the chapter and observing how to create the chapter application, the Guided Program Development section takes you through building the chapter project step by step. As you perform each task, you can refer to Hint Screens that remind you how to complete a step or use a particular technique. If you need further help, some steps include references to figures shown earlier in the chapter — you can revisit these figures to review exactly how to perform a task. Each step ends with a results figure, so you can make sure your application is on the right track. A complete program listing also appears at the end of the Guided Program Development section, which you can use to check your work.

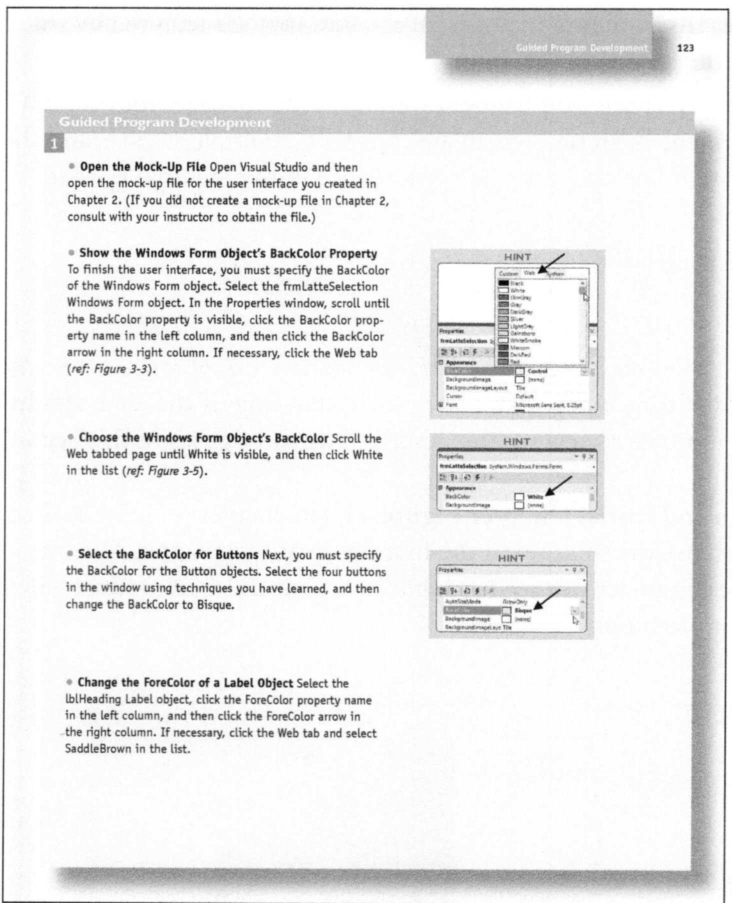

Guided Program Development 123

Guided Program Development

1

- **Open the Mock-Up File** Open Visual Studio and then open the mock-up file for the user interface you created in Chapter 2. (If you did not create a mock-up file in Chapter 2, consult with your instructor to obtain the file.)

- **Show the Windows Form Object's BackColor Property** To finish the user interface, you must specify the BackColor of the Windows Form object. Select the frmLatteSelection Windows Form object. In the Properties window, scroll until the BackColor property is visible, click the BackColor property name in the left column, and then click the BackColor arrow in the right column. If necessary, click the Web tab (*ref: Figure 3-3*).

HINT

- **Choose the Windows Form Object's BackColor** Scroll the Web tabbed page until White is visible, and then click White in the list (*ref: Figure 3-5*).

HINT

- **Select the BackColor for Buttons** Next, you must specify the BackColor for the Button objects. Select the four buttons in the window using techniques you have learned, and then change the BackColor to Bisque.

HINT

- **Change the ForeColor of a Label Object** Select the lblHeading Label object, click the ForeColor property name in the left column, and then click the ForeColor arrow in the right column. If necessary, click the Web tab and select SaddleBrown in the list.

Marginal Boxes Marginal elements include Heads Up boxes, which offer tips and programming advice, In the Real World boxes, which indicate how professional developers use Visual Basic 2017 tools, Watch Out For boxes, which identify common errors and explain how to avoid them, and Critical Thinking boxes, which help you go beyond the reading to think critically about the development process.

HEADS UP

Unlike some programming languages, the capitalization of object names, properties, property values, and other values is not important in Visual Basic. Therefore, the object name picPumpkin is equivalent to the object name picpumpkin. Capitalization is used within the object name to make the name easier to read.

IN THE REAL WORLD

Some developers use the AutoSize property for a Button object to ensure that the button always is large enough for the text. By setting the AutoSize property for a Button object to True in the Properties window, the Button object will expand or contract when you change the text so it fits precisely in the button.

WATCH OUT FOR

When you click an object to select it, you might double-click it accidentally. If you do, a tabbed page with programming code opens. To return to the form and continue developing the user interface, click the [Design] tab for your form, such as the frmLatteSelection.vb [Design] tab.

CRITICAL THINKING

Does every If statement need an End If coordinating statement?
Yes. Multiple nested If statements can be confusing to confirm that you have the correct number of End If statements. If you have 9 If statements, double-check that the code also contains 9 End If statements. Aligning each If statement with its coordinating End If statement helps you keep track of the nested statements.

Knowledge Check To verify you've learned the essential information in the chapter, you can work through the Knowledge Check exercises. Use these short exercises to test your knowledge of concepts and tools and to prepare for longer programming assignments.

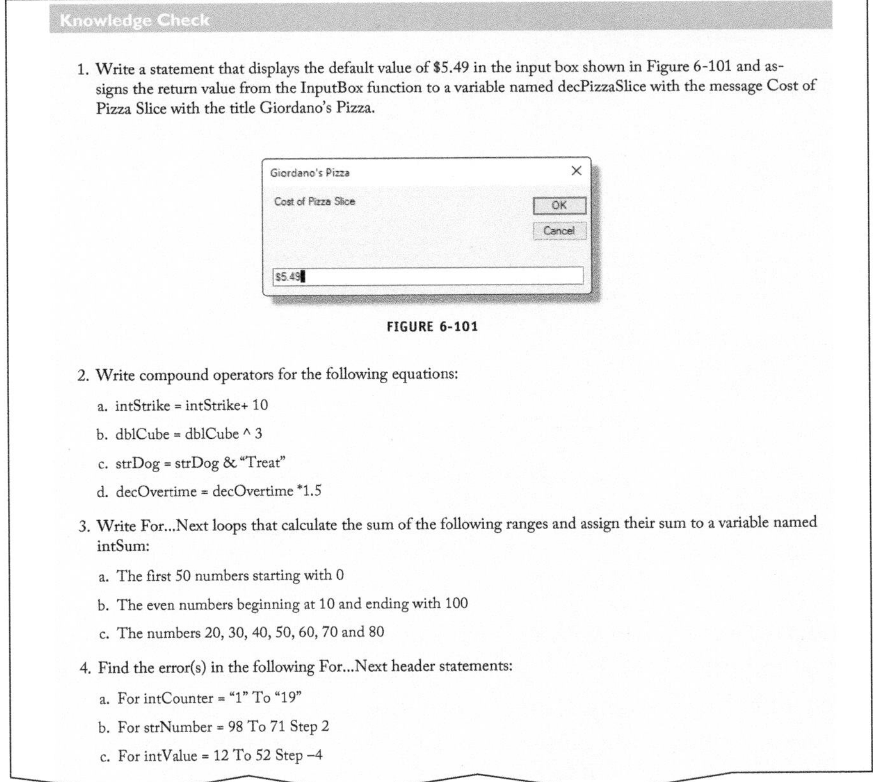

Knowledge Check

1. Write a statement that displays the default value of $5.49 in the input box shown in Figure 6-101 and assigns the return value from the InputBox function to a variable named decPizzaSlice with the message Cost of Pizza Slice with the title Giordano's Pizza.

FIGURE 6-101

2. Write compound operators for the following equations:
   a. intStrike = intStrike+ 10
   b. dblCube = dblCube ^ 3
   c. strDog = strDog & "Treat"
   d. decOvertime = decOvertime *1.5
3. Write For...Next loops that calculate the sum of the following ranges and assign their sum to a variable named intSum:
   a. The first 50 numbers starting with 0
   b. The even numbers beginning at 10 and ending with 100
   c. The numbers 20, 30, 40, 50, 60, 70 and 80
4. Find the error(s) in the following For...Next header statements:
   a. For intCounter = "1" To "19"
   b. For strNumber = 98 To 71 Step 2
   c. For intValue = 12 To 52 Step –4

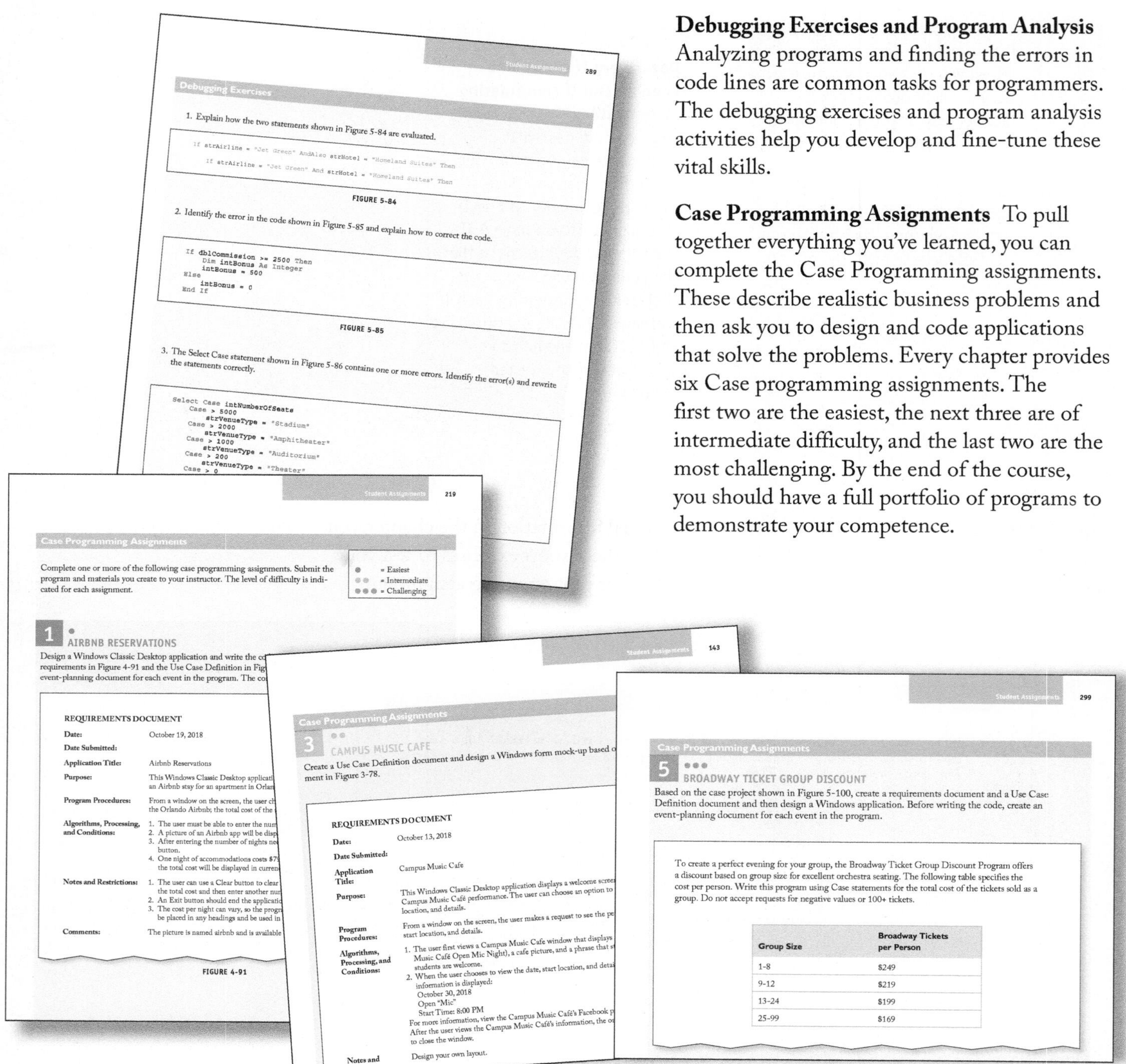

Debugging Exercises and Program Analysis Analyzing programs and finding the errors in code lines are common tasks for programmers. The debugging exercises and program analysis activities help you develop and fine-tune these vital skills.

Case Programming Assignments To pull together everything you've learned, you can complete the Case Programming assignments. These describe realistic business problems and then ask you to design and code applications that solve the problems. Every chapter provides six Case programming assignments. The first two are the easiest, the next three are of intermediate difficulty, and the last two are the most challenging. By the end of the course, you should have a full portfolio of programs to demonstrate your competence.

Acknowledgments

To Tim, my husband, for sharing this wonderful world filled with moments under the Northern Lights of Tromso. To Liam, Lochlan, Colin, and Jackson, my grandsons, without whose loving attention this book would have been finished in half the time. To my six children Timothy, Brittany, Ryan, Daniel, Bre, and Eric, who are no longer children but my dear friends. To Lisa Ruffolo, my editor, for being the motivating master of her detailed craft. And lastly, to my mother, who will be remembered for her tenacity, strength, and hard work.

—Corinne Hoisington

CHAPTER 1

Introduction to Visual Basic 2017 Programming

OBJECTIVES

You will have mastered the material in this chapter when you can:

- Understand software and computer programs
- State the role of a developer in creating computer programs
- Specify the use of a graphical user interface and describe an event-driven program
- Specify the roles of input, processing, output, and data when running a program on a computer
- Explain the logical operations a computer program can perform
- Define and describe the use of a database
- Identify the use of a computer programming language in general and Visual Basic 2017 in particular
- Explain the use of Visual Studio 2017 when developing Visual Basic 2017 programs
- Specify the programming languages available for use with Visual Studio 2017
- Explain .NET Framework 4.6.2
- Explain RAD
- Describe classes, objects, and the .NET Framework class libraries
- Explain ADO.NET, ASP.NET, MSIL, and CLR
- Specify the types of Visual Basic 2017 applications

Introduction

A computer is an electronic device that completes tasks under the direction of a sequence of instructions to produce useful results for people. Computers include desktop models, laptops, tablets, and smartphones. The set of instructions that directs a computer to perform tasks is called **computer software**, or a **computer program**. A computer program on a mobile device or on a Windows 10 computer is also called an **app**. In addition, programs are being developed for wearable devices, augmented reality headsets, smart TVs, automobiles, and smart devices (Internet of Things) such as home thermostats and refrigerators.

When controlled by programs, computers and mobile devices can accomplish a wide variety of activities. For example, computers can interpret and display a webpage, compute and write payroll checks for millions of employees, display video and play audio from the web, post to a social network on a smartphone, and engage in an augmented reality experience using a virtual reality headset such as the HoloLens (Figure 1-1).

FIGURE 1-1

Source: Microsoft

Two vital components of a computer must interact with each other for any activity to be performed. These components are computer hardware and computer software. **Computer hardware** is the physical equipment associated with a computer. It includes the keyboard (traditional or on-screen), mouse, touch screen or monitor, central processing unit (CPU), random access memory (RAM), and hard disk (Figure 1-2). A **mobile device** is portable computer hardware such as a smartphone, tablet computer, or wearable device such as a smart watch or headset.

A computer program, or app, is a set of electronic instructions that directs the hardware to perform tasks such as displaying a character on the screen when a key is pressed on the keyboard, adding an employee's regular pay and overtime pay to

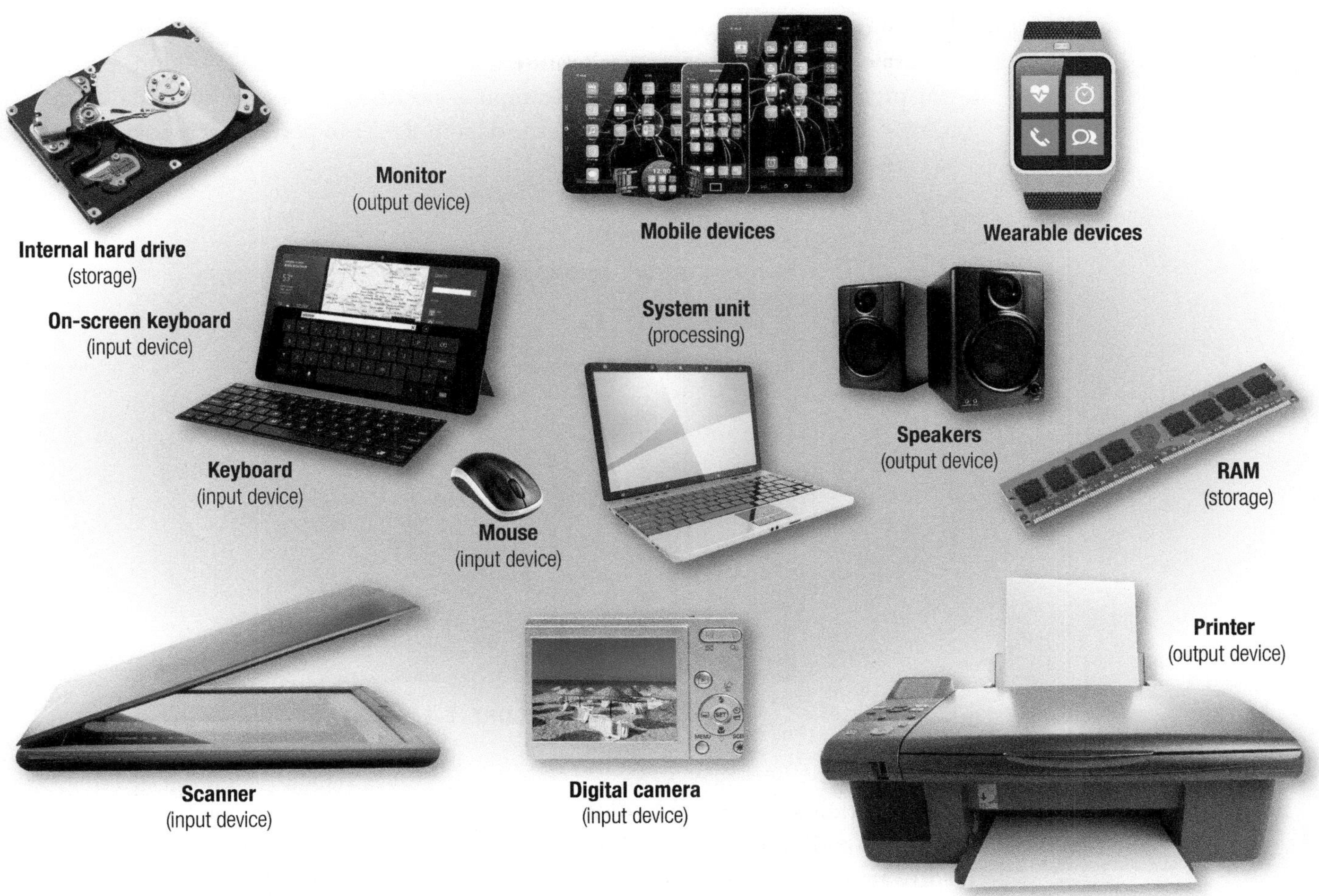

FIGURE 1-2

iStockphoto.com/Korovin; iStockphoto.com/Chesky_W; iStockphoto.com/Szemeno; iStockphoto.com/vladru; iStockphoto.com/AlexMax; iStockphoto.com/4X-image; iStockphoto.com/TPopova; iStockphoto.com/scorpion26; iStockphoto.com/muratkoc; iStockphoto.com/camillawisbauer; iStockphoto.com/George Manga

calculate the employee's total pay, or displaying a picture from an attached digital camera. Computer hardware cannot perform any activity unless an instruction directs that hardware to act. In most cases, the instruction is part of a computer program a developer has created to carry out the desired activity. A third component required is data. **Data** includes words, numbers, videos, graphics, and sound that programs manipulate, display, and otherwise process. The basic function of many programs is to accept some form of data (sometimes called **input data**), manipulate the data in some manner (sometimes called **processing**), and create some form of data that is usable by people or other computers (sometimes called **output data**, or **information**). In short, many computer programs perform the following general steps: accept input data, process the data, and create output data. The data that acts as input to a program, the processing that occurs, and the output that is created vary with the requirements of the program.

In order for the computer to execute a program, both the program and the data must be placed in the computer's **random access memory (RAM)** (Figure 1-3). Once the program is stored in RAM, the computer's **central processing unit (CPU)** can access the program instructions and the data in RAM to perform activities as directed by the program.

FIGURE 1-3

iStockphoto.com/NorasitKaewsai

Another activity that hardware and software typically carry out is saving both the data and other software. **Saving**, or **storing**, data refers to placing the data or software electronically on a storage medium such as a hard disk or a Universal Serial Bus (USB) drive or saving to a cloud storage server. The software and data are stored so they can be accessed and retrieved at a later time. Stored local data is said to be **persistent** because it remains available even after the computer power is turned off.

Computer Programmers and Developers

A computer program is designed and developed by people known as **computer programmers**, or developers. **Developers** are people skilled in designing computer programs and creating them using programming languages. Some computer programs are small and relatively simple, but often a problem to be solved on a computer requires more than one program. Thus, developers speak of developing an **application**, which can mean several computer programs working together to solve a problem.

When designing a program, developers analyze the problem and determine how to solve it. Once a computer program or an application is designed, the developer must create it so it can be executed on a computer. In most cases, the developer creates the program by writing its code using a **programming language**, which is a set of words and symbols that can be interpreted by special computer software and eventually executed as instructions by a computer. In this book, you will learn the skills required both to design and to create computer programs and apps using the Visual Basic 2017 programming language (Figure 1-4).

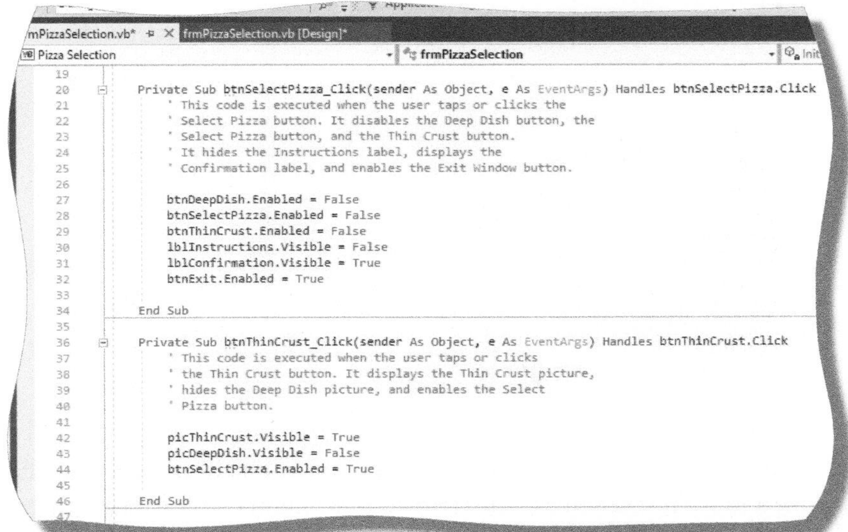

mPizzaSelection.vb* × frmPizzaSelection.vb [Design]*
Pizza Selection
frmPizzaSelection
Private Sub btnSelectPizza_Click(sender As Object, e As EventArgs) Handles btnSelectPizza.Click
' This code is executed when the user taps or clicks the
' Select Pizza button. It disables the Deep Dish button, the
' Select Pizza button, and the Thin Crust button.
' It hides the Instructions label, displays the
' Confirmation label, and enables the Exit Window button.
btnDeepDish.Enabled = False
btnSelectPizza.Enabled = False
btnThinCrust.Enabled = False
lblInstructions.Visible = False
lblConfirmation.Visible = True
btnExit.Enabled = True
End Sub
Private Sub btnThinCrust_Click(sender As Object, e As EventArgs) Handles btnThinCrust.Click
' This code is executed when the user taps or clicks
' the Thin Crust button. It displays the Thin Crust picture,
' hides the Deep Dish picture, and enables the Select
' Pizza button.
picThinCrust.Visible = True
picDeepDish.Visible = False
btnSelectPizza.Enabled = True
End Sub

FIGURE 1-4

CONSIDER THIS

Will I be able to find a job in computer programming?

According to Robert Half Technology, the following technology positions are in highest demand:

- Data scientists with a coding background
- Big data engineers
- Network security engineers
- Mobile application developers
- Software developers
- Software engineers

(www.roberthalf.com/technology/it-salary-center)

Event-Driven Computer Programs with a Graphical User Interface

Most Visual Basic 2017 programs are **event-driven programs** that communicate with the user through a **graphical user interface (GUI)**. The GUI usually consists of a window that contains a variety of objects and that can be displayed on various devices such as a computer monitor or a smartphone screen. Users employ GUI objects to select options, enter data, and cause events to occur. An **event** means the user has initiated an action that causes the program to perform a type of processing in response to that action. For example, a user might enter data into the program, and then click a button. The button action triggers an event, resulting in the program performing the appropriate processing in response.

To illustrate the process of entering data when using a GUI and then triggering an event, consider the window shown in Figure 1-5.

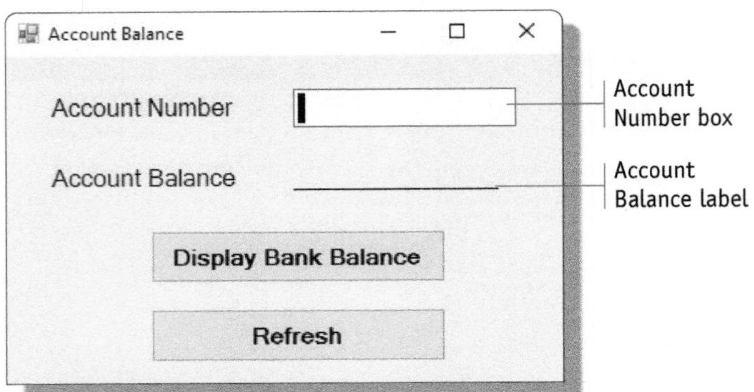

FIGURE 1-5

This window is part of a banking application. When it is displayed, the teller at the bank or a user on the web can enter an account number. Next, the user can click the Display Bank Balance button (which triggers an event) and the program displays the account balance. The following steps illustrate the dynamics of the interaction with the program:

STEP 1 The user enters the account number in the Account Number box.

The account number the user entered is displayed in the Account Number text box (Figure 1-6). The Account Balance label displays no information.

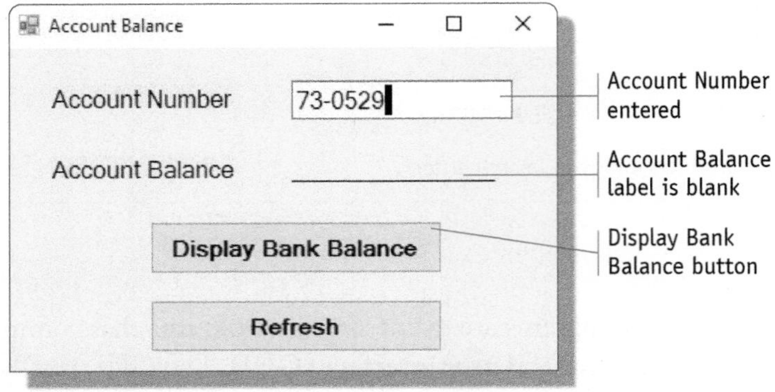

FIGURE 1-6

STEP 2 The user clicks the Display Bank Balance button.

The account balance is displayed in the Account Balance label (Figure 1-7). Clicking the Display Bank Balance button triggered the event that caused the program to determine and display the account balance based on data that the program accessed.

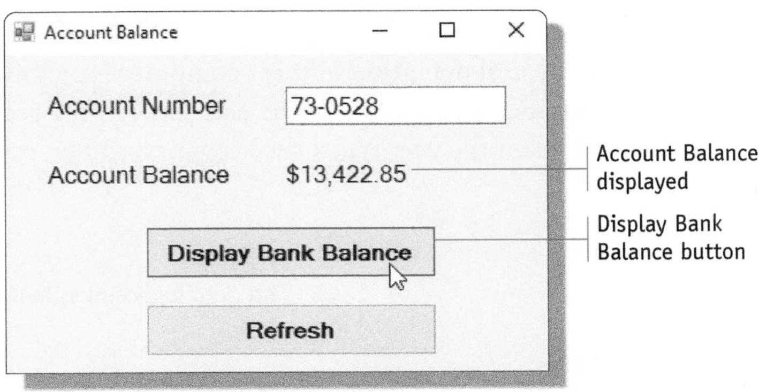

FIGURE 1-7

STEP 3 The user clicks the Refresh button to clear the text box and the label, and prepare the user interface for the next account number.

Clicking the Refresh button triggers another event. The text box and the label are cleared and the insertion point is placed in the Account Number text box (Figure 1-8). The user now can enter a new account number to determine the account balance.

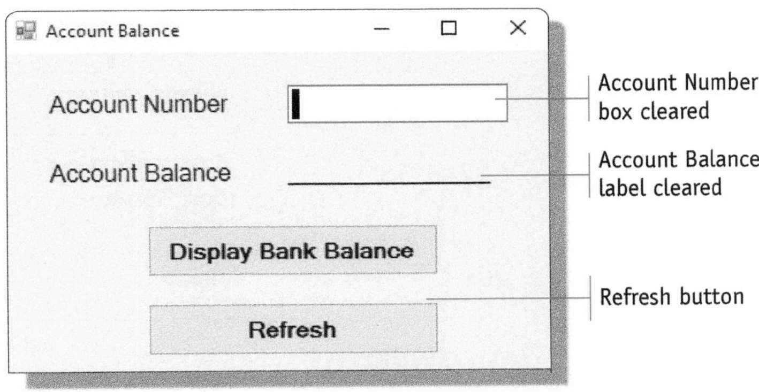

FIGURE 1-8

The events in the previous example consist of clicking the Display Bank Balance button and clicking the Refresh button. The program reacts to the events by performing specific actions (showing the account balance and resetting the text box and label). This is an example of an event-driven program. The Visual Basic developer designs the user interface and writes the program code that performs these event-triggered actions.

Basic Program Operations

All programs, regardless of their size and complexity, execute only a few fundamental operations: input, output, basic arithmetic operations, and logical operations. These operations can be combined in countless different ways to accomplish the tasks required of the program. The following pages describe these basic program operations.

Input Operation

As noted previously, a fundamental operation in most computer programs involves a user who enters data. For instance, in Figure 1-6, the user entered the account number. The steps that occurred when the user typed the account number are shown in Figure 1-9.

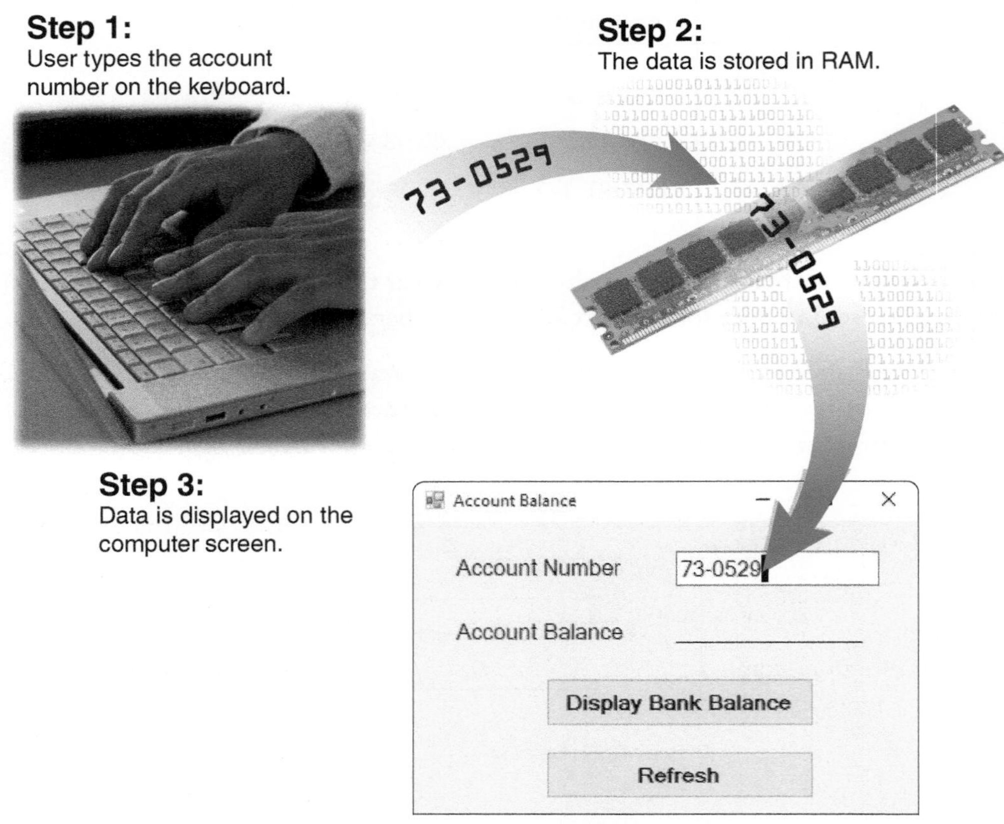

Step 1:
User types the account number on the keyboard.
Step 2:
The data is stored in RAM.
73-0529
73-0529
Step 3:
Data is displayed on the computer screen.
Account Balance
Account Number
73-0529
Account Balance
Display Bank Balance
Refresh

FIGURE 1-9

iStockphoto.com/Wesley Thornberry; iStockphoto.com/TPopova

In Figure 1-9, the banking computer program that processes the user's request is stored in RAM. The data entered by the user also is stored in RAM. Depending on the input device, the entered data might also be displayed on the computer screen. The input device used to enter data depends on the application. In Figure 1-9, the user typed the account number on a traditional keyboard or mobile device keyboard. Other applications might allow data to be entered with a scanner, touch screen, digital camera, video camera, mouse, or other device. In each instance, the data is stored in the computer's RAM. When the data is in RAM, instructions in the program can operate on the data.

Output Operation

The second basic program operation is creating output, or information. As you learned previously, a major goal of most computer programs is to create output data, or information, that is useful to people. In Figure 1-7 on page 7, the information requested of the program is the account balance. The process of creating output is shown in Figure 1-10.

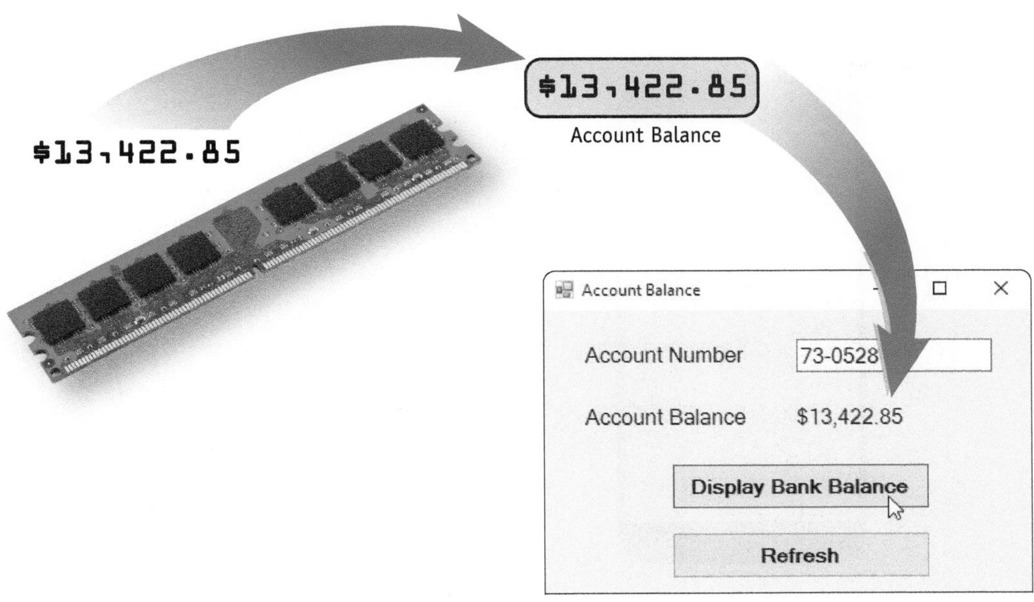

FIGURE 1-10

iStockphoto.com/TPopova

As always, the program must be stored in RAM to control the operations of the computer. In the example, the program sets the text of the Account Balance label equal to the account balance, and then displays it on the screen.

As with input operations, a variety of devices can present output. In addition to computer monitors, common output devices include printers, gaming console screens, and smartphone screens (Figure 1-11).

Basic Arithmetic Operations

After data is stored in main memory as a result of an input operation, the program can process it in some manner. In many programs, arithmetic operations (addition, subtraction, multiplication, and division) are performed on numeric data to produce useful output.

Prior to performing arithmetic operations, the numeric data used in calculations must be stored in RAM. Then, program instructions that also are stored in RAM can direct the computer to add, subtract, multiply, or divide the numbers. The answers from arithmetic operations can be used in additional calculations and processing, stored for future use, and used as output from the program.

Logical Operations

The ability of a computer to perform logical operations separates it from other types of calculating devices. Computers, through the use of programs, can compare numbers, letters of the alphabet, and special characters. Based on the result of these comparisons, the program can perform one processing task if the tested condition is true

FIGURE 1-11

iStockphoto.com/nixki; iStockphoto.com/guvendemir; iStockphoto.com/scorpion26

and another processing task if the condition is not true. Using a program to compare data and perform alternative operations allows the computer to complete sophisticated tasks such as predicting weather, formatting and altering digital photographs, editing digital video, and running high-speed games.

A program can perform the following types of logical operations:

- Comparing to determine if two values are equal
- Comparing to determine if one value is greater than another value
- Comparing to determine if one value is less than another value

Based on the results of these comparisons, the program can direct the computer to take alternative actions.

Saving Software and Data

When you develop and write a program, the code you write and other features, such as the GUI, must be saved on disk. Then, when you want the program to run, you can have the program loaded into RAM and executed. By saving the program on disk, you can execute the same program many times without rewriting it each time you want to run it.

The program you write, however, also can save data. This data, which can be generated from the processing in the program, can be saved on disk for future use. For example, in a banking application, a customer might open an account. The computer program that is used to open the account saves the customer's information, such as name, address, account number, and account balance, to a local file on the device or in the cloud on a remote server. Later, when the customer makes a deposit or withdrawal, the customer information will be retrieved and modified to reflect the deposit or withdrawal.

In most cases, data such as a customer's name and address is saved in a database. A **database** is a collection of data organized in a manner that allows access, retrieval, and use of that data. Once the data is saved in the database, any programs with permission can reference the data. You will learn more about databases and their use when programming using Visual Basic 2017 later in this textbook.

Visual Basic 2017 and Visual Studio 2017

To write a computer program, a developer uses a programming language. As you learned previously, a programming language is a set of written words, symbols, and codes, following a strict set of usage rules called the language **syntax**, that a developer uses to communicate instructions to a computer. An example of code statements in the Visual Basic 2017 programming language is shown in Figure 1-12.

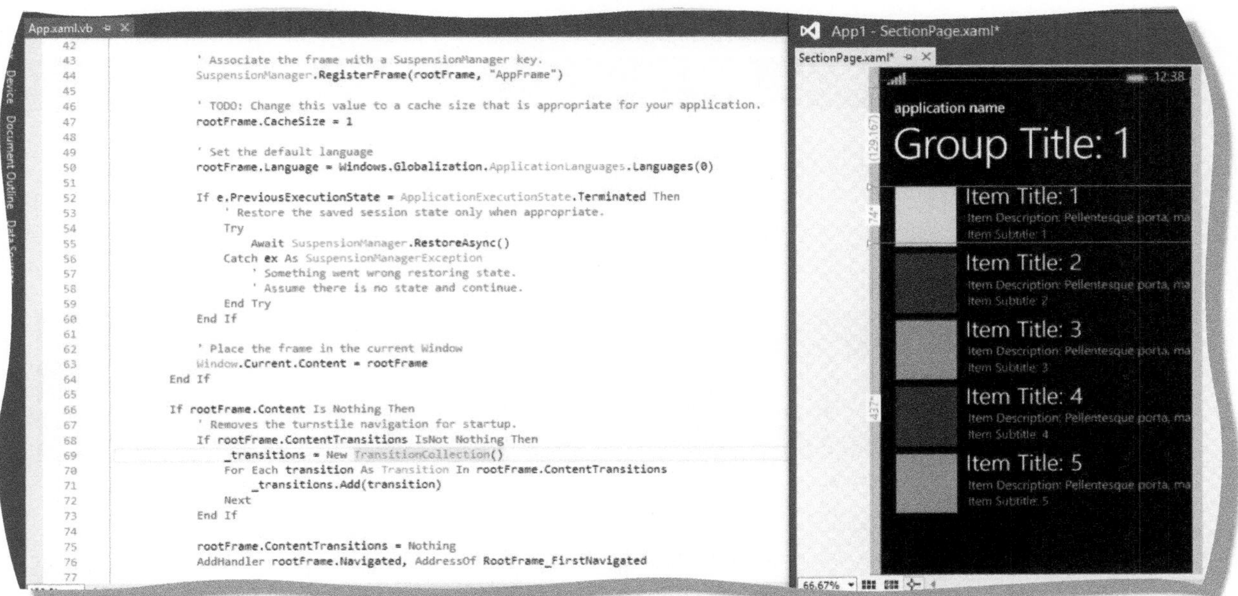

FIGURE 1-12

Each program statement causes the computer to perform one or more operations. When written, these instructions must conform to the rules of the Visual Basic 2017 language. Coding a program is a precise skill. The developer must follow the syntax, or **programming rules**, of the programming language precisely. Even a single coding error can cause a program to execute improperly. Therefore, the developer must pay strict attention to coding an error-free program.

When writing Visual Basic 2017 programs, most developers use a tool called Visual Studio 2017. **Visual Studio 2017** is a software application that allows you to develop Visual Basic 2017 programs using the code you write, code prewritten by others that can be incorporated into your program, and sophisticated tools that speed up the programming process significantly while building better executing and more reliable programs. In this book, you will use Visual Studio 2017 to write Visual Basic 2017 programs.

Visual Studio 2017 is a type of **integrated development environment (IDE)**, which provides services and tools that enable a developer to code, test, and implement a single program, or sometimes a series of programs that comprise an application. Visual Studio 2017, which was developed by Microsoft Corporation, works specifically with Visual Basic 2017 as well as other programming languages to develop program code.

Visual Basic, part of Visual Studio, can be installed on a computer running Windows 7 with Service Pack 1, Windows 8, Windows 10, or Windows Server 2016. Visual Studio 2017 can be installed on a 32-bit or 64-bit computer. Students, educators, and academic institutions can access a free copy of Visual Studio 2017 at *imagine.microsoft.com*. Microsoft Imagine (Figure 1-13) is a Microsoft program that supports technical education by providing access to Microsoft software for learning, teaching, and research purposes such as Visual Studio. This text uses the Microsoft Visual Studio 2017 Community version to present the programming topics. Microsoft Visual Studio Professional and Enterprise can also be used in teaching this textbook course.

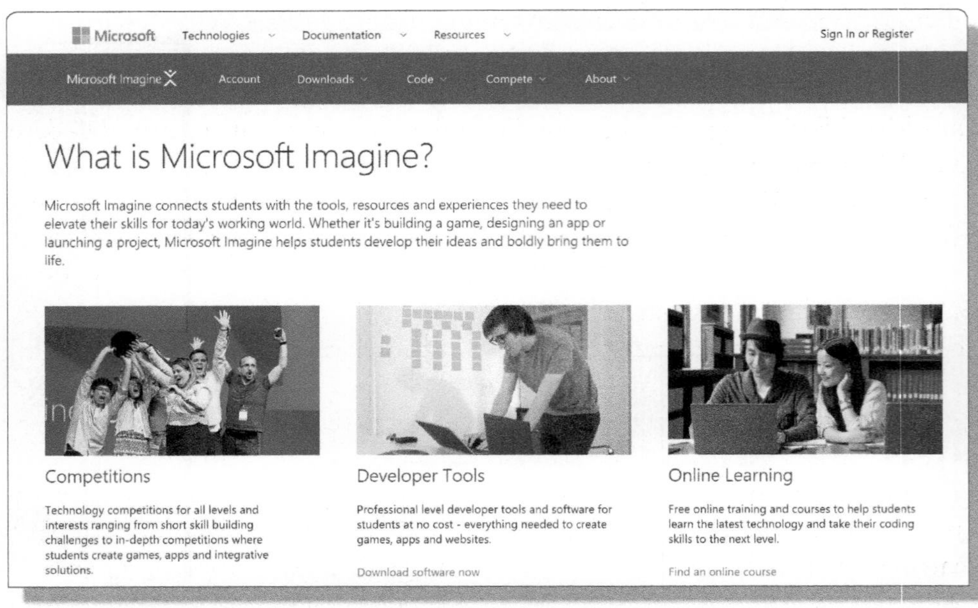

FIGURE 1-13

After you start the Visual Studio 2017 application, the Visual Studio 2017 window is displayed. In this window, you can develop and write your Visual Basic program, as shown in Figure 1-14.

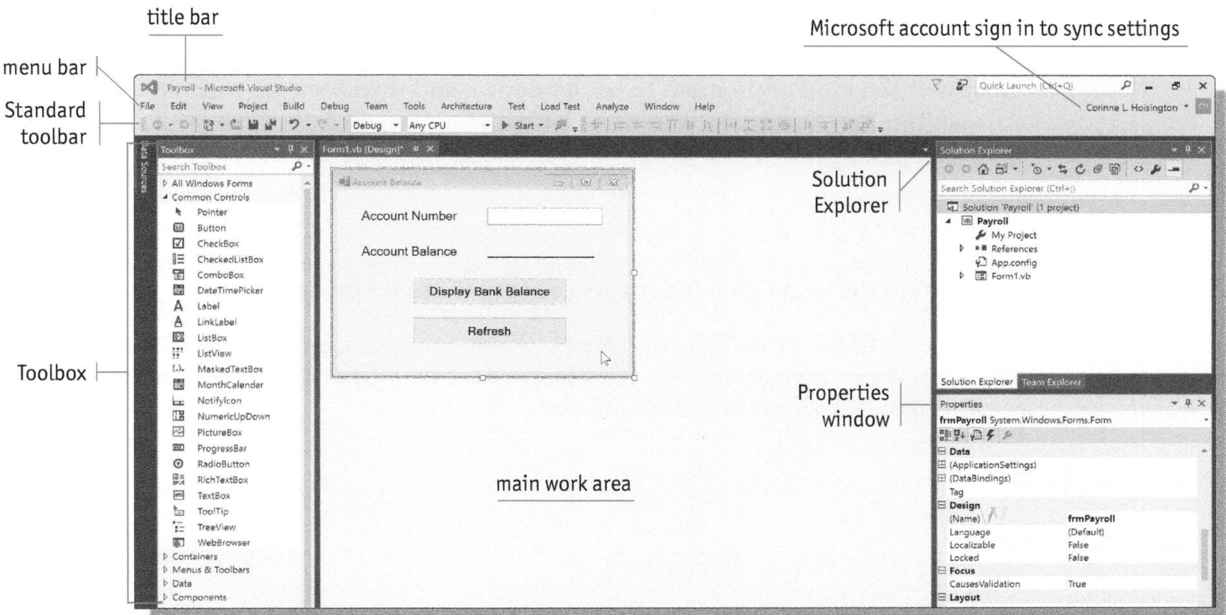

FIGURE 1-14

The following elements help you use the Visual Studio 2017 window. In subsequent chapters, you will learn to use each of the elements found in this window.

Title bar: The title bar identifies the window and the application open in the window. In Figure 1-14, the open application is named Payroll.

Menu bar: The menu bar displays the Visual Studio 2017 menu names. The menus contain lists of commands that allow you to create, edit, save, print, test, and run a Visual Basic program, and to perform other functions that are critical to developing Visual Basic programs.

Standard toolbar: The Standard toolbar contains buttons that execute frequently used commands such as Open Project, New Project, Save, Cut, Copy, Paste, and Undo.

Toolbox: The Toolbox contains **.NET components** that help you develop the GUI for your program. For example, you can use the Toolbox to place buttons, picture boxes, labels, radio buttons, and other Windows GUI objects in the windows of your program.

Main work area: The main work area contains the item you are currently developing. In Figure 1-14, this area contains the Account Balance window of the Payroll program.

Solution Explorer: The Solution Explorer window displays the elements of the Visual Basic **solution**, which is the name for the Visual Basic program and other items generated by Visual Studio to help the program execute properly. You will learn about these items and how to use the Solution Explorer window throughout this book.

Properties window: An item that is a visible part of a GUI, such as the Display Bank Balance button in Figure 1-14, is called an **object** or **control**. Each object in a Visual Basic program has a set of characteristics called the **properties** of the object. These properties, such as the size of the button and the text displayed within the button, can be set in the Properties window within Visual Studio. You will learn about the properties of many objects throughout this book.

To code a Visual Basic program, the developer starts the Visual Studio program, identifies the kind of program to be developed, and then uses the tools and features of Visual Studio to create the program.

Does Visual Studio Code contain the same developer tools as Visual Studio Professional and Community versions?

Microsoft Visual Studio Code is a free software IDE developed by Microsoft with multiple open source products that include lightweight versions of the Microsoft Visual Studio product line. The Visual Studio Code product line includes a subset of the full Visual Studio for the languages of C++, C#, Python, and PHP products.

Programming Languages

Several thousand programming languages exist today. Each language has its own rules and syntax for writing instructions. Languages often are designed for specific purposes, such as scientific applications, business solutions, or webpage development.

Visual Studio can be used to write programs in five languages: Visual Basic, Visual C++ (pronounced see plus plus and called C++ for short), Visual C# (pronounced see sharp and called C# for short), JavaScript, and Visual F# (pronounced eff sharp and called F# for short). You can develop a Windows Universal app for Windows 8/10 or a Windows smartphone coded with Visual Basic, C++, or C#. Each of these languages is described in the following sections.

Visual Basic

Visual Basic is a programming language that allows developers to easily build complex Windows and web programs, as well as other software tools. Visual Basic 2017 is based on the Visual Basic programming language that Microsoft developed in the early 1990s. Visual Basic was created from the BASIC (Beginner's All-purpose Symbolic Instructional Code) language, which was developed in the 1960s.

Visual Basic's popularity evolved from the wide range of productivity features that enabled developers to quickly generate high-quality software applications for Windows. Today, Visual Basic is one of the most widely used programming languages in the world because it is English-like and is considered one of the easier enterprise-level programming languages to learn. Visual Basic is the only language in Visual

Studio that is not case sensitive, which makes it easy for entry-level programmers. It is as powerful as the other programming languages in the Visual Studio suite, such as C++ or C#. An example of Visual Basic 2017 code is shown in Figure 1-12 on page 11.

In this book, you will learn to become a proficient Visual Basic developer.

Visual C++

C++ is a derivative of the programming language C, which originally was developed at Bell Labs in the 1970s. It gives developers exacting control of their applications through optimized code and access to system-provided services. It contains powerful language constructs, though at the price of added complexity. C++ provides unrivaled performance and precision for applications that require a high degree of control.

Visual C#

Introduced in 2001 by Microsoft, Visual C# offers a synthesis of the elegance and syntax of C++ with many of the productivity benefits enjoyed in Visual Basic. Visual C# can be used to create both Windows and Web applications, as well as other types of software tools. Microsoft designed Visual C# to overcome some of the limitations of C++ while still providing the depth of control that C++ developers demand. The language includes aspects of several other programming languages, such as C++, Java, and Delphi, with a strong emphasis on code simplification.

JavaScript

Fully included in the Visual Studio 2017 version, JavaScript (JS) is an open-source client-side scripting language that enhances web browser user interfaces and dynamic websites. Visual Studio 2017 provides complete IntelliSense and debugging support for all the JavaScript objects and its methods.

Visual F#

A Microsoft .NET object-oriented language that debuted with Visual Studio 2010 is called F#. A multipurpose language similar to Visual Basic and C#, the F# language is known for its math-intensive focus, making it perfect for heavy-duty scientific programming applications. The language is relatively new and is just beginning to gain popularity in the business and science environments.

.NET Framework 4.6.2

In the year 2000, Microsoft announced a set of software technologies and products under the umbrella name of .NET. The .NET technologies and products were designed to work together to allow businesses to connect information, people, systems, and devices through software. Much of this connection occurs over the Internet.

The software environment in which programs and applications can be developed for .NET is called the **.NET Framework**, which provides tools and processes developers can use to produce and run programs. The .NET Framework is a development platform for building apps for Windows, Windows Phone, Windows Server, and Windows Azure (the Microsoft professional cloud computing platform). The most recent version is called **.NET Framework 4.6.2**. Visual Studio 2017 provides the development environment for the developer to have access to the .NET Framework 4.6 tools and processes.

Major features of .NET Framework 4.6.2 include the .NET class library, ADO.NET (provides the ability to read and write data in databases), ASP.NET (provides the ability to develop web applications across desktop, tablet, and mobile browsers), Azure Cloud, Windows services, and the Common Language Runtime (CLR: allows programs to run on different computers under different operating systems). Each of these features is explained in the following sections.

.NET Class Library

As you have learned, most programs written using Visual Basic 2017 are event-driven programs in which a user performs an action, such as clicking a button, and the program executes the appropriate instructions. The instructions a program executes when a user clicks a button are normally written by the Visual Basic developer and are unique to the processing required by the program. For example, when a user clicks a button in one program, the overtime pay is calculated for an employee, whereas in another program parking fees are calculated. Each program responds to the events triggered by users with unique processing based on the requirements of the program.

In many programs, however, much of the programming code that must be developed is common for all the programs. For example, in all the programs you have seen in this chapter, a button was used to trigger an event in the program. The button appears in a window on a screen and senses when it has been clicked through the use of program instructions.

When code is common to multiple programs, the best approach is to write the code once and then reuse it when appropriate. For example, when a button is required in the GUI of a program, it is more efficient to use common programming code to insert the button than to require a developer to write all the code for a button each time one is required. When a common task must be performed or a new object such as a button is required, a developer can write the code once and save it as a class. That class can then be referenced by all other programs when the task or object is required.

In short, the coding required for a button can be placed in a class. A **class** is a named group of program code. Once the class is coded, it can be stored in a **class library**, which makes the class available to all developers who need to use it. For example, when you as a developer need to place a button in the user interface, you can use the Button class stored in a class library to create the button without writing all the programming code associated with the button (Figure 1-15).

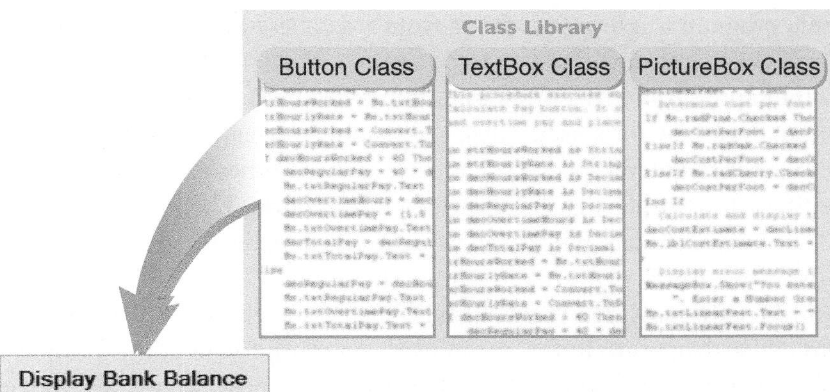

FIGURE 1-15

A button created from a class is called an **object**, or sometimes an **instance** of a class. In programming terminology, the process of creating a Button object from the Button class is called **instantiation.** In other words, a class acts as a general template, while an object is a specific item that is generated based on the class template. Thus, all buttons can be generated, or instantiated, from the Button class. The Display Bank Balance button in Figure 1-15 is a specific Button object instantiated from the Button class.

To create a Button object from the Button class in Visual Studio 2017, you only need to drag the Button .NET component from the Toolbox to a Windows Form object, as you will learn in Chapter 2.

A button in a GUI is only a single example of using classes and class libraries. The .NET Framework class library contains thousands of classes and many class libraries for Visual Basic developers who use Visual Studio to create programs.

With so many classes available in .NET Framework, developers use a method of program development called rapid application development. **Rapid application development (RAD)** refers to the process of using prebuilt classes to make application development faster, easier, and more reliable. Throughout this book, you will gain a further understanding of classes and their use in modern computer programming, and will see how the classes in the .NET Framework class libraries can be used for RAD.

ADO.NET

Often, programs you write must access data stored in a database. A set of prewritten classes called ADO.NET (ADO stands for ActiveX Data Objects) provides the functionality for a program to perform the four primary tasks required when working with a database: getting the data, examining the data, editing the data, and updating the data.

Getting the data refers to retrieving it from the database and making it available to the program. Once the data is retrieved from the database, ADO.NET provides the tools for the program to examine the data and determine how to use it. For example, a program might retrieve data from a database to create a printed report. The program can examine the data to determine its use for the report.

In other applications, the program might examine the data to determine if it is appropriate to display for a user. Thus, in a payroll application the program might require the user to enter a special value, such as her mother's maiden name, to verify her identity before displaying the requested information. The program, using ADO.NET classes, can compare the special value to the data retrieved from the database to determine if the user is permitted to access the data.

A third facility provided by ADO.NET is the ability to edit the data, which means to make changes to it. For example, if you change your address or telephone number, those values should be changed in your account database information. ADO.NET supports the ability to make those changes.

Finally, once changes have been made to data, ADO.NET enables a program to update the database with the new information by writing the data into the database.

ASP.NET

The Internet and the web are integral technological resources. Modern websites provide services from selling products to sharing the latest medical research on any known disease. The development and maintenance of these websites is a constant requirement and consumes many developer hours.

Recognizing the importance of the web, Microsoft developed .NET Framework 4.6.2 to include a programming framework called ASP.NET. Developers can use this framework through Visual Studio 2017 to build powerful and sophisticated web applications on a web server. Using ASP.NET classes, Visual Basic 2017 programmers can create websites that perform any function available on the web today. In addition to traditional websites, you can automatically adapt web applications to target mobile devices with enhanced ASP.NET support for mobile browsers. ASP.NET is designed for cloud technologies and server-side applications. **Cloud computing** is the connection of remote servers hosted on the Internet to store and process data, instead of storing the information locally on a personal computer or device.

ASP.NET offers several advantages for developers. First, almost all the objects available in the .NET framework, such as buttons, text boxes, and picture boxes, are available in ASP.NET. So, developers can use the same techniques to create a web application that they use to create Windows applications such as those shown in this chapter. In addition, ASP.NET is dedicated to mobile-first and cloud-first development. The code footprint for mobile webpages have been slimmed down to open quickly within mobile browsers. The ASP.NET within Visual Studio provides tools to develop interactive HTML5 web applications easily and efficiently with JavaScript and jQuery. Instead of coding separate webpages for each type of mobile device, a single programming model is available for designing webpages and services.

Important web requirements such as performance and security are enhanced and maximized through use of the tools offered with ASP.NET. In short, ASP.NET offers a complete solution for developing modern web applications and cloud services for computers, tablets, and smartphones.

Microsoft Intermediate Language and Common Language Runtime

After a developer writes a program in a programming language such as Visual Basic 2017 using Visual Studio 2017, the programming statements must be translated into a collection of instructions that eventually can be understood by the electronics of the computer. These electronic instructions are executed by the computer to carry out the tasks of the program. This process of translation is called **program compilation**.

Program compilation for a Visual Basic 2017 program creates a set of electronic code expressed in an intermediate language called the **Microsoft Intermediate Language (MSIL)**. When the program is executed, a portion of .NET called the **Common Language Runtime (CLR)** reads the MSIL and causes the instructions within the program to be executed (Figure 1-16).

In Figure 1-16, the Visual Basic program written by a developer is compiled, which translates the human-readable statements in Visual Basic into MSIL, the set of electronic code that forms the input to CLR. Then, when the program is ready for execution, the CLR reads the MSIL in RAM in a form that allows the computer's CPU to execute the instructions in the program.

The use of MSIL and CLR offers multiple benefits that provide speed and flexibility for both the development and execution environments of a program. Utmost among these benefits is that a program written using Visual Studio 2017 and compiled into MSIL can be executed on any computer using any operating system, as long as .NET Framework is available on the computer. So, with no changes to a program you write, the program could be executed on a Dell computer running Windows 10, a mobile smartphone, an older operating system, or an IBM computer using the Linux operating system. This ability to execute programs on different computers running different operating systems is a primary benefit of using .NET Framework.

Types of Visual Basic 2017 Applications

When you begin creating a new Visual Basic 2017 program in Visual Studio 2017, you must choose the type of application you will be developing. Based on your choice, Visual Studio 2017 provides the classes, tools, and features required for that type of application.

Five major types of applications are Windows Classic Desktop applications, Universal Windows apps, Web/Cloud applications, database applications, and HoloLens headset apps. A **Windows Classic Desktop application** means the program will run on a computer or other device that supports the Windows GUI. You can run Windows Classic Desktop applications on a variety of computers.

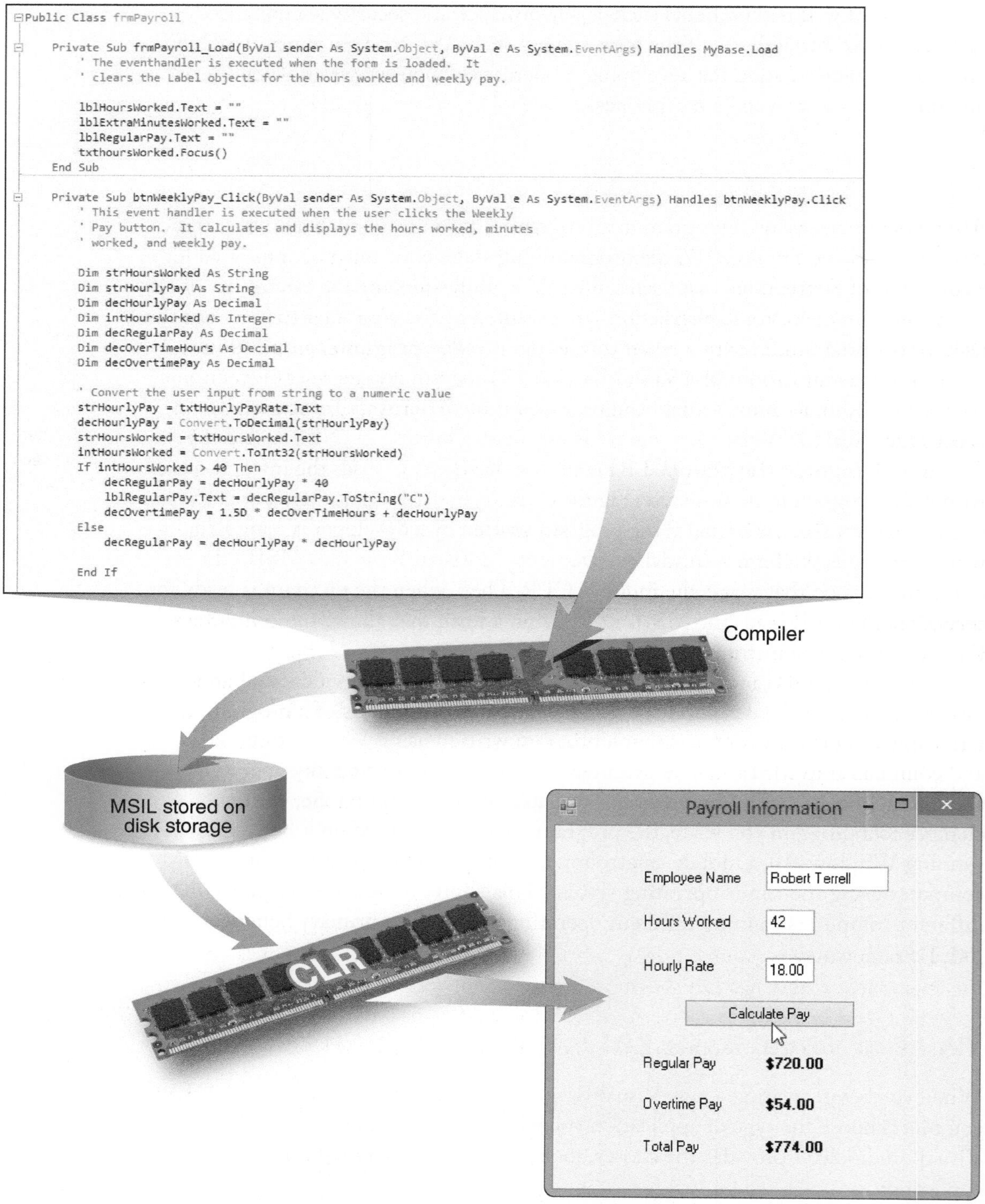

```
Public Class frmPayroll

    Private Sub frmPayroll_Load(ByVal sender As System.Object, ByVal e As System.EventArgs) Handles MyBase.Load
        ' The eventhandler is executed when the form is loaded.  It
        ' clears the Label objects for the hours worked and weekly pay.

        lblHoursWorked.Text = ""
        lblExtraMinutesWorked.Text = ""
        lblRegularPay.Text = ""
        txthoursWorked.Focus()
    End Sub

    Private Sub btnWeeklyPay_Click(ByVal sender As System.Object, ByVal e As System.EventArgs) Handles btnWeeklyPay.Click
        ' This event handler is executed when the user clicks the Weekly
        ' Pay button.  It calculates and displays the hours worked, minutes
        ' worked, and weekly pay.

        Dim strHoursWorked As String
        Dim strHourlyPay As String
        Dim decHourlyPay As Decimal
        Dim intHoursWorked As Integer
        Dim decRegularPay As Decimal
        Dim decOverTimeHours As Decimal
        Dim decOvertimePay As Decimal

        ' Convert the user input from string to a numeric value
        strHourlyPay = txtHourlyPayRate.Text
        decHourlyPay = Convert.ToDecimal(strHourlyPay)
        strHoursWorked = txtHoursWorked.Text
        intHoursWorked = Convert.ToInt32(strHoursWorked)
        If intHoursWorked > 40 Then
            decRegularPay = decHourlyPay * 40
            lblRegularPay.Text = decRegularPay.ToString("C")
            decOvertimePay = 1.5D * decOverTimeHours + decHourlyPay
        Else
            decRegularPay = decHourlyPay * decHourlyPay

        End If
```

Compiler

MSIL stored on disk storage

CLR

Payroll Information

Employee Name: Robert Terrell

Hours Worked: 42

Hourly Rate: 18.00

Calculate Pay

Regular Pay **$720.00**

Overtime Pay **$54.00**

Total Pay **$774.00**

iStockphoto.com/TPopova

FIGURE 1-16

You can also create **Windows Universal apps** that are designed to run on Windows 8 or Windows 10 computers and mobile devices such as smartphones and tablets. Windows Universal apps have a new look and feel; run on a variety of devices such as a desktop, Windows tablet, or Windows phone; and can be sold in the Windows Store. To develop a Windows Universal app, you must have Visual Studio 2017 installed on a Windows 8 or Windows 10 computer. You cannot develop Windows Universal apps on Windows 7 or Windows Server products. You must obtain a free developer license to develop and test Windows Universal apps before the Windows Store can certify them. The free developer license is provided on a per-machine basis and for a fixed amount of time using a Microsoft account.

When you open Visual Studio 2017 to create any type of application, you can sign in to Visual Studio with a Microsoft account to enable features such as synchronized settings that roam with you to your other Visual Studio devices. If you do not have a Microsoft account, Visual Studio provides the opportunity to sign up for an account for free.

In addition to Visual Studio's Universal App development, Microsoft has a separate app development platform, **Xamarin**, which enables you to develop a mobile app and deploy it to Android, iOS, and Windows devices. Microsoft Xamarin builds native apps for any platform in C#.

You create a **Web application** using ASP.NET. The application runs on a web server. It produces HTML5 code that is downloaded to the client computer, where the browser interprets the HTML and displays the contents of a webpage in a traditional or mobile browser. In a web application, the developer can include items such as security and forms processing to provide all the cloud and local services required of a modern website on a computer or mobile device.

A **database application** is written using ADO.NET to reference, access, display, and update data stored in a database. The Visual Basic 2017 developer writes the code to process the data.

CRITICAL THINKING

Do you have a great idea for an app for the App Store? Creating a mobile app and selling it in the Windows Store provides an exciting way to make money online. You do not need a storefront to sell your idea or worry about distribution. To create an income stream, you need to come up with a unique idea and make that idea a reality by learning to build an app.

Microsoft HoloLens Development

Display technology is rapidly moving beyond two dimensions. **HoloLens** is the augmented reality headset shown in Figure 1-1 on page 2 that places 3-D holographic images in your scope of vision. HoloLens apps are being developed using Visual Studio to select car options at Volvo dealerships, create a custom kitchen at Lowe's Home Centers, explore other planets at NASA, and replace a flat screen TV with a much larger holographic display. Holographic apps in the Windows Store can be monetized in the same way that all other apps are sold.

Microsoft Visual Studio works with Unity software to build HoloLens apps and test them on a built-in HoloLens emulator (Figure 1-17) without the need for a physical HoloLens headset. The emulator uses a Hyper-V virtual machine to run the app. The human and environmental inputs that would usually be read by the sensors on the HoloLens are instead simulated using your keyboard, mouse, or Xbox controller.

FIGURE 1-17

Source: Microsoft

Summary

In this chapter, you have learned the fundamentals of computer programming and have been introduced to the Visual Studio 2017 and Visual Basic 2017 program development environments. In subsequent chapters, you will learn to use Visual Studio 2017 and Visual Basic 2017 to create Windows Classic Desktop applications, Windows Universal apps, database applications, Web/Cloud applications for computer and mobile devices, and HoloLens apps.

Knowledge Check

1. The basic functions of many programs are: a. ____________________; b. ____________________; c. ____________________.
2. Explain the differences between computer hardware and computer software.
3. Match the following terms and their definitions:

a. Developer	1. A headset designed to view augmented reality
b. Persistent data	2. Someone skilled in designing computer programs and implementing them in programming languages
c. Programming language	3. A window with a variety of objects that can be displayed on a variety of devices
d. Graphical user interface	4. Data that is stored on a storage medium
e. HoloLens	5. The process of using prebuilt classes to make application development faster, easier, and more reliable
f. Database	6. A collection of data organized in a manner that allows access, retrieval, and use of that data
g. Rapid application development (RAD)	7. The connection of remote servers hosted on the Internet to store and process data instead of storing the information locally on a personal computer or device
h. Cloud computing	8. A set of words and symbols that can be interpreted by special computer software and eventually can be executed as instructions by a computer

4. Explain what an event is in the context of event-driven programs. Give two examples.
5. Give examples of the differences between an input operation and an output operation.
6. Describe three different databases where you think information about yourself might be stored.
7. What is programming language syntax? Why is it important?
8. What is a Toolbox in Visual Studio 2017? Why is it valuable?
9. Name two properties that a Button object can possess.
10. What are the five programming languages you can use with Visual Studio 2017?
11. Where can you sell the Windows Universal apps that you develop?
12. State three reasons that Visual Basic is one of the most widely used programming languages in the world.
13. Name two purposes of creating a Microsoft account for use in Visual Studio 2017.
14. Why is a class developed? How are classes organized and stored?

(continues)

Knowledge Check *continued*

15. Differentiate between a class and an object. Give three examples each of classes and objects.
16. What is the primary use of ADO.NET?
17. What do you call the process of translating statements written by a developer? What is the result of this process?
18. What are five types of applications you can create in Visual Basic 2017?
19. Find three YouTube videos that give an excellent overview of different HoloLens examples. Copy and the paste the URL of each of these videos and write a sentence after each URL explaining the video.
20. Research the cost of a HoloLens device and list the specifications.

CHAPTER 2

Program and Graphical User Interface Design

OBJECTIVES

You will have mastered the material in this chapter when you can:

- Create a Visual Basic 2017 Windows Classic Desktop application project
- Name and set the title bar text in a Windows Form object and resize a Windows Form object
- Add a Label object to a Windows Form object, name the Label object, set the text in the Label object, and change the Font properties of the text in the Label object
- Add a PictureBox object to the Windows Form object, name the PictureBox object, and resize the PictureBox object
- Add a Button object to the Windows Form object, name the Button object, set the text in the Button object, and change the Button object's size
- Align objects on the Windows Form object
- Save, close, and open Visual Basic projects
- Understand and implement design principles of the graphical user interface
- Understand and implement the first two phases of the program development life cycle

Introduction

IN THE REAL WORLD

The position of software engineer has the largest number of job openings among the top 25 best jobs listed on Glassdoor, and offers a median pay of $95,000.

Before a program can be coded using Visual Basic 2017, it must be designed. Designing a program can be compared to constructing a building. Before cement slabs are poured, steel beams are put in place and walls are built. Architects and engineers must design a building to ensure it will perform as required and be safe and reliable. The same holds true for a computer program or app. Once the program is designed, it can be implemented through the Visual Basic 2017 programming language to perform its intended functions.

To illustrate the process of creating a computer program in Visual Basic 2017 using **Visual Studio 2017** as the integrated development environment, you will design and implement the application shown in Figure 2-1 throughout this chapter and Chapter 3.

The application in Figure 2-1 could be part of a larger menu application used to select a coffee latte order at your favorite coffee shop. The program that creates the window in Figure 2-1 will run on a personal computer using the Windows operating system. Similar design principles for desktop computers and mobile devices taught in

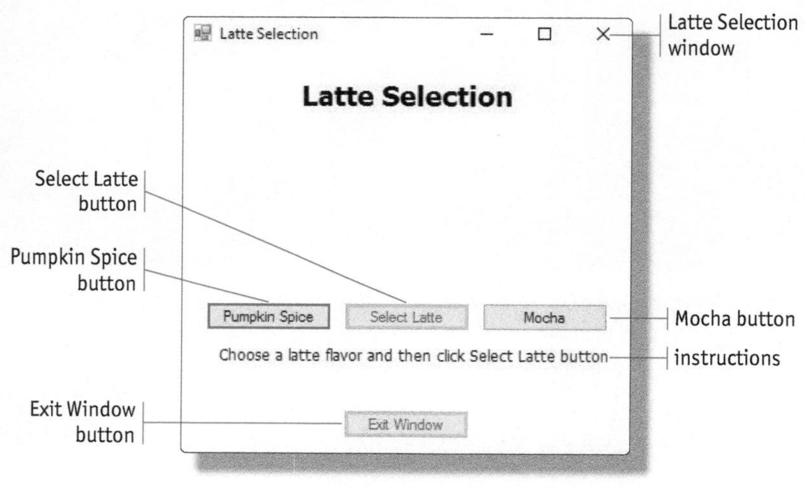

FIGURE 2-1a

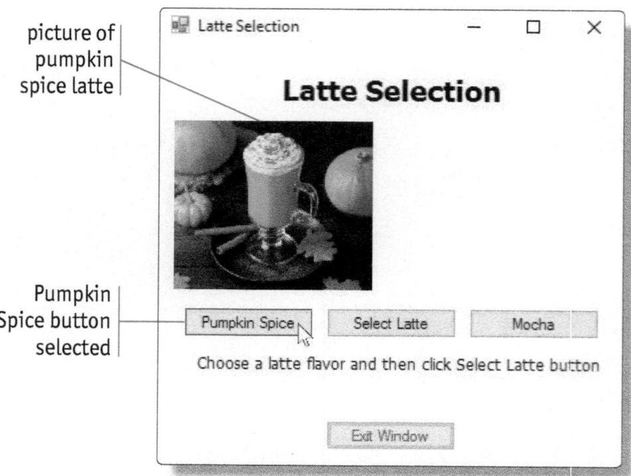

FIGURE 2-1b

Anna_Pustynnikova/Shutterstock.com

this chapter assist with graphic and text layout on any user interface to deliver a consistent experience across touch screens or a desktop's keyboard and mouse interaction. The program will allow customers to select their favorite latte type between the two options of pumpkin spice latte and mocha latte.

In Figure 2-1a, the program begins by displaying the Latte Selection window. The program provides instructions for the user to choose the latte flavor by clicking the Pumpkin Spice or Mocha button, and then to complete the selection by clicking the Select Latte button. If the user clicks the Pumpkin Spice button, a picture of a pumpkin spice latte is displayed (Figure 2-1b). If the user clicks the Mocha button, a picture of a mocha latte is displayed (Figure 2-1c). After choosing a latte flavor, the user can click the Select Latte button and the program informs the user that a flavored latte has been selected (Figure 2-1d). To close the window and exit the program, the user can click the Exit Window button after making a latte selection.

By the end of Chapter 3, you will have completed the design and implementation of this program.

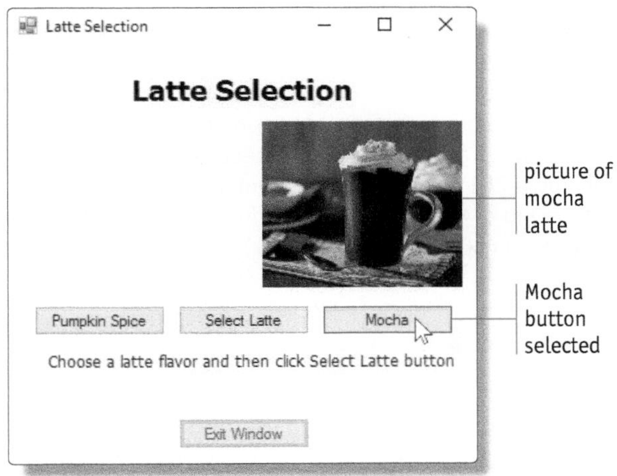

FIGURE 2-1c

Africa Studio/Shutterstock.com

FIGURE 2-1d

Africa Studio/Shutterstock.com

Using Visual Studio 2017

HEADS UP

Visual Basic 2017 can run on Windows 7, 8, or 10. In this book, the default operating system is Windows 10 with a screen resolution of 1366×768, but Windows Classic Desktop applications such as the program in this chapter work in all three operating systems.

When designing an event-driven program that uses a graphical user interface (GUI), such as the program in this chapter, one of the first steps after defining the purpose for the program is to design the user interface itself. Recall that the user interface is the window that appears on the screen when the program is running. The user interface includes a variety of objects such as buttons that are displayed in the window. Before beginning to design the user interface, however, the developer should know how to use Visual Studio and Visual Basic **rapid application development (RAD)** tools in the design process. For example, you use the Visual Studio tools to place a button on the window. Before starting the design of the program shown in Figure 2-1, you should know how to accomplish the Visual Studio tasks described on the following pages. In this text, you can complete steps by tapping if you are using a touch screen or by clicking if you are using a mouse or touchpad.

CONSIDER THIS

Can I store code and other files in the Visual Studio Cloud?

Microsoft provides an online storage cloud for the Visual Studio 2017 community. This optional storage space allows you to store your code, collaborate with team server members, test your code in the cloud, and sync your personal settings such as themes or keyboard shortcuts across various computers. The first time Visual Studio 2017 is launched, your Microsoft account sign-in and password information is requested. If you do not have a Microsoft account, you can create one for free at outlook.com. Signing into your Microsoft account is optional for Windows Classic Desktop applications, but is necessary for creating a Windows Store app. After signing into your Microsoft account, Visual Studio 2017 requests the user interface settings and color theme. These options can be changed at a later time in the Options menu of Visual Studio. To confirm that you are connected to your Microsoft account, check the profile name in the upper-right corner of Visual Studio.

Create a New Visual Basic 2017 Windows Classic Desktop Project

A **project** is equivalent to a single program created using Visual Studio. A **Windows Classic Desktop project** is a program that includes a user interface whose windows are created using the Windows operating system. When the program is executed, the user interacts with the program by using its windows and components (the user interface).

To create a new project using Visual Studio, you must specify the programming language you want to use and the type of program or application you will create. To create a new Visual Basic Windows Classic Desktop project, you can complete the following steps:

STEP 1 In Windows 10, click the Start button on the Windows taskbar, type `Visual Studio`, and then click Visual Studio 2017 in the search results. When the Start Page opens, click the New Project button on the Standard toolbar.

Visual Studio opens the New Project window (Figure 2-2). The New Project window on your computer might be displayed differently, depending on selections made when Visual Studio was installed on your computer. The left pane contains the programming languages and other types of templates available in Visual Studio. The middle pane contains the types of applications you can create within each programming language. The right pane displays a description of the selected application. At this point, you want to create a Windows Classic Desktop project using Visual Basic.

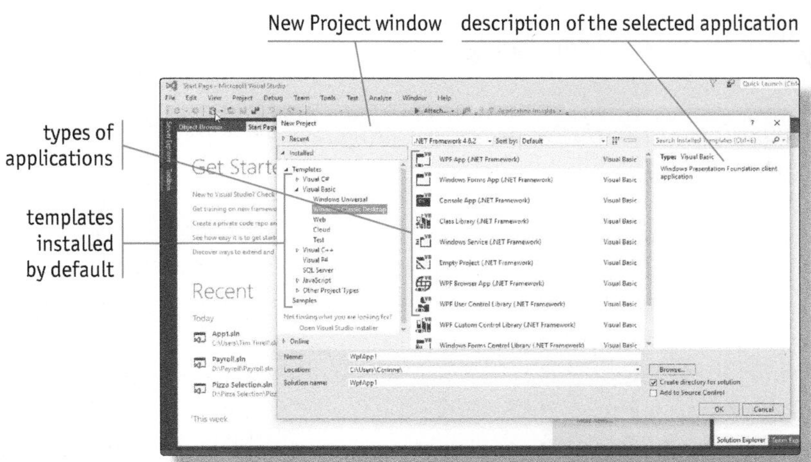

FIGURE 2-2

STEP 2 If necessary, expand Visual Basic and Windows in the left pane, and then click Windows Classic Desktop so it is selected. If necessary, click Windows Forms App in the middle pane.

Windows Classic Desktop is highlighted in the left pane and the types of Windows Classic Desktop projects you can create using Visual Basic are listed in the middle pane. Windows Forms App is selected in the middle pane (Figure 2-3). By making this selection, you specify you are creating a program that runs under the Windows operating system using the Windows Classic Desktop GUI.

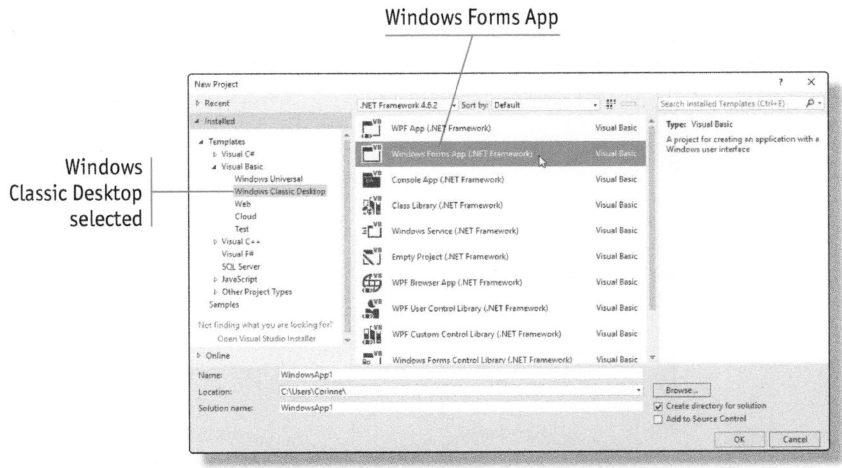

FIGURE 2-3

STEP 3 Type the project name. For this example, you could type `Latte Selection` as the name.

The project name appears in the Name text box (Figure 2-4).

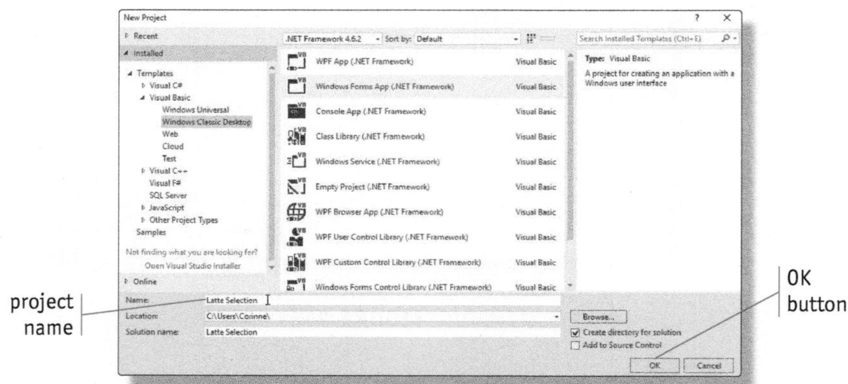

FIGURE 2-4

STEP 4 Click the OK button in the New Project window.

Visual Studio creates a new project (Figure 2-5). The project name is displayed in the title bar of the window.

IN THE REAL WORLD

Program names can contain spaces and some special characters, but by convention most developers use a name with capital letters at the beginning of each word. This naming convention is called camel case.

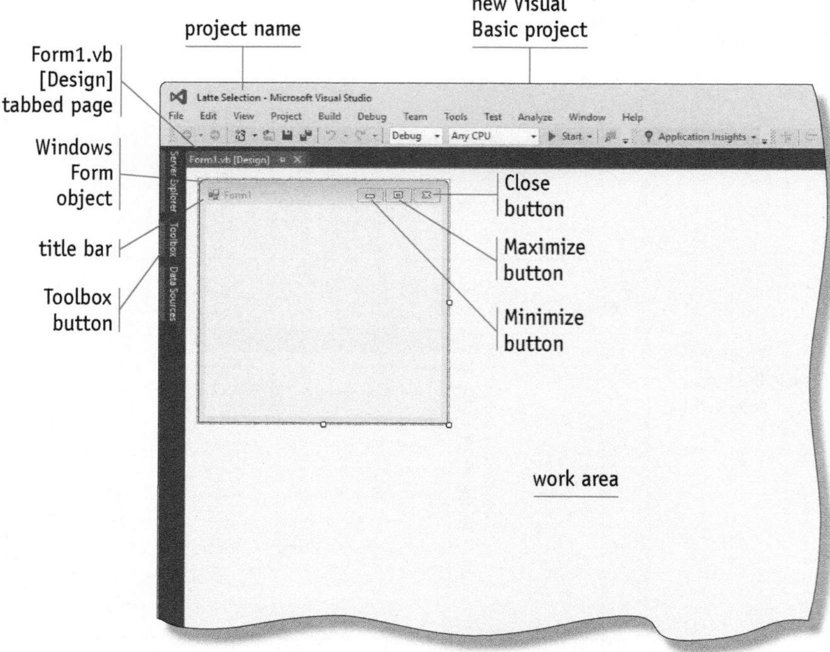

FIGURE 2-5

The Visual Studio window contains several important features you should know. First, in the portion of the window known as the **work area**, a tabbed page named Form1.vb [Design] contains a Windows Form object called Form1. A **Windows Form object** is the window you will use to build the program and then display it on your screen when you execute the program. The Windows Form object is the fundamental object in the GUI you will create using Visual Studio tools. Notice in Figure 2-5 that the Windows Form object contains a title bar, a window title (Form1), a Minimize button, a Maximize button, and a Close button.

A second important element is displayed on the left side of the window. Depending on the settings in Visual Studio, the left portion of the window will appear as shown in Figure 2-5 or Figure 2-6. In Figure 2-5, the left margin contains the Toolbox button. The Toolbox button also appears on the Standard toolbar.

Display the Toolbox

You can use the **Toolbox button** to display the Toolbox. The **Toolbox** is the primary tool you use to place objects such as buttons on the Windows Form object. Items in the Toolbox are grouped into sections called **tabs.** To display the Toolbox, you can complete the following steps:

STEP 1 If the window does not already display the Toolbox, click the Toolbox button in the left margin of the window. If necessary, click Common Controls to display the Common Controls tab.

When you point to the Toolbox button, the Toolbox is displayed on the window (Figure 2-6). Notice that the Toolbox hides the Form1 Windows Form object.

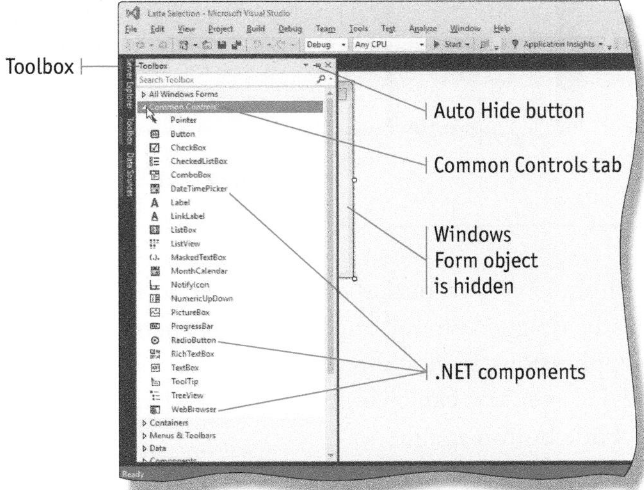

FIGURE 2-6

WATCH OUT FOR

In Figure 2-6, the Common Controls category of tools is open and all its tools are visible. If the Common Controls tab is not expanded, a right triangle appears to the left of the Common Controls tab. To open the tab, click the right triangle.

Among other things, the Toolbox contains many graphical elements called **controls** that you can place on the Windows Form object as GUI objects. For example, the Toolbox contains buttons that can be placed on the Windows Form object. You will learn how to perform this activity in the next section of this chapter.

Permanently Display the Toolbox

When you click outside the Toolbox, it no longer is displayed. When you are designing the GUI, normally it helps to display the Toolbox at all times. To always display the Toolbox, you can complete the following step:

STEP 1 If necessary, click the Toolbox button in the left margin of the window to display the Toolbox. Then, click the Auto Hide button (Pushpin icon) on the Toolbox title bar.

When you click the Auto Hide button, the Pushpin icon on the button changes from being horizontal, which indicates Auto Hide, to vertical, which indicates the Toolbox has been pinned to the window and will remain there (Figure 2-7). Form1 is moved to the right so you can see both the Toolbox and all of Form1.

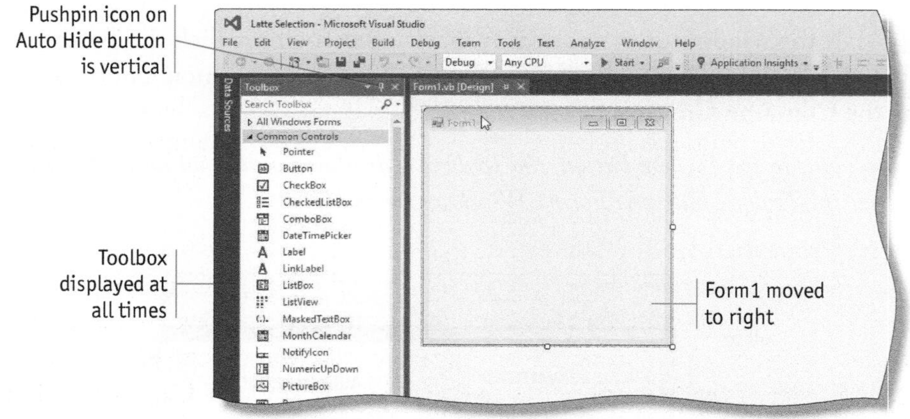

FIGURE 2-7

When the Pushpin icon is vertical, the Toolbox is said to be in Dockable mode, which means it can be dragged around and placed anywhere within the Visual Studio window. In most applications, it should remain on the left side of the window, as shown in Figure 2-7. Later, you can change the Toolbox back to Auto Hide mode by clicking the Auto Hide button again.

HEADS UP

If the Solution Explorer window is not displayed on your screen, you can display the window by completing the following steps:

1. Click View on the menu bar.
2. Click Solution Explorer on the View menu. The Solution Explorer window will be displayed in the location shown in Figure 2-8.

View Object Properties

Every object you create in the user interface, including the Windows Form object, has properties. **Properties** can describe a multitude of characteristics about the object, including its color, size, name, and position on the screen. You will learn about the properties of all the objects you create using the Toolbox.

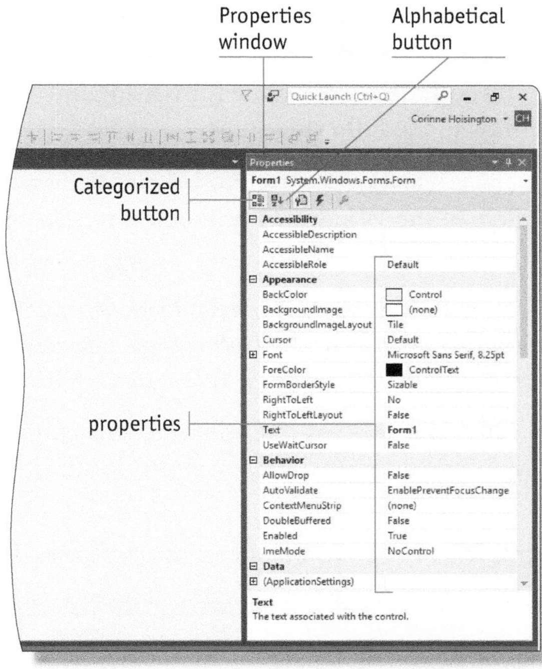

FIGURE 2-8

To view the properties for an object in Visual Studio, you use the Properties window. By default, the Properties window is displayed in the right section of the Visual Studio window (Figure 2-8). Your window might display the Solution Explorer window above the Properties window.

In the **Properties window** shown in Figure 2-8, the property names in the left list appear in Alphabetical view. Many developers find the Alphabetical view the easiest to use when searching for properties. Some developers, however, prefer the Categorized view, in which properties are organized according to type. You can change the order of the properties to Categorized if you click the Categorized button on the Properties window toolbar (see Figure 2-8). In this book, the properties are shown in Alphabetical view, which you select by clicking the Alphabetical button on the Properties window toolbar.

HEADS UP

If you want to reset your Visual Basic window to its original installed layout, you can complete the following steps:

1. Click Window on the menu bar.
2. Click Reset Window Layout on the Window menu.

Name the Windows Form Object

Visual Studio assigns a default name to every object in a Visual Basic GUI. For example, the first Windows Form object in a project is named Form1. In virtually every instance, a developer should assign a meaningful name to an object so the program can reference it if required. The name of an object should reflect the object's use. For example, a good name for the Latte Selection window might be frmLatte-Selection. Notice in the name that each word is capitalized and the remaining letters are lowercase. You should always follow this naming method when naming objects.

No spaces or other special characters are allowed in the object name. Also, by convention, each object name should begin with a prefix that identifies the type of object. For Windows Form objects, the prefix is frm. Therefore, the complete name for the Windows Form object would be frmLatteSelection. The form name should be changed from Form1 to a more descriptive name in the Solution Explorer.

To give the name frmLatteSelection to the form using the Solution Explorer in Figure 2-8, you can complete the following steps:

STEP 1 Click anywhere in the Windows Form object to select it and then click View on the menu bar.

When you click within any object, including a Windows Form object, it is selected (Figure 2-9). Sizing handles and a heavier border surround the selected object. In addition, the Properties window displays the properties of the selected object. When you click View on the menu bar, the View menu is displayed (Figure 2-9).

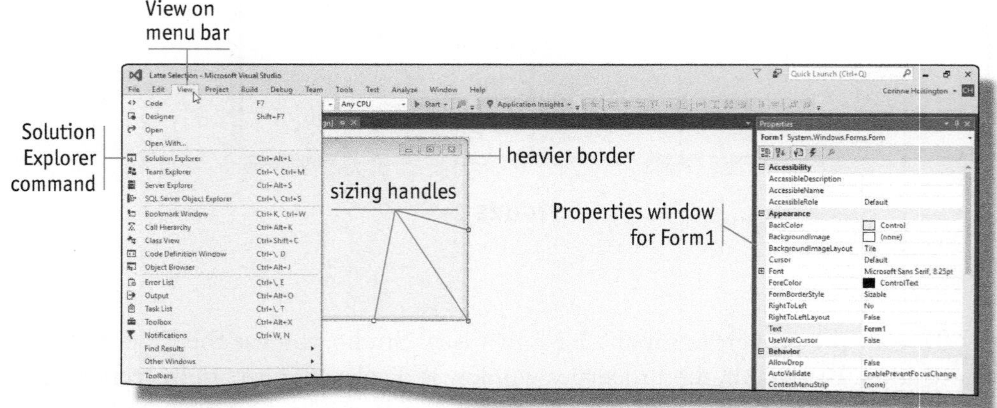

FIGURE 2-9

STEP 2 If necessary, click Solution Explorer on the View menu to display the Solution Explorer. In the Solution Explorer window, right-click the Form1.vb file name to display a shortcut menu with the Rename command.

The shortcut menu for the Form1.vb file appears in the Solution Explorer (Figure 2-10).

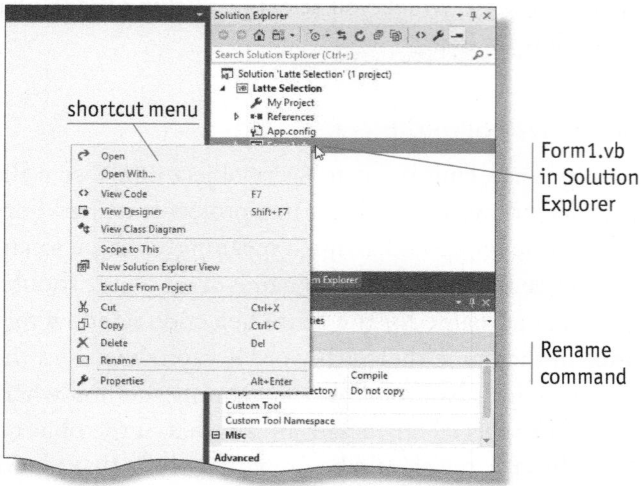

FIGURE 2-10

STEP 3 Click Rename. Type `frmLatteSelection.vb` and press the ENTER key.

The Form1.vb form file is given the new name frmLatteSelection.vb in the Solution Explorer window (Figure 2-11).

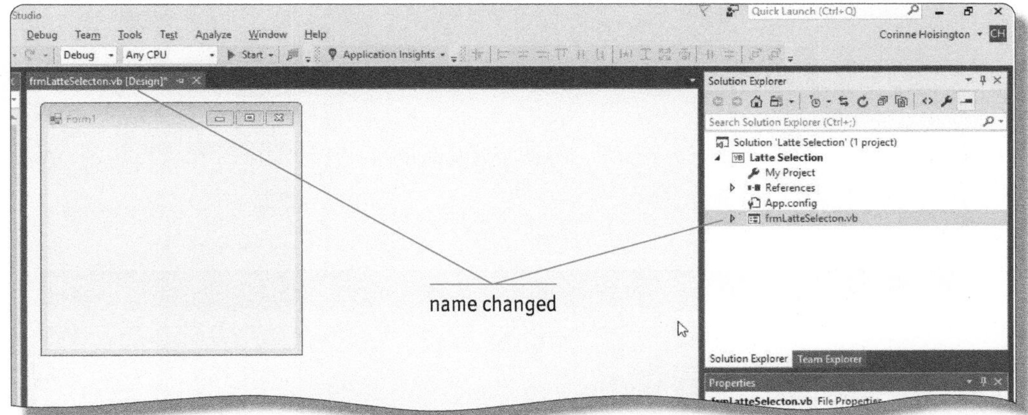

FIGURE 2-11

CONSIDER THIS

Why should you name the Form object?
Later in this text, you add multiple Form objects. It can become confusing if you do not have unique identifying names for each of the Form objects within the project.

Set the Title Bar Text in a Windows Form Object

After you name the Windows Form object, often the next step in GUI design is to change the title bar text to reflect the function of the program. In this example, the name used is Latte Selection. The **Text property** in the Properties window for the Windows Form object contains the value displayed in the title bar of the window. You can set the Text property using the following steps:

STEP 1 Click the Windows Form object and then scroll in the Properties window as necessary until you find the Text property. (Remember that the properties are in alphabetical order.) Then, double-click the Text property in the right column.

The text, Form1, is selected in the Properties window (Figure 2-12). Form1 is the default text value for the first Windows Form object created in a project. Whenever a property is selected, you can change it.

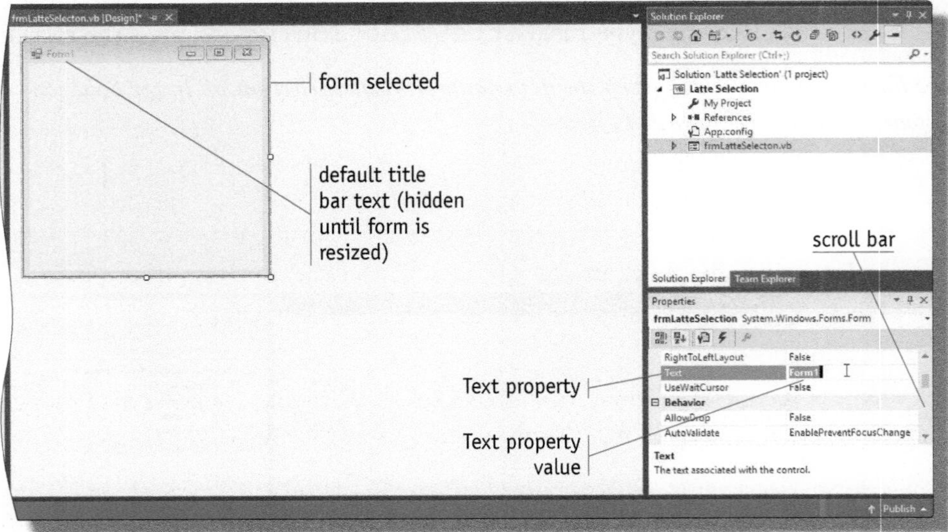

FIGURE 2-12

STEP 2 Type `Latte Selection` and then press the ENTER key. Resize the Form object to view the text at the top.

The value Latte Selection is displayed for the Text property in the Properties window and is partially displayed in the title bar of the Windows Form object (Figure 2-13). You can enter any value you like for the Text property of the Windows Form object.

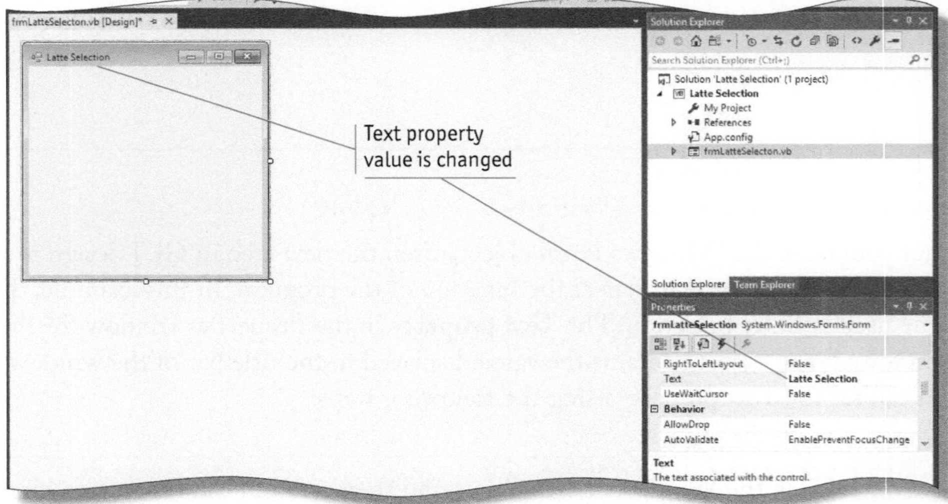

FIGURE 2-13

You can change many of the properties for any object in the GUI using the techniques just illustrated.

Resize a Form

To resize a Windows Form object, you can change the **Size property** in the Properties window to the exact number of horizontal and vertical pixels you desire. As an alternative, you can drag the vertical border to change the width of the window and the horizontal border to change the height. Another way to change the size is to drag a corner sizing handle, which allows you to change the width and height at the same time.

The following step illustrates how to change the Size property of the Windows Form object shown in Figure 2-14:

STEP 1 With the Windows Form object selected, double-click the Size property in the right column. Type 730, 700 and then press the ENTER key.

The Windows Form object has been resized (Figure 2-14). The exact size of the Windows Form object is shown on the status bar as (number of horizontal pixels, number of vertical pixels). In Figure 2-14, the size of the Windows Form object is 730 pixels horizontally by 700 pixels vertically.(Figure 2-14).

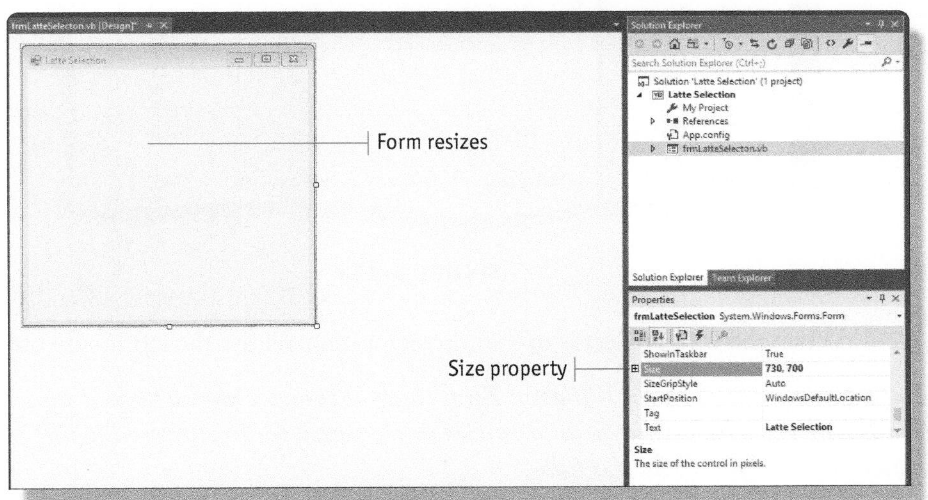

FIGURE 2-14

Adding GUI Objects

After setting up the Windows Form object as necessary for a project, you continue working on the user interface design by adding GUI objects to the form, such as labels, picture boxes, and buttons. Format and position the objects to make the form appealing and easy to use.

Add a Label Object

After sizing the Windows Form object, you can use the Toolbox to add other GUI objects as required. For example, a GUI often displays a message or labels an item in the window. To accomplish this, you can use the **Label .NET component** in the

IN THE REAL WORLD

In addition to dragging a .NET component from the Toolbox to the Windows Form object, you can place an object on the Windows Form object by double-clicking the .NET component in the Toolbox. You can move and resize the object after placing it on the Windows Form object. You also can click the .NET component in the Toolbox and then click the Windows Form object at the desired location for the object. The object will be placed where you clicked. Developers use the technique they find most convenient.

Toolbox to place a **Label object** on the Windows Form object. To add a Label object to a Windows Form object, you can complete the following steps:

STEP 1 Drag the Label .NET component from the Common Controls tab in the Toolbox over the Windows Form object to the approximate location where you want to place the Label object.

The pointer changes to a crosshair and small rectangle when you place it over the Windows Form object (Figure 2-15). The Label object will be placed on the form at the location of the small rectangle in the pointer.

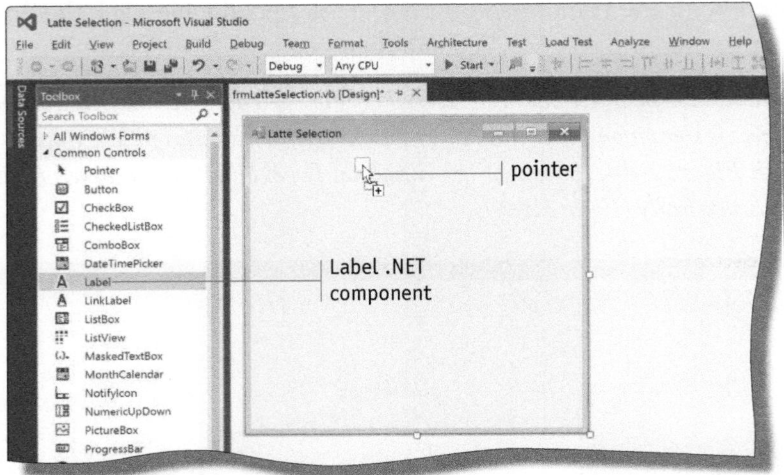

FIGURE 2-15

STEP 2 When the Label object is in the correct location, release the left mouse button.

The Label object is placed on the Windows Form object at the location you selected (Figure 2-16). The label is selected, as identified by the dotted border surrounding it. The default text within the label is Label1.

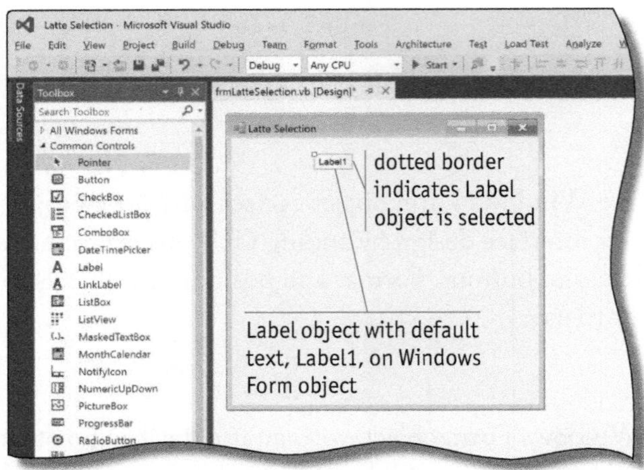

FIGURE 2-16

Name the Label Object

As with most objects you place on the Windows Form object, the first step after creating the object should be to name it. To give the Label object the name Heading with the Label prefix lbl, complete the following step:

STEP 1 With the Label object selected, scroll in the Properties window until you find the (Name) property. Then, double-click the (Name) property in the right column. Type the new name as `lblHeading` and then press the ENTER key.

The name you entered is displayed in the (Name) property in the Properties window (Figure 2-17). You now can reference the Label object by its name in other parts of the program.

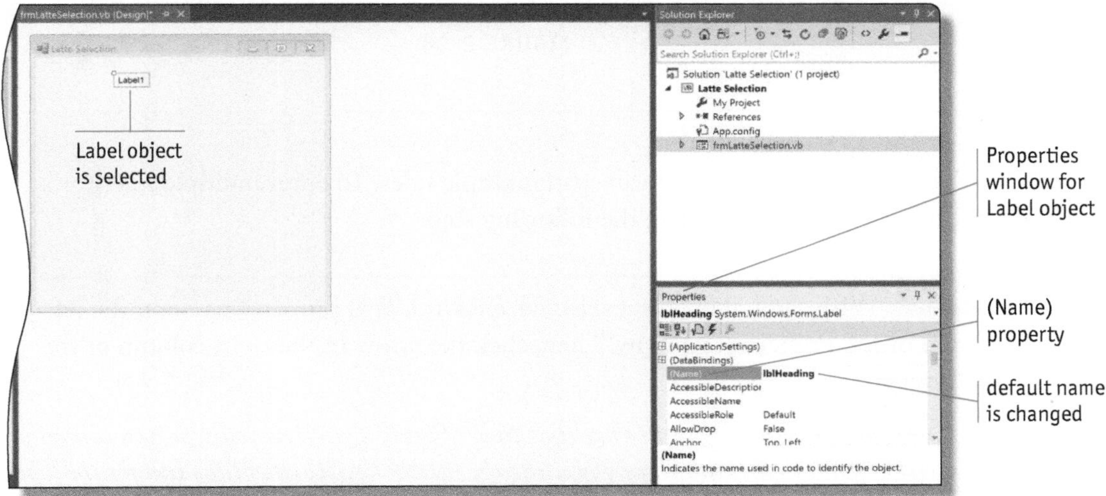

FIGURE 2-17

Change the Text in a Label Object

The default text in a Label object, Label1, normally is not the text you want to display in the label. Therefore, you should change the Text property for the Label object to the value you want. To change the text on the label in Figure 2-16 to Latte Selection, you can complete the following step:

STEP 1 With the Label object selected, scroll in the Properties window until you find the Text property. Then, double-click the value for the Text property in the right column. Type `Latte Selection` for the Text property and press the ENTER key.

The text you entered, Latte Selection, is displayed in the Text property and in the label itself (Figure 2-18). By default, the font size of the text is approximately 8 points. The Label object automatically expanded horizontally to accommodate the text you typed. By default, Label objects change to be the right size for the text in the Text property.

WATCH OUT FOR

If you make an error while typing a property value, such as the name, you can press the BACKSPACE key to erase your mistake and then type the correct data. You also can double-click the property you want to change and start over.

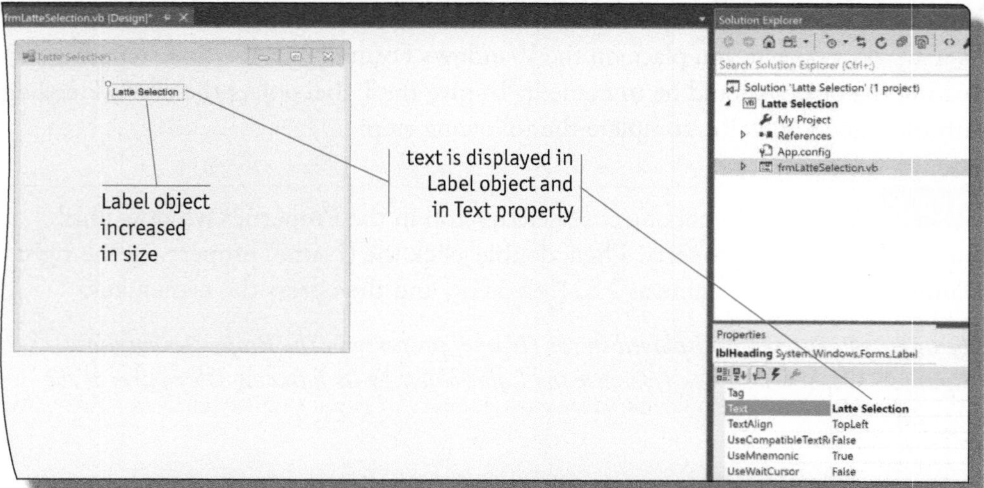

FIGURE 2-18

The text in a Label object can span multiple lines. To enter multiple lines for a Label object, you can complete the following step:

STEP 1 With the Label object selected, click the Text property name in the left column of the Properties window. Then, click the arrow in the right column of the Text property.

A box opens in which you can enter multiple lines (Figure 2-19). As you type, you can move the insertion point to the next line by pressing the ENTER key. To accept the text for the label, press CTRL+ENTER. (In other words, hold down the CTRL key, press the ENTER key, and then release both keys.)

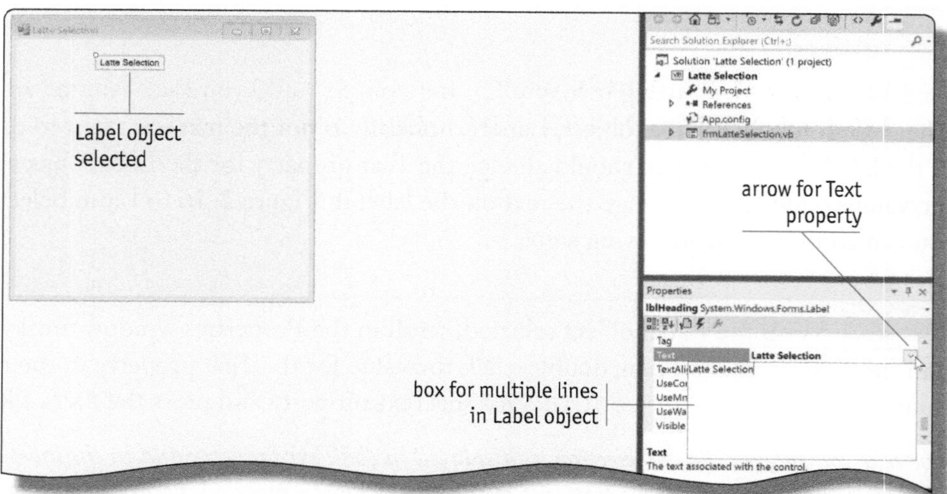

FIGURE 2-19

Change the Label Font, Font Style, and Font Size

The default font, font style, and font size of the text in a Label object often must be changed to reflect the purpose of the label. For example, in a label used as a heading for a window, the text should be larger than the default 8-point font size used for Label objects, and it should be bold to stand out as a heading. To change the font, font style, and font size of a label, you can select the label and then use the **Font property** to make the changes. To change the text in the lblHeading label to Tahoma font, make the font bold, and increase the font size to 16 points, you can complete the following steps:

WATCH OUT FOR

When you click an object to select it, you might double-click it accidentally. If you do, a tabbed page with programming code opens. To return to the form and continue developing the user interface, click the [Design] tab for your form, such as the frmLatteSelection.vb [Design] tab.

STEP 1 Click the Label object to select it. Scroll until you find the Font property in the Properties window. Click the Font property in the left column of the Properties window. Click the ellipsis button for the Font property.

When you click the Font property in the Properties window, a button with an ellipsis (three dots) is displayed in the right column. In the Properties window, an ellipsis button indicates that multiple choices for the property will be made available when you click the button. The Font dialog box is displayed (Figure 2-20). Using the Font dialog box, you can change the font, font style, and size of the text in the Label object.

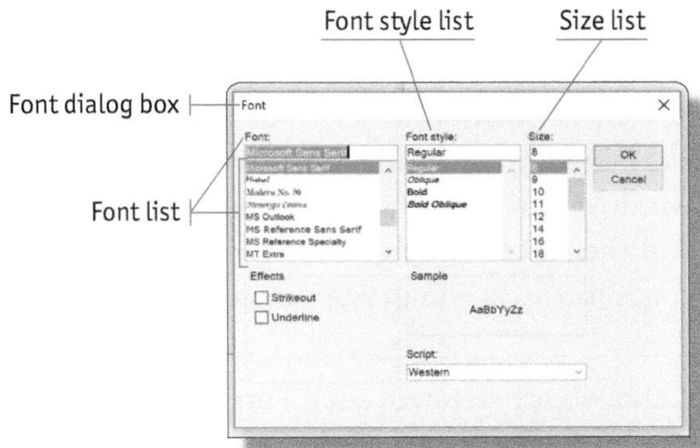

FIGURE 2-20

STEP 2 In the Font dialog box, scroll in the Font list until you find Tahoma and then click it. Click Bold in the Font style list. Click 16 in the Size list.

The selections are highlighted in the Font dialog box (Figure 2-21).

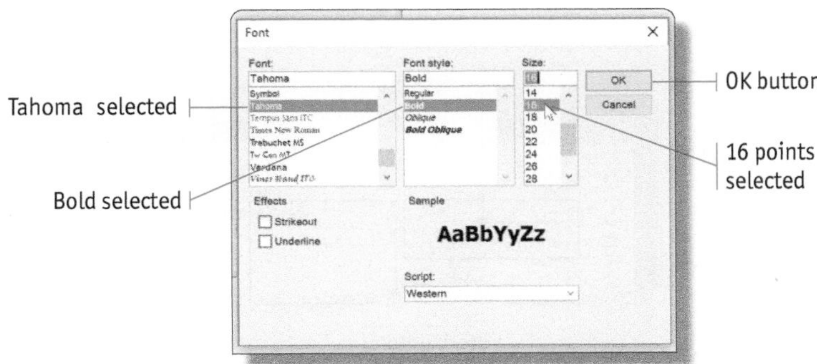

FIGURE 2-21

STEP 3 Click the OK button.

The font, font style, and font size in the Label object are changed as specified in the Font dialog box (Figure 2-22). The Label object automatically expands to accommodate the changed font. The changes also are made for the Font property in the Properties window.

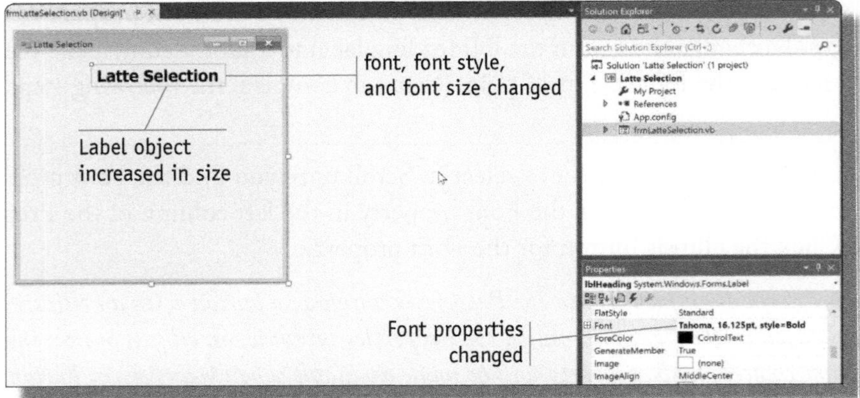

FIGURE 2-22

Center a Label Object in the Windows Form Object

When you place an object on the Windows Form object, your object may not be located in precisely the correct position, so you must align the object in the window. A single label often is centered horizontally in the window; that is, the distance from the left frame of the window to the beginning of the text should be the same as the distance from the end of the text to the right frame of the window. To horizontally center the label that contains the heading, you can complete the following steps:

STEP 1 With the Label object selected, click Format on the menu bar and then point to Center in Form on the Format menu.

The Format menu is displayed and the pointer is located on the Center in Form command (Figure 2-23). The Center in Form submenu also is displayed. The two choices on the Center in Form submenu are Horizontally and Vertically. Horizontally means the label will be centered between the left and the right edge of the window. Vertically means the label will be centered between the top edge and the bottom edge of the window.

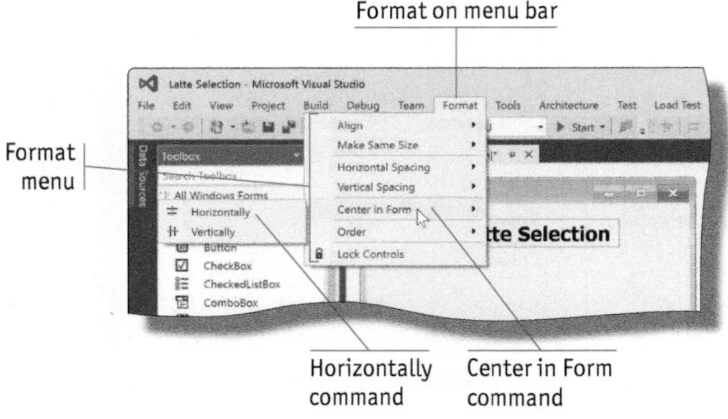

FIGURE 2-23

STEP 2 Click Horizontally on the Center in Form submenu.

The Label object is centered horizontally in the window (Figure 2-24).

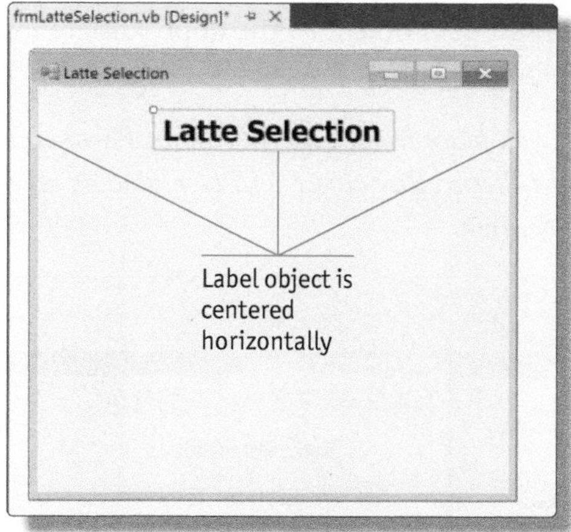

FIGURE 2-24

Aligning objects is an important aspect of user interface design because it makes objects and the interface easy to use. Centering within the Windows Form object is the first of several alignments you will make in this chapter.

Delete GUI Objects

In some instances, you might add an object to the Windows Form object and later discover you do not need the object in the user interface. When this occurs, you should delete the object from the Windows Form object. Visual Studio provides two primary ways to delete an object from the Windows Form object: the keyboard and a shortcut menu. An object can be selected and then deleted by pressing the Delete key on the keyboard.

A second way to delete an object is to use a shortcut menu. To do so, right-click the object to be deleted and then select Delete on the shortcut menu.

Use the Undo Button on the Standard Toolbar

As you work in Visual Studio to create a GUI, you might delete an object or perform another activity that you realize was an error. You can undo an action you just performed by clicking the Undo button on the Standard toolbar.

Add a PictureBox Object

When you want to display a picture in a window, such as the latte pictures shown in Figure 2-1b and Figure 2-1c on pages 26 and 27, respectively, you must place a PictureBox object on the Windows Form object. Then, you place the picture in the PictureBox object. In this section, you will learn to add a PictureBox object to the Windows Form object. In Chapter 3, you will learn how to place a picture in the PictureBox object.

A **PictureBox** is an object much like a label. To add a PictureBox object to the window, you can use the Toolbox, as shown in the following steps:

STEP 1 With the Toolbox visible, drag the PictureBox .NET component on the Toolbox over the Windows Form object to the approximate location where you want the PictureBox object to be displayed.

The pointer changes when you place it over the Windows Form object (Figure 2-25). The upper-left corner of the PictureBox object will be placed on the form at the location of the small square in the pointer.

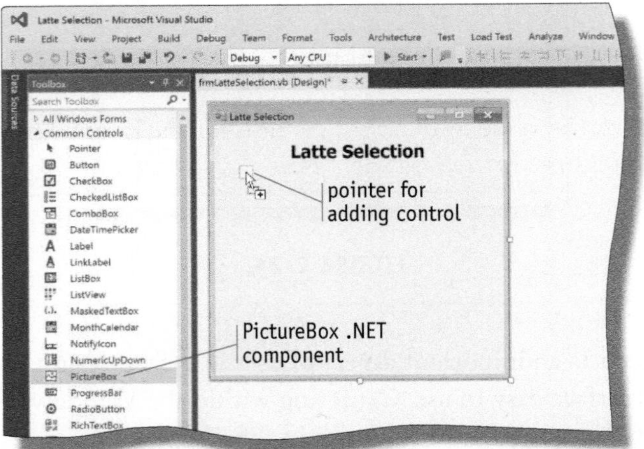

FIGURE 2-25

STEP 2 When the pointer is in the correct location, release the left mouse button.

A PictureBox object is placed on the Windows Form object in the default size (Figure 2-26). The PictureBox object is selected, as indicated by the sizing handles and the heavier border. Notice that when the pointer is inside the PictureBox object, it changes to a crosshair with four arrowheads. This indicates you can drag the PictureBox object anywhere on the Windows Form object.

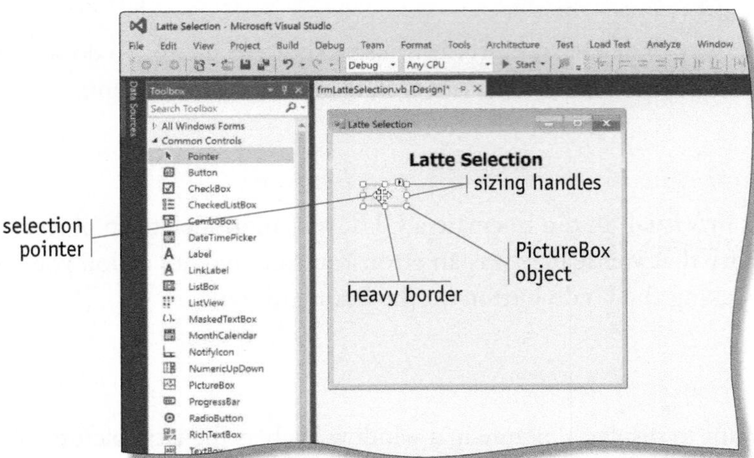

FIGURE 2-26

As you can see, placing a PictureBox object on the Windows Form object is similar to placing a Label object on the Windows Form object. You can use the same technique for most objects within the Toolbox.

Name a PictureBox Object

When you add an object to the Windows Form object, your next action should be to name the object. The technique for naming a PictureBox object is identical to that for a Label object, except that the prefix for a PictureBox object is pic. For example, to give the name picPumpkin to the PictureBox object just added to the form, you can complete the following steps:

Step 1: Select the PictureBox object.
Step 2: Locate the (Name) property in the Properties window for the PictureBox object.
Step 3: Double-click the value in the right column for the (Name) property, type picPumpkin as the name, and then press the ENTER key.

Resize a PictureBox Object

When you place a PictureBox object on the Windows Form object, it often is not the size required for the application. You can resize a PictureBox object using the same technique you used to resize the Windows Form object. Complete the following step to resize the PictureBox object:

STEP 1 Double-click to the right of the Size property of the PictureBox object, type `300, 250`, and then press the ENTER key.

When you change the Size property, the width and height of the PictureBox object are changed. In Figure 2-27, the width and height of the PictureBox object are increased. The actual size of the PictureBox object in pixels (300 horizontal pixels, 250 vertical pixels) is shown on the status bar.

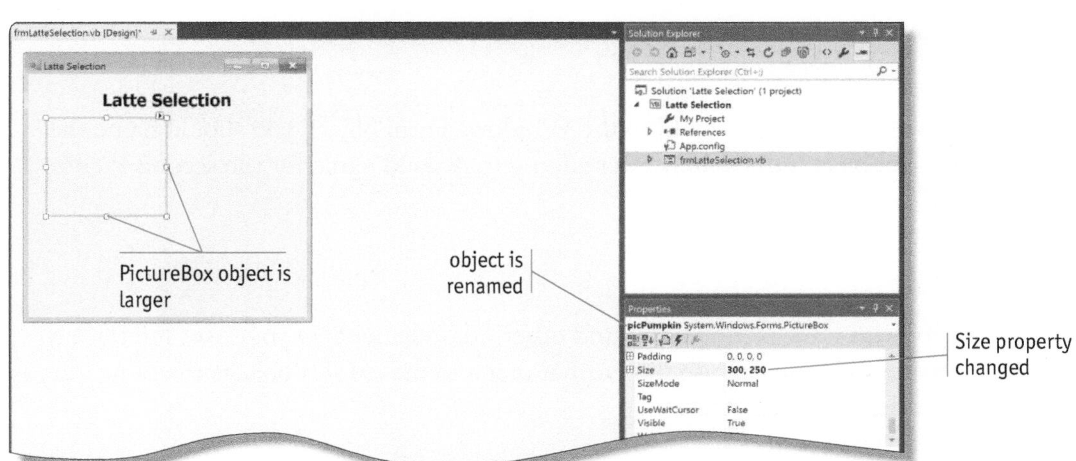

FIGURE 2-27

CRITICAL THINKING

If I want to place an image as the background of a Form object, should a PictureBox object be stretched to cover the entire form?
Instead of placing a form-sized image as the background, click the Form object and select the BackgroundImage property.

HEADS UP

The Size property will change to the new size in the Properties window. If you know the exact size you want, you can enter it directly in the Size property for that object.

Add a Second PictureBox Object

You can add a second PictureBox object to the Windows Form object by performing the same technique you used previously, as in the following step:

STEP 1 Drag the PictureBox .NET component in the Toolbox to any location in the Windows Form object, and then release the left mouse button.

The PictureBox object is placed on the Windows Form object (Figure 2-28). Notice that the PictureBox objects in Figure 2-28 are of different sizes. If you see a blue line as you drag the PictureBox object onto the Windows Form object, ignore it. You will learn about these lines later in this chapter.

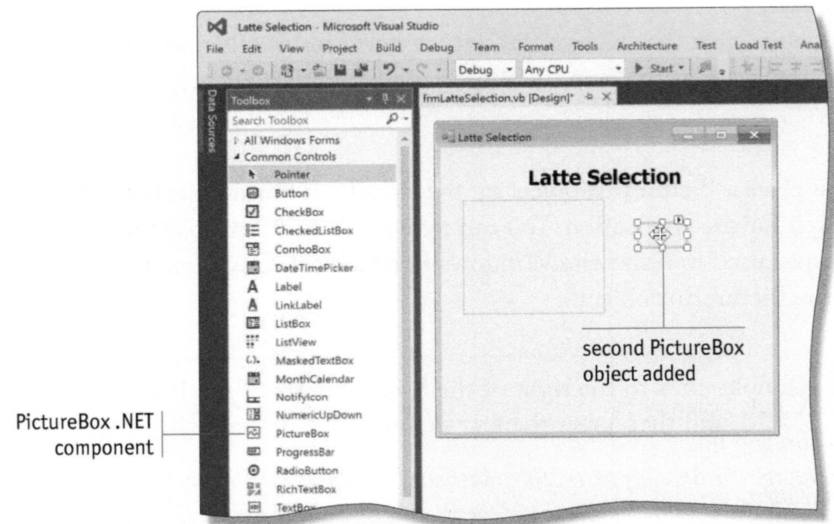

FIGURE 2-28

> **HEADS UP**
> When you want to select multiple objects, you can hold down the CTRL key as you click each object. Objects you previously selected will remain selected and the objects you click will be selected as well.

As with all objects you add to the Windows Form object, you should name the PictureBox object immediately after adding it. A good name for the second PictureBox object is picMocha.

Make Objects the Same Size

Often you will want picture boxes and other GUI elements in your user interface to be the same size. You can use the Format menu to make GUI objects the same size, as shown in the following steps:

STEP 1 Select the object whose size you want to duplicate (in this example, the left PictureBox object in the window), hold down the CTRL key, and then click the object you want to resize (the right PictureBox object in the window).

The left and right PictureBox objects are selected (Figure 2-29). The left PictureBox object is surrounded by white sizing handles and the right PictureBox object is surrounded by black sizing handles, which indicates the left PictureBox object is the controlling object when sizing or alignment commands are executed. The first object selected always is the controlling object.

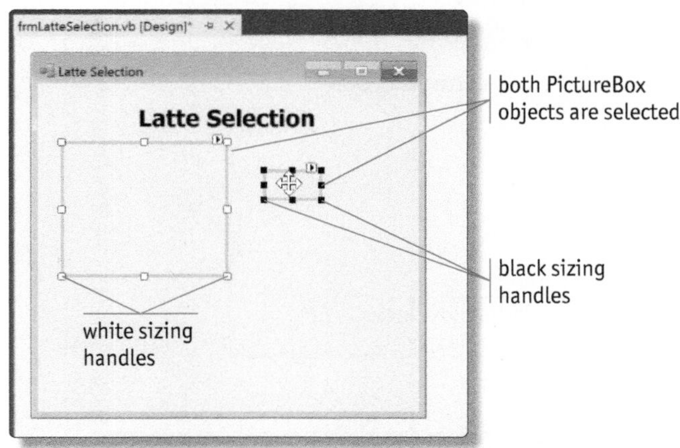

FIGURE 2-29

STEP 2 Click Format on the menu bar and then point to the Make Same Size command on the Format menu.

The Format menu and the Make Same Size submenu are displayed (Figure 2-30). The Make Same Size submenu provides commands to make the width, height, or both dimensions the same as the controlling object.

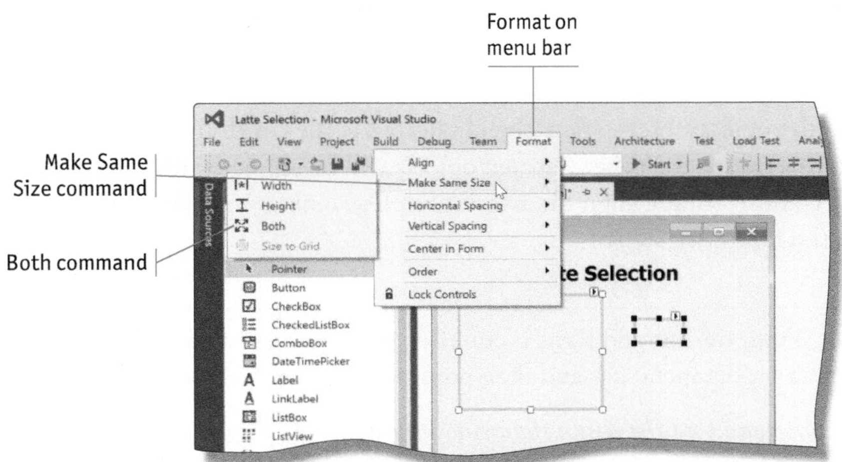

FIGURE 2-30

STEP 3 Click Both on the Make Same Size submenu.

Visual Studio changes the size of the right PictureBox object to match the size of the left PictureBox object (Figure 2-31). Both the width and the height of the right PictureBox object are changed.

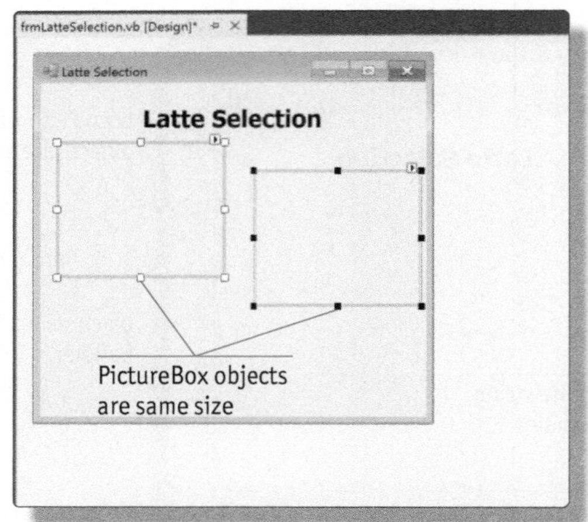

FIGURE 2-31

Align the PictureBox Objects

Notice in Figure 2-31 that the left PictureBox object is higher in the form than the right PictureBox object. When designing a GUI, you should consider aligning the elements to create a clean, uncluttered look for the user. **Alignment** means one element in the GUI is lined up horizontally (left and right) or vertically (up and down) with another element in the window. For example, in Figure 2-31 the GUI would look better if the PictureBox objects were aligned horizontally so their tops and bottoms were even across the window.

When you want to align objects that are already on the Windows Form object, select the objects to align and then specify the alignment you want. As you saw when changing the object size, the first object selected is the controlling object; when aligning, this means the other selected objects will be aligned with the first object selected. To horizontally align the two PictureBox objects in Figure 2-31, you can perform the following steps:

STEP 1 With the left and right PictureBox objects selected, as shown in Figure 2-31, click Format on the menu bar and then point to Align on the Format menu.

The Format menu and the Align submenu are displayed (Figure 2-32). The left PictureBox object is the controlling object, as indicated by the white sizing handles, so the right PictureBox object will be aligned horizontally with the left PictureBox object.

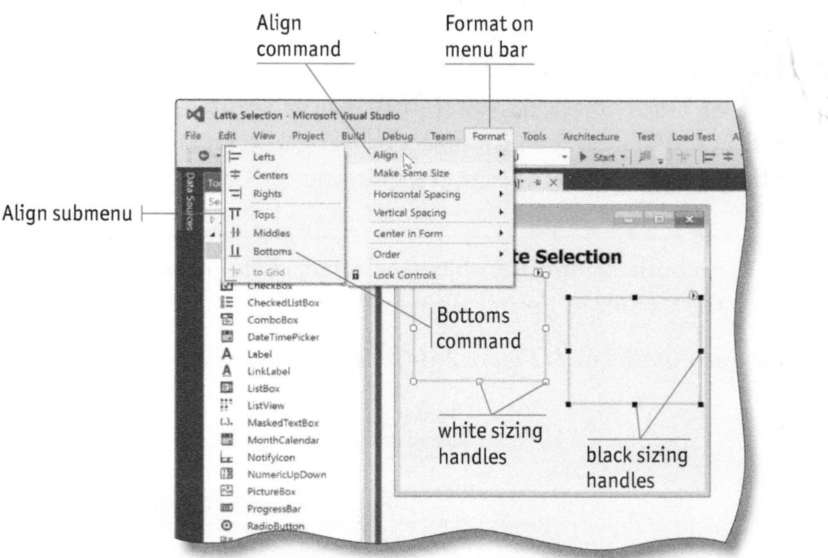

FIGURE 2-32

STEP 2 Click Bottoms on the Align submenu.

The bottom of the right PictureBox object is aligned horizontally with the bottom of the left PictureBox object (Figure 2-33). Because the PictureBox objects are the same size, the tops also are aligned.

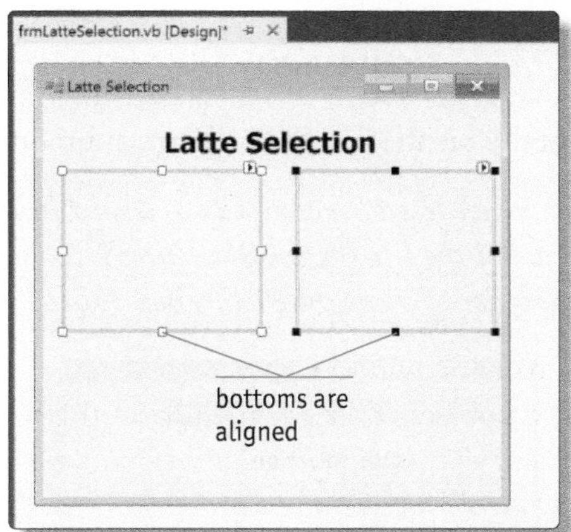

FIGURE 2-33

Notice on the Align submenu in Figure 2-32 that Visual Studio offers seven choices for alignment. When you are aligning objects horizontally, you should choose from the Tops, Middles, and Bottoms group. When you are aligning objects vertically, you should choose from the Lefts, Centers, and Rights group. You will learn how to align to a grid later in this book.

Center Multiple Objects Horizontally in the Window

From Figure 2-33, you can see that the PictureBox objects are not centered horizontally in the Windows Form object. As you learned, you can center one or more objects horizontally within the Windows Form object by using a command from the Format menu. To center the two PictureBox objects as a unit, you can complete the following steps:

STEP 1 With both PictureBox objects selected, click Format on the menu bar and then point to the Center in Form command.

The Format menu is displayed (Figure 2-34). The Center in Form submenu also is displayed.

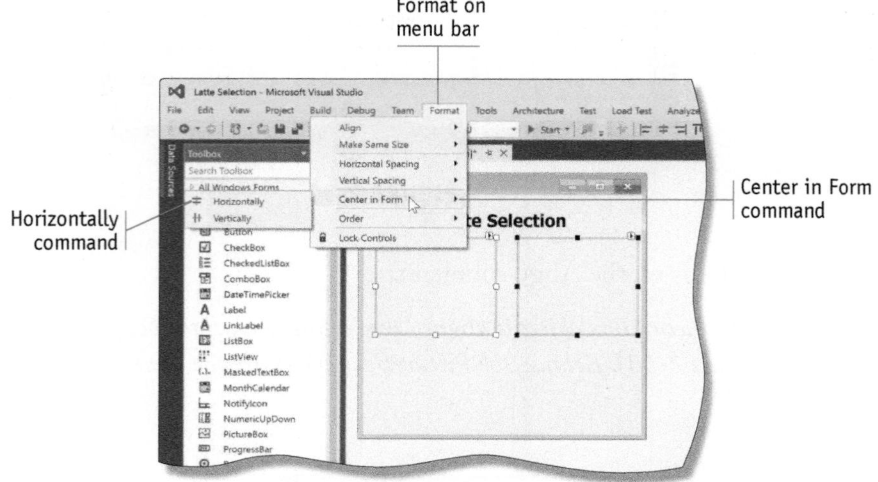

FIGURE 2-34

STEP 2 Click Horizontally on the Center in Form submenu.

The two PictureBox objects are centered horizontally as a unit in the Windows Form object (Figure 2-35). The left border of the left PictureBox object is the same distance from the window frame as the right border of the right PictureBox object.

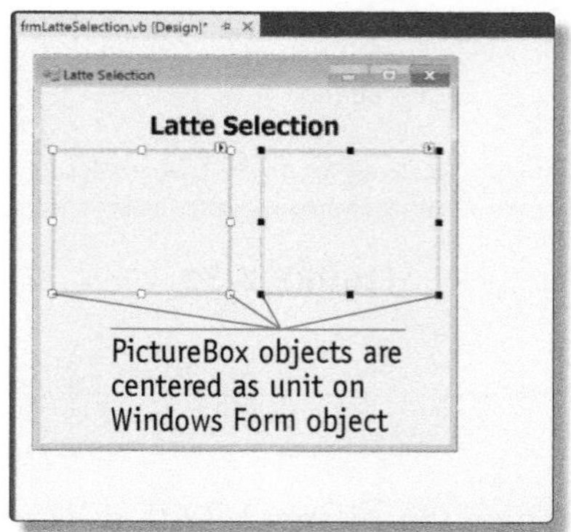

FIGURE 2-35

Adding an object, naming it, sizing it, and aligning it are basic to GUI design.

Add a Button Object

A **Button object** is commonly used in a GUI. For example, you probably are familiar with the OK button used in many applications. Generally, when the program is executing, buttons are used to cause an event to occur. To place a Button object on the Windows Form object, you use the Toolbox. To create a Button object, you can complete the following steps:

STEP 1 With the Toolbox displayed in the Visual Studio window, drag the Button control in the Toolbox over the Windows Form object to the position where you want to place the button below the first PictureBox object.

When you drag the button over the Windows Form object, the pointer changes (Figure 2-36). The upper-left corner of the Button object will be placed at the lower-left corner of the rectangle.

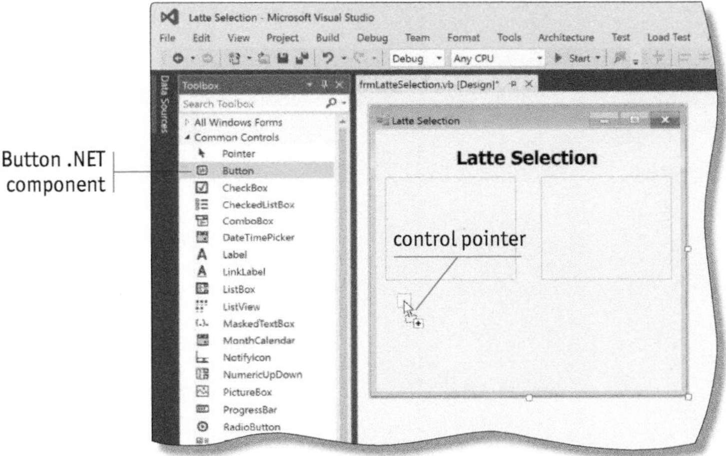

FIGURE 2-36

STEP 2 When the pointer is positioned properly, release the left mouse button.

A standard-sized Button object is added to the Windows Form object (Figure 2-37). The text on the button is the default, Button1. The button is selected, as indicated by the heavier border and sizing handles.

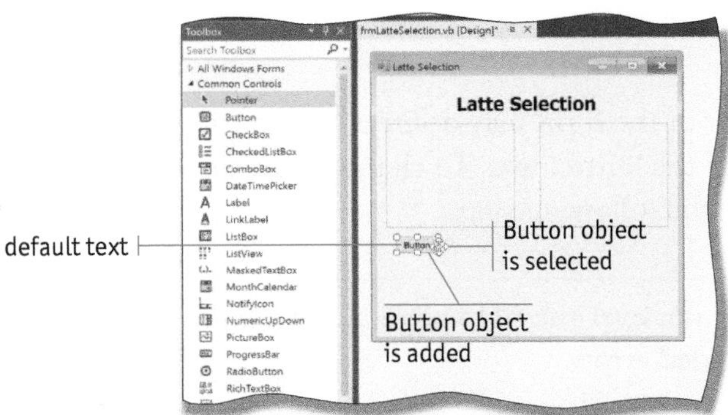

FIGURE 2-37

> **HEADS UP**
>
> In this chapter, you have named four different objects: a Windows Form object, a Label object, a PictureBox object, and a Button object. As you learned, each object name should have a prefix that identifies the type of object. In this chapter, the prefixes are:
>
> | Type of Object | Name Prefix |
> |---|---|
> | Windows Form object | frm |
> | Label object | lbl |
> | PictureBox object | pic |
> | Button object | btn |

Name and Set Text for a Button Object

As with other objects you add to the Windows Form object, the first step after adding the Button object is to name it. A Button object name should begin with the prefix btn. For example, the name for the button you just added could be btnPumpkin.

In most cases, you also will change the text that appears on the Button object. To change the text on the btnPumpkin button, you can do the following:

STEP 1 With the Button object selected, scroll in the Properties window until you find the Text property. Double-click the Text value in the right column, type `Pumpkin Spice`, and then press the ENTER key.

The text for the Pumpkin Spice button is changed on the button and in the Properties window (Figure 2-38). Notice that the text in the button is not fully displayed.

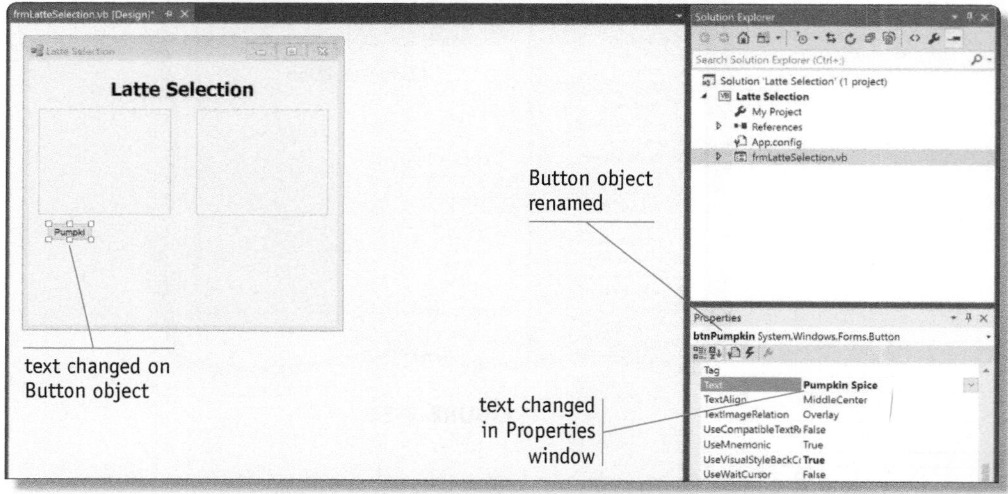

FIGURE 2-38

Change a Button Object's Size

Sometimes, the designer of the form may desire a large button or the button may not be big enough to display the button text. To change a Button object's size to a larger width, you can perform the following steps:

STEP 1 Place the pointer over the right edge of the Button object until the pointer changes to a double-headed arrow.

The pointer changes to a double-headed arrow, which indicates you can drag the border of the button to increase or decrease its size (Figure 2-39).

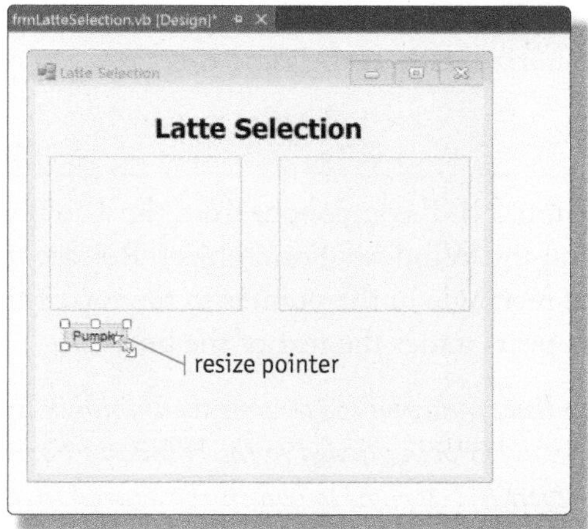

FIGURE 2-39

STEP 2 Drag the pointer to the right to increase the button's width, and then release the left mouse button.

As you drag the pointer to the right, the button becomes wider (Figure 2-40).

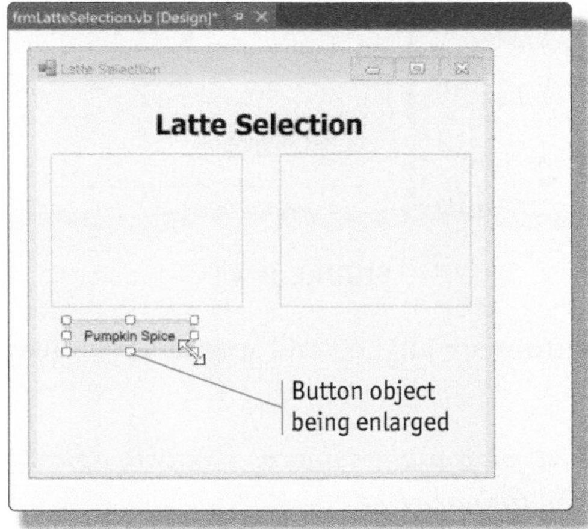

FIGURE 2-40

To move a Button object, first place the pointer on the button; when the pointer changes to a crosshair with four arrowheads, drag the button to any location on the Windows Form object. You can move other objects on the Windows Form object using the same technique.

> **IN THE REAL WORLD**
>
> Some developers use the AutoSize property for a Button object to ensure that the button always is large enough for the text. By setting the AutoSize property for a Button object to True in the Properties window, the Button object will expand or contract when you change the text so it fits precisely in the button.

Add and Align a Second Button

Often, a window requires more than one button. When a second button is added to the window, a normal requirement is to align the buttons. As with PictureBox objects, you can align Button objects horizontally or vertically.

With the PictureBox objects, you saw that you can align objects after placing them on the Windows Form object. You also can align objects when you place them on the Windows Form object. To add a second button to the Windows Form object in Figure 2-40 and align it horizontally at the same time, you can complete the following steps:

STEP 1 Drag the Button .NET component from the Toolbox to the right of the Pumpkin Spice button on the Windows Form object. Release the mouse button, and then align the top of the rectangle in the pointer to the top of the Pumpkin Spice button until a red line appears under the text of the buttons.

*The red line, called a **snap line**, indicates the text on the Pumpkin Spice button is aligned with the text on the Button object being added to the Windows Form object (Figure 2-41). You can drag the Button object left or right to obtain the desired spacing between the buttons. If the red line disappears while you are dragging, move the pointer up or down until the red line reappears, signaling the objects are aligned horizontally.*

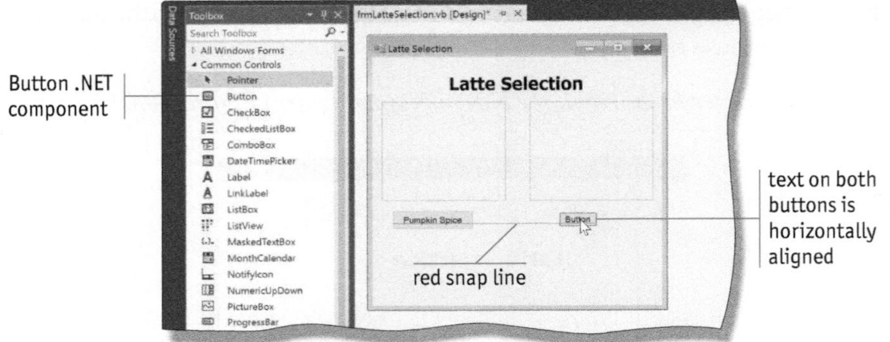

FIGURE 2-41

STEP 2 When the buttons are aligned and spaced as you like, release the left mouse button.

The Button object is aligned horizontally with the Pumpkin Spice button (Figure 2-42). The text of each button is on the same line.

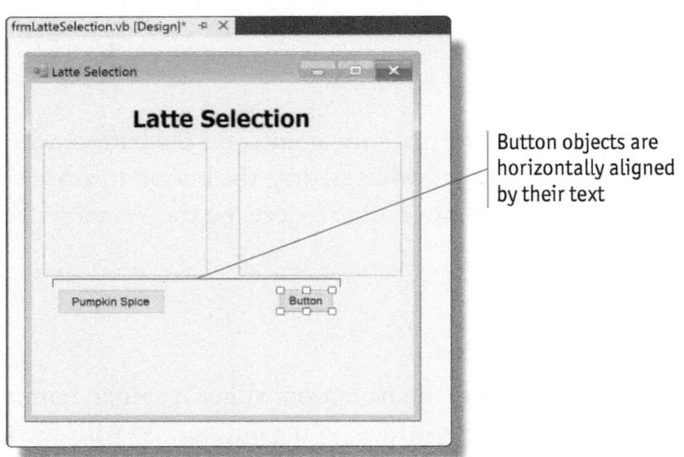

FIGURE 2-42

After adding the second Button object, you should name it, change the text as needed, and size the Button object if necessary. Assume you have named the second Button object btnMocha, changed the button text to Mocha, and made the two buttons the same size. Recall that you can make the Mocha button the same size as the Pumpkin Spice button by completing the following steps:

Step 1: Click the Pumpkin Spice button and then, while holding down the CTRL key, click the Mocha button.
Step 2: Click Format on the menu bar, point to Make Same Size on the Format menu, and then click Both on the Make Same Size submenu.
Step 3: To deselect the Button objects, click anywhere on the Windows Form object except on another object.

Align Objects Vertically

The buttons in Figure 2-42 are aligned horizontally, but they also can be aligned vertically. To illustrate this point and to use snap lines to align objects that are already on the Windows Form object, assume that the Pumpkin Spice and Mocha buttons are aligned vertically on the left side of the Windows Form object, with the Pumpkin Spice button above the Mocha button. To align the Button objects vertically, you can complete the following steps:

STEP 1 If necessary, click anywhere in the Windows Form object to deselect any other objects. Then, slowly drag the Mocha button below the Pumpkin Spice button until vertical blue snap lines are displayed.

*As you drag, **blue snap lines** indicate when the sides of the objects are aligned vertically. In Figure 2-43, the buttons are the same size, so when the left side of the Pumpkin Spice button is aligned with the left side of the Mocha button, the right sides are aligned as well. As a result, two blue vertical lines are displayed. If you drag the button a little more to the left or right, the buttons will not be aligned and the blue lines will disappear.*

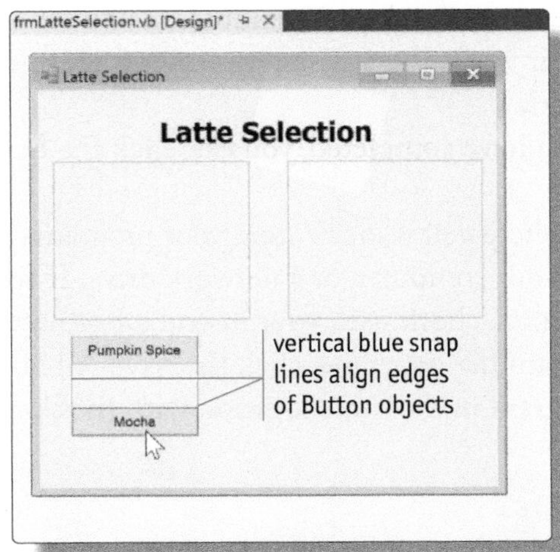

FIGURE 2-43

STEP 2 When the blue lines appear, indicating the buttons are aligned vertically, drag the Mocha button up or down to create the proper spacing between the buttons, and then release the left mouse button.

The proper vertical distance between the buttons is a judgment call based on the needs of the application, the size of the Windows Form object, and the number of other elements in the window (Figure 2-44). As with many aspects of GUI design, the eye of the developer is critical when placing objects in the window.

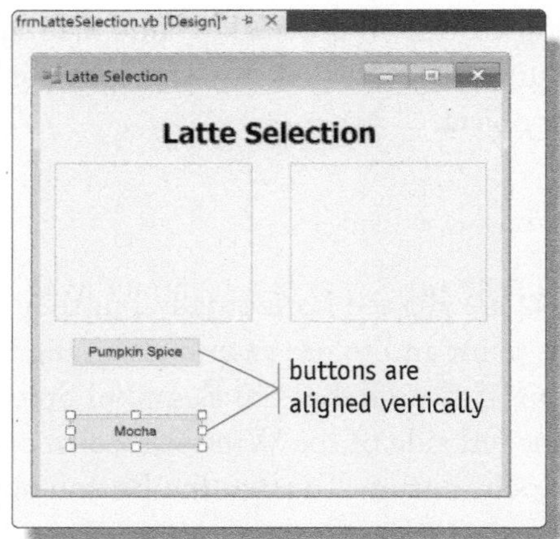

FIGURE 2-44

The use of red and blue snap lines allows you to align objects on the Windows Form object by dragging instead of selecting the objects and using the Format menu.

Visual Studio offers a variety of tools to create and align elements in the GUI, and to make the user interface as effective and useful as possible.

Saving, Closing, and Opening a Visual Basic Project

As you are working on a Visual Basic project, you must save your work on a regular basis. Some developers save every 10 to 20 minutes, while others might wait for a natural break to save their work. Regardless, it is important to develop the habit of regularly saving your work.

To save the work you have comp can click the Save All button on the Standard toolbar.

Select the location where you want to store your program. You might use a USB drive, the hard drive on your computer, or a network drive. If you have questions about where to store your program, check with your instructor or network administrator. After you save the program the first time, click the Save All button on the Standard toolbar to save your program in the same location with the same name.

Close Visual Studio 2017

To close Visual Studio, you can click the Close button to the right of the title bar in the Visual Studio window.

Open a Visual Basic Project

After you save a project and close Visual Studio, you often will want to open the project and work on it again. To open a saved project, you can use one of several methods:

Method 1: Double-click the solution file in the folder where it is stored. This method opens the solution and allows you to continue your work.

Method 2: With Visual Studio open, click the Open File button on the Standard toolbar, locate the solution file, and open it in the same manner you do for most Windows programs.

Method 3: With Visual Studio open, click File on the menu bar and then point to Recent Projects and Solutions on the File menu. A list of recent projects is displayed. Click the name of the project you want to open. This method might not work well if you are not using your own computer because other projects might be listed.

After using one of these methods, you can continue working on your project.

WATCH OUT FOR

Sometimes when you open a Visual Basic project, the Form1.vb[Design] tabbed page is not displayed. (This page is renamed frmLatteSelection.vb in your project.) To display the page, double-click Form1 or the new name of this project, frmLatteSelection.vb, which appears in the Solution Explorer window in the upper-right section of the Visual Studio window.

Program Development Life Cycle

Now that you have learned the necessary skills to design a user interface in Visual Studio and Visual Basic, you are ready to learn about the program development life cycle. The **program development life cycle** is a set of phases and steps that developers follow to design, create, and maintain a computer program. The phases of the program development life cycle are as follows:

1. **Gather and Analyze the Program Requirements** — The developer must obtain information that identifies the program requirements and then document these requirements.
2. **Design the User Interface** — After the developer understands the program requirements, the next step is to design the user interface. The user interface provides the framework for the processing that will occur within the program.
3. **Design the Program Processing Objects** — A computer program consists of one or more processing objects that perform the tasks required by the program. The developer must determine what processing objects are required and then determine the requirements of each object.
4. **Code the Program** — After a processing object has been designed, the object must be implemented in program code. **Program code** is the set of instructions, written using a programming language such as Visual Basic 2017, that a computer executes.
5. **Test the Program** — As the program is being coded, and after the coding is completed, the developer should test the program code to ensure it is executing properly. The testing process is ongoing and includes a variety of stages.
6. **Document the Program/System** — As a program is being designed and coded, and after the process is completed, the developer should document the program. **Documenting a program** means using a prescribed method to write down the instructions for using the program, the way the program performs its tasks, and other items that users, developers, and management might require.

7. **Maintain the Program/System** — After a program is put into use, it probably will have to be modified in the future. For example, if a third type of latte is added to the Latte Selection program, it must be changed to reflect the new latte type. The process of changing and updating programs is called **program and system maintenance**.

The program development life cycle rarely is accomplished in a linear fashion, with one phase completed before the next phase starts. Rather, programs are developed iteratively, which means phases and steps within phases might have to be repeated several times before the program is completed. For example, the requirements for a program might change after the developer has begun coding the program. If so, the developer must return to Phase 1 and gather and document the new requirements. Then, changes might be needed to the user interface or other parts of the program to accommodate the updated requirements. This process of moving back and forth within the program development cycle is normal when developing a computer program.

The next sections in this chapter explain Phase 1 and Phase 2 of the program development life cycle in more detail. The remaining phases are explained in Chapter 3.

Phase 1: Gather and Analyze the Program Requirements

An old programming adage states, "If you don't understand the problem to be solved, you will never develop a solution." While this seems self-evident, too often a program does not perform as desired because the designer did not understand the problem to be solved. Before beginning the user interface design, it is mandatory that the developer understands the problem.

In many programming projects, the developer is responsible for gathering program requirements by interviewing users, reviewing current procedures, and completing other fact-gathering tasks. The emphasis in this book is on learning to program using the Visual Basic 2017 language, so the process of gathering program requirements is beyond the scope of the book. You will be given the program requirements for each program in this book.

When the requirements have been determined, they must be documented so the developers can proceed to design and implement the program. The exact form of the requirements documentation can vary significantly. The format and amount of documentation might be dictated by the application itself or by the documentation standards of the organization for which the program is being developed. For Windows Classic Desktop applications in this book, two types of requirements documentation will be provided for you. The first is the requirements document.

A **requirements document** identifies the purpose of the program being developed, the application title, the procedures to be followed when using the program, any equations and calculations required by the program, any conditions within the program that must be tested, notes and restrictions that the program must follow, and any other comments that would be helpful to understanding the problem.

Recall that the program being developed in this chapter and Chapter 3 is the Latte Selection program (see Figure 2-1 on pages 26 and 27). The requirements document for the Latte Selection program is shown in Figure 2-45.

REQUIREMENTS DOCUMENT

Date Submitted:	January 23, 2019
Application Title:	Latte Selection
Purpose:	The Latte Selection program will allow a user to select a type of latte.
Program Procedures:	From a window on the screen, the user should view two different latte types and then make a latte selection.
Algorithms, Processing, and Conditions:	1. The user must be able to view choices for a pumpkin spice and mocha latte until the user selects a latte type. 2. When the user chooses a latte type, a picture of the selected type should appear in the window. 3. Only one picture should be displayed at a time, so if a user chooses pumpkin spice latte, only its picture should be displayed. If a user then chooses mocha latte, its picture should be displayed instead of pumpkin spice latte. 4. When the user makes a latte selection, a confirming message should be displayed. In addition, the user should be prevented from identifying a latte flavor after making the latte selection. 5. After the user makes a latte selection, the only allowable action is to exit the window.
Notes and Restrictions:	The user should be able to make a latte selection only after choosing a latte type.
Comments:	The pictures shown in the window should be selected from pictures available on the web.

FIGURE 2-45

The requirements document contains all the information a developer needs to design the program. In an event-driven program such as the Latte Selection program, however, one additional document often is needed to clarify for the developer what should occur in the program. This document is the Use Case Definition.

A **use case** is a sequence of actions a user will perform when using the program. The **Use Case Definition** specifies each of these sequences by describing what the user will do and how the program will respond. The Use Case Definition for the Latte Selection program is shown in Figure 2-46.

IN THE REAL WORLD

The general term *users* in this text can refer to widely different groups of people. In some cases, actual users of the program, such as bank tellers and their management for a banking application, must approve the user interface design. Not every teller must approve the design, of course, but a representative group should be involved in the process.

In other cases, *users* might refer to people who represent the actual users. For example, in the Latte Selection program in this chapter, not all the people who might order at a coffee shop have to approve the user interface design. The coffee shop chain might select certain customers to participate in a focus group, review the user interface, and make their comments.

The important point is that actual users or their representatives should review the interface. Then, management can give the final approval.

USE CASE DEFINITION

1. User clicks Pumpkin Spice or Mocha button.
2. Program displays a picture of the latte chosen by the user and enables the latte selection button.
3. User clicks latte flavor buttons to view the flavors of latte as desired.
   Program displays the picture of the chosen latte flavor.
4. User clicks the Select Latte button.
5. Program displays a latte selection confirmation message, and disables both latte flavor buttons and the Select Latte button. The Exit Window button becomes active.
6. User exits the program by clicking the Exit Window button.

FIGURE 2-46

As you can see, the Use Case Definition specifies the actions that the user performs and the actions the program must take in response.

The Use Case Definition is an important part of the requirements documentation for two reasons: (1) It defines for the developer exactly what will occur as the user operates the program. (2) It allows users to review the requirements documentation and ensure that the specifications are correct before the developer begins designing the program.

When gathering and documenting the program requirements, it is critical that users be involved. After all, the program is being developed for their use. When the users concur that the requirements documentation is correct, the developer can move forward into the design phases of the program with confidence that it will fulfill users' needs.

For the programs you will design in this book, the program requirements, including the requirements document and the Use Case Definition, will be provided to you. However, be aware that in many cases in the industry, an experienced developer must gather the requirements as well as implement them in a program.

Phase 2: Design the User Interface

Virtually all programs developed for a GUI are driven by the user's actions within the interface. These actions dictate the processing that the program should execute. Therefore, by designing the user interface, the developer will obtain a foundation for designing the rest of the program. By designing the user interface early in the design process, the developer also can interact with users and ensure that the interface will fulfill their requirements.

Expert program developers recognize the importance of the GUI. These developers spend 25 to 40 percent of program design on the user interface, which sometimes is called the **presentation layer** of the program because it is so critical to the program's success. Mobile devices use small screens, so an easy-to-follow user interface assists in clear navigation that relies on fingers instead of keyboard input.

In the past, developers would draw the user interface on paper and present the drawings to users for their approval. When using Visual Studio 2017, however, the developer should use the program's rapid application development tools to create the user interface. The interface is created with no functionality; that is, none of the buttons or other GUI elements will cause processing to occur. Often, these interface designs are called **mock-ups** because they are provided only for approval of the design. When the users or others approve the interface design, the developer can design the program elements required to implement the functions of the program.

An additional benefit of using Visual Studio to design the user interface is that you can use the completed design in the actual program; you do not have to re-create the design using other software.

CONSIDER THIS

My boss at my programming job asked me to design a prototype for the layout of the user interface. What is a prototype?
A prototype is a model of a software product or information system built for customer approval. It is similar to a mock-up of a user interface.

Principles of User Interface Design

Because the presentation layer of the program is so important, a number of principles and guidelines have been developed over the years for user interface design. **User experience design (UX)** is the process of enhancing user satisfaction by improving the usability and accessibility provided in the interaction between the user and the program or website. While the intent of this book is not to create experts in user interface design, you should understand some of the principles so you can develop programs that are useful and usable. The following are some **design principles** you should incorporate into your user interface designs:

1. The most important principle to remember is that the user's ability to operate the program effectively depends on the design of the interface. If the GUI is easy to use and follow, the user will have a productive and enjoyable experience. On the other hand, if the user struggles to figure out how to enter data or which button to click, the user interface design is defeating the purpose of the program.
2. If the user interface is not easy to use, the user will not be satisfied with the application regardless of how well it works.
3. The user interface includes the windows, graphics, and text shown on the screen, as well as the methods that interact with your program and cause operations to occur. Four primary means of interacting with a user interface are the keyboard, a pointing device such as a mouse, a touch interface, and voice input. The correct use of these tools significantly increases the probability of success for a traditional or touch-based user interface.

4. Using the interface should feel natural and normal. The developer must be aware of who the user is and how the user is accustomed to working. For example, the interface for a banking program in which a teller enters account information will be different from that of a graphic arts program that allows manipulation of graphics and photographs. Each must reflect the needs of the user.
5. Visual Studio contains a wide variety of objects, many of which can be used for similar purposes in the GUI. A good user interface provides the most appropriate object for each requirement. You will learn about all these objects and their correct use throughout this text.
6. Once an object is used for a particular purpose in the user interface, such as a button that causes a particular action, the object should be used for the same purpose throughout the program interface.
7. Objects must be arranged in the sequence in which they are used so the user can move from item to item on the screen in a logical, straightforward manner. Following this principle helps create an interface that is clean and easy to use. Again, the developer must understand the needs of the user.
8. The interface should be kept as simple as possible while containing all required functionality. Generally, the simpler the interface is, the more effective it will be. Consider using colors that are easy on the eyes to prevent eye fatigue.
9. When implemented, the user interface should be intuitive, which means the user should be able to use it with little or no instruction. In fact, the user should feel that no other interface could have been designed because the one they are using is the most natural.

By following these principles, you will create user interfaces that assist the user. The success of your program can depend on the user interface you design.

Sample Program

As you learned earlier, the Latte Selection program is the sample program for this chapter and Chapter 3 (see Figure 2-1 on pages 26 and 27). The requirements document for this program is shown in Figure 2-45 on page 59, and the Use Case Definition is shown in Figure 2-46 on page 60. With these documents in hand, the first phase of the program development cycle is complete.

Sample Program — Phase 2: Design the User Interface

When beginning the design of the user interface, the primary sources of reference are the requirements document and the Use Case Definition for the program. Using these documents, the developer must analyze the program requirements and determine which elements are required in the user interface.

On a line-for-line basis, the analysis of the requirements document in Figure 2-45 on page 59 could proceed as follows:

1. The application will be presented in a window on the screen, so a Windows Forms App using a Windows Form object is the appropriate means for creating the program.

2. The user will review the choices — a pumpkin spice or a mocha latte — and then make a selection. When a latte flavor is selected, a picture of the latte should be displayed. To choose each latte, the program uses a Button object, a common tool that is familiar to users. When a user clicks a button, the user has made a choice and the program responds appropriately. In this application, a good design decision is to use buttons so the user can decide between latte types and then make a latte selection. When the user clicks the Pumpkin Spice button, a picture of pumpkin spice latte will be displayed. When the user clicks the Mocha button, a picture of mocha latte will be displayed. The user then clicks the Select Latte button to make the selection.
3. Two pictures must be displayed in the user interface — a pumpkin spice picture and a mocha picture. Although it is possible to display two different pictures in a single PictureBox object depending on the user's choice, you can develop a simpler and more easily understood user interface if a PictureBox object and a button work together. In other words, when the user clicks the Pumpkin Spice button, the pumpkin spice picture is displayed in the Pumpkin Spice PictureBox object; when the user clicks the Mocha button, the mocha picture is displayed in the Mocha PictureBox object. In this way, the user can associate a button with a picture box location and the user interface is intuitive and easy to use.
4. When the user makes a latte selection by clicking the Select Latte button, a message must be displayed to confirm the latte selection. Therefore, a Label object must be included for the confirmation message.
5. After the user makes a latte selection, the only action available to the user is to exit the window, so an Exit Window button is required.
6. In addition to the requirements in the program requirements document, standard procedure usually dictates that a heading should appear in the program window. Also, it is common practice to include simple instructions in the window so the user is not confused while using the interface. The heading and instructions can be included as Label objects.
7. As a result of this analysis, the user interface should include the following items: a Windows Form object that will contain all the other objects, two PictureBox objects to contain pictures of pumpkin spice and mocha lattes, four Button objects (Pumpkin Spice button, Mocha button, Select Latte button, and Exit Window button), and three Label objects (Heading, Instructions, and Latte Selection Confirmation).

After determining the elements required for the user interface, the developer can use Visual Studio 2017 to create a mock-up of the user interface. The exact placement of objects in the window is a creative process, and is guided by the principles of user interface design you have learned. Usually, no right answer exists because each developer will see a slightly different solution, but you must adhere to the principles of a good user interface design. Figure 2-47 shows the mock-up created for the Latte Selection program.

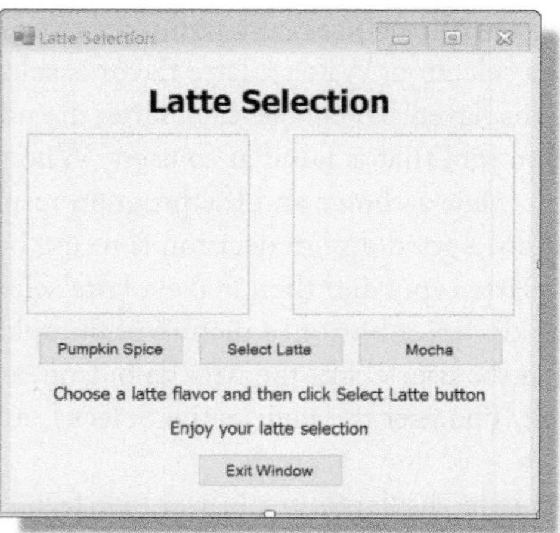

FIGURE 2-47

Guided Program Development

This section on guided program development takes you step by step through the process of creating the sample program in this chapter. To create the mock-up shown in Figure 2-48, complete the steps on the following pages.

HEADS UP

To create the mock-up of the GUI, you should complete all the tasks within the steps shown on the following pages. Many of the tasks include a reference to a figure identified by *ref:* after the instructions. This referenced figure was shown earlier in the text; it explains the technique required to complete the task. If you are not comfortable completing the task, refer to the figure to refresh your understanding of the techniques to use.

NOTE TO THE LEARNER

In the following activity, you should complete the tasks within the specified steps. Each of the tasks is accompanied by a Hint Screen. The purpose of the Hint Screen is to indicate where you should perform the activity in the Visual Studio window and to remind you which method to use. If you need further help completing a step, refer to the figure identified by *ref:*.

Guided Program Development

1

- **Open Visual Studio 2017** Open Visual Studio and sign in to your Microsoft account if necessary. Change your Development settings to Visual Basic, and then maximize the Visual Studio window, if necessary.

HEADS UP

While developing the program, you should save it periodically to keep from losing your work.

- **Create a New Visual Basic Windows Forms App** Create a new Visual Basic Windows Forms App project by clicking the New Project button, selecting Windows Classic Desktop in the left pane, selecting Windows Forms App in the middle pane, naming the project `Latte Selection`, and then clicking the OK button in the New Project window *(ref: Figure 2-2)*.

- **Keep the Toolbox Visible** If necessary, click the Auto Hide button to keep the Toolbox visible *(ref: Figure 2-7)*.

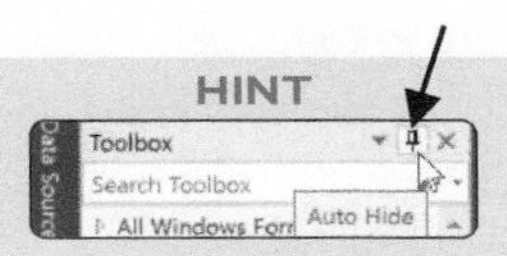

The Visual Studio application opens and a new project is displayed in the window (Figure 2-48). The Toolbox remains visible regardless of the location of the pointer.

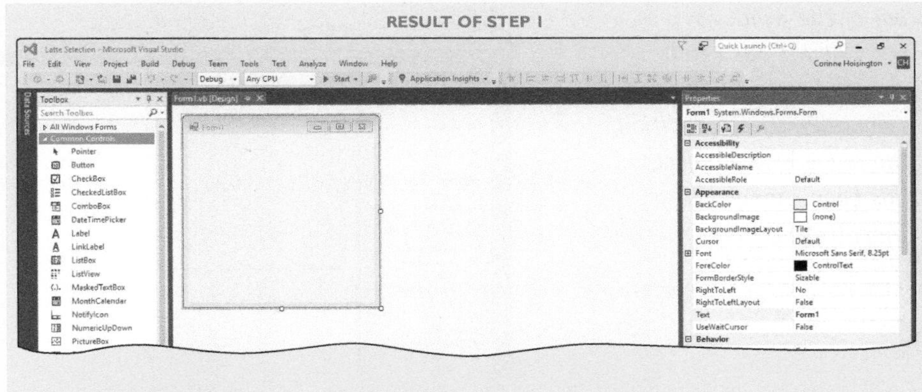

FIGURE 2-48

(continues)

Guided Program Development *continued*

2

- **Name the Windows Form Object** Click View on the menu bar and select Solution Explorer to display the Solution Explorer. In the Solution Explorer window, right-click Form1.vb. On the shortcut menu, click Rename. Name the form `frmLatteSelection` *(ref: Figure 2-11)*.

HINT

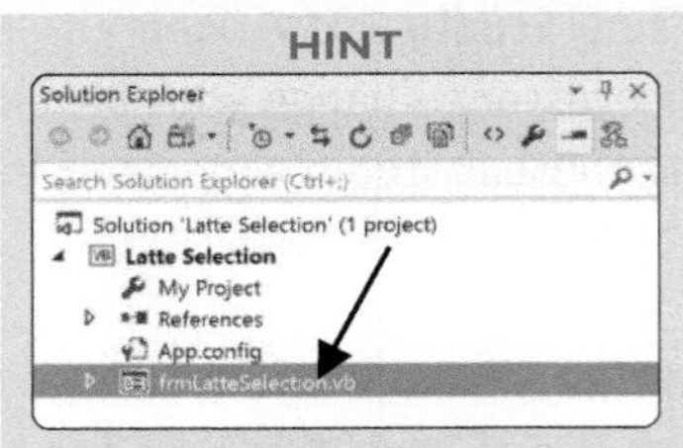

- **Change the Windows Form Object Text Property** With the Windows Form object selected, double-click the text value for the Windows Form object in the Text property of the Properties window. Change the title bar text for the Windows Form object to `Latte Selection` *(ref: Figure 2-13)*.

The text in the title bar of the Windows Form object has been changed to Latte Selection (Figure 2-49). In addition, the name of the object has been changed to frmLatteSelection.

RESULT OF STEP 2

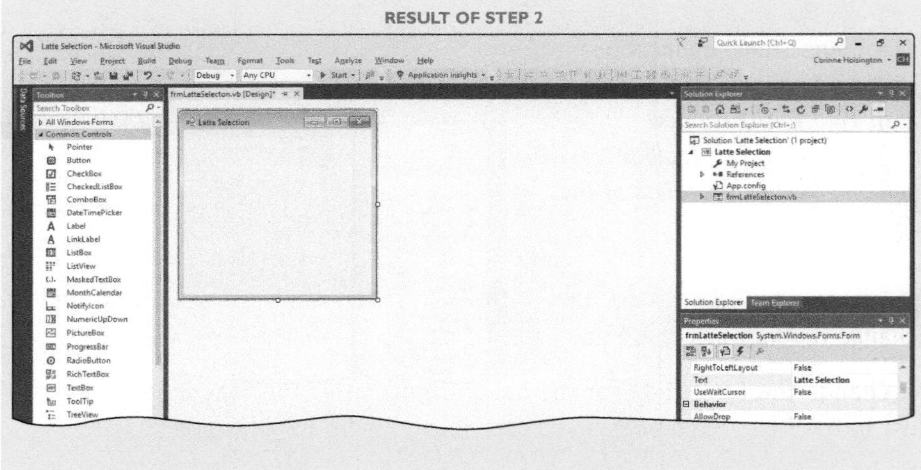

FIGURE 2-49

Guided Program Development *continued*

3

- **Resize the Windows Form Object** Resize the Windows Form object to the approximate size shown in Figure 2-47 (730 × 700) by changing the Size property in the Properties window to `730, 700` *(ref: Figure 2-14)*.

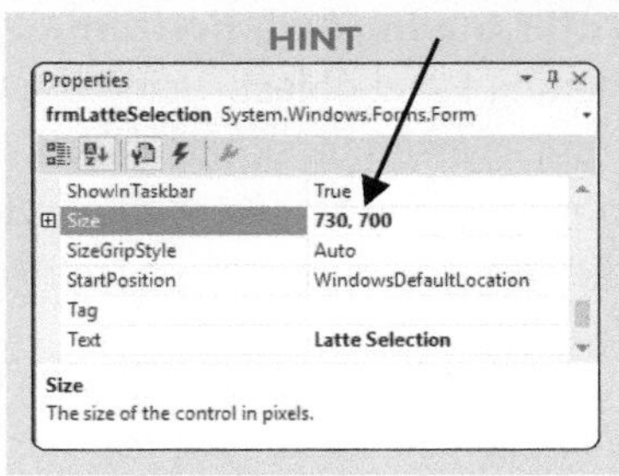

4

- **Add a Label Object** Add a Label object by dragging the Label .NET component from the Toolbox to the Windows Form object. Place the label near the center and top of the Windows Form object.

- **Name the Label Object** Change the name of the Label object to `lblHeading` by using the (Name) property in the Properties window for the Label object *(ref: Figure 2-17)*.

- **Change the Label Object Text Property** Double-click the text value for the Label object in the Text property of the Properties window, and then change the Text property of the lblHeading Label object to `Latte Selection` *(ref: Figure 2-18)*.

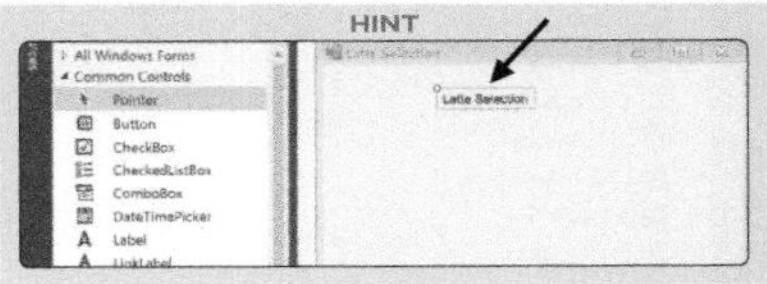

- **Open the Font Dialog Box** Click the Font property for the Label object in the Properties window, and then click the ellipsis button (...) for the Font property *(ref: Figure 2-20)*.

- **Change the Font for the Label Object** In the Font list of the Font dialog box, change the font in the lblHeading Label object to Tahoma *(ref: Figure 2-21)*.

- **Change the Font Style for the Label Object** Using the Font style list in the Font dialog box, change the font style in the lblHeading Label object to Bold *(ref: Figure 2-21)*.

- **Change the Size for the Label Object** Using the Size list in the Font dialog box, change the font size in the lblHeading Label object to 16 points *(ref: Figure 2-21)*.

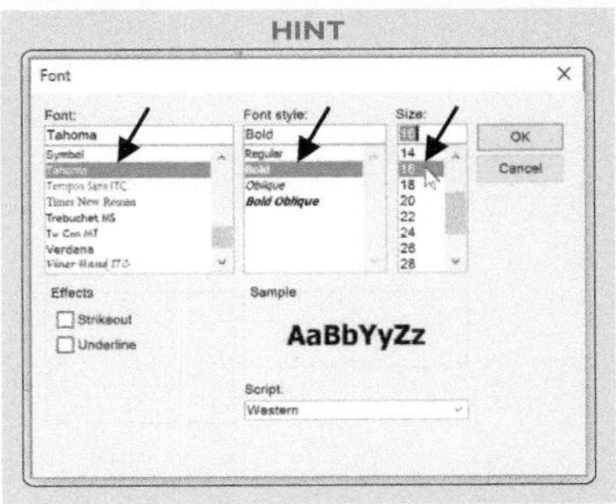

(continues)

Guided Program Development *continued*

- **Center the Heading Horizontally** If necessary, select the lblHeading Label object. Using the Center in Form command on the Format menu, click the Horizontally command on the Center in Form submenu to center the lblHeading Label object horizontally on the Windows Form object *(ref: Figure 2-23)*.

The lblHeading Label object text has been changed and the label object is centered horizontally on the Windows Form object (Figure 2-50). The vertical placement of the label (that is, the distance from the top of the window frame) depends on the eye of the developer, the size of the Windows Form object, and the other objects in the GUI.

RESULT OF STEPS 3 AND 4

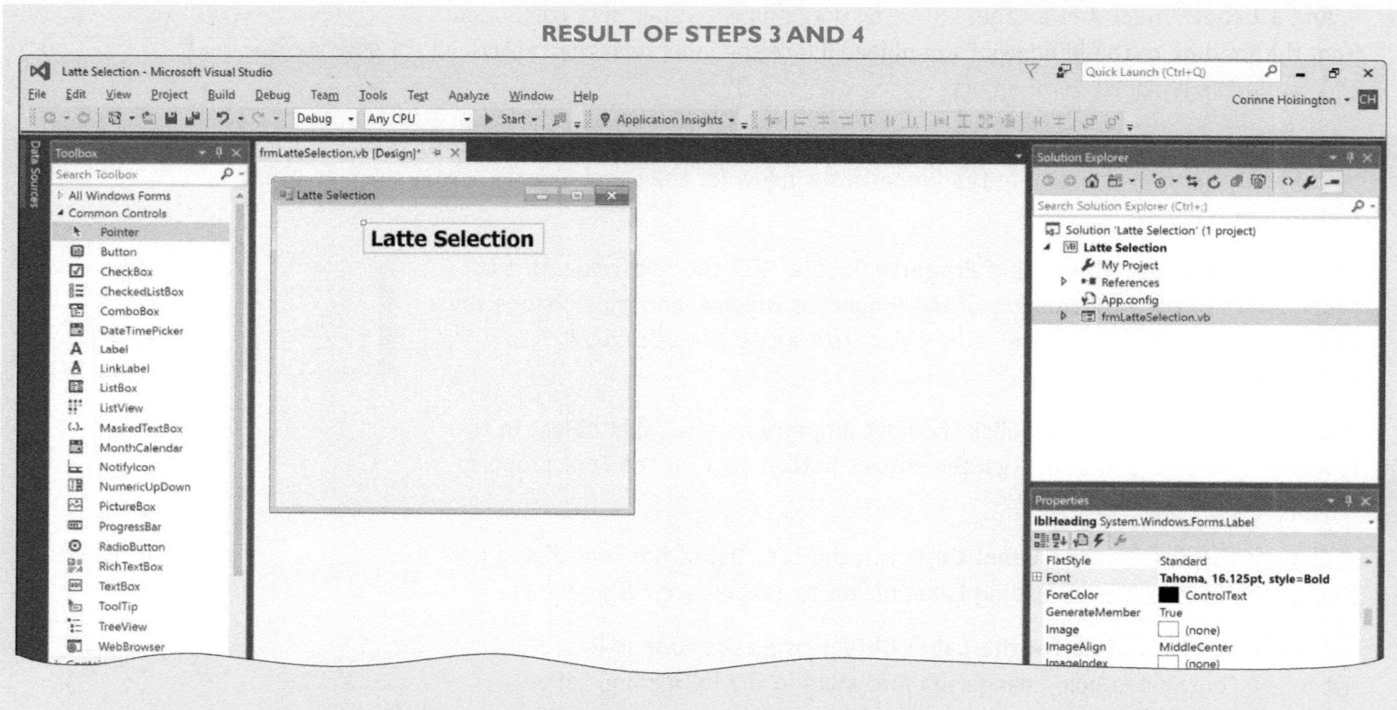

FIGURE 2-50

Guided Program Development *continued*

5

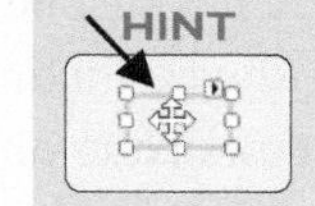

- **Add a PictureBox Object** Add a PictureBox object to the Windows Form object by dragging a PictureBox .NET component from the Toolbox to the Windows Form object. Place the PictureBox object below and to the left of the heading label, as shown in Figure 2-51 *(ref: Figure 2-26)*.
- **Name the PictureBox Object** Using the (Name) property in the PictureBox Properties window, name the PictureBox object `picPumpkin`.
- **Resize the PictureBox Object** Resize the PictureBox object by changing its Size property to `300, 250` *(ref: Figure 2-27)*.

A properly sized PictureBox object is displayed in the Windows Form object (Figure 2-51). This PictureBox object will display a picture of a pumpkin spice latte when the program is completed in Chapter 3.

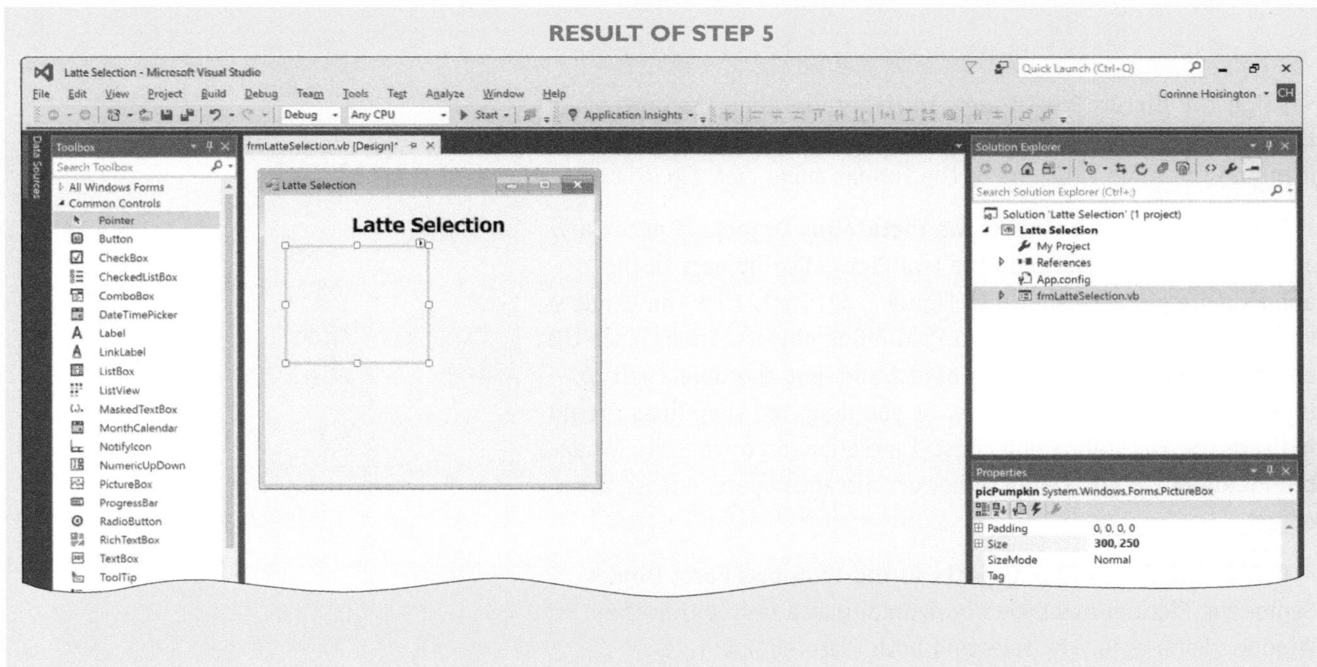

FIGURE 2-51

(continues)

Guided Program Development *continued*

6

- **Add a PictureBox Object** Add a second PictureBox object to the Windows Form object by dragging a PictureBox .NET component from the Toolbox to the Windows Form object. Place it to the right of the first PictureBox object in the Windows Form object *(ref: Figure 2-28)*.

- **Name the PictureBox Object** Using the (Name) property in the PictureBox Properties window, name the PictureBox object `picMocha`.

- **Size the PictureBox Object** Make the second PictureBox object on the Windows Form object the same size as the first by using the Both command on the Make Same Size submenu of the Format menu *(ref: Figure 2-31)*.

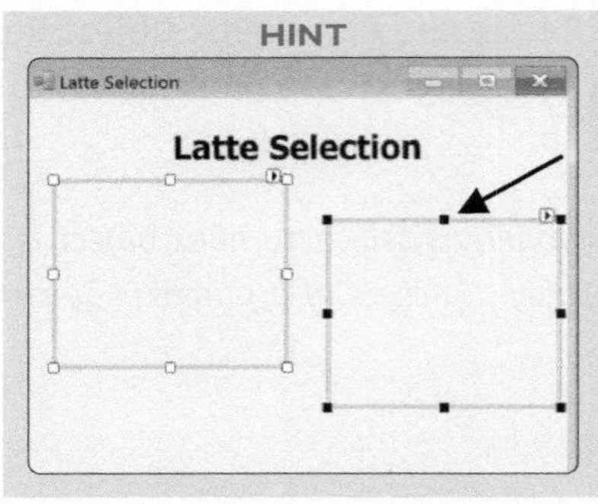

- **Align the PictureBox Objects Horizontally** Align the bottoms of the two PictureBox objects horizontally by using the Bottoms command on the Align submenu of the Format menu *(ref: Figure 2-33)*.

- **Set the Distance Between the PictureBox Objects** If necessary, adjust the distance between the two PictureBox objects to the approximate distance shown in Figure 2-52. First, click the Windows Form object to deselect the two PictureBox objects. Then, place the pointer in the right PictureBox object and drag the object left or right to set the correct distance. As you drag, red snap lines should indicate the PictureBox objects still are aligned horizontally. When the PictureBox objects are the correct distance apart, release the object.

- **Center the PictureBox Objects in the Windows Form Object** Center the PictureBox objects horizontally as a unit within the Windows Form object by selecting both PictureBox objects, displaying the Center in Form command on the Format menu, pointing to the Center in Form command, and then clicking Horizontally on the Center in Form submenu *(ref: Figure 2-35)*.

Guided Program Development *continued*

The PictureBox objects are sized and located properly within the Windows Form object (Figure 2-52).

RESULT OF STEP 6

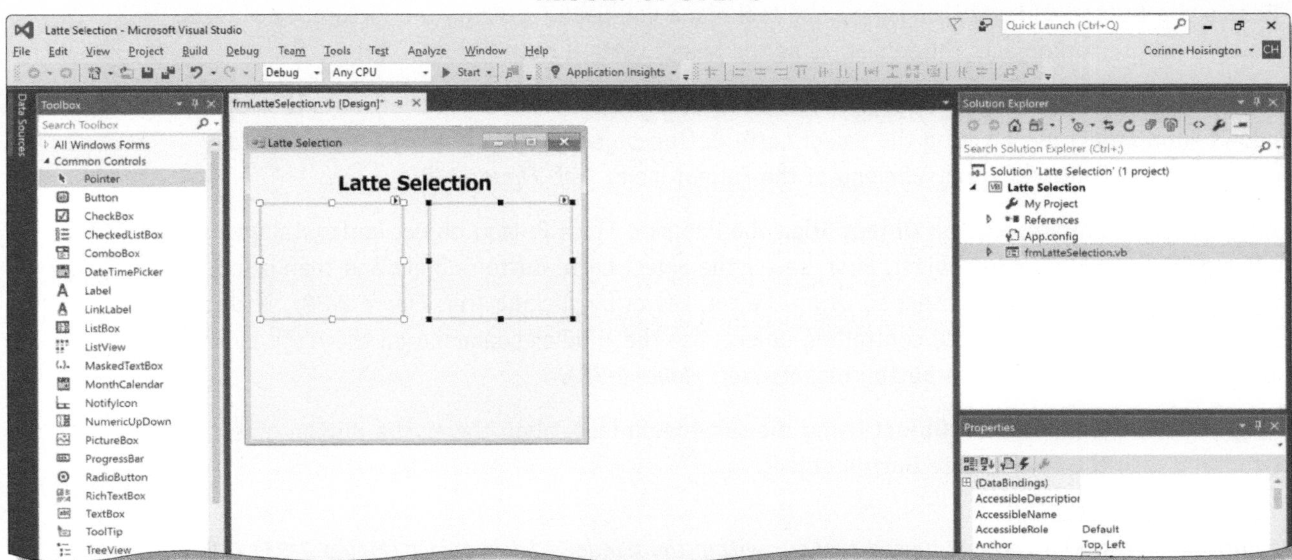

FIGURE 2-52

7

- **Add Three Button Objects to the Windows Form Object** Add three Button objects by dragging them onto the Windows Form object. Align them horizontally below the PictureBox objects at about the same locations shown in Figure 2-47 on page 64. Use red snap lines to align horizontally the buttons on the Windows Form object as you drag them onto the form *(ref: Figures 2-36 and 2-41).*

- **Name the Three Button Objects** Using the (Name) property in the Properties window, name the left Button object `btnPumpkin`, the center Button object `btnSelect`, and the right Button object `btnMocha`.

- **Change the Text Property for the Three Button Objects** Using the Text property in the Properties window, change the text for the left Button object to `Pumpkin Spice`, the text for the middle Button object to `Select Latte`, and the text for the right Button object to `Mocha` *(ref: Figure 2-47).*

(continues)

Guided Program Development *continued*

- **Change the Button Object Size** Change the size of the Select Latte button to accommodate the Select Latte text with extra room on each side of the text *(ref: Figure 2-39).*

- **Resize the Button Objects** Using the same technique you used for sizing the PictureBox objects, make all three Button objects the same size as the Select Latte Button object.

- **Center the btnSelect Button Object** Center the Select Latte Button object horizontally within the Windows Form object by selecting the Select Latte Button object and then using the Horizontally command on the Center in Form submenu of the Format menu *(ref: Figure 2-24).*

- **Align the btnPumpkin Button Object** Align the Pumpkin Spice Button object horizontally with the Pumpkin Spice PictureBox object. First, select the Select Latte Button object and then select the Pumpkin Spice Button object, either by using the CTRL key or by clicking *(ref: Figure 2-29)*. With the Select Latte Button object as the controlling object, use the Middles command on the Align submenu of the Format menu to align the Button objects *(ref: Figure 2-32).*

- **Align the btnMocha Button Object** Using the same technique, align the Mocha Button object horizontally with the Select Latte Button object.

The Button objects are sized and placed properly within the Windows Form object (Figure 2-53). All three buttons are the same size. The three buttons are aligned horizontally, and the Select Latte button is centered in the Windows Form object.

RESULT OF STEP 7

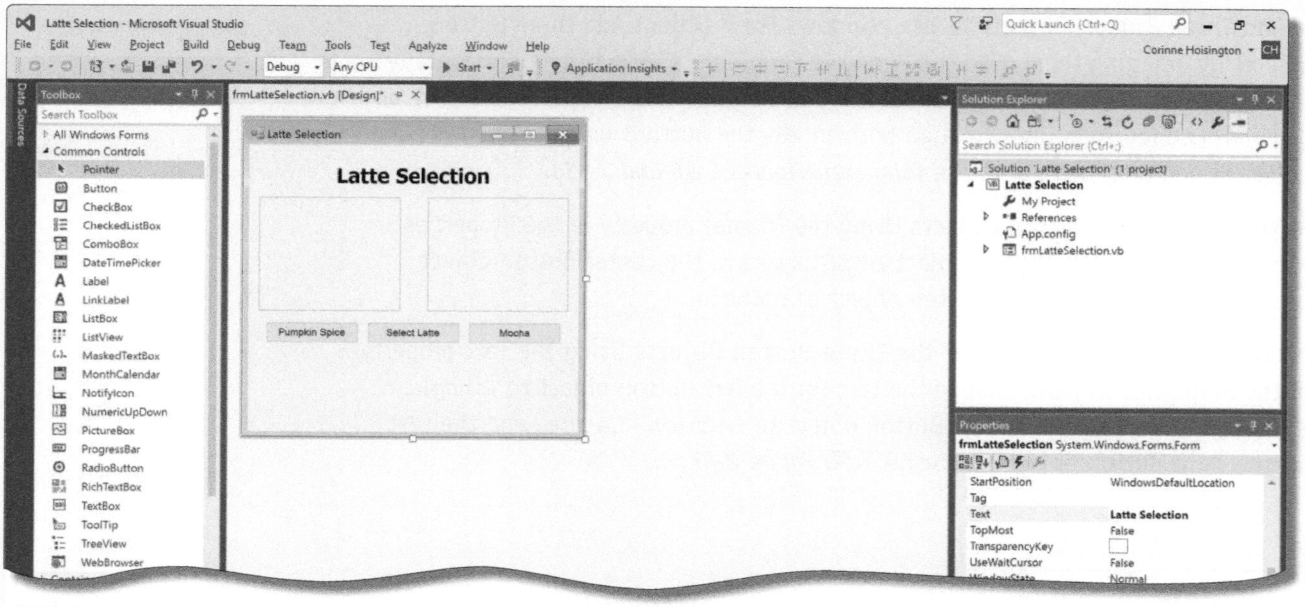

FIGURE 2-53

Guided Program Development *continued*

8

- **Add a Label Object** Add the instructions Label object to the Windows Form object by dragging a Label .NET object from the Toolbox to the Windows Form object. Place it below the Button objects at the approximate location shown.

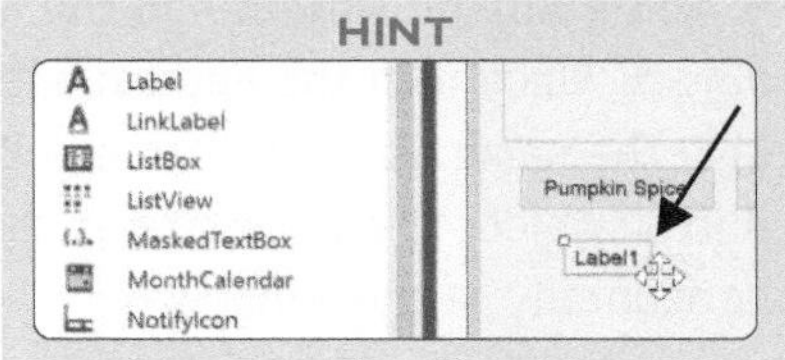

- **Name a Label Object** Using the techniques you have learned, name the Label object `lblInstructions`.

- **Change the Label Object Text Property** Using the techniques you have learned, change the text in the lblInstructions Label object to `Choose a latte flavor and then click Select Latte button`.

- **Change the Label Object Font** Using the techniques you have learned, change the font for the lblInstructions Label object to Tahoma, change the font style to Regular, and change the size to 9 points.

- **Center the Label Object** Using the techniques you have learned, center the lblInstructions Label object horizontally within the Windows Form object.

- **Add a Label Object** Using the techniques you have learned, add the final message Label object to the Windows Form object. The text of the label should read `Enjoy your latte selection`. Place the Label object in the location shown in Figure 2-54. Name it `lblConfirmation`. Change the font to Tahoma, the font style to Regular, and the size to 9 points. Center the Label object within the Windows Form object.

The two Label objects contain the correct text and are centered horizontally in the Windows Form object (Figure 2-54).

RESULT OF STEP 8

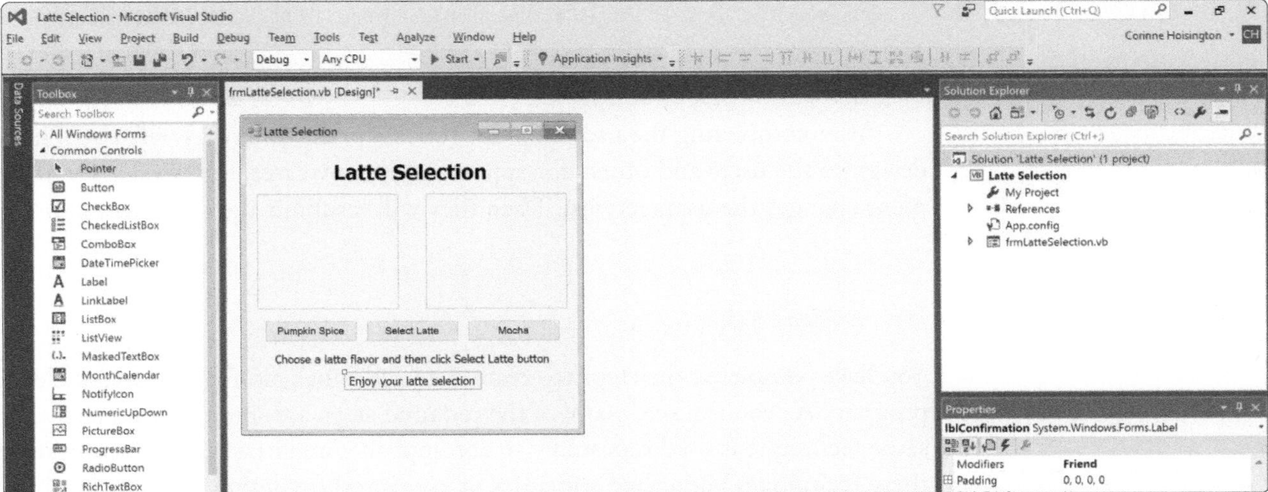

FIGURE 2-54

(continues)

Guided Program Development *continued*

9

- **Add a Button Object** Add the Exit Window Button object by dragging a Button control onto the Windows Form object. Place it in the approximate location shown in Figure 2-55. Then, using the techniques you have learned, give the name `btnExit` to the Button object, change its text to `Exit Window`, make the Exit Window Button object the same size as the other Button objects in the window, and center the Exit Window Button object horizontally in the window.

The user interface mock-up is complete (Figure 2-55).

RESULT OF STEP 9

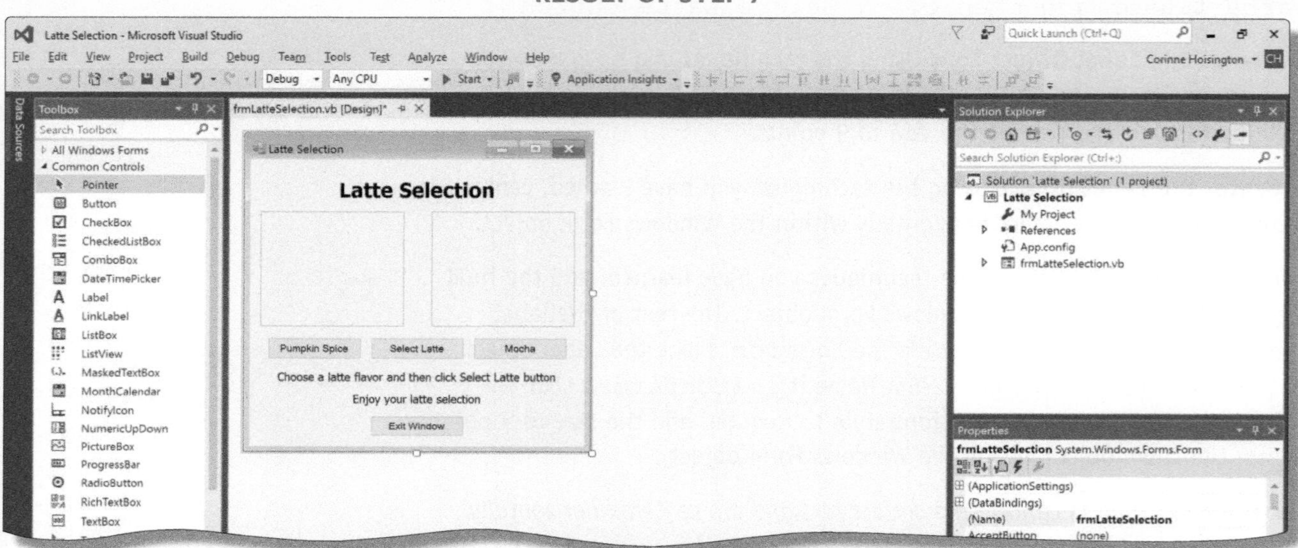

FIGURE 2-55

After completing the user interface mock-up, the designers will distribute the design to the users and others for approval. In many cases, the developers must implement changes the users request. Then they will resubmit the design for approval.

Summary

You have completed the steps to create the GUI mock-up for the Latte Selection program. As you can see, many of the required steps are somewhat repetitive; the same technique is used repeatedly to accomplish similar tasks. When you master these techniques and other principles of user interface design, you will be able to design user interfaces for a variety of programs.

Knowledge Check

1–5. Label the following parts of the window shown in Figure 2-56:

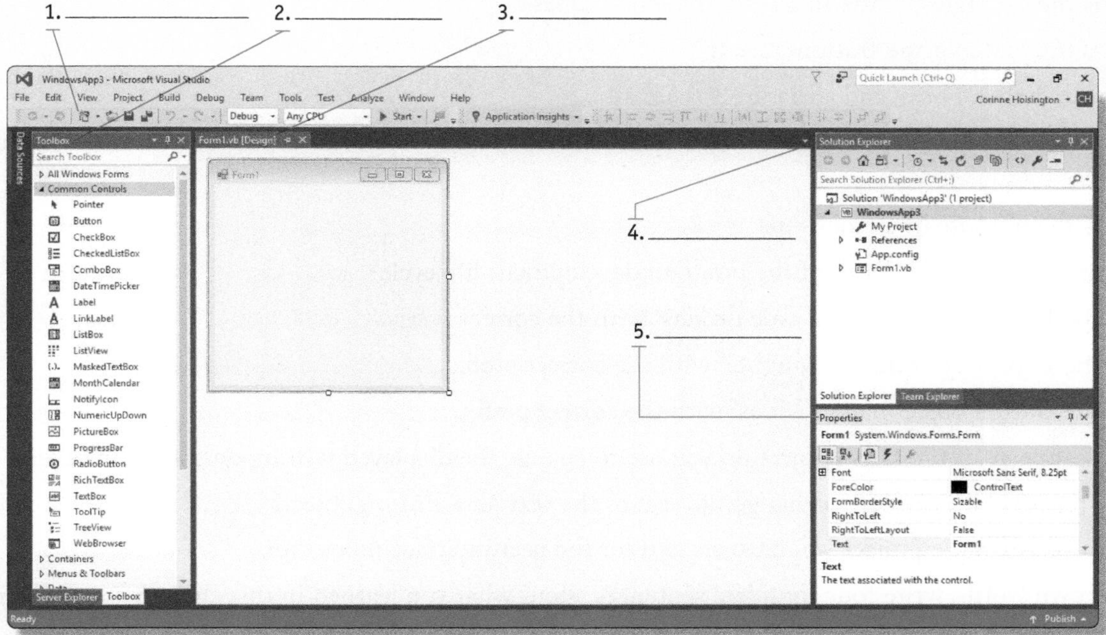

FIGURE 2-56

(continues)

Knowledge Check *continued*

6. Why would you sign in with a Microsoft account when opening Visual Studio?
7. What does RAD stand for?
8. What is the difference between red and blue snap lines?
9. What is the prefix of the Button object?
10. A Button, Label, Form, and a PictureBox are all _____________.
11. How do you select three PictureBox objects on the Windows Form object at the same time for alignment purposes?
12. What is the purpose of a mock-up?
13. What are the first two phases of the program development life cycle?
14. Write the Form object name "CastleTickets" with the correct prefix.
15. Write the Label object name "Knights" with the correct prefix.
16. Write the Button object name "Moat" with the correct prefix.
17. Which property of the Label object do you use to change the displayed writing on the Form object?
18. Which property do you use to change the size of the text on a Button object?
19. How do you save the project you have created for the user interface mock-up?
20. In your own words, write four complete sentences about what you learned in this chapter about UX design.

Debugging Exercises

1. List the steps required to change the poorly aligned buttons on the left (Figure 2-57a) to the properly aligned buttons on the right (Figure 2-57b).

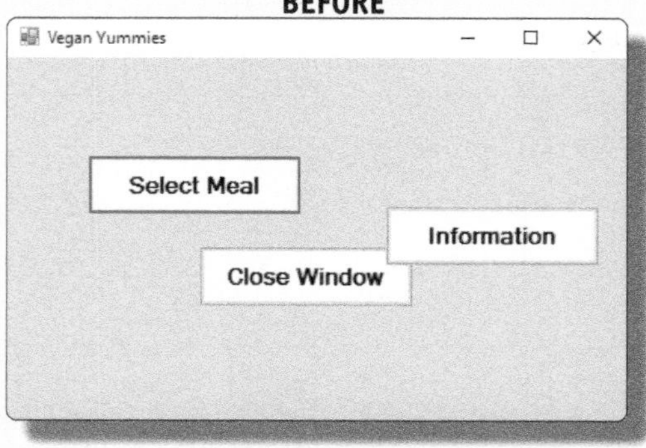

FIGURE 2-57a

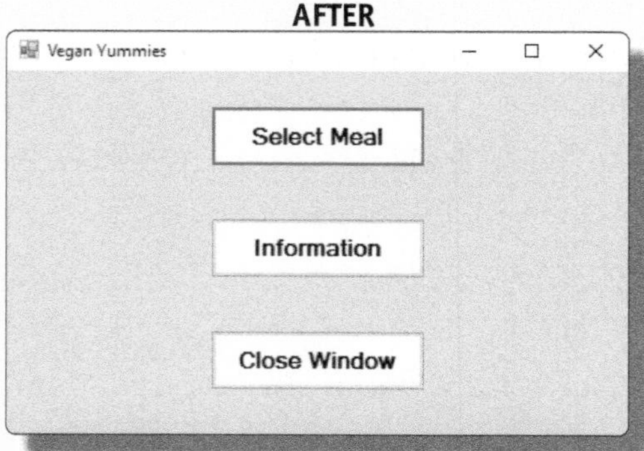

FIGURE 2-57b

Debugging Exercises *continued*

2. Change the order of the numbered Use Case Definition steps to correspond to the following problem definition: A college provides every incoming freshman with a gift card for a choice of two specialty restaurants within the cafeteria. Students should select one specialty restaurant they want. A program opens a window that displays each specialty restaurant one picture at a time when a student clicks the corresponding button. After making a decision, the student should click the Select Restaurant button. After selecting a restaurant, the student should exit the application.

USE CASE DEFINITION

1. User clicks the Select Restaurant button.
2. User clicks the Teppanyaki button or Sushi button.
3. User exits the program by clicking the Close button.
4. User clicks the button not selected in Step 2.
5. Program displays a confirmation message and disables both restaurant type buttons. The Close button becomes active.
6. Program displays a picture of the first selected specialty restaurant selected by the user and enables the Select Restaurant button.
7. Program displays a picture of the second selected specialty restaurant selected by the user.

Program Analysis

1. After you have placed objects on the Windows Form object (Figure 2-58), list the steps you would follow to change the font for the Order Cupcakes label to Tahoma font, Bold style, 20 points.
2. List the steps you would perform to center the Order Cupcakes label horizontally.
3. List the steps you would perform to center the PictureBox object horizontally on the Windows Form object in Figure 2-58.
4. List the steps you would perform to change the font for the Purchase Now button in Figure 2-58 to Tahoma, 14 points.
5. List the steps you would perform to align the two Button objects horizontally by the bottoms of the buttons.
6. List the steps you would perform to make the Purchase Now button the same size as the Close Window button.
7. In the real world, why is it important to have a user interface mock-up approved before proceeding with the rest of the project?

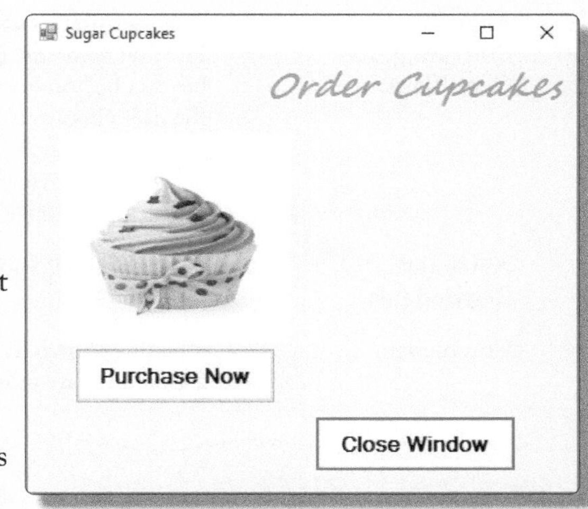

FIGURE 2-58

Ruth Black/Shutterstock.com

Case Programming Assignments

Complete one or more of the following case programming assignments. Submit the program and materials you create to your instructor. The level of difficulty is indicated for each assignment.

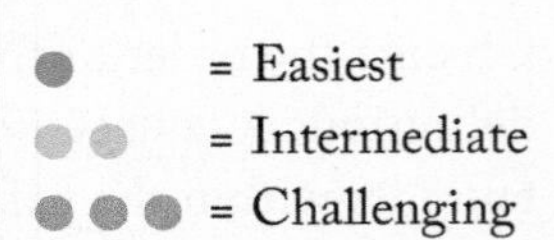

1 VIRTUAL REALITY HEADSETS

Create a Windows form mock-up for the requirements document shown in Figure 2-59 and the Use Case Definition shown in Figure 2-60. The Windows Form object and the other objects in the user interface are shown in Figure 2-61.

REQUIREMENTS DOCUMENT

Date: October 13, 2018

Date Submitted:

Application Title: Virtual Reality Headsets

Purpose: This Windows Classic Desktop application displays an order screen for two types of virtual reality headsets. The user can choose either a crown VR headset or earbud VR headset.

Program Procedures: From a window on the screen, the user makes a request to see one of the two VR headset types.

Algorithms, Processing, and Conditions:

1. The user first views a Virtual Reality Headset window that displays the VR Headset company (VR Forward). When the user chooses to click the first headset button for the Crown VR, the crown.jpg image is displayed. When the user chooses to view the second headset for the Earbud VR, the earbud.jpg image is displayed.
2. After the user views one of the two images, the user can select the other image or exit the window.

Notes and Restrictions: The images should not be displayed at the same time.

Comments: The picture shown in the window can be found on CengageBrain.com. The name of the pictures are crown and earbud. Images will be added in Chapter 3.

FIGURE 2-59

Case Programming Assignments *continued*

Virtual Reality Headsets

USE CASE DEFINITION

1. The window opens, displaying the name of the company. The two VR image buttons are enabled.
2. User clicks either the VR Crown or VR Earbud button.
3. The user can continue to click each VR button.
4. The Exit Window button is enabled after the user views an image. User clicks the Exit Window button to exit the application.

FIGURE 2-60

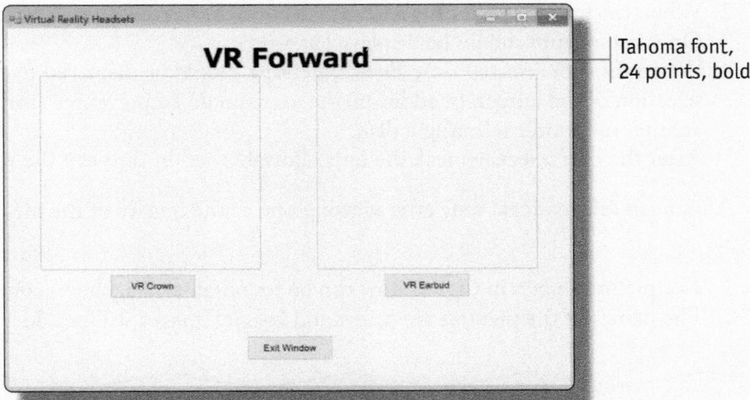

FIGURE 2-61

Case Programming Assignments

2 BURGER SPECIALS

Create a Windows Form mock-up for the requirements document in Figure 2-62 and the Use Case Definition shown in Figure 2-63. The Windows Form object and the other objects in the user interface are shown in Figure 2-64.

REQUIREMENTS DOCUMENT

Date:	January 10, 2019
Date Submitted:	
Application Title:	Burger Specials
Purpose:	This Windows Classic Desktop application displays the burger specials for a restaurant named Farm Burger. The user can select one of two specials: Prime Beef or Veggie.
Program Procedures:	From a window on the screen, the user orders one of two special burgers and the program confirms the order with a message.
Algorithms, Processing, and Conditions:	1. The user must be able to identify the Prime Beef or Veggie burger special name as many times as necessary until making a decision. 2. When the user identifies the special, a picture of that meal appears in the window. 3. Only one picture should be displayed at a time. 4. When the user selects Prime Beef, a message should be displayed to confirm the selection of the burger. In addition, the user should be prevented from identifying another meal after selecting a dish. 5. After the user selects a meal, the only allowable action is to exit the window.
Notes and Restrictions:	A user can select a meal only after viewing one of the images of the meals.
Comments:	1. The picture shown in the window can be found on cengagebrain.com. 2. The names of the pictures are prime and veggie. Images will be added in Chapter 3.

FIGURE 2-62

Case Programming Assignments *continued*

Burger Specials

USE CASE DEFINITION

1. User clicks the Prime Beef button or Veggie button.
2. Program displays a picture of the burger identified by the user and enables the burger selection button.
3. User clicks meal buttons to view meals as desired. Program displays the picture of the identified burger.
4. User clicks the Select Meal button.
5. Program displays a meal confirmation message and disables both burger buttons and the Select Meal button.
6. The Exit Window button becomes active. User exits the program by clicking the Exit Window button.

FIGURE 2-63

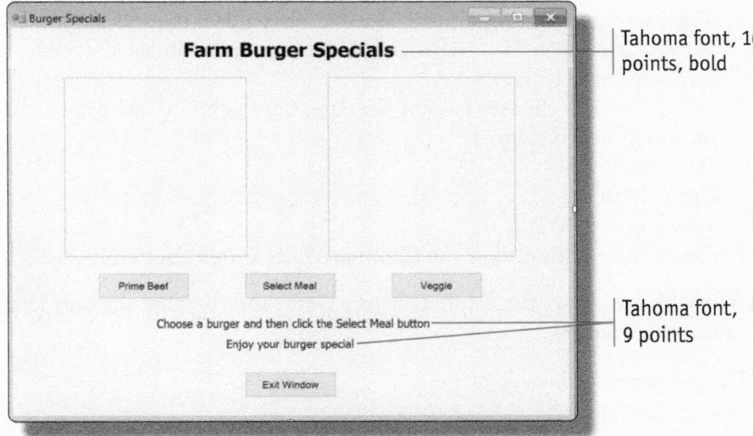

FIGURE 2-64

Case Programming Assignments

3 CAMPUS MUSIC CAFE

Create a Use Case Definition document and design a Windows form mock-up based on the requirements document in Figure 2-65.

REQUIREMENTS DOCUMENT

Date:	October 13, 2018
Date Submitted:	
Application Title:	Campus Music Cafe
Purpose:	This Windows Classic Desktop application displays a welcome screen to market the Campus Music Café performance. The user can choose an option to view the date, start location, and details.
Program Procedures:	From a window on the screen, the user makes a request to see the performance's date, start location, and details.
Algorithms, Processing, and Conditions:	1. The user first views a Campus Music Cafe window that displays the title (Campus Music Café Open Mic Night), a cafe picture, and a phrase that states that all college students are welcome. 2. When the user chooses to view the date, start location, and details, the following information is displayed: October 30, 2018 Open "Mic" Start Time: 8:00 PM For more information, view the Campus Music Café's Facebook page. After the user views the Campus Music Café's information, the only allowable action is to exit the window.
Notes and Restrictions:	Design your own layout.
Comments:	Locate your own image online for use in Chapter 3.

FIGURE 2-65

Case Programming Assignments

4 ●● SPRING BREAK TRAVEL SPECIALS

Create a Use Case Definition document and design a Windows Form mock-up based on the requirements document in Figure 2-66.

REQUIREMENTS DOCUMENT

Date:	March 21, 2018
Date Submitted:	
Application Title:	Spring Break Travel Specials
Purpose:	The Student Center on campus has created special Spring Break travel specials on three trips. A student can choose one of three Spring Break trips. The program must display each of the Spring Break travel specials upon request. The student can then select a trip for purchase.
Program Procedures:	From a window on the screen, the user selects one of three trips. A picture of the selected trips is displayed in the window. The user then can choose a trip for purchase.
Algorithms, Processing, and Conditions:	1. The user selects a trip. Then, a picture of the trip location is displayed in the window. 2. The user can select any of the three trips. Only the picture of the selected trip should be displayed. 3. The user can select trips as many times as necessary and display the pictures of the destinations. 4. The user finds a trip, chooses it for purchase, and clicks the Book Trip button. 5. After the user chooses a trip, a message stating "Enjoy your trip" should be displayed. 6. After the user chooses a trip, the only allowable action is to exit the window.
Notes and Restrictions:	The user should not be able to choose a trip until viewing at least one trip image.
Comments:	1. The available trips are to Myrtle Beach, Key West, or Venice Beach. Select your own pictures online. Images will be added in Chapter 3.

FIGURE 2-66

Case Programming Assignments

5 ●●● INTERNATIONAL SNACKS

Create a requirements document and a Use Case Definition document and then design a Windows Form mock-up based on the case project shown in Figure 2-67.

The international club on campus requests a computer application that will run on a kiosk during the International Festival where students can select a healthy international snack. The application should request which free snack you would like, display the choices as buttons, and then display an image of the snack you select. Another button allows you to make your final snack selection and display a confirmation message.

Snack
Bean Burrito
Falafel
Greek Yogurt
Spring Rolls

FIGURE 2-67

6 ●●● COSTUME SHOP

Create a requirements document and a Use Case Definition document and then design a Windows Form mock-up based on the case project shown in Figure 2-68.

A costume shop requests a computer application that advertises costume rentals. This week's costume rental specials are as follows:

Destination	Price
Renaissance Fair	$40 week rental
Stormtrooper	$49 week rental
Batman/Batgirl	$36 week rental
Pirate	$29 week rental

Write an application that allows the user to select any of the five costume rental specials. When the user selects a costume, the corresponding cost and a picture of the costume should be displayed. Clear each prior price and picture when the user selects a different costume. After selecting a costume, the user should be able to book the costume rental and then exit the window.

FIGURE 2-68

CHAPTER 3

Program Design and Coding

OBJECTIVES

You will have mastered the material in this chapter when you can:

- Change the color properties of an object
- Add images to a PictureBox object
- Locate and save an image from the web
- Import an image into the Program Resources folder
- Size an image
- Set the Visible property in the Properties window
- Set the Enabled property in the Properties window
- Run a Visual Basic 2017 program
- Enter Visual Basic 2017 code
- Understand Visual Basic 2017 code statement formats
- Use IntelliSense to enter Visual Basic 2017 code statements
- Use code to set the Visible property of an object
- Use code to set the Enabled property of an object
- Enter comments in Visual Basic 2017 code
- Correct errors in Visual Basic 2017 code
- Write code to use the Close() procedure
- Print code
- Prepare an event-planning document

Introduction

In Chapter 2 you completed the design of a graphical user interface (GUI) mock-up. While users and others can approve the mock-up as being functional, the developer normally must make a variety of changes to the GUI to prepare it for the actual production version of the program. Among these changes are the following:

- Adding color to the interface to make it more visually appealing
- Acquiring and including images that are required for the program
- Setting interface object properties in accordance with the needs of the program

Once these tasks have been completed, Phase 2 of the program development life cycle (PDLC) is complete.

The next two phases of the PDLC are as follows:

- Phase 3: Design the program processing objects
- Phase 4: Code the program

This chapter will provide the skills and knowledge necessary to complete Phase 2 of the PDLC and then complete Phases 3 and 4.

Sample Program

You will recall that the sample program for Chapter 2 and this chapter is the Latte Selection program. Windows for the program are shown in Figure 3-1.

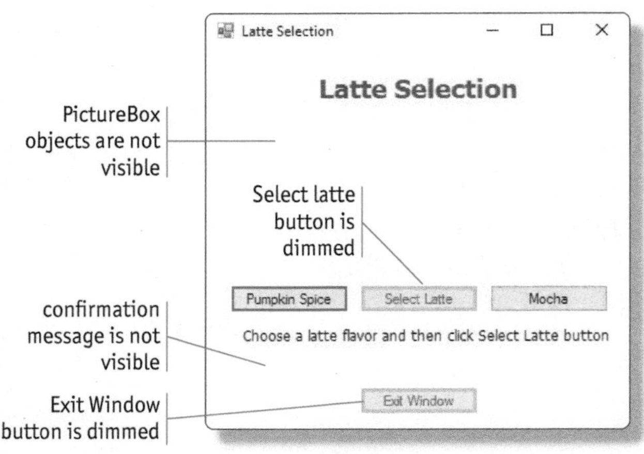

FIGURE 3-1a

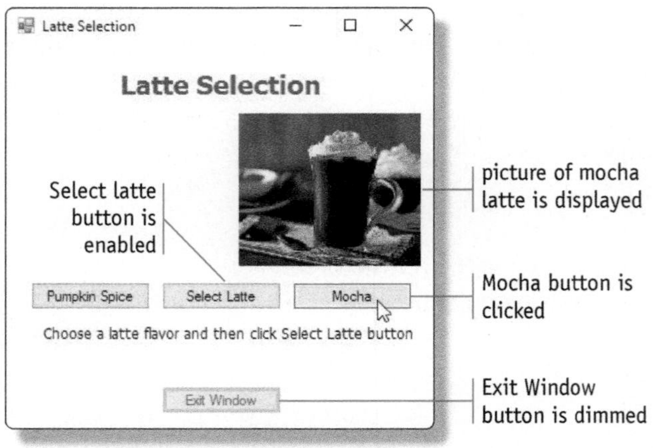

FIGURE 3-1b

Africa Studio/Shutterstock.com

FIGURE 3-1c
Africa Studio/Shutterstock.com

In the opening window (Figure 3-1a), no images appear in the PictureBox objects, and the Select Latte button and Exit Window button are dimmed, which means they are disabled (visible, but not available for selection) when the program begins. In Figure 3-1b, the user clicked the Mocha button, so the picture is displayed. In addition, the Select Latte button is enabled. The Exit Window button still is dimmed. In Figure 3-1c, the user has selected a flavored latte, so the latte selection confirmation message is displayed. The Pumpkin Spice, Select Latte, and Mocha buttons are dimmed and the Exit Window button is enabled. When the program runs, each of these changes occurs through the use of Visual Basic code you enter into the program, as you will discover later in this chapter.

Fine-Tune the User Interface

You learned about some properties of Visual Basic objects in Chapter 2, including the Name property and the Text property. As you probably noted while viewing the Properties window in Chapter 2, more properties are available for each of the objects in a GUI. In many cases, you set these properties to fine-tune the user interface and make it more usable. In the sample program, the BackColor and ForeColor properties make the user interface more attractive and effective.

BackColor and ForeColor Properties

The **BackColor** of an object is the color displayed in its background. For example, in Figure 3-1 on pages 86 and 87 the BackColor of the Windows Form object is white instead of the default gray color, and the BackColor of the Button objects is a Bisque shade. You can select the BackColor of an object by using the **BackColor property** in the Properties window. The **ForeColor** of an object is the color displayed in the text of the object. The heading Label object that displays the Latte Selection text uses a text color called Firebrick. To change the BackColor of a Windows Form object from its default color of Control (gray) to White, you can complete the following steps:

STEP 1 Click the Windows Form object to select it. (Do not click any of the objects on the Windows Form object.)

The Windows Form object is selected, as indicated by the thick border and the sizing handles (Figure 3-2).

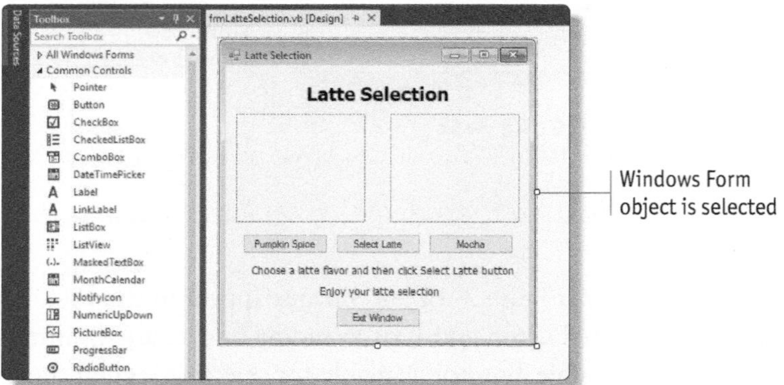

FIGURE 3-2

STEP 2 If necessary, scroll in the Properties window until the BackColor property is displayed, and then click the right column of the BackColor property.

The BackColor property is selected, and the BackColor arrow is displayed (Figure 3-3).

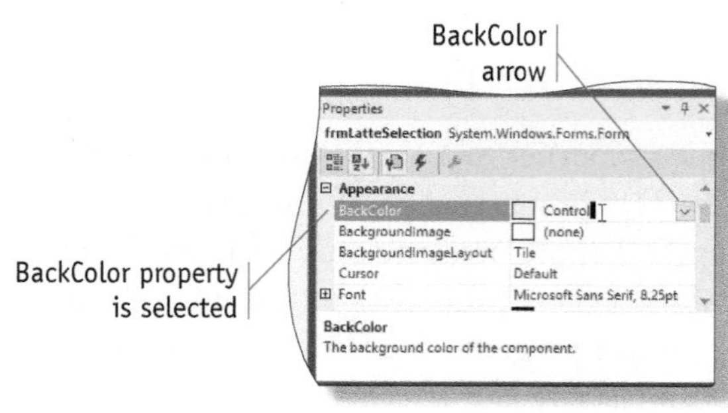

FIGURE 3-3

STEP 3 Click the BackColor arrow. Then, click the Web tab to display the Web tabbed page.

The color window opens within the Properties window (Figure 3-4). The Web tabbed page contains more than 100 named colors you can display as the BackColor for the selected object, which in this case is the Windows Form object.

IN THE REAL WORLD

Visual Studio 2017 offers three palettes for BackColors and ForeColors: the Custom palette, the Web palette, and the System palette. In the Custom palette, 48 colors are available for selection; in addition, 16 white color chips are available. You can select your own color by pressing and holding or right-clicking a chip and then identifying the color you want in the Define Color window. Be aware that some colors you select from the Define Color window might not be displayed properly on all computers. When the Web palette is open, you can choose from 141 colors that are guaranteed to be displayed properly on every computer. The System palette contains fewer colors; it lists only those that correspond to colors selected in other areas of the computer.

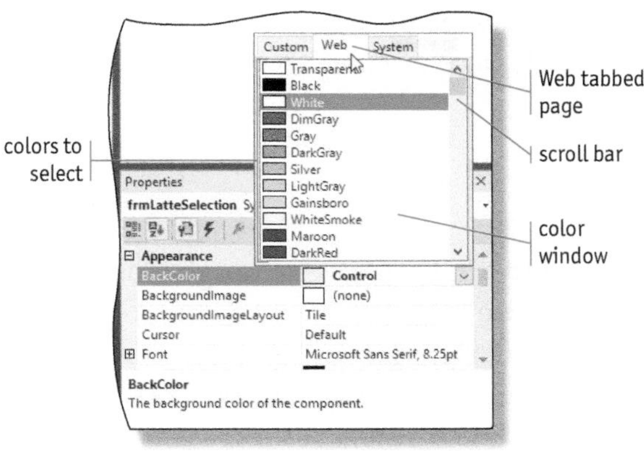

FIGURE 3-4

STEP 4 If necessary, scroll until White is displayed in the list of colors.

The name and a sample of the White color are displayed (Figure 3-5).

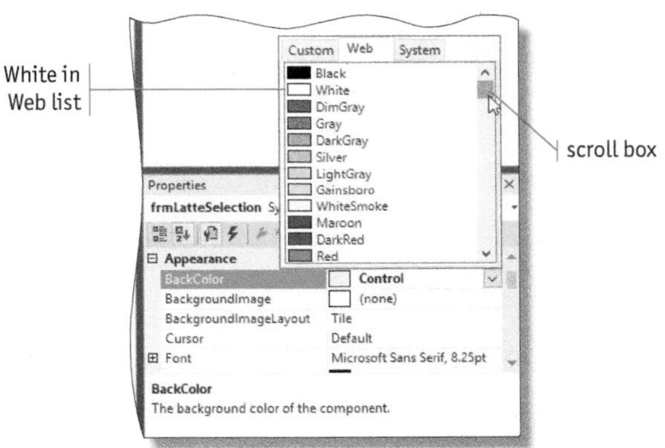

FIGURE 3-5

STEP 5 Click White on the color list.

The background color in the Windows Form object is changed to White (Figure 3-6).

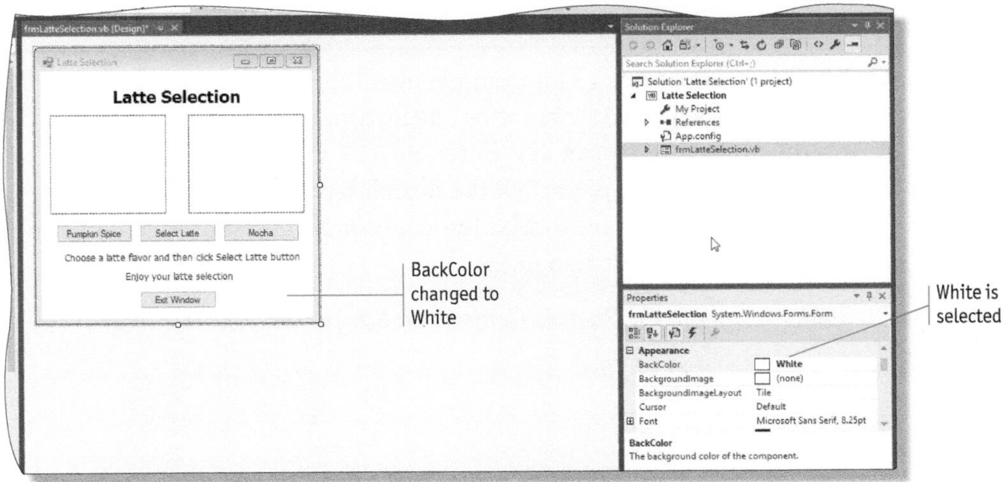

FIGURE 3-6

HEADS UP

Carefully consider your choice for the BackColor of a window. Generally, use light colors so objects in the window are easily visible. In some instances, you might choose a darker color for the BackColor, but then you should use lighter colors for the objects within the window. If you choose a darker BackColor and the object contains text, such as a Button or Label object, then the text color should be light. You specify text colors with the **ForeColor property.** The choice of a BackColor can be critical to the usability of the window.

You can use the same technique to change the BackColor or ForeColor of any object that contains the BackColor or ForeColor properties, including Button and Label objects.

Add Images to a PictureBox Object

> **HEADS UP**
>
> While many websites offer images you can select, three sites are particularly useful: bing.com/images, www.google.com/images, and www.webshots.com. When you visit sites, not all images are available for free download. In some cases, the images are copyrighted and you must acquire rights to use them. In addition, some sites require a fee before the image can be used. Therefore, you should download only images for which you have paid and acquired the rights to use or that are free of copyright restrictions and available to everyone.

PictureBox objects are used to display a graphic image. The sample program can display pictures of a pumpkin spice latte and a mocha latte. You must specify the image that will be displayed in a particular PictureBox object. Before specifying the image, however, you must locate the image and then place it in the Resources folder that is linked to the application. The general steps for displaying an image in a PictureBox object are as follows:

1. Locate the image to be displayed in the PictureBox object. You might locate this image on the web, in which case you must store the image in a folder on your computer, or the image might already be stored on your computer or a local school network.
2. Import the image into the **Resources folder**. This step makes the image available for display within the PictureBox object. Multiple images can be placed in the Resources folder.
3. Specify the image to be displayed within the PictureBox object.

Each of these steps will be explained on the following pages.

Locate and Save an Image from the Web

Images are available from a multitude of sources, from your own digital camera to millions of publicly available images on the web. If you work for a company, it might have photos and graphic logo images that can be used in company applications.

In this book, you can use the Student Companion Site to retrieve an image. For example, to retrieve the pumpkin image from this site, you can complete the following steps:

STEP 1 Open your web browser. (This example uses Internet Explorer; steps for other browsers might vary slightly.) Enter `www.cengagebrain.com` in the Address box, and then press the ENTER key. Enter `9781337102117` (the book's ISBN) in the Search text box, and then click the Search button. Select the Free Materials tab, and then click the Save to MyHome button. If necessary, click Student Companion to display your student resources.

The browser window opens and the Student Companion Site for this book is displayed (Figure 3-7).

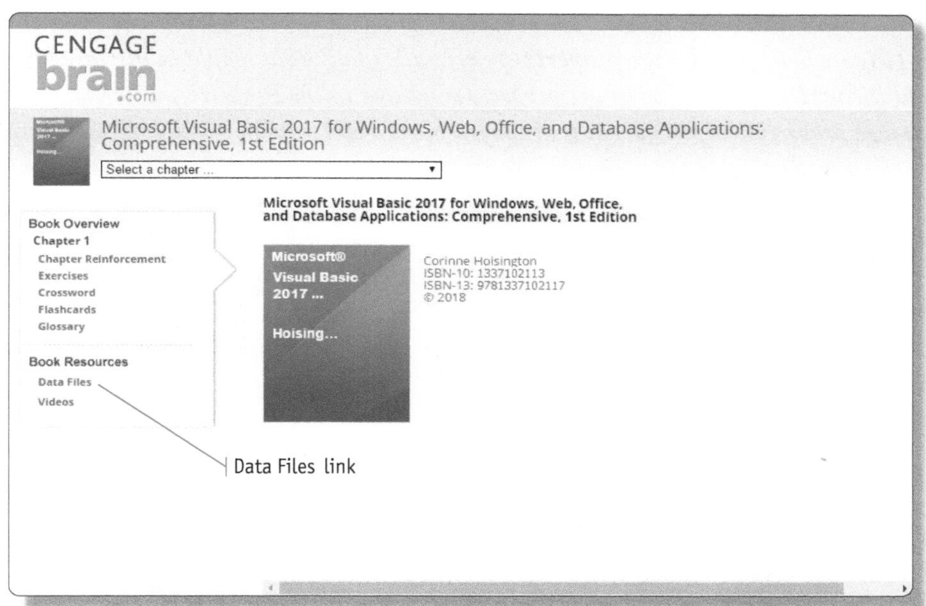

FIGURE 3-7

STEP 2 In the left pane, click Data Files. Click the Download Now link, click Save as, and then navigate to the location on your computer where you store downloaded files. Click the Save button to save the zipped file. Navigate to the location of the downloaded file, and then click the file. Click the Extract all button on the Extract tab to extract the files to the selected folder. Click the Browse button, navigate to the folder where you want to store files for this book, and then click the Extract button. Open the extracted folder for Chapter 3 to display its contents.

In the Save As dialog box you must identify the drive and folder in which you want to store the zipped files containing the Data Files. The location depends on your computer and drives. The image files for Chapter 3 are displayed in a folder window. Remember where you save the images because later you must locate and import them into the Resources folder for use in the program. In all sample programs in this book, images are stored on a USB drive that is designated as drive E. Image file names should not contain spaces.

WATCH OUT FOR

Webpages change frequently, so the pages displayed in your browser might differ from the ones shown here.

HEADS UP

When selecting an image, you should choose one that is the same approximate size of the PictureBox object where you will place the image. You can determine the size (in pixels) of a selected PictureBox object by looking at the Size property in the Properties window. To determine the size of the image on the web, press and hold or right-click the image and then click Properties on the menu. The size in pixels is displayed in the Properties dialog box. By choosing an image of the same approximate size, you minimize image distortion when it is fitted into the PictureBox object. If you cannot find an image of the same size, less distortion will occur if you select a larger image with approximately the same relative dimensions as the PictureBox object. In general, avoid selecting an image that is considerably smaller than the PictureBox object.

Import the Image into the Program Resources Folder

After you have saved an image on a storage device that is available to your computer, you should import the image into the program's Resources folder so the image is available for use. To import the Pumpkin image into the Resources folder, you can complete the following steps:

STEP 1 If necessary, open Visual Studio 2017 and the Latte Selection Visual Basic program. Select the picPumpkin PictureBox object by clicking it. Scroll in the PictureBox Properties window until the Image property is visible. Click the Image property name in the left list of the Properties window.

*With the PictureBox object selected, the Properties window displays all the properties of the object (Figure 3-8). The **Image property** specifies the image that should be displayed in the selected PictureBox object. The Image property is selected in the Properties window. The Image property's ellipsis button is displayed in the right column of the Image property.*

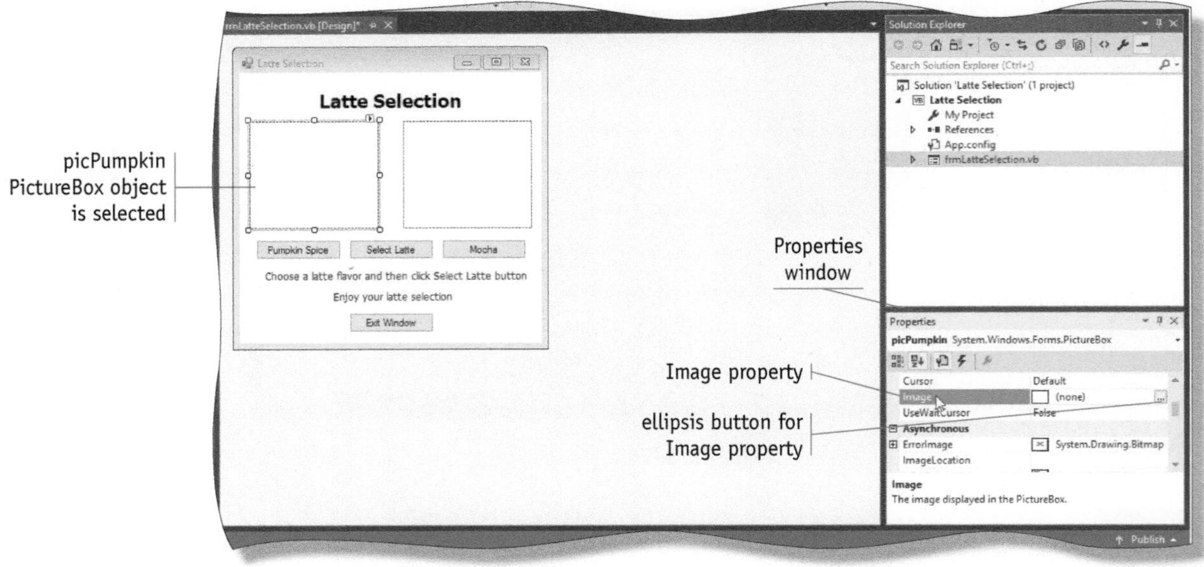

FIGURE 3-8

STEP 2 Click the ellipsis button in the right column of the Image property.

*The **Select Resource dialog box** opens (Figure 3-9) and displays the resources that have been imported for the program. In Figure 3-9, no resources have been imported.*

FIGURE 3-9

STEP 3 Click the Import button in the Select Resource dialog box. Use the features of the Open dialog box to locate the file you want to import into the program. In this case, you want to import the pumpkin.jpg file stored on drive E, which is a USB drive. Select pumpkin.jpg. Click the Open button in the Open dialog box.

The Select Resource dialog box is displayed again, but now the pumpkin image is identified in the Project resource file list (Figure 3-10). The image appears in the preview window. This means the image is now part of the resources for the program. You no longer need to locate the image on the USB drive to include the image in a Picture Box object.

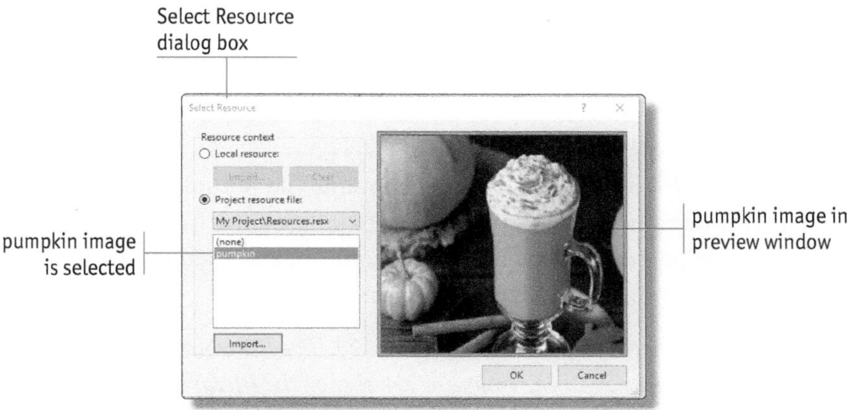

FIGURE 3-10
Anna_Pustynnikova/Shutterstock.com

STEP 5 With the pumpkin file name selected in the Project resource file list, click the OK button in the Select Resource dialog box.

The pumpkin image is displayed in the picPumpkin PictureBox object (Figure 3-11). In addition, the Resources folder is added to the Solution Explorer window, indicating the Resources folder now is part of the program.

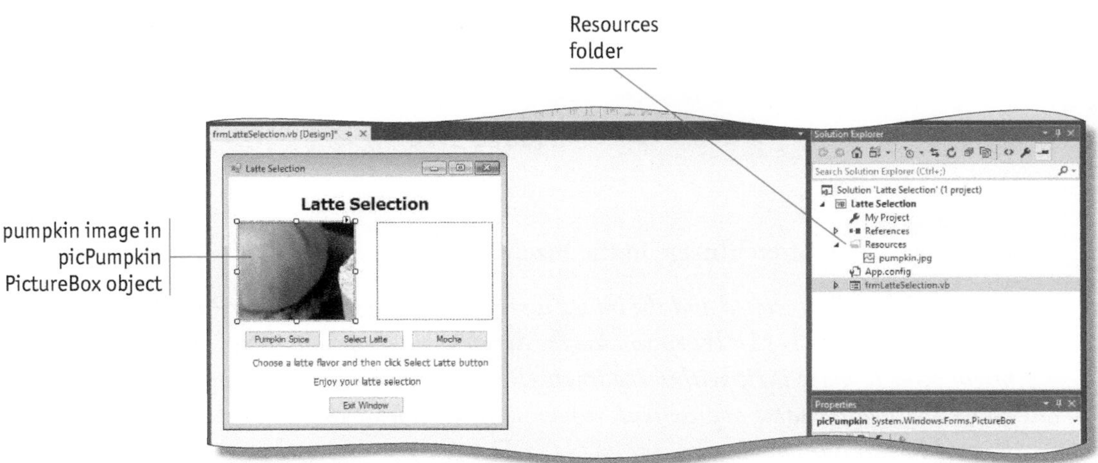

FIGURE 3-11
Anna_Pustynnikova/Shutterstock.com

HEADS UP

In the example, StretchImage is selected in the SizeMode list in the Properties window for PictureBox objects (see Figure 3-12). The other choices and their actions are as follows:

- **Normal —** No changes are made to the image size or the size of the PictureBox object. Visual Studio places the image in the PictureBox object and aligns the upper-left corner of the image with the upper-left corner of the PictureBox object.
- **AutoSize —** Visual Studio increases or decreases the size of the PictureBox object to accommodate the size of the image. The entire image is visible and fits precisely in the PictureBox object.
- **CenterImage —** No changes are made to the image size or the size of the PictureBox object. Visual Studio places the image in the PictureBox object and aligns the center of the image with the center of the PictureBox object.
- **Zoom —** The image size is either reduced or enlarged to fit in the PictureBox object. The fit can be left and right or up and down, depending on the dimensions of the image and the PictureBox object. If the image and PictureBox object are not exactly proportional to each other, the image will not fill out the entire PictureBox object.

Size an Image

In most cases, when you import an image into a program, the image will not fit in the PictureBox object perfectly because the two items have different sizes or dimensions. The developer must adjust the size of the image to fit in the PictureBox object or adjust the size of the PictureBox object to accommodate the image.

By comparing the images in Figures 3-10 and 3-11, you can see that the image is larger than the PictureBox object. Because the PictureBox object must remain its current size, the image must be adjusted using the **SizeMode property**. To adjust an image's size to fit in a PictureBox object, you can complete the following steps:

STEP 1 Select the PictureBox object that contains the pumpkin image, and then scroll in the picPumpkin Properties window until you see the SizeMode property. Click the SizeMode property name in the left column, and then click the SizeMode arrow in the right column of the SizeMode property.

The SizeMode property list is displayed (Figure 3-12). The list contains five choices you can use to change either the size of the image or the size of the PictureBox object. Normal is selected because it is the default value.

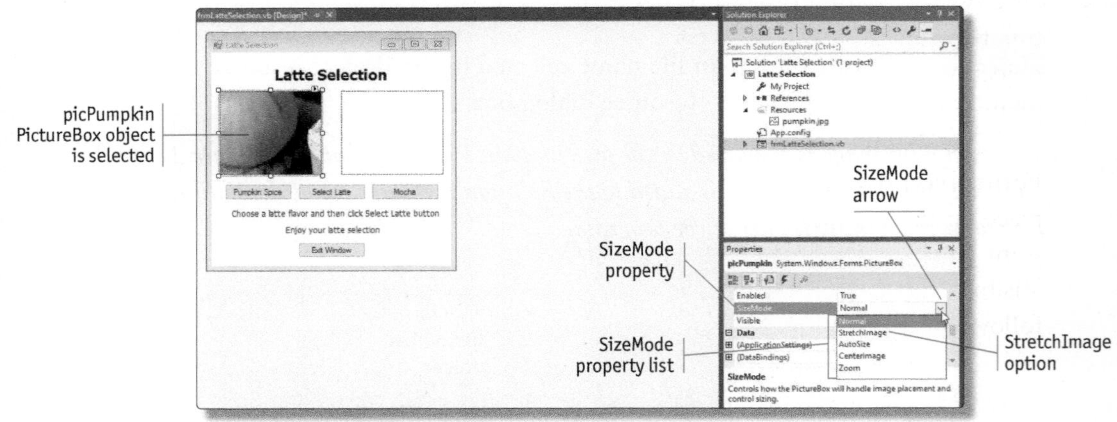

FIGURE 3-12

Anna_Pustynnikova/Shutterstock.com

STEP 2 Click StretchImage in the SizeMode list.

The SizeMode list is closed and the image is resized to fit within the picPumpkin PictureBox object (Figure 3-13). When you use the ***StretchImage option****, some image distortion might occur to make it fit within the PictureBox object. Therefore, you should select an image that has the same approximate dimensions (or at least the same aspect ratio) as the selected PictureBox object.*

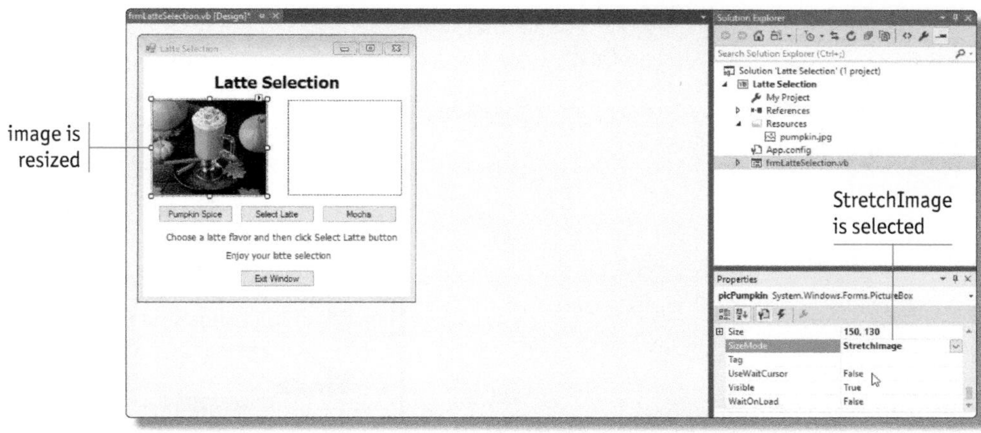

FIGURE 3-13

Anna_Pustynnikova/Shutterstock.com

Set the Visible Property

As you have learned, when the Latte Selection program begins, neither of the two latte types is pictured in the window. When the user clicks the Pumpkin Spice button, the program displays the appropriate picture in the Pumpkin Spice PictureBox object. When the user clicks the Mocha button, the program displays the appropriate picture in the other PictureBox object.

The **Visible property** controls whether an object is displayed on the Windows Form object. By default, the Visible property is set to True so that any object you place on the Windows Form object is displayed when the program runs. If you do not want an object to be displayed, you must set the Visible property to False. To set the Visible property to False for the picPumpkin PictureBox object, you can complete the following steps:

STEP 1 If necessary, select the picPumpkin PictureBox object. Scroll in the Properties window until the Visible property is displayed. Click the Visible property name in the left column, and then click the Visible arrow in the right column of the Visible property.

When you click the Visible arrow, the list displays the options True and False (Figure 3-14). To make the object visible when the program starts, select True. If you do not want the object to be visible when the program starts, select False.

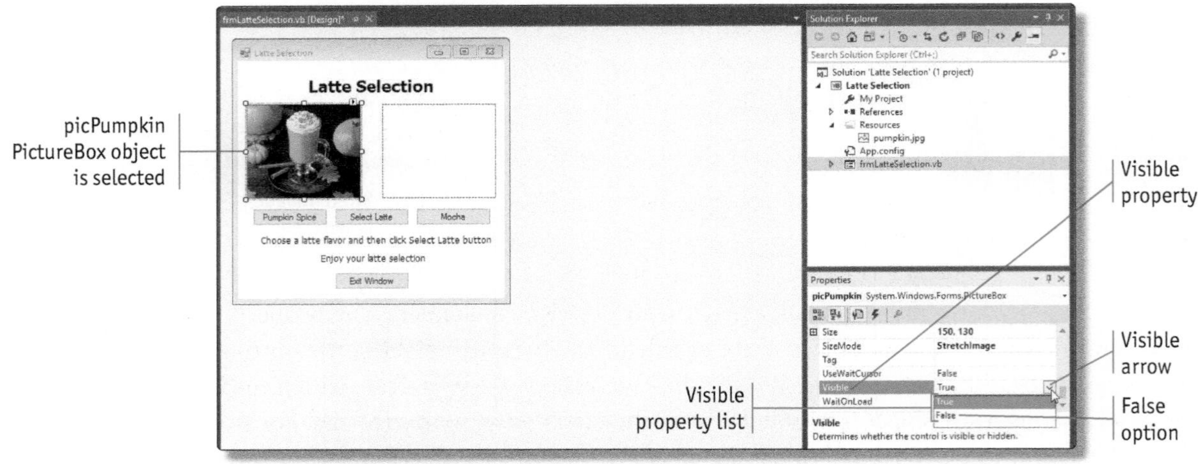

FIGURE 3-14

Anna_Pustynnikova/Shutterstock.com

STEP 2 Click False in the Visible property list.

The Visible property is set to False (Figure 3-15). When the program begins, the pumpkin picture will not be displayed on the Windows Form object. Note that the image and object are displayed on the frmLatteSelection.vb [Design] tabbed page regardless of the Visible property setting.

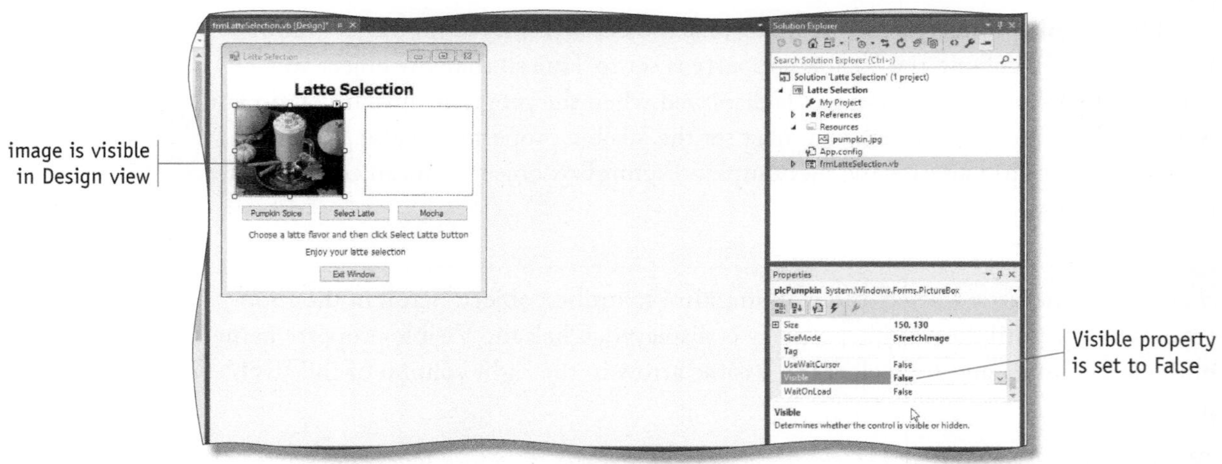

FIGURE 3-15

Anna_Pustynnikova/Shutterstock.com

Once you have set an object's Visible property to False, the only way to display the object on the Windows Form object while the program is running is to set the Visible property to True. You can do this by writing code, as you will see later in this chapter.

Set the Enabled Property

In an event-driven program, objects such as Button objects can be used to make events occur. For example, when you click the Pumpkin Spice button, a picture of a pumpkin spice latte is displayed in the PictureBox object. In addition, the Select Latte Button object becomes **enabled,** which means it can be clicked to make an event occur. When the program begins, however, the Select Latte button is **disabled,** which means nothing will happen when you click the button. A disabled button is displayed as dimmed (see Figure 3-1a on page 86).

The **Enabled property** controls when a Button object is enabled. The property also controls when a Button object is not enabled, which means clicking the button causes no action. The default selection for the Enabled property is True, which means the associated Button object is enabled. To set the Enabled property to False for the Select Latte button, you can complete the following steps:

STEP 1 Select the btnSelect object. Scroll in the Properties window until the Enabled property is displayed. Click the Enabled property name in the left column, and then click the Enabled arrow in the right column of the Enabled property.

When you click the Enabled arrow, the list contains the words True and False (Figure 3-16). To make the object enabled when the program starts, select True. If you do not want the object to be enabled when the program starts, select False.

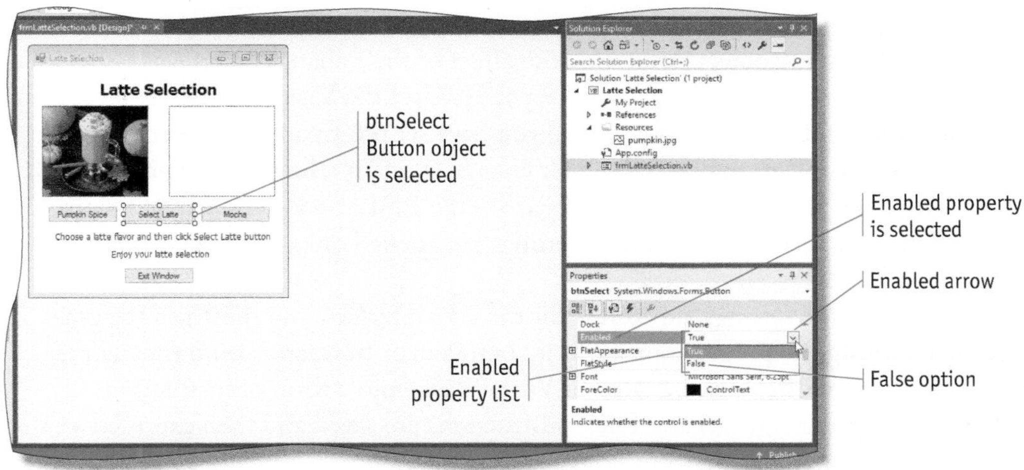

FIGURE 3-16

Anna_Pustynnikova/Shutterstock.com

STEP 2 Click False in the Enabled property list.

The Enabled property is set to False (Figure 3-17). When the program begins, the btnSelect Button object will not be enabled on the Windows Form object.

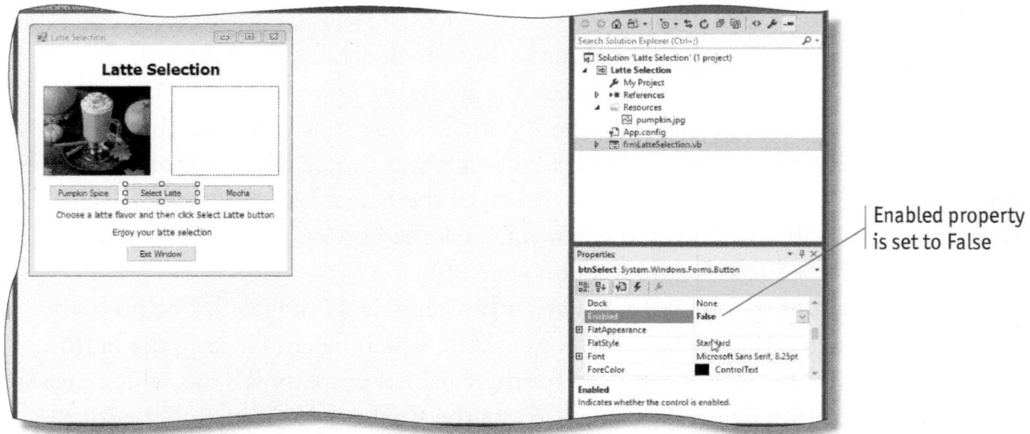

FIGURE 3-17

Anna_Pustynnikova/Shutterstock.com

Once you have set the Enabled property to False, the only way to enable a Button object on the Windows Form object while the program is running is to set the Enabled property to True. You can do this by writing code, as you will see later in this chapter.

Run a Program

When you set some object properties, the effect of their changes might not be evident until you run the program. For example, you have set the Visible property to False for the picPumpkin PictureBox object, and you have set the Enabled property to False for the btnSelect Button object. Neither change is evident, however, when you view the Latte Selection Windows Form object on the frmLatteSelection.vb [Design] tabbed page in Visual Studio. These settings are applied only when you actually run the program.

To ensure the settings are correct for the user interface, you must run the program. **Running the program** means it is compiled, or translated, from the instructions you have written or generated in Visual Basic into a form of instructions that the computer can execute. These instructions are saved and then executed as a program.

To run the program you have created, you can click the Start button on the Standard toolbar, as shown in the following steps:

STEP 1 Point to the Start button on the Standard toolbar.

The pointer appears over the Start button (Figure 3-18).

FIGURE 3-18

Anna_Pustynnikova/Shutterstock.com

STEP 2 Click the Start button on the Standard toolbar.

The program is compiled and saved, and then it runs on the computer. When the program runs, the Latte Selection window is displayed on the screen (Figure 3-19). Notice that the pumpkin image is not displayed in the window because the Visible property was set to False for the picPumpkin PictureBox object (see Figure 3-15). Notice also that the Select Latte button is dimmed, which indicates its Enabled property is set to False. The Diagnostic Tools button pane opens on the right.

FIGURE 3-19

Once you start running the program, it continues to run until you exit it. To exit a program, click the Close button on the right side of the window title bar (see Figure 3-19).

After you set all the properties for the objects in the user interface, the design of the user interface is complete. You now are ready to move to the next phase of the PDLC — designing the program processing objects.

Visual Basic Program Coding

Before beginning to design the program processing objects, the developer must understand certain program coding principles and techniques. **Program code** is the set of instructions written by the developer that direct the program to carry out its required processing. The following sections explain the Visual Basic 2017 code required for the Latte Selection program.

Enter Visual Basic Code for Event Handling

As you have learned, most processing in an event-driven program occurs when the user triggers an event. For example, when a user clicks a button on the GUI, the activity can trigger an event and the program performs the required processing. The developer writes program code to carry out the processing. This code is placed in a section of the program called an **event handler** — it *handles* the event that the user action triggers by executing code that performs the required processing.

To write the code for an event handler, the developer first must identify the GUI object that will be used to trigger the event. For example, when the Pumpkin Spice button is clicked in the sample program, the Pumpkin picture should appear in the picPumpkin PictureBox object. To write the code that will display the pumpkin picture, the developer must inform Visual Studio that the Pumpkin Spice button is the object for which the code is being written and that an event handler must be created for the click event. You can create the event handler using the following steps:

STEP 1 If necessary, open Visual Studio 2017 and the Latte Selection program and make the frmLatteSelection.vb [Design] tabbed window visible. If necessary, close the Output pane at the bottom of the screen. Point to the Pumpkin Spice Button object in the Windows Form object.

The pointer appears over the Pumpkin Spice Button object (Figure 3-20). The four-headed arrow pointer indicates you can drag the Button object to another location in the window.

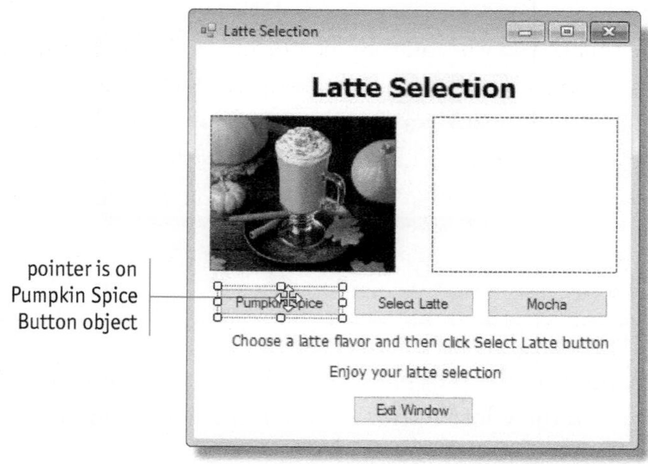

FIGURE 3-20

Anna_Pustynnikova/Shutterstock.com

STEP 2 Double-click the Pumpkin Spice Button object.

The code window is displayed on the frmLatteSelection.vb tabbed page (Figure 3-21). The code in the window is generated by Visual Studio. This code identifies an event handler, which is the code that executes when an event is triggered. When the Pumpkin Spice button is clicked, the program will execute the code in this event handler. The list box at the top of the tabbed page identifies the object for which the event handler will execute — in this case, the btnPumpkin object. The list box in the upper-right corner of the tabbed page identifies the event that must occur to execute the code in the event handler. The event identified in Figure 3-21 is "Click." When the user clicks the Pumpkin Spice button, the program executes the code between the Private Sub statement and the End Sub statement. The insertion point is located where the developer should begin entering the code that executes when the user clicks the btnPumpkin Button object.*

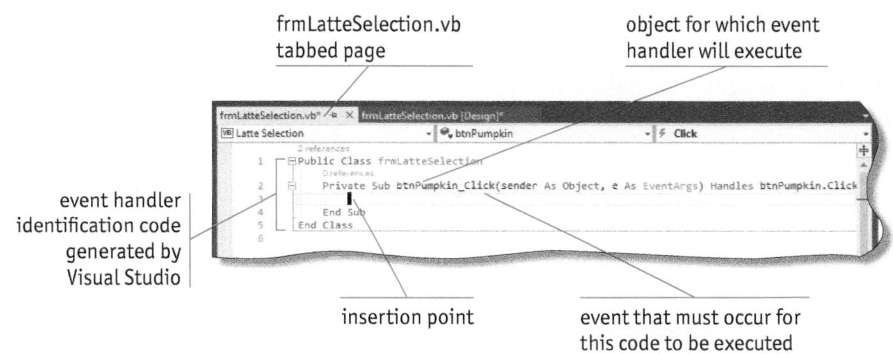

FIGURE 3-21

Visual Basic 2017 Coding Statements

A Visual Basic 2017 coding statement contains instructions that the computer eventually executes. Visual Basic has a set of rules, or **syntax**, that specifies how each statement must be written.

When the user clicks the Pumpkin Spice button while the Latte Selection program is running, the pumpkin image should be displayed in the picPumpkin PictureBox object. Figure 3-22 shows a Visual Basic coding statement that sets the Visible property to True for the picPumpkin PictureBox object so the image is displayed in the picture box after the statement executes.

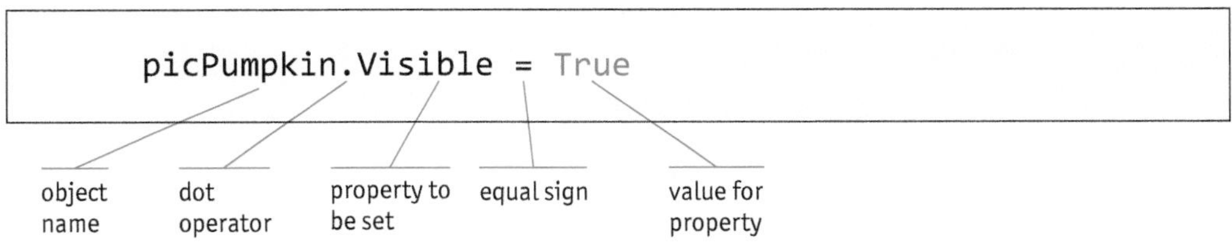

FIGURE 3-22

The first part of the statement, picPumpkin, identifies the object that contains the property to set. The name of the object is followed by the **dot operator** (period) with no intervening spaces. The dot operator separates the name of the object from the next entry in the statement and is required.

Following the dot operator is the name of the property to set. In Figure 3-22 on page 101, the name of the property is Visible. You will recall that the Visible property determines whether an image is displayed in the PictureBox object when the program is running. In Figure 3-15 on page 96, the Visible property was set to False for the picPumpkin PictureBox object so the image would not be displayed when the program started. This statement sets the Visible property to True so the image will be displayed.

The property name is followed by a space and then an equal sign. The space is not required, but good coding practice dictates that elements within a statement should be separated by a space so the statement is easier to read. One or more spaces can be used, but most developers use only one space. The equal sign is required because it indicates that the value to be used for setting the property follows. A space follows the equal sign for readability.

The word *True* follows the space. The value True in the Visible property indicates that the image should be displayed in the PictureBox object. When the program is running and the Visible property is set to True, the image appears in the picture box.

Each entry within the program statement must be correct or the program will not compile. This means the object name must be spelled properly, the dot operator must be placed in the correct location, the name of the property must be spelled properly, the equal sign must be present, and a valid entry for the property must follow the equal sign. For the Visible property, the only valid entries are True and False.

General Format of a Visual Basic Statement

The general format of the Visual Basic statement shown in Figure 3-22 appears in Figure 3-23.

General Format: Property Value Assignment Statement

```
objectname.property = propertyvalue
```

EXAMPLE	*RESULT*
picPumpkin.Visible = True	Picture is visible
btnSelectLatte.Enabled = False	Button is dimmed

FIGURE 3-23

In the general format, the object name always is the first item in the Visual Basic statement. The object name is the name you specified in the (Name) property of the Properties window. In Figure 3-22, the object name is picPumpkin because that name was given to the pumpkin PictureBox object.

The dot operator (period) is required. It follows the object name with no space between them. Immediately following the dot operator is the name of the property that will be set by the statement. The property name must be spelled correctly and must be a valid property for the object named in the statement. Valid properties that can be specified in the statement are identified in the Properties window associated with the object.

The equal sign must follow the property name in the statement. Visual Basic statements do not require spaces, nor is there a limit to how many spaces you can place between elements in the statement. The equal sign identifies the statement as an **assignment statement,** which means the value on the right side of the equal sign is assigned to the element on the left side of the equal sign. When setting properties, the element on the left side of the equal sign is the property.

The property value specified in the assignment statement must be a valid value for the property identified on the left side of the equal sign. You can see the valid values for a given property by looking in the Properties window for the object whose property you are setting.

After you have entered the property value, the Visual Basic statement is complete. Because correct programming protocol dictates that only one statement should appear on a line, the next step is to press the ENTER key to move the insertion point to the next line in the code window.

The general statement format shown in Figure 3-23 is used for all statements in which the code sets the value of an object property.

HEADS UP

Unlike some programming languages, the capitalization of object names, properties, property values, and other values is not important in Visual Basic. Therefore, the object name picPumpkin is equivalent to the object name picpumpkin. Capitalization is used within the object name to make the name easier to read.

IntelliSense

In Figure 3-21 on page 101, the insertion point is located in the code window. To enter the statement shown in Figure 3-22 into the program using the code window, you can type the entire statement. Visual Studio, however, provides help so that you will be less prone to make a typing error when entering the statement. This help feature is called IntelliSense.

IntelliSense displays all allowable entries you can make in a Visual Basic statement each time a dot (period), an equal sign, or another special character is required for the statement. When you type the prefix pic as shown in Figure 3-24, an IntelliSense window opens with all the objects that begin with the prefix. Instead of possibly misspelling the object name, you can select it from the IntelliSense list. The complete Visual Basic statement is shown in Figure 3-24.

```
picPumpkin.Visible = True
```

FIGURE 3-24

When you type the first few letters of the object name, IntelliSense displays a list of all the objects and other entries that can be specified in the statement.

IN THE REAL WORLD

Microsoft created IntelliSense in response to the demands of rapid application development so statements can be entered accurately and easily. Most developers use IntelliSense; it is the standard within the software industry.

Enter a Visual Basic Statement

To enter the Visual Basic statement in Figure 3-24 using IntelliSense, you can complete the following steps:

STEP 1 With the code window open and the insertion point positioned as shown in Figure 3-21 on page 101, type `pic`.

The characters "pic" are displayed in the code window (Figure 3-25). IntelliSense displays a list of all the entries that can follow the prefix in the statement. Sometimes the selected entry is correct for the statement you are entering, but often it is not. Therefore, you must identify the correct statement in the list before entering it.

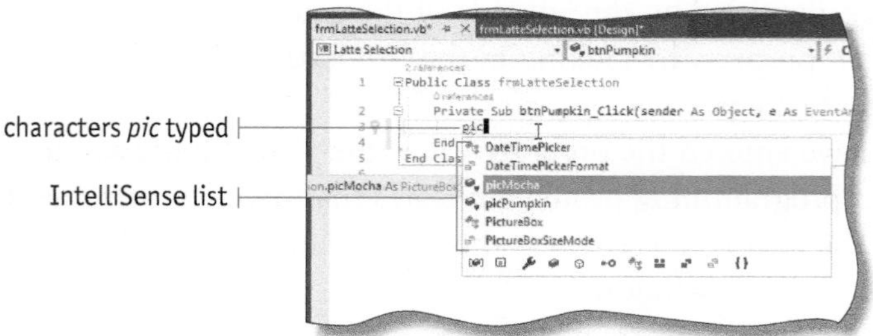

FIGURE 3-25

STEP 2 To identify the correct entry, type its next letter until the entry is selected. In this case, type `p`.

As you type, IntelliSense highlights an entry in the list that begins with the letters you enter (Figure 3-26). When you enter picp, IntelliSense highlights the only term in the list that begins with picp, which is picPumpkin. This is the object name you want to enter into the Visual Basic statement.

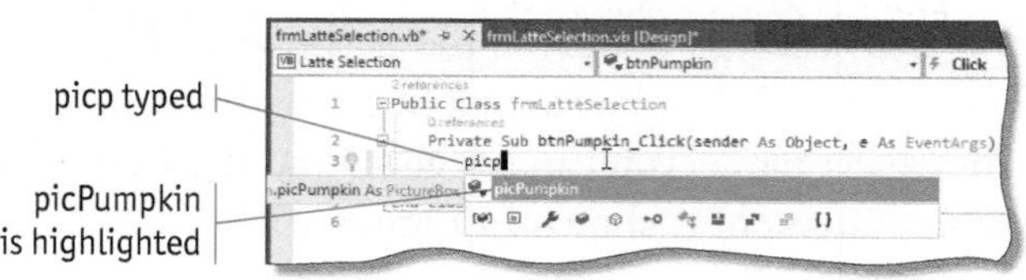

FIGURE 3-26

STEP 3 When IntelliSense highlights the correct object name, press the key corresponding to the entry that follows the object name. In this case, press the PERIOD key.

IntelliSense automatically enters the entire object name into the Visual Basic statement and the period you typed following the object name (Figure 3-27). In addition, IntelliSense realizes that the dot you entered means more information is required in the statement, so it displays a list of the allowable entries following the dot.

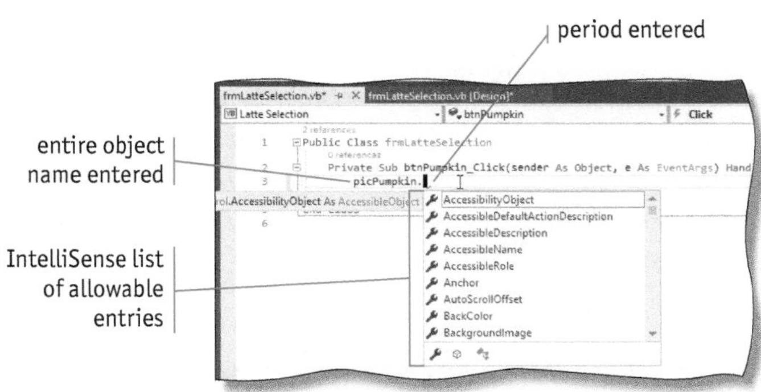

FIGURE 3-27

STEP 4 As with the object name in Step 2, the next step is to enter one or more characters until IntelliSense highlights the desired property in the list. Type the letter v for the Visible property.

IntelliSense highlights the properties in the list that begin with the letter v (Visible) (Figure 3-28). Because the Visible property is highlighted, no further action is required to select it. The red curly line below the code indicates that the line of code is not complete.

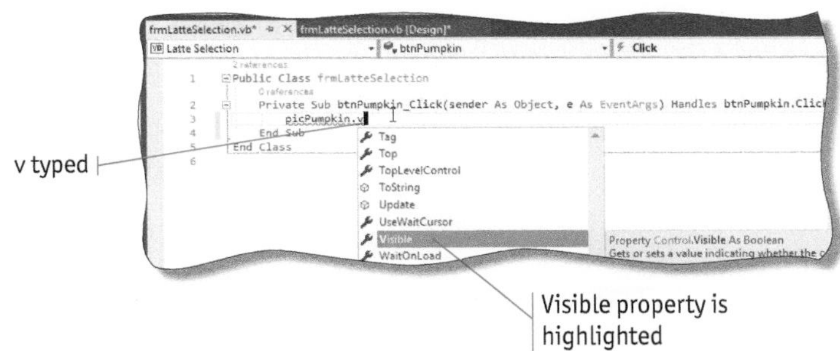

FIGURE 3-28

STEP 5 Press the key for the character that follows the property name. In this case, press the SPACEBAR.

IntelliSense enters the highlighted property name (Visible) followed by the space you typed (Figure 3-29). The space indicates to Visual Basic that the object name and property name entry is complete. In Figure 3-29, the statement gets or sets a value indicating whether the control is displayed. This means the Visible property indicates whether the picPumpkin PictureBox object is displayed.

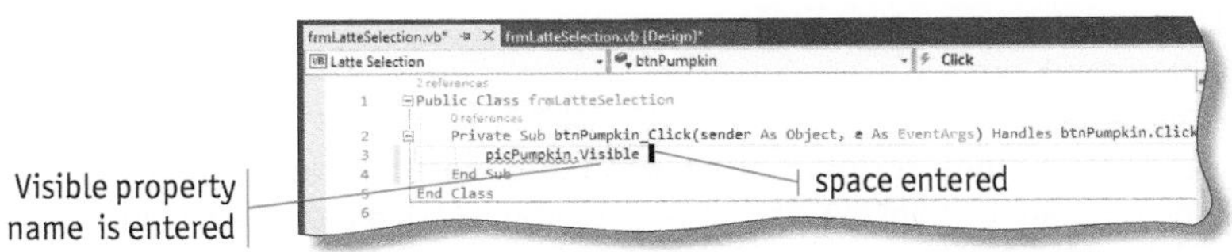

FIGURE 3-29

IN THE REAL WORLD

When you enter a statement using IntelliSense, it will format the statement by default after you press the ENTER key. If you had not entered spaces in the statement before and after the equal sign, IntelliSense would have inserted the spaces when you pressed the ENTER key. You can choose whether to enter spaces as you type the statement or let IntelliSense insert the spaces when you press the ENTER key.

IN THE REAL WORLD

You can highlight entries in the lists that IntelliSense displays in a variety of ways. In the previous example, you typed the first character of the entry. Other ways to highlight an entry include pressing the UP ARROW key and DOWN ARROW key, and scrolling in the list until the entry is visible and then clicking the entry.

To enter the item selected in the list, the example illustrates how to press the key for the character that follows the entry from the list. Other methods include pressing the Tab key and double-tapping or double-clicking the entry in the list. In both cases, you still must enter the next character in the statement, but in the example, that character is entered when you press the corresponding key to select the IntelliSense entry from the list.

STEP 6 Press the EQUAL SIGN key and then press the SPACEBAR and the letter t.

The equal sign and a space are displayed and then IntelliSense displays a list of the entries you can make (Figure 3-30). For the Visible property, the correct entries following the equal sign are False and True. An entry of False indicates the PictureBox object should not be visible; True indicates the opposite. IntelliSense highlights the True entry.

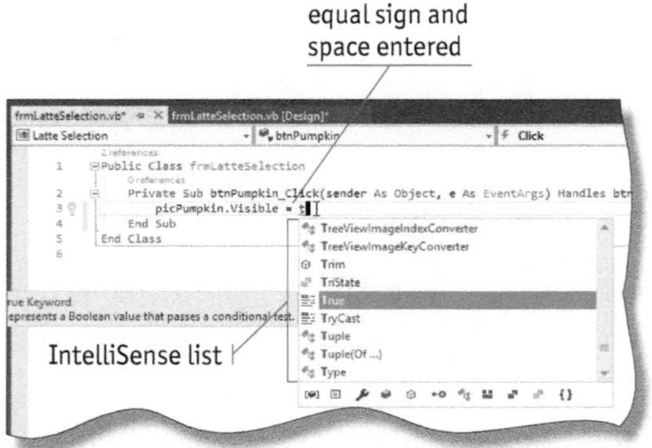

FIGURE 3-30

STEP 8 Press the key for the character that follows the True entry. In this case, press the ENTER key.

Because you pressed the ENTER key, IntelliSense enters True into the statement and then Visual Studio moves the indented insertion point to the next line (Figure 3-31). The Visual Basic statement now is entered completely.

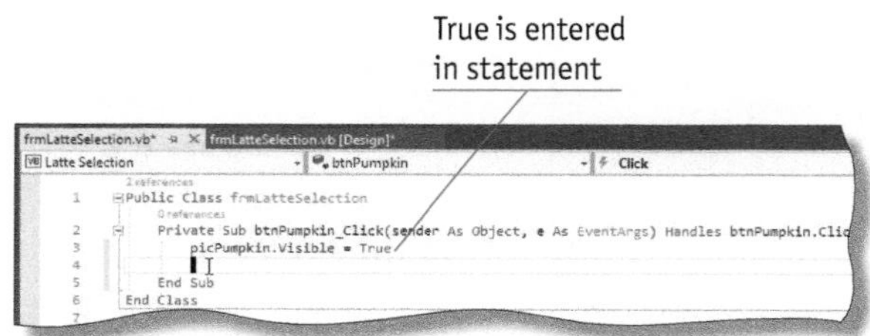

FIGURE 3-31

CONSIDER THIS

Can I turn on line numbers to receive assistance while creating my program?

Line numbers help identify each line of code in the code window. If line numbers do not appear in the code window on your computer, you can display them by completing the following steps:

1. Click Tools on the menu bar.
2. Click Options on the Tools menu.
3. If necessary, click the triangle next to Text Editor in the Options dialog box.
4. If necessary, click the triangle next to Basic in the list below Text Editor.
5. Click General in the list below Basic.
6. Place a check mark in the Line numbers check box.
7. Click the OK button in the Options dialog box.

Do professional programming teams immediately sit down at a laptop and start typing in code?

Professional programmers first design the program by thinking about the numerous ways the problem's solution may be found. One of the most common is called top-down design. Top-down design divides the program into sub-tasks. Each sub-task is a smaller problem that must be solved.

Visual Studio and IntelliSense automatically create the indentations in the program statements in Figure 3-31 because indentations make the statements easier to read and understand. As programs become more complex, proper indentation of program statements can be an important factor in developing error-free programs.

The following general steps summarize the procedure for using IntelliSense to enter a Visual Basic statement that sets a property:

1. In the IntelliSense list, type the first letter(s) of the name of the object whose property will be set.
2. When the object name is selected in the list, press the PERIOD key.
3. Type the first letter(s) of the name of the property to be set until the name is highlighted in the IntelliSense list.
4. Press the SPACEBAR to complete the first portion of the statement.
5. Press the EQUAL SIGN key.
6. Press the SPACEBAR.
7. Press the first letter(s) of the entry you want to select in the list until the entry is highlighted. If IntelliSense does not display a list, type the value for the property.
8. Press the ENTER key.

Using IntelliSense to enter a Visual Basic statement provides two significant advantages. First, it is faster to enter a statement using IntelliSense than it is to type the statement. Second, using IntelliSense drastically reduces the number of errors when entering statements. By using only the entries in the IntelliSense lists, the developer seldom will make an invalid entry. In addition, because the entry is chosen from a list, it cannot possibly be misspelled or mistyped.

Entering a programming statement is a fundamental skill for a Visual Basic programmer. You should thoroughly understand how to enter a programming statement using IntelliSense.

Set the Visible Property to False

In Figure 3-31, the programming statement set the Visible property to True for the picPumpkin PictureBox object, which will display the image in the picture box when the statement is executed. The statement will execute when the user clicks the Pumpkin Spice button because the statement is part of the btnPumpkin_Click event handler.

When the user clicks the Pumpkin Spice button, the Visible property also must be set to False for the picMocha PictureBox so the mocha picture is not displayed alongside the Pumpkin picture. To set the Visible property to False for the picMocha PictureBox object, you can complete the following steps:

STEP 1 Click the Close button to close the Toolbox. With the insertion point on the next line of the code window for the Pumpkin Spice button click event, type `pic`.

The letters you typed are displayed in the code window and the IntelliSense list shows the valid entries you can choose (Figure 3-32). The entry picPumpkin is highlighted because it is the last entry that was selected from this list.

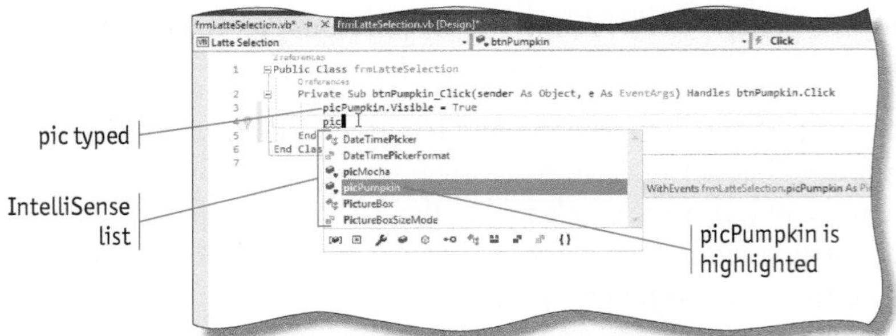

FIGURE 3-32

STEP 2 Type m to highlight the picMocha entry in the IntelliSense list.

IntelliSense highlights picMocha in the list because it is the only entry that starts with the characters "picm" (Figure 3-33).

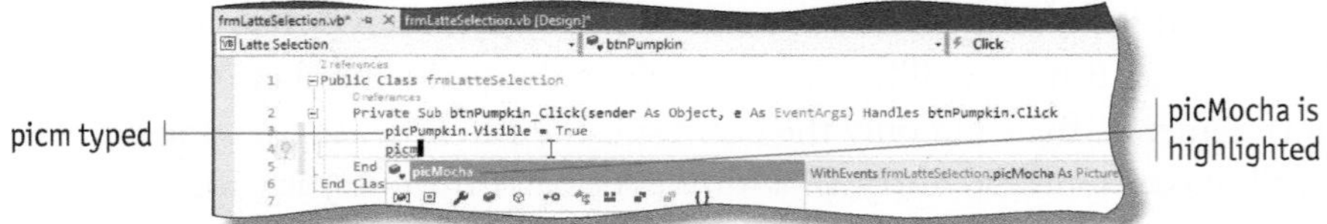

FIGURE 3-33

STEP 3 Press the key for the character that follows the object name. In this case, press the PERIOD key and type a v to highlight Visible.

The picMocha entry is placed in the statement followed by the dot operator (period) you typed. The Visible entry is highlighted in the list (Figure 3-34).

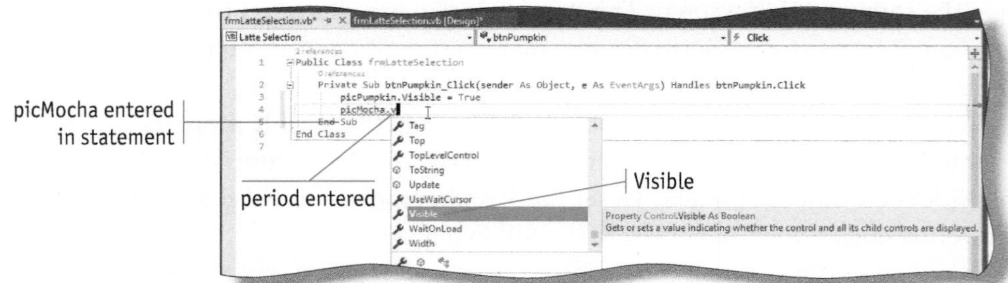

FIGURE 3-34

STEP 4 Press the SPACEBAR, press the EQUAL SIGN key, and then press the SPACEBAR.

IntelliSense places the Visible entry in the statement (Figure 3-35). Next, the space you typed appears, followed by the equal sign and the second space you typed. When you typed the equal sign, IntelliSense displayed the list of allowable entries following the equal sign.

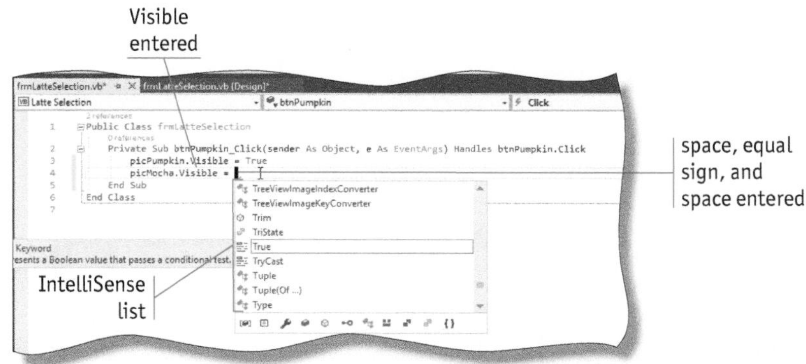

FIGURE 3-35

STEP 5 Type `f` and then press the ENTER key.

When you type the letter f, IntelliSense highlights False in the list. When you press the enter key, IntelliSense inserts False at the insertion point (Figure 3-36).

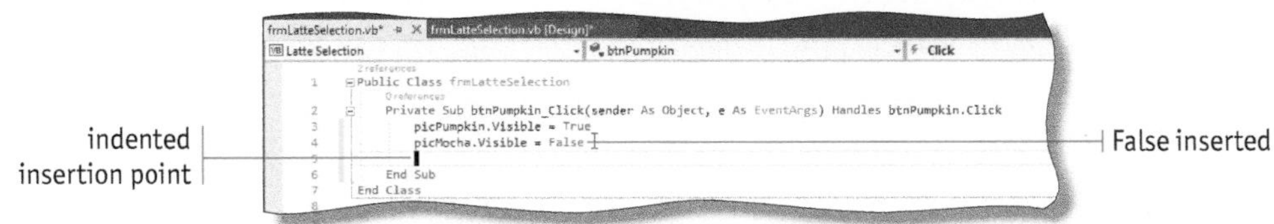

FIGURE 3-36

Again, using IntelliSense to enter a Visual Basic programming statement results in a correct statement entered in minimal time with a reduced chance of errors.

Set the Enabled Property

You learned earlier that if the Enabled property is True for a Button object, the click event code will be executed for the button when the user clicks it. If the Enabled property is False for a Button object, the event code for the button will not be executed. In Figure 3-17 on page 98, the Enabled property was set to False for the Select Latte button so that the button is not active when the program begins. When the user clicks a picture button such as the Pumpkin Spice button, however, the Enabled property must be set to True so the Select Latte button is active. To set the Enabled property to True, the developer must enter a coding statement for the btnSelect Button object. To enter the coding statement into the btnPumpkin_Click event handler, you can complete the following steps:

STEP 1 Type `btns` to display the IntelliSense list until IntelliSense highlights the btnSelect entry in the list.

IntelliSense highlights btnSelect, the only entry that starts with the characters "btns" (Figure 3-37). Sometimes, the correct entry will be highlighted before you type all the distinguishing characters. If so, you need not type more characters.

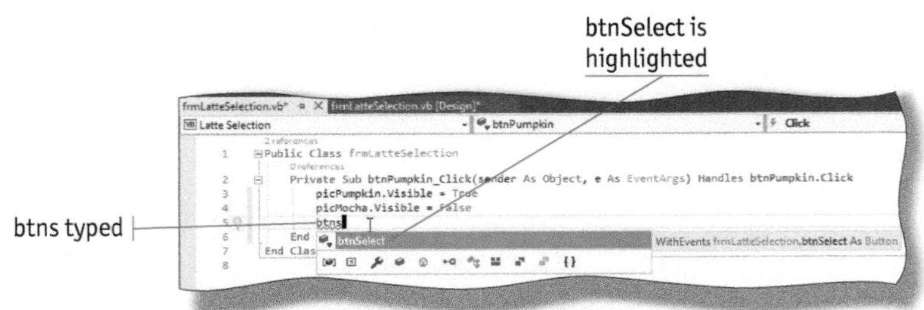

FIGURE 3-37

STEP 2 Type a period, type `e`, press the SPACEBAR, press the EQUAL SIGN key, press the SPACEBAR again, and then type `t` to select True in the IntelliSense list.

IntelliSense places the highlighted entry (btnSelect) in the statement and displays a list of the next allowable entries. When you typed e, Enabled was selected in the list. Pressing the SPACEBAR caused IntelliSense to place Enabled and then the space in the statement. When you typed the equal sign and second space, IntelliSense inserted both and displayed the list of entries that can follow the equal sign (Figure 3-38).

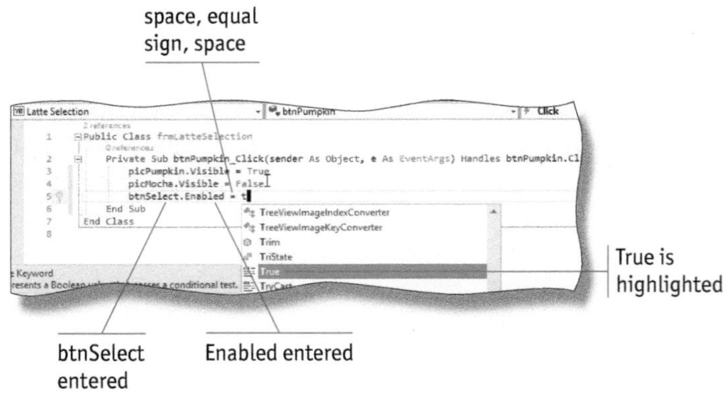

FIGURE 3-38

STEP 3 Press the ENTER key to enter the completed statement and place the insertion point on the next line.

IntelliSense enters True in the statement (Figure 3-39). Pressing the ENTER key completes the statement and moves the indented insertion point to the next line.

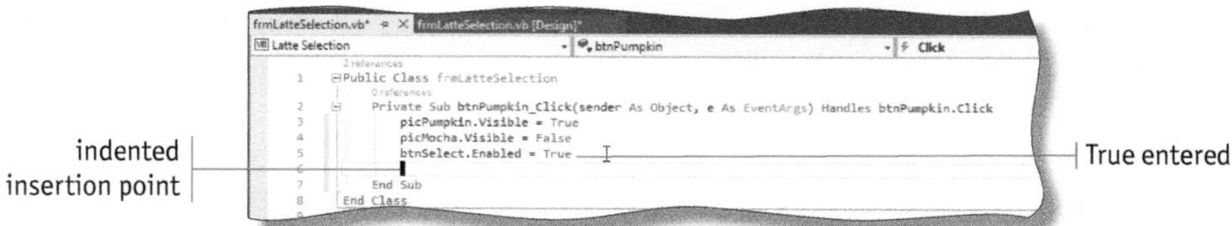
indented insertion point
True entered

FIGURE 3-39

Learning how to enter program statements using IntelliSense is fundamental to writing programs using the Visual Basic 2017 language.

Comments in Program Statements

A well-written Visual Basic program normally contains **comment statements** within the code itself to document what the code is doing. The general purpose of comments is to help code readers understand the code and how it accomplishes its tasks. An example of comment statements used in code is shown in Figure 3-40.

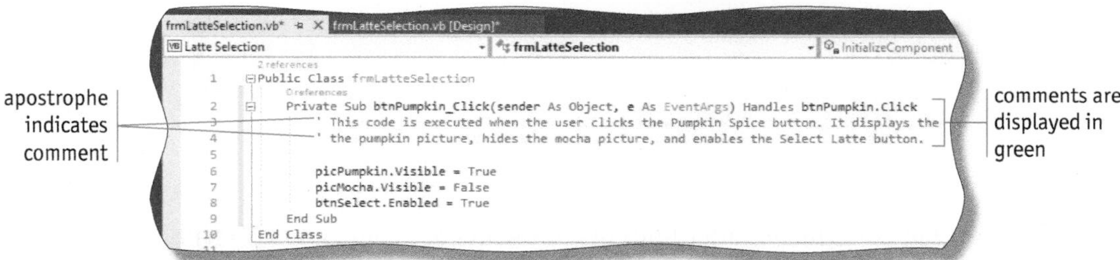
apostrophe indicates comment
comments are displayed in green
Public Class frmLatteSelection
Private Sub btnPumpkin_Click(sender As Object, e As EventArgs) Handles btnPumpkin.Click
' This code is executed when the user clicks the Pumpkin Spice button. It displays the
' the pumpkin picture, hides the mocha picture, and enables the Select Latte button.
picPumpkin.Visible = True
picMocha.Visible = False
btnSelect.Enabled = True
End Sub
End Class

FIGURE 3-40

A comment is preceded by an apostrophe. Whenever the Visual Basic compiler encounters an apostrophe in the code, it ignores the remaining characters on the line. To the compiler, it's as if the comments do not exist.

The comments in the code are displayed in green text and describe the processing that will occur in the code that follows. Because comments are ignored by the Visual Basic compiler, developers must not include programming language syntax in the comments. Any letters or characters are allowed within comments.

To enter comments, first type an apostrophe in the code. All characters following the apostrophe on a line of code are considered a comment. To enter the comment code shown in Figure 3-40, you can complete the following steps:

STEP 1 To insert a blank line following the event code generated by Visual Studio that begins with the word Private, click anywhere in that line and then press the END key. Press the ENTER key.

Visual Studio inserts a blank line in the code and then moves the insertion point to the blank line (Figure 3-41). The comments can be inserted on the blank line.

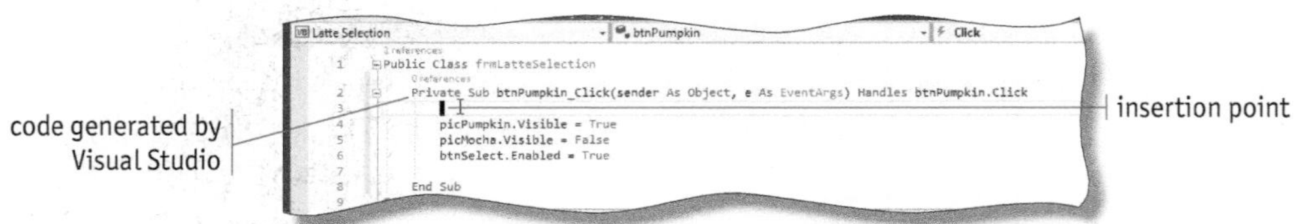

FIGURE 3-41

STEP 2 Type the first line of the comments, beginning with an apostrophe as shown in Figure 3-40, and then press the ENTER key. Type the next line of comments, and then press the ENTER key.

The apostrophe identifies the rest of the line as a comment. The comment lines are displayed in green text (Figure 3-42).

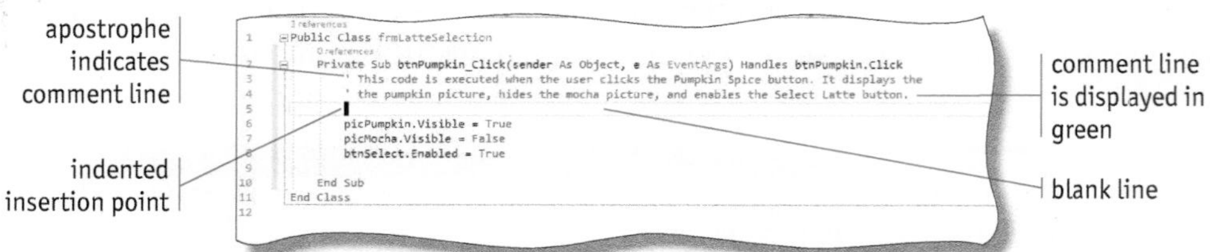

FIGURE 3-42

You can continue to enter lines of comments by typing an apostrophe and the comment and then pressing the ENTER key until all comments are completed.

Same-Line Comments

Because the Visual Basic compiler treats all characters following an apostrophe as comments, it is possible to place a comment on the same line as executable code. In Figure 3-43, a comment is shown on the same line as the statement that sets the btnSelect Enabled property to True.

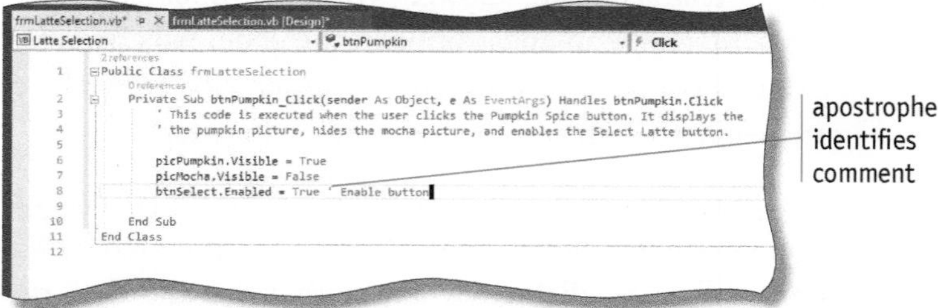

FIGURE 3-43

In Figure 3-43, the apostrophe specifies that subsequent characters on the line are to be treated as comments. Therefore, the Enable button text is displayed in green and is treated as a comment. To enter a comment on any line, enter an apostrophe and then type the comment. Remember that all characters after an apostrophe are treated as comments on a line of code.

Introductory Comments

Every program should begin with comments that state the name of the program, the developer's name, the date, and the purpose of the program. These introductory comments should precede all code in the program — even the code generated by Visual Studio (Figure 3-44).

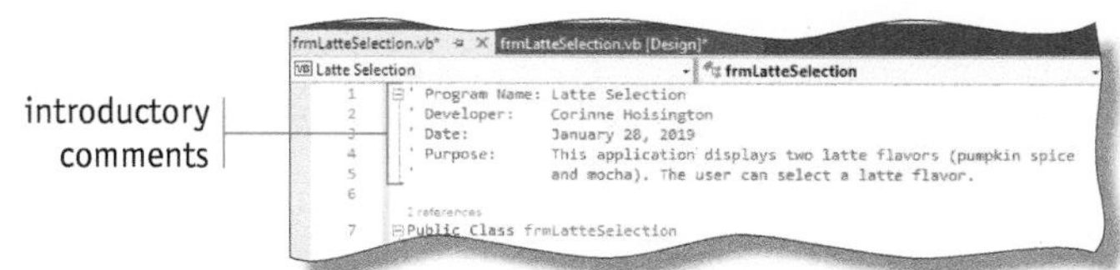

FIGURE 3-44

To enter introductory comments, you can complete the following steps:

STEP 1 Click to the left of the word Public on line 1 of the program to place the insertion point on that line. Press the ENTER key and then press the UP ARROW key.

When you press the ENTER key, Visual Studio inserts a blank line on line 1 of the code and moves the line that begins with the words Public Class down to line 2 (Figure 3-45). Visual Studio also moves the insertion point to line 2 when you press the ENTER key. When you press the UP ARROW key, the insertion point moves to the first line, which is blank.

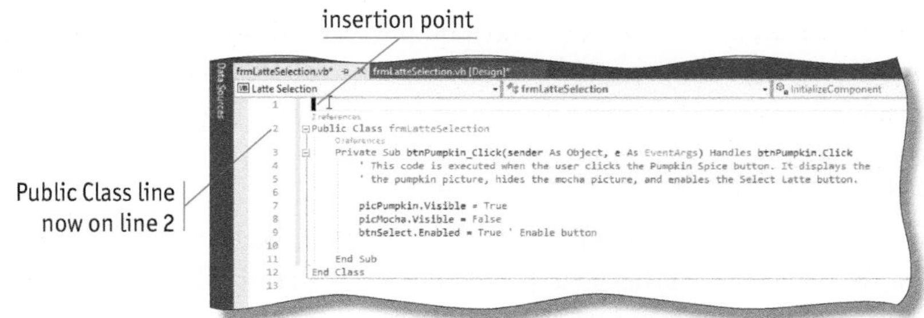

FIGURE 3-45

STEP 2 Type an apostrophe, a space, the text `Program Name:`, and then press the TAB key.

The apostrophe identifies all characters and words that follow as comments, so those characters are displayed in green (Figure 3-46). The first line of introductory comments normally specifies the name of the program. Pressing the TAB key moves the insertion point to the right.

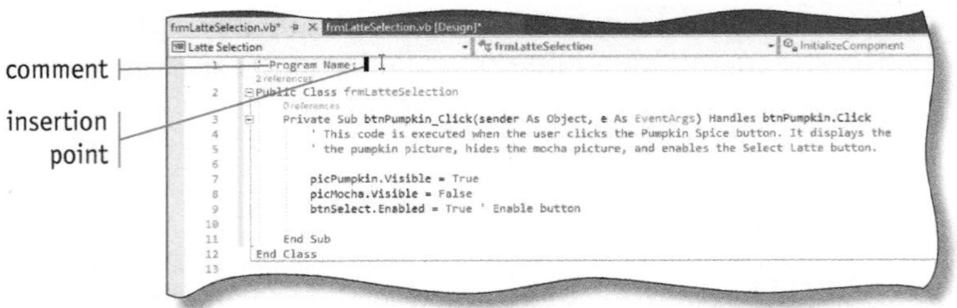

FIGURE 3-46

STEP 3 Type `Latte Selection` as the name of the program, and then press the ENTER key.

The program name appears in the first line of comments and the insertion point is moved to line 2 (Figure 3-47).

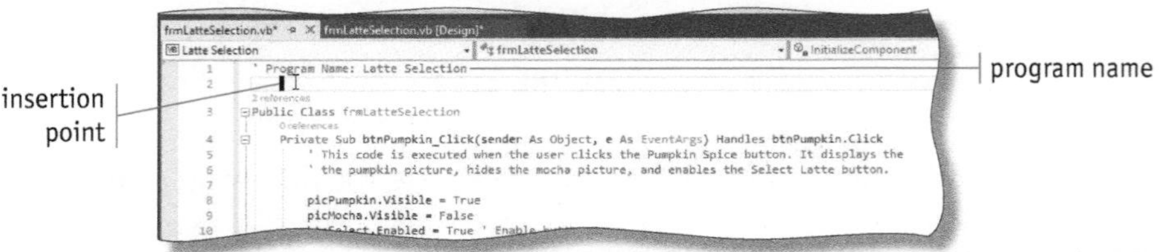

FIGURE 3-47

CONSIDER THIS

What do the yellow and green lines to the left of the code represent?
The yellow lines indicate lines of code that have not been saved. The green lines indicate the changes in code that have been saved. The yellow and green lines are a method of tracking your most recent changes in code.

You can enter the remaining comments using the same techniques. Press the TAB key one or more times to vertically align the paragraphs on the right so they appear as shown in Figure 3-44 on page 113.

Correct Errors in Code

Using IntelliSense to help you enter code reduces the likelihood of coding errors considerably. Nevertheless, because you could create errors when entering code, you should understand what to do when a coding error occurs.

One possible error would be to forget an apostrophe in a comment statement. In Figure 3-48, a comment was entered without a leading apostrophe.

In Figure 3-48, the comment words are displayed in black and red text, which indicates an error because comment characters normally are displayed in green text. Visual Studio gives no other indication that an error has occurred.

From the point where the error occurred, the developer might take any course of action. For example, she might immediately run the program. Or she might click anywhere in the window to move the insertion point, or press the ENTER key to insert a blank line. If the program in Figure 3-48 is executed immediately by clicking the Start button on the Standard toolbar, the window shown in Figure 3-49 will be displayed.

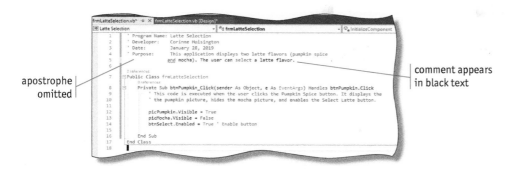

apostrophe omitted

comment appears in black text

FIGURE 3-48

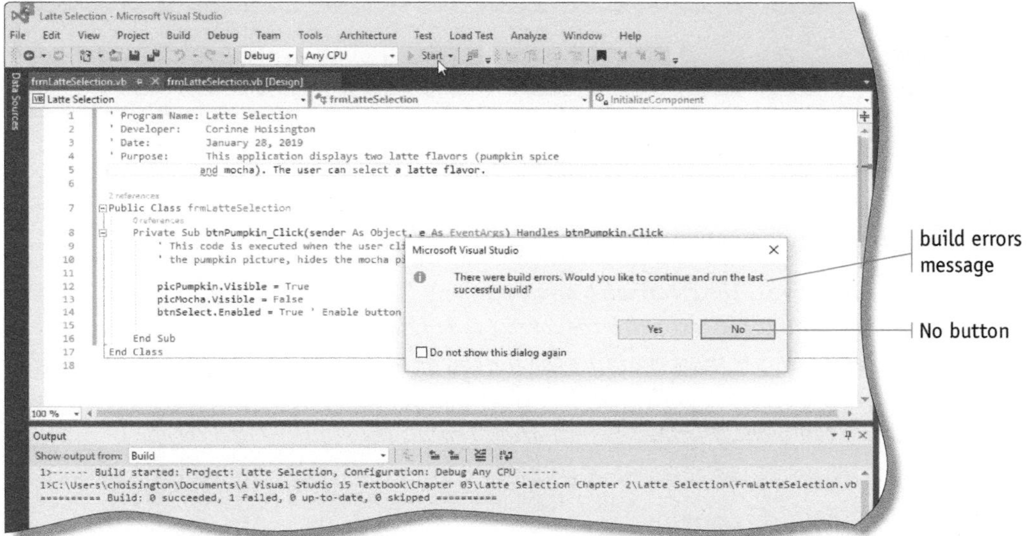

FIGURE 3-49

The **build errors message** means the Visual Basic compiler detected a coding error in the program. An absolute requirement when creating Visual Basic programs is that when you see the build errors message, you *always click the No button*. Under no circumstances should you click the Yes button in the dialog box. When you click the No button, you can perform the following steps to make corrections in your program:

STEP 1 Click the No button in the Microsoft Visual Studio dialog box that informs you of a build error (Figure 3-49).

When you click the No button, Visual Studio displays the program code and the Error List window (Figure 3-50). The ***Error List window*** *identifies the number of errors that occurred and displays descriptions of the errors. For example, the Syntax error means Visual Studio expected to find a different type of statement. The window also contains the file name in which the error occurred (frmLatteSelection.vb) and the line number of the statement in error (5). In the code window, the location of the error is noted by a red squiggly line.*

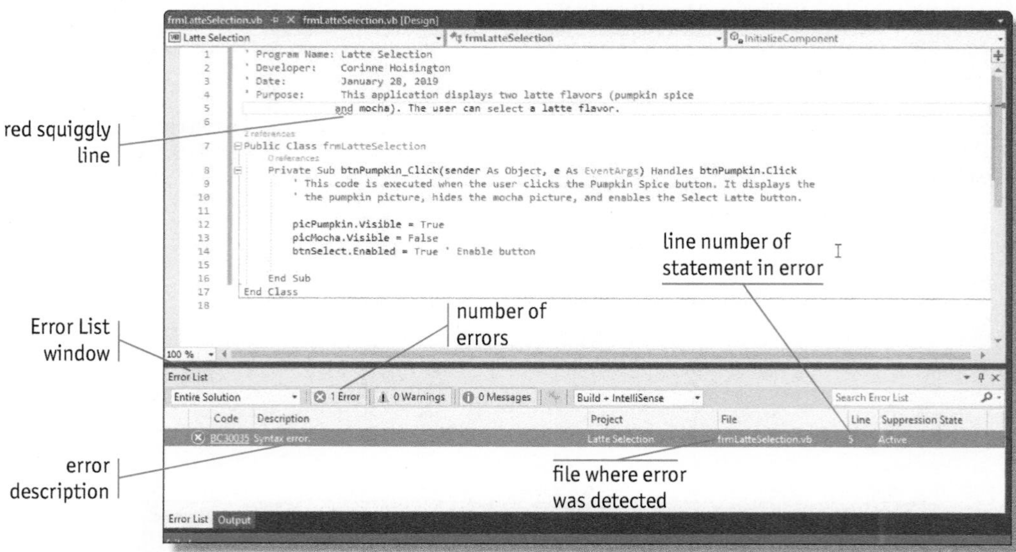

FIGURE 3-50

STEP 2 Double-click anywhere on the error line.

Visual Studio highlights the error with a red squiggly line. The developer can type and replace the highlighted text with the correct code (Figure 3-51). With the error highlighted, the developer must examine the statement to determine the error. By looking at line 5, where a word is highlighted, it is clear that the developer created a line that was intended to be a comment. Further examination reveals the required apostrophe is missing.

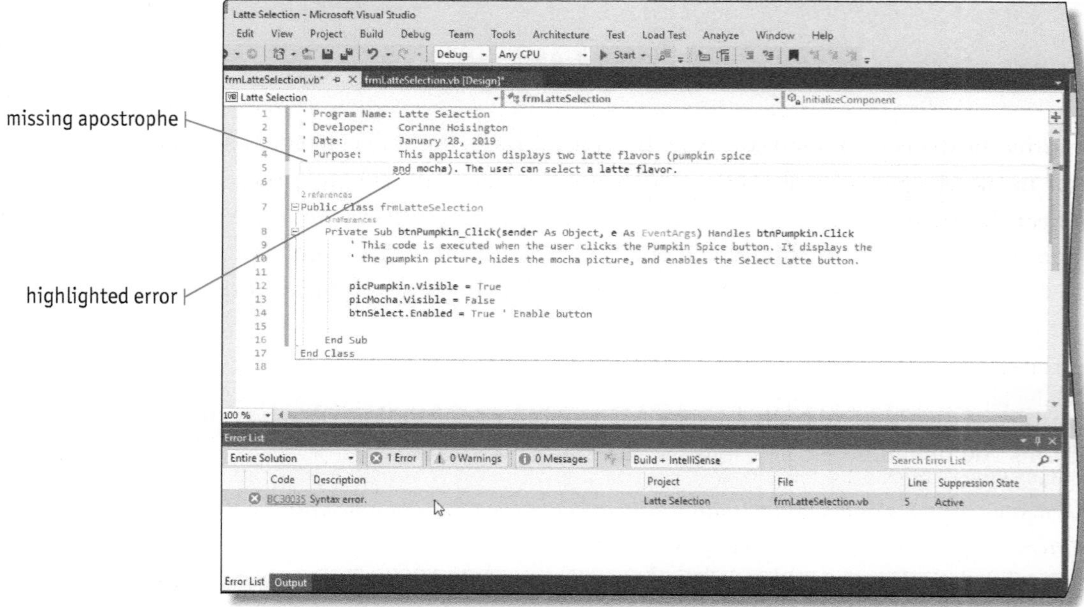

FIGURE 3-51

STEP 3 Click in the far left column on line 5 to place the insertion point there. Type an apostrophe.

The apostrophe is placed in the first column on line 5 of the program (Figure 3-52). If the statement has been corrected, the error line is removed from the Error List window, and the number of errors is reduced by one. The number of errors now is zero because the one error found in the program has been corrected. Multiple errors can be detected when the program is compiled.

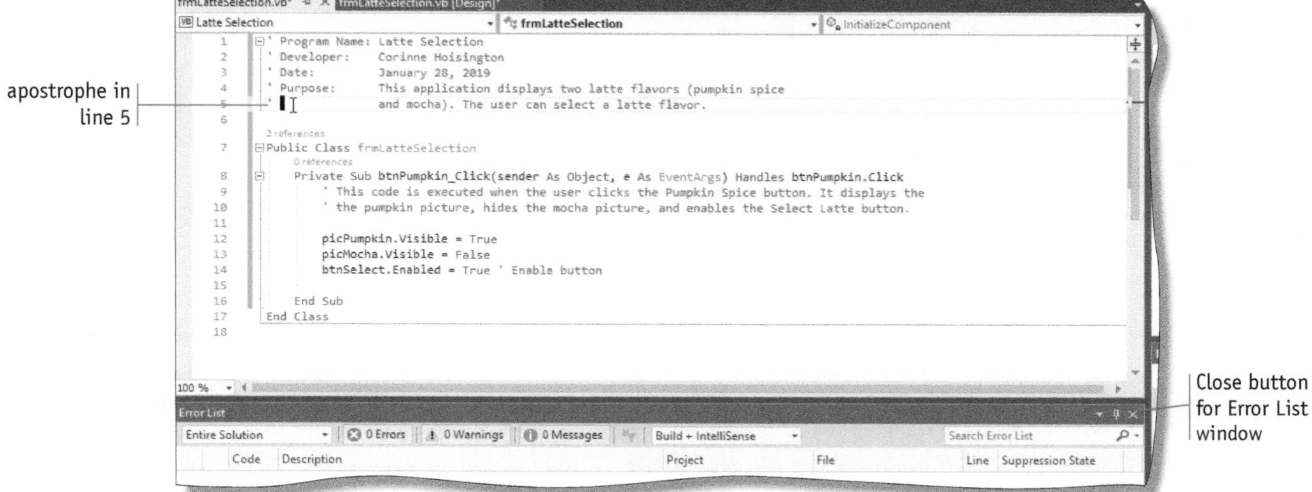

FIGURE 3-52

You can close the Error List window by clicking its Close button (see Figure 3-52).

In Figure 3-49 on page 115, the example assumed that the developer made an error and then immediately ran the program. If the developer moved the insertion point to another part of the program or clicked any other element in the window before running the program, then Visual Studio would provide a visual cue that an error occurred by displaying a red squiggly line under the error (Figure 3-50). You do not have to run the program to find coding errors. If a red squiggly line appears, you must correct the error.

> **CRITICAL THINKING**
>
> **When a program displays an error and a line number, is it possible that the error is on another line?**
>
> Yes. When an error is detected, review the line of code before the statement in error.

Additional Click Events

In the sample program in this chapter, multiple buttons can trigger events. For example, when the user clicks the Exit Window button, the program window should close and the program should terminate. To indicate that clicking the Exit Window button will trigger an event, and to prepare to write the code for the event, complete the same steps for the Exit Window button that you learned for the Pumpkin Spice button, as shown in the following example:

STEP 1 On the frmLatteSelection.vb [Design] tabbed page, double-click the Exit Window Button object.

Visual Studio opens the code window and displays the frmLatteSelection.vb tabbed page (Figure 3-53). Visual Studio also inserts the event handler code for the click event on the btnExit object. One horizontal line separates the event handler code for the btnExit object from code for other event handlers that might be in the program. The developer must write the code that will be executed when the click event occurs. The insertion point is located in the proper place to begin writing code.

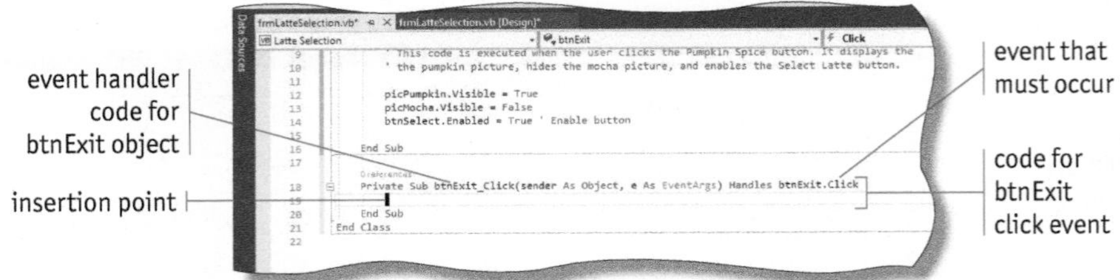

FIGURE 3-53

CRITICAL THINKING

Can the Exit Window button's Visible property be set to False and hidden until the latte flavor is selected?
Yes. A PictureBox, Label, or Button object can be hidden by setting the Visible property to False.

Enter Comments

As you have learned, you can enter code in the code window using the IntelliSense tools. The first code written for an event, however, should be comment code that identifies the event and the processing that will occur. The comment code for the Exit Window event handler is shown in Figure 3-54.

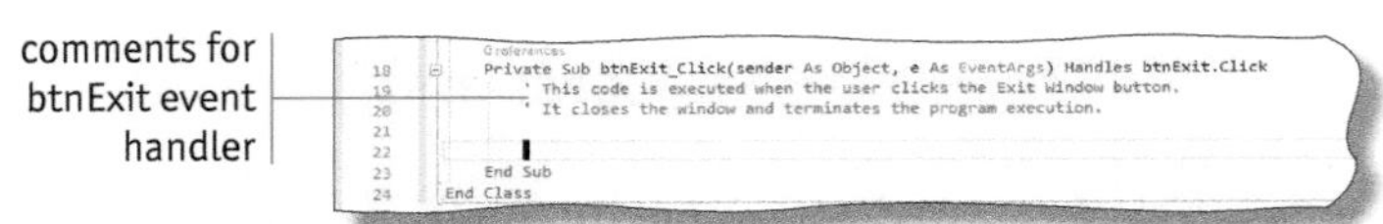

FIGURE 3-54

Close Procedure

The Visual Basic statement to close the window and terminate the program calls a procedure that performs the actual processing. A **procedure** is a set of prewritten code that can be called by a statement in the Visual Basic program. When the procedure is called, the program processes the code. The procedure used to close a window and terminate a program is the Close procedure.

You can use the statement in Figure 3-55 to call the Close procedure.

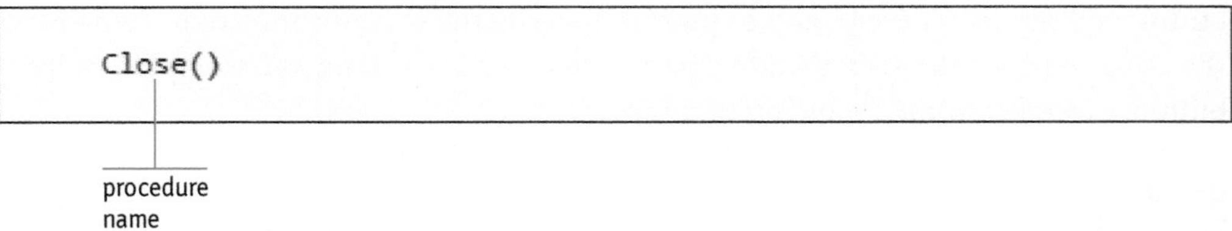

FIGURE 3-55

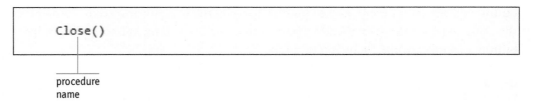

The word Close specifies the name of the procedure to be called. The left and right parentheses immediately following the procedure name identify the Visual Basic statement as a **procedure call statement**.

When the statement in Figure 3-55 is executed, the Close procedure will be called and control will be given to the prewritten programming statements in the Close procedure. These statements will close the window and end the application.

To enter the Close statement into the program, you can type "clo" and then select Close in the IntelliSense list, as shown in the following steps:

STEP 1 With the insertion point positioned as shown in Figure 3-54, type `clo` to highlight Close in the IntelliSense list.

When you type the letters "clo," IntelliSense highlights the word Close in the IntelliSense list (Figure 3-56).

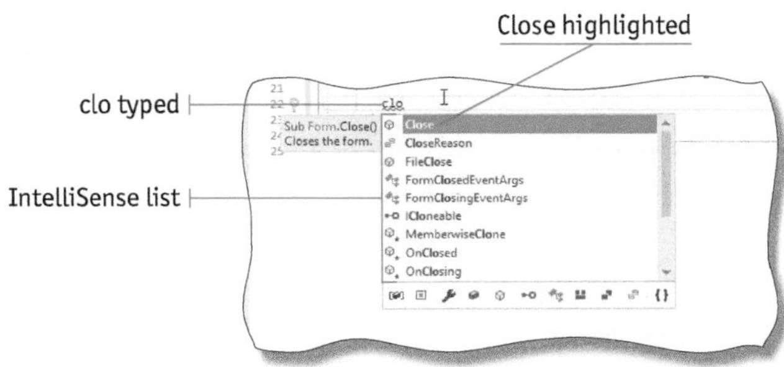

FIGURE 3-56

STEP 2 Press the ENTER key.

IntelliSense enters Close in the statement and, because it knows Close is a procedure call, automatically appends the open and closed parentheses to the statement (Figure 3-57). Then, Visual Studio returns the insertion point to the next line.

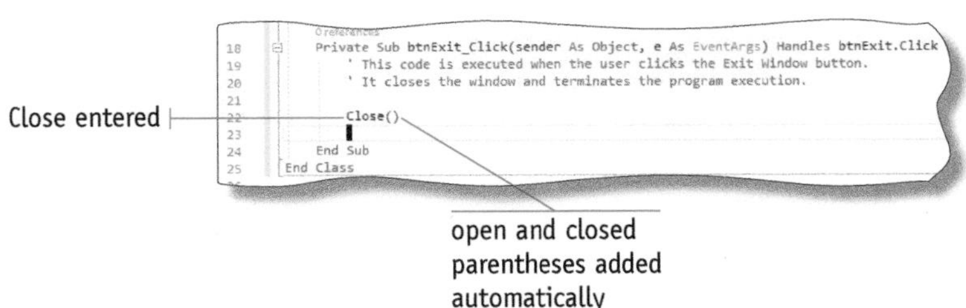

FIGURE 3-57

Prewritten procedures are an important element when using rapid application development in Visual Basic and Visual Studio because the developer is not required to write the procedure code. The developer merely writes a single statement to call the procedure. You will use many procedures in this book for a variety of reasons.

IN THE REAL WORLD

Developers can write their own procedures to perform required processing and then store them in a library so they and other programmers can use the procedures. You will learn more about using procedures throughout this book.

Print Code

In some instances, you will need to print the code in the program. While reviewing code, you might find it easier to read and understand the code on a printed page rather than on your computer screen. In other cases, you might want to share the code with another developer; the printed page often is a better tool for sharing than a monitor screen. To print the code in a program, you can complete the following steps:

1. Click File on the menu bar to display the File menu.
2. Click Print on the File menu to display the Print dialog box.
3. Make any other needed selections in the Print dialog box.
4. Click the OK button in the Print dialog box to print the code.

If you have a color printer, the code will be printed with correct color. Otherwise, shades of gray will represent the colors shown in the code window. If a line of code extends beyond one printed line, an arrow will appear at the end of the first line to indicate it continues to the next printed line.

Coding Summary

Writing code is the essence of programming in Visual Basic 2017. Much of the emphasis in this book will be on writing the code required to implement applications of all kinds.

Once you understand coding and the statements shown in this chapter, you are ready to continue the process of designing and implementing the Latte Selection program.

HEADS UP

Visual Studio 2017 does not provide a tool to print the user interface designed on the frmLatteSelection.vb [Design] tabbed page. You can implement a workaround to print the user interface using the following steps: (1) open Microsoft Word; (2) make Visual Studio 2017 the active program window; (3) with the user interface displayed on the frmLatteSelection.vb [Design] tabbed page, hold down the ALT key and then press the PRINT SCREEN key; (4) make Microsoft Word the active window; (5) click the Paste button on the Word Home tab. The screen shot created in Step 3 will be pasted into the Word document; (6) print the Word document. The Snipping Tool is another option to take a screen shot.

Phase 3 — Design the Program Processing Objects

The next phase in the PDLC requires determining the processing objects for the program and creating the event-planning document. In the Latte Selection program and programs of similar complexity, the designer need not be concerned about determining the processing objects. The only processing object required for the program is the Windows Form object. In more complex programs, determining processing objects will become important.

For the Latte Selection program, the next task is to design the event-planning document.

Event-Planning Document

As you have learned, programs written using a GUI normally are event-driven programs. An **event** means the user has initiated an action that causes the program to perform the appropriate type of processing in response. Once the mock-up has been created for the user interface, the developer must document the events that can occur based on the user interface.

The **event-planning document** is a table that specifies objects in the user interface that will cause events, the actions taken by the user to trigger the events, and the event processing that must occur. The event-planning document for the Latte Selection program is shown in Figure 3-58.

EVENT PLANNING DOCUMENT

Program Name:	**Developer:**	**Object:**	**Date:**
Latte Selection	Corinne Hoisington	frmLatteSelection	January 28, 2019
Object	**Event Trigger**	**Event Processing**	
btnPumpkin	Click	Display the pumpkin picture Hide the mocha picture Enable the Select Latte button	
btnSelect	Click	Disable the Pumpkin Spice button Disable the Select Latte button Disable the Mocha button Hide the Instructions label Display the Confirmation Message label Enable the Exit Window button	
btnMocha	Click	Display the mocha picture Hide the pumpkin picture Enable the Select Latte button	
btnExit	Click	Close the window and exit the program	

FIGURE 3-58

The left column in the event-planning document identifies the object in the GUI that can trigger an event. In the Latte Selection program, each of the four Button objects can be used to trigger an event, so each must be included in the event-planning document. Notice each Button object is identified by its name. Using this technique ensures that the documentation is precise and provides little room for error when the developer creates the code to implement these events.

The middle column identifies the event trigger, which is the action a user takes to cause the event. In all four event cases in Figure 3-58, clicking a button triggers the event. As you will learn in this book, users can perform a variety of acts to trigger an event. For example, a user might point to an object, right-click the object, or double-click the object. Each event trigger could trigger a different event.

The right column in the event-planning document specifies the event processing that the program must perform when the event occurs. This list of tasks for each event is a critical element in the program design. It must be precise and accurate. No processing step that must occur should be left out of the event-processing column. The tasks should be listed in the same sequence as they will be performed in the program.

For example, the first task for the btnPumpkin_Click event is to display the pumpkin picture. This is the primary task for the Pumpkin Spice button. However, several other tasks must be completed. When the program begins, the mocha picture is not visible, but if the user clicks the Mocha button, then the picture is displayed. When the user clicks the Pumpkin Spice button, however, the mocha picture should not be visible. Therefore, each time the user clicks the Pumpkin Spice button, the processing must hide the mocha picture.

You also will recall that when the program begins, the Select Latte button is dimmed (disabled). After the user clicks a latte flavor button, the Select Latte button must be enabled. For example, each time the user clicks the Pumpkin Spice button, the Select Latte button must be enabled.

As you review the event-planning document in Figure 3-58, be sure you understand the processing that must occur for each event.

You should note that the event-processing tasks in the right column identify *what* processing must be done when the event occurs. *How* these tasks will be accomplished is not identified specifically, although the information in the event-planning document must be precise enough that the developer can easily write the code to implement the specified tasks.

Phase 4 — Code the Program

After the events and tasks within the events have been identified, the developer is ready to code the program. As you have learned in this chapter, coding the program means entering Visual Basic statements to accomplish the tasks specified in the event-planning document. As the developer enters the code, she also will implement the logic to carry out the required processing.

Guided Program Development

To fine-tune the user interface in the Latte Selection program and enter the code required to process each event in the program, complete the following steps to create the program shown in Figure 3-1 on pages 86 and 87.

NOTE TO THE LEARNER

In the following activity, you should complete the tasks within the specified steps. Each of the tasks is accompanied by a Hint Screen. The purpose of the Hint Screen is to indicate where you should perform the activity in the Visual Studio window and to remind you which method to use. If you need further help completing a step, refer to the figure identified by *ref:*.

Guided Program Development

1

- **Open the Mock-Up File** Open Visual Studio and then open the mock-up file for the user interface you created in Chapter 2. (If you did not create a mock-up file in Chapter 2, consult with your instructor to obtain the file.)

- **Show the Windows Form Object's BackColor Property** To finish the user interface, you must specify the BackColor of the Windows Form object. Select the frmLatteSelection Windows Form object. In the Properties window, scroll until the BackColor property is visible, click the BackColor property name in the left column, and then click the BackColor arrow in the right column. If necessary, click the Web tab (*ref: Figure 3-3*).

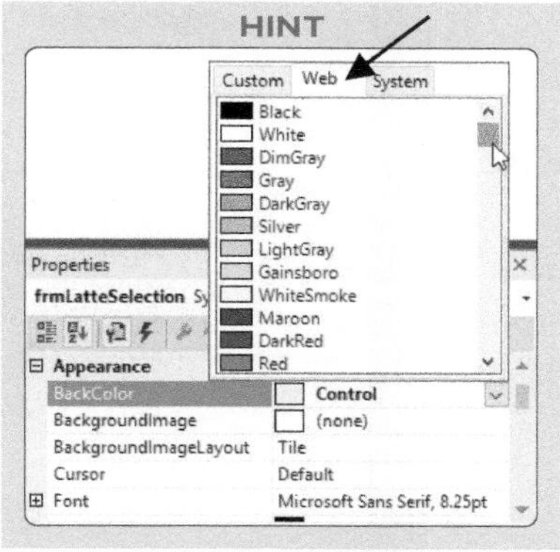

- **Choose the Windows Form Object's BackColor** Scroll the Web tabbed page until White is visible, and then click White in the list (*ref: Figure 3-5*).

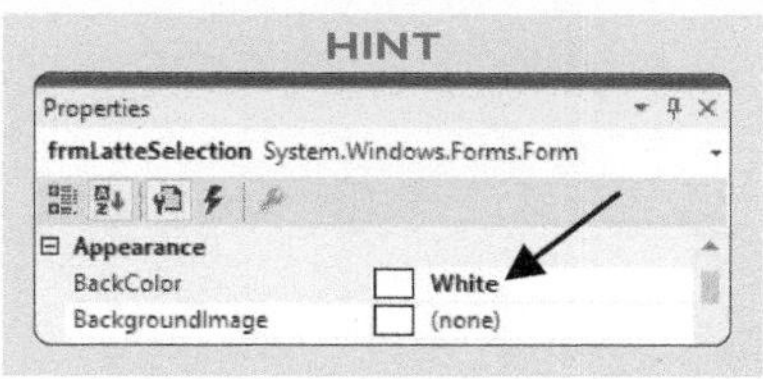

- **Select the BackColor for Buttons** Next, you must specify the BackColor for the Button objects. Select the four buttons in the window using techniques you have learned, and then change the BackColor to Bisque.

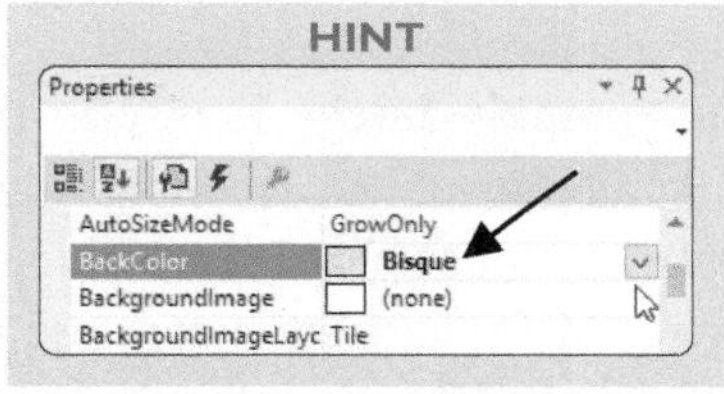

- **Change the ForeColor of a Label Object** Select the lblHeading Label object, click the ForeColor property name in the left column, and then click the ForeColor arrow in the right column. If necessary, click the Web tab and select SaddleBrown in the list.

(continues)

Guided Program Development *continued*

1

The BackColor for the Windows Form object is changed to White, the ForeColor of the heading is changed to SaddleBrown, and the BackColor for the buttons in the window is changed to Bisque (Figure 3-59).

RESULT OF STEP 1

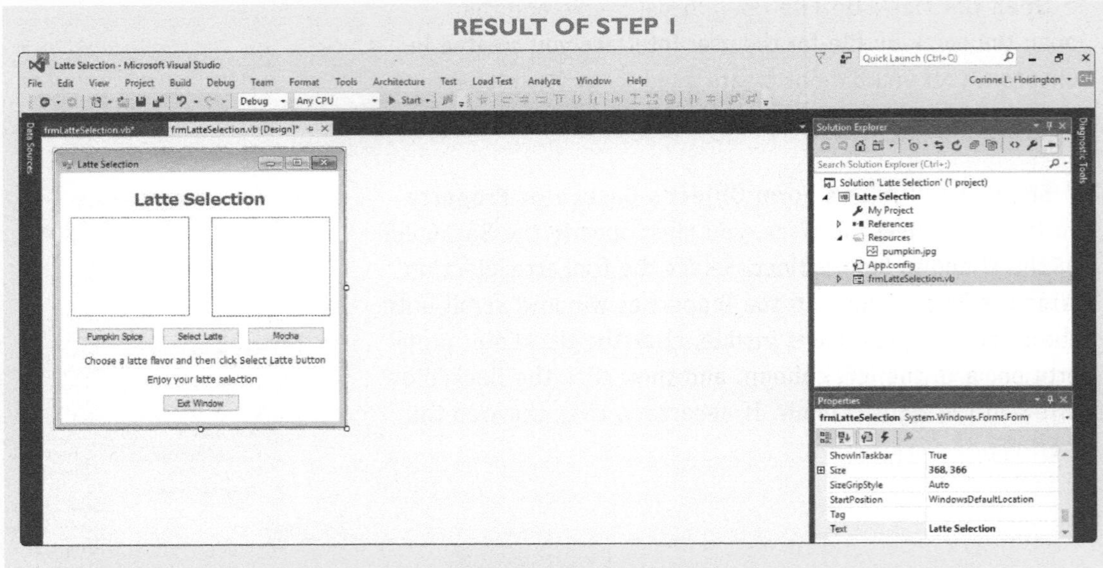

FIGURE 3-59

2

- **Download the Pumpkin Image** To display the pictures in the PictureBox object, you might need to use your web browser to download the pictures from the book's webpage at CengageBrain.com and store them on your computer. After downloading the files for Chapter 3, save the pumpkin image on a USB drive or other available storage media on your computer.

- **Download the Mocha Image** Save the mocha image on a USB drive or other storage media on your computer.

Guided Program Development *continued*

3

- **Display the Select Resource Dialog Box** After acquiring the pictures, you must import them into the Resources folder and specify the PictureBox object where they will be displayed. Select the picPumpkin PictureBox object. In the Properties window, click Image and then click the ellipsis button in the right column (*ref: Figure 3-8*).

- **Import the Pumpkin Image** In the Select Resource dialog box, click the Import button, import the pumpkin image from its saved location, and then click the OK button (*ref: Figure 3-9*).

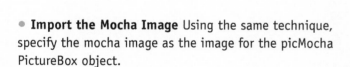

Anna_Pustynnikova/Shutterstock.com

- **Import the Mocha Image** Using the same technique, specify the mocha image as the image for the picMocha PictureBox object.

- **Set the SizeMode Property to StretchImage for the Pumpkin Image** When you import a picture, normally you must resize it or the PictureBox object so the picture is displayed properly. To resize the pumpkin image, select the picPumpkin PictureBox object. In the Properties window for the picPumpkin PictureBox object, click the SizeMode property name, click the SizeMode arrow, and then set the property to StretchImage (*ref: Figure 3-12*).

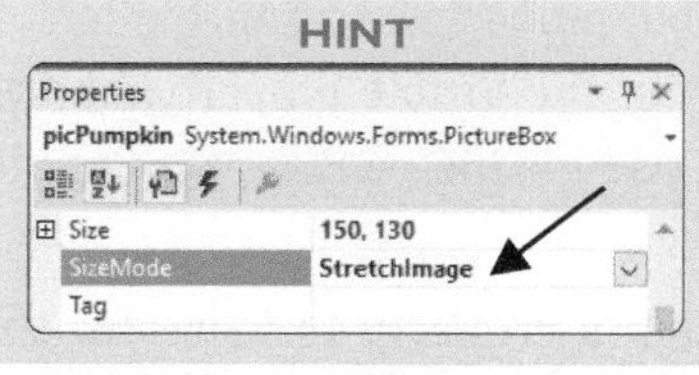

- **Set the SizeMode Property to StretchImage for the Mocha Image** Using the same technique, set the SizeMode property to StretchImage for the picMocha PictureBox object.

(continues)

Guided Program Development *continued*

The images are displayed in the correct PictureBox objects (Figure 3-60).

RESULT OF STEPS 2 & 3

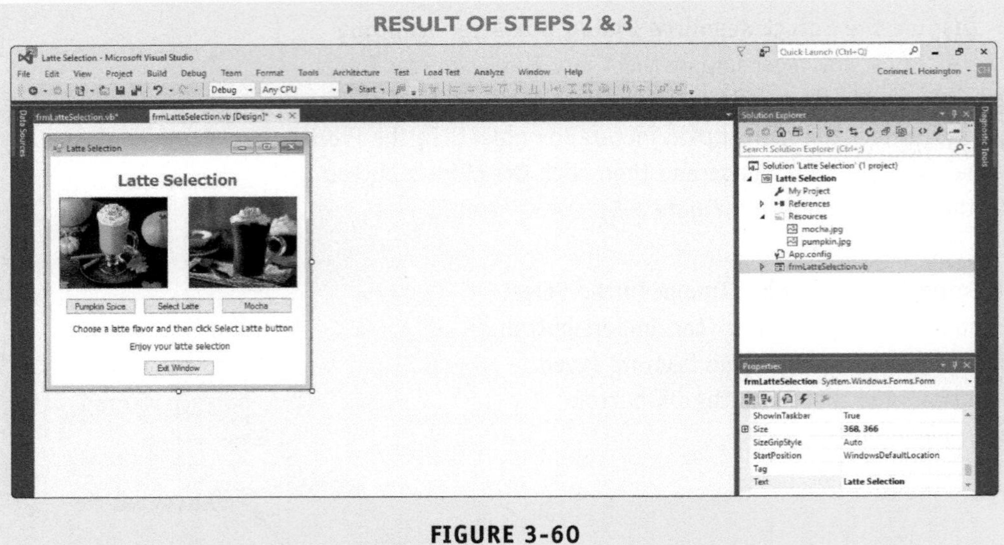

FIGURE 3-60

Anna_Pustynnikova/Shutterstock.com, Africa Studio/Shutterstock.com

4

- **Set the Visible Property to False for the Pumpkin Image** When the program begins, the pictures are not displayed in the window, so you must set their Visible property to False. In the Properties window for the picPumpkin PictureBox object, click the Visible property name in the left column, click the Visible arrow for the Visible property, and then set the Visible property to False for the picPumpkin PictureBox object (*ref: Figure 3-14*).
- **Set the Visible Property to False for the Mocha Image** Using the same technique, set the Visible property to False for the picMocha PictureBox object (*ref: Figure 3-14*).

HINT

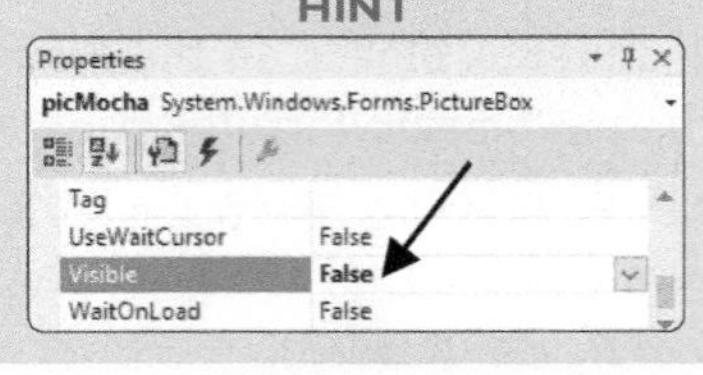

- **Set the Visible Property to False for the Confirmation Message** The confirmation message is not displayed when the program begins, so you must set its Visible property to False. In the Properties window, set the Visible property to False for the lblConfirmation Label object (*ref: Figure 3-14*).
- **Run the Program** After you make changes to a program, you should run it to ensure your changes work properly and are correct (*ref: Figure 3-18*).

Guided Program Development *continued*

In Figure 3-61, the latte pictures are not displayed. In addition, the confirmation message is not displayed.

RESULT OF STEP 4

FIGURE 3-61

5

- **Set the Select Latte Button's Enabled Property to False** Initially, the Select Latte button and the Exit Window button must be dimmed. In the Properties window for the btnSelect object, click the Enabled property name, click the Enabled arrow, and then set the Enabled property to False for the btnSelect Button object (*ref: Figure 3-16*).

HINT

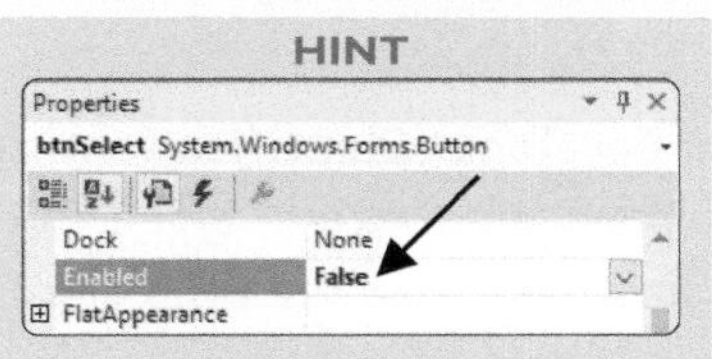

- **Set the Exit Window Button's Enabled Property to False** Using the same technique, set the Enabled property to False for the btnExit Button object (*ref: Figure 3-16*).
- **Run the Program** Again, after you make changes, always ensure the changes are correct. Run the program.
- *Both the Select Latte button and the Exit Window button are dimmed, indicating the Enabled property for both buttons is False (Figure 3-62).*

RESULT OF STEP 5

Latte Selection

Latte Selection

Pumpkin Spice | Select Latte | Mocha

Choose a latte flavor and then click Select Latte button

Exit Window

FIGURE 3-62

(continues)

Guided Program Development *continued*

6

- **Open the Code Window for the btnPumpkin Event Handler** The user interface now is complete, so you should begin writing the code for the program. To write code, you must open the code window. Double-click the Pumpkin Spice button to open the code window for the btnPumpkin_Click event (*ref: Figure 3-20*).
- **Position the Insertion Point** Close the Toolbox window. When you begin writing the code for a program, the first step is to write the introductory comments. Click in the far left position of the first line of code (Public Class)
- **Create a Blank Line and Position the Insertion Point** Press the ENTER key and then press the UP ARROW key (*ref: Figure 3-45*).
- **Enter the First Line of the Introductory Comments** The introductory comments provide the code reader with important information about the program. The first line normally specifies the name of the program. Type an apostrophe, press the SPACEBAR, type `Program Name:`, press TAB, type `Latte Selection`, and then press the ENTER key and the BACKSPACE key to return to the left position (*ref: Figure 3-47*).

HINT

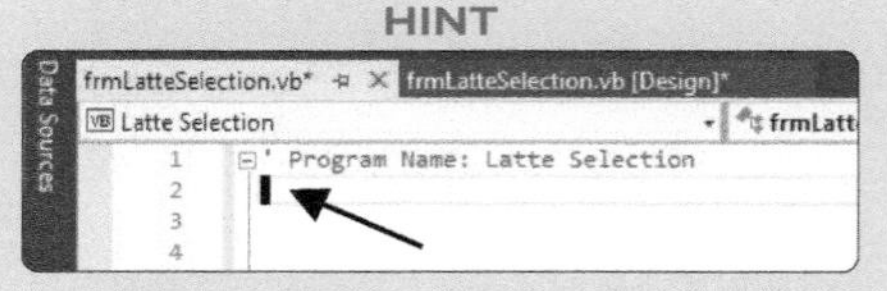

- **Enter the Developer Identification Comment Line** Type an apostrophe, press the SPACEBAR, type `Developer:`, press TAB, type your name, and then press the ENTER key.
- **Enter the Date Comment Line** Type an apostrophe, **press** the SPACEBAR, type `Date:`, press TAB three times, enter the current date, and then press the ENTER key.
- **Enter the First Program Purpose Comment Line** Type an apostrophe, press the SPACEBAR, type `Purpose:`, press TAB two times, enter the first line of your own comments about the program, and then press the ENTER key.
- **Enter the Remaining Program Purpose Comment Lines** Insert additional lines of comments about the purpose of the program as you see fit.

The comments appear at the top of the program code (Figure 3-63).

RESULT OF STEP 6

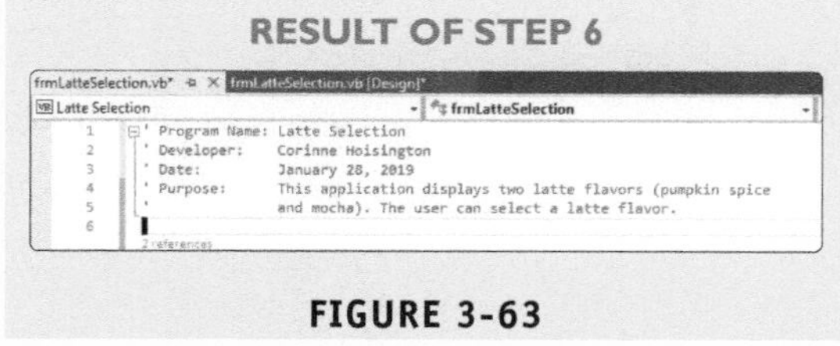

FIGURE 3-63

Guided Program Development *continued*

7

- **Position the Insertion Point Inside the Click Event Handler** With the insertion point located on the line above the line of code that begins with Public Class (see Figure 3-63), press the DOWN ARROW key three times and then press TAB two times to position the insertion point in the btnPumpkin_Click event handler

- **Enter the First Line of the Event Handler Comments** Each event handler should begin with comments describing what the event handler accomplishes. Type an apostrophe, press the SPACEBAR, and then enter the first line of comments for the btnPumpkin_Click event handler. Press the ENTER key (*ref: Figure 3-42*).

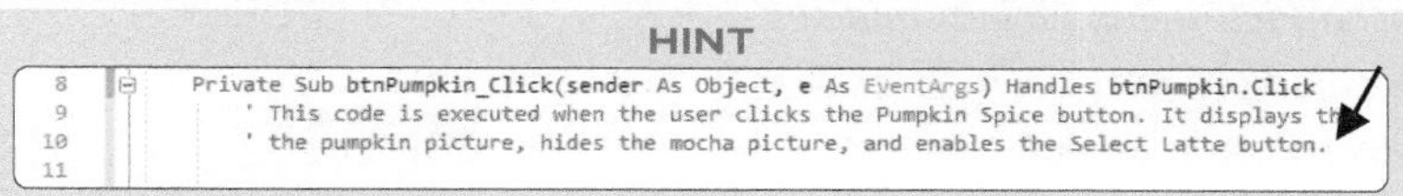

- **Enter the Remaining Event Handler Comments** Enter the remaining comments for the btnPumpkin_Click event handler.

- **Make the Pumpkin Spice PictureBox Object Visible** The first executable line of code in the Pumpkin Spice Button object click event handler must make the Pumpkin Spice PictureBox object visible. Using IntelliSense, enter the Visual Basic code statement to set the Visible property to True for the picPumpkin PictureBox object (*ref: Figure 3-28*).

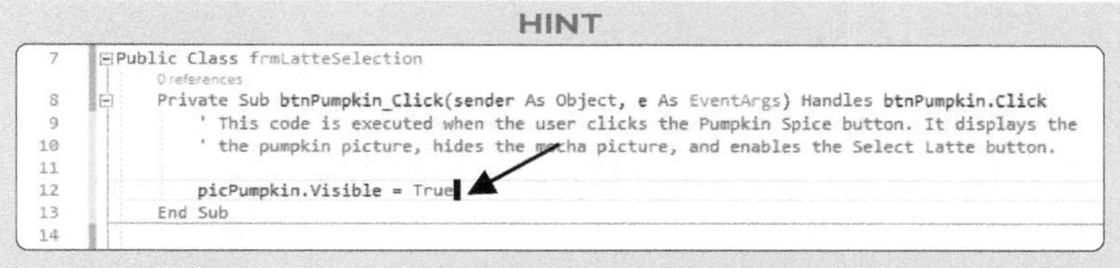

HINT
Public Class frmLatteSelection
0 references
Private Sub btnPumpkin_Click(sender As Object, e As EventArgs) Handles btnPumpkin.Click
' This code is executed when the user clicks the Pumpkin Spice button. It displays the
' the pumpkin picture, hides the mocha picture, and enables the Select Latte button.
picPumpkin.Visible = True
End Sub

- **Make Sure the Mocha PictureBox Object is Not Visible** As documented in the event-planning document, the next task is to make sure the mocha picture is not visible in the window. Using IntelliSense, enter the Visual Basic code statement to set the Visible property to False for the picMocha PictureBox object (*ref: Figure 3-35*).

- **Enable the Select Latte Button Object** The last task for the btnPumpkin_Click event handler is to enable the Select Latte button. Using IntelliSense, enter the Visual Basic code statement to set the Enabled property to True for the btnSelect Button object (*ref: Figure 3-38*).

(continues)

Guided Program Development *continued*

The lines of code are entered in the Pumpkin Spice Button object's click event handler (Figure 3-64). The code will set the Visible property to True for the picPumpkin PictureBox object, set the Visible property to False for the picMocha PictureBox object, and set the Enabled property to True for the btnSelect Button object.

RESULT OF STEP 7

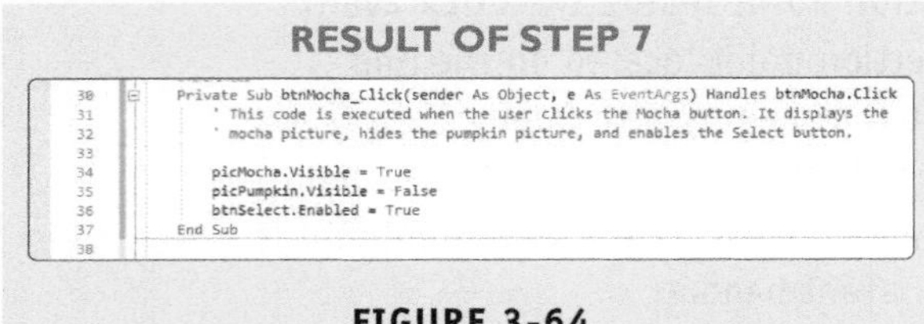

```
Private Sub btnMocha_Click(sender As Object, e As EventArgs) Handles btnMocha.Click
    ' This code is executed when the user clicks the Mocha button. It displays the
    ' mocha picture, hides the pumpkin picture, and enables the Select button.

    picMocha.Visible = True
    picPumpkin.Visible = False
    btnSelect.Enabled = True
End Sub
```

FIGURE 3-64

HEADS UP

As you enter executable code, you should refer to the event-planning document to ensure the code implements the identified tasks. The event-planning document is the guide to the code you write in each event handler.

8

- **Run the Program** When the code for an event handler is complete, good practice dictates that you should run the program to ensure the event handler code works properly. Run the program. Click the Pumpkin Spice button.

When you click the Pumpkin Spice button, the pumpkin picture is displayed, the mocha picture is not displayed, and the Select Latte button is enabled (Figure 3-65). These are the correct results. Note that if you click any of the other buttons in the window, nothing happens because you have not yet written the event handler code for these objects.

RESULT OF STEP 8

FIGURE 3-65

Guided Program Development *continued*

9

- **Display the Design Window** When the code for an event handler is completed, the next task is often to write the code for another event handler. To do so, you must go to the Design tabbed page and indicate the object for which the code will be written. Click the frmLatteSelection.vb [Design] tab to return to the Design tabbed page.

- **Open the Code Window for the btnSelect Event Handler** You must open the code window for the btnSelect Button object to enter code for the event handler. Double-click the Select Latte button to open the code window for the btnSelect_Click event (*ref: Figure 3-20*).

- **Enter Event Handler Comments** When beginning the code for an event handler, the first step is to enter the event handler comments. Enter the comments that describe the processing in the btnSelect_Click event handler.

- **Disable the btnPumpkin Button Object** According to the event-planning document (Figure 3-58 on page 121), the next task is to disable the Pumpkin Spice button. Using IntelliSense, enter the Visual Basic code statement to set the Enabled property to False for the btnPumpkin Button object (*ref: Figure 3-37*).

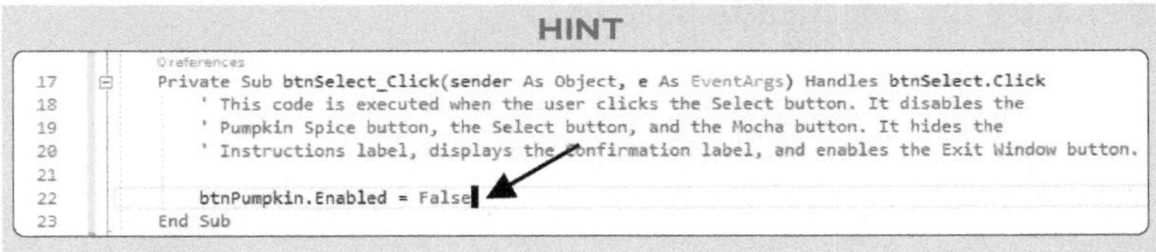

- **Disable the btnSelect Button Object** The next task is to disable the Select Latte button. Using IntelliSense, enter the Visual Basic code statement to set the Enabled property to False for the btnSelect Button object (*ref: Figure 3-37*).

- **Disable the btnMocha Button Object** Using IntelliSense, enter the Visual Basic code statement to set the Enabled property to False for the btnMocha Button object (*ref: Figure 3-37*).

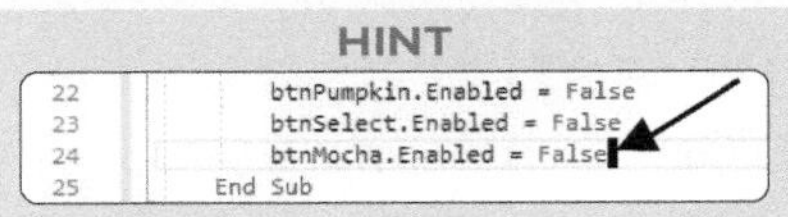

HINT
btnPumpkin.Enabled = False
btnSelect.Enabled = False
btnMocha.Enabled = False
End Sub

- **Hide the Instructions Label Object** When the Select Latte button is clicked, the instructions should not be displayed. Using IntelliSense, enter the Visual Basic code statement to set the Visible property to False for the lblInstructions Label object (*ref: Figure 3-28*).

(continues)

Guided Program Development *continued*

- **Display the Confirmation Message** The confirmation message must be displayed when the user clicks the Select Latte button. Using IntelliSense, enter the Visual Basic code statement to set the Visible property to True for the lblConfirmation Label object (*ref: Figure 3-30*).

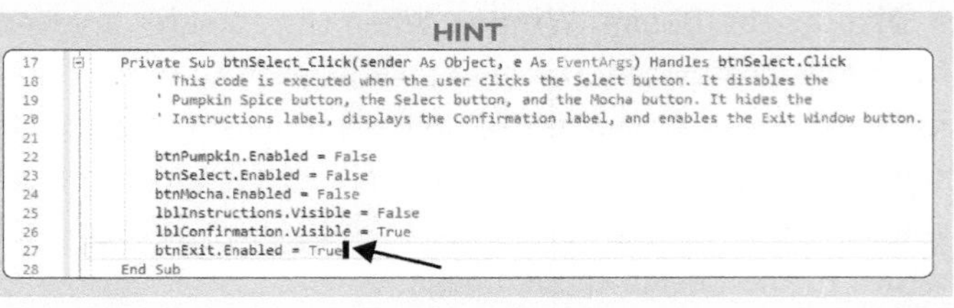
HINT
Private Sub btnSelect_Click(sender As Object, e As EventArgs) Handles btnSelect.Click
' This code is executed when the user clicks the Select button. It disables the
' Pumpkin Spice button, the Select button, and the Mocha button. It hides the
' Instructions label, displays the Confirmation label, and enables the Exit Window button.
btnPumpkin.Enabled = False
btnSelect.Enabled = False
btnMocha.Enabled = False
lblInstructions.Visible = False
lblConfirmation.Visible = True
btnExit.Enabled = True
End Sub

- **Enable the Exit Window Button** After the user clicks the Select Latte button, the only allowable action is to click the Exit Window button and exit the application. Therefore, the Exit Window button must be enabled. Using IntelliSense, enter the Visual Basic code statement to set the Enabled property to True for the btnExit Button object (*ref: Figure 3-37*).

- **Run the Program** Save and then run the program to ensure that it works correctly. Click the Pumpkin Spice button and then click the Select Latte button.

After clicking the two buttons, the Pumpkin picture is displayed; the Pumpkin Spice, Select Latte, and Mocha buttons are disabled; the Instructions label is not displayed; the Confirmation Message label is displayed; and the Exit Window button is enabled (Figure 3-66).

RESULT OF STEP 9
Latte Selection
Latte Selection
Pumpkin Spice
Select Latte
Mocha
Enjoy your latte selection
Exit Window

FIGURE 3-66

Anna_Pustynnikova/Shutterstock.com

Guided Program Development *continued*

10

- **Display the Design Window** The next task is to write the code for the btnMocha event handler. To return to the Design tabbed page so you can select the Mocha button, click the frmLatteSelection.vb [Design] tab.

- **Open the Code Window for the btnMocha Event Handler** Double-click the Mocha button to open the code window for the btnMocha_Click event (*ref: Figure 3-20*).

- **Enter the Event Handler Comments** Using the techniques you have learned, enter the comments that describe the processing in the btnMocha_Click event handler.

- **Make the Mocha PictureBox Object Visible** According to the event-planning document, the next task is to make the mocha picture visible. Using IntelliSense, enter the Visual Basic code statement to set the Visible property to True for the picMocha PictureBox object (*ref: Figure 3-30*).

- **Make Sure the Pumpkin Picture Is Not Visible** Using IntelliSense, enter the Visual Basic code statement to set the Visible property to False for the picPumpkin PictureBox object (*ref: Figure 3-36*).

- **Enable the Select Latte Button** Using IntelliSense, enter the Visual Basic code statement to set the Enabled property to True for the btnSelect Button object (*ref: Figure 3-39*).

- **Run the Program** Run the program and then click the Mocha button to ensure your code works correctly.

The completed code for the Select Latte button event handler and the Mocha button event handler is shown in Figure 3-67.

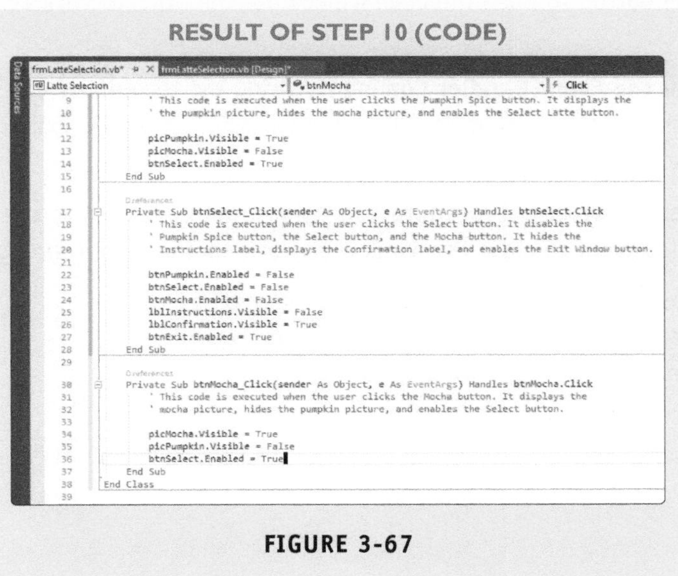
RESULT OF STEP 10 (CODE)
frmLatteSelection.vb*
frmLatteSelection.vb [Design]*
Latte Selection
btnMocha
Click
' This code is executed when the user clicks the Pumpkin Spice button. It displays the
' the pumpkin picture, hides the mocha picture, and enables the Select Latte button.
picPumpkin.Visible = True
picMocha.Visible = False
btnSelect.Enabled = True
End Sub
Private Sub btnSelect_Click(sender As Object, e As EventArgs) Handles btnSelect.Click
' This code is executed when the user clicks the Select button. It disables the
' Pumpkin Spice button, the Select button, and the Mocha button. It hides the
' Instructions label, displays the Confirmation label, and enables the Exit Window button.
btnPumpkin.Enabled = False
btnSelect.Enabled = False
btnMocha.Enabled = False
lblInstructions.Visible = False
lblConfirmation.Visible = True
btnExit.Enabled = True
End Sub
Private Sub btnMocha_Click(sender As Object, e As EventArgs) Handles btnMocha.Click
' This code is executed when the user clicks the Mocha button. It displays the
' mocha picture, hides the pumpkin picture, and enables the Select button.
picMocha.Visible = True
picPumpkin.Visible = False
btnSelect.Enabled = True
End Sub
End Class

FIGURE 3-67

(continues)

Guided Program Development *continued*

When you click the Mocha button, the mocha picture is displayed, the Pumpkin picture is not displayed, and the Select Latte button is enabled (Figure 3-68). The program is working properly.

RESULT OF STEP 10 (PROGRAM EXECUTION)

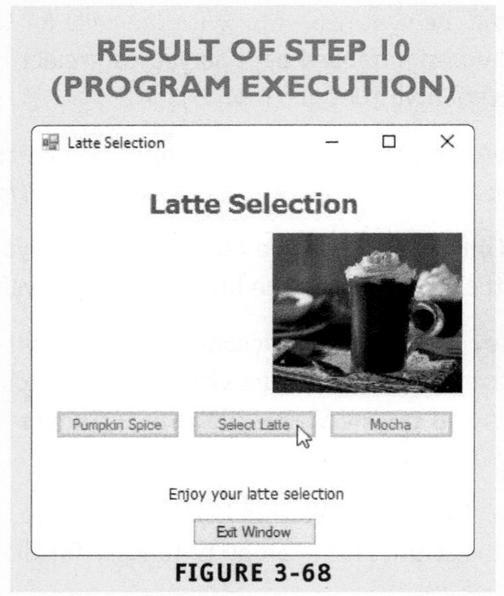
Latte Selection
Latte Selection
Pumpkin Spice
Select Latte
Mocha
Enjoy your latte selection
Exit Window

FIGURE 3-68

Africa Studio/Shutterstock.com

11

- **Display the Design Window** Click the frmLatteSelection.vb [Design] tab to return to the Design tabbed page.
- **Open the Code Window for the btnExit Event Handler** Double-click the Exit Window button to open the code window for the btnExit_Click event (*ref: Figure 3-20*).
- **Enter the Event Handler Comments** Using the techniques you have learned, enter the comments that describe the processing in the btnExit_Click event handler.
- **Enter the Close() Procedure Call** Using IntelliSense, enter the Visual Basic code statement to close the window and exit the program (*ref: Figure 3-57*).

The Close() procedure call statement is entered (Figure 3-69). When the procedure call is executed, the application will be closed.

RESULT OF STEP 11

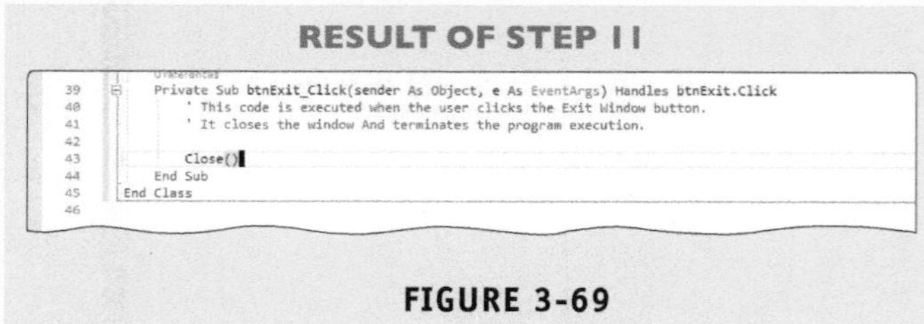
Private Sub btnExit_Click(sender As Object, e As EventArgs) Handles btnExit.Click
' This code is executed when the user clicks the Exit Window button.
' It closes the window And terminates the program execution.
Close()
End Sub
End Class

FIGURE 3-69

12

- **Run the Program** Run the program to ensure that it works correctly. Click the Pumpkin Spice button, the Mocha button, the Select Latte button, and the Exit Window button.

Code Listing

The complete code for the sample program is shown in Figure 3-70.

Summary

In this chapter you have learned to fine-tune a GUI to maximize its usefulness and to enter code for object event handlers.

```
Latte Selection                                    frmLatteSelection
' Program Name: Latte Selection
' Developer:    Corinne Hoisington
' Date:         January 28, 2019
' Purpose:      This application displays two latte flavors (pumpkin spice
'               and mocha). The user can select a latte flavor.

2 references
Public Class frmLatteSelection
    0 references
    Private Sub btnPumpkin_Click(sender As Object, e As EventArgs) Handles btnPumpkin.Click
        ' This code is executed when the user clicks the Pumpkin Spice button. It displays the
        ' the pumpkin picture, hides the mocha picture, and enables the Select Latte button.

        picPumpkin.Visible = True
        picMocha.Visible = False
        btnSelect.Enabled = True
    End Sub

    0 references
    Private Sub btnSelect_Click(sender As Object, e As EventArgs) Handles btnSelect.Click
        ' This code is executed when the user clicks the Select button. It disables the
        ' Pumpkin Spice button, the Select button, and the Mocha button. It hides the
        ' Instructions label, displays the Confirmation label, and enables the Exit Window button.

        btnPumpkin.Enabled = False
        btnSelect.Enabled = False
        btnMocha.Enabled = False
        lblInstructions.Visible = False
        lblConfirmation.Visible = True
        btnExit.Enabled = True
    End Sub

    0 references
    Private Sub btnMocha_Click(sender As Object, e As EventArgs) Handles btnMocha.Click
        ' This code is executed when the user clicks the Mocha button. It displays the
        ' mocha picture, hides the pumpkin picture, and enables the Select button.

        picMocha.Visible = True
        picPumpkin.Visible = False
        btnSelect.Enabled = True
    End Sub

    0 references
    Private Sub btnExit_Click(sender As Object, e As EventArgs) Handles btnExit.Click
        ' This code is executed when the user clicks the Exit Window button.
        ' It closes the window and terminates the program execution.

        Close()
    End Sub
End Class
```

FIGURE 3-70

Knowledge Check

1. When the Latte Selection program was executed, was the Enabled property of the Mocha button set to True or False?
2. Which property controls the background color of the Button object?
3. Which property controls the text color of a Label object?
4. Which color palette is guaranteed to be displayed properly on every computer?
5. When a PictureBox object is placed on the form, what is the default SizeMode property setting?
6. When you place a PictureBox object on a Windows form, in which project folder is the image stored in the Solution Explorer?
7. Which option should be selected in the SizeMode property to align the center of the image with the center of the PictureBox object?
8. Which option should be selected in the SizeMode property to make the image fit within the PictureBox object?
9. Which property has been set to False if a PictureBox object is hidden in a window when the program begins?
10. Which property has been set to False if a Button object is dimmed when you run the application?
11. What two options can you select for the Visible property in the Properties window?
12. Write a line of code that would set the Visible property to False for a PictureBox object named picCaptainAmerica.
13. Write a line of code that would set the Enabled property to True for a Button object named btnSuperman.
14. Write a line of code that would set the Visible property to True for a PictureBox object named picWonderWoman.
15. Write a comment line of code that states, "This code displays the superhero images."
16. What color is used to display comments in the code window of Visual Basic 2017?
17. Write a line of code that will close an application window and exit the application.
18. What does a red squiggly line mean in the code window?
19. Which symbol is associated with the assignment statement?
20. Why is it best to use IntelliSense when you enter code in the code window? List two reasons.

Debugging Exercises

1. Fix the following line of code to set the Enabled property to True for the btnCharacter Button object.

```
btnCharacter.Enable.True
```

2. Fix the following line of code to change the visibility of the btnExitProgram Button object so that you can view it when the program runs.

```
btnExitProgram.Visibilty = Yes
```

3. Fix the following line of code to set the Visible property to False for the lblGotham Label object.

```
lblGotham.Visible = ' False
```

4. Fix the following comment line of code.

```
The ' following line of code makes the Batman logo visible
```

5. Fix the following line of code.

```
Close;
```

6. Examine the code below. Then, write a line of code to replace the erroneous line.

```
btnMarvelProgram.Enabled = True
picSpiderman.Visibilty = Enable
picThor.Visible = False
```

Program Analysis

1. For the Yellowstone National Park application shown in Figure 3-71, write the Visual Basic 2017 coding statement to view the picture when the user clicks the btnParkImage button, assuming the Visible property had been set to False for the picParkBison PictureBox object in the Properties window.

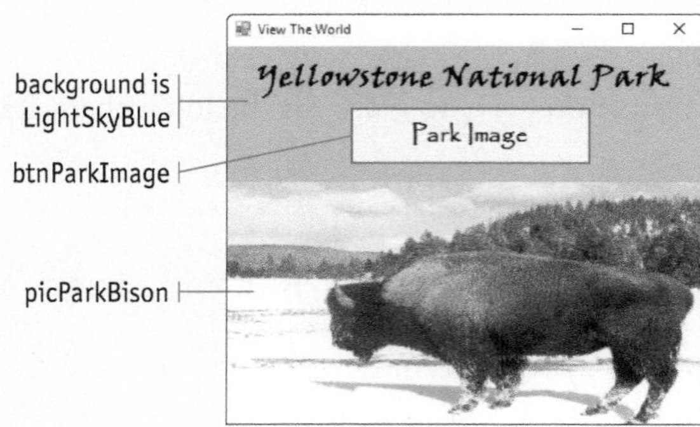

FIGURE 3-71

Photo courtesy of Corinne Hoisington

2. Which property in the Properties window controls whether the picParkBison image is displayed when the program begins? Which option for the property would you select to make the button dimmed when the program begins?
3. When you import the picture into the Resources folder and select the image to use in the picParkBison PictureBox object, which SizeMode property option would you select to view the complete picture?
4. Write the Visual Basic coding statement for the btnParkImage click event that would cause the image to be displayed.
5. To change the window background color to LightSkyBlue as shown in Figure 3-71, what property should you modify?
6. What property is used to display the text "View the World" in the window title bar?

Case Programming Assignments

Complete one or more of the following case programming assignments. Submit the program and materials you create to your instructor. The level of difficulty is indicated for each assignment.

● = Easiest
●● = Intermediate
●●● = Challenging

1 ● VIRTUAL REALITY HEADSETS

Create a Windows form mock-up for the requirements document shown in Figure 3-72 and the Use Case Definition shown in Figure 3-73. The Windows Form object and the other objects in the user interface are shown in Figure 3-74.

REQUIREMENTS DOCUMENT

Date:	October 13, 2018
Date Submitted:	
Application Title:	Virtual Reality Headsets
Purpose:	This Windows Classic Desktop application displays an order screen for two types of virtual reality headsets. The user can choose either a crown VR headset or earbud VR headset.
Program Procedures:	From a window on the screen, the user makes a request to see one of the two VR headset types.
Algorithms, Processing, and Conditions:	1. The user first views a Virtual Reality Headset window that displays the VR Headset company (VR Forward). When the user chooses to click the first headset button for the Crown VR, the crown.jpg image is displayed. When the user chooses to view the second headset for the Earbud VR, the earbud.jpg image is displayed. 2. After the user views one of the two images, the user can select the other image or close the window.
Notes and Restrictions:	The images should not be displayed at the same time.
Comments:	The pictures shown in the window can be found on CengageBrain.com. The name of the pictures are crown and earbud.

FIGURE 3-72

(continues)

Case Programming Assignments *continued*

Virtual Reality Headsets

USE CASE DEFINITION

1. The window opens, displaying the name of the company. The two VR image buttons are enabled.
2. User clicks either the VR Crown or VR Earbud button.
3. The user can continue to click each VR button.
4. The Exit Window button is enabled after the user views an image. User clicks the Exit Window button to exit the application.

FIGURE 3-73

In Figure 3-74a, no button has been clicked. In Figure 3-74b, the user has clicked the VR Crown button.

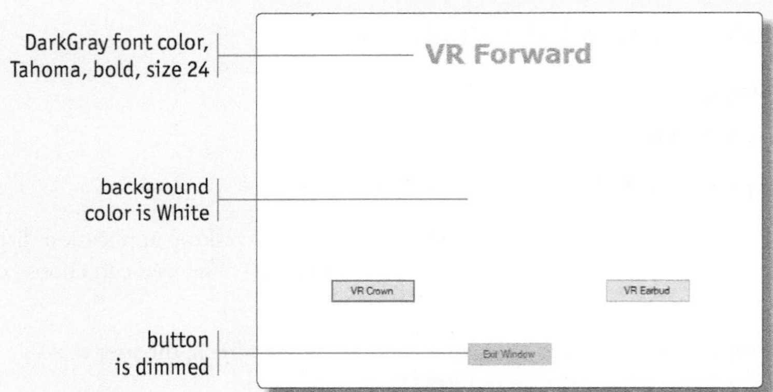

FIGURE 3-74a

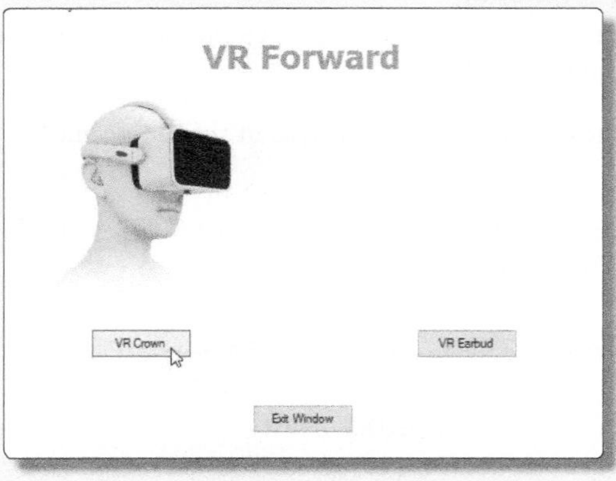

FIGURE 3-74b

Chesky/Shutterstock.com

Case Programming Assignments

2 • BURGER SPECIALS

Create a Windows form mock-up for the requirements document shown in Figure 3-75 and the Use Case Definition shown in Figure 3-76. The Windows Form object and the other objects in the user interface are shown in Figure 3-77.

REQUIREMENTS DOCUMENT

Date:	January 10, 2019
Date Submitted:	
Application Title:	Burger Specials
Purpose:	This Windows Classic Desktop application displays the burger specials for a restaurant named Farm Burger. The user can select one of two specials: Prime Beef or Veggie.
Program Procedures:	From a window on the screen, the user orders one of two special burgers and the program confirms the order with a message.
Algorithms, Processing, and Conditions:	1. The user must be able to identify the Prime Beef or Veggie burger special name as many times as necessary until making a decision. 2. When the user identifies the special, a picture of that meal appears in the window. 3. Only one picture should be displayed at a time. 4. When the user selects Prime Beef, a message should be displayed to confirm the selection of the burger. In addition, the user should be prevented from identifying another meal after selecting a dish. 5. After the user selects a meal, the only allowable action is to close the window.
Notes and Restrictions:	A user can select a meal only after viewing one of the images of the meals.
Comments:	1. The pictures shown in the window can be found on cengagebrain.com. 2. The names of the pictures are prime and veggie.

FIGURE 3-75

(continues)

Case Programming Assignments *continued*

Burger Specials

USE CASE DEFINITION

1. User clicks the Prime Beef button or Veggie button.
2. Program displays a picture of the burger identified by the user and enables the burger selection button.
3. User clicks burger buttons to view burgers as desired. Program displays the picture of the identified burger.
4. User clicks the Select Meal button.
5. Program displays a meal confirmation message and disables both burger buttons and the Select Meal button.
6. The Exit Window button becomes active. User exits the program by clicking the Exit Window button.

FIGURE 3-76

In Figure 3-77a, no button has been clicked. In Figure 3-77b, the user has clicked the Veggie button. In Figure 3-77c, the user has clicked the Select Meal button.

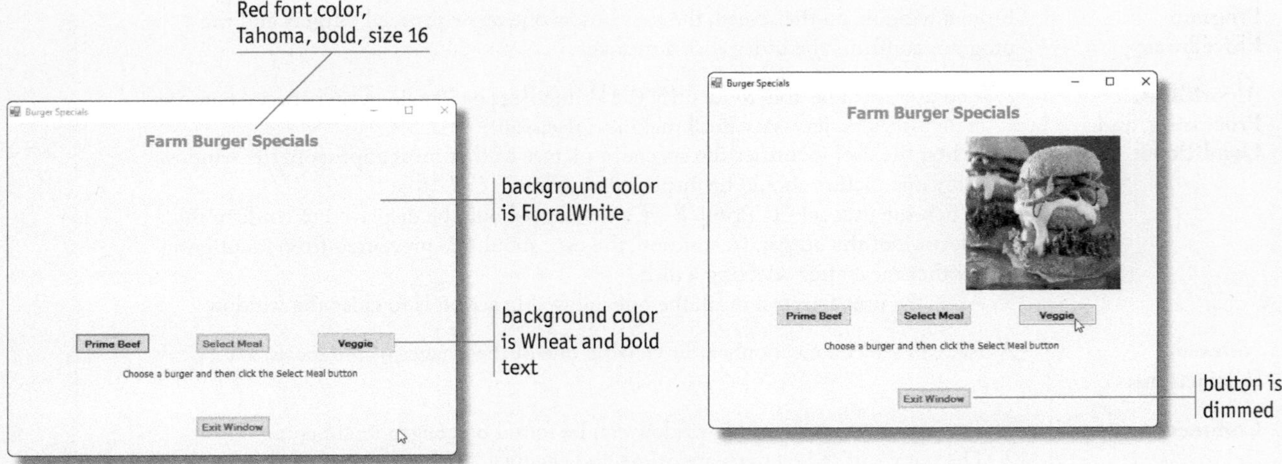

FIGURE 3-77a

FIGURE 3-77b
Olga Miltsova/Shutterstock.com

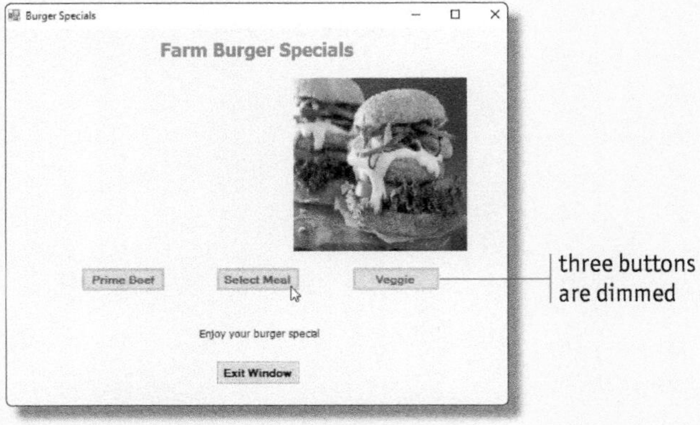

FIGURE 3-77c
Olga Miltsova/Shutterstock.com

Case Programming Assignments

3 ●● CAMPUS MUSIC CAFE

Create a Use Case Definition document and design a Windows form mock-up based on the requirements document in Figure 3-78.

REQUIREMENTS DOCUMENT

Date:	October 13, 2018
Date Submitted:	
Application Title:	Campus Music Cafe
Purpose:	This Windows Classic Desktop application displays a welcome screen to market the Campus Music Café performance. The user can choose an option to view the date, start location, and details.
Program Procedures:	From a window on the screen, the user makes a request to see the performance's date, start location, and details.
Algorithms, Processing, and Conditions:	1. The user first views a Campus Music Cafe window that displays the title (Campus Music Café Open Mic Night), a cafe picture, and a phrase that states that all college students are welcome. 2. When the user chooses to view the date, start location, and details, the following information is displayed: October 30, 2018 Open "Mic" Start Time: 8:00 PM For more information, view the Campus Music Café's Facebook page. After the user views the Campus Music Café's information, the only allowable action is to close the window.
Notes and Restrictions:	Design your own layout.
Comments:	Locate your own image online.

FIGURE 3-78

Case Programming Assignments

4 SPRING BREAK TRAVEL SPECIALS

Create a Use Case Definition document and design a Windows form mock-up based on the requirements document in Figure 3-79.

REQUIREMENTS DOCUMENT

Date:	March 21, 2019
Date Submitted:	
Application Title:	Spring Break Travel Specials
Purpose:	The Student Center on campus has created special Spring Break travel specials on three trips. A student can choose one of three Spring Break trips. The program must display each of the Spring Break travel specials upon request. The student can then select a trip for purchase.
Program Procedures:	From a window on the screen, the user selects one of three trips. A picture of the selected trip is displayed in the window. The user then can choose a trip for purchase.
Algorithms, Processing, and Conditions:	1. The user selects a trip. Then, a picture of the trip location is displayed in the window. 2. The user can select any of the three trips. Only the picture of the selected trip should be displayed. 3. The user can select trips as many times as necessary and display the pictures of the destinations. 4. The user finds a trip, chooses it for purchase, and clicks the Purchase button. 5. After the user chooses a trip, a message stating "Enjoy your trip!" should be displayed. 6. After the user chooses a trip, the only allowable action is to close the window.
Notes and Restrictions:	The user should not be able to choose a trip until viewing at least one trip image.
Comments:	The available trips are to Myrtle Beach, Key West, or Venice Beach. Select your own pictures online.

FIGURE 3-79

Case Programming Assignments

5 ●●● HEALTHY SNACK SELECTION

Create a requirements document and a Use Case Definition document and then design a Windows form mock-up based on the case project shown in Figure 3-80:

The international club on campus requests a computer application that will run on a kiosk during the International Festival where students can select a healthy international snack. The application should request which free snack you would like, display the choices as buttons, and then display an image of the snack you select. Another button allows you to make your final snack selection and display a confirmation message.

Snack
Bean Burrito
Falafel
Greek Yogurt
Spring Rolls

FIGURE 3-80

Case Programming Assignments

6 COSTUME PARTY RENTALS

Create a requirements document and a Use Case Definition document and then design a Windows form mock-up based on the case project shown in Figure 3-81:

A costume shop requests a computer application that advertises costume rentals. This week's costume rental specials are as follows:

Costume	Price per Week
Renaissance Fair	$40
Stormtrooper	$49
Batman/Batgirl	$36
Pirate	$29

Write an application that allows the user to select any of the five costume rental specials. When the user selects a costume, the corresponding cost and a picture of the costume should be displayed. Clear each prior price and picture when the user selects a different costume. After selecting a costume, the user should be able to book the costume rental and then close the window.

FIGURE 3-81

CHAPTER 4

Variables and Arithmetic Operations

OBJECTIVES

You will have mastered the material in this chapter when you can:

- Create, modify, and program a TextBox object
- Use code to place data in the Text property of a Label object
- Use the AcceptButton and CancelButton properties
- Understand and declare String and Numeric variables
- Use assignment statements to place data in variables
- Use literals and constants in coding statements
- Understand scope rules for variables
- Convert string and numeric data
- Understand and use arithmetic operators and arithmetic operations
- Format and display numeric data as a string
- Create a form load event
- Create a concatenated string
- Debug a program

Introduction

In the Latte Selection program you developed in Chapter 2 and Chapter 3, you clicked buttons in the user interface to trigger events, but you did not enter data. In many applications, users must enter data that the program then uses in its processing.

When processing data entered by a user, a common requirement is to perform arithmetic operations on the data to generate useful output. Arithmetic operations include adding, subtracting, multiplying, and dividing numeric data.

To illustrate user data input and arithmetic operations, the application in this chapter allows the user to specify a number of bikes to rent from a beach bike rental program. The application then calculates the total cost of renting the bikes. The user interface for the program is shown in Figure 4-1.

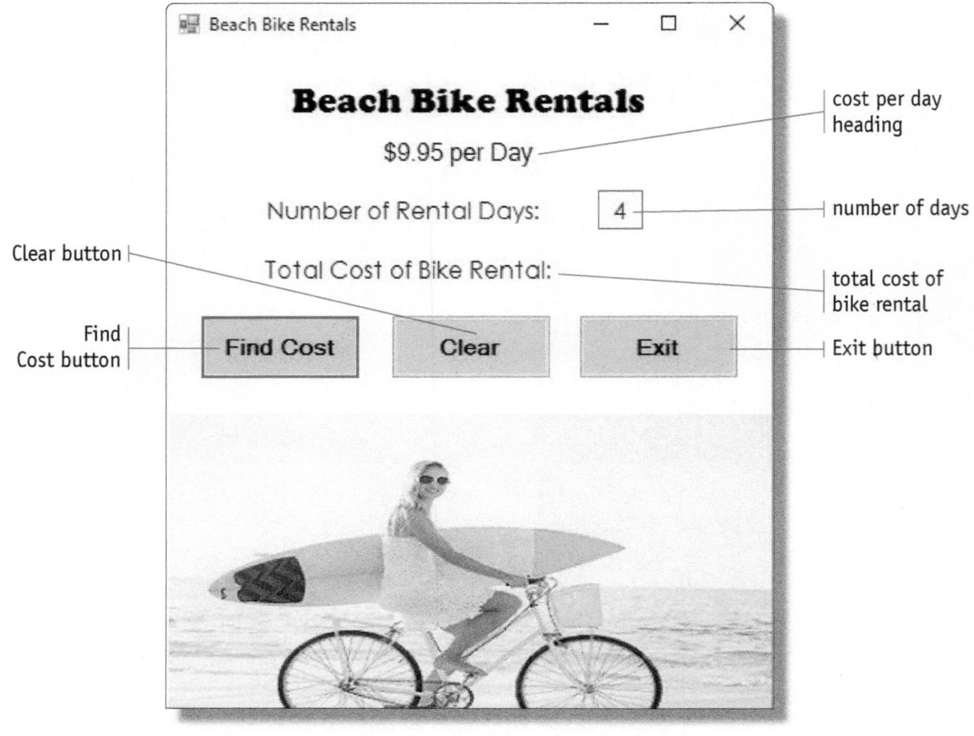

FIGURE 4-1

iStockphoto.com/Wavebreakmedia

In Figure 4-1, the user entered 4 as the number of days to rent the beach bike while on vacation. The minimum rental time is 1 day. When the user clicks the Find Cost button, the program multiplies 4 (days) by the cost per bike rental for a day ($9.95) and then displays the result as the total cost of the rental for a single bike. When the user clicks the Clear button, the values for the number of days and the total cost of the bike rental are cleared so the next user can enter a value. Clicking the Exit button closes the window and ends the program.

To create this application, the developer must understand how to perform the following processes, among others:

1. Define a text box for data entry
2. Define a label to hold the results of arithmetic operations
3. Convert data in a text box to data that can be used for arithmetic operations
4. Perform arithmetic operations on data entered by a user

The following pages describe the tools and techniques required to create the program shown in Figure 4-1.

Design the User Interface

As you have learned in Chapter 2 and Chapter 3, the next step after completing the program requirements document for an application is to define the graphical user interface. In this chapter, three new elements are introduced:

- TextBox objects
- Labels intended for variable text property values
- Accept buttons

Each of these elements is described in the following sections.

TextBox Objects

A **TextBox object** allows users to enter data into a program. In Figure 4-2, the user can enter a value into the text box.

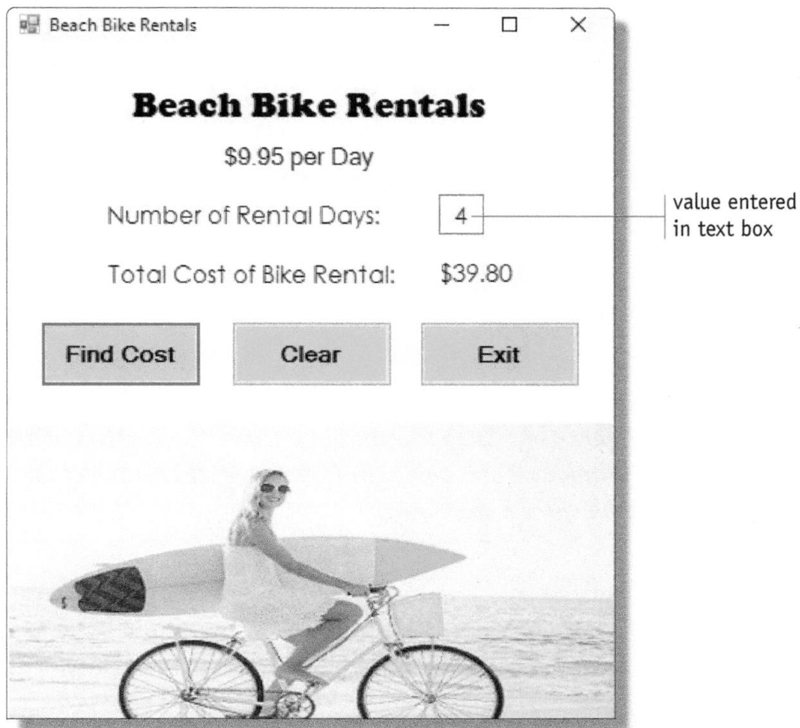

FIGURE 4-2

iStockphoto.com/Wavebreakmedia

In Figure 4-2, the TextBox object is placed on the Windows Form object. A TextBox object automatically allows the user to enter data in the text box. To place a TextBox object on the Windows Form object, you can complete the following steps. (Note that the examples in this chapter illustrate new objects in the user interface. Portions of the user interface have already been completed for you. You should not expect to *click along* with these examples unless you create all the elements or follow the steps using an unformatted user interface.)

STEP 1 With Visual Studio open, the Beach Bike Rentals Windows Classic Desktop application created, and the frmBike.vb [Design] tabbed page visible, point to the TextBox .NET component in the Toolbox.

The TextBox .NET component is highlighted in the Toolbox (Figure 4-3).

FIGURE 4-3

iStockphoto.com/Wavebreakmedia

STEP 2 Drag the TextBox .NET component onto the Windows Form object at the desired location.

While you drag, the pointer changes to indicate a TextBox object will be placed on the Windows Form object (Figure 4-4). Snap lines indicate where the TextBox object aligns with other objects on the Windows Form object. In Figure 4-4, the bottom of the TextBox object aligns with the bottom of the Label object.

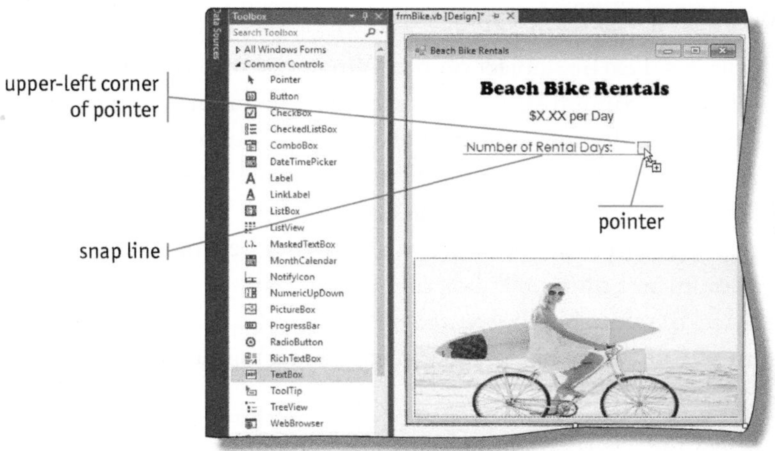

FIGURE 4-4

iStockphoto.com/Wavebreakmedia

STEP 3 When the upper-left corner of the pointer is located where you want to place the TextBox object's upper-left corner, release the TextBox object.

Visual Studio places the TextBox object at the location identified by the pointer (Figure 4-5). The default size of the TextBox object is 100 pixels wide by 20 pixels high. Notice that by default the TextBox object contains no text. You can change that by entering text in the Text property of the TextBox object.

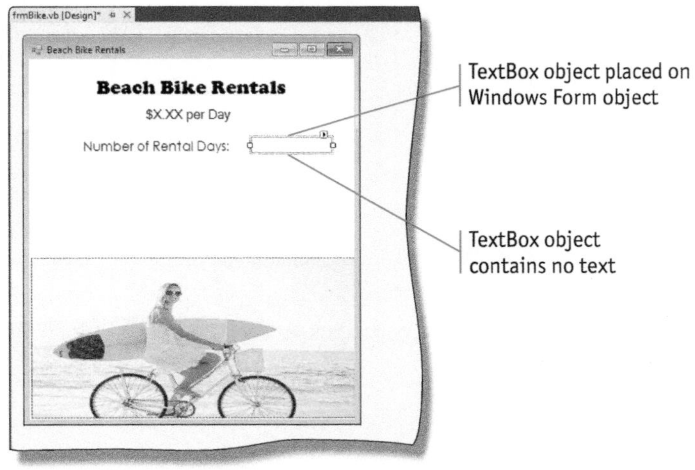

FIGURE 4-5

iStockphoto.com/Wavebreakmedia

As you have learned, whenever you place an object on the Windows Form object, you must name the object. When naming a TextBox object, the prefix should be txt. Therefore, the name of the TextBox object in Figure 4-5 could be txtNumberOfDays.

Size and Position a TextBox Object

To properly place a TextBox object on the Windows Form object, you need to know the minimum and maximum size of the text box. The minimum size normally is determined by the maximum number of characters the user will enter into the text box. For example, if the user can enter 99 in the sample program as the maximum number of days, the minimum size of the text box must be large enough to display two numbers. Although it can be larger, it should not be smaller.

The maximum size of the text box often is determined by the design of the user interface; that is, the size should *look and feel good* in the user interface. To determine the minimum size of the text box, you can use the technique in the following steps:

STEP 1 Select the TextBox object. Select the (Name) property and name the TextBox object `txtNumberOfDays`. Scroll in the Properties window until the Text property is visible and then click the right column for the Text property.

The TextBox object is selected, as shown by the thick border and sizing handles (Figure 4-6). The TextBox object is named txtNumberOfDays. The Text property for the TextBox object is highlighted and the insertion point indicates you can enter text for the Text property.

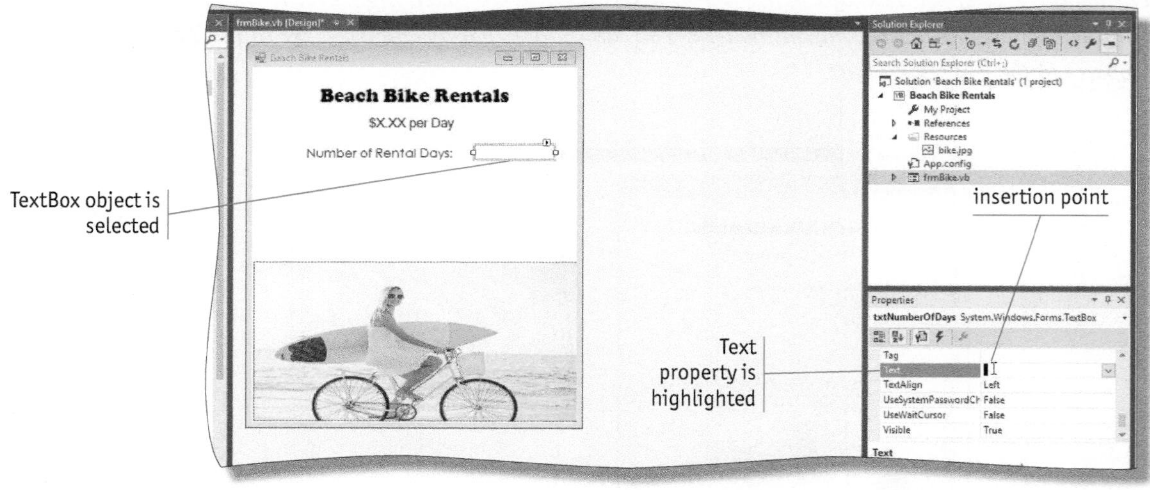

iStockphoto.com/Wavebreakmedia

FIGURE 4-6

STEP 2 Using the Properties window, change the Font property to the correct font and font size. For this application, change the font to Century Gothic and change the font size to 12. Type the maximum number of characters the user normally will enter into the text box and then press the ENTER key. Programmers often use the digit 8 in this situation because it is wider than other digits. This example uses the value 88 because two digits is the maximum number the user normally will enter for the number of days.

When the value is entered in the Text property of the TextBox object, the value is displayed in the TextBox object (Figure 4-7).

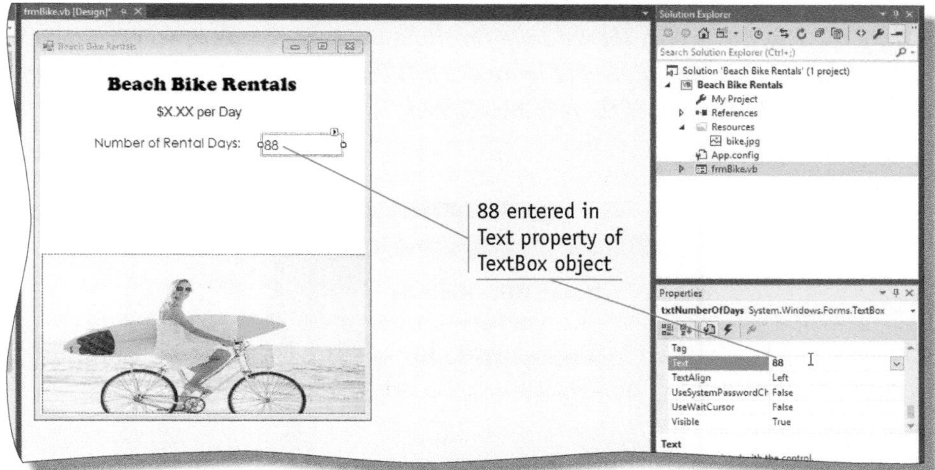

iStockphoto.com/Wavebreakmedia

FIGURE 4-7

STEP 3 Drag the right edge of the TextBox object and resize it to be slightly wider than the 88 entry.

As you drag, the size of the TextBox object changes (Figure 4-8). When you release the TextBox object, the text box will be resized.

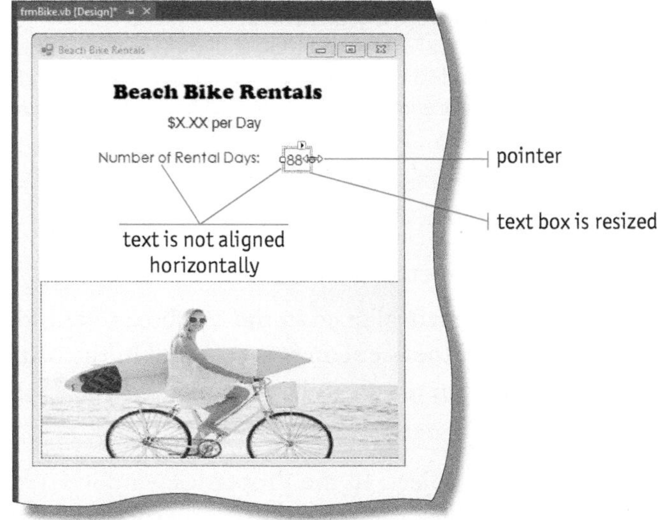

FIGURE 4-8

iStockphoto.com/Wavebreakmedia

STEP 4 To horizontally align the text in the label and the text in the text box, drag the text box up until a red snap line indicates the bottoms of the text are aligned (Figure 4-9). Then, release the left mouse button.

As you drag the TextBox object, the red snap line indicates when the bottoms of the text in the label and the text box are aligned (Figure 4-9). When you release the TextBox object, it will be placed so the bottoms of the text are aligned.

FIGURE 4-9
iStockphoto.com/Wavebreakmedia

CONSIDER THIS

Are details such as alignment important in design and programming?
The user interface is more important than ever with Windows application and mobile design. Many colleges teach entire courses on interface design (UX). Remember, your users respond to consistency in your design layout. Language is another interface element that should be consistent. A consistent interface enables your users to have a better understanding of how the application works and increases their efficiency.

Align Text in a TextBox Object

In Figure 4-9, the numbers are left-aligned in the text box. Often, the user interface will be more useful if the value the user enters is centered in the text box. To align the text in a TextBox object, you can use the following method:

STEP 1 Select the TextBox object. In the Properties window, scroll until the TextAlign property is visible, click the TextAlign property in the left column, and then click the list arrow in the right column of the TextAlign property.

The TextAlign property list contains the values Left, Right, and Center (Figure 4-10).

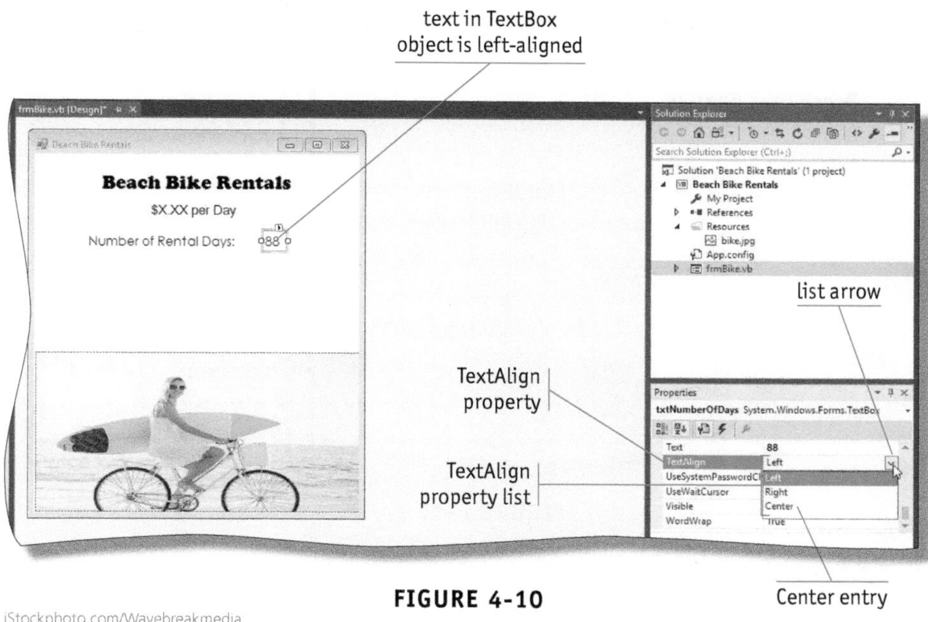

FIGURE 4-10

iStockphoto.com/Wavebreakmedia

STEP 2 Click Center in the TextAlign property list.

The text in the TextBox object is centered (Figure 4-11). When a user enters data in the text box, the data also will be centered.

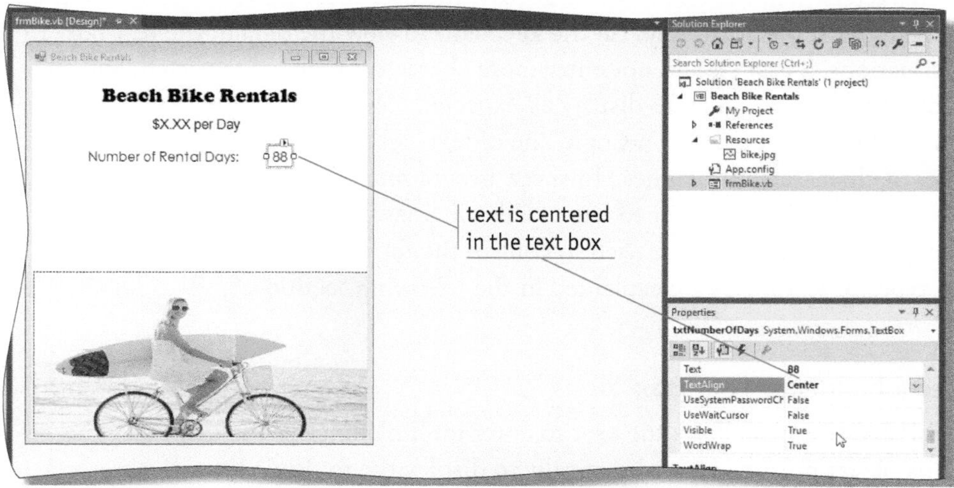

FIGURE 4-11

iStockphoto.com/Wavebreakmedia

STEP 3 Because the TextBox object is sized properly, remove the digits in the TextBox object. Select the characters 88 in the Text property, press the DELETE key, and then press the ENTER key.

The TextBox object contains no text and is ready for use in the user interface (Figure 4-12).

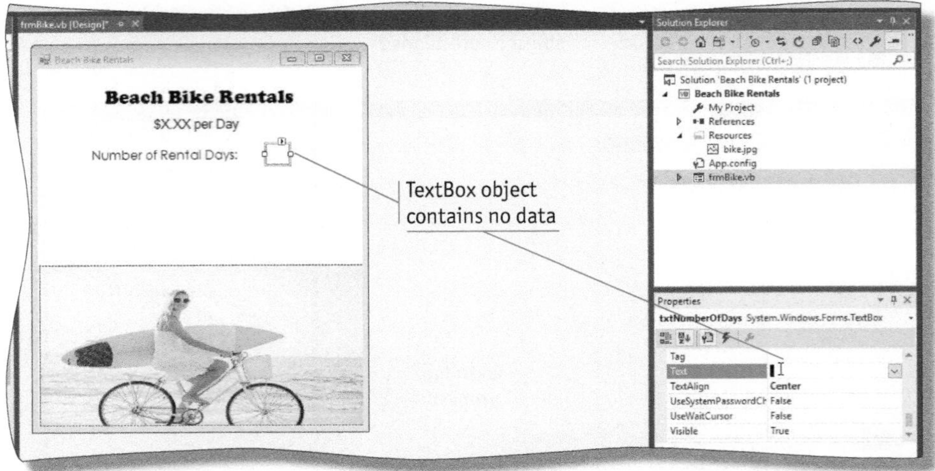

FIGURE 4-12

iStockphoto.com/Wavebreakmedia

Enter Data in a TextBox Object

When the program is executed, the user can enter data in the text box. Users can enter letters, numbers, and other characters. If the user enters more characters than the text box can display, the characters that have already been entered scroll to the left and no longer are visible. A text box does not contain a scroll bar, so if a user enters more characters than the text box can display, the user must move the insertion point left or right with the arrow keys on the keyboard to view the data in the text box. In most situations, a user should not enter more characters than are expected, and the text box should be designed to display all expected characters.

In a default text box, only a single line of text can be entered regardless of the number of characters in the line. However, programmers can select a special option for a text box to allow the user to enter multiple lines of text. Additionally, the MaskedTextBox object can be used to control the format of data that a user enters. These types of text boxes are explained in the following sections.

Create a MultiLine Text Box

A MultiLine text box allows the user to enter multiple lines in the text box. The TextBox object must be resized vertically to display the multiple lines. To create a TextBox object that can accept multiple lines, you can complete the following steps:

STEP 1 Select the TextBox object, click the Action tag, and then point to the MultiLine check box.

The TextBox Tasks list is displayed with the MultiLine check box (Figure 4-13). When you click the MultiLine check box, the TextBox object will be able to accept multiple lines.

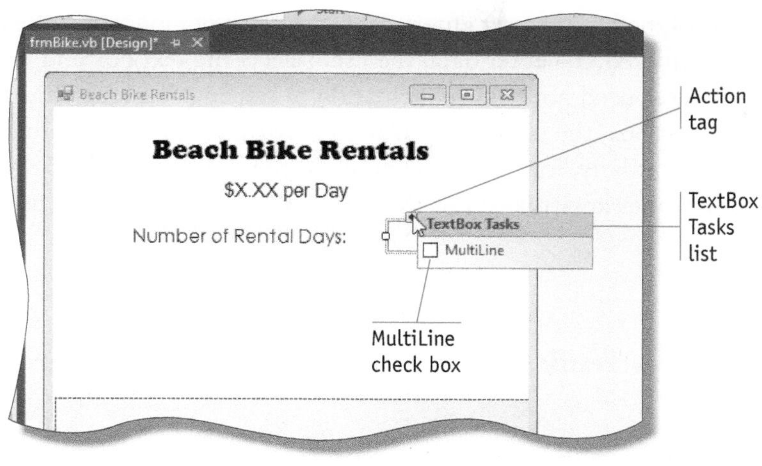

FIGURE 4-13

iStockphoto.com/Wavebreakmedia

STEP 2 Click the MultiLine check box.

The text box is enabled to accept multiple lines.

In addition to enabling multiple lines, you should increase the vertical size of the TextBox object so the multiple lines will be visible when the user enters them.

Create a MaskedTextBox Object

The MaskedTextBox object allows you to specify the data format of the value typed into the text box. Using the MaskedTextBox object removes confusion about which format should be used for data the user enters. The term *mask* refers to a predefined layout for the data. Figure 4-14 shows three examples of the MaskedTextBox used for the Short date input mask, the Phone number input mask, and the Social Security number input mask.

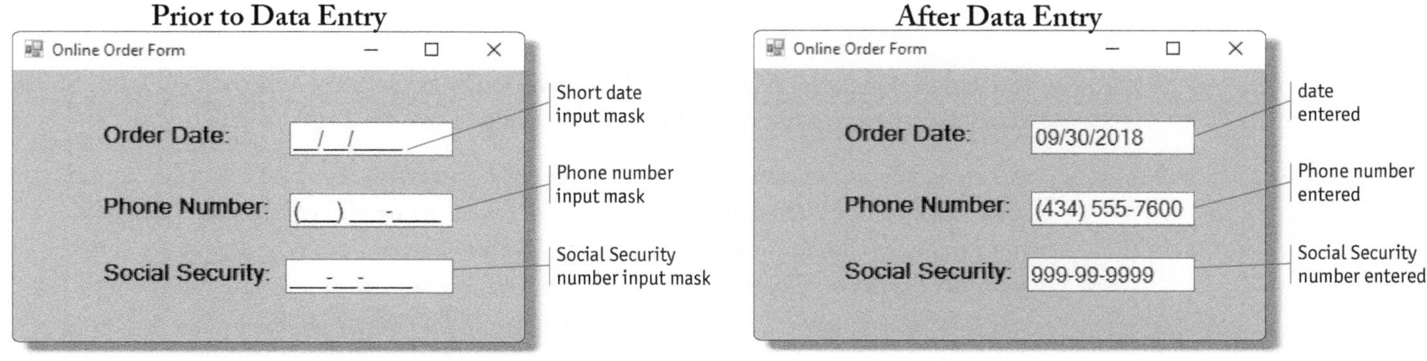

FIGURE 4-14

In Figure 4-14, before the user enters data, the mask demonstrates the format of the data to be entered. To enter data, the user selects the text box and then types data into it. The user need not enter punctuation or spacing. To enter the date in the Order Date text box, the user typed 09302018 with no spaces, punctuation, or other keystrokes. Similarly, for the phone number, the user typed 4345557600, again with no spaces or other keystrokes. For the Social Security number, the user typed 999999999.

To place a MaskedTextBox object on the Windows Form object, you can complete the following steps:

STEP 1 Drag a MaskedTextBox .NET component from the Toolbox to the Windows Form object. Then, click the Action tag on the TextBox object and point to the Set Mask command.

The MaskedTextBox object is placed on the Windows Form object (Figure 4-15). When the Action tag is clicked, the MaskedTextBox Tasks list is displayed. The Set Mask command is the only command in the list.

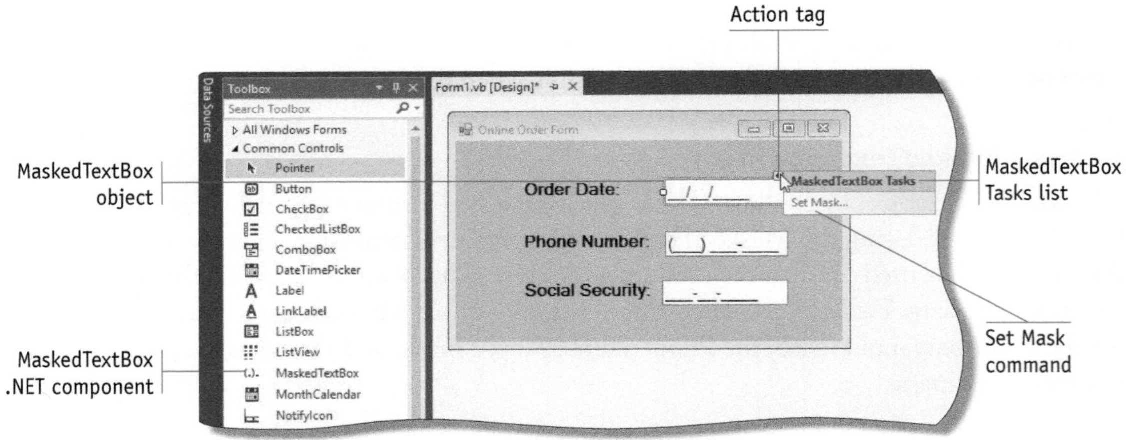

FIGURE 4-15

STEP 2 Click Set Mask on the MaskedTextBox Tasks list and then click the Short date mask description in the Input Mask dialog box.

Visual Studio displays the Input Mask dialog box (Figure 4-16). The Mask Description column contains all the masks that can be used for the MaskedTextBox object. The Short date mask description is highlighted. In the Preview box, you can type data to see how the mask will perform when it is used in the MaskedTextBox object. The Use Validating Type check box is selected to verify that the user entered valid numeric data.

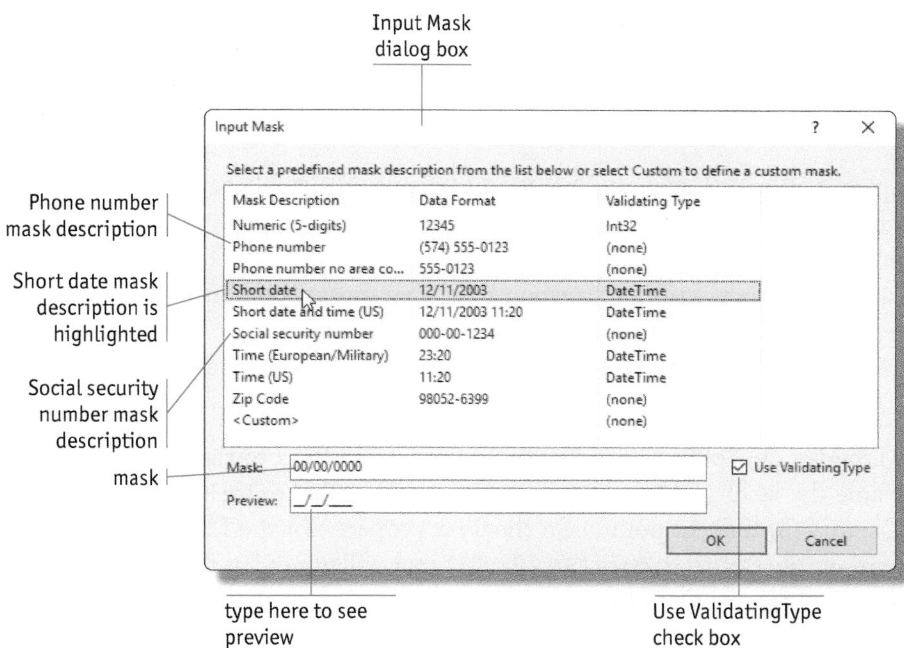

FIGURE 4-16

STEP 3 Click the OK button in the Input Mask dialog box and then click anywhere in the Windows Form object.

The mask is placed in the MaskedTextBox object (Figure 4-17).

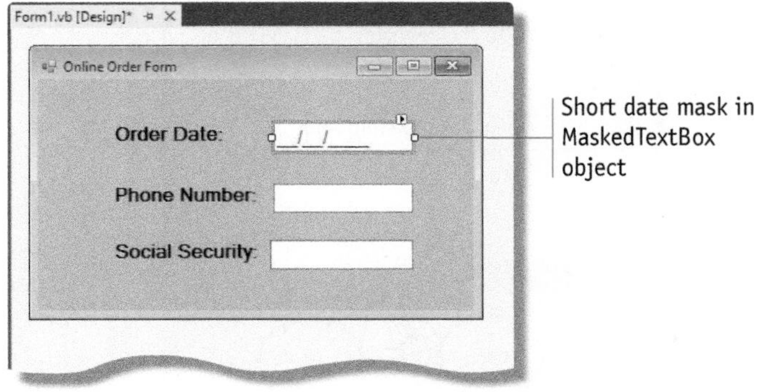

FIGURE 4-17

You can use the same technique to place the phone number and Social Security number in the MaskedTextBox.

Label Objects

In the sample program, a Label object is used to display the total cost of the bike rental (see Figure 4-1 on page 148). The developer must accomplish two tasks to prepare the label for this purpose: place the label on the Windows Form object in the correct location, and then ensure that when the Label object contains its maximum value, its location will work within the user interface design.

To accomplish these two tasks, you can complete the following step:

STEP 1 Drag a Label object onto the Windows Form object to the correct location. Name the label `lblTotalCost`. Change the label to the appropriate font and size (Century Gothic, 12 points). In the Text property for the Label object, enter the maximum number of characters (`$888.88`) that will appear in the label during execution of the program. Drag the Label object up until the red snap line appears (Figure 4-18). Then release the Label object.

The properly sized characters appear in the label. The label is aligned (Figure 4-18).

FIGURE 4-18
iStockphoto.com/Wavebreakmedia

When program execution begins, the label that will contain the total cost of the bike rental should be blank. In Figure 4-18, however, it contains the value in the Text property of the Label object ($888.88). If the Text property in a Label object is set to hold no content, it will not be displayed in the Windows Form object during the design phase, which makes the Label object difficult to work with in Design mode. Therefore, most designers place a value in the Text property of the Label object and leave it there during user interface design. Then, when the program begins, the label Text property will be set to blank. You will learn to perform this task later in the chapter.

Accept Button in Form Properties

Computer users often press the ENTER key to enter data in a text box and cause processing to occur. For instance, in the sample program for this chapter, users might prefer to type the number of rental days and press the ENTER key instead of typing the number and clicking the Find Cost button.

You can assign a button to be an Accept button in the user interface, which means the program will carry out the event handler processing associated with the button if the user clicks it or presses the ENTER key. To assign the Find Cost button as the Accept button, you can complete the following steps:

STEP 1 After the Button objects are added, click a blank area in the Windows Form object to select it. Scroll in the Properties window until the AcceptButton property is visible. Click the AcceptButton property name in the left column and then click the AcceptButton property list arrow in the right column.

The AcceptButton property list displays the names of the Button objects on the selected Windows Form object (Figure 4-19). Any of these buttons can be specified as the Accept button.

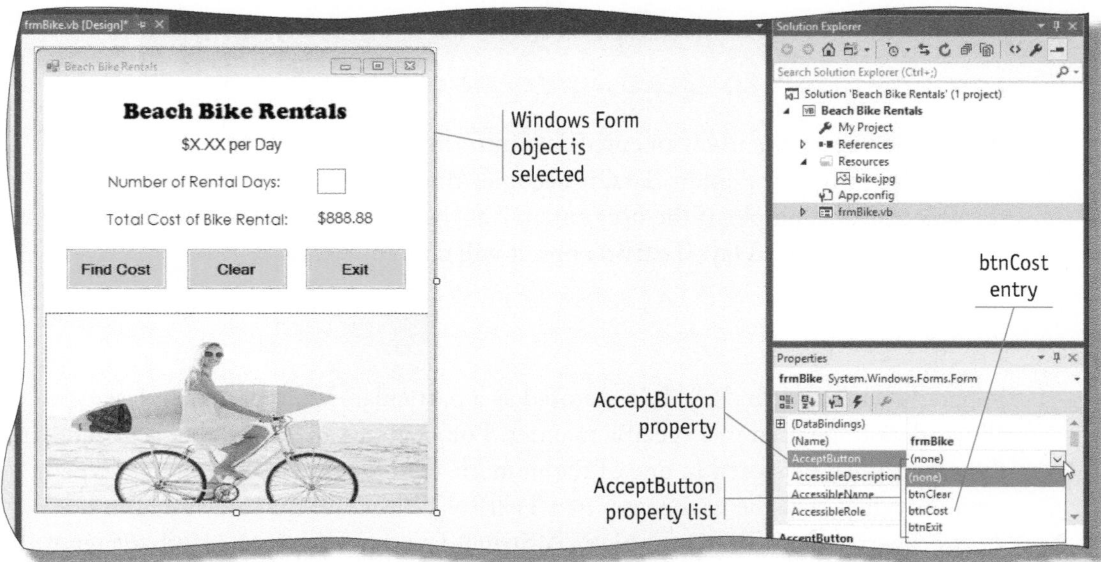

FIGURE 4-19

iStockphoto.com/Wavebreakmedia

STEP 2 Click btnCost in the AcceptButton property list.

The btnCost Button object is designated as the Accept button. When the program is running, the user can press the ENTER key after entering data to execute the event handler processing for the Find Cost button. Notice the border of the Find Cost button displays a blue edge to identify that the AcceptButton property is set.

Cancel Button in Form Properties

In the same manner as the Accept button, you can designate a Cancel button for the Windows Form object. When the user presses the ESC key, the event handler processing will be executed for the button identified as the Cancel button. In the sample program, the Cancel button will be used to clear the text box and the total cost of bikes rented and to place the insertion point in the text box. Thus, it performs the same activity that occurs when the user clicks the Clear button. To specify the Cancel button for the sample program, you complete the following steps:

Step 1: Click a blank area in the Windows Form object to select it.
Step 2: Click the CancelButton property name in the left column of the Properties window for the Windows Form object, and then click the CancelButton list arrow.
Step 3: Click the button name (btnClear) in the CancelButton property list.

When the program is executed, the user can press the ESC key to perform the same processing as when the Clear button is clicked.

> **CRITICAL THINKING**
>
> **Why does a developer have to test every possible input and action that a user may perform while running an application?**
> Users do not always follow the *expected path*. They enter data incorrectly. They decide they need to go back and change something they have already entered. They discover they need to learn more about what the application is asking of them and require more detailed assistance. By adding properties such as the AcceptButton and others, you will eliminate any actions that may crash the program.

Introduction to Data Entry and Data Types

As you have seen, the user can enter data into the program by using the TextBox object. When the user enters data, it becomes the value stored in the Text property of the object. For example, if the user enters 7 as the number of days, the Text property for the txtNumberOfDays TextBox object will contain the value 7.

String Data Type

When data is stored in RAM, it is stored as a particular data type. Each data type allows data to be used in a specific manner. For example, to add two values together, the values must be stored in one of the numeric data types. The **String** data type is used for values that the user enters in a TextBox object and that are stored in the Text property of the TextBox object. A String data type can store any character available on the computer.

When the user enters data into a TextBox object, it is good programming style to copy the entered value from the Text property of the TextBox object to a String variable. A **variable** is a named location in RAM where data is stored. A **String variable** is a named location in RAM that can store a string value. Thus, a person's name, a dollar amount, a phone number, or the number of bikes rented can be stored in a String variable.

The programmer defines a variable during the coding of the program. The statement in Figure 4-20 defines a string.

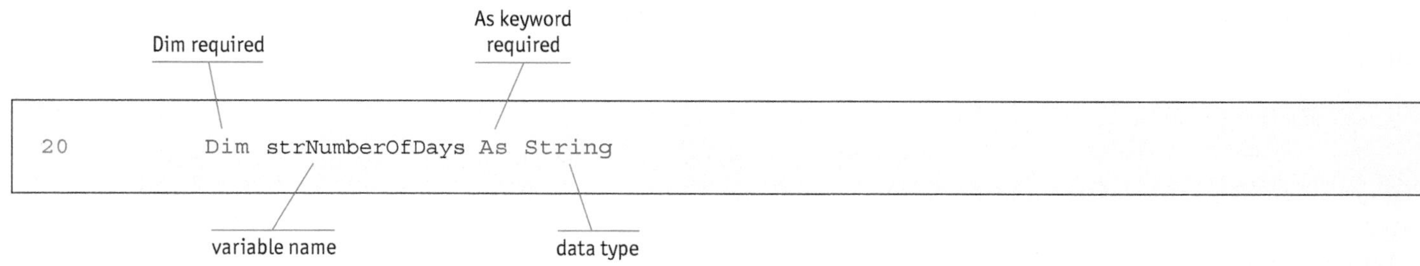

FIGURE 4-20

To begin the statement, the keyword Dim is required. This keyword stands for *variable dimension*. It indicates to the Visual Basic compiler that the entries after Dim are defining a variable.

The next entry is the variable name. Every variable must have a name so it can be referenced in other statements within the program. By convention, every String variable name begins with the letters str followed by a descriptive name. The name in Figure 4-20 (strNumberOfDays) indicates a String variable that will contain the number of days entered by the user.

The keyword As must follow the name of the variable, as shown in Figure 4-20. If it is not included, a compilation error will occur. Following the word As is the declaration for the variable's data type. In Figure 4-20, the data type is specified as String.

As a result of the statement in Figure 4-20, when the program is compiled, the Visual Basic compiler will allocate an area in RAM that is reserved to contain the value in the string.

The general format to define a variable is shown in Figure 4-21.

VARIABLE NAME RULES

Variable names in Visual Basic must follow a few simple rules. The name must begin with a letter or an underline symbol (_). The name can contain letters, numbers, and the underline symbol. It cannot contain spaces or other special characters. Reserved words in Visual Basic cannot be used for variable names; reserved words appear in blue in the code window.

General Format: Define a Variable

```
Dim VariableName As DataType
```

EXAMPLE	*RESULT*
`Dim strNumberOfDays`	`String variable`
`Dim intNumberOfDays`	`Integer variable`
`decTotalCost As Decimal`	`Decimal variable`

FIGURE 4-21

HEADS UP

When defining variables, good programming practice dictates that the variable names should reflect the actual values to be placed in the variable. That way, anyone reading the program code can easily understand the use of the variable. For example, a good name for a String variable that contains an employee's last name would be strEmployeeLastName. You should not use names like strXXX, strLN, strEmp, or strName. Each of these names is imprecise and potentially misleading. You should consider the people who will read your code when you name the variables in your program. Your goal must be to make their task as clear and easy as possible.

The Integer and Decimal variables defined as examples in Figure 4-21 are numeric variables. You will learn about numeric variables shortly.

Assignment Statements

When a variable is defined as shown in Figure 4-20, the variable does not contain any data. One method used to place data in the variable is an **assignment statement**. The assignment statement shown in Figure 4-22 will copy the data from the Text property of the txtNumberOfDays TextBox object into the strNumberOfDays String variable.

The variable name to the left of the assignment statement (strNumberOfDays) identifies the variable to which a value will be copied. The equal sign indicates to the Visual Basic compiler that the statement is an assignment statement. The equal sign is required.

The value to the right of the equal sign will be copied to the variable to the left of the equal sign. In Figure 4-22, the value in the Text property of the txtNumberOfDays TextBox object will be copied to the strNumberOfDays variable.

To enter the definition of the strNumberOfDays variable and then enter the assignment statement in Figure 4-22 using IntelliSense, you can complete the following steps:

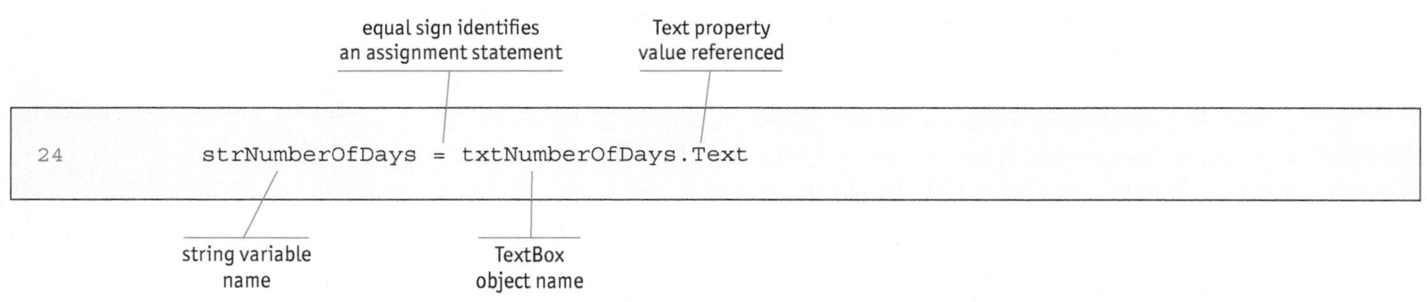

FIGURE 4-22

STEP 1 With Visual Studio open to the code window and the insertion point located in the desired column, type `Dim` followed by a space. Then, type the name of the String variable you want to define, `strNumberOfDays`.

The Dim keyword and the String name you typed are displayed in the code window (Figure 4-23). Notice that Dim is blue to indicate it is a keyword. The green curly line indicates that the keyword has not been assigned a value in the program.

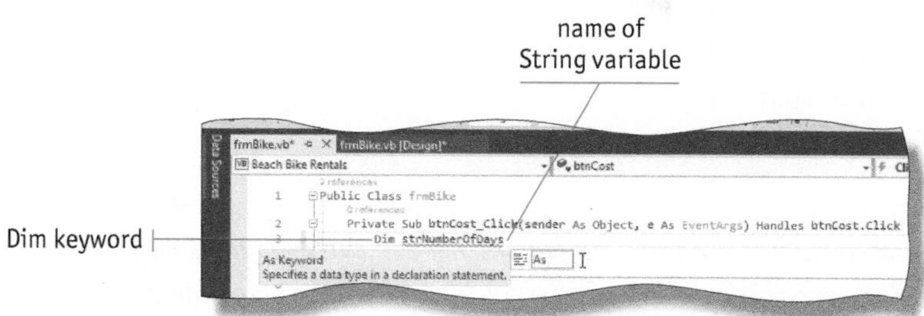

FIGURE 4-23

STEP 2 Press the SPACEBAR, type the word As, and then press the SPACEBAR again.

The letters you typed are entered. When you typed the space following the word As, IntelliSense displayed a list (Figure 4-24). The list contains all the allowable entries that can follow the As keyword. To define a String variable, the correct entry is String.

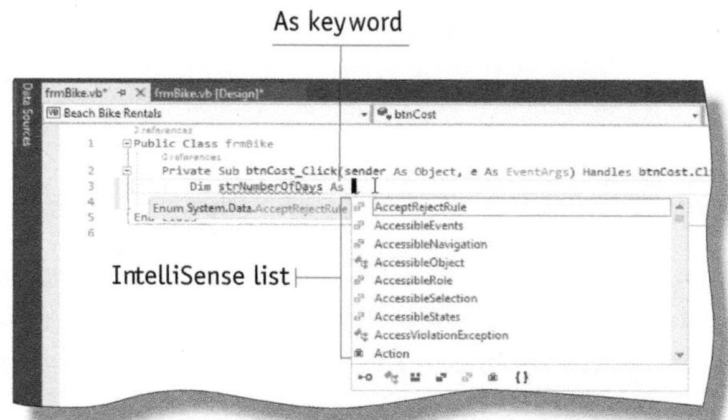

FIGURE 4-24

STEP 3 Because the correct entry is String, type str and press the ENTER key.

IntelliSense highlights String in the list. The Dim statement is entered (Figure 4-25). The green squiggly underline indicates the variable is not referenced within the program. Visual Studio will remove the underline when the variable is used in an assignment statement or other statement.

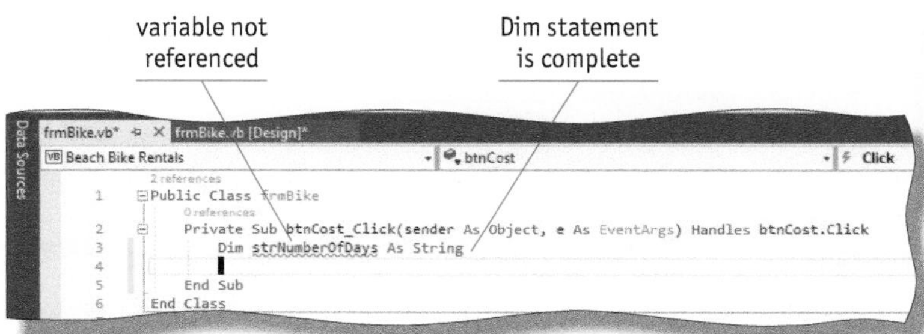

FIGURE 4-25

STEP 4 To begin the assignment statement, type `strn`. IntelliSense displays the only variable name that starts with the letters strn, which is the String variable strNumberOfDays.

IntelliSense displays a list of allowable entries for the statement (Figure 4-26). Whenever you want to reference a variable name in a statement, you can type the first few letters of the name to have IntelliSense display a list of allowable entries. The variable name strNumberOfDays is highlighted because you typed strn.

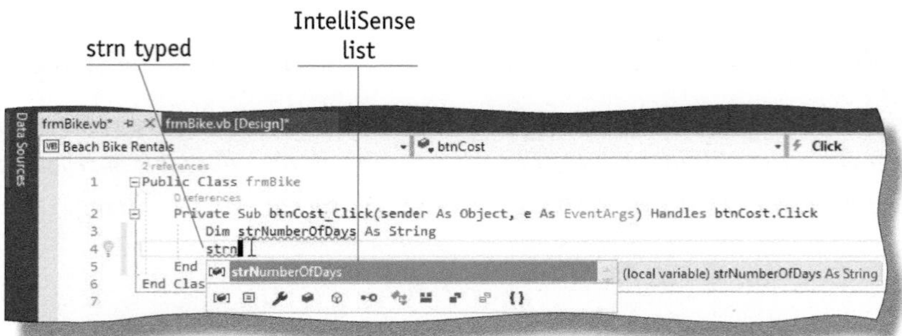

FIGURE 4-26

STEP 5 Press the SPACEBAR, press the EQUAL SIGN key, and then press the SPACEBAR.

IntelliSense enters the highlighted variable name, the spaces, and the equal sign you typed (Figure 4-27). The spaces are not required in Visual Basic but should be included in the statement for ease of reading. An IntelliSense list automatically appears and displays the possible valid entries.

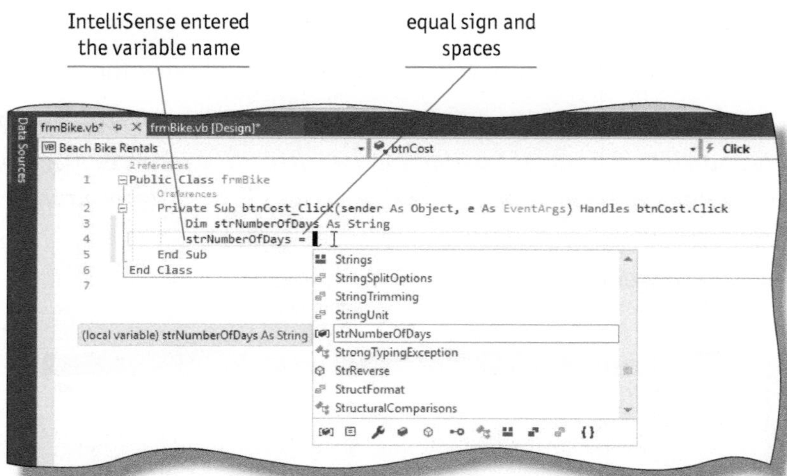

FIGURE 4-27

STEP 6 Type `txt` to display the IntelliSense list of Form objects, and then type `n` to identify the txtNumberOfDays TextBox object in the IntelliSense list.

The IntelliSense list contains the valid entries for the statement; in this case, only one object has the prefix of txt. The TextBox object txtNumberOfDays is highlighted in the list (Figure 4-28).

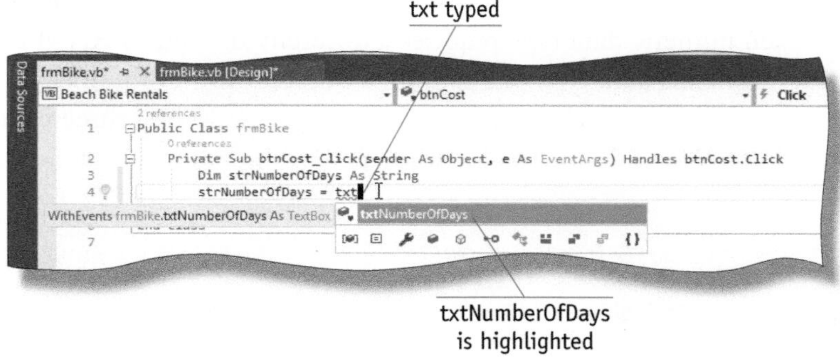

FIGURE 4-28

STEP 7 Press the PERIOD key. If necessary, type `te` to highlight the Text entry in the IntelliSense list. Press the ENTER key.

After the dot operator (period) and the txtNumberOfDays object name are entered, Visual Studio displays the IntelliSense list. When you typed te, the Text entry was highlighted in the IntelliSense list. The assignment statement is entered (Figure 4-29). When the statement is executed, the value in the Text property of the txtNumberOfDays TextBox object will be copied to the location in memory identified by the strNumberOfDays variable name. Notice also that the green squiggly lines in the Dim statement are removed because the variable now is referenced in a statement.

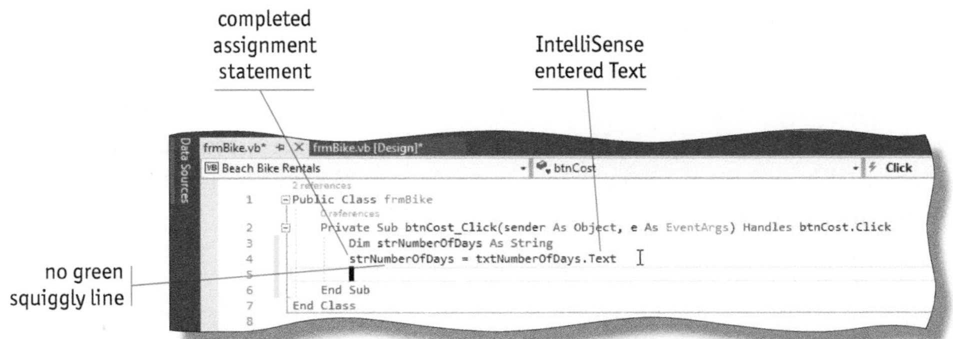

FIGURE 4-29

For any variable you define within a program, you can use the method shown in the previous steps to declare a variable name and include it in assignment statements. IntelliSense works the same with each variable name, regardless of the variable type.

HEADS UP

IntelliSense has different rules for entering object names and variable names into a Visual Basic statement. To enter the name of an object that has been defined in the user interface, type the prefix. To enter a variable name you have declared in the program, type the first few letters of the variable name. In each case, IntelliSense will display a list of the allowable entries.

Numeric Data Types

As you will recall, the String data type can contain any character that can be entered or stored on a computer. String data types, however, cannot be used in arithmetic operations. A **numeric data type** must be used in arithmetic operations. To multiply two values, for example, the values must be stored in one of the numeric data types.

Visual Basic allows a variety of numeric data types depending on the need of the application. Each numeric data type requires a different amount of RAM to store the numeric value, and each data type can contain a different form of numeric data and a different maximum range of values. The table in Figure 4-30 lists three widely used numeric data types. These data types are explained in the following sections.

Data Type	Sample Value	Memory Allocation	Range of Values
Integer	48	4 bytes	−2,147,483,648 to +2,147,483,647
Decimal	3.14519	16 bytes	Decimal values that may have up to 28 significant digits
Double	5.3452307 or 673.6529	8 bytes	−1.79769313486232e308 to +1.79769313486232e308

FIGURE 4-30

Integer Data Type

An **Integer data type** holds a nondecimal whole number in Visual Basic. As you can see from Figure 4-30, an Integer data type can store a value that is greater or less than 2 billion. Examples of integers include the number of bikes to be rented, the number of credit hours you are taking in a semester, and the number of points your favorite football team scored. Notice that each of these examples is a whole number.

Normally, an Integer data type is stored in an Integer variable. An **Integer variable** identifies a location in RAM where an integer value is stored. To define an Integer variable and place a value in the variable, you can use the Dim statement and the assignment statement, as shown in Figure 4-31.

```
Dim intNumberOfDays As Integer
intNumberOfDays = 4
```

FIGURE 4-31

The Dim statement in Figure 4-31 is similar to the Dim statement used to define the String variable (Figure 4-24 on page 165), except that the variable name begins with the prefix int and the word Integer follows the word As. Four bytes of RAM will be reserved for any value that is stored in the intNumberOfDays Integer variable as a result of the Dim statement in Figure 4-31.

The definition in Figure 4-31 will not place a value in the intNumberOfDays variable. To place a value in the variable, you can use an assignment statement. Enter the intNumberOfDays variable that will hold the value on the left side of the equal sign, and enter the value to be placed in the variable (4) on the right side of the equal sign. When the statement is executed, the value 4 will be copied to the RAM location identified by the variable name intNumberOfDays.

You also can place an initial value in the variable. For example, to define an Integer variable to hold the number of credit hours you are taking and to place the value 12 in that variable, you could write the Dim statement in Figure 4-32.

HEADS UP

Visual Basic 2015 now allows you to omit the data type without causing an error. For example, entering Dim intValue = 1 does not produce an error because the compiler infers that the value of intValue is an Integer data type. This feature is called type inference. While you are learning how to write programs, it is best to use the data types so you can understand the changes as you convert one data type to another.

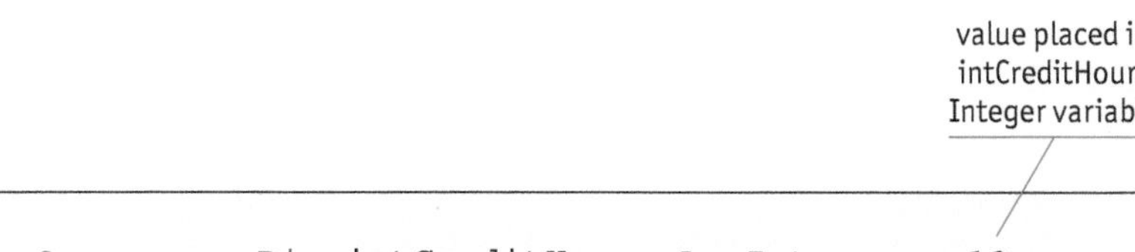


```
        Dim intCreditHours As Integer = 12
```

FIGURE 4-32

The statement in Figure 4-32 defines the Integer variable named intCreditHours. The equal sign after the word *Integer* indicates to the Visual Basic compiler that the value to the right of the equal sign should be placed in the variable. The value 12 will be placed in the intCreditHours Integer variable when the program is compiled.

Decimal Data Type

A **Decimal data type** accurately represents large or very precise decimal numbers. It is ideal for use in the accounting and scientific fields to ensure that numbers keep their precision and are not subject to rounding errors. The Decimal data type can be accurate to 28 significant digits. (Significant digits are those that contribute to the precision of a number.) Often, Decimal data types are used to store dollar amounts. For example, to define the Decimal variable for the total cost of the bike rental in the sample program, you can use the statement in Figure 4-33.

HEADS UP

A Double data type represents numbers in a way that might not be precisely correct. For example, the value 0.07875 might be represented as 0.078749999999 in the Double data type. Therefore, when exact precision is required, the Decimal data type is preferred over the Double data type. The Double data type does have advantages, however; it can store a much larger or much smaller number than the Decimal data type, and it requires only 8 bytes of memory for each variable as opposed to 16 bytes for each Decimal variable.

```
        Dim decTotalCost As Decimal
```

FIGURE 4-33

The Dim statement is used to define the Decimal variable. The dec prefix is used for all Decimal variable names. When the compiler processes the statement in Figure 4-33, 16 bytes of RAM will be reserved for a value to be placed in the decTotalCost variable. Initially, no value will be present in the variable unless you specify a value, as shown in Figure 4-32. You can use an assignment statement to place data into the decTotalCost variable.

Double Data Type

A **Double data type** can represent huge positive numbers and very small negative numbers that can include values to the right of the decimal point. Sometimes, a Double data type is said to represent floating-point numbers, which means the decimal point can be anywhere within the number. The Dim statement in Figure 4-34 declares a Double variable that could be used in a tax application.

```
Dim dblTaxRate As Double
dblTaxRate = 0.07875
```

FIGURE 4-34

In Figure 4-34, the dblTaxRate Double variable is declared and then the assignment statement places the value 0.07875 in the memory location identified by the variable name. Note that a Double variable begins with the dbl prefix.

Other Data Types

Visual Basic supports other data types that are used for more specialized situations. Two widely used data types are Char and Boolean (Figure 4-35).

Data Type	Sample Value	Memory Allocation	Range of Values
Char	A single character such as ? or M	2 bytes	Any single character
Boolean	True or False	2 bytes	True or False

FIGURE 4-35

Char Data Type

The **Char data type** represents a single keystroke such as a letter of the alphabet, a punctuation mark, or a symbol. The prefix for a Char variable name is chr. When you assign a value to a Char variable, you must place quotation marks around the value. For example, in Figure 4-36, the value A is assigned to the chrTopGrade Char variable.

```
        Dim chrTopGrade As Char
        chrTopGrade = "A"
```

FIGURE 4-36

The value A in the assignment statement has quotation marks around it. In addition, Visual Studio displays the letter and the quotation marks in red text, indicating they are not Visual Basic keywords, variable names, or object names. In fact, the value is called a literal. You will learn more about literals shortly.

Visual Studio allows 65,534 different characters in a program. These characters consist of numbers, letters, and punctuation symbols. In addition, a wide variety of technical characters, mathematical symbols, and worldwide textual characters are available, which allows developers to work in almost every known language, including Korean (Figure 4-37). These characters are represented by a coding system called Unicode. To learn more about Unicode, visit www.unicode.org.

유니코드에 대해 ?

어떤 플랫폼,
어떤 프로그램,
어떤 언어에도 상관없이
유니코드는 모든 문자에 대해 고유 번호를 제공합니다.

FIGURE 4-37

Even though you can assign a number to a Char variable, it cannot be used in arithmetic operations. A number to be used in an arithmetic operation must be assigned a numeric variable.

Boolean Data Type

A Boolean data variable can contain a value that Visual Basic interprets as either true or false. A Boolean variable name begins with the bln prefix. If a variable in your program should represent whether a condition is true or not true, then the variable should be Boolean. In Figure 4-38, a Boolean variable called blnFullTimeStudent is declared and then the assignment statement sets the Boolean variable to True.

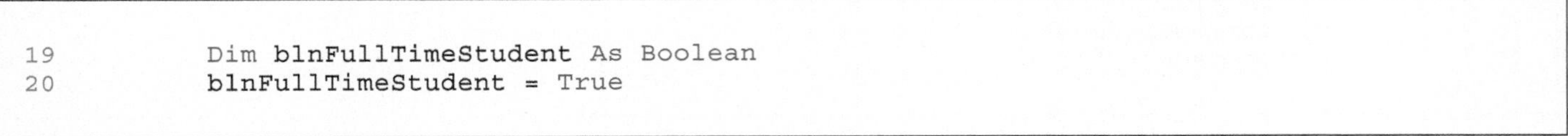

```
Dim blnFullTimeStudent As Boolean
blnFullTimeStudent = True
```

FIGURE 4-38

In Figure 4-38, the Dim statement is used to declare the blnFullTimeStudent Boolean variable. The assignment statement sets the Boolean variable to True. This variable can be checked in the program to determine whether it is true or false, and appropriate processing can occur as a result.

Miscellaneous Data Types

Visual Basic has several other data types that are used less often than the ones you have seen so far. These data types are summarized in the table in Figure 4-39.

Data Type	Sample Value	Memory Allocation	Range of Values
Byte	A whole number such as 7	1 bytes	0 to 255
Date	April 22, 2014	8 bytes	Dates and times
Long	A whole number such as 342,534,538	8 bytes	−9,223,372,036,854,775,808 through +9,223,372,036,854,775,807
Object	Holds a reference	4 bytes	A memory address
Short	A whole number such as 16,546	2 bytes	−32,786 through 32,767
Single	A number such as 312,672.3274	4 bytes	−3.4028235E+38 through 1.401298E−45 for negative values; and from 1.401298E−45 through 3.4028235E+38 for positive values

FIGURE 4-39

As a review, the prefixes for each of the data type variable names are shown in Figure 4-40.

Data Type	Prefix
String	str
Integer	int
Decimal	dec
Double	dbl
Char	chr
Boolean	bln
Byte	byt
Date	dtm
Long	lng
Short	shr
Single	sng

FIGURE 4-40

Literals

When an assignment statement includes a value like the one in Figure 4-34 on page 170 or Figure 4-36 on page 171, the value is called a **literal** because it literally is the value required by the assignment statement. It is not a variable. The Visual Basic compiler determines the data type of the value you use for a literal based on the value itself. For example, if you type *Chicago*, the compiler treats the literal as a String data type, and if you type 49.327, the compiler treats the literal as a Double data type. The table in Figure 4-41 displays the default literal types as determined by the Visual Basic compiler.

Standard Literal Form	Default Data Type	Example
Numeric, no fractional part	Integer	104
Numeric, no fractional part, too large for Integer data type	Long	3987925494
Numeric, fractional part	Double	0.99 8.625
Enclosed within double quotes	String	"Bre Pauley"
Enclosed within number signs	Date	#3/17/2017 3:30 PM#

FIGURE 4-41

Forced Literal Types

Sometimes you might want a literal to be a different data type than the Visual Basic default type. For example, you may want to assign the number 9.95 to a Decimal data variable to take advantage of the precision of the Decimal data type. As you can see in Figure 4-41, Visual Basic will consider the value 9.95 a Double data type by default. To define the literal as a Decimal literal, you must use a special character to force Visual Basic to use a data type other than the default. Specifically, you place the literal-type character at the end of the literal value. The table in Figure 4-42 shows the available literal-type characters and examples of their use.

Literal-Type Character	Data Type	Example
S	Short	Dim shoAge As Short shoAge = 40S
I	Integer	Dim intHeight as Integer intHeight = 76I
D	Decimal	Dim decPricePerDay As Decimal decPricePerDay = 9.95D
R	Double	Dim dblWeight As Double dblWeight = 8491R
C	Char	Dim chrNumberOfDays As Char chrNumberOfDays = "7"C

FIGURE 4-42

In the first example, the value 40 will be processed by Visual Basic as a Short data type literal, even though the value would be considered an Integer value by default. In the second example, the literal-type character confirms that the value should be treated as an Integer data type. In the third example, the value 9.95 will be processed as a Decimal data type, even though it would be considered a Double data type by default. In the next example, the value 8491 would be considered an Integer data value by default, but because the R literal-type character is used, Visual Basic will treat it as a Double data type. In the final example, the value 7 will be treated as a Char data type.

Constants

Recall that a variable identifies a location in memory where a value can be stored. By its nature, the value in a variable can be changed by statements within the program. For instance, in the sample program in this chapter, one user might request 4 bike rentals and another user might request 12 bike rentals for a large group; the value in the strNumberOfDays variable can change based on the user's needs. In some instances, however, you might not want the value to be changed. For example, the cost of renting a bike in the sample program is $9.95 per day. This value will not change, regardless of how many bikes were rented.

When a value will remain the same throughout the execution of the program, you should assign a meaningful name to a value. A **constant** contains one permanent value throughout the execution of the program. It cannot be changed by any statement within the program. To define a constant value, you can use the code in Figure 4-43.

```
Const _cdecPricePerDay As Decimal = 9.95D
```

FIGURE 4-43

The following rules apply to a constant:

1. The declaration of a constant begins with the letters Const, not the letters Dim.
2. You must assign the value to be contained in the constant on the same line as its definition. In Figure 4-43, the value 9.95D is assigned to the constant on the same line as the Const definition.
3. You cannot attempt to change the value of the constant anywhere in the program. If you do, you will produce a compiler error.
4. The letter c often is placed before the constant name to identify it throughout the program as a variable that cannot be changed.
5. Other than the letter c, constant names are formed using the same rules and techniques as other variable names.

Using a named constant instead of a literal provides significant advantages:

6. The program becomes easier to read because the value is identified by the name. For example, instead of using the value 9.95D in a literal, you can use it in a constant called _cdecPricePerDay. This variable name describes the use of the value 9.95D and makes the program easier to read.
7. If you discover that a value must be changed in the code, it is much easier and more reliable to change the value one time in the constant as opposed to changing every occurrence of the value in a literal.

Reference a Variable

You learned earlier that when a variable is declared, it is underlined with a green squiggly line until it is referenced in a statement. This feature of Visual Basic is intended to ensure that you do not declare a variable and then forget to use it. It also helps ensure that you do not waste memory by declaring an unnecessary variable.

When using a variable in a program, it is mandatory that you define the variable before using the variable name in a statement. For example, the statements in Figure 4-44 *will cause an error* because the variable is used in an assignment statement before it is declared.

```
25        strNumberOfDays = txtNumberOfDays.Text
26        Dim strNumberOfDays As String
```

FIGURE 4-44

In the code in Figure 4-44, the variable strNumberOfDays is referenced in an assignment statement (line 25) before it is defined (line 26). This creates a compile error. The Visual Basic IDE indicates a compile error with a the blue squiggly line. In this case, the compile error occurs with the variable name strNumberOfDays on line 25. If you attempt to compile the statements on lines 25 and 26, you will receive a build error. Always define a variable before it is used in a statement.

Scope of Variables

When you declare a variable in Visual Basic, you not only declare the data type of the variable but also implicitly define its scope. The **scope of a variable** specifies where the variable can be referenced in a Visual Basic statement within the program. In larger programs with multiple classes and forms, scope becomes critical, but it is important that you understand the concept at this point.

You declare a variable in a region within a program. For instance, in the sample program in this chapter, you can declare a variable in the click event handler for the Find Cost button. You could declare another variable in the click event handler for the Clear button. Scope determines where each of these variables can be referenced and used in the Visual Basic program. *The rule is: A variable can be referenced only within the region of the program where it is defined.* A region in the programs you have seen thus far in the book is the code between the Sub statement and the End Sub statement in the event handlers. The code between the Sub statement and the End Sub statement is a **procedure**.

Therefore, if you declare a variable within the click event handler for the Find Cost button, that variable cannot be referenced in the click event handler for the Clear button, and vice versa. A variable that can be referenced only within the region of the program where it is defined is called a **local variable**. This variable is defined in one region of the program and cannot be changed by a statement in another region of the program.

In addition, when a variable is defined in a procedure and the procedure ends, the values of the local variables within the procedure are destroyed. Thus, local variables have a certain **lifetime** in the program. They are only *alive* from the time the procedure begins until it ends. If the procedure is executed again, the value the variable once contained no longer is present. One execution of the procedure is a variable's lifetime. Therefore, if a user clicks the Find Cost button, the values in the variables are valid until the click event is completed. When the user clicks the Find Cost button again, all values from the first click are gone.

You can also define variables that can be used in multiple regions of a Visual Basic program. These variables are called **global variables**. In most programs, local variables should be used because they cause fewer errors than global variables.

Understanding the scope of a variable is important when developing a program. You will learn more about the scope of variables later in this chapter and throughout this book.

Convert Variable Data

Variables used in arithmetic statements in a Visual Basic program must be numeric. String variables cannot be used in an arithmetic statement. If you attempt to use them, you will create a compilation error.

A user often enters data in a text box. Data in the Text property of a TextBox object is treated as String data. Because String data cannot be used in an arithmetic statement, the String data entered by a user must be converted to numeric data before it can be used in an arithmetic statement.

For instance, in the sample program in this chapter, the user enters the number of days to rent bikes. Before this number can be used in an arithmetic statement to determine the total cost of bike rentals, the value must be converted to an Integer data type.

Visual Basic includes several procedures that allow you to convert one data type to another data type. You will recall that a procedure is a prewritten set of code that can be called by a statement in the Visual Basic program. When the procedure is called, it performs a particular task. In this case, the task is to convert the String value the user entered into an Integer data type that can be used in an arithmetic operation. One procedure that converts a String data type to an Integer data type is named ToInt32. The number 32 in the procedure name identifies that the representation of the integer will require 32 bits or 4 bytes, which is the amount of memory required for the Integer data type. The procedure is in the Convert class, which is available in a Visual Studio 2017 class library.

Use a Procedure

When you need to use a procedure to accomplish a task in your program, you must understand what the procedure does and how to code the procedure call in a program statement. A procedure can operate in one of two ways: It can perform its task and return a value, or it can perform its task without returning a value. You will recall in the Chapter 3 sample program that the Close() procedure closed the window and ended the program. The procedure performed its task but did not return a value. A procedure of this type is called a **Sub procedure**.

In the Beach Bike Rentals program in this chapter, the requirement is to convert the String value for the number of bikes the user enters into an Integer data type. Then, it can be used in an arithmetic operation. Therefore, the procedure must return a value (the Integer value for the number of days). A procedure that returns a value is called a **Function procedure**, or a **function**.

In addition, a procedure might require data to be passed to it when called in order to carry out its processing. In the sample program in this chapter, the Function procedure to convert a String variable to an Integer variable first must be able to access the String variable. Therefore, in the statement that calls the Function procedure, the variable name for the String variable to be converted must be passed to the procedure. A value is passed to a procedure through the use of an argument.

An **argument** identifies a value required by a procedure. To pass the argument to the procedure, include its name within parentheses following the name of the procedure in the calling statement. For example, to pass the value stored in the strNumberOfDays variable to the ToInt32 procedure, you could use the statement in Figure 4-45.

FIGURE 4-45

The name of the procedure is ToInt32. The argument is strNumberOfDays, which is the String variable that contains the value to be converted to an Integer data type by the ToInt32 procedure. Notice that the argument is enclosed within parentheses.

Every procedure is part of a class in Visual Basic. You will recall from Chapter 1 that a **class** is a named grouping of program code. When the calling statement must call a procedure, it first must identify the class that contains the procedure. Thus, in Figure 4-45 the calling statement is incomplete because the class name is not included. The class that contains the ToInt32 procedure is the Convert class. To complete the procedure call statement, the class must be added, as shown in Figure 4-46.

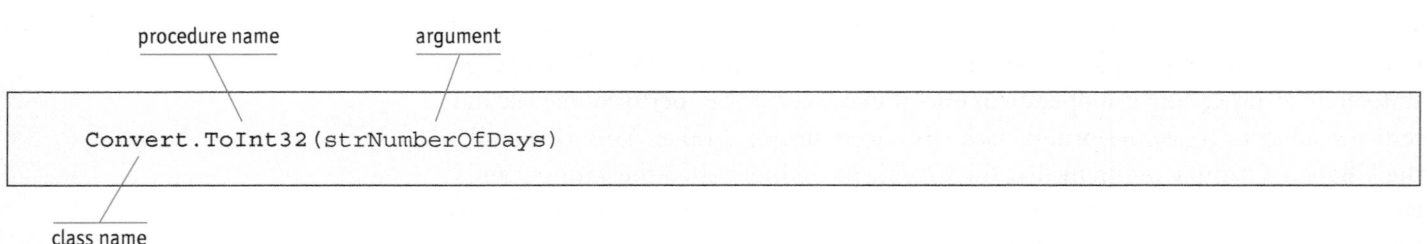

FIGURE 4-46

In Figure 4-46, the class name Convert begins the procedure call. A dot operator separates the class name from the procedure name (ToInt32). The argument (strNumberOfDays) within the parentheses completes the procedure call.

When a Function procedure returns a value, such as the ToInt32 procedure that returns an integer value, the returned value essentially replaces the Function procedure call in the assignment statement. In Figure 4-47, you can see that when the processing is completed within the Function procedure, the integer value is substituted for the procedure call in the assignment statement.

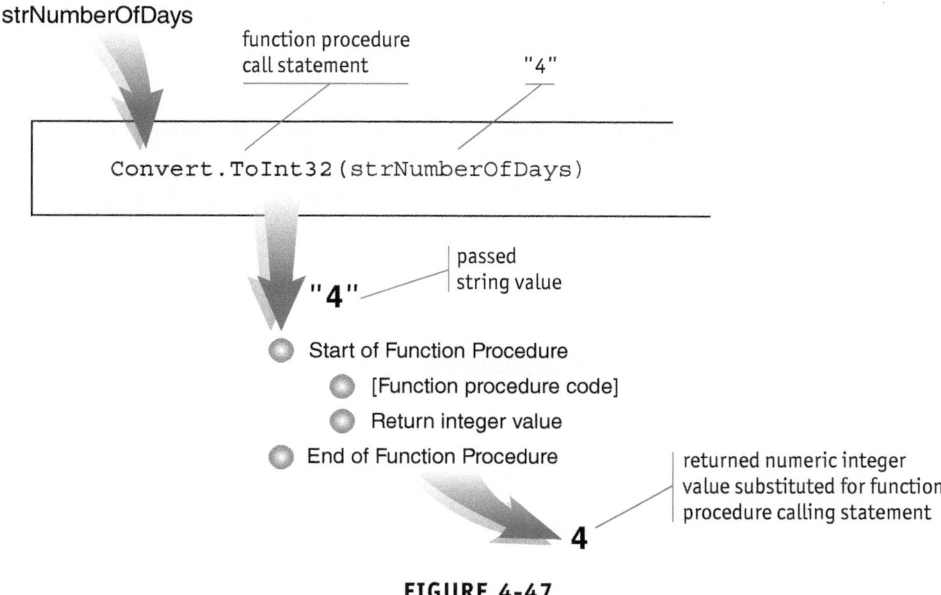

FIGURE 4-47

Figure 4-48 shows the complete assignment statement to convert the String data type in the strNumberOfDays variable to an Integer data type and place it in the intNumberOfDays variable.

The intNumberOfDays variable name to the left of the equal sign identifies the Integer variable where the converted value will be copied. The equal sign in the assignment statement is required. As a result of the assignment statement in Figure 4-48, the ToInt32 Function procedure in the Convert class will convert the value in the strNumberOfDays String variable to an integer value. The assignment statement will place that integer value in the intNumberOfDays variable.

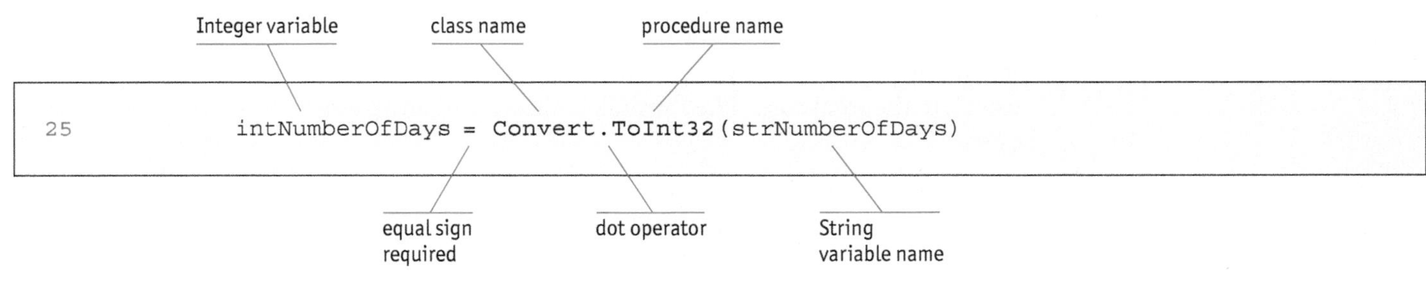

FIGURE 4-48

The use of Function procedures and arguments with procedure calls is common when programming in Visual Basic. You will encounter many examples of Function procedure calls throughout this book.

Option Strict On

In the previous section, you saw an example of how to explicitly change a value from one data type to another. By default, Visual Basic will automatically convert data types if the one on the right side of the equal sign in an assignment statement is different from the one on the left side of the equal sign. Quite often, however, the automatic conversion can introduce errors and produce an incorrect converted value. Therefore, allowing automatic conversion typically is not a good programming style.

To prevent automatic conversion of values, the developer must insert the Option Strict On statement in the program prior to any event handler code. In Figure 4-49, the Option Strict On statement is shown just after the introductory comments in the sample program for this chapter.

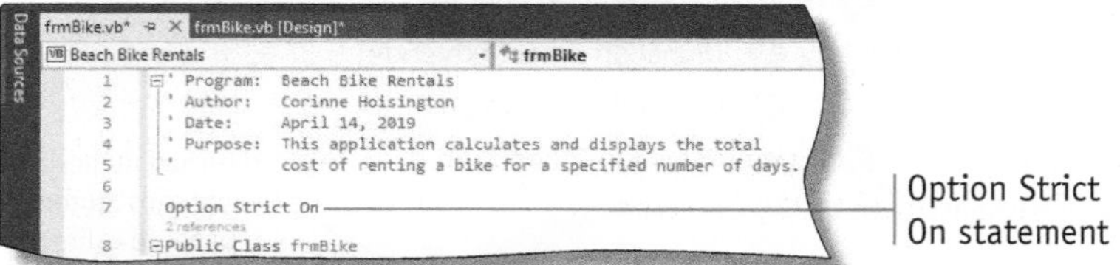

FIGURE 4-49

The Option Strict On statement explicitly prevents any default data type conversions that would cause data loss and prevents any conversion between numeric types and strings. Therefore, you must write explicit conversion statements to convert from one data type to another. This approach minimizes potential errors that can occur from data conversion.

Arithmetic Operations

The ability to perform arithmetic operations on numeric data is fundamental to computer programs. Many programs require arithmetic operations to add, subtract, multiply, and divide numeric data. For example, in the Beach Bike Rentals program in this chapter, the cost per day must be multiplied by the number of rental days to calculate the total cost. The formula is shown in Figure 4-50.

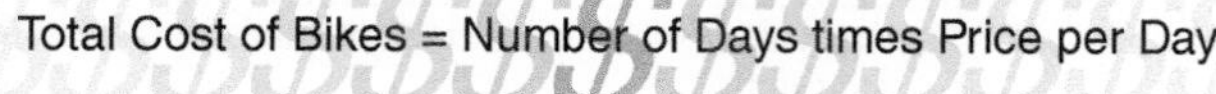

Total Cost of Bikes = Number of Days times Price per Day

FIGURE 4-50

An assignment statement is used in Visual Basic 2017 to perform the arithmetic operation shown in Figure 4-50. The statements used in the sample program and a depiction of the operation are shown in Figure 4-51.

In the code in Figure 4-51, the variable strNumberOfDays is assigned the user's entered value by the assignment statement on line 23. (See Figure 4-20 on page 163 for a detailed explanation of this statement.) The statement on line 24 converts the value in the strNumberOfDays variable to an integer and copies it to the

```
18
19          Dim strNumberOfDays As String
20          Dim intNumberOfDays As Integer
21          Dim decTotalCost As Decimal
22
23          strNumberOfDays = txtNumberOfDays.Text
24          intNumberOfDays = Convert.ToInt32(strNumberOfDays)
25          decTotalCost = intNumberOfDays * _cdecPricePerDay
26          lblTotalCost.Text = decTotalCost.ToString("C")
```

FIGURE 4-51

intNumberOfDays variable. (See Figure 4-48 on page 179 for an explanation of this statement.)

The statement on line 25 multiplies the integer value in the intNumberOfDays variable by the constant value in the _cdecPricePerDay variable, and then copies the result to the decTotalCost variable. For example, if the user enters 4 as the number of rental days, the value 4 is multiplied by 9.95 (the value in the _cdecPricePerDay variable), and the result (39.80) is copied to the decTotalCost variable.

Arithmetic Operators

The asterisk (*) is an important element on the right side of the equal sign in the assignment statement on line 25. This asterisk is the multiplication **arithmetic operator**. Whenever the compiler encounters this operator, the value to the left of the operator is multiplied by the value to the right of the operator, and these values are replaced in the assignment statement by the product of the two numbers. Thus, in Figure 4-51 on page 181, the arithmetic expression intNumberOfDays * _cdecPricePerDay is replaced by the value 39.80. Then, the assignment statement places the value 39.80 in the decTotalCost variable.

The multiplication arithmetic operator is only one of the arithmetic operators available in Visual Basic 2017. The table in Figure 4-52 lists the arithmetic operators in Visual Basic 2017, describes their use, and provides an example of their use.

Arithmetic Operator	Use	Assignment Statement Showing Use
+	Addition	decTotal = decPrice + decTax
–	Subtraction	decCost = decRegularPrice – decDiscount
*	Multiplication	decTax = decItemPrice * decTaxRate
/	Division	decClassAverage = decTotalScores / intNumberOfStudents
^	Exponentiation	intSquareArea = intSquareSide ^ 2
\	Integer Division	intResult = 13 \ 5
Mod	Modulus Arithmetic (remainder)	intRemainder = 13 Mod 5

FIGURE 4-52

The arithmetic operators shown in Figure 4-52 are explained in the following paragraphs:

Addition

The **addition arithmetic operator** (+) adds the numeric values immediately to the left and right of the operator and replaces the arithmetic expression in the assignment statement. For example, in Figure 4-53, the value in the decPrice variable is added to the value in the decTax variable.

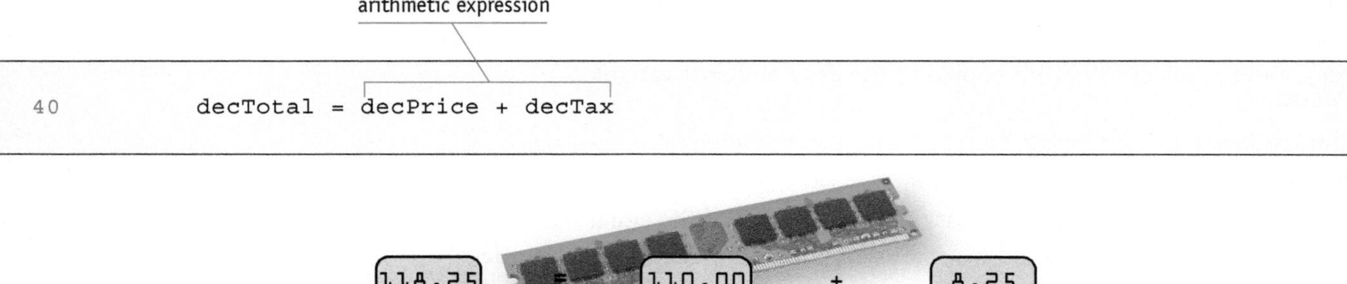

FIGURE 4-53

iStockphoto.com/Tpopova

In Figure 4-53, the arithmetic expression (decPrice + decTax) is evaluated, and then the assignment statement copies the sum to the decTotal variable in RAM.

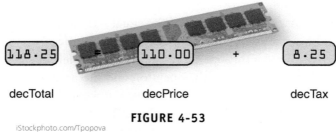

An arithmetic expression that uses the addition operator can contain more than two numeric values to be added. For example, in Figure 4-54, three variables are used in the arithmetic expression.

```
        decTotalPay = decRegularPay + decOvertimePay + decBonusPay
```

FIGURE 4-54

In Figure 4-54, the value in decRegularPay is added to the value in decOvertimePay. The result then is added to decBonusPay, and that sum is copied to the decTotalPay variable. Visual Basic imposes no limit on the number of variables in an arithmetic expression.

In addition to variables, arithmetic expressions can contain literals. The assignment statement in Figure 4-55 uses a literal.

```
decTicketCost = decInternetTicketCost + 10.25
```

FIGURE 4-55

In Figure 4-55, the value 10.25 is added to the value in the decInternetTicketCost variable, and that sum is placed in the decTicketCost variable. Generally, literals should not be used in arithmetic expressions unless you know that the value will not change. For example, if the extra cost for the ticket could change in the future, good program design would dictate that the value be placed in a variable (perhaps even a constant).

Subtraction

To subtract one value from another in an assignment statement, Visual Basic 2017 uses the **subtraction arithmetic operator** (–), as shown in Figure 4-56.

```
decNetProfit = decRevenue - decCosts
```

FIGURE 4-56

In Figure 4-56, the value in the decCosts variable is subtracted from the value in the decRevenue variable. The result then is copied into the decNetProfit variable. If the value in decCosts is greater than the value in decRevenue, the value placed in the decNetProfit variable will be negative.

Use Arithmetic Results

After an arithmetic operation has been performed using an assignment statement, the values used in the operation and the resulting answer can be used in subsequent arithmetic operations or for other purposes within the program. For example, the result of one operation can be used in a subsequent calculation (Figure 4-57).

```
decComputerCost = decMonitorCost + decSystemUnitCost
decNetComputerCost = decComputerCost - decSystemDiscount
```

FIGURE 4-57

In Figure 4-57, the statement on line 67 determines the computer cost by adding the costs of the monitor and the system unit. The statement on line 68 calculates the net computer cost by subtracting the system discount from the computer cost calculated on line 67. Whenever a value is stored in a variable, it can be used in other statements within the program.

Multiplication

Multiplication is accomplished through the use of an assignment statement and the multiplication operator (*), as shown in Figure 4-58.

```
intLandPlotArea = intLandPlotLength * intLandPlotWidth
```

FIGURE 4-58

In Figure 4-58, the value in the intLandPlotLength variable is multiplied by the value in the intLandPlotWidth variable. The product of the multiplication is placed in the intLandPlotArea variable.

If two positive numbers are multiplied, the answer is positive. If two negative numbers are multiplied, the answer is positive. If one positive number and one negative number are multiplied, the answer is negative.

When two numbers are multiplied, you must be aware of the size of the result. The largest number of digits that can appear as a result of multiplication is the sum of the number of digits in the values being multiplied. If the product is greater than the value that can be stored in the variable to the left of the assignment statement, an overflow error can occur and the program will be ended.

CONSIDER THIS

How should I test my program to make sure it works properly?

When you allow user input, be sure to test every possible entry by the user. If a decimal value is entered instead of an expected integer value, your program may stop functioning. As you learn more about coding in the next chapters, error validation will become an important part of developing your program.

Division

Visual Basic 2017 provides three arithmetic operators for division and related calculations: the slash (/), the backslash (\), and the MOD operator.

You use the slash for normal division. For example, in Figure 4-59, the value in the decTestScores variable is divided by 3 to obtain the average test score.

```
        decAverageTestScore = decTestScores / 3
```

FIGURE 4-59

You use the backslash (\) for integer division. With integer division, the quotient returned from the division operation is an integer. If the division operation produces a quotient with a remainder, the remainder is dropped, or truncated. The examples in Figure 4-60 illustrate the use of the integer division arithmetic operator.

WATCH OUT FOR

The divisor is the number to the right of the division operator. Make sure the divisor is not zero. If you attempt to divide by zero, your program will be ended with an error.

Division Operation	Result
12\5	2
25\4	6
30\7	4

FIGURE 4-60

Notice in each example in Figure 4-60 that the result is a whole number with the remainder truncated.

The MOD operator divides the number to the left of the operator by the number to the right of the operator and returns an integer value that is the remainder of the division operation. Integer division and the MOD operator often are used together, as shown in Figure 4-61.

```
86        intHours = intTotalNumberOfMinutes \ 60
87        intMinutes = intTotalNumberOfMinutes Mod 60
```

FIGURE 4-61

In Figure 4-61, the operation on line 86 will return only the integer value of the division. For example, if the intTotalNumberOfMinutes variable contains 150, a result of 2 (2 = 150\60) will be placed in the intHours variable. The operation on line 87 will place the remainder in the intMinutes variable. The remainder in the example is 30; 150 divided by 60 is 2, with a remainder of 30.

Exponentiation

Exponentiation means raising a number to a power. It is accomplished in Visual Basic 2017 using the exponentiation arithmetic operator (^), as shown in Figure 4-62.

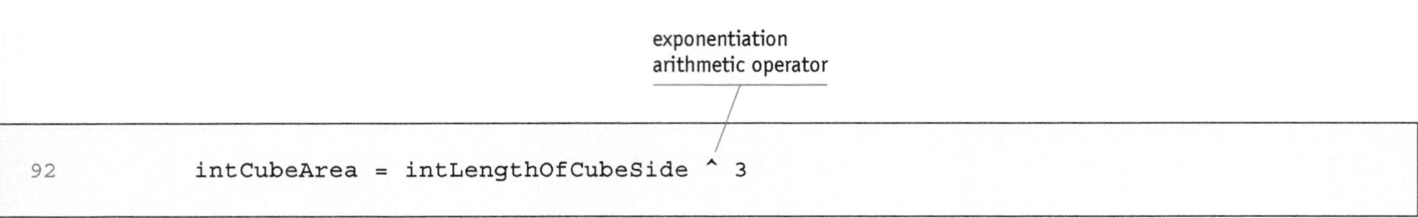

FIGURE 4-62

In Figure 4-62, the arithmetic expression is the same as intLengthOfCubeSide * intLengthOfCubeSide* intLengthOfCubeSide. Therefore, the value is cubed and copied to the intCubeArea variable.

The exponent used in the operation can be a fraction. If so, the root is taken (Figure 4-63).

```
intLengthOfCubeSide = intCubeArea ^ (1 / 3)
```

FIGURE 4-63

In Figure 4-63, the cube root of the value in the intCubeArea variable is calculated and the result is copied to the intLengthOfCubeSide variable. Thus, if the area of the cube is 64, the value calculated for the length of the cube side would be 4 (4 * 4 * 4 = 64). The fractional exponent can never be negative, and it must be placed within parentheses.

Multiple Operations

A single assignment statement can contain multiple arithmetic operations. In Figure 4-64, the addition and subtraction operators are used to calculate the new balance in a savings account by adding the deposits to the old balance and subtracting withdrawals.

```
decNewBalance = decOldBalance + decDeposits - decWithdrawals
```

FIGURE 4-64

When the assignment statement is executed in Figure 4-64, the value in the decOldBalance variable is added to the value in the decDeposits variable. Then, the value in the decWithdrawals variable is subtracted from that sum and the result is copied to the decNewBalance variable.

Notice in Figure 4-64 that the calculations proceed from left to right in the arithmetic expression.

Hierarchy of Operations

When multiple operations are included in a single assignment statement, the sequence for performing the calculations is determined by the following rules:

1. Exponentiation (^) is performed first.
2. Multiplication (*) and division (/) are performed next.
3. Integer division (\) is next.
4. MOD then occurs.
5. Addition (+) and subtraction (–) are performed last.
6. Within each of the preceding five steps, calculations are performed from left to right.

As a result of this predetermined sequence, an arithmetic expression such as decBonus + decHours * decHourlyRate would result in the product of decHours * decHourlyRate being added to decBonus.

An arithmetic expression such as decGrade1 + decGrade2 / 2 would cause the value in the decGrade2 variable to be divided by 2 and then the quotient to be added to the value in decGrade1 because division is performed before addition. However, this calculation probably was not intended. Instead, the intent probably was to add the values in decGrade1 and decGrade2 and then divide the sum by 2. To force certain operations to be performed before others, you can use parentheses. Any arithmetic expression within parentheses is evaluated before expressions outside the parentheses, as shown in Figure 4-65.

```
        decAverageGrade = (decGrade1 + decGrade2) / 2
```

FIGURE 4-65

In Figure 4-65, the addition operation is inside the parentheses, so it will be completed before the division operation. Therefore, the result of the arithmetic expression is that the value in decGrade1 is added to the value in decGrade2. That sum then is divided by 2 and the quotient is copied to the decAverageGrade variable.

If you want to make the sequence of operations explicitly clear, you can use parentheses around multiple arithmetic operations in an arithmetic expression even if the predetermined sequence of operations will produce the correct answer.

Display Numeric Output Data

As you have learned, the result of an arithmetic expression is a numeric value that typically is stored in a numeric variable. To display the numeric data as information in a graphical user interface, usually the data must be placed in the Text property of a

Label object or a TextBox object. The Text property of these objects, however, requires that the data be a String data type. Therefore, to display a numeric value in a label or a text box, the numeric data must be converted to a String data type.

Each of the numeric data types provides a function called ToString that converts data from a numeric data type to the String data type. The general format of the function call for a Decimal numeric variable is shown in Figure 4-66.

> **IN THE REAL WORLD**
>
> You know that a procedure is a collection of code that a program can call to perform a particular function, such as converting data stored in a numeric data type to data stored as a String data type. In some programming languages, a procedure is called a method. Therefore, as you search the index or other areas in Visual Studio Help, you might find the word *method* used. Just remember that the terms *method* and *procedure* are virtually synonymous.

General Format: ToString Function

```
decVariable.ToString()
```

FIGURE 4-66

The statement shown in Figure 4-66 consists of the name of the Decimal variable that contains data to be converted, the dot operator (.), and the name of the function (ToString). Notice that the function name is followed immediately by closed parentheses, which indicates to the Visual Basic compiler that ToString is a procedure name. When the function call is executed, the value returned by the ToString function replaces the call.

The function call normally is contained within an assignment statement to assign the returned string value to the Text property of a Label or TextBox object. The example in Figure 4-67 shows the assignment statement to convert the numeric value in the decTemperature variable to a String value that then is placed in the Text property of the lblTemperature Label object.

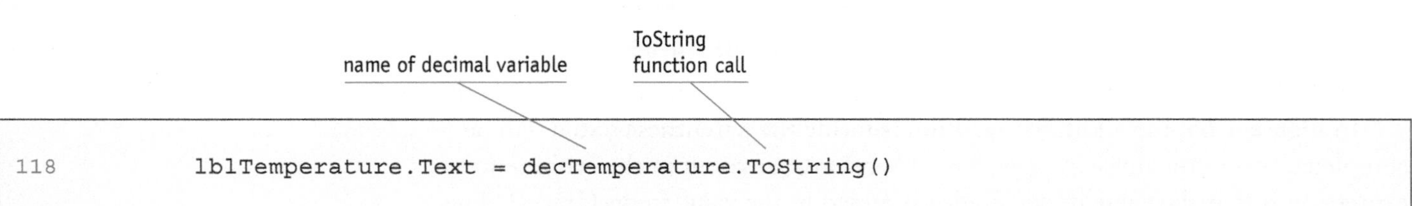

FIGURE 4-67

In Figure 4-67, the name of the Decimal variable (decTemperature) is followed by the dot operator and then the name of the function (ToString) with the required parentheses. When the statement on line 118 is executed, the ToString function is called. It converts the numeric value in the decTemperature variable to a String data type and returns the String data. The assignment statement then copies the returned String data to the Text property of the Temperature Label object.

Format Specifications for the ToString Function

In the example in Figure 4-67, the conversion from numeric value to String value is a straight conversion, which means the value is returned but not formatted in any manner. For example, if the numeric value in the Decimal variable was 47.235, then the same value was returned as a String value.

The ToString function, however, can convert numeric data to String data using a specified format. For example, the value 2317.49 could be returned as $2,317.49. The returned value is in the form of dollars and cents, or currency. To identify the format for the numeric data to be returned by the ToString function, the **format specifier** must be included as an argument in the parentheses following the ToString function name. The table in Figure 4-68 on page 189 identifies the commonly used format specifiers; in the examples, the value in the numeric field is 8976.43561.

In Figure 4-68, each format specifier is used as an argument within parentheses. The argument must be included in the quotation marks on each side of the format specifier, as shown. The letter for the format specifier can be uppercase or lowercase.

HEADS UP

Rounding is an important consideration when determining the formatting of a number. When using the ToString function, all values are rounded based on the digit after the last digit to be displayed. For example, if the value 729.837 is being converted to a Currency string from a numeric format, the returned result will be rounded up ($729.84). If the value to be converted is 575.371, the returned result will be rounded down ($575.37). Rounding also is used with the precision specifier.

Format Specifier	Format	Description	Output from the Function
General(G)	ToString("G")	Displays the number as is	8976.43561
Currency(C)	ToString("C")	Displays the number with a dollar sign, a thousands separator (comma), 2 digits to the right of the decimal and negative numbers in parentheses	$8,976.44
Fixed(F)	ToString("F")	Displays the number with 2 digits to the right of the decimal and a minus sign for negative numbers	8976.44
Number(N)	ToString("N")	Displays a number with a thousands separator, 2 digits to the right of the decimal and a minus sign for negative numbers	8,976.44
Percent(P)	ToString("P")	Displays the number multiplied by 100 with a % sign, a thousands separator, 2 digits to the right of the decimal and a minus sign for negative numbers	897,643.56%
Scientific(E)	ToString("E")	Displays the number in E-notation and a minus sign for negative numbers	8.976436E+03

FIGURE 4-68

Precision Specifier

Each format specifier has a default number of digits that will be returned to the right of the decimal point. You can use a precision specifier, however, to override this default number. The **precision specifier** is a number included within the quotation marks in the function call that identifies the number of positions that should be returned to the right of the decimal point. The examples in Figure 4-69 illustrate the use of the precision specifier; assume that the value in the decNumericValue variable is 8976.43561.

Statement	Copied to Text Property of lblOutput Label Object
lblOutput = decNumericValue.ToString("C2")	$8,976.44
lblOutput = decNumericValue.ToString("C3")	$8,976.436
lblOutput = decNumericValue.ToString("F1")	8976.4
lblOutput = decNumericValue.ToString("N4")	8,976.4356
lblOutput = decNumericValue.ToString("P0")	897,644%

FIGURE 4-69

As you can see, the precision specifier identifies the number of digits that should be displayed to the right of the decimal point in the string returned from the ToString function. Notice that if the precision specifier is 0, no digits are returned to the right of the decimal point.

As with all conversions, when the number of positions to the right of the decimal point in the returned string is less than the number of digits to the right of the decimal point in the numeric value being converted, the returned value is rounded to the specified number of decimal places.

Clear the Form — Clear Procedure and Focus Procedure

Earlier in this chapter, you learned that when the user clicks the Clear button in the Beach Bike Rentals program (see Figure 4-1 on page 148), the event handler for the Clear button must clear the results from the window and allow the user to enter the next number of rental days. To clear the results, the Clear button event handler must complete the following tasks:

1. Clear the Text property of the TextBox object
2. Clear the Text property of the Label object that displays the total cost of the bikes rented
3. Set the focus on the TextBox object, which means placing the insertion point in the text box

You will learn to accomplish these tasks in the following sections.

Clear Procedure

The Clear procedure clears any data in the Text property of a TextBox object. The general format of the Clear procedure is shown in Figure 4-70.

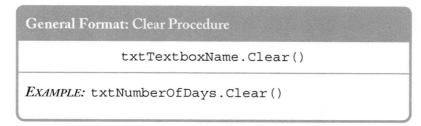

General Format: Clear Procedure

```
txtTextboxName.Clear()
```

EXAMPLE: `txtNumberOfDays.Clear()`

FIGURE 4-70

When the Clear procedure is executed, the Text property is cleared of data. As with every procedure call, the name of the procedure must be followed by parentheses.

Clear the Text Property of a Label

The Clear procedure cannot be used with a Label object. Instead, to clear the Text property of a Label object, you must write an assignment statement that assigns a null length string to the Text property. A null length string has no length, which means it is a string with no characters. A null length string is represented by two quotation marks with no character between them (""). To assign a null length string to the Text property, you can use the statement shown in Figure 4-71.

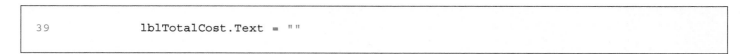

```
        lblTotalCost.Text = ""
```

FIGURE 4-71

In Figure 4-71, the null length string represented by the two empty quotation marks is assigned to the Text property of the lblTotalCost Label object. As a result of the assignment statement, the Text property is cleared.

Set the Focus

When the focus is on a TextBox object, the insertion point is located in the text box (Figure 4-72).

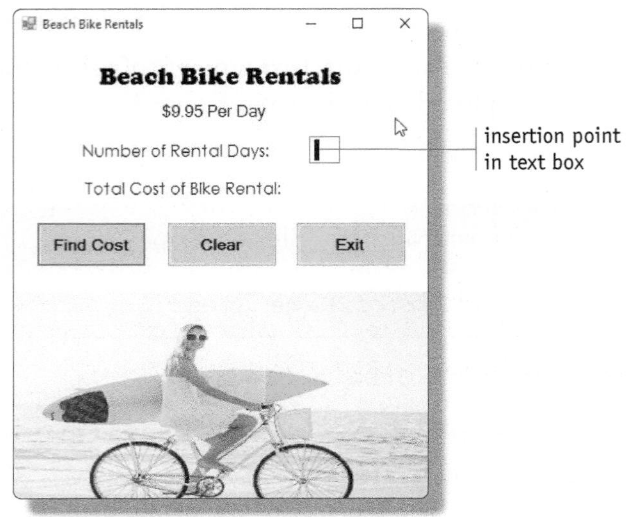

FIGURE 4-72

iStockphoto.com/Wavebreakmedia

When the user clicks a button or other item in the graphical user interface, the focus shifts to that item. Therefore, to place the focus on a text box, the user can click it. However, the programmer can use the Focus procedure to place the focus on a text box automatically without requiring the user to click it first, thus making it easier for the user to enter data in the text box (Figure 4-73).

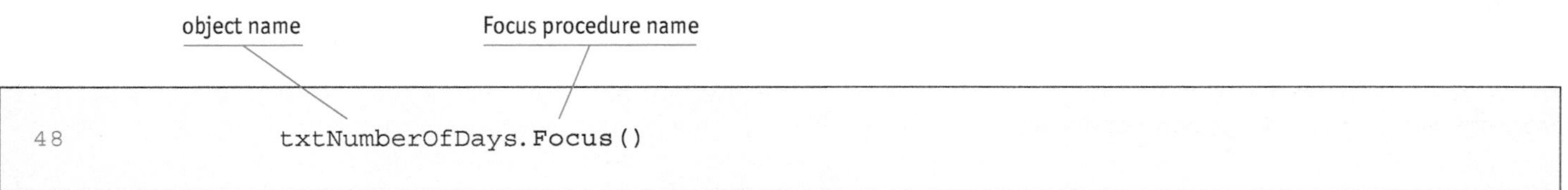

FIGURE 4-73

As with most procedure calls, the name of the object begins the statement, followed immediately by the dot operator (period). The name of the procedure (Focus) follows the dot operator. When the statement on line 48 is executed, the focus is placed on the txtNumberOfDays TextBox object, which means the insertion point is placed in the text box.

Form Load Event

In the sample programs in Chapter 3 and this chapter, you have seen that an event can occur when the user clicks a button. The user's action triggers the code to execute in the event handler for the button click. For example, in the Beach Bike Rentals program in this chapter, the user clicks the Find Cost button and the event handler code responds by multiplying the number of days the bike is rented by the price per day and displaying the result (see Figure 4-1 on page 148).

Clicking a button is not the only action that can trigger an event. For example, a form load event occurs each time a program is started and the Windows Form object is loaded into computer memory. For the program in this chapter, a form load event occurs when the program starts and the Beach Bike Rentals form is loaded. In some programs, an event handler is not written for this particular event and no processing occurs. In the Beach Bike Rentals program, however, a form loading event handler is required. This event handler completes the following tasks:

1. Displays the cost per day per bike heading
2. Clears the placeholder from the lblTotalCost Text property
3. Sets the focus on the txtNumberOfDays text box

Concatenation, Class Scope, and Debugging

To complete the chapter project, you need to use two new programming techniques: concatenation and assigning a variable so it has class scope. Finally, you need to debug the program by checking for errors common in programs that accept user entries.

Concatenation

In the Beach Bike Rentals program, the lblCostHeading Label object displays the cost per day. In the user interface design, the lblCostHeading Label contains placeholder information for the label, but does not contain the actual cost per day (Figure 4-74).

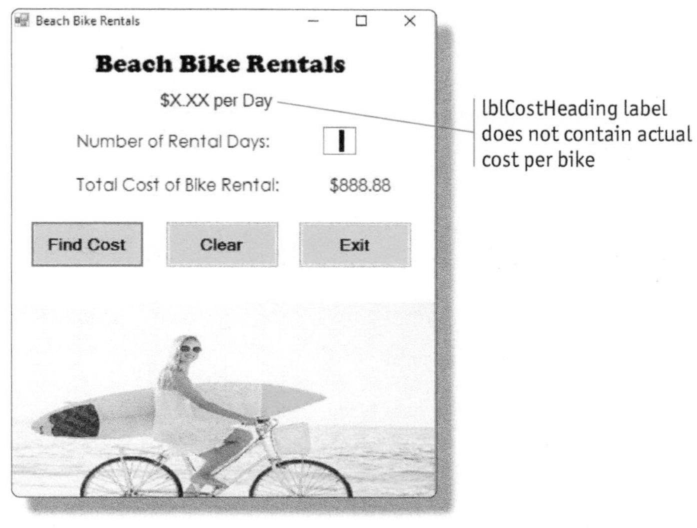

FIGURE 4-74
iStockphoto.com/Wavebreakmedia

In Figure 4-74, the programmer had two reasons for not placing the actual rental cost in the label during the design phase. First, in the original implementation of the program, the cost per day is $9.95. In the future, however, the cost might change for a holiday or permanently over time. Generally, data that might change should be placed in the Text property of a Label object during execution time, not at design time. Therefore, the cost per bike should be placed in the label by the form load event handler when the form opens. Second, the cost per bike is used in two places in the program — in the label and when the actual calculation is performed to determine the total cost (see Figure 4-51 on page 181). Instead of using the numeric value of 9.95 several times within the program, the value should be assigned to a variable. If the value must be changed in the future, only one change to the variable is necessary. For example, if the price per daily bike rental changes to $12.95, the price can be changed in the price per day variable and then it will be correct for all uses of the variable. To illustrate, the variable for the price per day is shown in Figure 4-75.

```
Const _cdecPricePerDay As Decimal = 9.95D
```

FIGURE 4-75

> **HEADS UP**
>
> In some instances, it is better to continue a line of code in the code window on a second line so that the entire line can be read without scrolling. To continue a line of code on a subsequent line, place a space in the statement and then place an underscore (_) character in the line of code. The underscore character indicates to the Visual Basic compiler that the line of code continues on the next line (Figure 4-76).

As you can see, the price per day is declared as a constant that cannot be changed during program execution. If the price changes in the future, the developer can make one change to this declaration and all elements of the program that use the value will be correct.

To create the heading for the Beach Bike Rentals program, the value in the variable declared in Figure 4-75 must be combined with the words *per Day* and the result must be placed in the Text property of the lblCostHeading Label object. The process of joining two different values into a single string is called **concatenation**. When you use concatenation, the values being concatenated must be String data types. Note in Figure 4-75 that the _cdecPricePerDay variable is a Decimal data type. Therefore, it must be changed to a String data type before being joined with the words in the heading.

The statement in Figure 4-76 converts the Decimal data type to a String data type, concatenates (or joins) the two strings together, and then places the result in the Text property of the lblCostHeading Label object.

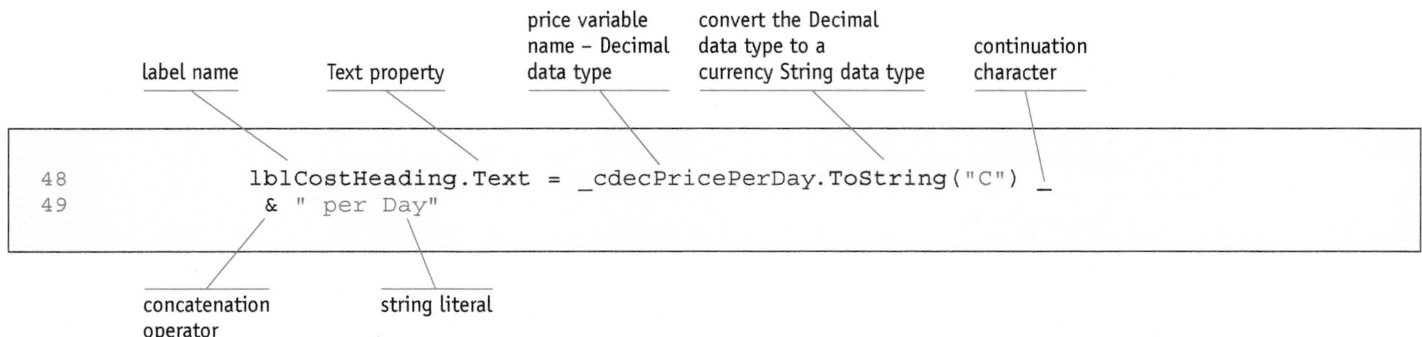

FIGURE 4-76

In Figure 4-76, the string generated to the right of the equal sign will be placed in the Text property of the lblCostHeading Label object. The first entry to the right of the equal sign is the price variable name (Figure 4-75). Following the dot operator is the ToString procedure name, followed by the currency argument within parentheses. Remember that the ToString procedure converts a numeric value to a String data type. When the currency argument ("C") is used, the String value returned is in a currency format.

Following the conversion statement is the **concatenation operator (&)**. When the Visual Basic compiler encounters this operator, the string to the left of the operator is joined with the String data to the right of the operator to create a single concatenated string. The resulting string then is placed in the Text property of the lblCostHeading Label object.

The process that occurs to the right of the equal sign is illustrated in Figure 4-77.

CRITICAL THINKING

Can I connect string text together with a plus sign as well?

Yes, for example the following two statements are allowed in Visual Basic:

```
Dim x As String =
"Con" & "caten" &
"ation"
```

```
Dim y As String =
"Con" + "caten" +
"ation"
```

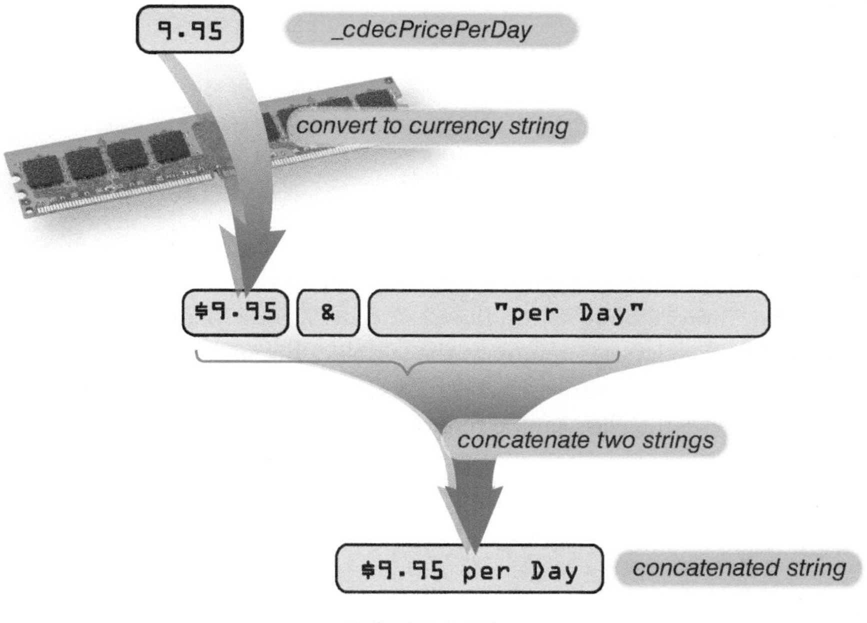

FIGURE 4-77

iStockphoto.com/Tpopova

As Figure 4-77 shows, to obtain the concatenated string, the Decimal value in the _cdecPricePerDay Decimal variable is converted to a currency String data type. Then, that value is combined with the string literal to create the concatenated string. In the assignment statement in Figure 4-76 on page 194, the concatenated string is assigned to the Text property of the lblCostHeading Label object.

Class Scope

Remember that when you declare a variable, you also define its scope. The scope of a variable identifies where within the program the variable can be referenced. For example, if a variable is declared within an event handler procedure, the variable can be referenced only within that procedure.

Sometimes, a variable must be referenced in multiple event handlers. In the Beach Bike Rentals program, the value in the _cdecPricePerDay variable is referenced in the Find Cost button event handler when the total cost is calculated (Figure 4-51 on page 181). The value also is referenced in the form load event when the heading is displayed (Figure 4-76 on page 194). Because the variable is referenced in two different event-handling procedures, it must be defined at the class level instead of the procedure (event handler) level. This means that the variable must be declared in the code before the first procedure in the program. As shown in Figure 4-78, the declaration of the _cdecPricePerDay variable follows the class definition statement but appears before the first event handler procedure.

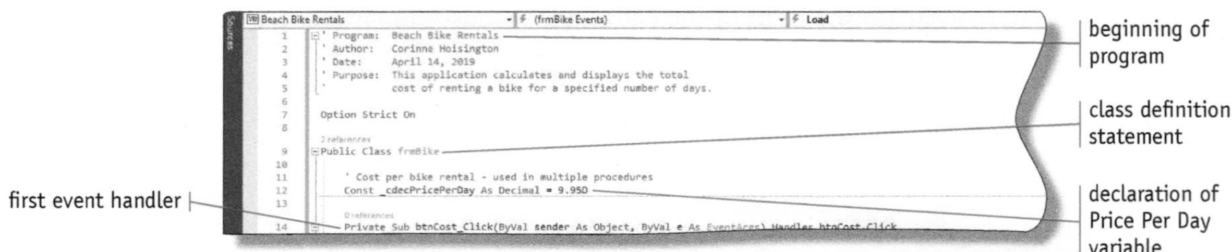
Beach Bike Rentals
(frmBike Events)
Load
' Program: Beach Bike Rentals
' Author: Corinne Hoisington
' Date: April 14, 2019
' Purpose: This application calculates and displays the total
' cost of renting a bike for a specified number of days.
Option Strict On
Public Class frmBike
' Cost per bike rental - used in multiple procedures
Const _cdecPricePerDay As Decimal = 9.95D
Private Sub btnCost_Click(ByVal sender As Object, ByVal e As EventArgs) Handles btnCost.Click
beginning of program
class definition statement
declaration of Price Per Day variable
first event handler

FIGURE 4-78

IN THE REAL WORLD

When a variable is declared for use throughout a class, the naming convention specifies that the name should begin with an underscore character (_). When you see a variable name that begins with the underscore character, you know the variable has class scope.

As a result of the code in Figure 4-78, the scope of the _cdecPricePerDay variable will be all procedures within the class; that is, code in any event handler procedure within the class can reference the variable. Because the variable is declared a constant, the value in the variable cannot be changed by code within the class; however, the value in the class can be referenced to calculate the total cost and to create the cost heading.

Debug Your Program

When your program processes numeric data entered by a user, you should be aware of several errors that can occur when the user enters data the program does not expect. The three errors that occur most often are Format Exceptions, Overflow Exceptions, and Divide By Zero Exceptions.

A **Format Exception** occurs when the user enters data that a statement within the program cannot process properly. In the Beach Bike Rentals program, the user must enter a numeric value for the number of bikes to rent. When the user clicks the Find Cost button, the program converts the entered value to an integer and then uses the numeric value in the calculation (Figure 4-48 on page 179). If the user enters a nonnumeric value, such as ab (Figure 4-79a), the conversion process cannot take place because the argument passed to the Convert class is not a numeric value. In this situation, a Format Exception error is recognized and the error box in Figure 4-79b is displayed.

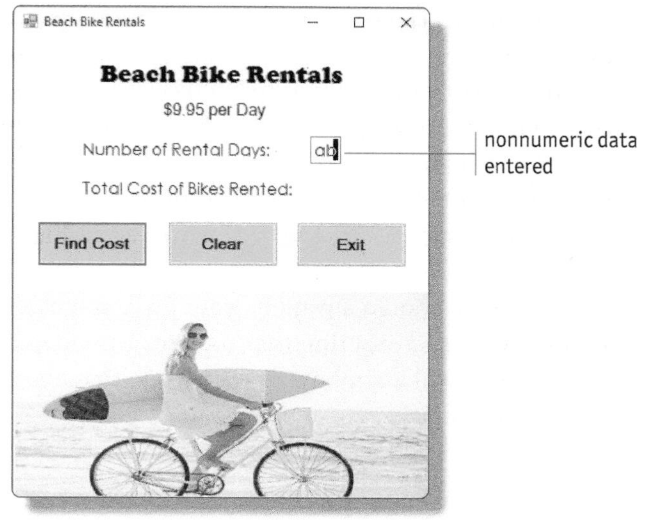

FIGURE 4-79a

iStockphoto.com/Wavebreakmedia

statement that caused the exception

```
        Dim strNumberOfDays As String
        Dim intNumberOfDays As Integer
        Dim decTotalCost As Decimal

        strNumberOfDays = txtNumberOfDays.Text
        intNumberOfDays = Convert.ToInt32(strNumberOfDays)
        decTotalCost = intNumberOfDays * _cdecPricePerDay
        lblTotalCost.Text = decTotalCost.ToString("C")
    End Sub

    0 references
    Private Sub btnClear_Click(ByVal sender As Object, ByV
        ' This event handler is executed when the user cli
        ' Clear button. It clears the number of day's text
        ' and the Text property of the Total Cost label.
```

Exception Unhandled

System.FormatException: 'Input string was not in a correct format.'

Details... | Copy

▸ Exception Settings

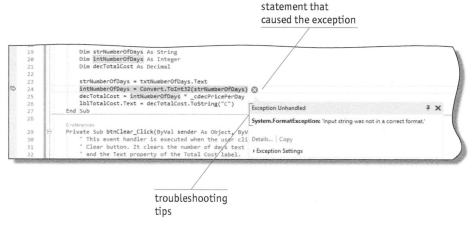

troubleshooting tips

FIGURE 4-79b

In Figure 4-79a, the user entered the value ab and then clicked the Find Cost button. When control was passed to the ToInt32 procedure to convert the String value in the text box to an integer, the Format Exception was triggered because the value in the strNumberOfDays variable was not numeric. When an exception occurs, the execution of the program is terminated. With Visual Studio running, click the Stop Debugging button on the Standard toolbar.

An **Overflow Exception** occurs when the user enters a value greater than the maximum value the statement can process. For example, in the Beach Bike Rentals program, if the user enters a value in the text box that is too large for the ToInt32 procedure to convert, an Overflow Exception occurs.

An Overflow Exception also can occur when a calculation creates a value larger than a procedure can process. For example, if two large but valid numbers are multiplied, the product of the multiplication might be too large to process.

The third type of common error is the **Divide By Zero Exception**. It is not possible to divide by zero, so if your program contains a division operation and the divisor is zero, the Divide By Zero Exception will occur.

Whenever an exception occurs, a window similar to that in Figure 4-79b will be displayed.

To avoid exceptions, which should always be your goal, you can use certain techniques for editing the data and ensuring that the user has entered valid data. In Chapter 5 and Chapter 6, you will learn how to write code that checks user input to ensure that exceptions do not occur.

Program Design

As you have learned, the requirements document identifies the purpose of the program being developed, the application title, the procedures to be followed when using the program, any required equations and calculations, any conditions within the program that must be tested, notes and restrictions that must be followed by the program, and any other comments that would be helpful to understanding the problem. The requirements document for the Beach Bike Rentals application is shown in Figure 4-80.

REQUIREMENTS DOCUMENT

Date:	April 14, 2019
Date Submitted:	
Application Title:	Beach Bike Rentals
Purpose:	The Beach Bike Rentals program allows the user to enter the number of days they intend to rent a bike. The program calculates the total cost of the bike rental based on a price of $9.95 per day.
Program Procedures:	In a Windows Classic Desktop application, the user enters the number of days to rent a bike. The program calculates the total cost of the bike rental. The user can clear the values on the screen and enter a new value for the number of days the bike is rented.

FIGURE 4-80 (continues)

Algorithms, Processing, and Conditions:	1. The user must be able to enter the number of days the bike is to be rented. 2. The user can initiate the calculation and display the total cost of the bike rented. 3. The application computes the total cost by multiplying the number of days by the cost per day ($9.95). 4. The total cost of the bike rental is displayed as a currency value. 5. The user should be able to clear the value entered for the number of days and the total cost of bike rental. 6. The user should be provided with a button to exit the program.
Notes and Restrictions:	n/a
Comments:	A graphic should depict a bike rental image. A graphic named bike is available on CengageBrain.com.

FIGURE 4-80 (continued)

The Use Case Definition for the Beach Bike Rentals program is shown in Figure 4-81.

USE CASE DEFINITION

1. The Windows Classic Desktop application opens with a text box in which the user can enter the number of days a bike is rented. The user interface includes the text box, an area to display the total cost of the bike rental, a Find Cost button, a Clear button, and an Exit button.
2. The user enters the number of days the bike is rented.
3. The user clicks the Find Cost button.
4. The program displays the total cost of the bike rental.
5. The user clicks the Clear button to clear the Number of Rental Days text box and remove the Total Cost of the Bike Rental amount.
6. The user can repeat Steps 2 through 5.
7. The user clicks the Exit button to end the application.

FIGURE 4-81

Event-Planning Document

You will recall that the event-planning document is a table that specifies which objects in the user interface will cause events, the action taken by the user to trigger each event, and the event processing that must occur. The event-planning document for the Beach Bike Rentals program is shown in Figure 4-82.

EVENT-PLANNING DOCUMENT

Program Name: Beach Bike Rentals	**Developer:** Corinne Hoisington	**Object:** frmBikes	**Date:** April 14, 2019
OBJECT	**EVENT TRIGGER**	**EVENT PROCESSING**	
btnCost	Click	Assign data entered in text box to a String variable Convert entered data to numeric integer Find total cost of bike rental (number of days * price per day) Display total cost of bikes rental	
btnClear	Click	Clear Number of Rental Days text box Clear Total Cost of Bike Rental label text Set focus on Number of Rental Days text box	
btnExit	Click	Close the window and end the program	
frmBike	Load	Display heading with price per bike rental Clear the placement digits for Total Cost of Bike Rental Label object Set focus on Number of Rental Days text box	

FIGURE 4-82

Code the Program

You are now ready to code the program by entering Visual Basic statements to accomplish the tasks specified in the event-planning document. You also will implement the logic to carry out the required processing.

Guided Program Development

To design the user interface for the Beach Bike Rentals program and enter the code required to process each event in the program, complete the following steps:

NOTE TO THE LEARNER

In the following activity, you should complete the tasks within the specified steps. Each of the tasks is accompanied by a Hint Screen. The purpose of the Hint Screen is to indicate where you should perform the activity in the Visual Studio window and to remind you which method to use. If you need further help completing a step, refer to the figure identified by *ref:*.

Guided Program Development

Phase I: Create the User Interface Mockup

1

- **Create a Windows Classic Desktop Application** Open Visual Studio and then click the New Project button on the Standard toolbar. If necessary, click Windows Classic Desktop in the left pane of the New Project window, click Windows Forms App in the center pane, and then type `Beach Bike Rentals` in the Name text box.

HINT

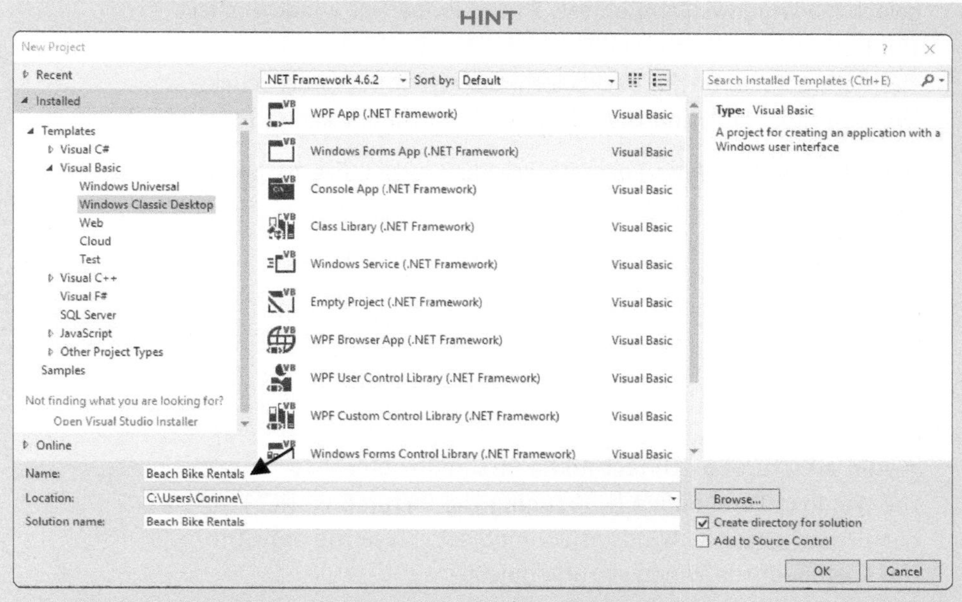

- **Display the Toolbox** Click the OK button in the New Project window, and then ensure that the Toolbox is displayed in the Visual Studio window. If it is not, click View on the menu bar and then click Toolbox. If necessary, click the triangle next to the Common Controls category name and then click the Auto Hide button to display the tools.

- **Name the Windows Form Object** In the Solution Explorer window, right-click the Form1.vb form file name and select Rename. Type `frmBike.vb` and then press the ENTER key.

HINT

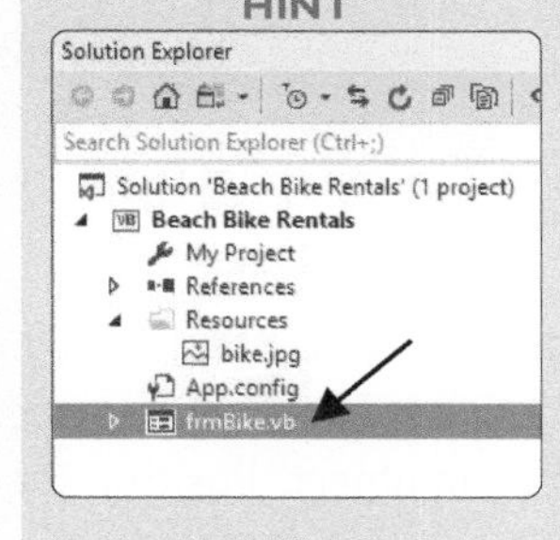

- **Change the Title on the Title Bar** To change the title on the Windows Form object, click the form, scroll in the Properties window until the Text property is displayed, double-click in the right column of the Text property, type `Beach Bike Rentals`, and then press the ENTER key.

(continues)

Guided Program Development *continued*

- **Set the BackColor Property for the Windows Form Object** To set the BackColor property to White for the user interface, select the Windows Form object. In the Properties window, click the BackColor property, and then click the BackColor arrow in the right column of the BackColor property. If necessary, click the Web tab. Scroll and then click White in the BackColor list.

- **Resize the Windows Form Object** Change the Size property of the form to `420,500`.

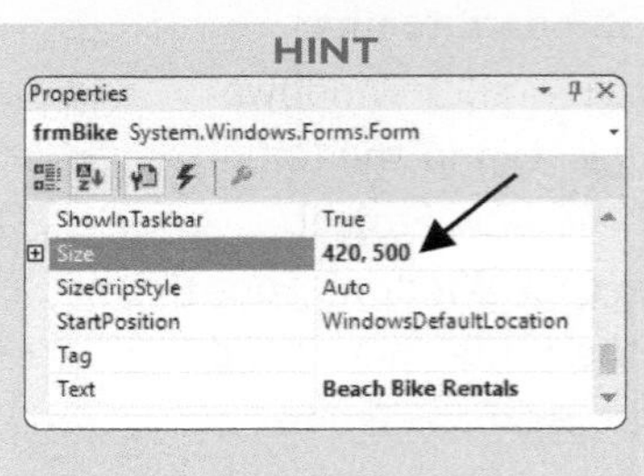

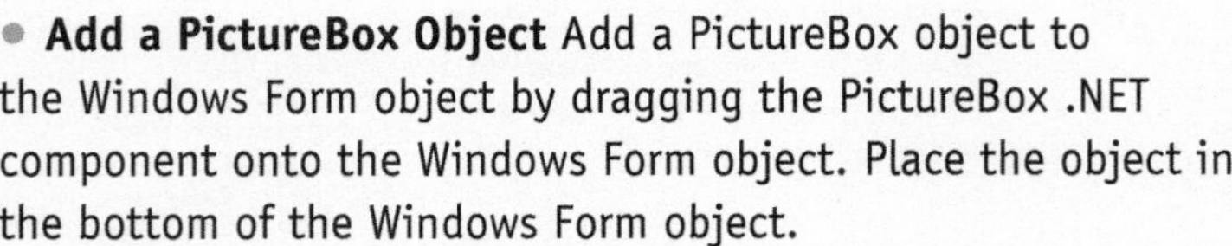

- **Add a PictureBox Object** Add a PictureBox object to the Windows Form object by dragging the PictureBox .NET component onto the Windows Form object. Place the object in the bottom of the Windows Form object.

- **Name the PictureBox Object** With the PictureBox object selected, scroll in the Properties window until the (Name) property is visible. Double-click in the right column of the (Name) property, type `picBikes`, and then press the ENTER key.

- **Resize the PictureBox Object** With the picBikes PictureBox object still selected, click to the right of the Size property and change it to `407,206`.

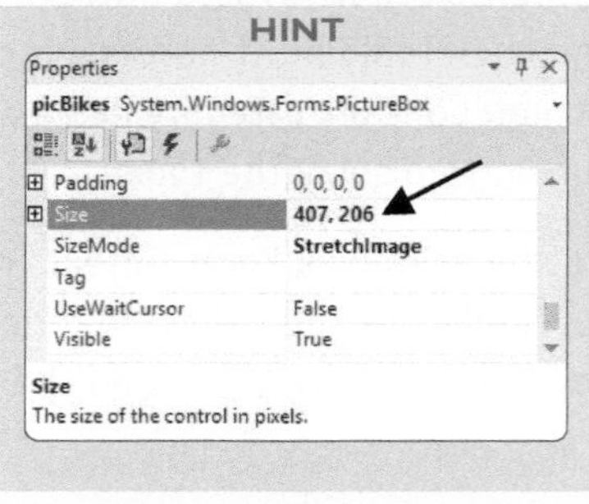

- **Add a Heading Label** To insert the Beach Bike Rentals heading label, drag the Label .NET component from the Toolbox to the Windows Form object. Position the Label object as shown in Figure 4-83.

- **Name the Label Object** Name the Label object `lblHeading` by scrolling to the (Name) property in the Properties window, double-clicking the (Name) property in the right column, typing `lblHeading`, and then pressing the ENTER key.

Guided Program Development *continued*

- **Change the Text of the Label Object** With the lblHeading Label object selected, scroll until the Text property is visible, double-click in the right column of the Text property, type `Beach Bike Rentals`, and then press the ENTER key.

HINT

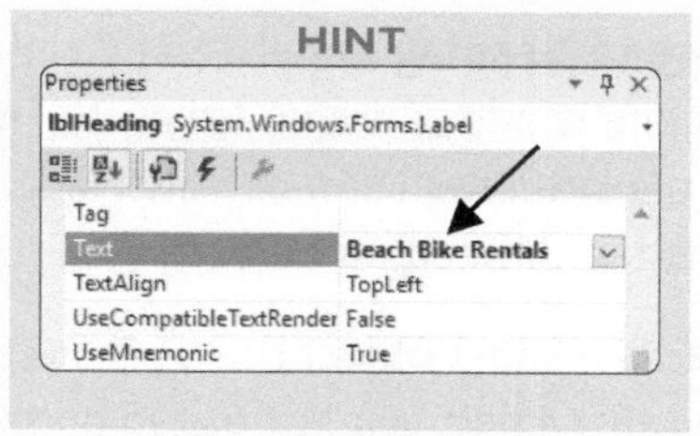

- **Change the Heading Font, Font Style, and Size** To make the heading stand out on the Windows form, its font should be larger and more prominent. To change the font to Cooper Black, its style to Black, and its size to 18, select the Label object and then scroll in the Properties window until the Font property is visible. Click the Font property in the right column, and then click the ellipsis button. In the Font dialog box, scroll if necessary, click Cooper Black (or a similar font) in the Font list, click Black in the Font style list, and then click 18 in the Size list. Click the OK button in the Font dialog box.

HINT

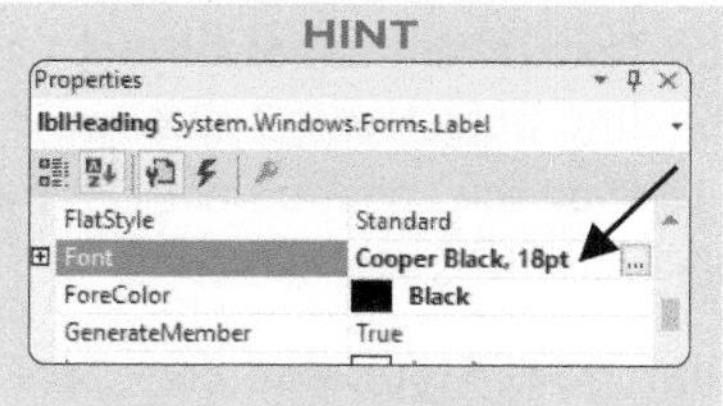

- **Horizontally Center the Label Object** The Label object should be centered horizontally in the form. Click Format on the menu bar, point to Center in Form on the Format menu, and then click Horizontally on the Center in Form submenu.

The PictureBox object and the Label object are placed on the resized Windows Form object (Figure 4-83). The font and font size for the Label object are appropriate for a heading in the window.

RESULT OF STEP 1

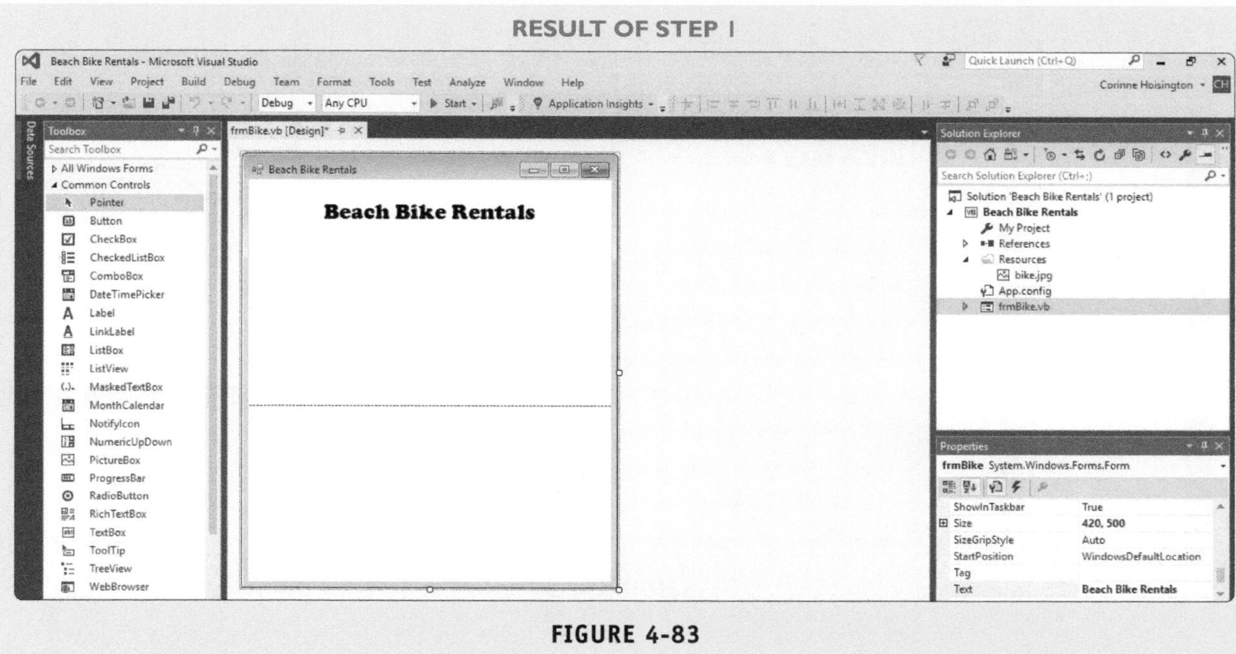

FIGURE 4-83

(continues)

Guided Program Development *continued*

2

- **Add a Second Heading Label** To add the second heading label required for the window, drag a Label .NET component from the Toolbox to the Windows Form object. Place the second Label object below the lblHeading object.

- **Name the New Label Object** Use `lblCostHeading` as the name of the Label object you just placed on the Windows Form object.

- **Change the Text in the Label Object** Change the text in the lblCostHeading object to `$X.XX per Day`. This text is a placeholder so that the Label object can be properly aligned and will be visible when it is not selected.

- **Set the Font, Font Style, and Font Size** Use the Font property and ellipsis button in the Properties window to display the Font dialog box, and then change the font to Microsoft Sans Serif, the style to Regular, and the size to 12 points for the lblCostHeading Label object.

HINT

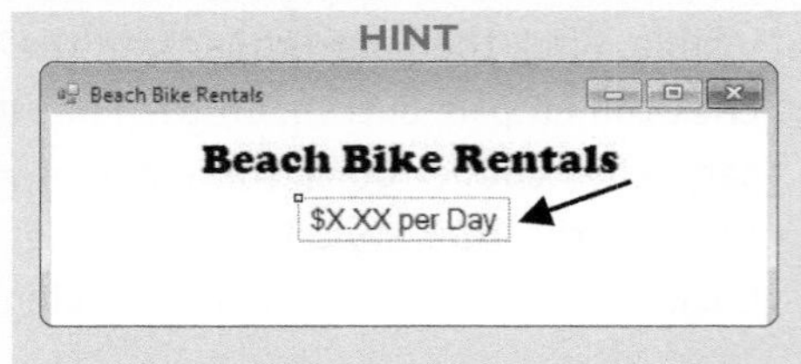

- **Center-Align the Label Object** Select the lblCostHeading label, click Format on the menu bar, point to Center in Form, and then click Horizontally.

The PictureBox object and the Label objects are properly aligned in the Windows Form object (Figure 4-84).

RESULT OF STEP 2

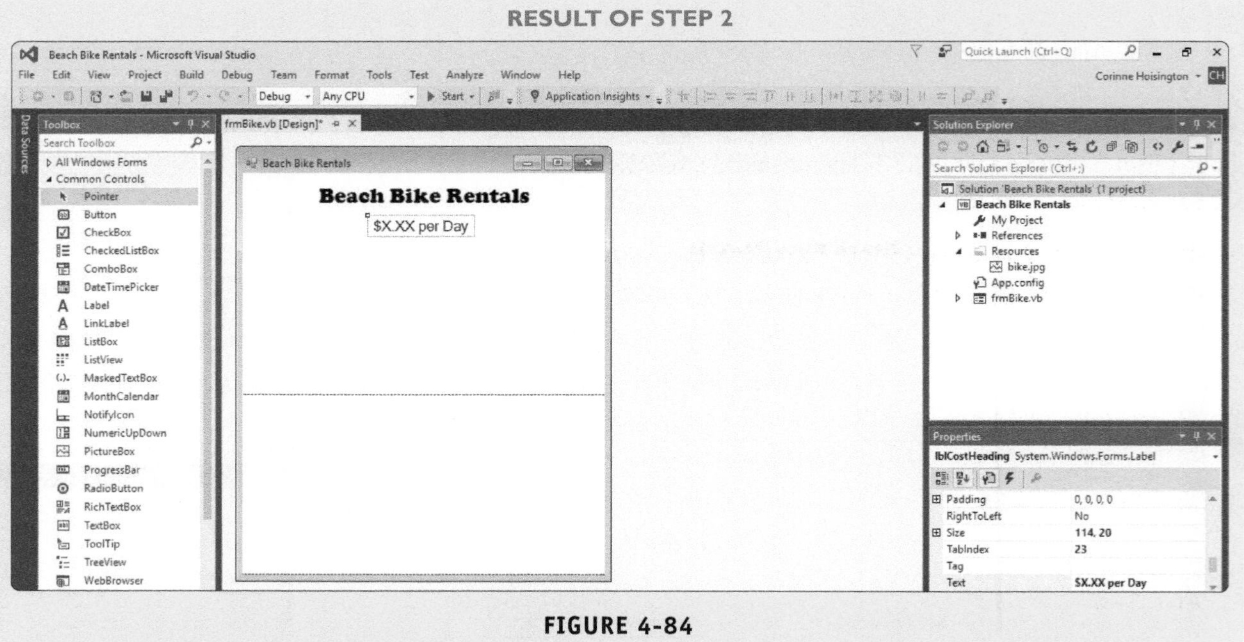

FIGURE 4-84

Guided Program Development *continued*

3

- **Add a Label for the Number of Rental Days** Add the Label object for the number of rental days by dragging it from the Toolbox. Place it below the two other Label objects.

- **Change the Name, Enter Text, and Change the Font for the Number of Rental Days Label** Using techniques you have learned previously, change the name of the Label object to `lblNumberOfDays`. In the Text property, enter `Number of Rental Days:`. Using the Font property in the Properties window, change the font to Century Gothic, Regular style, and 12-point size.

- **Add a TextBox Object for the Number of Rental Days** Drag a TextBox object to the Windows Form object. Name the TextBox object `txtNumberOfDays` *(ref: Figure 4-3)*.

HEADS UP

As you work through the development of your program, remember to save the program frequently. To save the program, you can click the Save All button on the Standard toolbar

HINT

- **Enter Data into the Text Property** As you learned in this chapter, even though the TextBox object will not contain text when the program begins, size it properly by entering text in the Text property of the TextBox object. Select the TextBox object, and then in the Properties window, change the Text property to `88` *(ref: Figure 4-7)*.

- **Change the Font and Size of the TextBox Object** Using the Properties window, change the font for the TextBox object to Century Gothic, Regular style, and 12-point size. Drag the right border of the TextBox object so the numbers fit properly in the text box *(ref: Figure 4-8)*.

- **Align the Resized TextBox Object** To realign the resized TextBox object, drag it up until the red snap line indicates the text in the TextBox object is bottom-aligned with the label *(ref: Figure 4-9)*.

- **Center-Align Text in the TextBox Object** To center-align the text in the TextBox object, select the TextBox object, scroll in the Properties window until the TextAlign property is visible, click the list arrow in the right column of the TextAlign property, and then click Center in the TextAlign property list *(ref: Figure 4-10)*.

(continues)

Guided Program Development *continued*

- **Remove Text from the TextBox Object** Because the TextBox object is sized properly, remove the digits from the TextBox object by selecting them in the Text property of the object and then pressing the DELETE key *(ref: Figure 4-12)*.

- **Add the Total Cost of Bikes Rented Label Objects** A label that reports the total cost of the bikes rented must be displayed as the Text property of a Label object. A second label actually identifies the total cost. Drag two labels onto the Windows Form object and place them on the same horizontal line using the blue snap lines. Vertically align the left side of the left label with the label above it. Vertically align the left side of the right label with the text box above it. Name the Label object on the left `lblTotalLabel`. Name the label on the right `lblTotalCost` *(ref: Figure 4-18)*.

- **Enter Text for the Labels and Change the Font** Select the lblTotalLabel Label object and then double-click the right column of the Text property for the label. Type `Total Cost of Bike Rental:` and then press the ENTER key. Select the lblTotalCost Label object and then double-click the right column of the Text property for the label. Enter the value `$888.88` to represent the widest expected value for the label. With the right label selected, hold down the CTRL key and then click the left label. With both labels selected, change the font to Century Gothic, Regular style, 12-point size. Select the lblNumberOfDays, txtNumberOfDays, lblTotalLabel, and lblTotalCost Label objects and Center in Form horizontally (Format menu) to center the four objects across the form.

HINT

- **Add Buttons** Three buttons are required for the user interface: the Find Cost button, the Clear button, and the Exit button. Drag three buttons onto the Windows Form object below the labels. Use blue snap lines to horizontally align the tops of the buttons. Using the (Name) property for each button, name the first button `btnCost`, the second button `btnClear`, and the third button `btnExit`.

- **Change the Button Text and the Font Style** Using the Text property for each button, change the text for the btnCost Button object to `Find Cost` and the text for the btnClear button to `Clear`. Change the text for the btnExit button to `Exit`. Select all three buttons by clicking the Find Cost button, holding down the ctrl key, and then clicking the other two buttons. Next, click the Font property, click the ellipsis button in the right column of the Font property, and then change the font style to Bold and size 11 in the Font dialog box.

Guided Program Development *continued*

- **Change Button Size** The btnCost button does not display the entire Text property, so it must be enlarged. Drag the right border of the btnCost button until the entire Text property is visible.

- **Change the Size of the Other Buttons** Click the btnCost button first, and then hold down the CTRL key and click the other two buttons to select all three buttons. Make these buttons the same size by clicking Format on the menu bar, pointing to Make Same Size on the Format menu, and clicking Both on the Make Same Size submenu.

- **Space and Center the Buttons** With all three buttons selected, display the Format menu, point to Horizontal Spacing on the Format menu, and then click Make Equal on the Horizontal Spacing submenu. Display the Format menu, point to Center in Form on the Format menu, and then click Horizontally on the Center in Form submenu to center all three buttons horizontally in the Windows Form object.

The mockup for the user interface is complete (Figure 4-85).

RESULT OF STEP 3

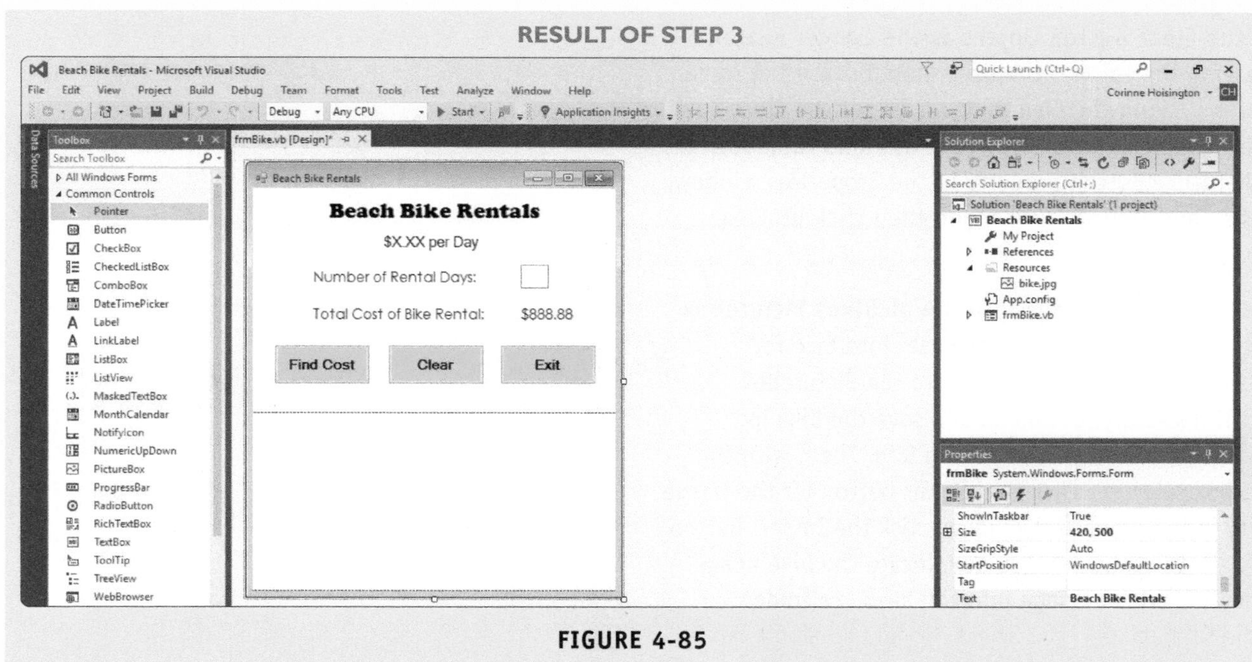

FIGURE 4-85

(continues)

Guided Program Development *continued*

Phase 2: Fine-Tune the User Interface

4

- **Set the BackColor for the Button Objects** To set the BackColor to Gold for the button objects, select all three buttons. Click the BackColor property in the Properties window, and then click the BackColor arrow in the right column of the BackColor property. Click the Web tab, if necessary. Scroll as required and then click Gold in the BackColor list.

- **Set the Find Cost Button Object as the Accept Button** When the user enters the number of days to rent a bike, she should be able to calculate the total cost by clicking the Find Cost button or by pressing the ENTER key. To assign the Find Cost button as the Accept button, first select the Windows Form object by clicking anywhere in the window except on another object. Scroll in the Properties window until the AcceptButton property is visible, click the AcceptButton property, click the AcceptButton property arrow, and then click btnCost *(ref: Figure 4-19)*.

HINT

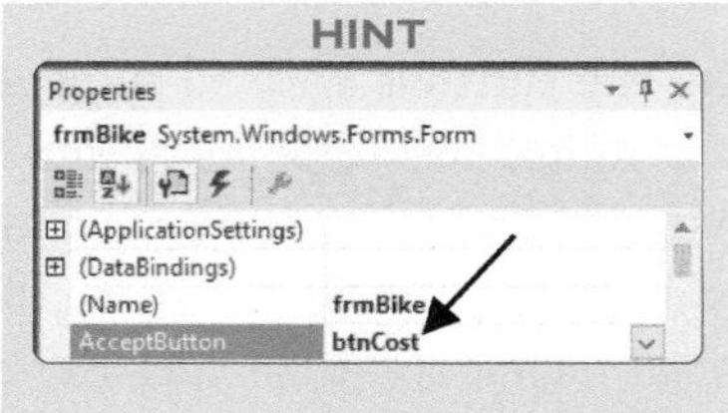

- **Set the Clear Button Object as the Cancel Button** By pressing the ESC key, the user should cause the same action as clicking the Clear button. To set the Clear button as the Cancel button, click the Windows Form object, click the CancelButton property in the Properties window, click the CancelButton arrow, and then click btnClear *(ref: page 162)*.

HINT

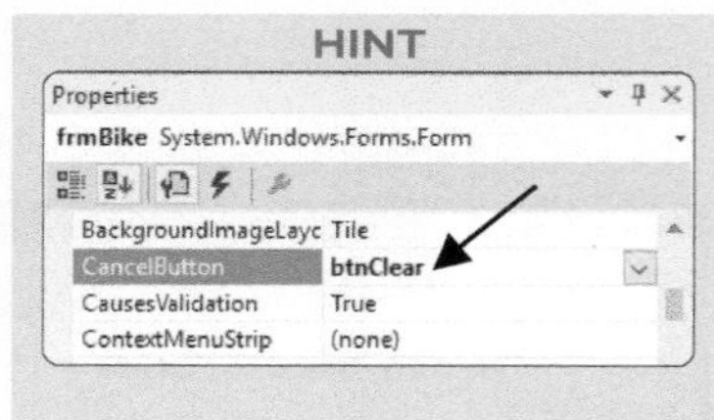

- **Insert the Bikes Image into the picBikes PictureBox Object** The last step to ready the user interface for execution is to insert the image into the PictureBox object. If necessary, download and save the bike.jpg image from the Student Companion Site. Then, with the picture box selected, click the ellipsis button for the Image property in the Properties window, click the Import button in the Select Resource dialog box, locate the bike image, and then import the image into the Resource folder. Click the OK button in the Select Resource dialog box.

HINT

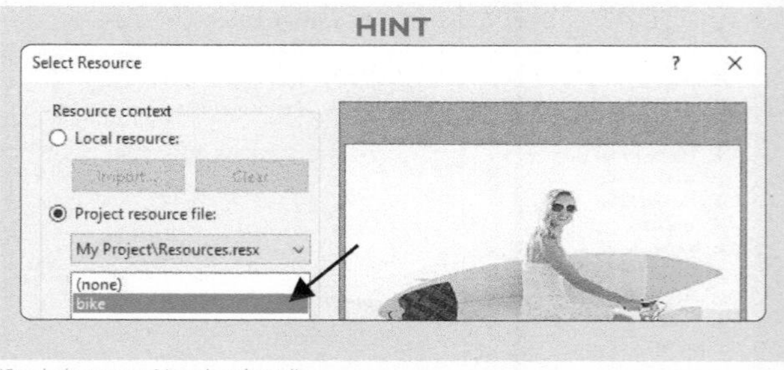

iStockphoto.com/Wavebreakmedia

- **Resize the Image** To resize the Bikes image, change the SizeMode property. With the picBikes PictureBox object selected, click the SizeMode property in the Properties window, click the SizeMode arrow in the right column, and then click StretchImage.

Guided Program Development *continued*

The user interface is complete (Figure 4-86).

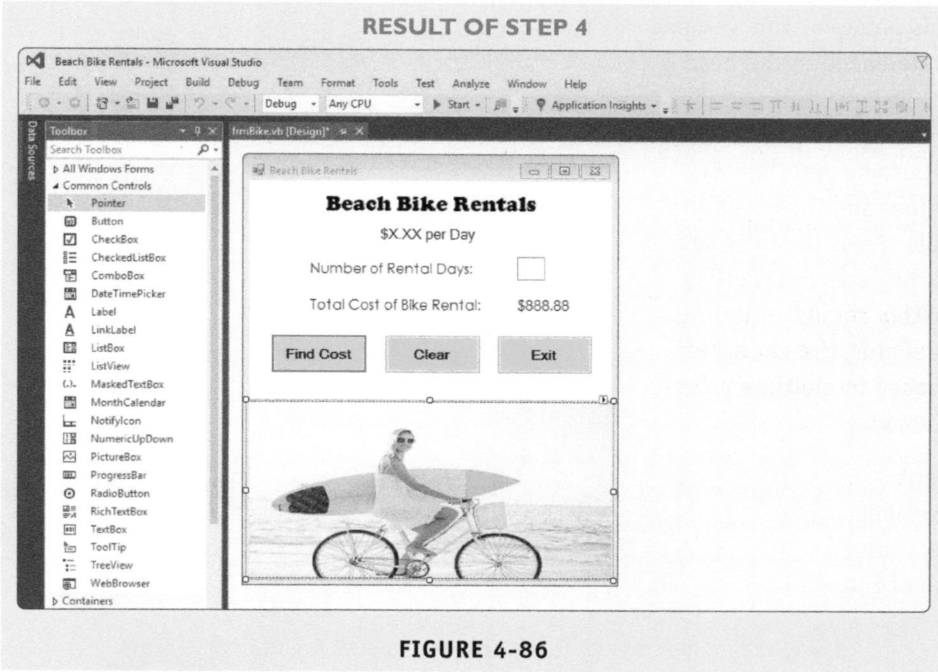
RESULT OF STEP 4
Beach Bike Rentals - Microsoft Visual Studio
Beach Bike Rentals
$X.XX per Day
Number of Rental Days:
Total Cost of Bike Rental:
$888.88
Find Cost
Clear
Exit

FIGURE 4-86

iStockphoto.com/Wavebreakmedia

Phase 3: Code the Application

5

• **Code the Comments** Double-click the btnCost Button object on the frmBike Windows Form object to open the code window and create the btnCost_Click event handler. Click the Close button on the Toolbox title bar to close the Toolbox. Click at the beginning of the first words, Public Class frmBike, and press the ENTER key to create a blank line. Press the UP ARROW key and then insert the first four standard comments. Insert the Option Strict On command at the beginning of the code to turn on strict type checking *(ref: Figure 4-49)*.

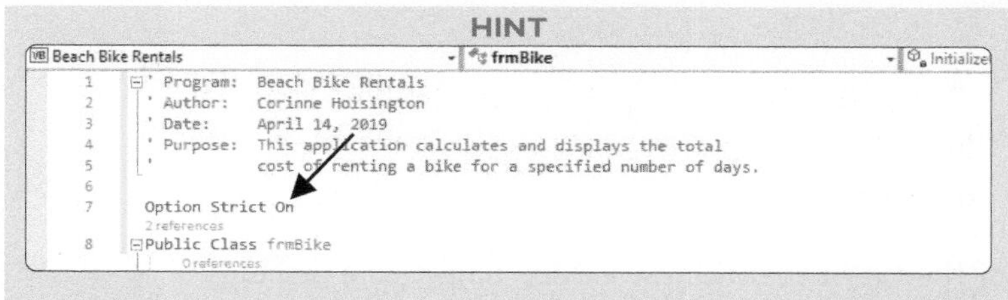
HINT
Beach Bike Rentals
frmBike
' Program: Beach Bike Rentals
' Author: Corinne Hoisington
' Date: April 14, 2019
' Purpose: This application calculates and displays the total
' cost of renting a bike for a specified number of days.
Option Strict On
Public Class frmBike

(continues)

Guided Program Development *continued*

- **Enter the _cdecPricePerDay Class Variable** The next step is to enter the class variable that is referenced in more than one event handler in this program. This variable contains the price per day and is referenced in the heading and to calculate the total cost. To enter this variable, press the DOWN ARROW key until the insertion point is on the blank line following the Public Class command (line 8). Press the ENTER key to add a blank line, and then type the comment that identifies the variable. Press the ENTER key and then write the declaration for the _cdecPricePerDay variable. The constant Decimal variable should contain the value 9.95. The underline character (_) in the name indicates a class variable that is referenced in multiple procedures within the class *(ref: Figure 4-43)*.

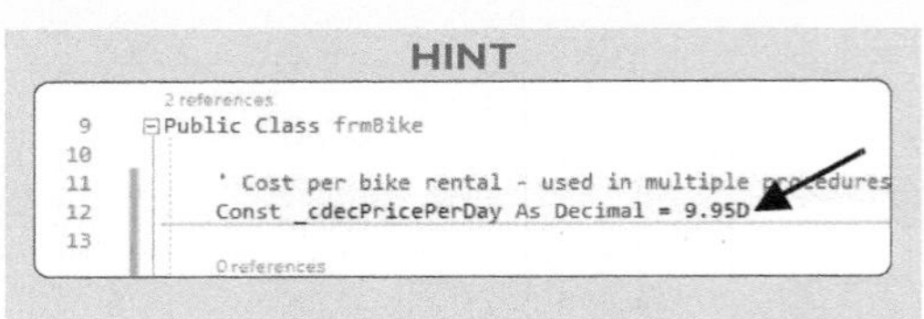

HINT
2 references
Public Class frmBike
' Cost per bike rental - used in multiple procedures
Const _cdecPricePerDay As Decimal = 9.95D
0 references

- **Comment the btnCost Click Event Handler** Following the Private statement for the btnCost_Click event handler, enter a comment to describe the purpose of the btnCost_Click event.

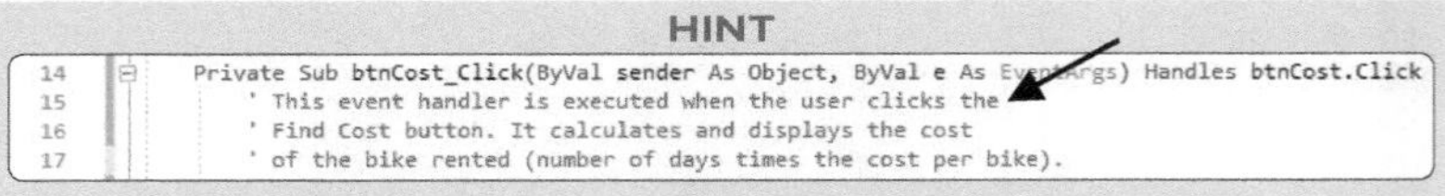

HINT
Private Sub btnCost_Click(ByVal sender As Object, ByVal e As EventArgs) Handles btnCost.Click
' This event handler is executed when the user clicks the
' Find Cost button. It calculates and displays the cost
' of the bike rented (number of days times the cost per bike).

- **Declare and Initialize the Variables** This event handler requires three variables: (1) strNumberOfDays, which holds the number of rental days entered by the user; (2) intNumberOfDays, which holds the integer value for the number of days entered by the user; and (3) decTotalCost, which holds the calculated total cost of the bike rental. Declare these three variables *(ref: Figure 4-20, Figure 4-31, Figure 4-34)*.

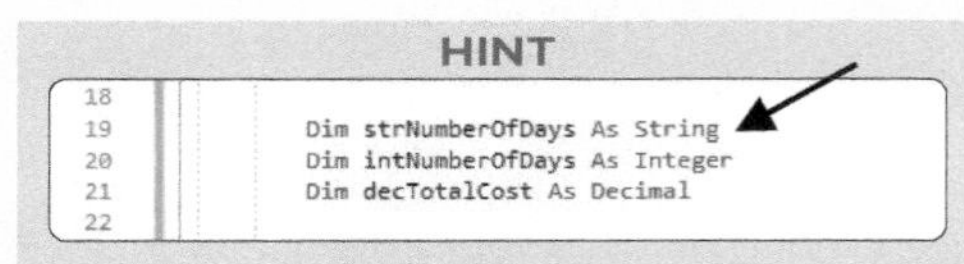

- **Write the Statements to Place the Number of Rental Days in a Variable and Convert the Value to an Integer** The first steps in the event handler are to move the number of the days value from the Text property of the txtNumberOfDays TextBox object to a String variable and then convert that value to an integer value. Using IntelliSense, write the code to complete these steps *(ref: Figure 4-26, Figure 4-48)*.

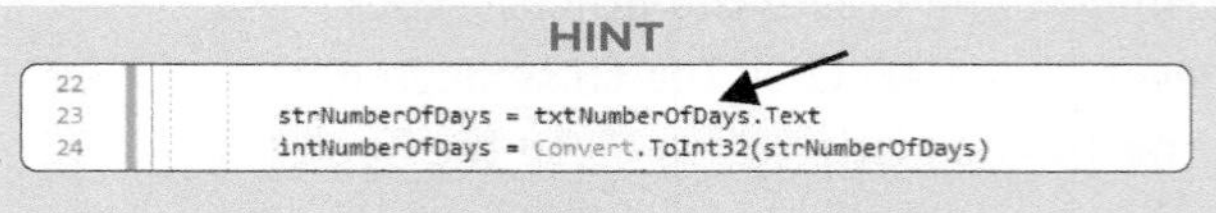

- **Find the Total Cost of the Bike Rented** To calculate the total cost of the bike rented and place the result in the decTotalCost variable, multiply the number of days by the price per day. Using IntelliSense, write the statement to perform this calculation *(ref: Figure 4-51)*.

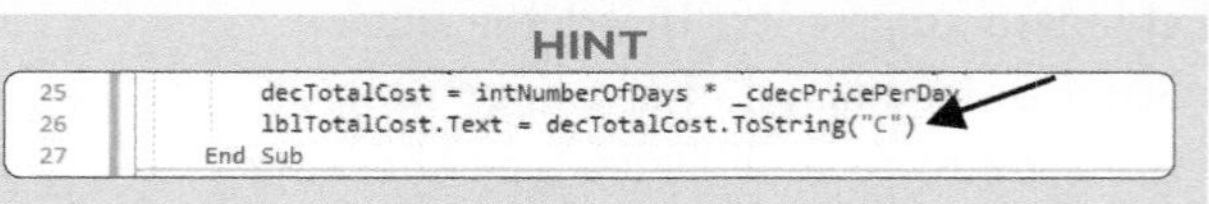

HINT
decTotalCost = intNumberOfDays * _cdecPricePerDay
lblTotalCost.Text = decTotalCost.ToString("C")
End Sub

Guided Program Development *continued*

- **Convert the Decimal Total Cost of the Bike Rental to a String Currency Value and Place It in the Text Property of the lblTotalCost Label Object** After calculating the total cost of the bike rental, the result must be converted from a Decimal value to a currency String value so it can be displayed as the value in the Text property of a Label object. Write the statement to perform this conversion and place the converted value in the Text property of the lblTotalCost Label object.

The coding for the btnCost_Click event handler is complete (Figure 4-87).

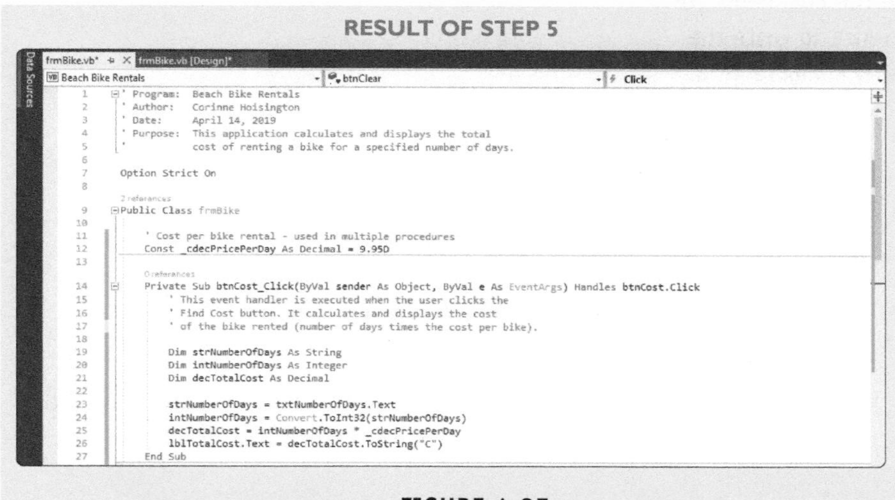
RESULT OF STEP 5
Data Sources
frmBike.vb*
frmBike.vb [Design]*
Beach Bike Rentals
btnClear
Click
' Program: Beach Bike Rentals
' Author: Corinne Hoisington
' Date: April 14, 2019
' Purpose: This application calculates and displays the total
'   cost of renting a bike for a specified number of days.
Option Strict On
2 references
Public Class frmBike
' Cost per bike rental - used in multiple procedures
Const _cdecPricePerDay As Decimal = 9.95D
0 references
Private Sub btnCost_Click(ByVal sender As Object, ByVal e As EventArgs) Handles btnCost.Click
' This event handler is executed when the user clicks the
' Find Cost button. It calculates and displays the cost
' of the bike rented (number of days times the cost per bike).
Dim strNumberOfDays As String
Dim intNumberOfDays As Integer
Dim decTotalCost As Decimal
strNumberOfDays = txtNumberOfDays.Text
intNumberOfDays = Convert.ToInt32(strNumberOfDays)
decTotalCost = intNumberOfDays * _cdecPricePerDay
lblTotalCost.Text = decTotalCost.ToString("C")
End Sub

FIGURE 4-87

6

- **Run the Application** After you enter code, you should run the application to ensure it is working properly. Run the Beach Bike Rentals application by clicking the Start button on the Standard toolbar. Enter 2 for the Number of Rental Days and then click the Find Cost button. The Total Cost of the Bike Rental should be $19.90. Enter 10 for the Number of Rental Days and then press the ENTER key.

When the number of rental days is 10, the total cost of the beach bike rental is $99.50 (Figure 4-88).

Beach Bike Rentals
Beach Bike Rentals
$9.95 per Day
Number of Rental Days:
10
Total Cost of Bike Rental:
$99.50
Find Cost
Clear
Exit

FIGURE 4-88

iStockphoto.com/Wavebreakmedia

(continues)

Guided Program Development *continued*

- **Write the Code for the Clear Button Event Handler** Click the frmBike.vb [Design] tab in the code window to return to the design window. Double-click the Clear button to create the event handler for the Clear button. The Clear button event handler must accomplish the following tasks: Clear the txtNumberOfDays text box; clear the value in the Text property of the lblTotalCost Label object; and set the focus to the txtNumberOfDays text box. Write the comments for the event handler and then use IntelliSense to write the code for the event handler *(ref: Figure 4-71, Figure 4-72, Figure 4-73)*.

HINT

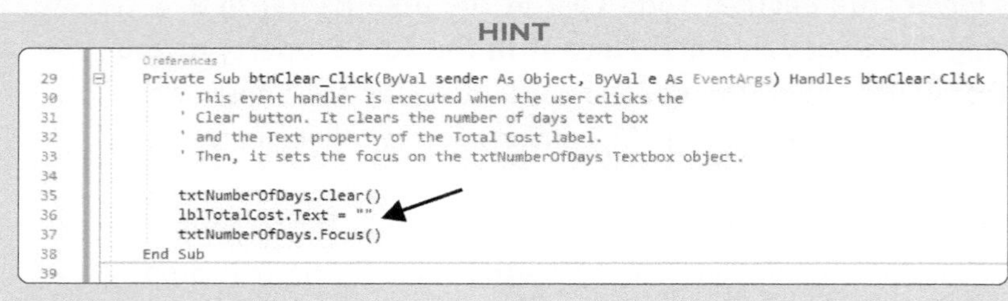

- **Write the Code for the Form Load Event Handler** Click the frmBike.vb [Design] tab in the code window to return to the design window. Double-click the Windows Form object to create the event handler for the Form Load event. The Form Load event handler must accomplish the following tasks: Using concatenation, create and display the Price per Day heading in the Text property of the lblCostHeading Label object; clear the Text property of the lblTotalCost Label object; and set the focus to the txtNumberOfDays TextBox object. Write the comments for the event handler and then use IntelliSense to write the code for the event handler *(ref: Figure 4-71, Figure 4-73, Figure 4-76)*.

HINT

```
0 references
Private Sub frmDigitalDownloads_Load(ByVal sender As Object, ByVal e As EventArgs) Handles MyBase.Load
    ' This event handler is executed when the form is loaded.
    ' It displays the cost heading, clears the Text property of the
    ' Total Cost label, and sets the focus on
    ' the txtNumberOfDays Textbox object.

    lblCostHeading.Text = _cdecPricePerDay.ToString("C") & " per Day"
    lblTotalCost.Text = ""
    txtNumberOfDays.Focus()
End Sub
```

- **Write the Code for the Exit Button Event Handler** Click the frmBike.vb [Design] tab in the code window to return to the design window. Double-click the Exit button to create its event handler. The Exit button event handler must close the window and end the application. Write the comments and code for this event handler.

HINT

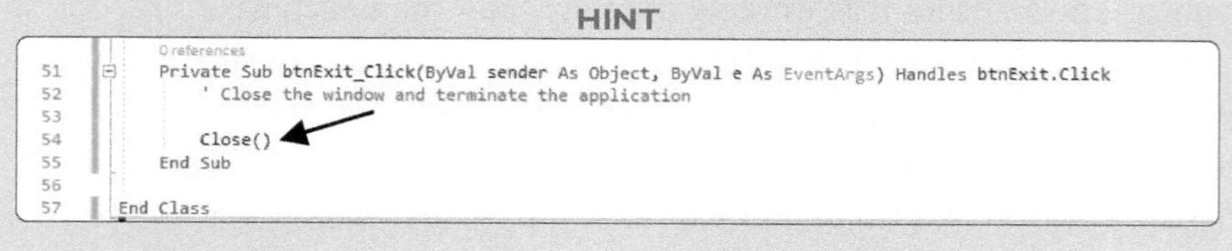

Guided Program Development *continued*

The coding is complete for the Clear button event handler, the Form load event handler, and the Exit button event handler (Figure 4-89).

RESULT OF STEP 6

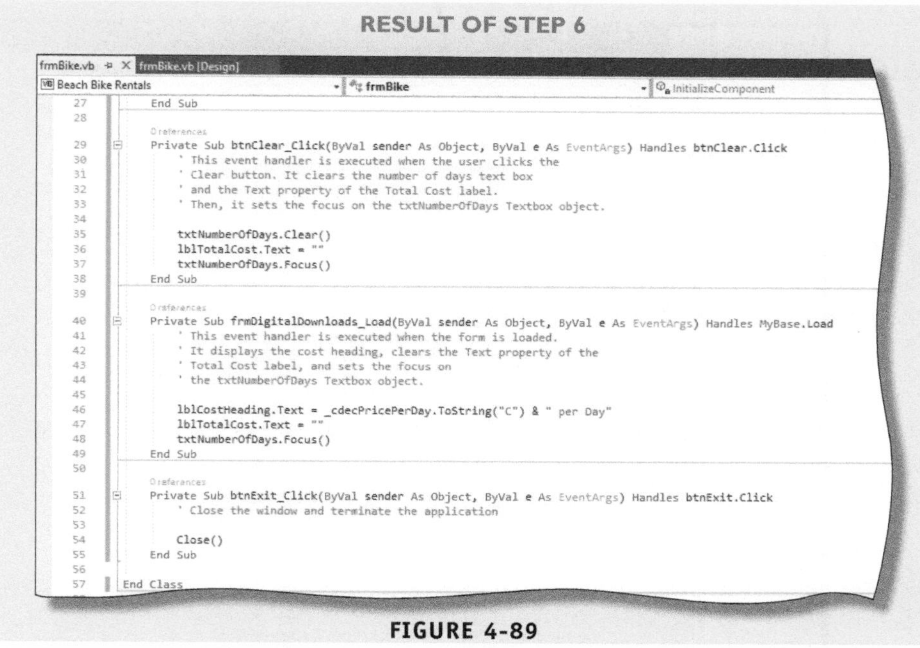

```
        End Sub

    Private Sub btnClear_Click(ByVal sender As Object, ByVal e As EventArgs) Handles btnClear.Click
        ' This event handler is executed when the user clicks the
        ' Clear button. It clears the number of days text box
        ' and the Text property of the Total Cost label.
        ' Then, it sets the focus on the txtNumberOfDays Textbox object.

        txtNumberOfDays.Clear()
        lblTotalCost.Text = ""
        txtNumberOfDays.Focus()
    End Sub

    Private Sub frmDigitalDownloads_Load(ByVal sender As Object, ByVal e As EventArgs) Handles MyBase.Load
        ' This event handler is executed when the form is loaded.
        ' It displays the cost heading, clears the Text property of the
        ' Total Cost label, and sets the focus on
        ' the txtNumberOfDays Textbox object.

        lblCostHeading.Text = _cdecPricePerDay.ToString("C") & " per Day"
        lblTotalCost.Text = ""
        txtNumberOfDays.Focus()
    End Sub

    Private Sub btnExit_Click(ByVal sender As Object, ByVal e As EventArgs) Handles btnExit.Click
        ' Close the window and terminate the application

        Close()
    End Sub

End Class
```

FIGURE 4-89

- **Test the Program** After finishing the coding, you should test the program to ensure it works properly. Run the Beach Bike Rentals application by clicking the Start button on the Standard toolbar. Enter 2 for the Number of Rental Days and then click the Find Cost button. The Total Cost of Bike Rental should be $19.90. Click the Clear button to clear the text box and the label that contains the total cost of the bike rental. Enter 5 for the Number of Rental Days and then press the ENTER key. The Total Cost of Bike Rental should be $49.75. Press the ESC key to clear the text box and the label that contains the total cost of the bike rental. Enter other values to test the program completely.

The program runs properly.

(continues)

Code Listing

The complete code for the sample program is shown in Figure 4-90.

```
frmBike.vb
Beach Bike Rentals                                    frmBike
' Program:  Beach Bike Rentals
' Author:   Corinne Hoisington
' Date:     April 14, 2019
' Purpose:  This application calculates and displays the total
'           cost of renting a bike for a specified number of days.

Option Strict On

2 references
Public Class frmBike

    ' Cost per bike rental - used in multiple procedures
    Const _cdecPricePerDay As Decimal = 9.95D

    0 references
    Private Sub btnCost_Click(ByVal sender As Object, ByVal e As EventArgs) Handles btnCost.Click
        ' This event handler is executed when the user clicks the
        ' Find Cost button. It calculates and displays the cost
        ' of the bike rented (number of days times the cost per bike).

        Dim strNumberOfDays As String
        Dim intNumberOfDays As Integer
        Dim decTotalCost As Decimal

        strNumberOfDays = txtNumberOfDays.Text
        intNumberOfDays = Convert.ToInt32(strNumberOfDays)
        decTotalCost = intNumberOfDays * _cdecPricePerDay
        lblTotalCost.Text = decTotalCost.ToString("C")
    End Sub

    0 references
    Private Sub btnClear_Click(ByVal sender As Object, ByVal e As EventArgs) Handles btnClear.Click
        ' This event handler is executed when the user clicks the
        ' Clear button. It clears the number of days text box
        ' and the Text property of the Total Cost label.
        ' Then, it sets the focus on the txtNumberOfDays Textbox object.

        txtNumberOfDays.Clear()
        lblTotalCost.Text = ""
        txtNumberOfDays.Focus()
    End Sub

    0 references
    Private Sub frmDigitalDownloads_Load(ByVal sender As Object, ByVal e As EventArgs) Handles MyBase.Load
        ' This event handler is executed when the form is loaded.
        ' It displays the cost heading, clears the Text property of the
        ' Total Cost label, and sets the focus on
        ' the txtNumberOfDays Textbox object.

        lblCostHeading.Text = _cdecPricePerDay.ToString("C") & " per Day"
        lblTotalCost.Text = ""
        txtNumberOfDays.Focus()
    End Sub

    0 references
    Private Sub btnExit_Click(ByVal sender As Object, ByVal e As EventArgs) Handles btnExit.Click
        ' Close the window and terminate the application

        Close()
    End Sub

End Class
```

FIGURE 4-90

Knowledge Check

1. Which data type should an ampersand (&) symbol be assigned?
2. Write a Dim statement for each of the following variables using the variable type and variable name that would be best for each value.

   a. The population of Alaska

   b. The smallest data type you can use for the age of a child

   c. A constant for the first initial of your first name

   d. The minimum wage

   e. The name of the street where you live

   f. The answer to a true/false question

3. Determine whether each of the following variable names is valid or invalid. Explain the error in each invalid variable name.

   a. #samtechnow

   b. first_Input_Value

   c. Orange-is-new-black

   d. 3CPO

   e. Close

   f. Name Of Cortana

   g. _cdecPi

4. List the steps that specify how you would perfectly align a group of TextBox objects along their left edges.
5. Which data type is best for currency amounts?
6. Explain the hierarchy for the order of operations.
7. What is the solution to each of the following arithmetic expressions?

   a. 6 + 7 * 2 - 1

   b. 48 / 6 * 2^2

   c. 40 - 6 ^ 2 / 3

   d. 74 Mod 9

   e. 9 \ 4 * 3

   f. 2 ^ 3 * (8 - 5)

   g. (15 Mod 2) + 5 * 3

(continues)

Knowledge Check *continued*

8. What is the difference between a method and a procedure?
9. What is the difference between a variable and a literal?
10. Correct the following statements:

    a. `Dim itHeight As Integr`

    b. `Dim dblDiscountAmount A Dbl`

    c. `Constant _cstrCollege As Sentence = "PVCC"`

    d. `Dim strSenatorName As Number`

    e. `strLastName = 'Prof. J Starks'`

    f. `1.5 * decPay = decOverTimePayRate`

11. Write a statement that sets the focus on the txtSeafood TextBox object.
12. Write a statement that removes the contents of the txtPrince TextBox object.
13. Write a statement that blanks the Text property of the lblEligibilityAge Label object.
14. Write a statement to convert the value in the String variable strNeckSize to an integer value and place the integer value in a variable named intNeckSize.
15. Write a statement to convert the value in the String variable strHourlyPay to a Decimal value and place the Decimal value in a variable named decGross.
16. Write a statement to close a form that currently is open.
17. Write a statement that declares a constant named _cdecInsuranceDeductible as a Decimal data type and set its value to 500.00.
18. Which Windows Form property allows the user to press the ESC key while the form is active and activate a button's event handler?
19. What is a local variable? How does its scope differ from that of a global variable?
20. When the following statements are executed, what would be displayed in the lblHourlyWage Label object

```
decHourlyWage = 13.837
lblHourlyWage.Text = decHourlyWage.ToString("C")
```

Debugging Exercises

1. Fix the following code:

```
Option Strict
Dim intDistance As Integer
intDistance = 17.5
```

2. Fix the following code:

```
Dim dblRegularPay As Double
Dim dblOvertimePay As Double
```

Debugging Exercises *continued*

```
intRegularPay = 783.87
intOvertimePay = 105.92
lbl.TotalPay = (dblRegularPay + dblOvertimePay).ToString ('C')
```

3. Analyze the code and then correct it.

```
Dim strCity as String = "Miami"
Dim strState as Double = "Florida"
Dim strLocation as String
strLoc = strCity + strState
```

Program Analysis

1. What will occur when the user clicks the btnSlope Button in the following code?

```
Private Sub btnSlope_Click(ByVal sender As System.Object, ByVal e As System.
EventArgs) Handles btnSlope.Click
 Dim decRise As Decimal
 Dim decRun As Decimal
 Dim decSlope As Decimal
 decRise = 12.3D
 decRun = 2.1D
 decSlope = decRise / decRun
 lblSlope.Text = "The Line Slope is" & decSlope.ToString("F1")
End Sub
```

2. How would the number .0456 be displayed if the format specifier ("P") is used in a Convert.ToString statement?
3. How would the number 3746.35555 be displayed if the format specifier ("F3") is used in a Convert.ToString statement?
4. If you want the user to enter her phone number with the area code, which .NET component would be best to use on the Windows Form object?
5. Using the format specifier with the ToString procedure, write the statement that would display:
   a. The value in the decDvdCost variable with a dollar sign and two places to the right of the decimal point in a label named lblDvd
   b. The value in the decWithholdingTaxRate variable with a percent sign and one place to the right of the decimal point in a label named lblWithholdingTaxRate
   c. The value in the decOilRevenue variable with commas as needed, two places to the right of the decimal point, and no dollar sign in a label called lblOilRevenue

(continues)

Program Analysis *continued*

6. Write a single line of code to declare a variable decWindSpeed as a Decimal data type and assign it the value 25.47. Use a forced literal to ensure that the compiler views this number as a Decimal data type.
7. What would the values of these variables be at the end of the code that follows?

   a. intParts

   b. intBoxes

   c. intLeftovers

```
Dim intParts As Integer
Dim intBoxes As Integer
Dim intLeftovers As Integer
intParts = 78
intPartsPerBox = 8
intBoxes = intParts \ intPartsPerBox
intLeftovers = intParts Mod intBoxes
```

8. Are the following statements written correctly? If not, how should they be written?

```
Dim dblPay as Double
lblPay.Text = dblPay.ToString("C2")
```

9. For a Button object named btnCalories, write the click event handler to implement the following requirements and calculate the number of calories burned during a run:

   a. Declare variables named strMilesRan, decCaloriesConsumed, and decMilesRan.

   b. Declare a constant named _cdecCaloriesBurnedPerHour and assign it the value 700. (Assume you burn 700 calories for every mile you run.)

   c. Allow the user to enter the number of miles she ran today.

   d. Convert the number of miles to a Decimal data type.

   e. Calculate the number of calories the user burned during her run.

   f. Display the result rounded to zero decimal places in a label named lblCaloriesBurned.

10. What would the output be when the user clicks the btnDrivingAge Button?

```
Private Sub btnDrivingAge_Click(ByVal sender As System.Object, ByVal e As
System.EventArgs) Handles btnDrivingAge.Click
  Dim intPresentAge As Integer
  Const cintDrivingAge As Integer = 16
  Dim intYearsToDrive As Integer
  intPresentAge = 13
  intYearsToDrive = cintDrivingAge - intPresentAge
  lblYearsLeft.Text = intYearsToDrive.ToString() & " year(s) until you can
 drive."
End Sub
```

Case Programming Assignments

Complete one or more of the following case programming assignments. Submit the program and materials you create to your instructor. The level of difficulty is indicated for each assignment.

● = Easiest
●● = Intermediate
●●● = Challenging

1 ● AIRBNB RESERVATIONS

Design a Windows Classic Desktop application and write the code that will execute according to the program requirements in Figure 4-91 and the Use Case Definition in Figure 4-92. Before writing the code, create an event-planning document for each event in the program. The completed program is shown in Figure 4-93.

REQUIREMENTS DOCUMENT

Date: October 19, 2018

Date Submitted:

Application Title: Airbnb Reservations

Purpose: This Windows Classic Desktop application allows a user to calculate the cost of an Airbnb stay for an apartment in Orlando, Florida.

Program Procedures: From a window on the screen, the user chooses the number of nights to stay at the Orlando Airbnb; the total cost of the accommodations is displayed.

Algorithms, Processing, and Conditions:

1. The user must be able to enter the number of nights.
2. A picture of an Airbnb app will be displayed throughout the entire process.
3. After entering the number of nights needed, the user clicks the Display Cost button.
4. One night of accommodations costs $79 for the full apartment each night; the total cost will be displayed in currency format.

Notes and Restrictions:

1. The user can use a Clear button to clear the number of nights entered and the total cost and then enter another number of nights.
2. An Exit button should end the application.
3. The cost per night can vary, so the program should allow a different price to be placed in any headings and be used in any calculations.

Comments: The picture is named airbnb and is available on CengageBrain.com.

FIGURE 4-91

(continues)

Case Programming Assignments *continued*

Airbnb Reservations

USE CASE DEFINITION

1. The Windows Classic Desktop application opens.
2. The user enters the number of nights.
3. The user clicks the Display Cost button.
4. The program displays the total cost for the Airbnb stay.
5. The user can click the Clear button and repeat Steps 2 through 4.
6. The user exits the program by clicking the Exit button.

FIGURE 4-92

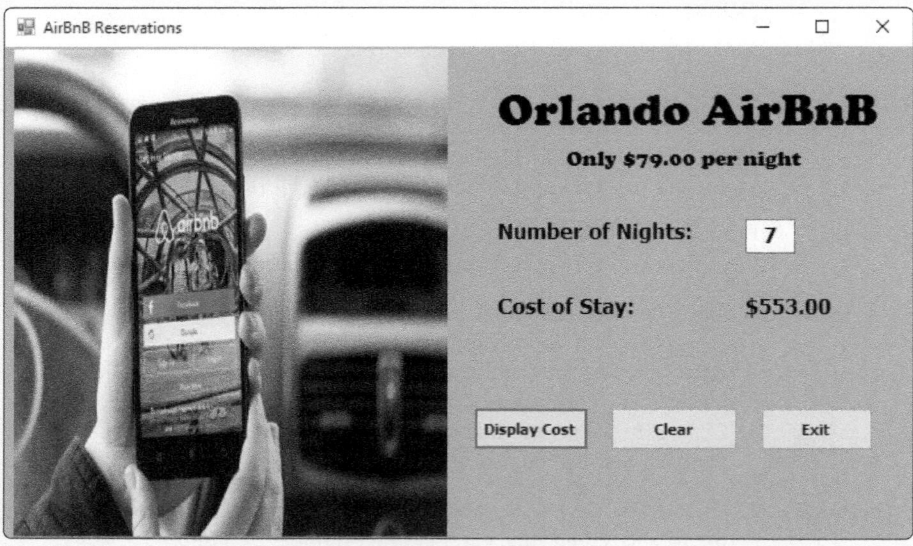

FIGURE 4-93

iStockphoto.com/GoodLifeStudio

Case Programming Assignments

2 • SEATTLE WALKING TOUR

Design a Windows Classic Desktop application and write the code that will execute according to the program requirements in Figure 4-94 and the Use Case Definition in Figure 4-95. Before writing the code, create an event-planning document for each event in the program. The completed program is shown in Figure 4-96.

REQUIREMENTS DOCUMENT

Date: February 19, 2018

Date Submitted:

Application Title: Seattle Walking Tour

Purpose: This Windows Classic Desktop application computes the cost of a Seattle walking tour.

Program Procedures: From a window on the screen, the user enters the number of tickets needed for a three-hour walking tour of the waterfront of Seattle. The program calculates and displays the cost of the tickets with an additional cost of $1.99 for booking using the app.

Algorithms, Processing, and Conditions:

1. The user must be able to enter the number of tickets for the Seattle Walking Tour.
2. The title of the program and an image of Seattle's skyline will be displayed throughout the entire process.
3. After entering the number of tickets, the user clicks the Display Cost button.
4. Each tour ticket is $14.99.
5. A one-time booking fee of $1.99 is charged regardless of the number of tickets purchased as a convenience charge of booking through the app.
6. The program displays the cost including the booking fee in currency format.

Notes and Restrictions:

1. The user can clear the number of tickets and make another entry.
2. An Exit button should end the application.

Comments: The Seattle image is named seattle and is available on CengageBrain.com.

FIGURE 4-94

(continues)

Case Programming Assignments *continued*

Seattle Walking Tour

USE CASE DEFINITION

1. The Windows Classic Desktop application opens.
2. The user enters the number of tour tickets needed.
3. The user clicks the Display Cost button.
4. The program displays the total cost of the Seattle Walking Tour tickets.
5. The user can click the Clear button and repeat Steps 2 through 4.
6. The user exits the program by clicking the Exit button.

FIGURE 4-95

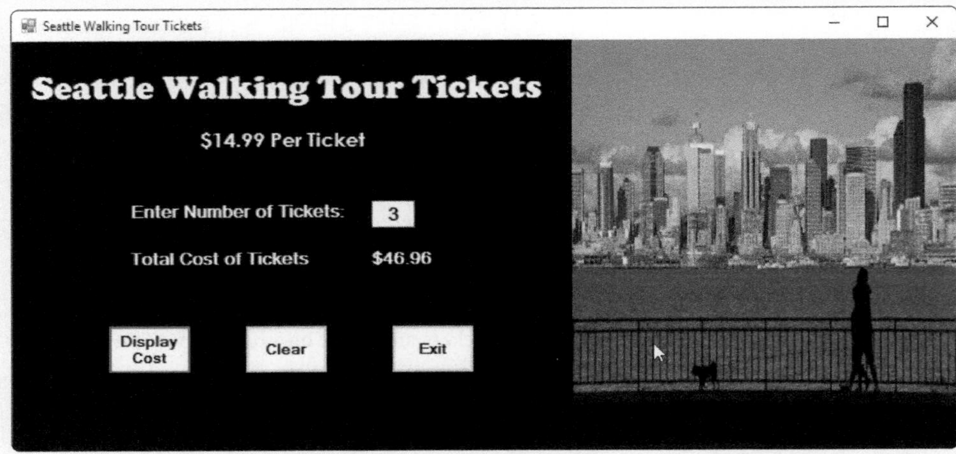

FIGURE 4-96

iStockphoto.com/LoweStock

Case Programming Assignments

3 ●● DRIVERLESS UBER CAR

Design a Windows Classic Desktop application and write the code that will execute according to the program requirements in Figure 4-97. Before designing the user interface, create a Use Case Definition. Before writing the code, create an event-planning document for each event in the program.

REQUIREMENTS DOCUMENT

Date:	October 20, 2018
Date Submitted:	
Application Title:	Driverless Uber Car
Purpose:	This Windows Classic Desktop application calculates the cost of a driverless Uber car fare.
Program Procedures:	From a window on the screen, a user enters the number of miles to the destination. The program displays the flat rate per mile and the total cost of the Uber fare.
Algorithms, Processing, and Conditions:	1. The user must be able to enter the number of miles to her destination. 2. A picture of a driverless Uber car will be displayed throughout the entire process. 3. After entering the number of miles driven, the user clicks the Display Fare button. 4. The cost per mile is $1.80 and a flat rate of $2.80 is charged at pickup. 5. The total cost for the fare is displayed using the currency format.
Notes and Restrictions:	1. The user can clear the miles entered by clicking a Clear button. The user can then can enter another mileage amount. 2. An Exit button should end the application.
Comments:	Locate an image for the app at Google or Bing images.

FIGURE 4-97

Case Programming Assignments

PAYROLL CALCULATOR

Design a Windows Classic Desktop application and write the code that will execute according to the program requirements in Figure 4-98. Before designing the user interface, create a Use Case Definition. Before writing the code, create an event-planning document for each event in the program.

REQUIREMENTS DOCUMENT

Date:	January 4, 2018
Date Submitted:	
Application Title:	Payroll Calculator
Purpose:	This Windows Classic Desktop application will compute and display the FICA tax, federal tax, and state tax for a two-week pay period.
Program Procedures:	From a window on the screen, the user enters her gross pay check for two weeks. The program estimates the FICA tax, federal tax, and state tax for a two week pay cycle.
Algorithms, Processing, and Conditions:	1. Users must be able to enter their biweekly income. 2. The FICA tax (7.65%), federal tax (22%), and state income tax (4%) are computed. 3. The tax amounts should be displayed on separate lines and in currency format, two places past the decimal point. 4. The net pay should be displayed after the tax amounts have been deducted.
Notes and Restrictions:	1. The user can clear the income and taxes and then enter new data. 2. The user can use an Exit button to exit the application.
Comments:	The designer should design the user interface, including the graphic and words displayed.

FIGURE 4-98

Case Programming Assignments

5 ●●● ICE SKATING RINK

Create a requirements document and a Use Case Definition document and then design a Windows application based on the case project shown in Figure 4-99. Before writing the code, create an event-planning document for each event in the program.

> Your local town is placing an indoor ice skating rink in the city center. Create a Windows application that allows you to compute how much cubic feet of ice that the ice rink will hold. The Windows application should request the length, width, and average depth (for example, most ice rinks have a depth of 2 feet of ice). The program then determines the volume of the playground in cubic feet of ice needed (volume = length * width * depth). Allow the user to enter values with decimal places. The user should be able to clear all entries and then reenter data. To exit the program, the user should be able to click a button.

FIGURE 4-99

Case Programming Assignments

6 ●●● FITNESS TRACKER APP

Create a requirements document and a Use Case Definition document and then design a Windows application based on the case project shown in Figure 4-100. Before writing the code, create an event-planning document for each event in the program.

A fitness tracker app company has asked you to write a Windows application that its users can use to determine the total number of hours someone has exercised during their lifetimes, assuming they exercise an average of 2.5 hours per week. All users should enter their first name, their birth date, and the current date. For both dates, ask for the month, day, and year separately in numeric form. To calculate the number of hours exercised, assume 365 days per year and 30 days per month. The program must display the user's name and the number of hours the user has exercised in his or her lifetime. The user can click a Clear button to clear all entries and results. An Exit button must be available to exit the application.

FIGURE 4-100

CHAPTER 5

Decision Structures

OBJECTIVES

You will have mastered the material in this chapter when you can:

- Use the GroupBox object
- Place RadioButton objects in applications
- Display a message box
- Make decisions using If . . . Then statements
- Make decisions using If . . . Then . . . Else statements
- Make decisions using nested If statements
- Make decisions using logical operators
- Make decisions using Case statements
- Insert code snippets
- Test input to ensure a value is numeric

Introduction

Developers can code Visual Basic applications to make decisions based on the input of users or other conditions that occur. Decision making is one of the fundamental activities of a computer program. In this chapter, you will learn to write decision-making statements in Visual Basic 2017.

Visual Basic allows you to test conditions and perform different operations depending on the results. You can test whether a condition is true or false and change the flow of what happens in a program based on the user's input.

The sample program in this chapter is called the Decking Cost Calculator application. It is written for homeowners and decking contractors who want to compare the costs of three different decking options for materials. The application compares the cost of pressure-treated lumber, redwood, and composite decking.

The application asks the user to enter the number of square feet for the decking required and the desired decking material. The application then computes the cost of the decking based on a rate of $2.35 per square foot for pressure-treated lumber, $7.75 per square foot for redwood, and $8.50 per square foot for composite. Figure 5-1 shows the user interface for the application.

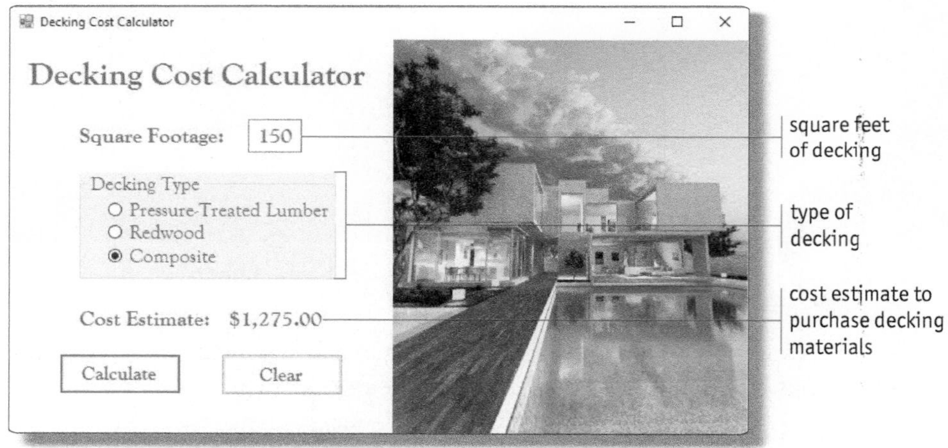

Franck Boston/Shutterstock.com

FIGURE 5-1

In Figure 5-1, the Decking Cost Calculator Windows application displays the text "Decking Cost Calculator" in the title bar. The square footage that the user enters in the TextBox object includes all decking materials for the job. The user chooses the decking type by selecting one of the following radio buttons: Pressure-Treated Lumber, Redwood, or Composite. After the user enters the number of square feet of decking and selects a type of building material, the user clicks the Calculate button to obtain the cost estimate. The calculation is the square feet multiplied by the cost of the selected decking. The cost estimate is displayed in currency format. In the example in Figure 5-1, the user entered 150 square feet for the deck size and selected Composite. After the user clicked the Calculate button, the application displayed a cost of $1275.00 (150 × $8.50).

Clicking the Clear button clears the square footage, resets the radio button selection to Pressure-Treated Lumber, which is the least expensive decking type, and clears the calculation result.

Checking the validity of data the user entered is a requirement of the sample program in this chapter. In Chapter 4, you learned that if you enter nonnumeric data and attempt to use it in a calculation, the program will be terminated. To check for invalid data, the Decking Cost Calculator application ensures that the user enters a numeric value greater than zero in the Square Footage TextBox object. A warning appears if the user leaves the TextBox blank or does not enter a valid number. Figure 5-2 displays the Input Error dialog box, called a Message Box, which directs the user to enter the square footage for the decking.

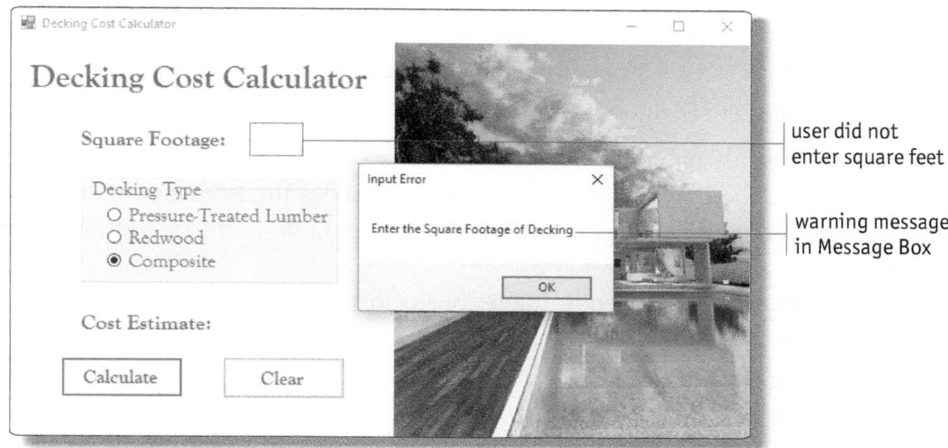

FIGURE 5-2

Franck Boston/Shutterstock.com

Checking input data for validity is an important task in Visual Basic programs. You will learn several data validation techniques in this chapter.

User Interface Design

The user interface for the Decking Cost Calculator application includes three new objects: a GroupBox, RadioButtons, and Message Boxes. The Message Boxes appear when the user enters a negative number or a nonnumeric value.

Use the GroupBox Object

The Decking Cost Calculator Form object requires a GroupBox object and RadioButton objects (Figure 5-3).

A **GroupBox** object associates items as a group, allowing the user to select one item from the group. It also includes caption text. RadioButton objects allow the user to make choices. In Figure 5-3, the GroupBox object groups the radio buttons for selecting the decking type. When RadioButton objects are contained in a group box,

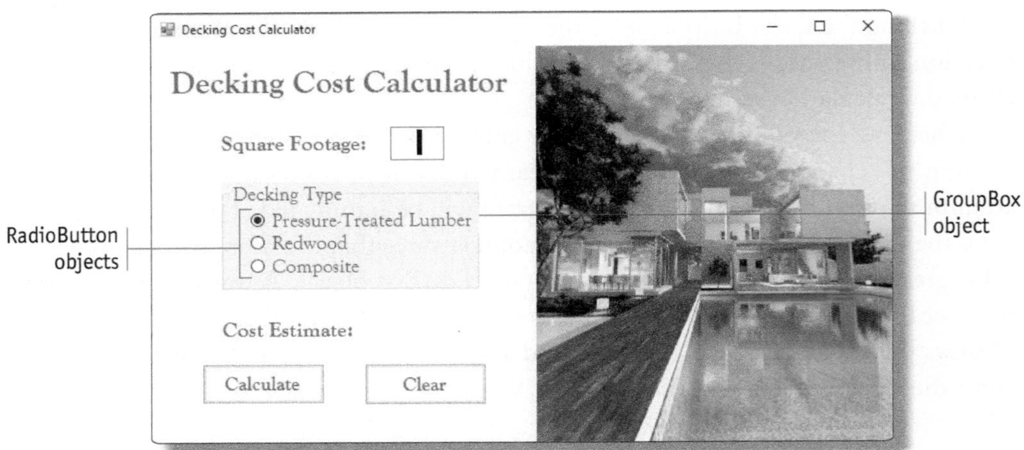

FIGURE 5-3

Franck Boston/Shutterstock.com

the user can select only one radio button. For example, in Figure 5-3, the Pressure-Treated Lumber radio button is selected. If the user clicks the Redwood radio button, it becomes selected, and the Pressure-Treated Lumber radio button is automatically deselected.

The GroupBox object shown in Figure 5-3 is displayed with the Text property of DeckingType as the caption text. The prefix for the GroupBox object (Name) property is grp. To place a GroupBox object on the Form object, you can complete the following steps:

STEP 1 Drag the GroupBox object from the Containers category of the Toolbox to the approximate location where you want to place the GroupBox object on the Form object.

The pointer changes when you place it over the Form object (Figure 5-4). The GroupBox object will be placed on the form at the location of the outline in the pointer.

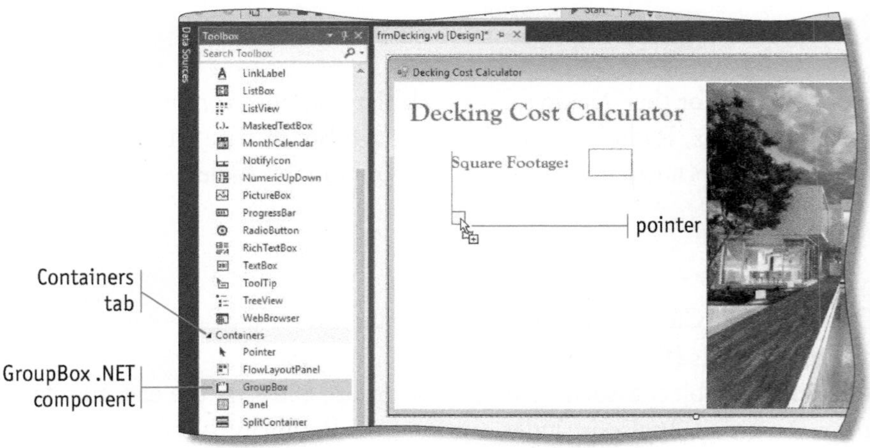

FIGURE 5-4

Franck Boston/Shutterstock.com

STEP 2 When the pointer is in the correct location, release the object. With the GroupBox object selected, scroll in the Properties window to the (Name) property. Double-click in the right column of the (Name) property and then enter the name `grpDeckType`. Double-click in the right column of the Text property to change the caption of the GroupBox object. Enter the text `Decking Type`. Change the BackColor property to the color AliceBlue and the ForeColor to Sienna. Click the right column of the Size property for the GroupBox object and enter `244, 106` as the size.

The name you entered is displayed in the (Name) property in the Properties window, the caption Decking Type is displayed, the background color is changed, and the object is resized (Figure 5-5).

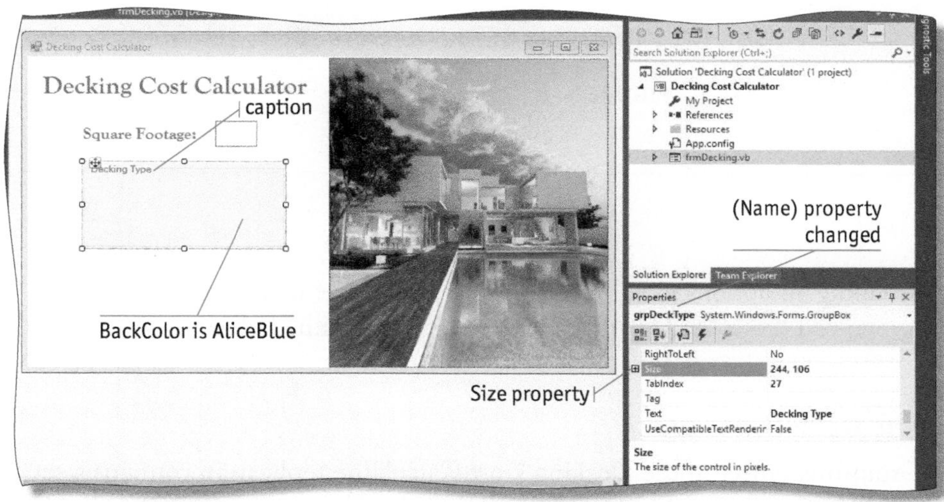

FIGURE 5-5

Franck Boston/Shutterstock.com

STEP 3 Change the Font property to Goudy Old Style, Regular, 14 points.

If you want to move the GroupBox to another location on the form, place the pointer over the drag box on the border of the GroupBox object and then drag it to the desired location. The Font property is set to Goudy Old Style (Figure 5-6).

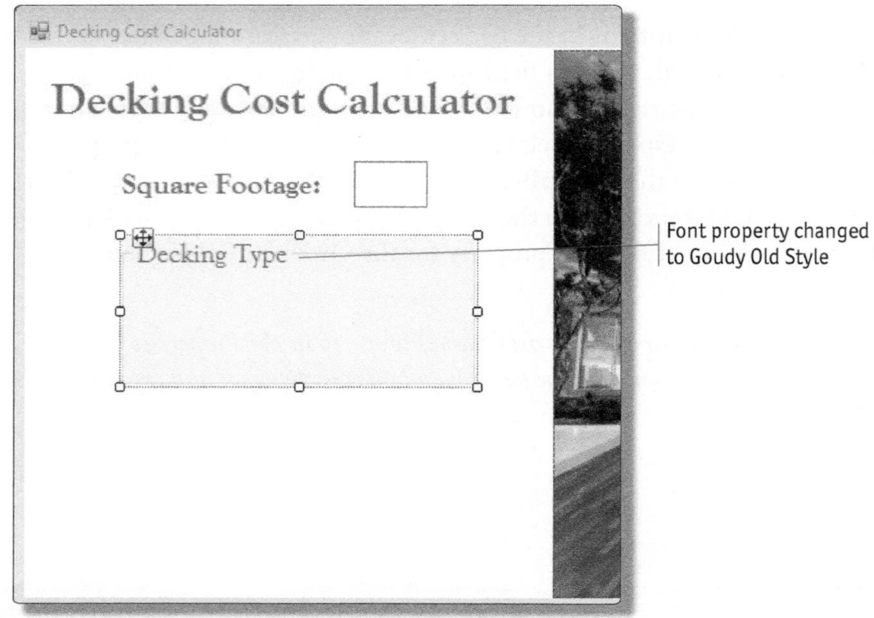

FIGURE 5-6

Franck Boston/Shutterstock.com

Grouping all options in a GroupBox object gives the user a logical visual cue. Also, when you move the GroupBox object, all its contained objects move as well.

Add the RadioButton Objects

The GroupBox object in the Decking Cost Calculator application contains a set of RadioButton objects (see Figure 5-3 on page 230). The user may select only one type of decking: pressure-treated lumber, redwood, or composite. To place RadioButton objects within the GroupBox object, you can complete the following steps:

STEP 1 Drag one RadioButton object from the Toolbox to the GroupBox object. Drag a second RadioButton object from the Toolbox into the GroupBox object, and use blue snap lines to align and separate the RadioButton objects vertically.

The second RadioButton object is aligned vertically with a blue snap line, which separates it vertically from the first RadioButton object (Figure 5-7).

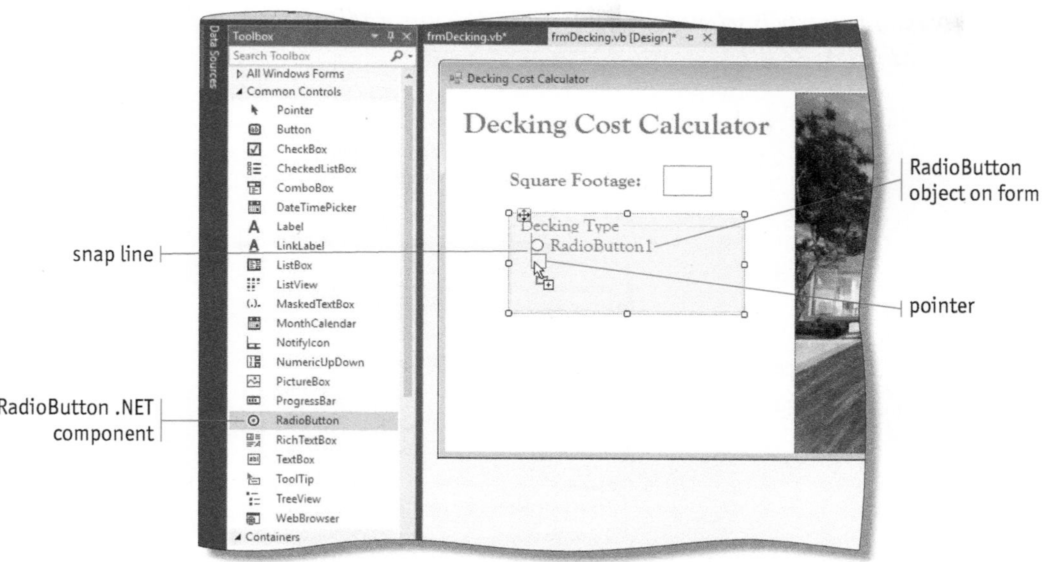

FIGURE 5-7

Franck Boston/Shutterstock.com

STEP 2 Release the RadioButton object to place it within the GroupBox object. Using the same technique, add a third RadioButton object.

Three RadioButton objects are placed on the form and aligned within the GroupBox object (Figure 5-8).

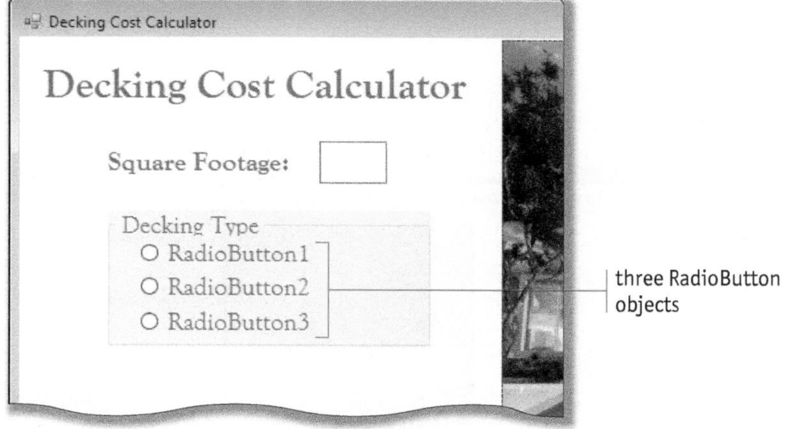

FIGURE 5-8

Franck Boston/Shutterstock.com

STEP 3 Name the RadioButton objects by selecting them one at a time, double-clicking in the right column of the (Name) property in the Properties window, and entering the name. The names for the radio buttons, from top to bottom, should be `radLumber`, `radRedwood`, and `radComposite`.

The (Name) property is selected. The names radLumber, radRedwood, and radComposite are entered (Figure 5-9).

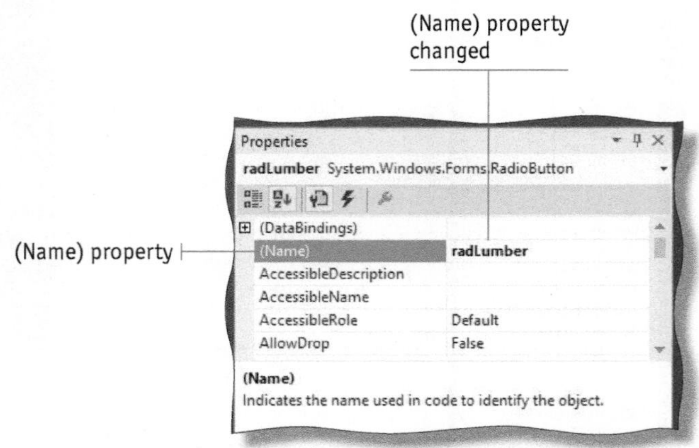

FIGURE 5-9

STEP 4 Change the Text property for each RadioButton object by double-clicking the right column of the Text property and typing `Pressure-Treated Lumber` for the first RadioButton, `Redwood` for the second RadioButton, and `Composite` for the third RadioButton.

The Text property is changed to the types of decking available: Pressure-Treated Lumber, Redwood, and Composite (Figure 5-10).

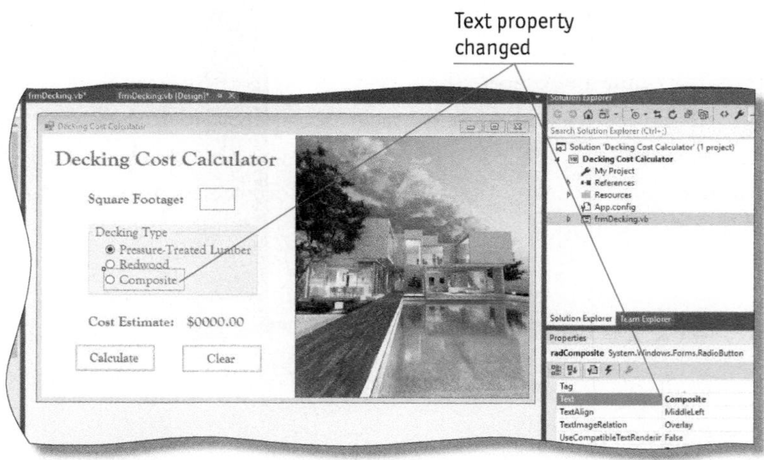

FIGURE 5-10

Franck Boston/Shutterstock.com

CONSIDER THIS

A RadioButton object is best used when you have only one selection per group. What type of object would you use to select more than one option?

CheckBox objects are used with lists of options in which the user may select any number of choices. In other words, each CheckBox object is independent of all other CheckBox objects in the list, so checking one box does not uncheck the others.

Use the Checked Property of RadioButton Objects

The RadioButton objects in the Decking Cost Calculator application allow the user to select one decking type. When the user selects Composite, as shown in Figure 5-11, the radio button is selected, and the small circle in the radio button is shaded. When the Composite radio button is selected, its Checked property changes from False (unselected) to True (selected).

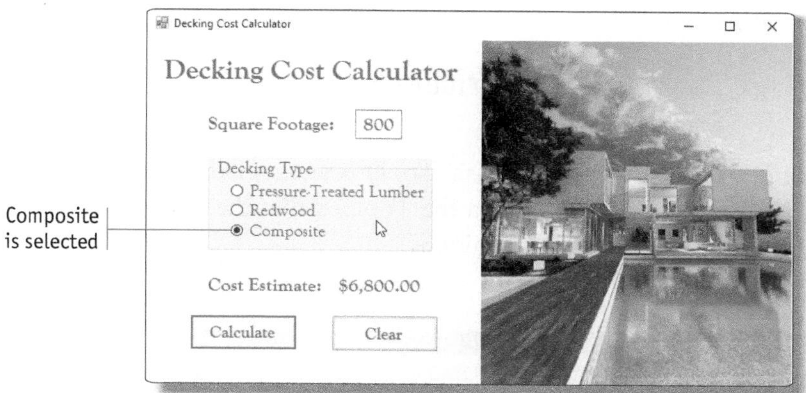

FIGURE 5-11

Franck Boston/Shutterstock.com

During design time, you usually set the Checked property to True for the most commonly selected radio button to save the user from having to select it. In the Decking Cost Calculator application, homeowners select Pressure-Treated Lumber most often due to the reduced cost. To cause the radLumber RadioButton object to appear selected (shaded) when the program begins, you change the Checked property for the radLumber RadioButton object from False to True (Figure 5-12).

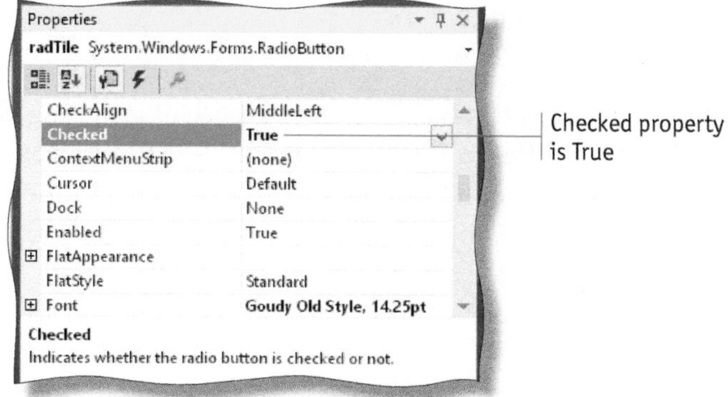

FIGURE 5-12

Windows Application Container Objects

The Panel object in a Windows application works like a GroupBox object. For Windows applications, Visual Basic provides four additional container objects: FlowLayoutPanel, SplitContainer, TabControl, and TableLayoutPanel. The GroupBox object is used most often; it provides several options that are not available with the Panel object. Figure 5-13 shows the differences between the GroupBox and Panel objects.

Option	GroupBox Object	Panel Object
Have a caption	Yes	No
Have scroll bars	Yes	No
Display a labeled border	Yes	No

FIGURE 5-13

Figure 5-14 shows the Visual Basic Toolbox and a GroupBox object and Panel object in a Windows Form. Notice in the Toolbox that the GroupBox and Panel objects are in a category called Containers.

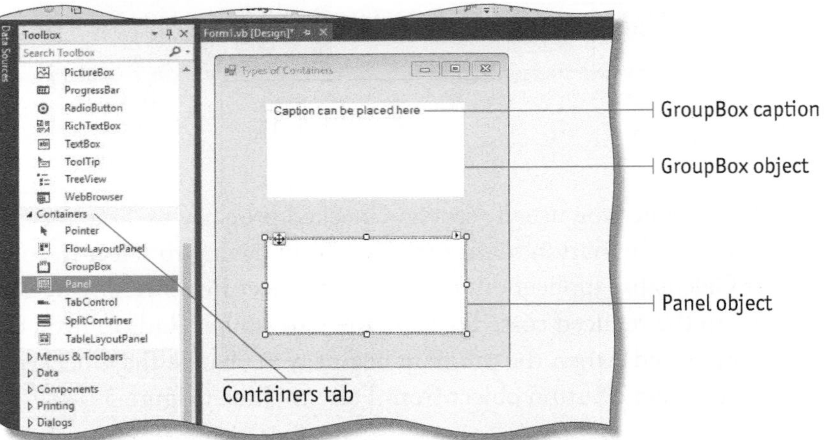

FIGURE 5-14

GroupBox and Panel objects have the same purpose of grouping RadioButtons and other objects, but they differ in their appearance. The GroupBox object in Figure 5-14 displays a border around its edges, with a text area in the upper-left portion for a caption. The Panel object has a black dashed border that does not appear when the application is executed.

Related sets of RadioButtons should be placed in separate container objects so that the user can select one radio button from each group. Always place the container object on the form first, and then drag the RadioButton objects into the container object.

The Course Sign-Up example in Figure 5-15 displays a Windows application that allows the user to sign up for a technology course. Notice the two separate groups of RadioButton objects. In the Choose Course Level GroupBox object, the user should select a course level. In the Choose Semester GroupBox object, the user should identify the semester for the course. As you can see, the user selects one radio button from the left group and one radio button from the right group.

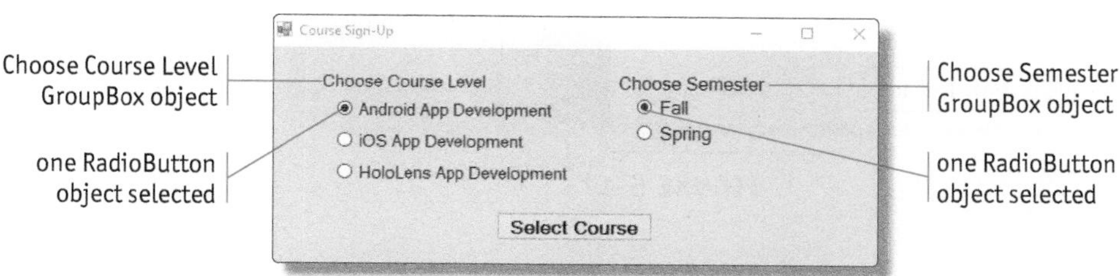

FIGURE 5-15

Display a Message Box

In the Decking Cost Calculator application, a message box, also called a dialog box, opens if the user does not enter the square footage of the decking correctly. The dialog box displays an error message if the user omits the square footage or enters nonnumeric data (Figure 5-16).

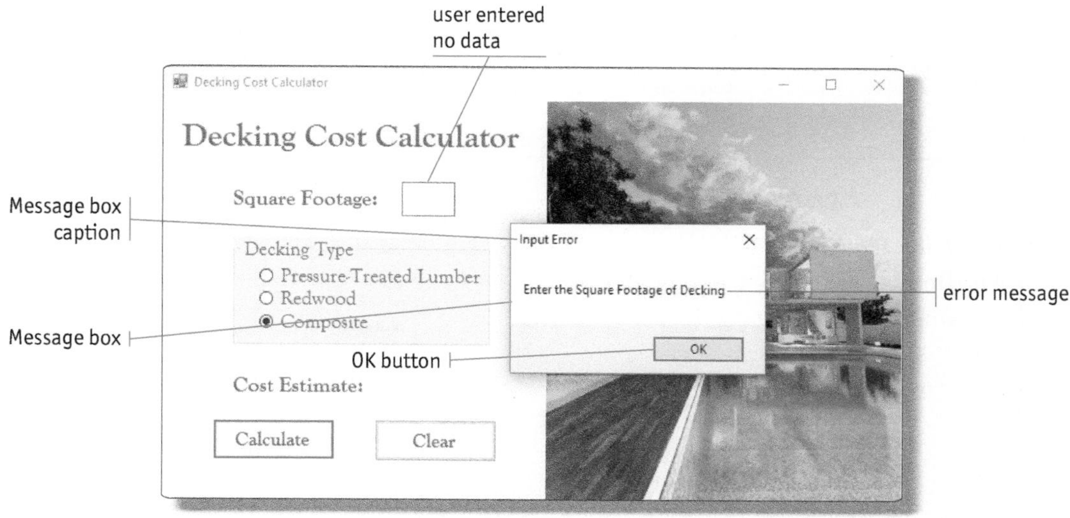

FIGURE 5-16

Franck Boston/Shutterstock.com

If the user enters a negative number for the square footage of the decking, a message box appears and indicates that a positive number is necessary (Figure 5-17).

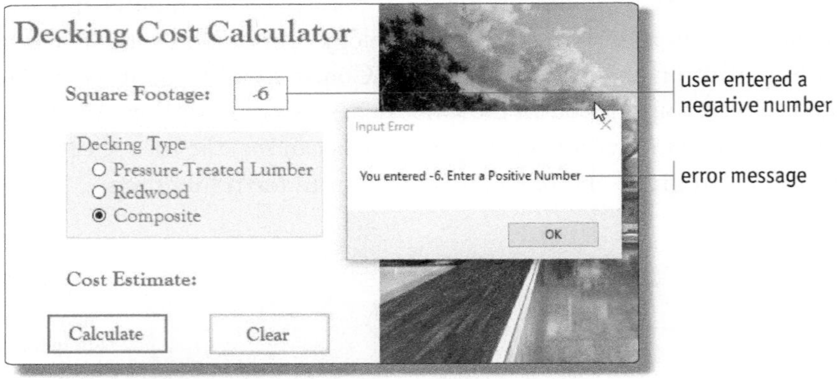

FIGURE 5-17

Franck Boston/Shutterstock.com

> **HEADS UP**
> You can create message boxes with two different commands: MessageBox.Show and MsgBox. This book focuses on the MsgBox command because it is shorter and easier to use.

This message box reminds the user to enter the square footage of the decking as a positive number. A message box must be closed before the application can continue. The user can continue the application by clicking the OK button in the message box.

In Visual Basic, the message in a message box window is displayed using a procedure named Show, which is found in the MessageBox class. The syntax for the statement that displays a message in a message box is shown in Figure 5-18.

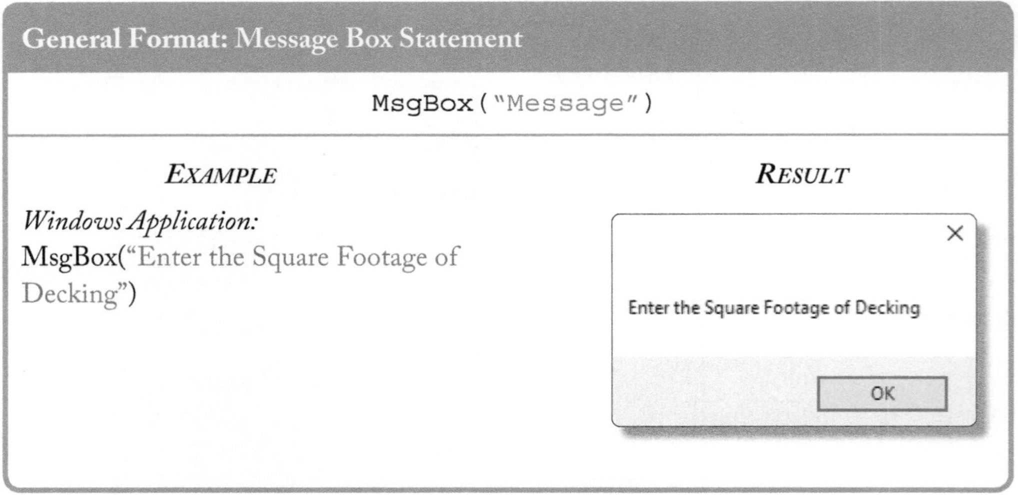

General Format: Message Box Statement
MsgBox("Message")
Example
Result
Windows Application:
MsgBox("Enter the Square Footage of Decking")
Enter the Square Footage of Decking
OK

FIGURE 5-18

The string message shown in the parentheses will appear in the message box when the code is executed. The string message is considered an argument of the procedure. You will recall that an argument is a value passed to a procedure. The first argument for the MsgBox command contains the message to be printed in the message box window during execution.

The example in Figure 5-19 illustrates the code that could be used in the Calculate button click event handler. This code could be executed if the user clicks the Calculate button without entering a numeric value in the Square Footage text box (Figure 5-16 on page 237).

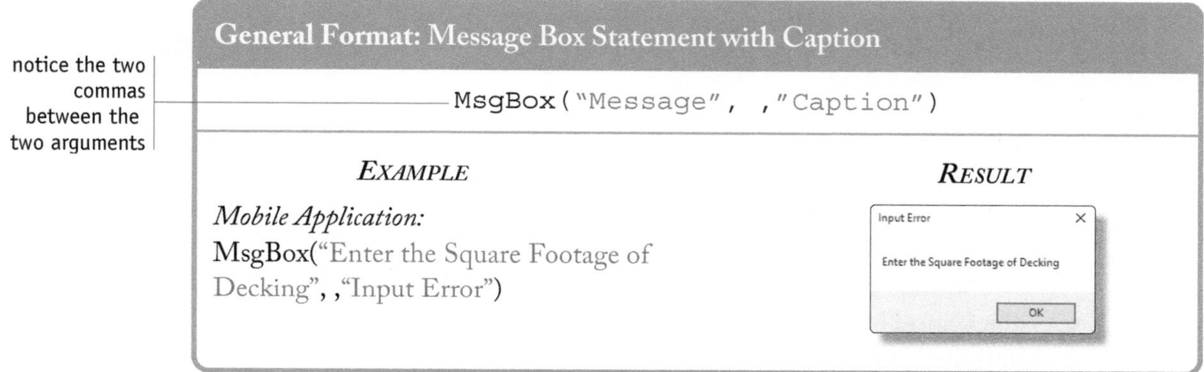

FIGURE 5-19

Display Message Box Captions

A message box can be displayed during execution with a variety of arguments. For example, by using the syntax shown in Figure 5-19, a message box can display a message and a caption in the title bar (two arguments with two commas between the arguments).

The title bar in the example in Figure 5-19 displays a caption and the message box displays a message. In many applications, the caption is used to give further information to the user.

Message Box Buttons

The general format for changing the button command from OK to another button type is shown in Figure 5-20. The button entry can be a command or a value representing a command.

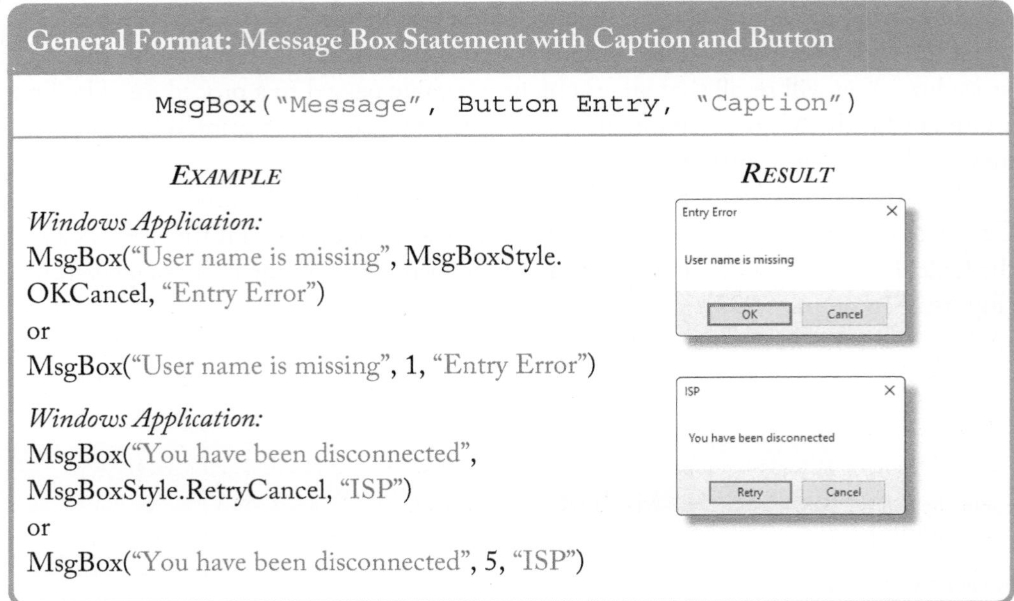
General Format: Message Box Statement with Caption and Button

```
MsgBox("Message", Button Entry, "Caption")
```

EXAMPLE

Windows Application:
MsgBox("User name is missing", MsgBoxStyle.OKCancel, "Entry Error")
or
MsgBox("User name is missing", 1, "Entry Error")

Windows Application:
MsgBox("You have been disconnected", MsgBoxStyle.RetryCancel, "ISP")
or
MsgBox("You have been disconnected", 5, "ISP")

RESULT

FIGURE 5-20

In the first example in Figure 5-20, the buttons specified are the OK button and the Cancel button. In the second example, the buttons shown are the Retry button and the Cancel button.

Figure 5-21 shows all the possible entries that can be placed in the Button Entry portion of the argument passed to the Show procedure.

MsgBoxButtons Arguments	Value	Use
MsgBoxStyle.OKOnly	0	Displays an OK button — default setting
MsgBoxStyle.OKCancel	1	Displays an OK and Cancel button
MsgBoxStyle.AbortRetryIgnore	2	After a failing situation, the user can choose to Abort, Retry, or Ignore
MsgBoxStyle.YesNoCancel	3	Displays Yes, No, and Cancel buttons
MsgBoxStyle.YesNo	4	Displays Yes and No buttons
MsgBoxStyle.RetryCancel	5	After an error occurs, the user can choose to Retry or Cancel

FIGURE 5-21

Message Box Icons

In the button entry portion of the argument (the second argument), you can add a message box icon (Figure 5-22). The word "or" connects the button entry to the icon entry.

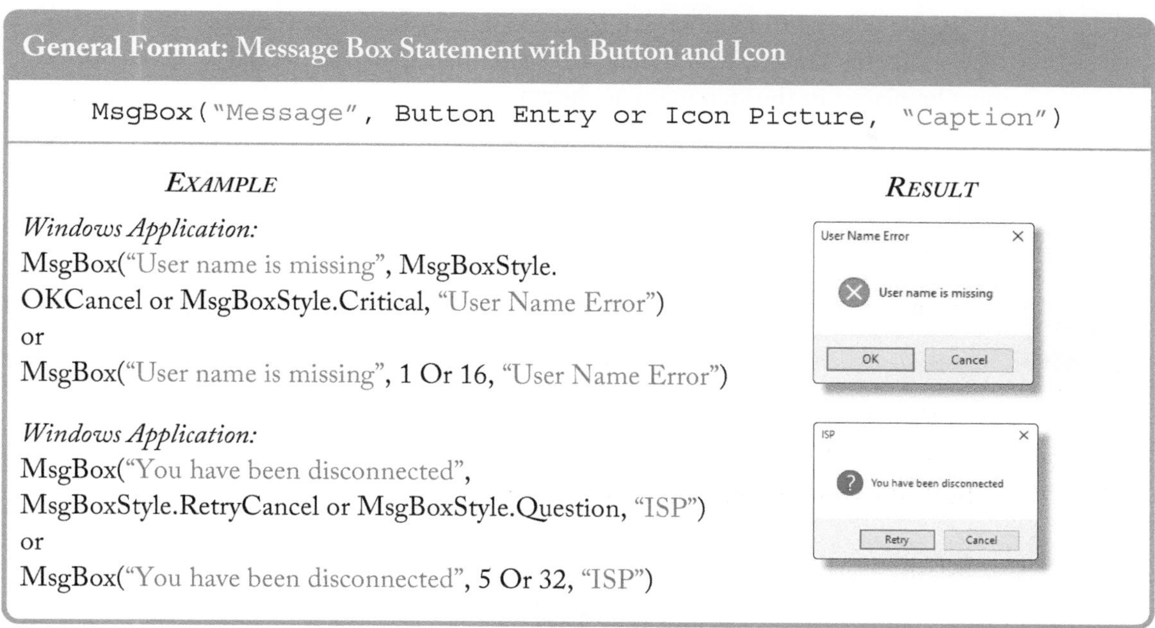

General Format: Message Box Statement with Button and Icon

```
MsgBox("Message", Button Entry or Icon Picture, "Caption")
```

EXAMPLE

Windows Application:
MsgBox("User name is missing", MsgBoxStyle.
OKCancel or MsgBoxStyle.Critical, "User Name Error")
or
MsgBox("User name is missing", 1 Or 16, "User Name Error")

Windows Application:
MsgBox("You have been disconnected",
MsgBoxStyle.RetryCancel or MsgBoxStyle.Question, "ISP")
or
MsgBox("You have been disconnected", 5 Or 32, "ISP")

RESULT

FIGURE 5-22

The picture icon represents the MsgBoxStyle that can be displayed as a graphic icon in the message box. Both examples in Figure 5-22 show an icon added to the message box.

The picture icon in the second argument can contain any of the entries shown in Figure 5-23.

MsgBoxStyle Icons	Value	Icon	Use
MsgBoxStyle.Critical	16		Alerts the user to an error
MsgBoxStyle.Question	32		Displays a question mark
MsgBoxStyle.Exclamation	48		Alerts the user to a possible problem
MsgBoxStyle.Information	64		Displays an information icon

FIGURE 5-23

In the general formats shown for a message box, you must follow the syntax of the statements exactly, which means the commas, quotation marks, and parentheses must be placed in the statement as shown.

You can also add values to display both the buttons and a picture icon. In Figure 5-24, the value of the message button type AbortRetryIgnore is 2 and the value of the critical icon is 16. If you add 16 plus 2, the result is 18.

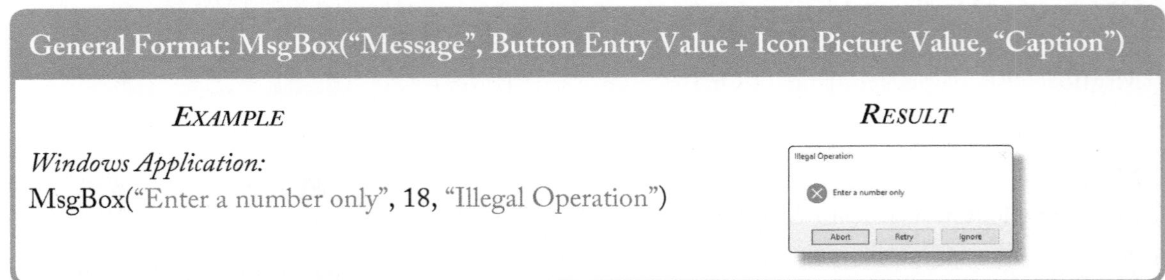

General Format: MsgBox("Message", Button Entry Value + Icon Picture Value, "Caption")

EXAMPLE	*RESULT*
Windows Application: MsgBox("Enter a number only", 18, "Illegal Operation")	

FIGURE 5-24

Message Box IntelliSense

When you enter the code for a message box, IntelliSense can assist you. For example, the message box you create in the following steps contains a message, caption, and buttons. To use IntelliSense to enter the code, you can complete the following steps:

STEP 1 In the code window, inside the event handler you are coding, type msg to display MsgBox in the IntelliSense list.

IntelliSense displays a list of the allowable entries (Figure 5-25). When you type msg, MsgBox is selected in the IntelliSense list.

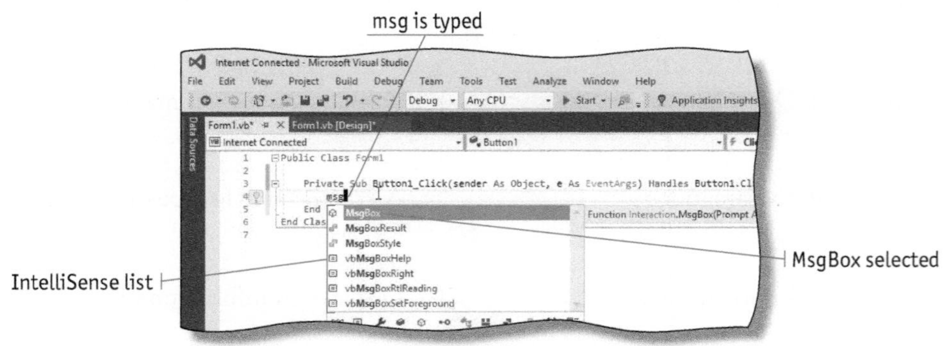

FIGURE 5-25

STEP 2 Press the TAB key to select MsgBox in the IntelliSense list. Type the following text: ("You have been disconnected from the Internet", m)

The first argument for the message box is entered (Figure 5-26). IntelliSense displays a list of allowable entries for the second argument.

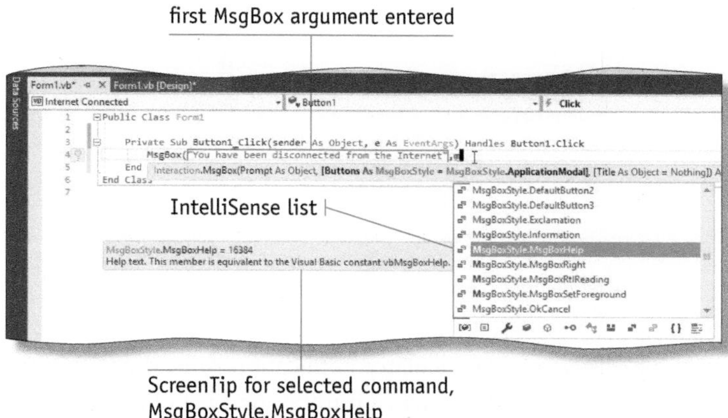

FIGURE 5-26

STEP 3 Select the MsgBoxStyle.AbortRetryIgnore argument by pressing the up arrow until the correct argument is highlighted. Type a comma, then type "ISP" and a right parenthesis.

The MsgBoxStyle.AbortRetryIgnore argument is selected. Next, the comma and the caption "ISP" are entered with a right parenthesis (Figure 5-27).

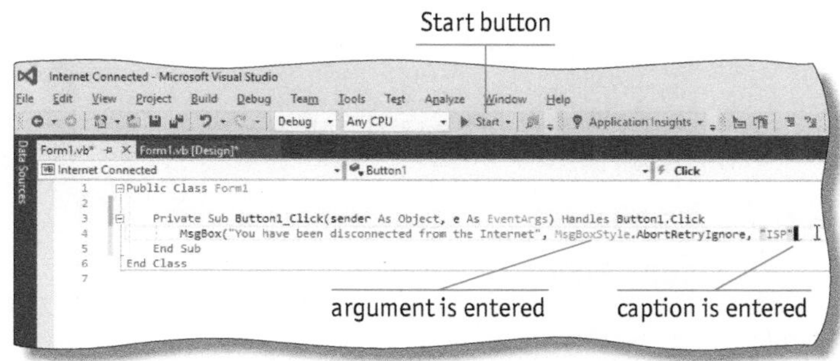

FIGURE 5-27

STEP 4 Click the Start button on the Standard toolbar.

The application runs, displaying the message box that shows the message, buttons, and caption (Figure 5-28).

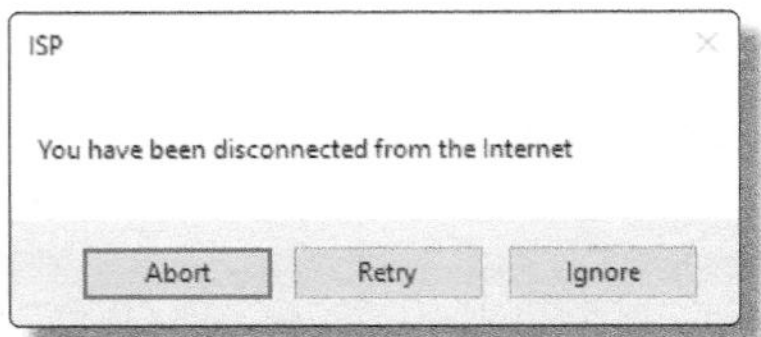

FIGURE 5-28

String Concatenation

Recall that when the Decking Cost Calculator application runs, the user enters the square footage of the deck. If the user enters a number that is not greater than zero, such as –6, a message box displays "You entered –6. Enter a Positive Number", as shown in Figure 5-29.

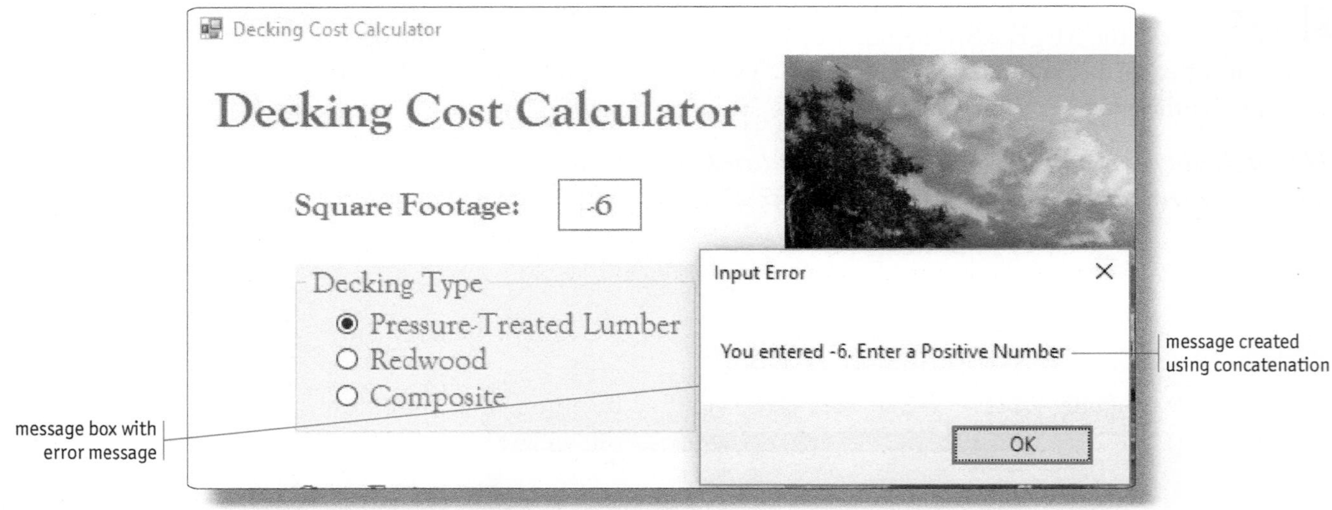

FIGURE 5-29

Franck Boston/Shutterstock.com

To create the message in the message box, you can use concatenation, which you learned about in Chapter 4. In Figure 5-29, the string message is constructed by joining a string ("You entered"), a variable named decFootage that contains the entered square footage (which must be converted to a string), and a string for the final part of the message (". Enter a Positive Number"). The code in Figure 5-30 creates the message box.

```
MsgBox("You entered " & decFootage.ToString() & ". Enter a Positive Number", , "Input Error")
```

FIGURE 5-30

You will recall that the operator to concatenate strings is the ampersand (&). When the statement is executed, the three string elements are joined together (concatenated) to form the one string that is displayed in the message box.

Make Decisions with Conditional Statements

In the Decking Cost Calculator application, users can select one of three types of decking: pressure-treated lumber, redwood, or composite. The price per square foot is based on the user's choice of decking. To select the decking type, the user must click one of three radio buttons titled Pressure-Treated Lumber, Redwood, and Composite. Then, based on the choice, the application uses a different decking cost.

> **HEADS UP**
>
> In older versions of Visual Basic, the plus (+) sign was used to concatenate strings instead of the ampersand (&) symbol. The + sign still functions for concatenation, but it can be confusing because it looks like the plus sign used in addition. You should always use the ampersand.

Visual Basic uses decision structures to deal with the different conditions that occur based on the values entered into an application. A **decision structure** is one of the three fundamental control structures used in computer programming. For example, if the user clicks the Redwood radio button, the decking cost is set to $7.75 per square foot. The statement that tests the radio button is called a **conditional statement**. The condition to check is whether the Redwood radio button is selected. If so, the decking cost is set to $7.75. The cost of the decking only includes the materials and not the installation.

When a condition is tested in a Visual Basic program, the condition is either true or false. For example, when checking to determine if the Redwood radio button is selected, the condition can be either true (the button is checked) or false (is not checked). All conditional statements result in the tested condition being either true or false.

To implement a conditional statement and the statements that are executed when a condition is true or false, Visual Basic uses the If statement and its variety of formats. You will learn about the If statement in the following sections.

Use the If . . . Then Statement

In the sample program, an If . . . Then statement is used to determine the cost of the decking. The simplest form of the If . . . Then statement is shown in Figure 5-31.

```
5        If condition Then
6            Statement(s) executed when condition is true
7        End If
8
```

FIGURE 5-31

In Figure 5-31, when the condition tested in the If statement on line 5 is true, the statement(s) between the If and the End If keywords will be executed. If the condition is not true, no statements between the If and End If keywords will be executed, and program execution will continue with the statement(s) after the End If statement.

HEADS UP

If Visual Basic does not automatically indent the code in an If . . . Then statement, follow these steps: (1) click Tools on the menu bar and then click Options; (2) if necessary, expand Text Editor in the left panel; (3) if necessary, expand Basic in the left panel; (4) if necessary, click Advanced in the left panel; (5) ensure that the "Pretty listing (reformatting) of code" check box contains a check mark; (6) click the OK button in the Options dialog box.

Visual Basic automatically indents statements to be executed when a condition is true or not true to indicate which lines of code are within the conditional If . . . Then structure. This is why the statement on line 6 in Figure 5-31 on the previous page is indented. The End If keywords terminate the If . . . Then block of code. After executing the If . . . Then block, execution continues with any statements that follow the closing End If statement.

Relational Operators

In Figure 5-31, the condition portion of the If . . . Then statement means a condition is tested to determine if it is true or false. The conditions that can be tested are as follows:

1. Is one value equal to another value?
2. Is one value not equal to another value?
3. Is one value greater than another value?
4. Is one value less than another value?
5. Is one value greater than or equal to another value?
6. Is one value less than or equal to another value?

To test these conditions, Visual Basic provides relational operators that are used within the conditional statement to express the relationship being tested. Figure 5-32 shows these relational operators.

Relational Operator		Meaning	Example	Resulting Condition
1	=	Equal to	8 = 8	True
2	<>	Not equal to	6 <> 6	False
3	>	Greater than	7 > 9	False
4	<	Less than	4 < 6	True
5	> =	Greater than or equal to	3 > = 3	True
6	< =	Less than or equal to	7 < = 5	False

FIGURE 5-32

A condition tested using a relational operator is evaluated as true or false. Example 1 tests whether 8 is equal to 8. Because they are equal, the resulting condition is true. Example 2 tests whether 6 is not equal to 6. Because they are equal, the resulting condition is false. Similarly, Example 5 tests whether 3 is greater than or equal to 3. Because they are equal, the resulting condition is true.

As an example of using a relational operator, consider the following problem in which an If statement is used to determine if someone is old enough to vote. If the value in the intAge variable is greater than or equal to 18, then the person is old enough to vote. If not, the person is not old enough to vote. The If . . . Then statement to test this condition is shown in Figure 5-33.

```
        If intAge >= 18 Then
            lblVotingEligibility.Text = "You are old enough to vote"
        End If
```

FIGURE 5-33

In Figure 5-33, if the value in the intAge variable is greater than or equal to 18, the string value "You are old enough to vote" is assigned to the Text property of the lblVotingEligibility Label object. If not, then no processing occurs based on the conditional statement, and any statement(s) following the End If keywords will be executed.

You can see in Figure 5-33 that several keywords are required in an If . . . Then statement. The word If must be the first item. Next, the condition(s) to be tested are stated, followed by the word Then. This keyword is required in an If statement.

The End If keywords follow the statements to be executed when the condition is true. This entry is also required. It signals to the Visual Basic compiler that the statements following it must be executed regardless of the result of the conditional statement; that is, the End If keywords are the last element within the If block, and no subsequent statements depend on the If block for execution.

To enter the If . . . Then statement shown in Figure 5-33, you can complete the following steps:

STEP 1 With the insertion point in the correct location in the code, type if and then press the SPACEBAR.

The statement begins with the word If (Figure 5-34). The If command is displayed in blue because it is a Visual Basic keyword. You can type uppercase or lowercase letters.

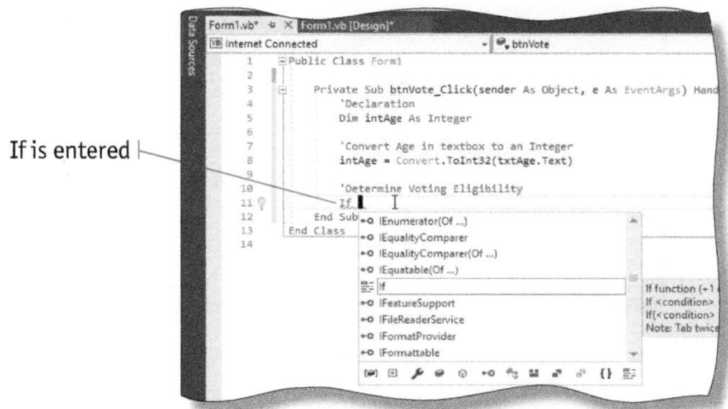

FIGURE 5-34

HEADS UP

Always place the words If and Then on the same programming line. If you use IntelliSense, this is done automatically for you. The End If statement, which terminates the decision structure, also should be on a line by itself.

STEP 2 Type `inta` to select the variable named intAge in the IntelliSense list. Type `>=18` as the condition to be tested. Press the ENTER key.

The If... Then statement is entered in the code window (Figure 5-35). When the ENTER key is pressed, Visual Basic adds the keyword Then to the end of the If statement line of code and inserts spaces between the elements of the statement for ease of reading. In addition, Visual Basic inserts the End If keywords following a blank line. Notice the keywords Then and End If are capitalized and displayed in blue.

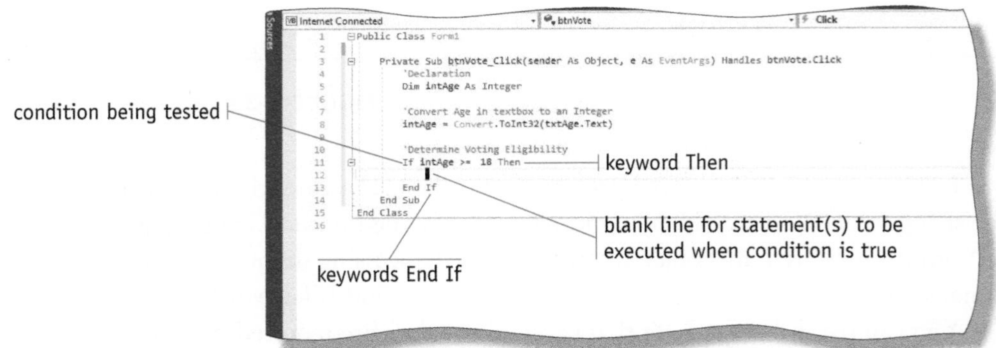

FIGURE 5-35

STEP 3 On the blank line (line 12 in Figure 5-35), enter the statement that should be executed when the condition is true. To place the message "You are old enough to vote" in the Text property of the lblVotingEligibility Label object, insert the code shown in Figure 5-33 on the previous page. Remember to use IntelliSense to reference the lblVotingEligibility Label object.

The resulting statement is entered between the If and End If keywords (Figure 5-36). Notice that Visual Basic automatically indents the line for ease of reading. The blank line allows you to enter more statements. If you have no further statements, you can press the delete key to delete the blank line in the If... Then statement.

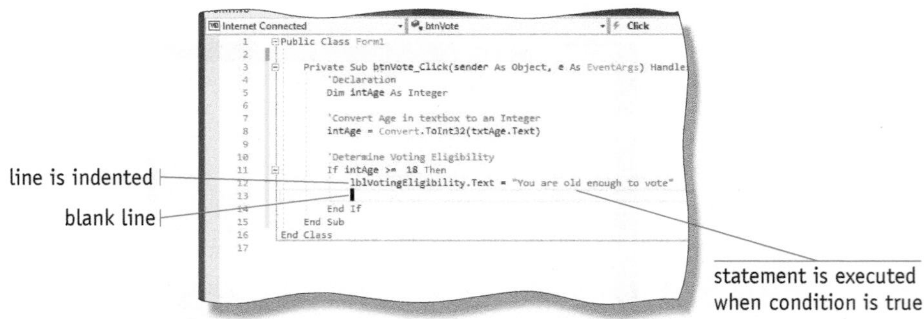

FIGURE 5-36

Compare Strings

You also can write an If . . . Then statement to compare string values using the relational operators shown in Figure 5-32 on page 246. A string value comparison compares each character in two strings, starting with the first character in each string. For example, in the two strings in Figure 5-37, the comparison begins with the first character (a) in each string. Because the characters are equal, the comparison continues with the second character in each string, which is b. Because these characters are equal, the comparison continues with the third character in each string, c. Because all three characters are equal, the strings are considered equal, and the resulting condition from the If statement is true.

```
        Dim String1 As String = "abc"
        Dim String2 As String = "abc"

        If String1 = String2 Then
              lblStringTest.Text = "Equal"
        End If
```

FIGURE 5-37

All characters found in strings, including letters, numbers, and special characters, are in a sequence based on how the characters are coded internally on the computer. In Visual Studio 2017, characters are stored and sequenced in Unicode, which is a coding methodology that can accommodate more than 60,000 characters. Appendix A shows the Unicode sequence for the standard keyboard characters. You will find that numbers have lower Unicode values than uppercase letters and uppercase letters have lower values than lowercase letters.

Using the If . . . Then statement, the following comparisons produce the following resulting conditions:

Example 1:

```
Dim String1 As String = "Powder"
Dim String2 As String = "Power"

If String1 < String2 Then
```

Resulting Condition: True because in the fourth character position, the letter d is less than the letter e.

Example 2:

```
Dim String1 As String = "6"
Dim String2 As String = "T"

If String1 < String2 Then
```

Resulting Condition: True because in a string comparison, a number is less than an uppercase letter.

CRITICAL THINKING

How do you determine if this statement is true or false: If #hashtag < @samtechnow Then?
By using Appendix A, you can see the # symbol is assigned to the Unicode decimal value of 35 and the @ symbol is assigned to the Unicode decimal value of 64. The value of the # symbol is less than that of the @ symbol, making this statement true. To keep up with the latest technology, follow the author Corinne Hoisington on Twitter at @samtechnow.

Example 3:

```
Dim String1 As String = "12"
Dim String2 As String = "9"

If String1 < String2 Then
```

Resulting Condition: True because in a string comparison, the characters in the first position of the string are compared first. Because the value 1 in String1 is less than the value 9 in String2, the entire value in String1 is considered less than the value in String2.

Example 4:

```
Dim String1 As String = "anchor"
Dim String2 As String = "Anchorline"

If String1 > String2 Then
```

Resulting Condition: True because a lowercase letter (the a in the first position of String1) is considered greater than an uppercase letter (the A in the first position of String2).

Compare Different Data Types

Every type of data available in Visual Basic can be compared. Different numeric types can be compared to each other using an If statement. A single string character can be compared to a Char data type. The following examples illustrate some of the allowable comparisons.

Example 1: Decimal compared to Double

```
If decQuarterlySales > dblSalesQuota Then
```

If decQuarterlySales = 110,324.54 and dblSalesQuota = 112,435.54, the condition is false.

Example 2: Decimal compared to Integer

```
If decTirePressureReading > intTirePressureMaximum Then
```

If decTirePressureReading = 30.21 and intTirePressure-Maximum = 30, the condition is true.

Example 3: Double compared to Integer

```
If dblCurrentTemperature >= intHeatDanger Then
```

If dblCurrentTemperature = 94.543 and intHeatDanger = 98, the condition is false.

Example 4: String compared to Char

```
If strChemistryGrade < chrPassingGrade Then
```

If strChemistryGrade = "B" and chrPassingGrade = "C", the condition is true.

Visual Basic allows comparisons between most data types. If you are unsure whether a comparison can be made, write an If statement to ensure that the comparison is working properly.

Use the If . . . Then . . . Else Statement

An If . . . Then statement executes a set of instructions if a condition is true. If the condition is false, the instructions between the If statement and the End If statement are not executed and program execution continues with the statement(s) following the End If statement.

In many applications, the logic requires one set of instructions to be executed if a condition is true and another set of instructions to be executed if a condition is false. For example, a program requirement could specify that if a student's test score is 70 or greater, the message "You passed the examination" should be displayed, while if the test score is less than 70, the message "You failed the examination" should be displayed.

To execute one set of instructions if a condition is true and another set of instructions if the condition is false, you can use the If . . . Then . . . Else statement. Figure 5-38 illustrates the syntax of the If . . . Then . . . Else statement.

```
If condition Then
    Statement(s) executed if condition is true
Else
    Statement(s) executed if condition is false
End If
```

FIGURE 5-38

If the condition tested by the If statement is true, the statement(s) between the Then keyword and the Else keyword will be executed. If the condition tested is false, the statement(s) between the Else keyword and the End If keywords will be executed.

The example in Figure 5-39 shows the use of the If . . . Then . . . Else statement to calculate student fees by testing the student's status.

statement is executed if student is a graduate

```
If strStudentStatus = "Graduate" Then
    decStudentFees = decGraduateFee * intNumberOfUnits
Else
    decStudentFees = decUndergraduateFee * intNumberOfUnits
End If
```

statement is executed if student is not a graduate

FIGURE 5-39

HEADS UP

A condition cannot be true and false at the same time, so both statements for a true condition and statements for a false condition cannot be executed based on a single comparison.

If the student is in graduate school, the student fees are calculated by multiplying the graduate fee by the number of units. If the student is not a graduate student, the student fees are calculated by multiplying the undergraduate fee by the number of units. Notice that a student cannot be both an undergraduate and a graduate student, so either the statement following the Then keyword will be executed or the statement following the Else keyword will be executed.

Compare to an Arithmetic Expression

An If statement can compare an arithmetic expression to a constant or other data type. For example, in Figure 5-40, the withdrawals from a bank account are compared to the value obtained by adding the current balance to deposits and then subtracting account charges.

```
If decWithdrawals > decCurrentBalance + decDeposits - decAccountCharges Then
    lblAccountStatus.Text = "Overdrawn"
Else
    lblAccountStatus.Text = "Balance is Positive"
End If
```

FIGURE 5-40

In Figure 5-40, if the value in the decWithdrawals variable is greater than the current balance plus the deposits minus the account charges, the Text property of the lblAccountStatus Label object is set to Overdrawn. If the value in decWithdrawals is less than or equal to the value from the arithmetic expression, the message “Balance is Positive” is placed in the Text property of the lblAccountStatus Label object. Notice that the arithmetic expression is evaluated prior to the comparison. If the condition is true, the statement between the Then and Else keywords is executed. If the condition is false, the statement between the Else and End If keywords is executed.

Use the If . . . Then . . . ElseIf Statement

Complex logic problems might require a more complex structure than the If . . . Then . . . Else logic structure. For example, consider the following logical problem that must be solved in a computer program:

An online store charges a shipping fee based on the dollar amount of the order being shipped. The rules are as follows:

1. If the order amount is above $500, the shipping cost is $30.
2. If the order amount is more than $400 and not greater than $500, the shipping cost is $25.
3. If the order amount is more than $200 and not greater than $400, the shipping cost is $20.
4. If the order amount is equal to or less than $200, the shipping cost is $15.

When one of the conditions is found to be true, the rest of the conditions are not tested because the correct condition has been found. To solve this problem, you should think this way:

1. If the order amount is greater than $500.00, then the shipping cost is $30.00, and no more processing is needed to determine the shipping cost.
2. If, however, the order amount is not greater than $500.00, you must check further to see if it is greater than $400.00 (400.01 through 500.00). If so, the shipping cost is $25.00.
3. If the order amount is not greater than $400.00, the next step is to check whether it is greater than $200.00. In other words, check within the range of $201.00 to $400.00. If this is true, the shipping cost is $20.00.
4. If none of the above is true, then the order amount must be less than or equal to $200. In this case, the shipping cost is $15.00.

As you can see, a simple If . . . Then . . . Else statement could not solve this logic problem because the structure tests only a single condition and specifies the processing based on whether the condition is true or false. For a problem in which multiple conditions must be tested, the If . . . Then . . . ElseIf statement might be appropriate. The general format of the If . . . Then . . . ElseIf statement is shown in Figure 5-41.

```
105         If decOrderAmount > 500D Then
106             Statement(s) executed if condition is true
107         ElseIf decOrderAmount > 400D Then
108             Statement(s) executed if condition is true
109         ElseIf decOrderAmount > 200D Then
110             Statement(s) executed if condition is true
111         ElseIf decOrderAmount > 0D Then
112             Statement(s) executed if condition is true
113         End If
```

FIGURE 5-41

Once a condition is true in the code in Figure 5-41 on the previous page, Visual Basic bypasses the rest of the ElseIf statements. For example, assume the order amount is $455. The first condition tests whether the order amount is greater than 500. The first condition would test false because 455 is not greater than 500.

Next, the ElseIf entry will test whether 455 is greater than 400. Because the value 455 is greater than 400, the condition is true and the statement(s) on line 108 will be executed. The remaining ElseIf statements will not be evaluated because the true condition has been found.

Separate If . . . Then statements are not used in the example in Figure 5-41 because each condition would have to be tested even though a condition had already been found to be true. When using an If . . . Then . . . ElseIf statement, any remaining conditions are not tested after a condition is found to be true, making the process faster and more efficient.

HEADS UP

When testing conditions like those in the example in Figure 5-41, make sure that you do not leave a number out of the range of numbers being tested. For example, if one ElseIf statement tests decOrderAmount > 400.00 and the next ElseIf statement tests < 400.00, the value 400.00 has not been tested and the program will not properly process the value 400.00.

Trailing Else Statements

You may want to include a trailing Else statement at the end of an If . . . Then . . . ElseIf conditional statement to handle a condition that does not meet any of the previous conditions tested. In the example in Figure 5-42, the code is determining whether the user is eligible for Social Security benefits. If the user's age is greater than or equal to 65, the user receives full benefits. If the user's age is between 0 and 65, the user is not eligible for benefits.

```
115         If intAge >= 65 Then
116             lblSocialSecurity.Text = "Full Benefits"
117         ElseIf intAge > 0 Then
118             lblSocialSecurity.Text = "Not Eligible for Benefits"
119         Else
120             lblSocialSecurity.Text = "Invalid Age"
121         End If
```

FIGURE 5-42

In Figure 5-42, the statement on line 120 that follows the trailing Else statement on line 119 is executed if the number in the intAge variable does not meet the conditions stated in the previous If statements. For example, if the intAge variable contains a negative value such as –12, the Text property of the lblSocialSecurity Label object will be set to "Invalid Age."

Nested If Statements

At times, more than one decision has to be made to determine what processing must occur. For example, if one condition is true, a second condition may need to be tested before the correct code is executed. To test a second condition only after determining that a first condition is true (or false), you must place an If statement within another If statement. When you place one If statement within another one, the inner If statement is said to be nested within the outer If Statement. The syntax of a nested If statement is shown in Figure 5-43.

In Figure 5-43, if the first condition tested is true, the statements following the keyword Then are executed. The statement to be executed when the first condition is true is another If statement (line 124) that tests the second condition. This second If statement is said to be a nested If statement or an inner If statement. If the second condition is true, the program executes the statement(s) on line 125 following the keyword Then for the first inner If statement. If the second condition is not true, the program executes the statement(s) on line 127 following the keyword Else for the first inner If statement. The End If entry (line 128) follows the first inner If statement, indicating the end of the effect of the first inner If statement.

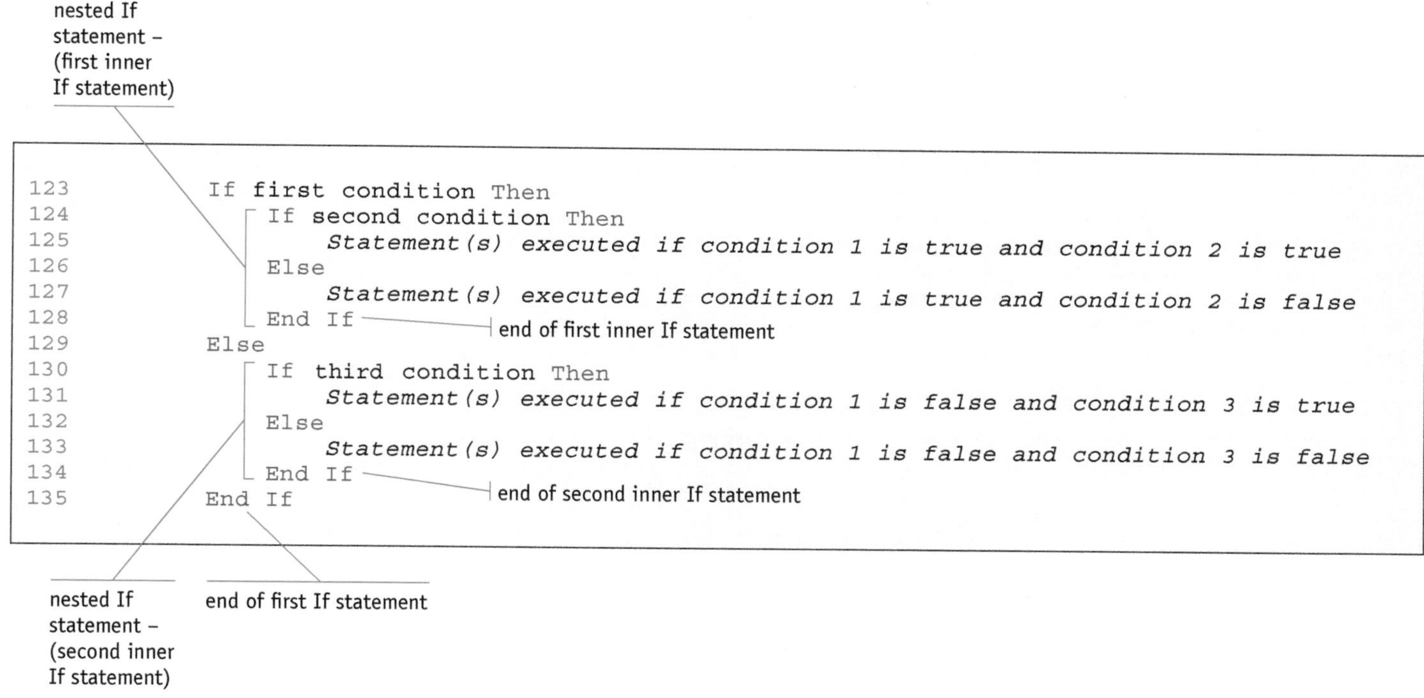


```
123    If first condition Then
124        If second condition Then
125            Statement(s) executed if condition 1 is true and condition 2 is true
126        Else
127            Statement(s) executed if condition 1 is true and condition 2 is false
128        End If
129    Else
130        If third condition Then
131            Statement(s) executed if condition 1 is false and condition 3 is true
132        Else
133            Statement(s) executed if condition 1 is false and condition 3 is false
134        End If
135    End If
```

FIGURE 5-43

If the first condition is not true, then the program executes the statements following the keyword Else on line 129 for the first If statement. The statement to be executed when the first condition is not true is an If statement that tests the third condition (line 130). If the third condition is true, the program executes the statement(s) on line 131 following the Then keyword of the second inner If statement. Finally, if the second inner If statement that tests the third condition is false, the statements on line 133 are executed.

To illustrate a nested If statement, assume a college has the following admissions policy: If an applying student has a GPA (grade point average) greater than 3.5 and a score greater than 1000 on the SAT college entrance exam, then that student is granted admission. If an applying student has a GPA greater than 3.5 but an SAT score of 1000 or lower, the student is advised to retake the SAT exam. If an applying student has a GPA of 3.5 or lower but an SAT score greater than 1200, the student is granted probationary admission, which means she must achieve a 2.5 GPA in the first semester of college. If an applying student has a GPA of 3.5 or lower and an SAT score of 1200 or lower, the student is denied admission. The nested If statement to process this admission policy is shown in Figure 5-44.

Notice in Figure 5-44 that the test for greater than 1000 on the SAT (line 141) must take place only after the test for a GPA greater than 3.5 (line 140), because the test for greater than 1000 is required only after the program determines that the GPA is greater than 3.5. Therefore, a nested If statement is required. In addition, the test for greater than 1200 (line 147) should occur only after the program determines that

CRITICAL THINKING

Does every If statement need an End If coordinating statement?

Yes. Multiple nested If statements can be confusing to confirm that you have the correct number of End If statements. If you have 9 If statements, double-check that the code also contains 9 End If statements. Aligning each If statement with its coordinating End If statement helps you keep track of the nested statements.

```
If decGPA > 3.5D Then
    If intSatScore > 1000 Then
        lblAdmissionStatus.Text = "You have earned admission"
    Else
        lblAdmissionStatus.Text = "Retake the SAT exam"
    End If
Else
    If intSatScore > 1200 Then
        lblAdmissionStatus.Text = "You have earned probationary admission"
    Else
        lblAdmissionStatus.Text = "You have been denied admission"
    End If
End If
```

FIGURE 5-44

the GPA is 3.5 or lower. As you can see, you should use a nested If statement when a condition must be tested only after another condition has been tested.

Other Nested If Configurations

You can use nested If statements in a variety of forms. Assume, for example, that a school's admissions policy is as follows: If an applying student has a GPA greater than 3.5 and an SAT score greater than 1100, then that student is granted admission. If an applying student has a GPA greater than 3.5 but an SAT score of 1100 or lower, the student is advised to retake the SAT exam. If an applying student has a GPA of 3.5 or lower, the student is denied admission. The nested If statement in Figure 5-45 solves this logic problem.

```
154         If decGPA > 3.5D Then
155             If intSatScore > 1100 Then
156                 lblAdmissionStatus.Text = "You have earned admission"
157             Else
158                 lblAdmissionStatus.Text = "Retake the SAT exam"
159             End If
160         Else
161             lblAdmissionStatus.Text = "You have been denied admission"
162         End If
```

FIGURE 5-45

In Figure 5-45, if the GPA is greater than 3.5, then the first inner If statement on line 155 is executed to determine if the SAT score is greater than 1100. If so, the person has earned admission. If not, the person is advised to retake the SAT exam. If the GPA is not greater than 3.5, the student is denied admission. Notice that an If statement does not follow the Else keyword on line 160. An inner If statement need not follow both the If and the Else keywords.

Sometimes, after a condition is found to be true, a statement must be executed before the inner If statement is executed. For example, assume that if a student's GPA is greater than 3.5, then the student should be informed that her GPA is acceptable for admission. The code in Figure 5-46 implements this condition.

```
164         If decGPA > 3.5D Then
165             lblGPAStatus.Text = "Your GPA is acceptable"
166             If intSatScore > 1100 Then
167                 lblAdmissionStatus.Text = "You have earned admission"
168             Else
169                 lblAdmissionStatus.Text = "Retake the SAT exam"
170             End If
171         Else
172             lblGPAStatus.Text = "Your GPA is not acceptable"
173             lblAdmissionStatus.Text = "You have been denied admission"
174         End If
```

FIGURE 5-46

On line 165 in Figure 5-46, the message "Your GPA is acceptable" is assigned to the Text property of the lblGPAStatus Label object before checking the SAT score. As you can see, after the first condition has been tested, one or more statements can be executed prior to executing the inner If statement. This holds true for the Else portion of the If statement as well.

Match If, Else, and End If Entries

When you write a nested If statement, the inner If statement must be fully contained within the outer If statement. To accomplish this, you must ensure that each Else entry has a corresponding If entry, and an inner If statement must be terminated with an End If entry before either the Else entry or the End If entry for the outer If statement. If you code the nested If statement incorrectly, one or more of its entries will be shown with a blue squiggly line, indicating an error in the structure of the statement.

You also must place the correct executing statements with the If and Else statements within the nested If statement. For example, in Figure 5-47, the code is incorrect because the statements following the Else statements have been switched.

```
If decGPA > 3.5D Then
    lblGPAStatus.Text = "Your GPA is acceptable"
    If intSatScore > 1100 Then
        lblAdmissionStatus.Text = "You have earned admission"
    Else
        lblAdmissionStatus.Text = "You have been denied admission"
    End If
Else
    lblGPAStatus Text = "Your GPA is not acceptable"
    lblAdmissionStatus.Text = "Retake the SAT exam"
End If
```


FIGURE 5-47

You must be precise when placing the executing statements in the nested If statement. It is easy to miscode a nested If statement.

Nest Three or More Levels of If Statements

If statements are not limited to two levels of nesting. Three or more levels can be included in a nested If statement, although the statement can become difficult to understand and code. If more than two levels are required to solve a logic problem, great care must be taken to prevent errors such as the one shown in Figure 5-47.

Test the Status of a RadioButton Object in Code

In the Decking Cost Calculator application, the user selects one RadioButton in the GroupBox object to select the decking type. The code must check each RadioButton to determine if it has been selected by the user. When the user selects a radio button, its Checked property is changed from False to True. In addition, the Checked property for other RadioButton objects in the GroupBox object is set to False. This Checked property can be tested in an If statement to determine if the RadioButton object has been selected.

To test the status of the Checked property for the radLumber RadioButton object, a programmer can write the general statement shown in Figure 5-48.

```
        If radLumber.Checked Then
            Statement(s) to be executed if radio button is checked
        End If
```

FIGURE 5-48

Notice in Figure 5-48 that the RadioButton property is not compared using a relational operator. Instead, when a program tests a property that can contain only True or False, only the property must be specified in the If statement. When the property contains True, then the If statement is considered true, and when the property contains False, then the If statement is considered false.

Test Radio Buttons with the If . . . Then . . . ElseIf Statement

When a program contains multiple RadioButton objects in a Panel object or a GroupBox object, only one of the radio buttons can be selected. The If . . . Then . . . ElseIf statement is used to check multiple radio buttons because once the checked radio button is detected, checking the remaining radio buttons is unnecessary.

In the Decking Cost Calculator application, the user clicks one of three radio buttons (Pressure-Treated Lumber, Redwood, or Composite) to select the type of decking used. When using an If . . . Then . . . ElseIf statement to check the status of the radio buttons, the most likely choice should be checked first. Thus, the fewest number of tests are performed. Therefore, the first If statement should test the status of the Pressure-Treated Lumber radio button (radLumber). If the radLumber button is checked, the Cost Per Square Foot should be set to the value in the decLumberCost variable, which is 2.35. No further testing should be done (Figure 5-49).

```
If decFootage > 0 Then
    ' Determine cost per square foot
    If radLumber.Checked Then
        decCostPerSquareFoot = decLumberCost
    ElseIf radRedwood.Checked Then
        decCostPerSquareFoot = decRedwoodCost
    ElseIf radComposite.Checked Then
        decCostPerSquareFoot = decCompositeCost
    End If
    ' Calculate and display the cost estimate
    decCostEstimate = decFootage * decCostPerSquareFoot
    lblCostEstimate.Text = decCostEstimate.ToString("C")
Else
```

FIGURE 5-49

If the radLumber button is not checked, then the radRedwood button should be tested. If radRedwood is checked, the Cost Per Square Foot should be set to the value in the decRedwoodCost variable (7.75), and no further testing should be done. If the radRedwood button is not checked, then the radComposite button should be tested. If the other two buttons are not checked, then the radComposite button must be checked because one of the three must be checked. The Cost Per Square Foot will be set to the value in the decCompositeCost variable (8.50).

As you learned earlier, during design time, you can set the Checked property to True for the most frequently selected RadioButton to save the user from having to select it. In the Decking Cost Calculator application, after the Cost Per Square Foot has been determined and the Cost Estimate has been calculated, the user can click the Clear button to clear the Square Footage text box, clear the Cost Estimate, and reset the radio buttons so that the Pressure-Treated Lumber button is selected. The code to reset the radio buttons is shown in Figure 5-50.

```
        radLumber.Checked = True
        radRedwood.Checked = False
        radComposite.Checked = False
```

FIGURE 5-50

In Figure 5-50, the Checked property for the radLumber RadioButton object is set to True using the same method you have seen in previous chapters for setting an object property. Similarly, the Checked property for the other two RadioButton objects is set to False. As a result of these statements, the Pressure-Treated Lumber radio button will be selected in the user interface, and the Redwood and Composite radio buttons will not be selected.

Block-Level Scope

In Chapter 4, you learned that the scope of a variable is defined by where it is declared within a program. For example, if a variable is declared within an event handler, then only code within that event handler can reference the variable. Code in one event handler within a program cannot reference a variable declared in another event handler.

Within an event handler, an If . . . Then . . . Else statement is considered a block of code. To review, this statement is the code beginning with the If keyword and ending with the corresponding Else keyword or the code beginning with the Else keyword and ending with the End If keywords. Variables can be declared within the block of code, but they can be referenced only within the block of code where they are declared. For example, variables defined within an If . . . Then block of code fall out of scope (cannot be referenced) outside that block of code. To illustrate this concept, the code in Figure 5-51 shows a variable named intYears declared within an If . . . Then block of code.

```
11          If intAge < 18 Then
12              Dim intYears As Integer
13              intYears = 18 - intAge
14              lblMessage.Text = "You can vote in " & intYears & " years(s)."
15          Else
16              lblMessage.Text = "You can vote!"
17          End If
```

FIGURE 5-51

On line 12 in Figure 5-51, the variable intYears is declared as an Integer variable. On line 13, the variable is used in an arithmetic statement to receive the result of the calculation 18 – intAge, which determines the number of years less than 18 that is stored in intAge. The result in intYears is concatenated with literals in the statement on line 14. The intYears variable can be referenced in any statement between the If keyword and the Else keyword. It cannot be referenced anywhere else in the program, not even in the Else portion of the If statement. When a statement referencing the intYears variable is written outside the area between the If keyword and the Else keyword, a compilation error will occur and the program will not compile and execute.

Although the scope of the intYears variable in Figure 5-51 is between the If keyword on line 11 and the Else keyword on line 15, you should realize that the variable itself perseveres during the execution of the event handler procedure. Therefore, if the If statement in Figure 5-51 is executed a second time, the value in the intYears variable will be the same as when the If statement was completed the first time. To avoid unexpected results when the If statement is executed the second time, you should initialize block variables at the beginning of the block. In Figure 5-51, the statement on line 13 sets the value in the intYears variable immediately after it is declared, which is a good programming technique.

Use Logical Operators

The If statements you have seen thus far test a single condition. In many cases, more than one condition must be true or one of several conditions must be true to execute the statements in the Then portion of the If . . . Then . . . Else statement. When more than one condition is included in an If . . . Then . . . Else statement, the conditions are called a **compound condition**. For example, consider the following business traveling rule: "If the flight costs less than $300 and the hotel is less than $120.00 per night, the business trip is approved." In this case, both conditions — flight less than $300 *and* hotel less than $120.00 per night — must be true for the trip to be approved. If either condition is not true, then the business trip is not approved.

To create an If statement that processes the business traveling rule, you must use a **logical operator**. The most common set of logical operators are listed in Figure 5-52.

Logical Operator	Meaning
And	All conditions tested in the If statement must be true
Or	One condition tested in the If statement must be true
Not	Negates a condition

FIGURE 5-52

For the business traveling rule, you should use the And logical operator.

Use the And Logical Operator

The **And logical operator** allows you to combine two or more conditions into a compound condition that can be tested with an If statement. If any of the conditions stated in the compound condition is false, the compound condition is considered false, and the statements following the Else portion of the If statement will be executed. The code in Figure 5-53 uses the And logical operator to implement the business traveling rule.

```
        If decFlightCost < 300D And decHotelCost < 120D Then
            lblTripMessage.Text = "Your business trip is approved"
        Else
            lblTripMessage.Text = "Your business trip is denied"
        End If
```

FIGURE 5-53

In Figure 5-53, both conditions in the compound condition (flight cost less than 300 and hotel cost less than 120) must be true for the business trip to be approved. If one of the conditions is false, then the compound condition is considered false and the If statement would return a false indication. For example, if the flight cost is 300 or more, the trip will not be approved regardless of the hotel cost. Similarly, if the hotel cost is 120 or more, the trip will not be approved regardless of the flight cost. This process is illustrated in Figure 5-54.

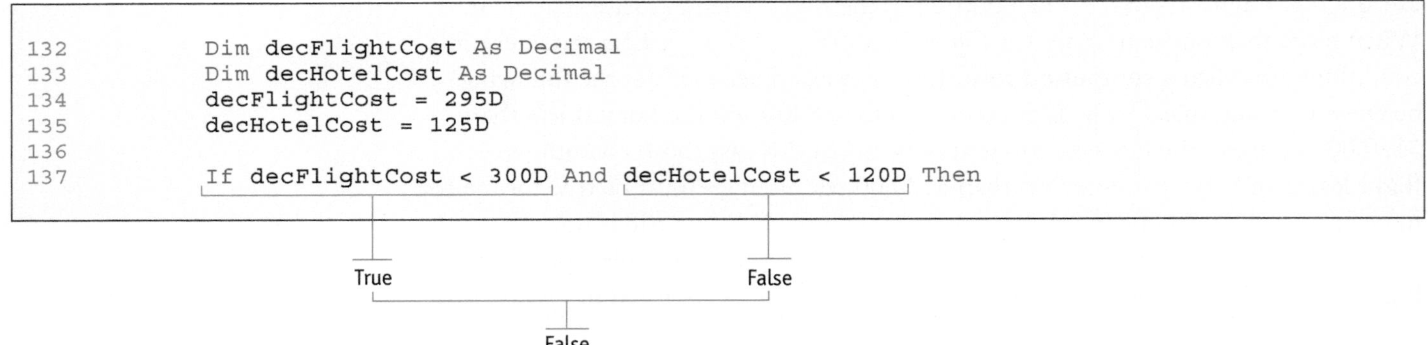

Dim decFlightCost As Decimal
Dim decHotelCost As Decimal
decFlightCost = 295D
decHotelCost = 125D
If decFlightCost < 300D And decHotelCost < 120D Then
True
False
False

FIGURE 5-54

In Figure 5-54, the flight cost is 295, so it is less than 300 and the first part of the compound condition is true. Following the And logical operator, the hotel cost (125) is not less than 120. Therefore, the second part of the compound condition is false. When either condition is false with the And logical operator, the If statement considers the compound condition to be false. The result of the If statement in Figure 5-54 is that the compound condition is considered to be false.

Use the Or Logical Operator

When the **Or logical operator** is used to connect two or more conditions, the compound condition is true if any tested condition is true. Even if four conditional statements are included in the compound condition, only one conditional statement in the compound condition must be true for the entire statement to be considered true.

As an example, assume a college requires each student to have either at least a 3.5 GPA or at least a 1080 score on the SAT exam to be accepted for enrollment. If the student meets one or both conditions, the student is accepted. The If statement in Figure 5-55, which uses the Or logical operator, will solve this problem.

```
If decGPA >= 3.5D Or intSATScore >= 1080 Then
    lblAcceptance.Text = "You have been accepted"
Else
    lblAcceptance.Text = "You are not accepted"
End If
```

FIGURE 5-55

In Figure 5-55, if the decGPA is 3.2 but the intSATScore is 1130, the compound condition would be considered true because at least one of its conditions (intSATScore >= 1080) is true (Figure 5-56).

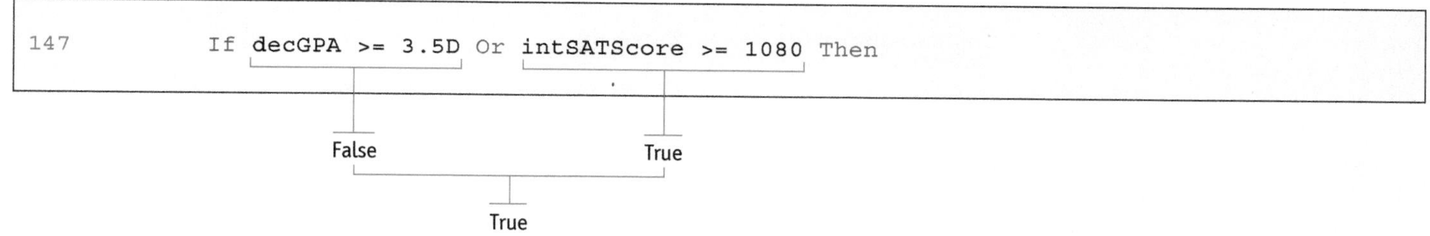

FIGURE 5-56

Use the Not Logical Operator

The **Not logical operator** allows you to state conditions that are best expressed in a negative way. In essence, the Not logical operator reverses the logical value of a condition on which it operates. For example, if a shoe store sells shoes under size 14 from its showroom but requires special orders for larger sizes, the code could use the Not logical operator shown in Figure 5-57 to negate the condition in the statement.

```
        If Not decShoeSize >= 14 Then
            lblOrderPolicy.Text = "Showroom shoe style available"
        Else
            lblOrderPolicy.Text = "Special order needed"
        End If
```

FIGURE 5-57

The statement in Figure 5-57 works, but the use of the Not logical operator makes the If statement somewhat difficult to understand. Generally, a statement that avoids using the Not logical operator is more easily understood. For example, the code in Figure 5-58 accomplishes the same task as the code in Figure 5-57 and is easier to understand.

```
        If decShoeSize < 14 Then
            lblOrderPolicy.Text = "Showroom shoe style available"
        Else
            lblOrderPolicy.Text = "Special order needed"
        End If
```

FIGURE 5-58

Other Logical Operators

The Visual Basic programming language provides three other logical operators, as shown in Figure 5-59.

IN THE REAL WORLD

Many developers avoid using the Not logical operator because it makes the code harder to understand. By removing the Not logical operator and reversing the relational operator, the statement becomes clearer.

Logical Operator	Meaning
Xor	When one condition in the compound condition is true, but not both, the compound condition is true
AndAlso	As soon as a condition is found to be false, no further conditions are tested and the compound condition is false
OrElse	As soon as a condition is found to be true, no further conditions are tested and the compound condition is true

FIGURE 5-59

Order of Operations for Logical Operators

You can combine more than one logical operator in the same If . . . Then statement. In an If statement, arithmetic operators are evaluated first, relational operators are evaluated next, and logical operators are evaluated last. The order of operations for logical operators is shown in Figure 5-60.

Logical Operator	Order
Not	Highest Precedence
And, AndAlso	Next Precedence
Or, OrElse, Xor	Last Precedence

FIGURE 5-60

In most cases, if a developer uses multiple relational or logical operators in an If statement, the order of precedence should be established through the use of parentheses to clarify the sequence of evaluation. As in arithmetic expressions, conditional expressions within parentheses are evaluated before conditional expressions outside parentheses.

Select Case Statement

In some programming applications, different operations can occur based on the value in a single field. For example, in Figure 5-61, the user enters the number of the

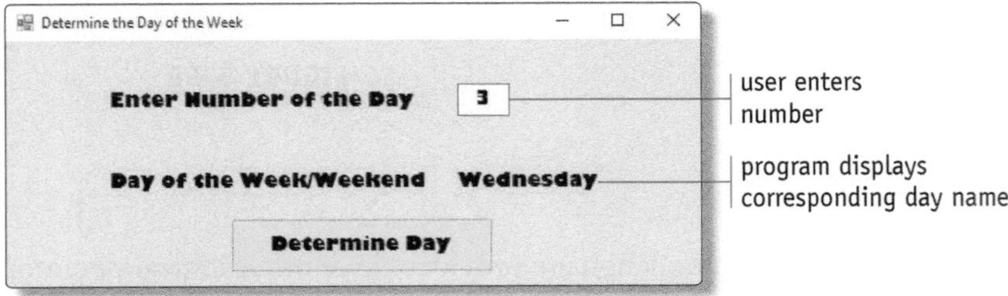

FIGURE 5-61

day in the week and the program displays the name of the day. The program must evaluate the number of the day value and display the name of the correct day.

In Figure 5-61, if the number of the day is 1, then the value Monday should be displayed. If the number of the day is 2, then the value Tuesday should be displayed, and so on. If the number of the day is 6 or 7, then the value Weekend should be displayed. If the user does not enter a value of 1 through 7, the user should be prompted to do so.

To solve this problem, a series of If . . . Then . . . ElseIf statements could be used, but an easier and clearer way to solve the problem is to use the Select Case statement.

When using a Select Case statement, the value in a single field, such as the day number, is evaluated. Based on the value in the field, a distinct action is taken. In this case, the name of the day is displayed.

A general example of the Select Case statement is shown in Figure 5-62.

```
Select Case Test Expression
    Case First Expression
        Statement(s) for First Case
    Case Second Expression
        Statement(s) for Second Case
    Case Third Expression
        Statement(s) for Third Case
    Case Else
        Statement(s) for when the Case Conditions do not match the
            test expressions above
End Select
```

FIGURE 5-62

The code for the Determine Day of Week application is shown in Figure 5-63.

```
Select Case intDayNumber
    Case 1
        lblDayOfWeek.Text = "Monday"
    Case 2
        lblDayOfWeek.Text = "Tuesday"
    Case 3
        lblDayOfWeek.Text = "Wednesday"
    Case 4
        lblDayOfWeek.Text = "Thursday"
    Case 5
        lblDayOfWeek.Text = "Friday"
    Case 6
        lblDayOfWeek.Text = "Weekend"
    Case 7
        lblDayOfWeek.Text = "Weekend"
    Case Else
        lblDayOfWeek.Text = "Enter 1 through 7"
End Select
```

FIGURE 5-63

The Select Case statement begins with the Select Case command. The test expression specifies the value or variable to be tested in the Select Case statement. In Figure 5-63, the variable is intDayNumber. So, when the Select Case statement is executed, each of the cases will be compared to the value in the intDayNumber variable.

Each Case statement specifies the value for which the test expression is checked. For example, the first Case statement on line 14 in Figure 5-63 specifies the value 1. If the value in the variable intDayNumber is equal to 1, the program executes the statement following the first Case statement up to the second Case statement (line 16). In Figure 5-63, the assignment statement on line 15 that sets the Text property of lblDayOfWeek to Monday is executed if the value in intDayNumber is equal to 1. More than one statement can follow a Case statement.

If the expression following the first Case statement is not true, then the next Case statement is evaluated. In Figure 5-63, the Case statement on line 16 checks if the value in intDayNumber is equal to 2. If so, the Text property of lblDayOfWeek is set to Tuesday. This process continues through the remainder of the Case statements.

The Case Else statement on line 28 is an optional entry that includes all conditions not specifically tested in the other Case statements. In Figure 5-63, if the value in the intDayNumber variable is not equal to 1 through 7, then the statement following the Case Else statement is executed. While not required, good programming practice dictates that the Case Else statement should be used so that all cases are accounted for and the program performs a specific action regardless of the value found in the test expression.

The End Select statement is required to end the Select Case statement. When you enter the Select Case statement in Visual Studio 2017, IntelliSense automatically includes the End Select statement.

Select Case Test Expressions

The example in Figure 5-63 on the previous page used an integer as the test expression value, but a value of any data type can be used in the test expression. For example, the test expression in Figure 5-64 uses the Text property of the txtStudentMajor TextBox object as a string value.

```
        Select Case txtStudentMajor.Text
            Case "Accounting"
                lblDepartment.Text = "Business"
            Case "Marketing"
                lblDepartment.Text = "Business"
            Case "Electrical Engineering"
                lblDepartment.Text = "Engineering"
            Case "Biochemistry"
                lblDepartment.Text = "Chemistry"
            Case "Shakespearean Literature"
                lblDepartment.Text = "English"
            Case "Web Design and E-Commerce"
                lblDepartment.Text = "CIS"
            Case Else
                lblDepartment.Text = "Other"
        End Select
```

FIGURE 5-64

In Figure 5-64, the Select Case statement is used to test the value in the Text property of the txtStudentMajor TextBox object and move the corresponding department name to the Text property of the lblDepartment object. The Case statements specify the values to be tested in the text box. The use of a string for the Select Case statement works in the same manner as other data types.

HEADS UP

If you forget to type the Is keyword in the Case Is statement, Visual Studio will insert it for you.

Use Relational Operators in a Select Case Statement

You can use relational operators in a Select Case statement, but you must use the keyword Is with the relational operator. For example, in Figure 5-41 on page 253, an If . . . Then . . . ElseIf statement was used to determine the shipping cost. That same processing could be accomplished using a Select Case statement, as shown in Figure 5-65.

```
        Select Case decOrderAmount
            Case Is > 500D
                decShippingCost = 30D
            Case Is > 400D
                decShippingCost = 25D
            Case Is > 200D
                decShippingCost = 20D
            Case Is > 0D
                decShippingCost = 15D
            Case Else
                decShippingCost = 0D
        End Select
```

FIGURE 5-65

Use Ranges in Select Case Statements

Another way to specify values in a Select Case statement is to use ranges. In Figure 5-66, the Case statements illustrate testing for six different conditions.

```
        Select Case intGradeLevel
            Case 1 To 3
                lblGradeLevelExam.Text = "Early elementary"
            Case 4 To 6
                lblGradeLevelExam.Text = "Late elementary"
            Case 7 To 8
                lblGradeLevelExam.Text = "Middle school"
            Case 9 To 10
                lblGradeLevelExam.Text = "Early high school"
            Case 11
                lblGradeLevelExam.Text = "Late high school"
            Case 12
                lblGradeLevelExam.Text = "Final exam"
            Case Else
                lblGradeLevelExam.Text = "Invalid grade level"
        End Select
```

FIGURE 5-66

As you can see, a range of values is specified in a Case statement by stating the beginning value, the word To, and then the ending value in the range. The Case statements will test the value in the intGradeLevel variable, and the appropriate statements will be executed.

You also can write Case statements so that more than one distinct value is tested. In Figure 5-67, the Case statement tests the individual values of 1, 3, 8, 11, and 17 against the value specified in the intDepartmentNumber variable.

```
        Select Case intDepartmentNumber
            Case 1, 3, 8, 11, 17
```

FIGURE 5-67

Notice in Figure 5-67 that each value in the Case statement is separated by a comma. The code in Figure 5-68 shows a combination of the two techniques, using both commas and a To statement.

```
        Select Case intDepartmentNumber
            Case 2, 4, 7, 12 To 16, 22
```

FIGURE 5-68

Select Which Decision Structure to Use

In some instances, you might need to determine if you should use the Select Case statement or the If . . . Then . . . ElseIf statement to solve a problem. Generally, the Select Case statement is most useful when more than two or three values must be tested for a given variable. For example, in Figure 5-64 on page 266, six different values are checked in the Text property of the txtStudentMajor TextBox object. This is a perfect example of when to use the Select Case statement.

The If . . . Then . . . ElseIf statement is more flexible because more than one variable can be used in the comparison. Programmers can also use compound conditions with the And, Or, and Not logical operators.

Use Code Snippets

Visual Basic includes a library of almost 500 pieces of code, called IntelliSense **code snippets**, that you can insert into an application. Each snippet consists of a complete programming task such as an If . . . Then . . . Else decision structure, sending an email message, or drawing a circle. Inserting these commonly used pieces of code is an effective way to enhance productivity. You also can create your own snippets and add them to the library.

In addition to inserting snippets in your program, you can display a code snippet to ensure that you understand the syntax and requirements for a given type of statement. To insert and display a code snippet for the If . . . Then . . . Else statement, you can complete the following steps:

STEP 1 Right-click the line in the code window where you want to insert the snippet.

Visual Studio displays a shortcut menu (Figure 5-69). It is important to right-click the code window in the exact location where you want the code snippet to appear. If you right-click outside this location, the shortcut menu might list customized choices for the wrong area of code. In addition, if you click in the wrong place, the snippet will be positioned in the incorrect location in your program.

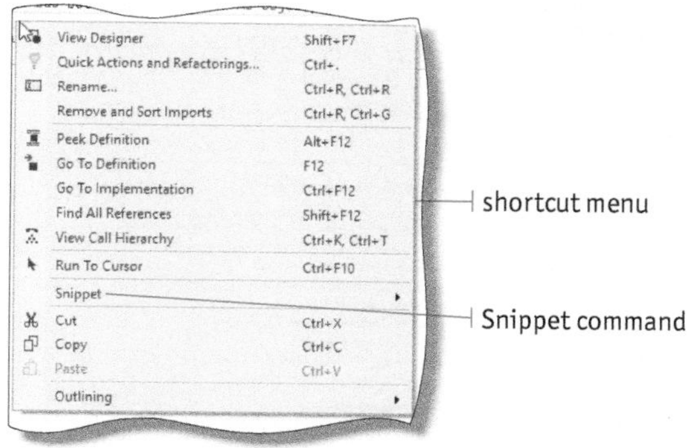

FIGURE 5-69

STEP 2 Click Snippet on the shortcut menu. Click Insert Snippet.

Visual Studio displays a menu of folders that contain snippets (Figure 5-70). The code snippets in each folder correspond to their folder titles.

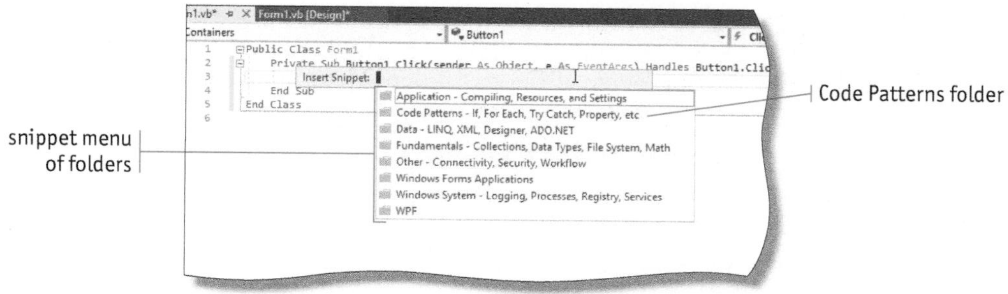

FIGURE 5-70

STEP 3 Double-click the folder named Code Patterns - If, For Each, Try Catch, Property, etc., which contains commonly used code such as the If . . . Then . . . Else statement.

Visual Studio displays a menu of folders for code patterns (Figure 5-71).

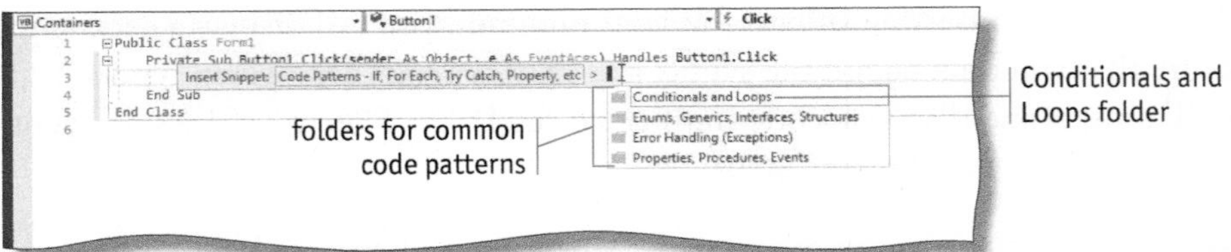

FIGURE 5-71

STEP 4 Double-click the Conditionals and Loops folder because an If . . . Then . . . Else statement is a conditional statement.

Visual Studio displays the list of Conditionals and Loops code snippets (Figure 5-72). Some of these statements will be unfamiliar until you complete Chapter 6, but you can see that the list of code snippets includes several different types of If statements.

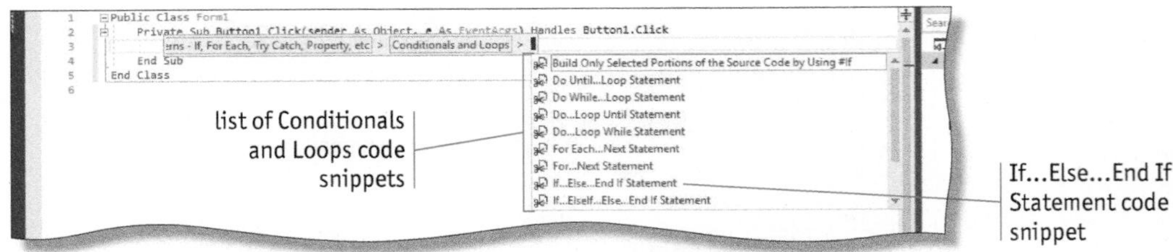

FIGURE 5-72

IN THE REAL WORLD

You can save time by inserting code snippets because you no longer need to search countless code examples just to find a similar piece of code to copy and paste into your solution code.

STEP 5 Double-click the If . . . Else . . . End If Statement code snippet.

The If . . . Else . . . End If Statement code snippet is inserted into the code on the line selected in Step 1 (Figure 5-73). The highlighted text must be replaced by the condition(s) to be tested in the If statement. The programmer must add the code to be executed when the condition is true and the code to be executed when the condition is false.

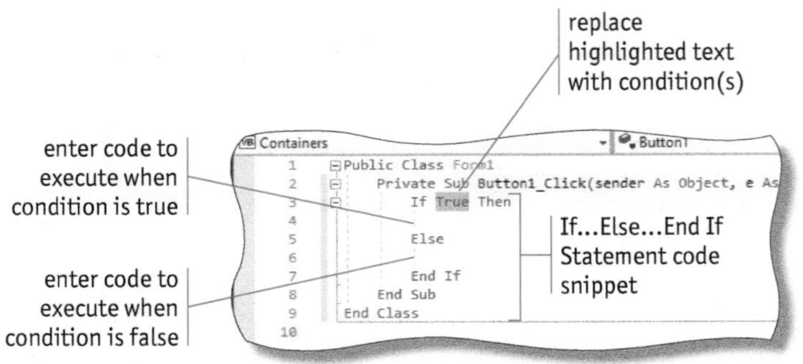

FIGURE 5-73

You must modify the code snippet shown in Figure 5-73 for the code to work properly. You may find that modifying a complicated code snippet is more work than using IntelliSense to enter the statement.

Code snippets are also helpful for learning or reviewing the format and syntax of a statement. For example, if you want to review the syntax of an If . . . Then . . . ElseIf statement, you could insert the statement into the code window and examine it. You could then either click the Undo button to remove the statement, or you could comment out the snippet code and keep it for your review. In many cases when checking syntax, reviewing a snippet is faster and clearer than consulting Visual Basic help.

Validate Data

Since the first days of computers, the phrase "garbage in, garbage out" has described the fact that allowing incorrect input data into a program produces incorrect output. Developers should anticipate that users will enter invalid data. Therefore, they must write code that prevents the invalid data from being used in the program to produce invalid output.

For example, in the Decking Cost Calculator application, the user is asked to enter the number of square feet for the decking. If the user enters a negative number or a letter or even leaves the text box blank, the program should inform the user of the input error and allow the user to reenter a proper value. If the program attempts to process invalid data, unexpected errors can occur, which is not the way a program should respond to invalid input data.

To properly check the square footage value entered by the user, two tests must be performed. First, the program must check the value to ensure it is numeric. Second, the numeric value entered by the user must be checked to ensure it is greater than zero. These tests are explained in the following sections.

Test Input to Determine If the Value Is Numeric

In the Decking Cost Calculator application, if no check is performed on the input data and the user accidentally enters a nonnumeric character such as an "a" or does not enter a value at all, the program will fail when Visual Basic attempts to convert that value to a number. An exception (error) screen will open, and the program will close. Therefore, the program must check the value entered by the user to ensure it is numeric. In addition, if the user enters a nonnumeric value, the program should inform the user of the error and request a valid numeric value.

The Visual Basic **IsNumeric function** can check the input value to determine if it can be converted into a numeric value such as an Integer or Decimal data type. If so, it returns a True Boolean value. If the value is not recognized as a numeric value, the IsNumeric function returns a False Boolean value.

For example, the IsNumeric function can check the value in the Text property of the Square Footage text box. If the user enters a letter such as "a" in the text box, the IsNumeric function will return a False Boolean value because the letter "a" is not numeric.

Because the IsNumeric function returns a Boolean value (True or False), it can be placed within an If statement as the condition to be tested. If the returned value is True, the condition in the If statement is considered true. If the returned value is False, the condition in the If statement is considered false. The code in Figure 5-74 uses an If statement to determine if the Text property of the txtFootage TextBox object is numeric.

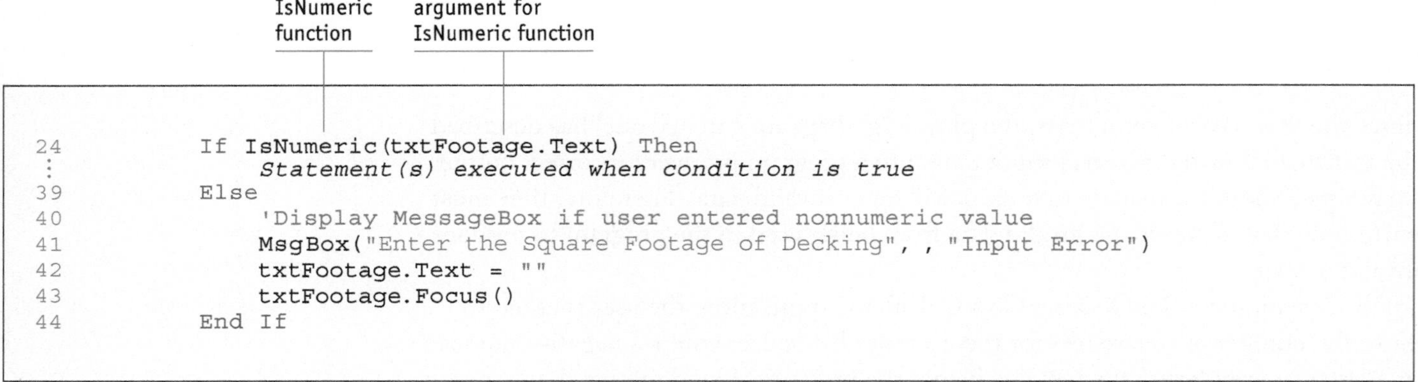


```
24        If IsNumeric(txtFootage.Text) Then
 :            Statement(s) executed when condition is true
39        Else
40            'Display MessageBox if user entered nonnumeric value
41            MsgBox("Enter the Square Footage of Decking", , "Input Error")
42            txtFootage.Text = ""
43            txtFootage.Focus()
44        End If
```

FIGURE 5-74

In Figure 5-74, the If statement on line 24 calls the IsNumeric function. The Text property of the txtFootage TextBox object is the argument for the IsNumeric function. As a result of this specification, the IsNumeric function will analyze the data in the Text property of the txtFootage TextBox object. If the data can be converted to a numeric data type, then the function will return a Boolean value of True. If the data cannot be converted to a numeric data type, the function will return a Boolean value of False.

Once the function has returned a Boolean value, the If statement tests the Boolean value. If it is true, the value in the Text property of the txtFootage TextBox object is numeric, and the appropriate statements are executed. If the condition is false, meaning the value is not numeric, the statements on lines 41-43 are executed. The statement on line 41 displays a message box telling the user to enter the square footage of the decking (see Figure 5-2 on page 229). The caption of the message box is "Input Error". The statement on line 42 clears the Text property. The statement on line 43 sets the focus on the text box so the user can reenter the value.

Check for a Positive Number

If the condition in Figure 5-74 on the previous page is true, the value in the Text property must be converted to a Decimal data type. Then, the program checks to ensure that the entered value is greater than zero. These statements are shown in Figure 5-75.

```
22
23              ' Did user enter a numeric value?
24              If IsNumeric(txtFootage.Text) Then
25                  decFootage = Convert.ToDecimal(txtFootage.Text)
26                  ' Is Square Footage greater than zero
27                  If decFootage > 0 Then
28                      ' Determine cost per square foot
29                      If radLumber.Checked Then
30                          decCostPerSquareFoot = decLumberCost
31                      ElseIf radRedwood.Checked Then
32                          decCostPerSquareFoot = decRedwoodCost
33                      ElseIf radComposite.Checked Then
34                          decCostPerSquareFoot = decCompositeCost
35                      End If
36                      ' Calculate and display the cost estimate
37                      decCostEstimate = decFootage * decCostPerSquareFoot
38                      lblCostEstimate.Text = decCostEstimate.ToString("C")
39                  Else
40                      ' Display error message if user entered a negative value
41                      MsgBox("You entered " & decFootage.ToString() & ". Enter a Positive Number", , "Input Error")
42                      txtFootage.Text = ""
43                      txtFootage.Focus()
44                  End If
45              Else
46                  ' Display error message if user entered a nonnumeric value
47                  MsgBox("Enter the Square Footage of Decking", , "Input Error")
48                  txtFootage.Text = ""
49                  txtFootage.Focus()
50              End If
51          End Sub
52
```

FIGURE 5-75

When the value in the Text property is numeric, it is converted to a Decimal value (line 25). On line 27, the Decimal value is compared to zero. If it is greater than zero, then the processing for a true statement is executed. If the value is not greater than zero, a message box is displayed to inform the user that an invalid entry was made (see Figure 5-29 on page 244). The user then can enter a valid value.

The process of validating input data is fundamental to programming when using a graphical user interface. A well-designed program must ensure that the user enters valid data.

> **CRITICAL THINKING**
>
> **Why is it so important to check that each input value is valid?** As devices become smaller and more mobile, data validation is more important because it is so easy to accidentally enter incorrect characters with your touch keyboard. Developers cannot have their programs and apps crash each time someone makes an erroneous keystroke. Keep in mind that your instructor will test each of your programs with all kinds of keyboard input to verify that your program will not fail.

Program Design

As you have learned, the requirements document identifies the purpose of the program being developed, the application title, the procedures to be followed when using the program, any required equations and calculations, any conditions that must be tested, notes and restrictions that must be followed by the program, and any other comments that would be helpful in understanding the problem. The requirements document for the Decking Cost Calculator application is shown in Figure 5-76. The Use Case Definition document is shown in Figure 5-77.

REQUIREMENTS DOCUMENT

Date: January 29, 2019

Date Submitted:

Application Title: Decking Cost Calculator

Purpose: This application calculates the estimated cost of decking for a job bid or homeowner installation.

Program Procedures: The user should enter the square footage of decking needed and select the type of decking. The estimated cost for the decking job will be displayed.

Algorithms, Processing, and Conditions:

1. The user must be able to enter the number of square feet of decking.
2. The user must be able to select one of three decking types: pressure-treated lumber, redwood, or composite.
3. The user can initiate the calculation and display the cost estimate for the decking.
4. The application computes the cost estimate of the decking based on the number of square feet and the cost of the decking. Pressure-treated lumber costs $2.35 per square foot of decking, redwood costs $7.75 per square foot, and composite costs $8.50 per square foot without the cost of installation.
5. The estimate calculation is square footage * cost per square foot.
6. The cost estimate is displayed in currency format.
7. The user should be able to clear the square footage entered, reset the decking type to pressure-treated lumber, and clear the cost estimate.

Notes and Restrictions:

1. If the user enters a nonnumeric value for the square footage or leaves the TextBox object empty, the user should be advised and asked for a valid entry.
2. If the user enters a negative number for the square footage, the user should be advised and asked for a valid entry.

Comments: The title of the Windows Form should be Decking Cost Calculator.

FIGURE 5-76

USE CASE DEFINITION

1. The window opens and displays the Decking Cost Calculator, a text box requesting the number of square feet for the decking, radio buttons to select the decking type, and two buttons labeled Calculate and Clear.
2. The user enters the square footage and selects one of the decking types.
3. The user clicks the Calculate button.
4. The user will be warned if a nonnumeric value is entered, the text box is left empty, or a negative number is entered.
5. The program displays the cost estimate for the decking materials cost.
6. The user clicks the Clear button to clear the Square Footage text box, set the decking choice to Pressure-Treated Lumber, and erase the cost estimate.
7. The user clicks the Close button to exit the application.

FIGURE 5-77

Event-Planning Document

You will recall that the event-planning document is a table that specifies which objects in the user interface will cause events, the action taken by the user to trigger each event, and the event processing that must occur. The event-planning document for the Decking Cost Calculator application is shown in Figure 5-78.

Event-Planning Document

Program Name: Decking Cost Calculator	**Developer:** Corinne Hoisington	**Object:** frmDecking	**Date:** January 29, 2019
OBJECT	**EVENT TRIGGER**	**EVENT PROCESSING**	
btnCalculate	Click	Ensure data entered is numeric Display error message if data is not numeric or text box is empty Convert data entered to numeric Ensure data entered is greater than zero Display error message if data is not greater than zero Assign decking cost per foot based on type of decking selection Calculate cost (square footage* cost per square foot) Display cost	
btnClear	Click	Clear input text box Clear cost estimate Set the Pressure-Treated Lumber radio button to checked Clear the Redwood radio button Clear the Composite radio button Set focus on input text box	
frmDecking	Load	Set focus on input text box Clear the placement zeros for cost	

FIGURE 5-78

Design and Code the Program

After identifying the events and tasks within the events, the developer is ready to create the program. As you have learned, creating the program means designing the user interface and then entering Visual Basic statements to accomplish the tasks specified in the event-planning document. As the developer enters the code, she also will implement the logic to carry out the required processing.

NOTE TO THE LEARNER

In the following activity, you should complete the tasks within the specified steps. Each of the tasks is accompanied by a Hint Screen. The purpose of the Hint Screen is to indicate where you should perform the activity in the Visual Studio window and to remind you which method to use. If you need further help completing a step, refer to the figure identified by *ref:*.

To design the user interface for the Decking Cost Calculator application and enter the code required to process each event in the program, complete the steps on the next few pages.

Guided Program Development

Phase I: Design the Form

1

- **Create a Windows Application** Open Visual Studio. Create a new Visual Basic Windows Application project by completing the following: Click the New Project button on the Standard toolbar; click Windows Classic Desktop in the left pane; select Windows Forms App; name the project by entering `Decking Cost Calculator` in the Name text box; then click the OK button in the New Project window.

HINT

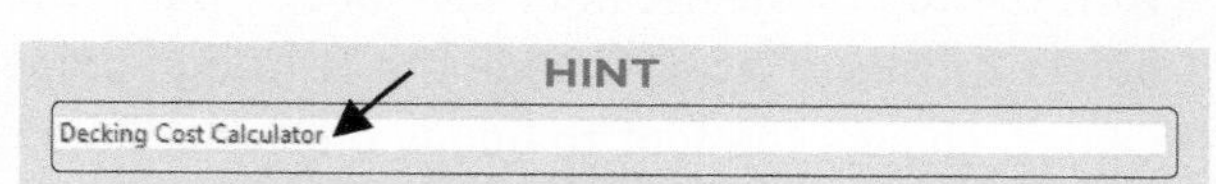

- **Name the Form** In the Solution Explorer pane, right-click Form1.vb and then click Rename. Type `frmDecking.vb` and then press the ENTER key. Click the Yes button to automatically change the form (Name) in the Properties window.

- **Change the Size Property** In the Properties window, change the Size property to `720, 431`.

- **Change the BackColor Property** In the Properties window, change the BackColor property to White.

- **Change the Text on the Title Bar** To change the text on the title bar, click the form, scroll down the Properties window until the Text property is displayed, double-click the right column of the Text property, type `Decking Cost Calculator`, and then press the ENTER key.

- **Add a Heading Label** Drag a label onto the form and name the label `lblHeading`. Set the Text property for the Label object to `Decking Cost Calculator`. Set the font to Goudy Old Style, Bold, 24 points.

HINT

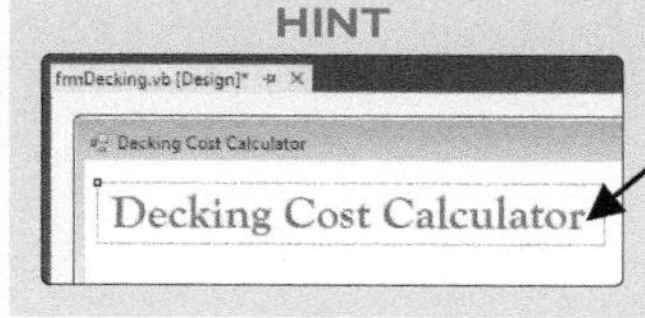

- **Add a Label** Drag a second label onto the frmDecking Form object and name the label `lblSquareFeet`. Set the Text property of the Label object to `Square Footage:`. Set the font to Goudy Old Style, Bold, 16 points.

(continues)

Guided Program Development *continued*

- **Add a TextBox Object** Drag a TextBox object onto the form. Using snap lines, align the top of the TextBox object with the top of the second Label object. Name the TextBox object `txtFootage`. Change the TextAlign property to Center. Change the font to Goudy Old Style, Bold, 16 points. Reduce the width of the TextBox object to closely resemble the one in Figure 5-79. Center the Label object and the TextBox object horizontally below the title label.

A title Label object is displayed on the first line of the form. A Label object and TextBox object occupy the second line of the frmDecking Form object (Figure 5-79). They are centered horizontally below the title label.

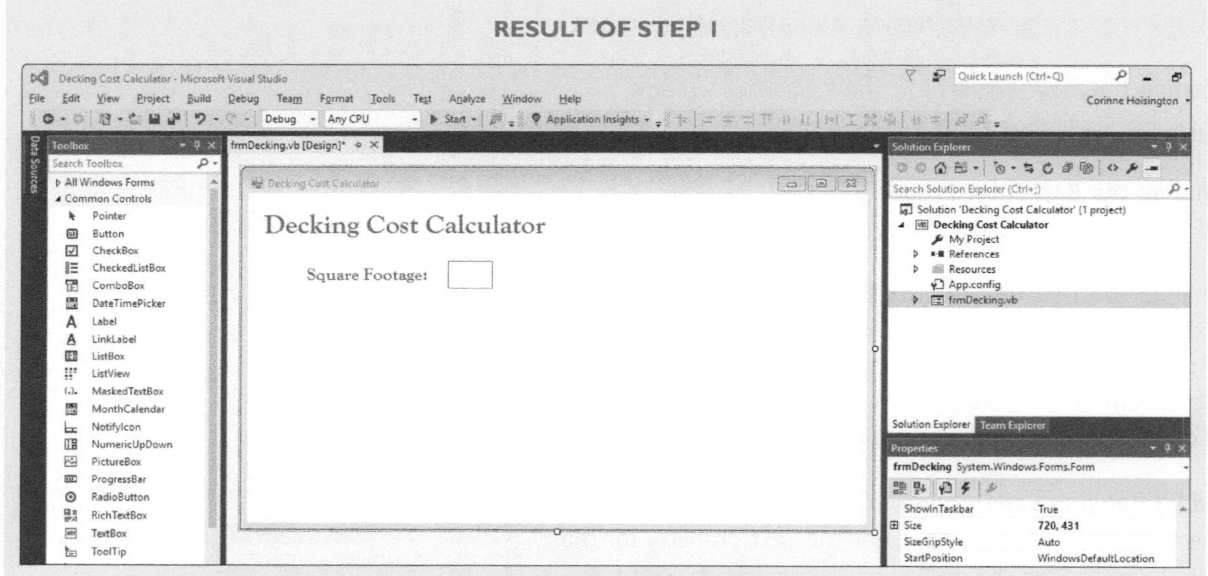

FIGURE 5-79

Guided Program Development *continued*

2

- **Add a GroupBox** Drag a GroupBox object from the Containers category of the Toolbox to the frmDecking Form object. Name the GroupBox `grpDeckType`. Change the Text property to `Decking Type`. Set the size of the GroupBox object to `244, 106`. Change the BackColor of the GroupBox object to AliceBlue. Center the GroupBox object horizontally below the title label object, and change the font to Goudy Old Style, Regular, 14 points (*ref: Figure 5-4*).

HINT

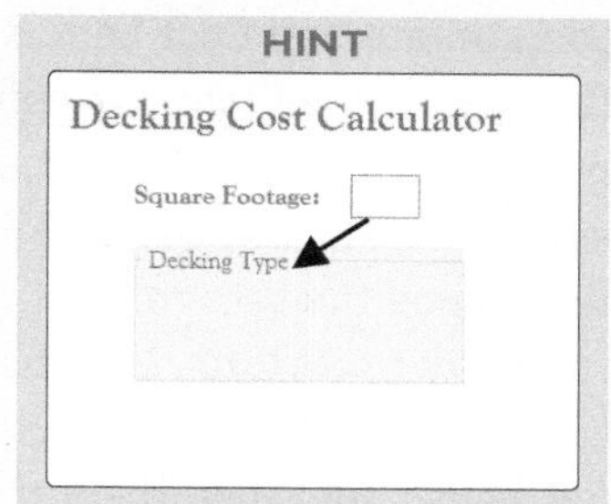

- **Add Radio Buttons** Place three RadioButton objects on the GroupBox object. Name the first RadioButton `radLumber` and change its Text property to `Pressure-Treated Lumber`. Name the second RadioButton `radRedwood` and change its Text property to `Redwood`. Name the third RadioButton `radComposite` and change its Text property to `Composite`. If necessary, select the three RadioButtons and change the font to Goudy Old Style, Regular, 14 points (*ref: Figure 5-7*).

- **Set Radio Button Properties** Click the radLumber RadioButton object and change its Checked property from False to True. Pressure-treated lumber is the decking most commonly used by homeowners (*ref: Figure 5-12*).

The group box and radio buttons are included on the frmDecking Form object (Figure 5-80). The radLumber radio button is selected because it is the most widely use decking type.

RESULT OF STEP 2

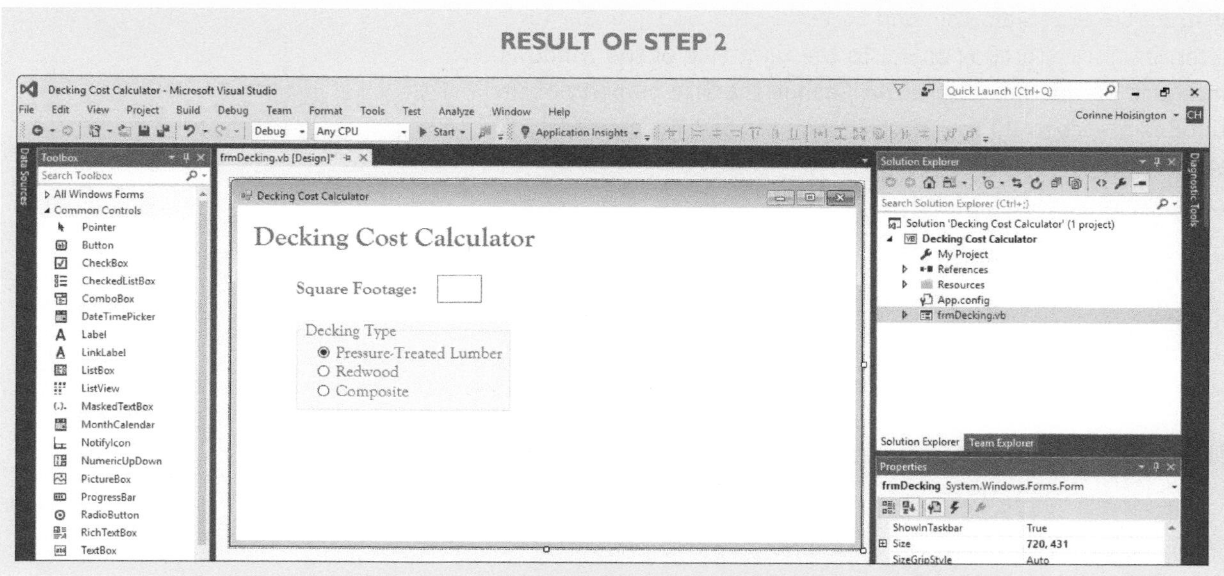

FIGURE 5-80

(continues)

Guided Program Development *continued*

3

- **Add Estimate and Cost Labels** Drag two more Label objects onto the form below the GroupBox object. Align these labels by their tops using snap lines. Name the first label `lblCost`, change its Text property to `Cost Estimate:`, and resize the Label object to view the text. Name the second label `lblCostEstimate` and set its Text property to `$0000.00`. These placement zeros allow you to view the Label object when it is not selected. The placement zeros will be cleared using code when the form is loaded. Change the font for both Label objects to Goudy Old Style, Bold, 16 points. Horizontally center the labels as a unit below the title label.

HINT

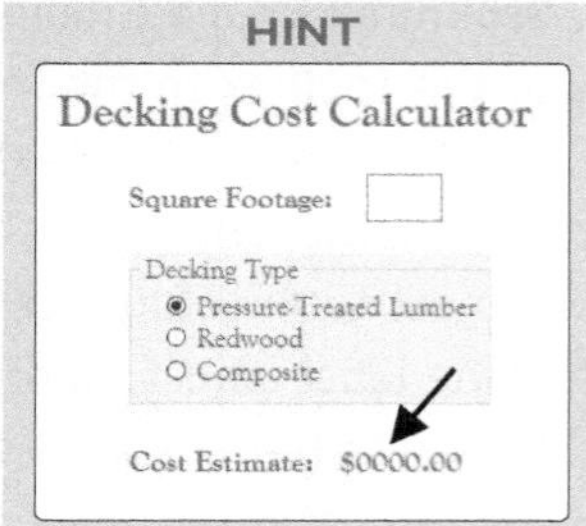

- **Add Calculate and Clear Buttons** Drag two Button objects onto the form. Align the tops of the Button objects using snap lines. Name the left Button object `btnCalculate` and change its Text property to `Calculate`. Name the right Button object `btnClear` and change its Text property to `Clear`. Change the font for these two buttons to Goudy Old Style, Bold, 14 points. Change the size of each button to `116, 41`. Change the BackColor property for each button to White.

- **Change the ForeColor Property** Select every object and change the ForeColor property to Sienna.

- **Add a Picture to the Windows Form** Download the deck.jpg picture by visiting CengageBrain.com and accessing the resources for this chapter. Drag a PictureBox object to the right side of the Windows Form. Name the picture `picDeck`. Change the Size property of the PictureBox object to `338, 390`. Change the SizeMode property to StretchImage.

Guided Program Development *continued*

The user interface is complete (Figure 5-81).

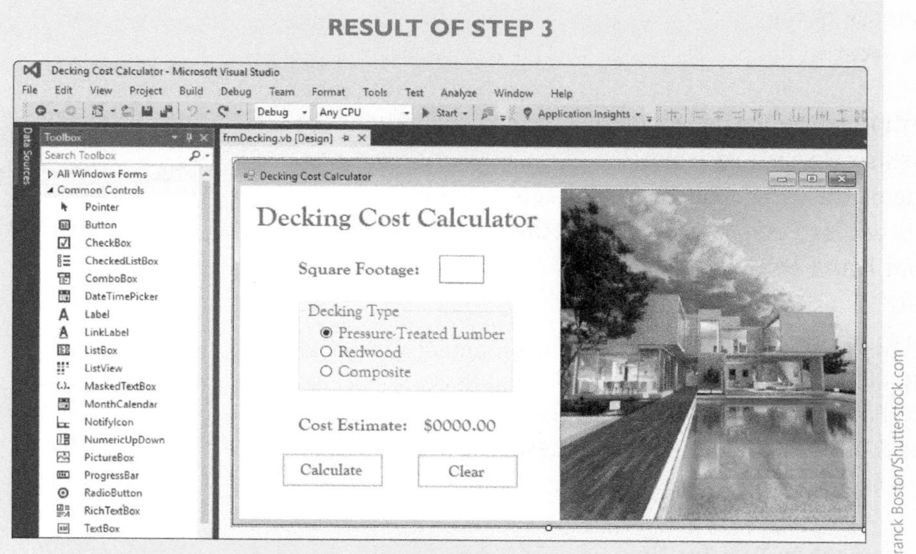

FIGURE 5-81

Phase 2: Code the Application

4

- **Code the Comments** Double-click the btnCalculate Button object on the frmDecking Form object to open the code window and create the btnCalculate_Click event handler. Close the Toolbox. Click before the first words, Public Class frmDecking, and then press the ENTER key to create a blank line. Insert the first four standard comments. Insert the Option Strict On command at the beginning of the code to turn on strict-type checking.

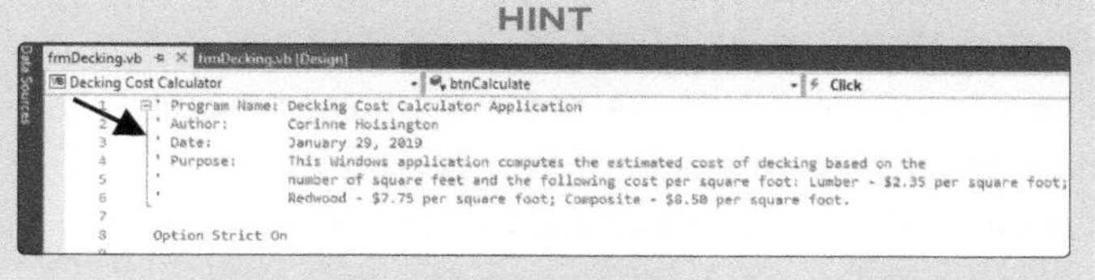

(continues)

Guided Program Development *continued*

- **Add Comments to the btnCalculate _Click Event Handler** Enter a comment to describe the purpose of the btnCalculate_Click event.

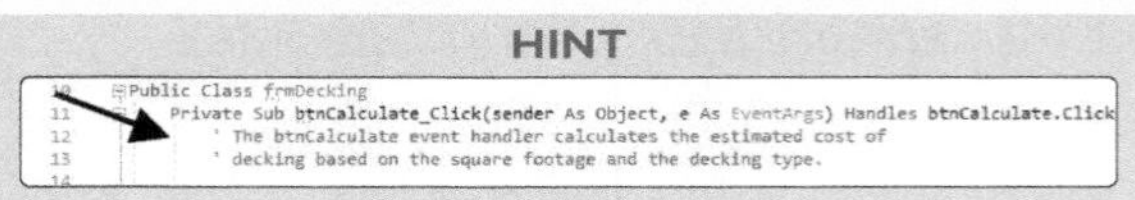

- **Declare and Initialize the Variables** This application requires six Decimal variables: (1) decFootage: Holds the estimated square footage of the decking; (2) decCostPerSquareFoot: Holds the cost per square foot based on the decking type; (3) decCostEstimate: Is assigned the calculated final estimated cost; (4) decLumberCost: Is assigned the value 2.35; (5) decRedwoodCost: Is assigned the value 7.75; (6) decCompositeCost: Is assigned the value 8.50. Declare and initialize these six variables.

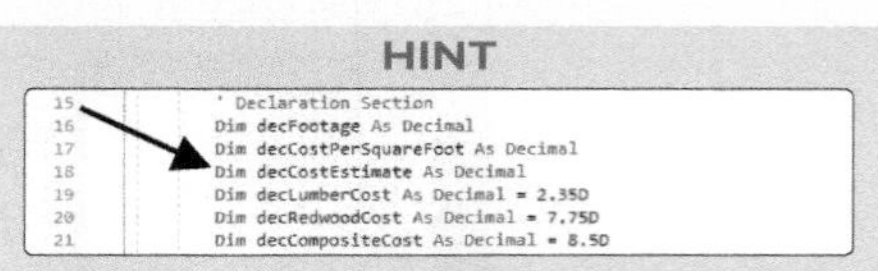

- **Write the If Statement to Test for Numeric Data** When the user clicks the Calculate button, the program must first ensure that the user entered a valid numeric value in the txtFootage TextBox object. If the user has entered a valid numeric value, the value must be converted from a string value into a Decimal data type. Write the If statement and conversion statement required for this process (*ref: Figure 5-74*).

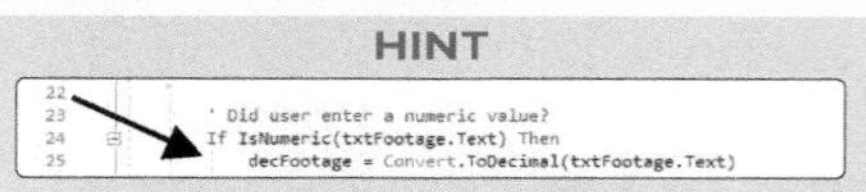

- **Write the If Statement to Test for a Positive Number** If the value in the txtFootage TextBox object is numeric, then the converted numeric value must be checked to ensure that it is a positive number. Write the If statement to check whether the converted numeric value is greater than zero (*ref: Figure 5-75*).

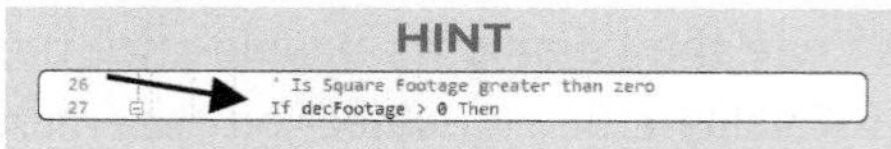

Guided Program Development *continued*

- **Write the If Statement to Determine the Cost Per Square Foot** When the value is greater than zero, the cost per square foot is determined by checking the status of the RadioButton objects and placing the appropriate cost per square foot in the decCostPerSquareFoot variable. Using the If . . . Then . . . ElseIf structure, write the statements to identify the checked radio button and place the appropriate cost in the decCostPerSquareFoot variable (*ref: Figure 5-49*).

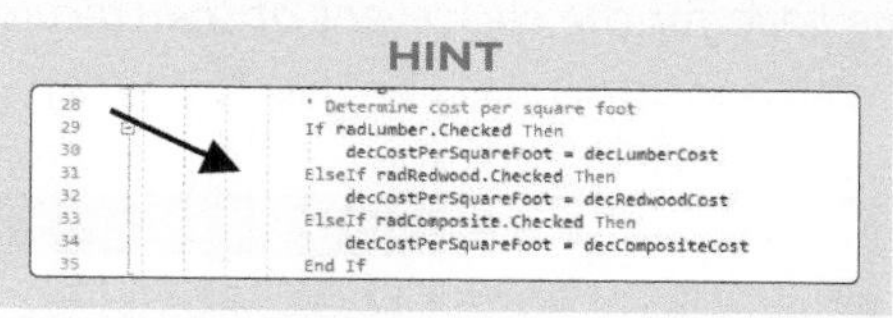

- **Calculate and Display the Cost Estimate** The next step is to calculate the cost estimate by multiplying the value in the decCostPerSquareFoot variable by the square footage. Next, display the cost estimate in the cost estimate label. Write the statements to calculate and display the cost estimate in the currency format.

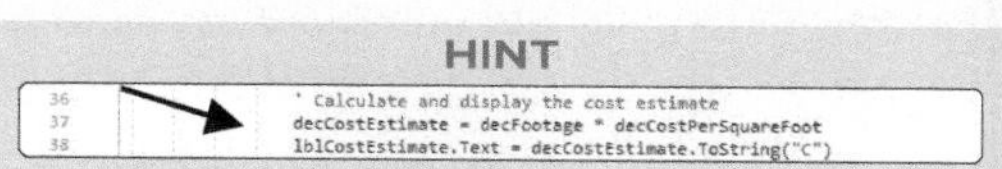

- **Display a Message Box If the Value Entered Is Not Greater Than Zero** After the processing is finished for the true portion of the If statements, the Else portion of the If statements must be written. Write the code to display the message box that contains the error message when the user enters a value that is not greater than zero (*ref: Figure 5-30*).

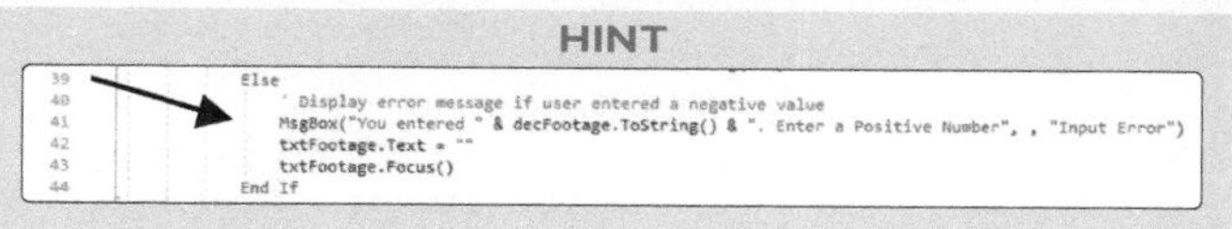

- **Display an Error Message If the Value Entered Is Not Numeric** Write the Else portion of the If statement to display an error message if the value entered by the user is not numeric (*ref: Figure 5-74*).

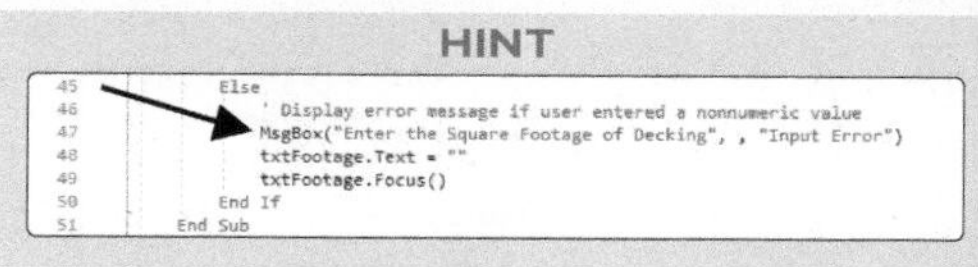

(continues)

Guided Program Development *continued*

The code for the click event of the Calculate button is completed (Figure 5-82).

RESULT OF STEP 4

frmDecking.vb

Decking Cost Calculator | btnCalculate

```
Public Class frmDecking
    Private Sub btnCalculate_Click(sender As Object, e As EventArgs) Handles btnCalculate.Click
        ' The btnCalculate event handler calculates the estimated cost of
        ' decking based on the square footage and the decking type.

        ' Declaration Section
        Dim decFootage As Decimal
        Dim decCostPerSquareFoot As Decimal
        Dim decCostEstimate As Decimal
        Dim decLumberCost As Decimal = 2.35D
        Dim decRedwoodCost As Decimal = 7.75D
        Dim decCompositeCost As Decimal = 8.5D

        ' Did user enter a numeric value?
        If IsNumeric(txtFootage.Text) Then
            decFootage = Convert.ToDecimal(txtFootage.Text)
            ' Is Square Footage greater than zero
            If decFootage > 0 Then
                ' Determine cost per square foot
                If radLumber.Checked Then
                    decCostPerSquareFoot = decLumberCost
                ElseIf radRedwood.Checked Then
                    decCostPerSquareFoot = decRedwoodCost
                ElseIf radComposite.Checked Then
                    decCostPerSquareFoot = decCompositeCost
                End If
                ' Calculate and display the cost estimate
                decCostEstimate = decFootage * decCostPerSquareFoot
                lblCostEstimate.Text = decCostEstimate.ToString("C")
            Else
                ' Display error message if user entered a negative value
                MsgBox("You entered " & decFootage.ToString() & ". Enter a Positive Number", , "Input Error")
                txtFootage.Text = ""
                txtFootage.Focus()
            End If
        Else
            ' Display error message if user entered a nonnumeric value
            MsgBox("Enter the Square Footage of Decking", , "Input Error")
            txtFootage.Text = ""
            txtFootage.Focus()
        End If
    End Sub
```

FIGURE 5-82

Guided Program Development *continued*

5

- **Create the Clear Button Click Event Handler** The Clear button click event includes the following processing: (1) clear the txtFootage Text property; (2) clear the lblCostEstimate Text property; (3) set the radLumber Checked property to True; (4) set the radRedwood and radComposite Checked properties to False; (5) set the focus in the txtFootage text box. To enter this code, click the frmDecking.vb [Design] tab and then double-click the Clear button. Using IntelliSense, enter the required code.

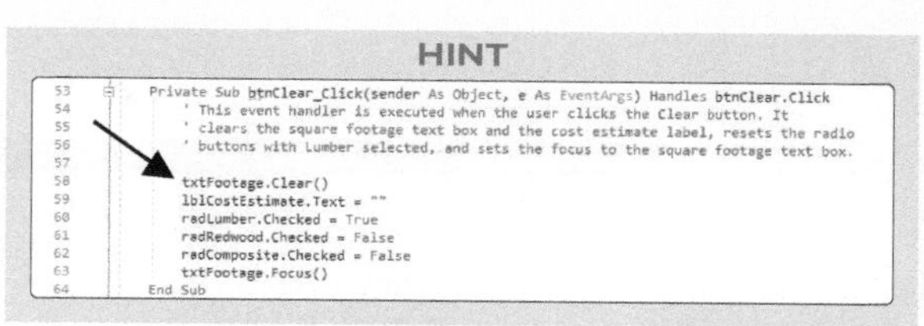

HINT
Private Sub btnClear_Click(sender As Object, e As EventArgs) Handles btnClear.Click
' This event handler is executed when the user clicks the Clear button. It
' clears the square footage text box and the cost estimate label, resets the radio
' buttons with Lumber selected, and sets the focus to the square footage text box.
txtFootage.Clear()
lblCostEstimate.Text = ""
radLumber.Checked = True
radRedwood.Checked = False
radComposite.Checked = False
txtFootage.Focus()
End Sub

- **Create the Form Load Event Handler** When the frmDecking Form object loads, the following processing should occur: (1) the focus is in the txtFootage text box; (2) the lblCostEstimate Text property is set to null. Click the frmDecking.vb [Design] tab to return to Design view and then double-click the form. Enter the code for the form load event handler.

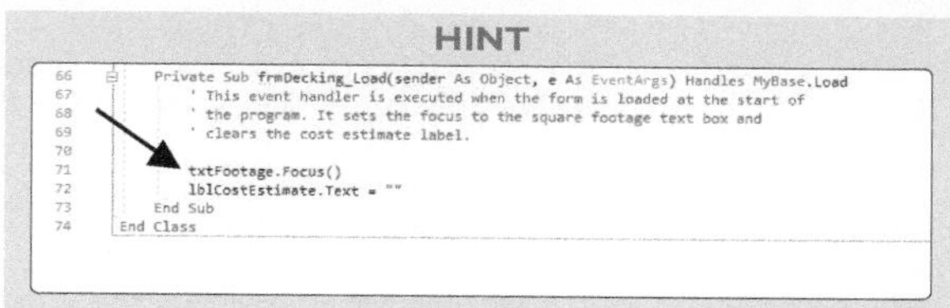

HINT
Private Sub frmDecking_Load(sender As Object, e As EventArgs) Handles MyBase.Load
' This event handler is executed when the form is loaded at the start of
' the program. It sets the focus to the square footage text box and
' clears the cost estimate label.
txtFootage.Focus()
lblCostEstimate.Text = ""
End Sub
End Class

6

- **Run the Application** After you have completed the code, you should run the application to ensure that it works properly.

- **Test the Application** Test the application with the following data: (1) square footage `250`, decking type Pressure-Treated Lumber; (2) square footage `210`, decking type Composite; (3) square footage `170`, decking type Redwood; (4) square footage `Fifteen` (use this word), decking type Composite; (5) square footage `-800`, decking type Pressure-Treated Lumber; (6) use other values to thoroughly test the program. After each test, click the Clear button before entering new data.

- **Close the Program** After testing the application, close the window by clicking the Close button in the title bar of the window.

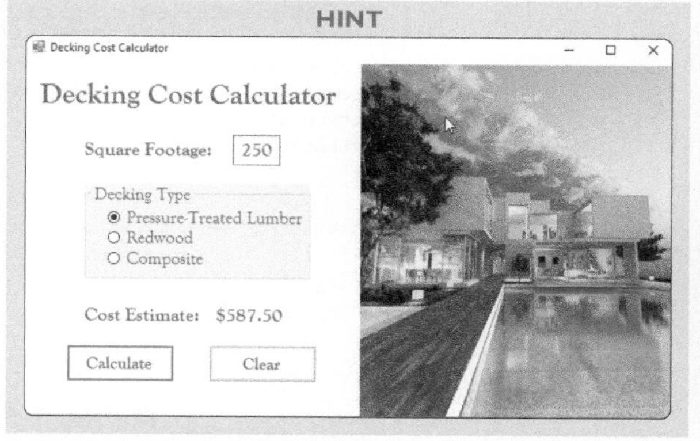

Franck Boston/Shutterstock.com

Code Listing

The complete code for the sample program is shown in Figure 5-83.

frmDecking.vb

Decking Cost Calculator | (frmDecking Events)

```
' Program Name: Decking Cost Calculator Application
' Author:       Corinne Hoisington
' Date:         January 29, 2019
' Purpose:      This Windows application computes the estimated cost of decking based on the
'               number of square feet and the following cost per square foot: Lumber - $2.35 per square foot;
'               Redwood - $7.75 per square foot; Composite - $8.50 per square foot.

Option Strict On

Public Class frmDecking
    Private Sub btnCalculate_Click(sender As Object, e As EventArgs) Handles btnCalculate.Click
        ' The btnCalculate event handler calculates the estimated cost of
        ' decking based on the square footage and the decking type.

        ' Declaration Section
        Dim decFootage As Decimal
        Dim decCostPerSquareFoot As Decimal
        Dim decCostEstimate As Decimal
        Dim decLumberCost As Decimal = 2.35D
        Dim decRedwoodCost As Decimal = 7.75D
        Dim decCompositeCost As Decimal = 8.5D

        ' Did user enter a numeric value?
        If IsNumeric(txtFootage.Text) Then
            decFootage = Convert.ToDecimal(txtFootage.Text)
            ' Is Square Footage greater than zero
            If decFootage > 0 Then
                ' Determine cost per square foot
                If radLumber.Checked Then
                    decCostPerSquareFoot = decLumberCost
                ElseIf radRedwood.Checked Then
                    decCostPerSquareFoot = decRedwoodCost
                ElseIf radComposite.Checked Then
                    decCostPerSquareFoot = decCompositeCost
                End If
                ' Calculate and display the cost estimate
                decCostEstimate = decFootage * decCostPerSquareFoot
                lblCostEstimate.Text = decCostEstimate.ToString("C")
            Else
                ' Display error message if user entered a negative value
                MsgBox("You entered " & decFootage.ToString() & ". Enter a Positive Number", , "Input Error")
                txtFootage.Text = ""
                txtFootage.Focus()
            End If
        Else
            ' Display error message if user entered a nonnumeric value
            MsgBox("Enter the Square Footage of Decking", , "Input Error")
            txtFootage.Text = ""
            txtFootage.Focus()
        End If
    End Sub
```

FIGURE 5-83 (continues)

```
    Private Sub btnClear_Click(sender As Object, e As EventArgs) Handles btnClear.Click
        ' This event handler is executed when the user clicks the Clear button. It
        ' clears the square footage text box and the cost estimate label, resets the radio
        ' buttons with Lumber selected, and sets the focus to the square footage text box.

        txtFootage.Clear()
        lblCostEstimate.Text = ""
        radLumber.Checked = True
        radRedwood.Checked = False
        radComposite.Checked = False
        txtFootage.Focus()
    End Sub

    Private Sub frmDecking_Load(sender As Object, e As EventArgs) Handles MyBase.Load
        ' This event handler is executed when the form is loaded at the start of
        ' the program. It sets the focus to the square footage text box and
        ' clears the cost estimate label.

        txtFootage.Focus()
        lblCostEstimate.Text = ""
    End Sub
End Class
```

FIGURE 5-83 (continued)

Summary

In this chapter, you have learned to make decisions based on the user's input.

Knowledge Check

1. If a form opens and the first of three RadioButtons is checked within a GroupBox object, what happens to the first RadioButton object when you click the second RadioButton object?
2. Write an If . . . Then statement that tests whether the value in the variable intRow is between 1 and 8. If the number is in that range, set the Text property for the lblCabin Label object to "First Class."
3. Name the six relational operators and state the purpose of each operator.
4. Write an If . . . Then . . . Else statement that assigns 70 to a variable named intSpeed if strInterstate is equal to "I40." Otherwise, assign 60 to intSpeed.
5. List the three most common logical operators and explain their meaning.
6. Rewrite the following line of code without a Not logical operator but keep the same logical processing:

   ```
   If Not decHoloLens <= 429.99 Then
   ```
7. The intent of the following statement is to check whether the radBusTicket RadioButton object is checked. What is the error in the statement? Rewrite the statement so it is correct.

   ```
   If radBusTicket = Checked Then
   ```
8. The intent of the following statement is to check whether the value in the intGrade variable is less than 0 or greater than 100. What is the error in the statement? Rewrite the statement so it is correct.

   ```
   If intGrade < 0 And intGrade > 100 Then
   ```
9. What is the most commonly used container object?
10. One of the most common mistakes when writing an If statement is writing one similar to this statement. Fix this statement.

    ```
    If decShoeSize > 5.5 and < 10.0 Then
    ```
11. What is the prefix for a RadioButton object and a GroupBox object?
12. Write a statement that opens a dialog box with the title "Escape Room" and the message "Group Size of Booking."
13. What is the difference between a Panel object and a GroupBox object?
14. What is the difference between the Or logical operator and the Xor logical operator?
15. Write a data validation statement that would check to ensure that the value in the intAge variable is between 1 and 115. If the age is not valid, display an error message box that states the age is invalid.
16. How many radio buttons in a group can be selected at one time?
17. Using the concatenation operator (&), write a statement that would create the compound word "reunion" from the following two strings: strClass1 = "re" and strClass2 = "union." Assign the compound word to the strCompound string variable.
18. Write a statement that would clear the radio button named radDrake.
19. Write a Select Case statement using the fewest Case statements possible to display the number of days in each month. The user enters the number of the month, such as 8, which is converted to an integer and assigned to the intMonth variable. The Select Case statement should display a message box that states the number of days in the month, such as "31 Days."
20. Which logical operator has the highest precedence in the order of operations?

Debugging Exercises

1. Explain how the two statements shown in Figure 5-84 are evaluated.

```
If strAirline = "Jet Green" AndAlso strHotel = "Homeland Suites" Then

    If strAirline = "Jet Green" And strHotel = "Homeland Suites" Then
```

FIGURE 5-84

2. Identify the error in the code shown in Figure 5-85 and explain how to correct the code.

```
If dblCommission >= 2500 Then
    Dim intBonus As Integer
    intBonus = 500
Else
    intBonus = 0
End If
```

FIGURE 5-85

3. The Select Case statement shown in Figure 5-86 contains one or more errors. Identify the error(s) and rewrite the statements correctly.

```
Select Case intNumberOfSeats
    Case > 5000
        strVenueType = "Stadium"
    Case > 2000
        strVenueType = "Amphitheater"
    Case > 1000
        strVenueType = "Auditorium"
    Case > 200
        strVenueType = "Theater"
    Case > 0
        strVenueType = "Club"
    Else Case
        strVenueType = "Error"
Select End
```

FIGURE 5-86

(continues)

Debugging Exercises *continued*

4. The Select Case statement shown in Figure 5-87 contains one or more errors. Identify the error(s) and rewrite the statements correctly.

```
Select Case charFlightCode
       Case 'F', 'A'
              lblFare.Text = 'First Class'
       Case 'B', 'Q'
              lblFare.Text = 'Business Class'
       Case 'Y', 'S', 'M'
              lblFare.Text = 'Full Fare Economy'
       Case 'K', 'C'
              lblFare.Text = 'Preferred Economy'
       Case 'U', 'J', 'P', 'G'
              lblFare.Text = 'Economy'
       Else
              lblFare.Text = 'Unknown'
End Select
```

FIGURE 5-87

5. The If . . . Then . . . Else statement shown in Figure 5-88 contains one or more errors. Identify the error(s) and rewrite the statements correctly.

```
If strShippingMethod = "Overnite" Then
    If strDeliveryTime = "Morning" Then
        decDeliveryCost = 29.00D
    Else
        decDeliveryCost = 24.00D
Else
    If strShippingMethod = "Two Days" Then
        decDeliveryCost = 14.00D
    Else
        decDeliveryCost = 4.00D
End If
```

FIGURE 5-88

Program Analysis

1. Write an If . . . Then decision structure to compare the two numbers in the decDeveloperPay and decWebDesignerPay variables. Display a message box that states decDeveloperPay is greater than decWebDesignerPay.
2. Write an If statement that displays the message box "A Day's Drive" if the value in the variable decMiles is within the range from 300 to 599.
3. Write an If . . . Then . . . Else statement that checks the value in the variable chrGender for the value M (Male) or F (Female) and assigns the information shown in Figure 5-89 to lblCollegeExpectation.Text based on the gender. If the variable chrGender contains a value other than M or F, assign the message "Invalid Gender" to lblCollegeExpectation.Text.

Gender	College Expectation
Male	75% plan to graduate from college
Female	85% plan to graduate from college

FIGURE 5-89

4. Write a Select Case statement that tests the user's age in a variable named intAge and assigns the generation name of that age group to the variable strGeneration, according to the information shown in Figure 5-90.

Age Group	Generation Name
50 and above	Baby Boomers
39–49	Generation X
18–38	Generation Y
Below 18	Millennials

FIGURE 5-90

5. Rewrite the Select Case statement shown in Figure 5-91 as an If . . . Then . . . Else statement.

```
Select Case chrDepartment
    Case "B", "b"
        strDept = "Baby / Infant Clothing"
    Case "T", "t"
        strDept = "Technology"
End Select
```

FIGURE 5-91

(continues)

Program Analysis *continued*

6. In each of the following examples, is the condition True or False?
   a. "CVCC" >= "GRCC"
   b. "G" >= "g"
   c. "Nerdy" < "Nerd"
   d. "Cool" <> "cool"
   e. "50" >= "Fifty"
   f. ("Paris" < "Barcelona") And ("Amsterdam" <= "Prague")
   g. ("Ford" > "Chevrolet") Or ("Toyota" < "Honda")
   h. 3 ^ 2 <= 3 * 4
   i. Not ("CNN" >= "ABC")
   j. Not ("Tim" > "Tom") And Not ("Great" <> "great")

Case Programming Assignments

Complete one or more of the following case programming assignments. Submit the program and materials you create to your instructor. The level of difficulty is indicated for each assignment.

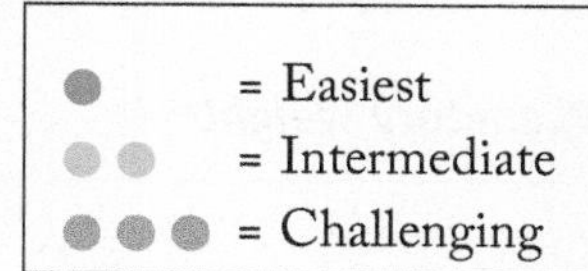

1 • PLANETARY WEIGHT

Design a Windows Classic Desktop application and write the code that will execute according to the program requirements in Figure 5-92. Before writing the code, create a Use Case Definition, as shown in Figure 5-93. Before writing the code, create an event-planning document for each event in the program. The completed Form object and other objects in the user interface are shown in Figure 5-94 on the next page.

REQUIREMENTS DOCUMENT

Date:	May 6, 2019
Date Submitted:	
Application Title:	Planetary Weight Application
Purpose:	This Windows Classic Desktop application calculates a user's weight in pounds and kilograms on Venus or on Mars.
Program Procedures:	The user enters her weight in pounds and selects either Venus or Mars. The application will determine the user's weight on Venus or Mars in pounds and kilograms.
Algorithms, Processing, and Conditions:	1. The user must be able to enter her weight in pounds and indicate that she wants to see her equivalent weight on Venus or Mars. 2. One pound on Earth is equivalent to 0.907 pounds on Venus. One pound on Earth is equivalent to 0.377 pounds on Mars. 3. One pound is equivalent to 0.454 kilograms. 4. The user must be able to initiate the calculation and the display of her weight on Venus or Mars. 5. The user must be able to clear her input and the results.
Notes and Restrictions:	1. If the user's weight entry is blank or nonnumeric, the user should be advised and asked for a valid entry. 2. The results should be displayed one place past the decimal point.
Comments:	Obtain an image for this program from CengageBrain.com. The name of the image file is planets.

FIGURE 5-92

(continues)

Case Programming Assignments *continued*

PLanetary Weight

USE CASE DEFINITION

1. The Windows Classic Desktop application window opens.
2. The user enters a weight in pounds and selects whether to convert it to the equivalent weight on Venus or Mars.
3. The user clicks the Display button to display the selected weight.
4. The user clears the input and the result by clicking the Clear button.
5. If desired, the user repeats the process.

FIGURE 5-93

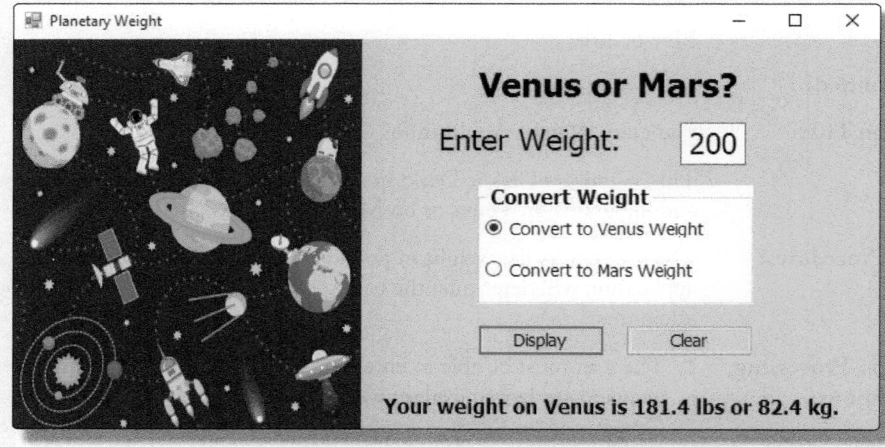

FIGURE 5-94

iStockphoto.com/Askold Romanov

Case Programming Assignments

2 ● COMIC CONVENTION

Design a Windows Classic Desktop application and write the code that will execute according to the program requirements in Figure 5-95 and the Use Case Definition in Figure 5-96. Before writing the code, create an event-planning document for each event in the program. The completed Form object and other objects in the user interface are shown in Figure 5-97.

REQUIREMENTS DOCUMENT

Date:	May 11, 2019
Date Submitted:	
Application Title:	Comic Convention
Purpose:	This Windows Classic Desktop application computes the registration cost of attending a Comic Convention.
Program Procedures:	The user enters the size of the group attending the Comic Convention. The application computes the registration cost for the group based on badge type.
Algorithms, Processing, and Conditions:	1. A user must be able to enter the size of the group and select the desired badge type. The user can select the following badge types: • Convention + Superhero Experience ($380) • Convention + Autographs ($275) • Convention ($209) 2. The user must be able to initiate the registration calculation and the display of the registration cost. 3. The user must be able to clear the entries and results.
Notes and Restrictions:	1. If the user enters a nonnumeric value for the group size or does not enter a group size, the user should be advised and asked for a valid entry. 2. If the user enters a negative group size, the user should be advised and asked for a valid entry. 3. If the value entered is greater than 20, the user should be advised and asked for a valid entry. 4. The registration cost should be displayed in currency format.
Comments:	Obtain an image for this program from CengageBrain.com. The name of the image file is comic.

FIGURE 5-95

(continues)

Case Programming Assignments *continued*

Comic Convention

USE CASE DEFINITION

1. The Windows Classic Desktop application window opens.
2. The user enters the group size and selects the type of convention badge.
3. The user clicks the Calculate button.
4. The program displays the cost of the convention tickets using currency format.
5. A MsgBox appears and displays a warning if the user enters a negative number for the group size.
6. A MsgBox appears and displays a warning if the user enters a value for the group size that exceeds 20.
7. The user can clear the input and the results by clicking the Clear button.

FIGURE 5-96

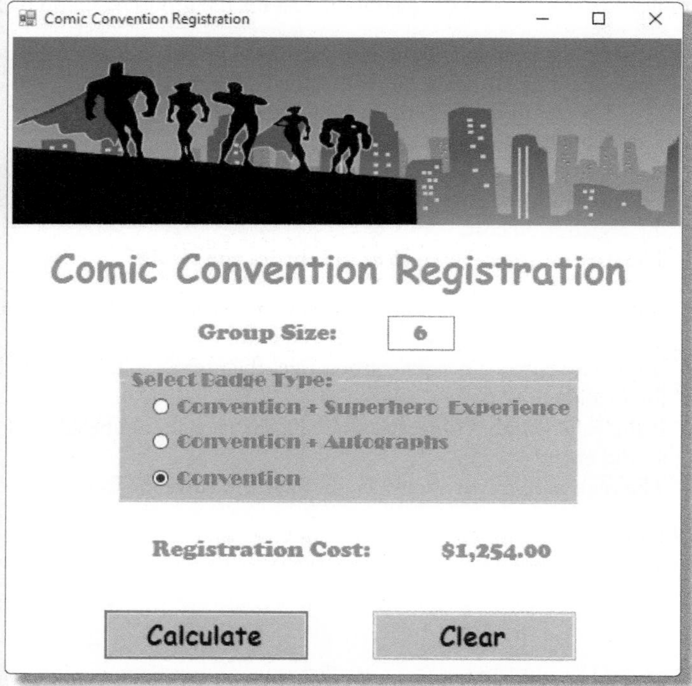

FIGURE 5-97

Case Programming Assignments

3 ●● LONDON TUBE TICKETS

Design a Windows Classic Desktop application and write the code that will execute according to the program requirements in Figure 5-98. Before designing the user interface, create a Use Case Definition. Before writing the code, create an event-planning document for each event in the program.

REQUIREMENTS DOCUMENT

Date: May 6, 2019

Date Submitted:

Application Title: London Tube Tickets

Purpose: This Windows Classic Desktop application calculates the cost of tickets on the London Tube.

Program Procedures: The user should enter the number of tickets and the zones of intended travel. The ticket cost will be computed and displayed for the entered number of tickets in U.S. dollars. The single-fare adult ticket costs in British pounds are as follows:

- Zones 1-3: £4.90
- Zones 1-5: £5.90
- Zones 1-6: £6.00

Algorithms, Processing, and Conditions:

1. The user must enter the number of single-fare tickets.
2. Based on the zones covered, the ticket cost is calculated and then converted to U.S. dollars using the conversion at the website xe.com.
3. The user should be able to clear the number of single-fare tickets, the number of zones, and the cost of the tickets in U.S. dollars.

Notes and Restrictions:

1. If the user enters a nonnumeric value for the number of single-fare tickets, the user should be advised and asked for a valid entry.
2. If the user enters a negative number of tickets or does not enter a number, the user should be advised and asked for a valid entry.
3. The default ticket type is Zones 1–3.

Comments: n/a

FIGURE 5-98

4 ●● BUILDING PLANS CONVERSION

Design a Windows Classic Desktop application and write the code that will execute according to the program requirements in Figure 5-99. Before designing the user interface, create a Use Case Definition. Before writing the code, create an event-planning document for each event in the program.

REQUIREMENTS DOCUMENT

Date:	May 6, 2019
Date Submitted:	
Application Title:	Building Plans Conversion
Purpose:	This Windows Classic Desktop application converts inches to meters or from meters to inches when building plans need to be converted between Imperial and Metric systems.
Program Procedures:	The user enters the number of inches or meters to be converted and selects either Imperial to Metric or Metric to Imperial.
Algorithms, Processing, and Conditions:	1. The user must be able to enter the measurement to be converted in inches or meters. 2. One inch is equivalent to 0.0254 meters. One meter is equivalent to 39.37008 inches. 3. The user must be able to initiate the calculation and the display of the conversion. 4. The user must be able to clear her input and the results.
Notes and Restrictions:	1. If the user's entry is blank or nonnumeric, the user should be advised and asked for a valid entry. 2. The results should be displayed three places past the decimal point.
Comments:	n/a

FIGURE 5-99

Case Programming Assignments

5 ●●● BROADWAY TICKET GROUP DISCOUNT

Based on the case project shown in Figure 5-100, create a requirements document and a Use Case Definition document and then design a Windows application. Before writing the code, create an event-planning document for each event in the program.

To create a perfect evening for your group, the Broadway Ticket Group Discount Program offers a discount based on group size for excellent orchestra seating. The following table specifies the cost per person. Write this program using Case statements for the total cost of the tickets sold as a group. Do not accept requests for negative values or 100+ tickets.

Group Size	Broadway Tickets per Person
1-8	$249
9-12	$219
13-24	$199
25-99	$169

FIGURE 5-100

Case Programming Assignments

PARTY PLATTERS

Based on the case project shown in Figure 5-101, create a requirements document and a Use Case Definition document and then design a Windows application. Before writing the code, create an event-planning document for each event in the program.

A local grocery store offers party platters made to order. The grocery store has asked you to create a Windows application that allows customers to enter their orders on a flat-screen computer. Create an application that allows the user to select one of five party platters. Create and display a list of platters of your own choice, along with a display of prices for each platter using radio buttons. A second radio button group should request if the customer will pre-pay or pay upon order pickup. The grocery store has a loyalty program that deducts 5 percent of the total order cost for every 10 points a customer has earned. Allow users to enter their total number of loyalty points and compute the cost of their order. Customers cannot receive money back if their loyalty points exceed the full cost of their order.

FIGURE 5-101

CHAPTER 6

Loop Structures

OBJECTIVES

You will have mastered the material in this chapter when you can:

- Add a MenuStrip object
- Use the InputBox function
- Display data using the ListBox object
- Add a Background Image
- Understand the use of counters and accumulators
- Understand the use of compound operators
- Repeat a process using a For... Next loop
- Repeat a process using a Do loop
- Avoid infinite loops
- Prime a loop
- Validate data
- Create a nested loop
- Select the best type of loop
- Debug using DataTips at breakpoints
- Publish a finished application using ClickOnce technology

Introduction

In Chapter 5, you learned about the decision structure, one of the major control structures used in computer programming. In this chapter, you will learn another major structure called the **looping structure**, or the **iteration structure**.

A fundamental process in a computer program is to repeat a series of instructions either while a condition is true (or not true) or until a condition is true (or not true). For example, if a company is processing electronic pay checks for 5,000 employees, it can use the same set of instructions to post an electronic deposit for each employee, varying only the name of the employee and amount paid for each check. This process would continue until all checks are deposited. Unique check deposit instructions for each employee in the company are not required.

The process of repeating a set of instructions while a condition is true or until a condition is true is called **looping**. When the program is executing those instructions, it is said to be in a loop. Another term for looping is **iteration**.

The programming project in this chapter uses a loop to obtain input data and produce output information. A large company challenged groups of eight employees to form weight loss fitness teams. The Human Resource department requested a Windows application that determines the average weight loss for each team. This application, called the Fitness Challenge application, computes the average weight loss for up to eight team members who enter the total number of pounds they lost during their weight loss challenge. The application uses a loop to request and display the weight loss amounts of the team members. The application then displays the average weight loss by the fitness team (Figure 6-1).

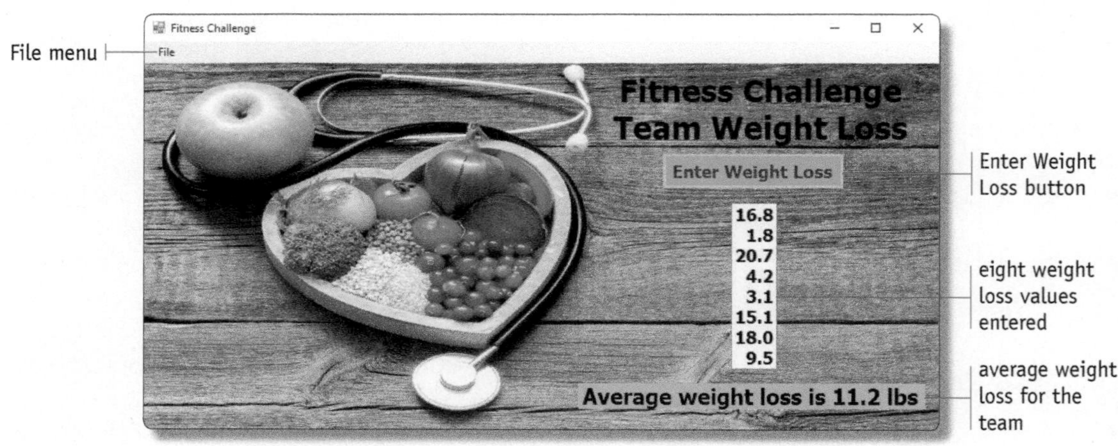

FIGURE 6-1

iStockphoto.com/udra

Figure 6-1 shows eight values the user entered in a list. After the user enters the weight loss values, the application calculates the average weight loss of the entire team.

When the Fitness Challenge application begins, the main window shows no weight loss values (Figure 6-2).

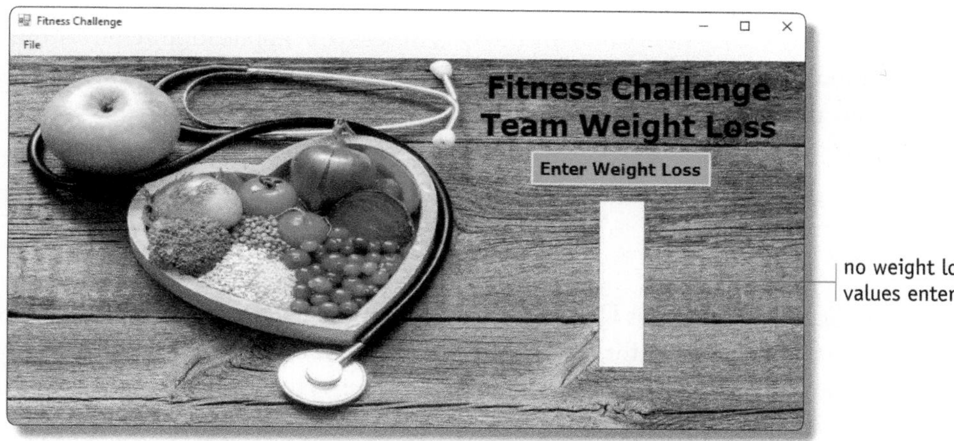

FIGURE 6-2

iStockphoto.com/udra

When the user clicks the Enter Weight Loss button, the Weight Loss dialog box opens (Figure 6-3), allowing the user to enter the weight loss of the first team member. This dialog box is called an **input box**.

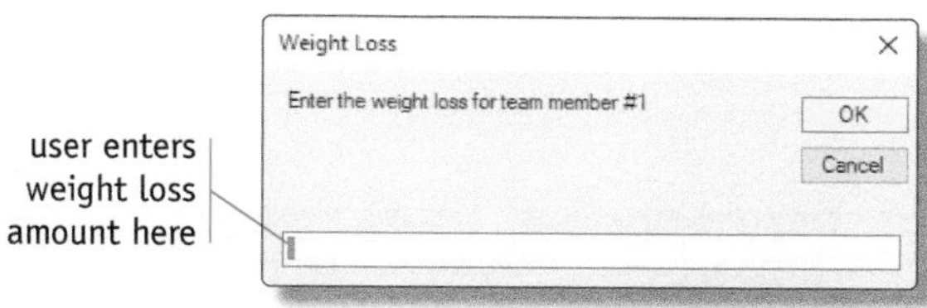

FIGURE 6-3

After entering the first weight loss value, the user clicks the OK button in the Weight Loss dialog box. The application lists the weight loss value in the main window and then displays the input box again, requesting the next team member's weight loss. This process repeats for up to eight team members and is implemented using a loop in the program. When the user is entering weight loss values, the program is said to be in a loop. The loop is terminated when the user enters the weight loss for the eighth team member or clicks the Cancel button in the Weight Loss dialog box. After the loop is terminated, the Fitness Challenge application displays the average weight loss for the team, as shown in Figure 6-1 on page 302.

The Fitness Challenge application has several other features. Figure 6-1 shows a menu bar containing the File menu at the top of the window. The File menu contains the Clear command, which clears the list and the average weight loss, and the Exit command, which closes the window and ends the application. In this chapter, you will learn to design and code a menu.

In addition, the application contains input validation. For example, if a user enters a nonnumeric or negative value for the weight loss, the application requests the weight loss amount again, until the user enters a reasonable value.

Finally, the application displays the average weight loss to one decimal place, such as 11.2 lbs.

User Interface Design

The user interface for the Fitness Challenge application includes three new elements: a menu, an input box, and a list for the weight loss values. The menu and the list of team member weight loss values are objects placed on the Windows Form object. The input box is created through the use of a function call in the program code. Each of these items is explained in the following sections.

Insert a MenuStrip Object

A **menu bar** is a strip across the top of a window that contains one or more menu names. A **menu** is a group of commands, or items, presented in a list. In the sample program, a File menu is created in the application window (Figure 6-4).

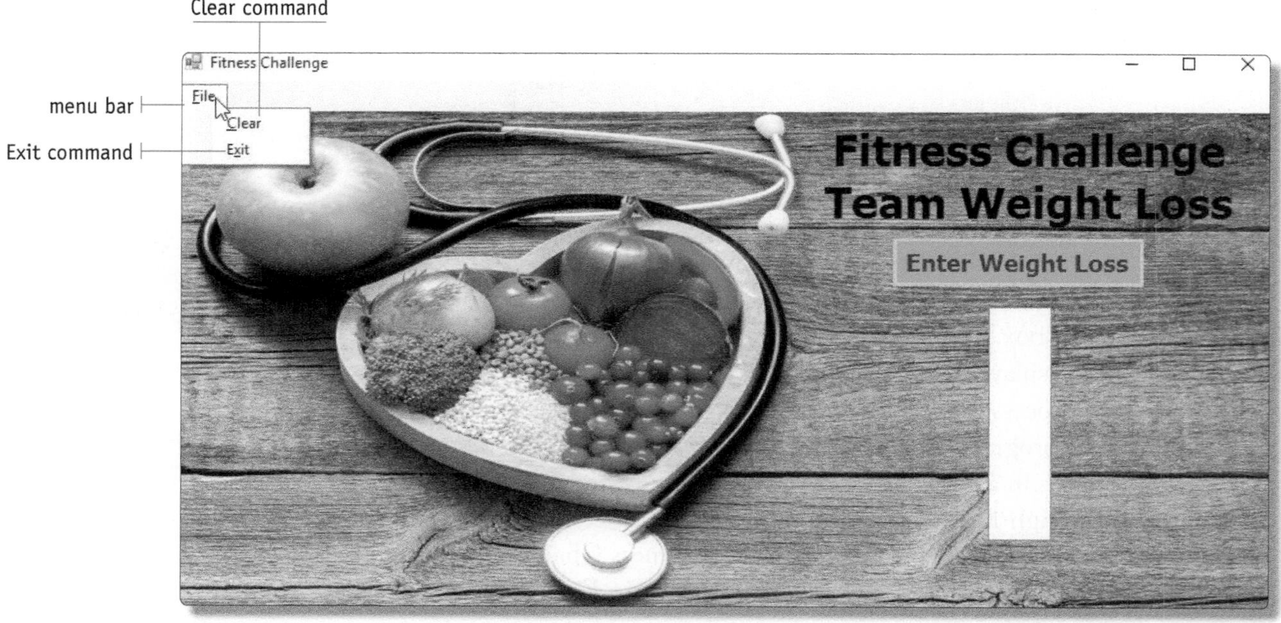

FIGURE 6-4

iStockphoto.com/udra

When the user clicks File on the menu bar during program execution, a menu appears with two commands: Clear and Exit. The user clicks the Clear menu command to clear the entered weight values and the results. Clicking the Exit menu command ends the application. An advantage of a menu is that it conserves space instead of cluttering the form with objects such as buttons.

Using Visual Studio 2017, you can place menus at the top of a Windows Form using the MenuStrip object. To place a MenuStrip object on a Windows Form, you can complete the following steps:

STEP 1 With a Windows Form object open in the Visual Studio window, scroll in the Toolbox to display the Menus & Toolbars category. If the category is not open, click the expand icon (the right-pointing triangle) next to the Menus & Toolbars category name. Drag the MenuStrip .NET component to the Windows Form object.

The pointer changes when you place it over the Windows Form object (Figure 6-5).

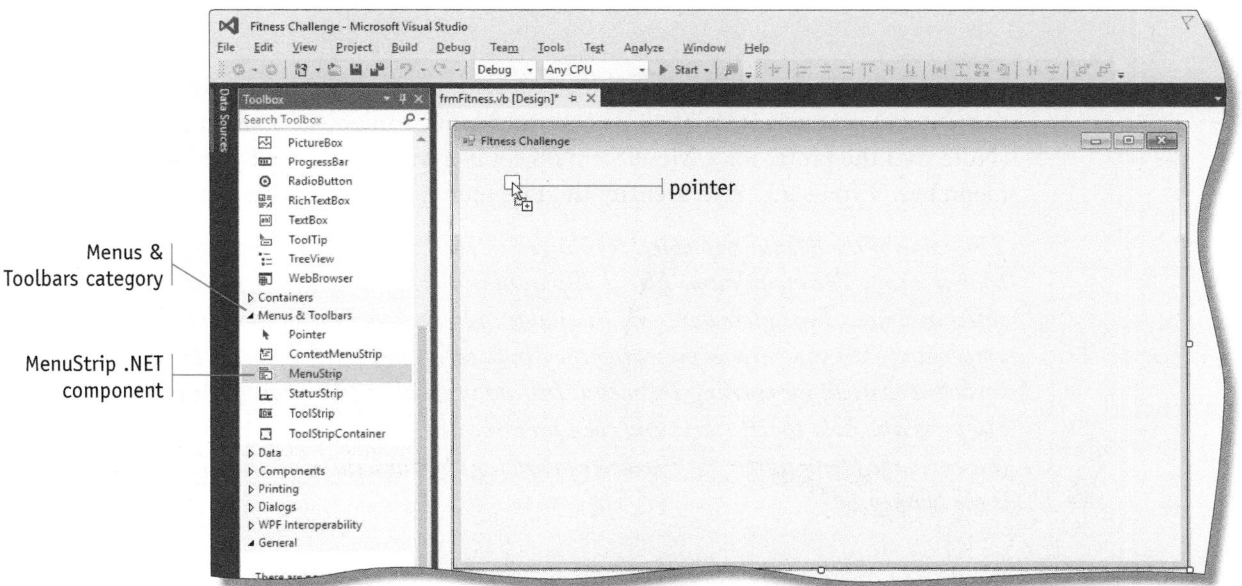

FIGURE 6-5

STEP 2 Release the object.

Visual Studio places the MenuStrip object at the top of the form regardless of where you released the object (Figure 6-6). The Component Tray, which is displayed below the form, organizes nongraphical Toolbox objects. It displays the MenuStrip1 object name.

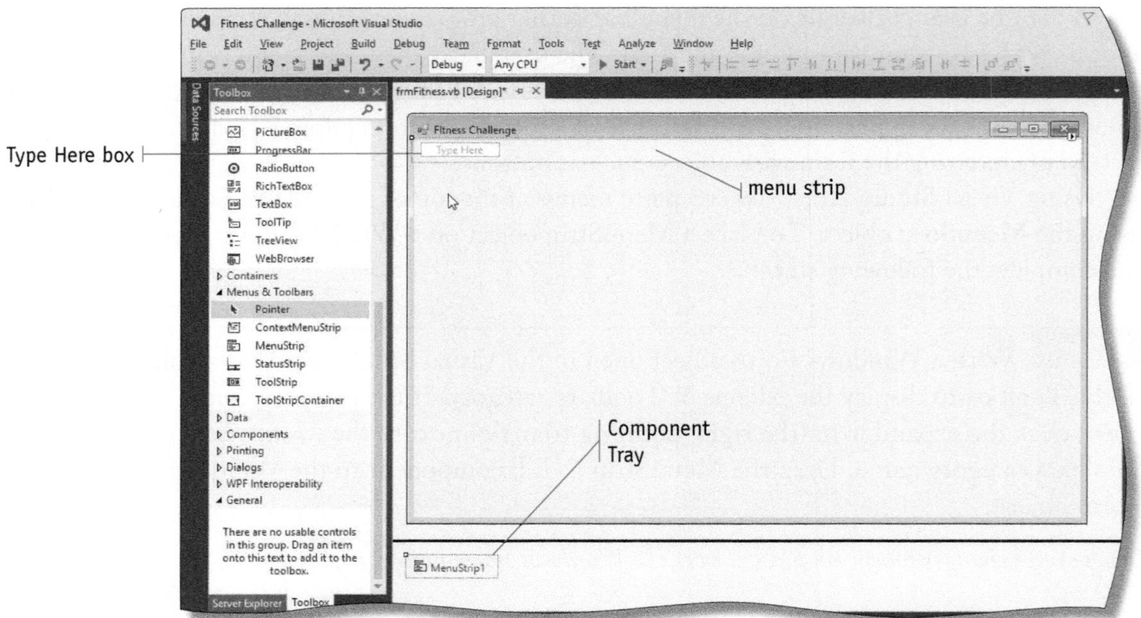

FIGURE 6-6

STEP 3 With the MenuStrip object selected, scroll in the Properties window until the (Name) property is visible. Change the MenuStrip object name to `mnuFitness`. (Note that the prefix for a MenuStrip object is mnu). Click the Type Here box on the menu bar. Type `&File` to identify the File menu, and then press the enter key.

The name of the MenuStrip object is changed in the Properties window and in the Component Tray. The menu name File is displayed in the upper-left corner of the MenuStrip object and new Type Here boxes are available to create other menu items (Figure 6-7). The ampersand (&) you entered preceding the f indicates that f is a hot key. A hot key provides a keyboard shortcut for opening the menu. Instead of clicking File to open the menu, the user can press and hold the ALT key, and then press the designated hot key, such as ALT+F. After you enter the menu name, the character following the ampersand is underlined to indicate it is the hot key.

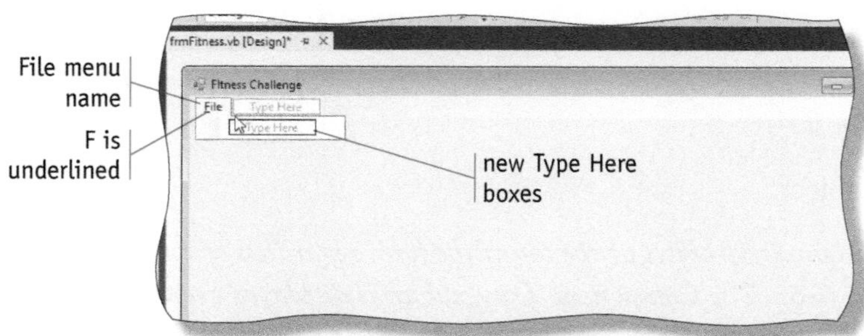

FIGURE 6-7

STEP 4 Click File in the MenuStrip object to select it, scroll in the Properties window to the (Name) property, and then change the name to `mnuFile`. To add a menu item to the File menu, click the Type Here box below the File menu name. Type `&Clear` and then press ENTER to create a new menu item named Clear with c as the hot key.

The name of the File menu is displayed in the (Name) property in the Properties window. The Clear menu item is displayed below the File menu (Figure 6-8). After you press the ENTER key, the character following the ampersand is underlined to indicate it is the hot key.

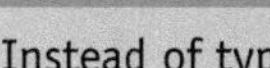

HEADS UP

Instead of typing the menu name on a MenuStrip object, you can choose to add a menu item, combo box, or text box to the menu bar. To do so, point to the Type Here box, click its list arrow, and then click MenuItem, ComboBox, or TextBox.

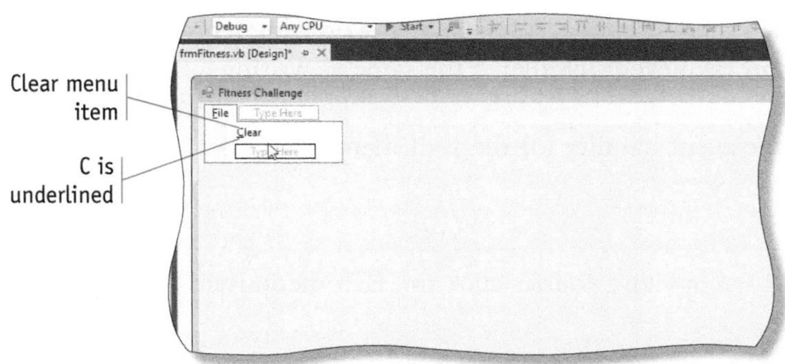

FIGURE 6-8

STEP 5 On the File menu, click Clear to select it, scroll in the Properties window until the (Name) property is visible, and then change the name to `mnuClear`.

The mnuClear name is displayed in the (Name) property in the Properties window (Figure 6-9).

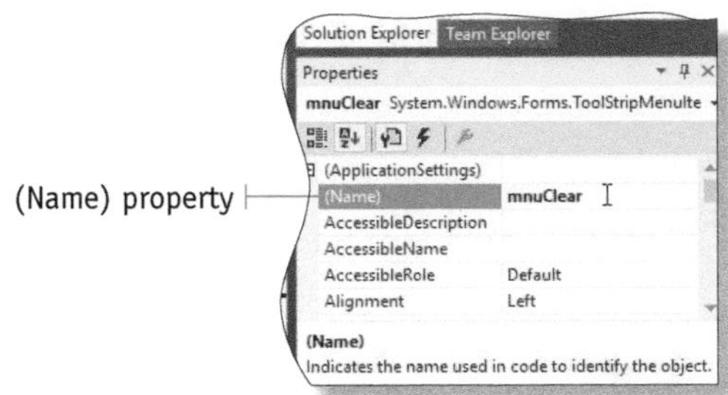

FIGURE 6-9

HEADS UP

As you work with MenuStrip objects and hot keys, keep in mind that all hot keys should be unique.

The letter representing a hot key appears underlined in the menu name, as shown in Figure 6-8. The first letter often is used for the hot key, but not always. For example, in the chapter project, the File menu includes the Exit item (see Figure 6-4 on page 304). The hot key typically used for the Exit item is the letter x. When entering the Exit menu item on the File menu, the developer can type E&xit, which assigns the letter following the & (x) as the hot key.

When assigning menu item hot keys, you should be aware that they are not case-sensitive. Therefore, you should not assign "T" to one menu item and "t" to another.

Event Handlers for Menu Items

Recall that the design of the user interface occurs before you write the code for event handlers. When you are ready to write code, however, you must write an event handler for each menu item because clicking it or using its hot key triggers an event. Writing a menu item event handler is the same as writing an event handler for a button click.

To code the event handler for the Exit menu item, you can complete the following steps:

STEP 1 In Design view, double-click the Exit menu item to open the code window.

The code window is displayed and the insertion point is located within the Exit item click event handler (Figure 6-10). When the user clicks the Exit item on the File menu, the code in the event handler will be executed.

FIGURE 6-10

STEP 2 Using IntelliSense, enter the Close procedure call to close the window and exit the application.

When executed, the Close procedure will close the window and the program (Figure 6-11).

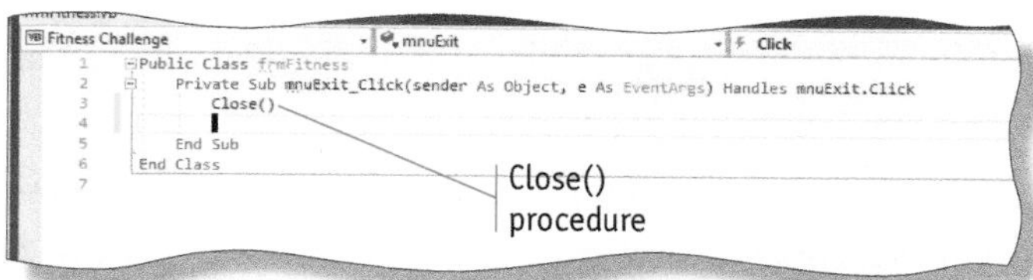

FIGURE 6-11

Insert Standard Items for a Menu

Developers often customize the MenuStrip object for the specific needs of an application. In addition, Visual Basic 2017 contains an **Action Tag** that allows you to create a full standard menu bar commonly provided in Windows programs, with File, Edit, Tools, and Help menus. In Visual Basic 2017, an Action Tag appears in the upper-right corner of many objects, including a MenuStrip. Action Tags provide a way for you to specify a set of actions, called **smart actions**, for an object as you design a form. For example, to insert a full standard menu, you can complete the following steps:

STEP 1 With a new Windows Form object open, drag the MenuStrip .NET component onto the Windows Form object. Click the Action Tag on the MenuStrip object.

The MenuStrip Tasks menu opens (Figure 6-12).

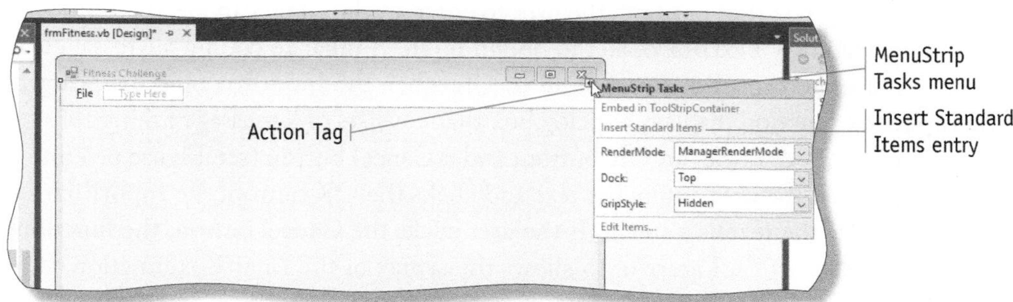

FIGURE 6-12

STEP 2 Click Insert Standard Items on the MenuStrip Tasks menu.

The MenuStrip object contains four menu names: File, Edit, Tools, and Help (Figure 6-13). These are the standard menus found in many Windows applications. Each menu contains the items typically listed on the menus.

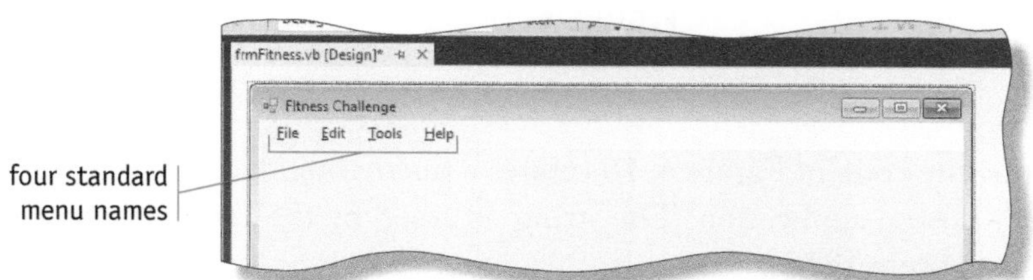

FIGURE 6-13

HEADS UP

In Microsoft Windows 7, 8, and 10, menus are de-emphasized as the focus switches to a more graphical layout such as the ribbon used in Microsoft Office, which includes images rather than menus for navigational control.

STEP 3 Click File on the menu bar to view the individual menu items, their associated icons, and their shortcut keys.

The standard File menu items (New, Open, Save, Save As, Print, Print Preview, and Exit) are displayed with their associated icons and shortcut keys (Figure 6-14). The other menus also contain standard items. You can code an event handler for each menu item by double-clicking the item.

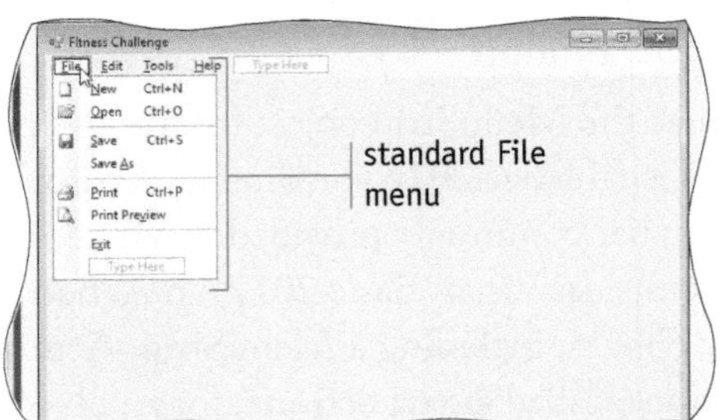

FIGURE 6-14

Use the InputBox Function

To calculate a team's weight loss, the Fitness Challenge application uses an InputBox object in which users enter the weight loss of each team member. The InputBox object is a dialog box that prompts the user to enter a value. You can use the InputBox function instead of a TextBox object to obtain input. Similar to coding a MessageBox object, you use the InputBox function to specify when the InputBox object appears. The InputBox function displays a dialog box that consists of a message asking for input, an input area, a title, an OK button, and a Cancel button (see Figure 6-3 on page 303). When the user enters the text and clicks the OK button, the InputBox function returns the text as a string. If the user clicks the Cancel button, the function returns a null string (""). Figure 6-15 shows the syntax of the InputBox function:

General Format: InputBox Function

```
strVariableName = InputBox("Question to Prompt User",
                           "Title Bar")
```

FIGURE 6-15

For example, the code in Figure 6-16 creates a dialog box that requests the user's age for a driver's license application. The string returned by the InputBox function is assigned to the strAge variable.

```
        Dim strAge As String

        strAge = InputBox("Please enter your age", "Driver's License Agency")
```

FIGURE 6-16

When the application runs, the InputBox object in Figure 6-17 opens, requesting that the user enter his or her age.

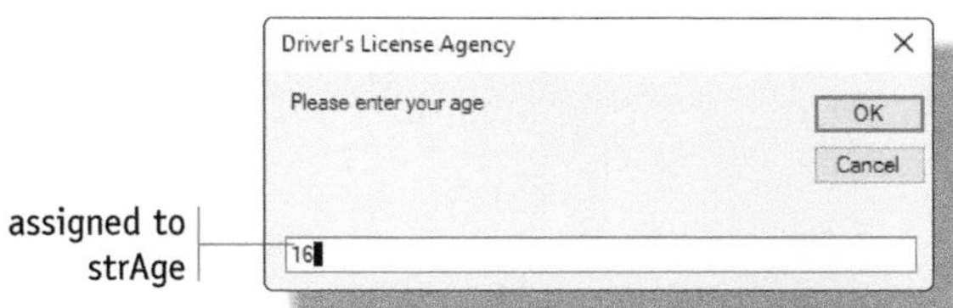

FIGURE 6-17

The InputBox object returns all data entered as a string, which then can be converted to the appropriate data type.

Display a Default Value in an InputBox Object

The InputBox object can be assigned a default value. For example, if a college application for admission requests the student's home state and the college or university is located in Ohio, the most likely state, Ohio, can be the default value in the InputBox, as shown in Figure 6-18.

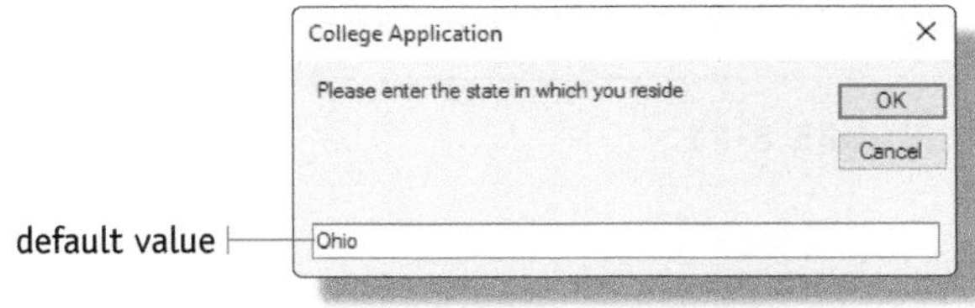

FIGURE 6-18

The code to produce this input box is shown in Figure 6-19.

```
        Dim strState As String

        strState = InputBox("Please enter the state in which you reside:", _
            "College Application", "Ohio")
```

FIGURE 6-19

As you can see, the third argument for the InputBox function call is the default value that is placed in the input box. It must be a String value and follow the syntax shown in Figure 6-19.

Create the InputBox Object for Fitness Challenge Application

The Fitness Challenge application uses an InputBox object that requests the weight loss amounts of team members numbered 1–8, as shown in Figure 6-20.

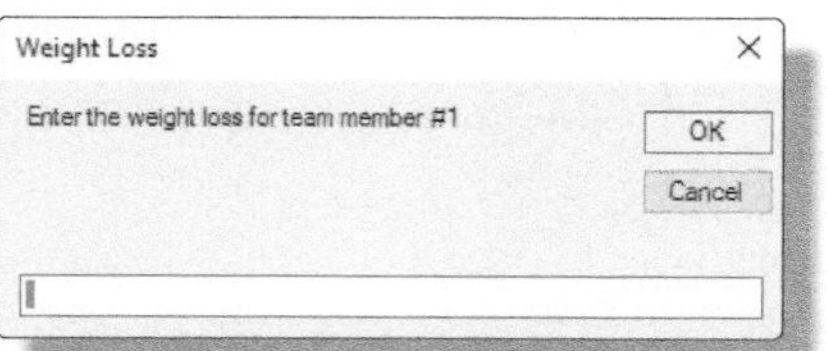

FIGURE 6-20

HEADS UP

An InputBox object allows you to gather data without placing a TextBox for the requested value on the Windows Form object.

The code for the Weight Loss InputBox is shown in Figure 6-21. Notice that the prompt message for the user is assigned to the strInputMessage variable, and the title bar text (Weight Loss) is assigned to the strInputHeading variable.

```
        Dim strWeightLoss As String
        Dim strInputMessage As String = "Enter the weight loss for team member #"
        Dim strInputHeading As String = "Weight Loss"
        Dim intNumberOfEntries As Integer = 1

        strWeightLoss = InputBox(strInputMessage & intNumberOfEntries, strInputHeading, " ")
```

FIGURE 6-21

The variable intNumberOfEntries identifies the team member's number. It is included in the prompt message through the use of concatenation. The variable intNumberOfEntries is incremented later in the code so that it refers to the correct team member each time the InputBox function call is executed.

In Figure 6-21, the default value is specified as a space (" "). When the input box is displayed, a space will be selected in the input area. This space is required so that if a user clicks the OK button without entering any data, the InputBox will not return a null character (" "), which indicates the user clicked the Cancel button. This normally is a good programming practice.

When the user clicks the Cancel button in an input box and the InputBox function returns a null character, the program can test for the null character to determine further processing.

Display Data Using the ListBox Object

In the Fitness Challenge application, the user enters weight loss values into the InputBox object, and the application displays the weight loss values in a list box (see Figure 6-1 on page 302). To create such a list, you use the ListBox object provided in the Visual Basic Toolbox. A ListBox object displays a group of values, called items, with one item per line. To add a ListBox object to a Windows Form object, you can complete the following steps:

STEP 1 Drag the ListBox object from the Toolbox to where you want to place the ListBox object on the Windows Form object. When the pointer is in the correct location, release the object.

The ListBox object is placed on the form (Figure 6-22).

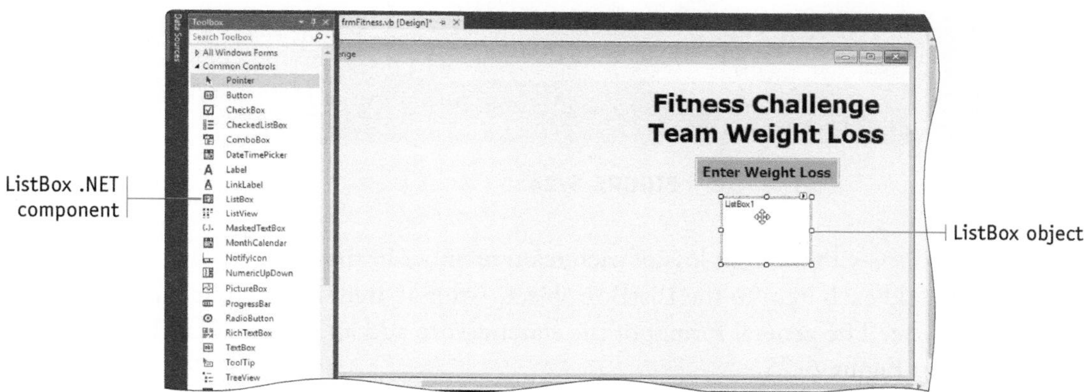

FIGURE 6-22

STEP 2 With the ListBox object selected, scroll in the Properties window to the (Name) property. Name the ListBox object `lstWeightLoss`.

The name you entered is displayed in the (Name) property in the Properties window (Figure 6-23). Notice a ListBox object name begins with lst (be sure to use a lowercase letter l, not the number one).

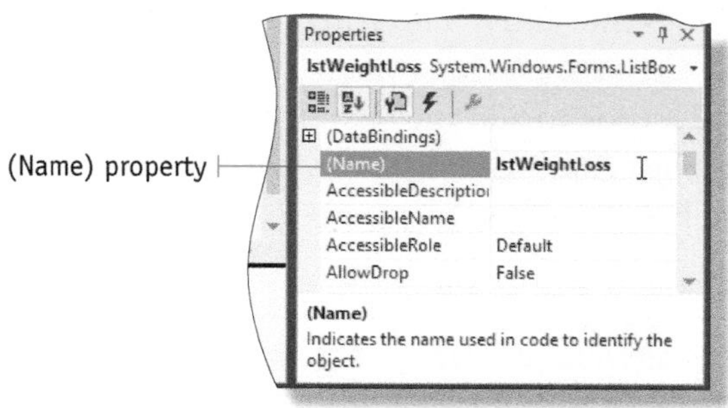

FIGURE 6-23

After placing a ListBox object on the Windows Form object, you can adjust the size by dragging the size handles. Be sure to resize the ListBox so that it is large enough to hold the application data. The ListBox object for the Fitness Challenge application is designed to be wide enough to hold three digits and a decimal point and long enough to hold eight numbers (Figure 6-24).

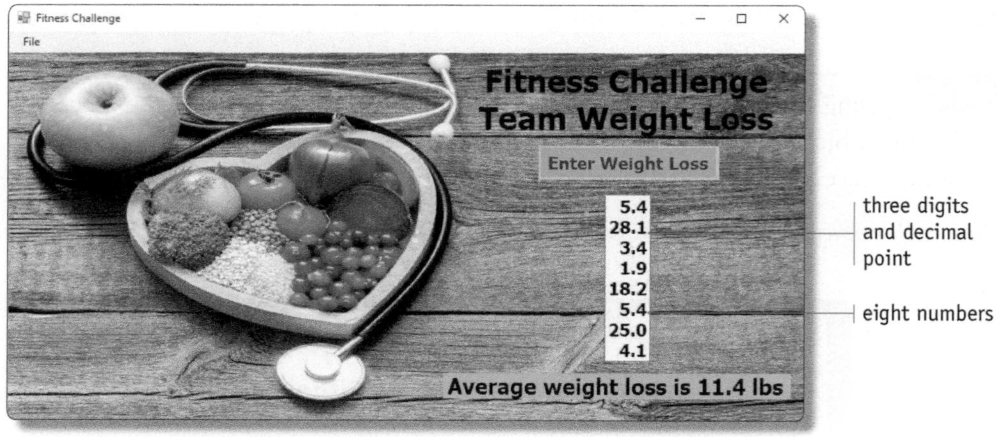

FIGURE 6-24

iStockphoto.com/udra

To display the weight loss of each team member in the list box, you must write code to add each item to the ListBox object. After an item is added, it is displayed in the list box. The general format of the statement to add an item to a ListBox object is shown in Figure 6-25.

General Format: Adding Items to a ListBox Object

```
lstListBoxName.Items.Add(Variable Name)
```

FIGURE 6-25

In Figure 6-25, the Add procedure will add the item contained in the variable identified by the Variable Name entry. The syntax for the statement must be followed precisely.

Figure 6-26 shows the code to add the team member weight loss values to the lstWeightLoss ListBox object and then display the weight loss of each team member (decWeightLoss) in the ListBox object.

```
lstWeightLoss.Items.Add(decWeightLoss)
```

FIGURE 6-26

If the number of items exceeds the number that can be displayed in the designated length of the ListBox object, a scroll bar automatically is added to the ListBox object, as shown in Figure 6-27.

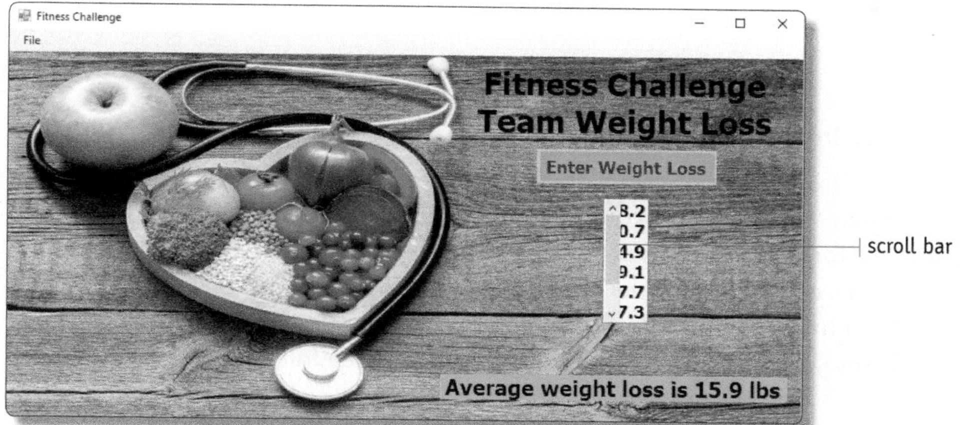

FIGURE 6-27

iStockphoto.com/udra

To clear the items in a ListBox object, the Clear method works as it does for the TextBox object. The syntax of the statement to clear the ListBox is shown in Figure 6-28.

General Format: Clear the ListBox Object

```
lstListBoxName.Items.Clear()
```

FIGURE 6-28

In the Fitness Challenge application, the user can select the Clear menu item to clear the form. The code in Figure 6-29 removes the items from the lstWeightLoss ListBox.

```
        lstWeightLoss.Items.Clear()
```

FIGURE 6-29

CONSIDER THIS

Can I control where the InputBox appears on the screen?
To control the position of the InputBox, you can add an optional X position and Y position representing the upper-left edge of the dialog box. The syntax of the InputBox with sample X and Y positions is as follows:
myValue = InputBox(message, title, defaultValue, 150, 100)
The 150 pixels represents the X position (horizontal) and the 100 pixels represents the Y position (vertical).

Add ListBox Items during Design

The Fitness Challenge application allows the user to add items to the ListBox object during program execution, but you can also add items to a ListBox object while designing the form. Adding items to the ListBox object during the design phase allows the user to select an item from the ListBox object during execution. For example, in an application to select a favorite clothing store, you can add items to a ListBox object named lstStores during the form design by completing the following steps:

STEP 1 Assume the lstStores ListBox object already has been placed and named on the Windows Form object. Select the ListBox object on the Windows Form object and then click the Items property in the Properties window.

The Items property in the Properties window is selected. An ellipsis button appears to the right of the (Collection) entry (Figure 6-30).

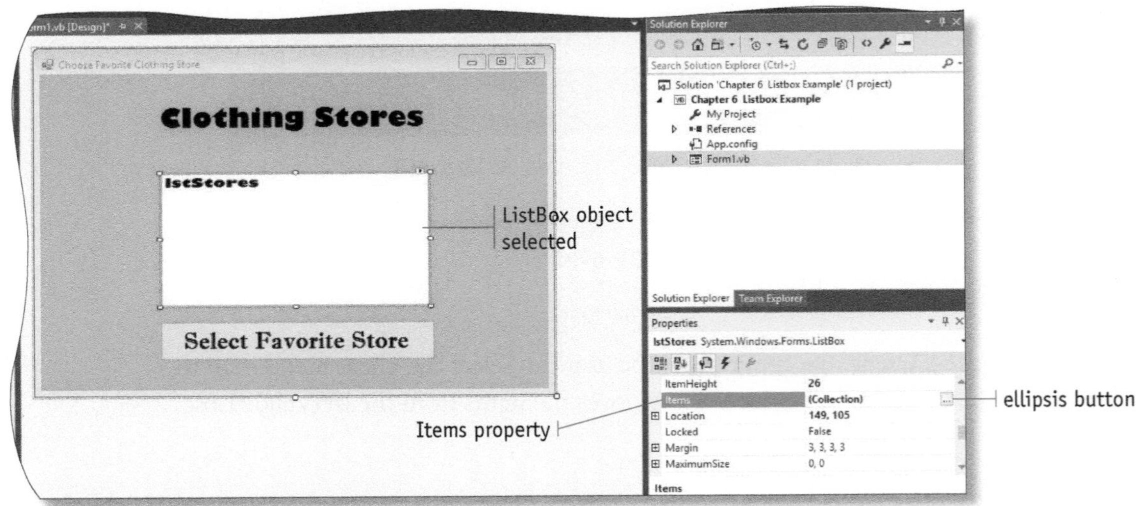

FIGURE 6-30

STEP 2 Click the ellipsis button in the right column of the Items property.

The String Collection Editor window opens, allowing you to enter items that will be displayed in the lstStores ListBox object (Figure 6-31).

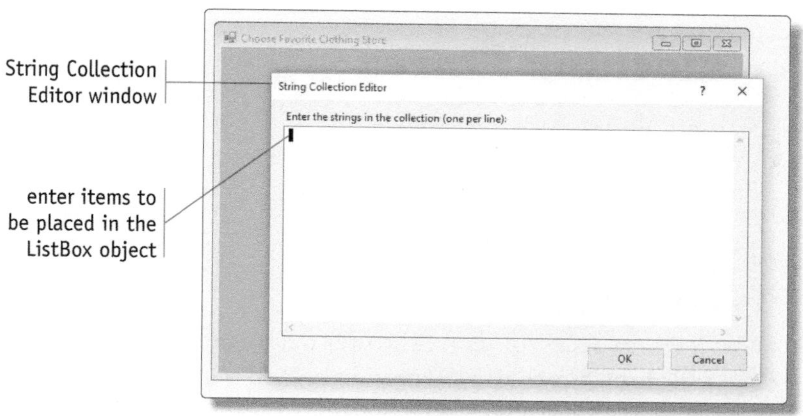

FIGURE 6-31

STEP 3 Click the String Collection Editor window. Type the following items to represent popular retail stores, and then press ENTER at the end of each line:

```
Abercrombie & Fitch
Anthropologie
Express
H & M
Urban Outfitters
```

The items representing favorite retail stores appear in the String Collection Editor window on separate lines (Figure 6-32).

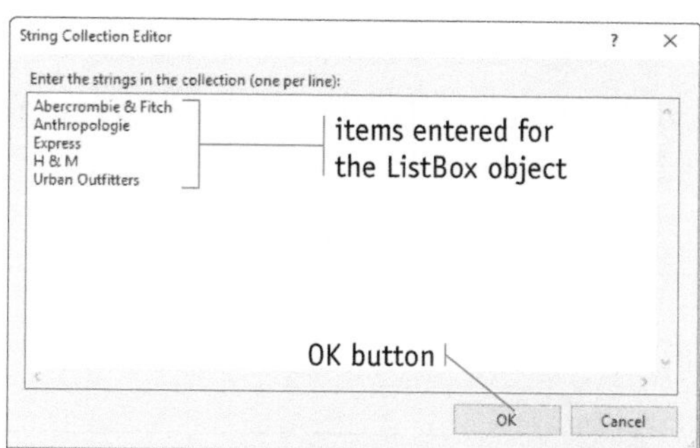

FIGURE 6-32

STEP 4 Click the OK button.

The Windows Form object displays the stores in the lstStores ListBox object (Figure 6-33). The user can select one of the items in the ListBox object during execution.

FIGURE 6-33

Use the SelectedItem Property

The SelectedItem property identifies which item in the ListBox is selected. An assignment statement assigns that property to a variable, as shown in Figure 6-34.

General Format: Assign the Selected Item in a ListBox Object

```
StrVariableName = lstListBoxName.selectedItem
```

FIGURE 6-34

Figure 6-35 shows the code to display the user's selection of his or her favorite store from the lstStores ListBox object in a message box.

```
        MsgBox("Your favorite store is "_
        &lstStores.SelectedItem & ".")
```

FIGURE 6-35

Add a Background Image

In addition to using background colors to design the Windows Form object, you may want to place a background image on the form itself. Background images are commonly displayed in your Facebook header and in mobile apps such as clouds in the background of the Weather Channel app. The **BackgroundImage** property of the Form object can set the background image to an imported image. The **Background ImageLayout** property can be used to control the appearance of the image on the form. By default the background image repeats the same picture in a tile pattern, but the BackgroundImageLayout property can be changed to Center, Stretch, or Zoom.

To change the background image on the form, you can complete the following steps, which assumes that you have downloaded the health image file from the CengageBrain site.

STEP 1 Click the Form object. In the Properties window, click the ellipsis button of the BackgroundImage property. Click the Import button and open the file location of the health image file. Click health.jpg and click the Open button.

The Select Resource window displays the imported background image file named health.jpg (Figure 6-36).

CRITICAL THINKING

Can I remove a background image from the Form object?
Yes. To remove the picture in the background of a form, in the Properties window press and hold or right-click the ellipsis button of the BackgroundImage property and select Reset.

FIGURE 6-36

iStockphoto.com/udra

STEP 2 Click the OK button.

The background image health.jpg is displayed in the frmFitness form (Figure 6-37).

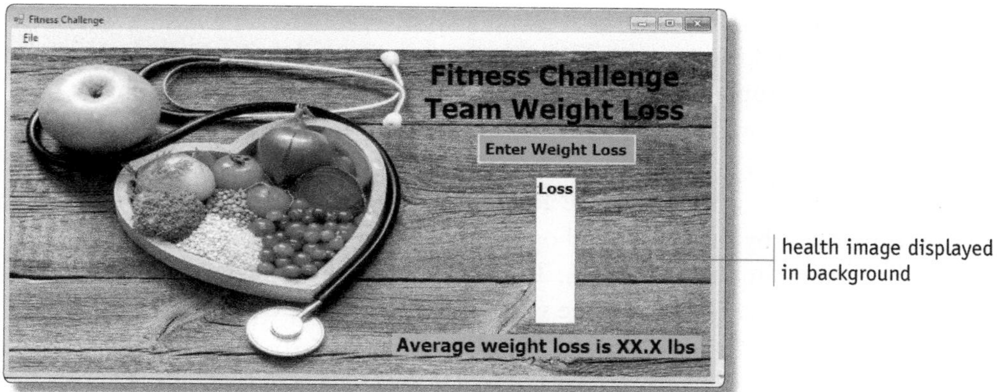

FIGURE 6-37

iStockphoto.com/udra

Use Accumulators, Counters, and Compound Operators

After the user enters the weight loss values of up to eight team members, the Fitness Challenge application calculates the average weight loss (see Figure 6-1 on page 302). The formula to calculate the average weight loss is: (total of all weight loss values entered) / (number of team members). For example, if the total of all the weight loss values entered is 145.2 and weight loss values were entered for eight team members, the average weight loss is 18.2 pounds.

To calculate the average, the program must add the weight loss of each team member to a variable. The variable that contains an accumulated value such as the total of all the weight loss values is called an **accumulator**.

To compute the average weight loss, the program must also keep track of how many weight loss values have been entered. The variable that keeps track of this value is called a **counter**. A counter always is incremented with a constant value. This value can be positive or negative. In the Fitness Challenge application, the counter is incremented by 1 each time the user enters a weight loss number for a team member. Only positive values that indicate how many pounds were lost are accepted; for example, 8.3 represents 8.3 pounds lost.

You can use one of two techniques to add a value to a variable and then update the value in the variable, as with an accumulator or a counter. The first technique is shown in Figure 6-38.

```
26        decTotalWeightLoss = decTotalWeightLoss + decWeightLoss
27        intNumberOfEntries = intNumberOfEntries + 1
```

FIGURE 6-38

On line 26 in Figure 6-38, the value in the decTotalWeightLoss variable is added to the value in the decWeightLoss variable and the result is stored in the decTotalWeightLoss variable. This statement accumulates the weight loss values in the decTotalWeightLoss accumulator. The statement in line 27 increments the number of entries counter by 1. The effect is that the value in the number of entries counter is increased by 1 each time the statement is executed.

A second method for accomplishing this task is to use a shortcut mathematical operator called a **compound operator** that allows you to add, subtract, multiply, divide, use modulus or exponents, or concatenate strings, storing the result in the same variable. An assignment statement that includes a compound operator begins with the variable that will contain the accumulated value, such as an accumulator or a counter, followed by the compound operator. A compound operator consists of an arithmetic operator and an equal sign. The last element in the assignment statement is the variable or literal containing the value to be used in the calculation.

CRITICAL THINKING

Why are accumulators typically found within a loop?

An accumulator calculates a running total. For example, at a basketball game, a three-point shot adds three points to the present score, so an accumulator of score += 3 adds three points to the existing score. The repetition of the game allows many three pointers to be scored, so each time the scorekeeper clicks the three-point button, the loop repeats and the score code statement within the loop accumulates three more points in its value.

An assignment statement using a compound operator such as:

```
intNumberOfEntries += 1
```

is the same as:

```
intNumberOfEntries = intNumberOfEntries + 1
```

The += compound operator adds the value of the right operand to the value of the left operand and stores the result in the left operand's variable. Similarly, the statement:

```
decTotalWeightLoss += decWeightLoss
```

is the same as:

```
decTotalWeightLoss = decTotalWeightLoss + decWeightLoss
```

The table in Figure 6-39 shows an example of compound operators used in code. Assume that intResult = 24, decResult = 24, and strSample = "tree".

Operation	**Example with Single Operators**	**Example with Compound Operator**	**Result**
Addition	intResult = intResult + 1	intResult + = 1	intResult = 25
Subtraction	intResult = intResult – 3	intResult – = 3	intResult = 21
Multiplication	intResult = intResult * 2	intResult * = 2	intResult = 48
Decimal Division	decResult = decResult / 5	decResult / = 5	decResult = 4.8
Integer Division	intResult = intResult \ 5	intResult \ = 5	intResult = 4
Exponents	intResult = intResult ^ 2	intResult ^ = 2	intResult = 576
Concatenate	strSample = strSample & "house"	strSample & = "house"	strSample = "tree house"

FIGURE 6-39

Developers often use compound operators in Visual Basic coding. The coding example in Figure 6-40 uses several compound operators and a MsgBox object. When the following code is executed, the result shown in the MsgBox object is "Final Result = 2."

```
Dim intTotal As Integer
intTotal = 7
intTotal += 6
intTotal *= 2
intTotal /= 13
MsgBox("Final Result = " & intTotal.ToString(), , "Compound Operators")
```

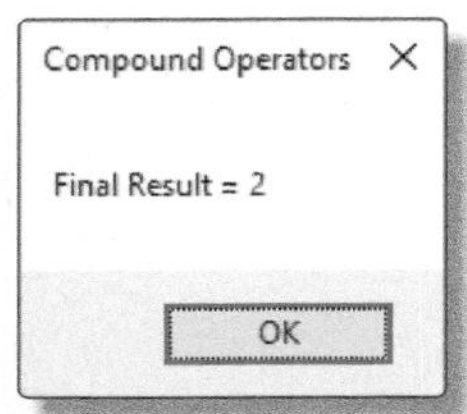

FIGURE 6-40

HEADS UP

The compound operators +=, -=, *=, /=, \=, ^=, and &= run faster than their regular longer equation counterparts because the statement is more compact.

Compound operators can also be used to connect two strings with the concatenation operator (&). The code in Figure 6-41 creates the phrase "To err is human!" in a MsgBox object by using compound operators to concatenate the strPhrase variable. Each compound operator joins another word to the end of the phrase assigned to the strPhrase variable.

```
Dim strPhrase As String
strPhrase = "To err"
strPhrase &= " is "
strPhrase &= "human!"
MsgBox(strPhrase, , "Compound Operators")
```

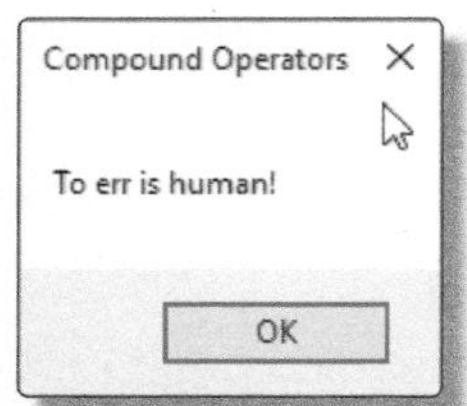

FIGURE 6-41

Use Loops to Perform Repetitive Tasks

In the Fitness Challenge application, the user enters weight loss values in an InputBox for up to eight team members. The repetitive process of entering eight weight loss values can be coded within a loop to simplify the task with fewer lines of code. Unlike If...Then statements that execute only once, loops repeat multiple times.

Each repetition of the loop is called an iteration. An iteration is a single execution of a set of instructions that are to be repeated.

Loops are powerful structures that repeat a section of code a certain number of times or until a particular condition is met. Visual Basic has two main types of loops: For...Next loops and Do loops.

Repeat a Process Using the For...Next Loop

You can use a For...Next loop when a section of code should be executed an exact number of times. The syntax of a For...Next loop is shown in Figure 6-42.

General Format: For...Next loop

```
For Control Variable = Beginning Numeric Value To Ending
                       Numeric Value

   ' Body of the Loop

 Next
```

FIGURE 6-42

In Figure 6-42, the For...Next loop begins with the keyword For. Following this keyword is the control variable, which is the numeric variable that keeps track of the number of iterations the loop completes. To begin the loop, the For statement places the beginning numeric value in the control variable. The program then executes the code between the For and Next statements, which is called the body of the loop.

Upon reaching the Next statement, the program returns to the For statement and increments the value of the control variable. This process continues until the value in the control variable is greater than the ending numeric value. The program then executes the statement(s) that follows the Next command.

Figure 6-43 shows a For...Next loop designed to execute four times. The control value is a variable named intNumber.

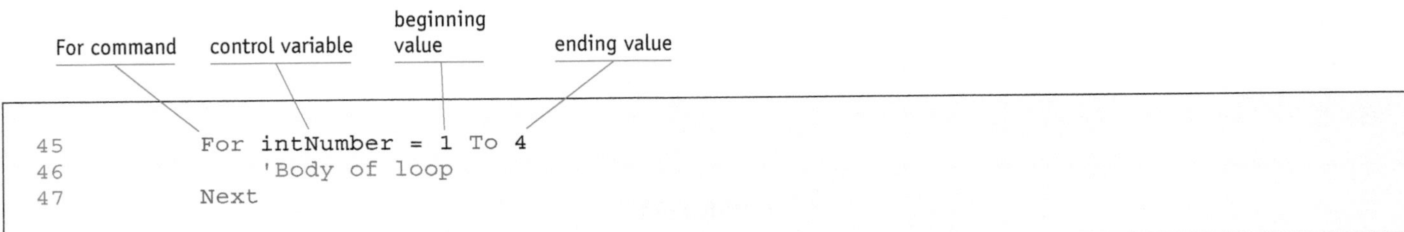

FIGURE 6-43

The first line in Figure 6-43 specifies that the control variable (intNumber) is assigned the value 1 because the literal 1 is the beginning value. Then the program executes the body of the loop. When the program encounters the Next statement, control returns to the For statement where, by default, the value 1 is added to the control variable. The code in the body of the loop is executed again. This process continues until the value in the control variable is greater than the ending value, which is 4 in this example. Then the program executes the statement(s) that follow the Next command. A loop never ends in the middle of the loop. The comparison is made to the upper limit of the For statement, and when the value exceeds the upper limit, the loop terminates. The table in Figure 6-44 illustrates the looping process.

Loop Iteration	Value of intNumber	Process
1	intNumber = 1	Executes the code inside the loop
2	intNumber = 2	Executes the code inside the loop
3	intNumber = 3	Executes the code inside the loop
4	intNumber = 4	Executes the code inside the loop
5 (exits the loop)	intNumber = 5	The control variable value exceeds the ending value, so the application exits the For...Next loop. This means the statement(s) following the Next command are executed.

FIGURE 6-44

Include a Step Value in a For...Next Loop

A Step value is the value in a For...Next loop that is added to or subtracted from the beginning value on each iteration of the loop. If you do not include a Step value in the For statement, as shown in Figure 6-45, by default the value in the control variable is incremented by 1 after each iteration of the loop.

Step value

```
For intNumber = 1 To 99 Step 2
    ' Body of loop
Next
```

FIGURE 6-45

In Figure 6-45, a Step value of 2 has been added to the For statement. The control variable intNumber is set to the initial value of 1, and the lines of code in the body of the loop are executed. After the first iteration of the loop, the Step value is added to the control variable, changing the value in the control variable to 3 (1 + 2 = 3). The For loop will continue until the value in intNumber is greater than 99.

The Step value can be negative. If so, the value in the control variable is decreased on each iteration of the loop. To exit the loop, you must specify an ending value that is less than the beginning value, as shown in Figure 6-46.

negative Step value

```
For intCount = 25 To -10 Step -5
    ' Body of loop
Next
```

FIGURE 6-46

In the first iteration of the For...Next loop in Figure 6-46, the control variable value is 25. The value in the intCount control variable is decreased by 5 each time the loop repeats. This repetition continues until the value in intCount is less than –10. Then the loop ends.

You can also assign decimal values to the control variable in a For...Next loop. For example, the For loop in Figure 6-47 has a starting value of 3.1. The loop ends when the value in the control variable is greater than 4.5. The Step value is 0.1, which means the value in decNumber increments by 0.1 on each pass through the loop.

decimal Step value

```
For decNumber = 3.1 To 4.5 Step 0.1
    ' Body of loop
Next
```

FIGURE 6-47

A For...Next loop can also include variables and mathematical expressions, as shown in Figure 6-48.

```
        For intNumber = intBegin To (intEnd * 2) Step intIncrement
            'Body of loop
        Next
```

FIGURE 6-48

In Figure 6-48, the intNumber control variable is initialized with the value in the intBegin variable. Each time the Next statement is encountered and control is returned to the For statement, the value in intNumber is incremented by the value in the intIncrement variable. The loop continues until the value in intNumber is greater than the product of the value in intEnd times 2.

Use IntelliSense to Enter the For...Next Loop Code

Suppose an application is designed to have a list box that displays the population growth for Alaska during the next six years. Assume that the current population of Alaska is 675,000 people and is expected to grow at 5 percent per year for the next six years. The code in Figure 6-49 accomplishes this processing.

```
        Dim intAlaskaPopulation As Integer = 675000
        Dim intYears As Integer

        For intYears = 1 To 6
            intAlaskaPopulation += (intAlaskaPopulation * 0.05)
            lstGrowth.Items.Add("Year " & intYears & " Population " & intAlaskaPopulation)

        Next
```

FIGURE 6-49

To use IntelliSense to enter the code shown in Figure 6-49, you can complete the following steps, which assume a lstGrowth ListBox object has been defined on a Windows Form object.

STEP 1 In the code window, type `Dim intAlaskaPopulation As Integer = 675000` and then press the ENTER key. Type `Dim intYears As Integer` and then press the ENTER key two times. Type `for` and a space to open an IntelliSense list.

When you press the SPACEBAR, For is capitalized because it is a reserved word (Figure 6-50).

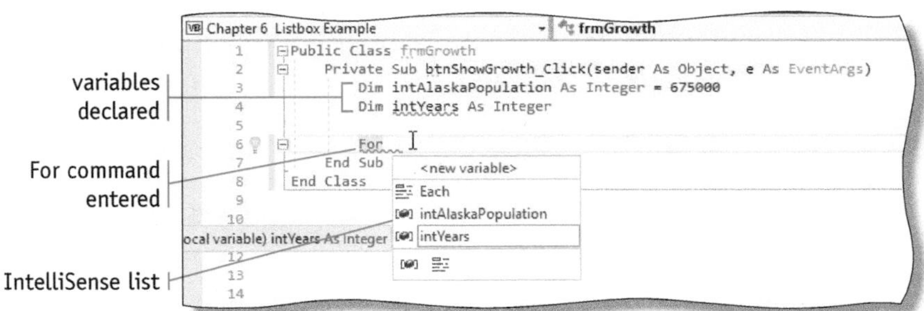

FIGURE 6-50

STEP 2 Type the first four letters of the intYears variable name (`intY`) to select intYears in the IntelliSense list. Type `= 1 to 6` and then press the ENTER key to specify the beginning value and ending value for the loop.

Visual Basic automatically inserts the Next statement in the code (Figure 6-51). For, To, and Next are blue to indicate they are keywords.

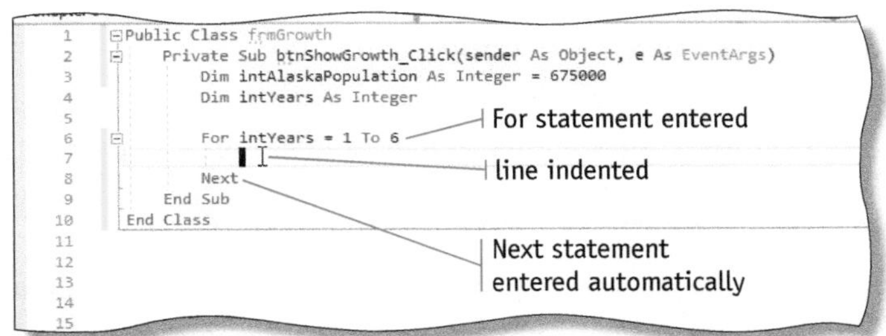

FIGURE 6-51

STEP 3 Use IntelliSense to select the appropriate variables. Enter the two new lines shown in Figure 6-52.

Each line of code automatically is indented between the For and Next statements (Figure 6-52).

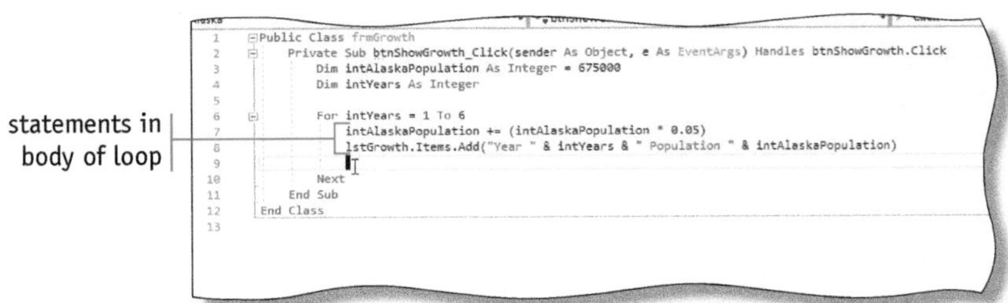

FIGURE 6-52

STEP 4 Run the program to see the results of the loop.

The loop calculates and displays the Alaskan population growth for six years based on 5 percent growth per year (Figure 6-53).

IN THE REAL WORLD

It is best to indent the body of the loop to clearly display what is being repeated. When you use IntelliSense to enter the loop, Visual Basic automatically indents the code properly. When other developers read the code, it is easy to identify the indented portion as the loop body.

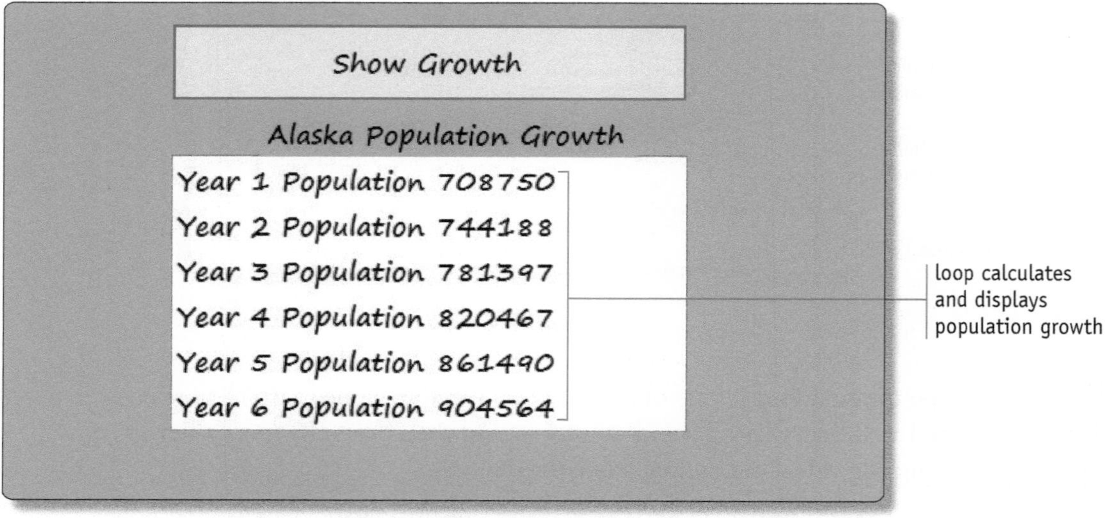

FIGURE 6-53

Handle User Input in a For...Next Loop

The beginning, ending, and Step values used in a For...Next loop can vary based on user input. For example, the Squared Values application shown in Figure 6-54 displays the squared values of a range of numbers the user enters. The user enters the beginning (minimum) and ending (maximum) range of values and then clicks the Calculate Values button to view the squares of the numbers in the range.

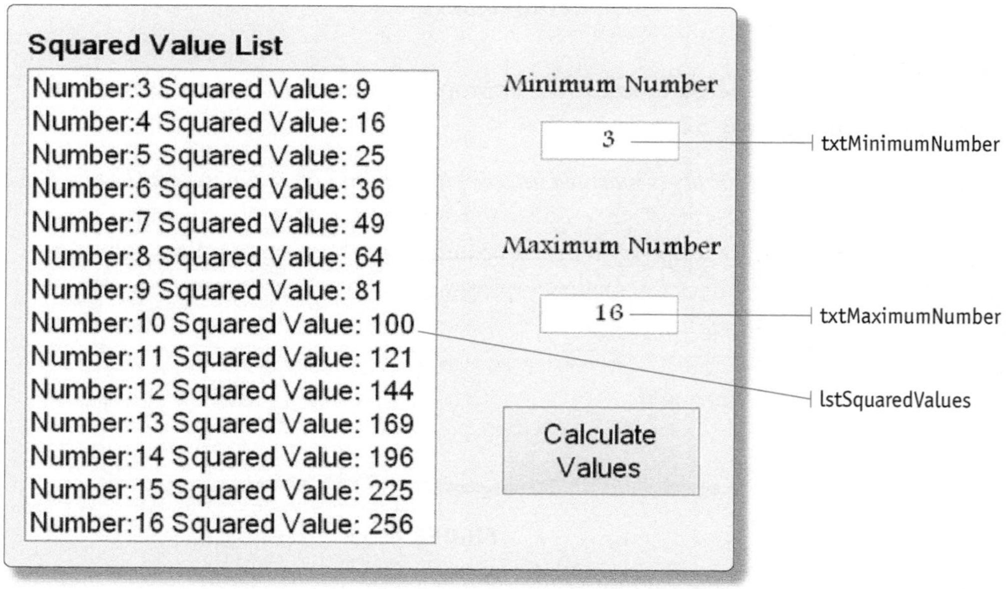

FIGURE 6-54

The code for the Squared Values application is shown in Figure 6-55.

```
 5      Dim intCount As Integer
 6      Dim intBegin As Integer
 7      Dim intEnd As Integer
 8
 9      intBegin = Convert.ToInt32(txtMinimumNumber.Text)
10      intEnd = Convert.ToInt32(txtMaximumNumber.Text)
11
12      For intCount = intBegin To intEnd
13          lstSquaredValues.Items.Add("Number: " & intCount & " Squared Value: " & (intCount ^ 2))
14      Next
15
16  End Sub
```

FIGURE 6-55

On line 9 in Figure 6-55, the minimum value the user entered is converted to an integer and placed in the intBegin variable. Similarly, on line 10, the maximum value the user entered is converted to an integer and assigned to the intEnd variable. On line 12, the value in intBegin is used as the beginning value in the For...Next loop, and the value in intEnd is used as the ending value. As you can see, the number of iterations for the loop is determined by values the user entered.

Within the loop, the value in intCount begins with the value in intBegin and is incremented by the default value of 1 each time through the loop. The application calculates the squared value from the number in intCount. As a result, the application calculates the squared values for all numbers beginning with the minimum number and ending with the maximum number.

Repeat a Process Using a Do Loop

You use a For...Next loop to repeat a process an exact number of times. In many applications, however, a loop should be repeated until a certain condition changes. For example, in the Fitness Challenge application, the user repeats the process of entering a weight loss value eight times and then stops entering values by clicking the Cancel button. The loop in the Fitness Challenge application continues until one of two conditions becomes true: either the count of the weight loss values entered reaches 8 or the user clicks the Cancel button on the InputBox object.

In a **Do loop**, the body of the loop is executed while or until a condition is true or false. The Do loop uses a condition similar to an If...Then decision structure to determine whether it should continue looping. In this way, you can use a Do loop to execute a body of statements an indefinite number of times. In the Fitness Challenge application, a Do loop can run an indefinite number of times because the user can end the loop at any time by clicking the Cancel button.

Visual Basic 2017 provides two types of Do loops: the Do While loop and the Do Until loop. Both Do loops execute statements repeatedly until a specified condition becomes true or false. Each loop examines a condition to determine whether the condition is true. The **Do While loop** executes as long as the condition is true. It is stated as, "Do the loop processing while the condition is true."

The **Do Until loop** executes until the condition becomes true. It is stated as, "Do the loop processing until a condition is true."

Do loops are either top-controlled or bottom-controlled, depending on whether the condition is tested before the loop begins or after the body of the loop has executed one time. A **top-controlled loop** is tested before the loop is entered. A top-controlled loop is also called a pre-test. The body of a top-controlled loop might not be executed at all because the condition being tested might be true before any processing in the loop occurs.

Bottom-controlled loops test the condition at the bottom of the loop, also called a post test, so the body of a bottom-controlled loop is executed at least once. Visual Basic provides top-controlled and bottom-controlled Do While and Do Until loops, meaning it can execute four types of Do loops.

Top-Controlled Do While Loops

You use a top-controlled Do While loop if you want the body of the loop to repeat as long as a condition remains true. Figure 6-56 shows the syntax of a top-controlled Do While loop.

General Format: Do While Loop (Top-Controlled)

```
Do While condition
    ' Body of loop
Loop
```

FIGURE 6-56

A top-controlled Do While loop begins with the keywords Do While. Next, the condition is specified. The condition is expressed using the same relational operators that are available with the If statements that you learned in Chapter 5. Any condition that can be specified in an If statement can be specified in a Do While condition. The condition can compare numeric values or string values.

The body of the loop contains the instructions that are executed as long as the condition is true. The Loop keyword indicates the end of the loop. Visual Basic inserts it automatically when you enter the Do While keywords.

A statement within the body of the Do While loop must cause the condition to change at some point so the loop ends. For example, consider the following statement:

```
Do While strColor = "Red"
```

The loop continues to process as long as the value in the strColor variable remains Red. Based on the processing in the body of the loop, at some point the value in the strColor variable must be changed from Red. If not, the loop will not end. A loop that does not end is called an **infinite loop**.

The code in Figure 6-57 is an example of a top-controlled Do While loop. It continues to add 1 to the variable intScore while intScore is less than 5. It is considered a top-controlled loop because the condition is checked at the top of the loop.

```
        Dim intScore As Integer = 0
        Do While intScore < 5
            intScore += 1
        Loop
```

FIGURE 6-57

The loop in Figure 6-57 begins by testing whether intScore is less than 5. Because intScore starts with the value 0, the condition tested is true: 0 is less than 5. Next, the variable intScore is incremented by 1, and the loop repeats. The table in Figure 6-58 displays the values that are assigned to intScore each time the condition is checked in the code in Figure 6-57.

Loop Iteration	Value of intScore	Result of Condition Tested
1	intScore = 0	True
2	intScore = 1	True
3	intScore = 2	True
4	intScore = 3	True
5	intScore = 4	True
6	intScore = 5	False

FIGURE 6-58

The loop in Figure 6-57 is executed five times because intScore is less than 5 during five iterations of the loop. As shown in Figure 6-57, if the value in the variable intScore is 5 or greater when the Do While statement is first executed, the body of the loop never will be executed because the condition is not true prior to the first iteration of the loop.

Enter a Do Loop Using IntelliSense

To use IntelliSense to enter the Do While loop shown in Figure 6-57, you can complete the following steps:

STEP 1 In the code window, enter the intScore variable declaration and then press the ENTER key. Type `Do While` and a space to display an IntelliSense list. Type `ints` to highlight intScore in the list.

The words Do While appear in blue because they are Visual Basic keywords (Figure 6-59). The IntelliSense list contains the valid entries and the intScore variable name is highlighted.

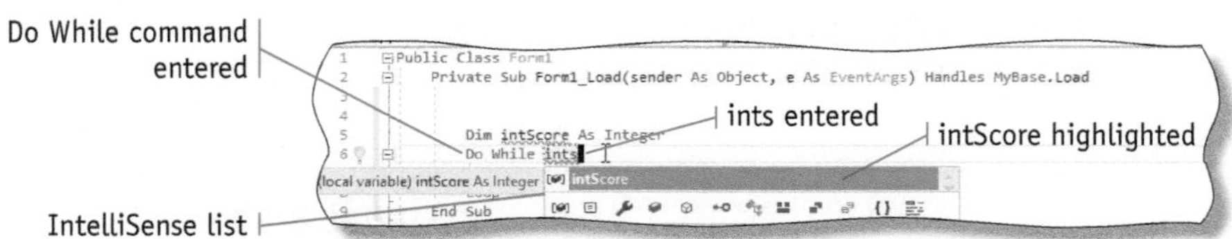

FIGURE 6-59

STEP 2 Type < `5` and then press the ENTER key.

Visual Basic automatically inserts the intScore variable name and the characters you typed (Figure 6-60). The keyword Loop is also inserted and the insertion point is located inside the loop, ready to enter the body of the loop.

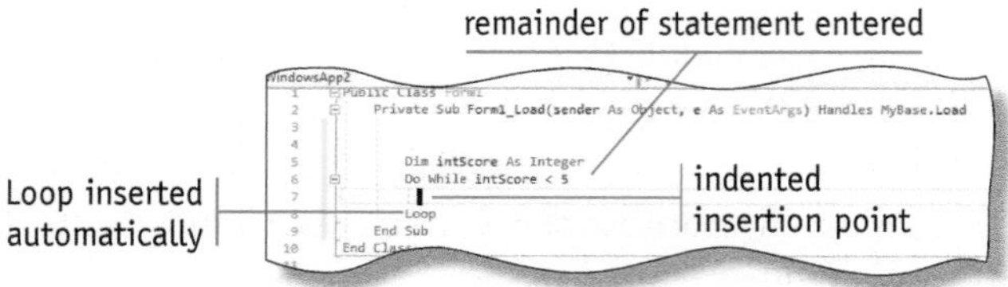

FIGURE 6-60

HEADS UP

Use a top-controlled loop if you want to test the condition before entering the body of the loop. Use a bottom-controlled loop if you want the body to execute one time and then test the condition to see if the loop continues.

STEP 3 Type `ints` to highlight the intScore variable. Complete the statement by typing += `1` and then pressing the ENTER key. Press the DELETE key to delete the blank line.

The statement automatically is indented between the Do While and Loop statements (Figure 6-61). The intScore += 1 statement uses a compound operator to increment the intScore variable.

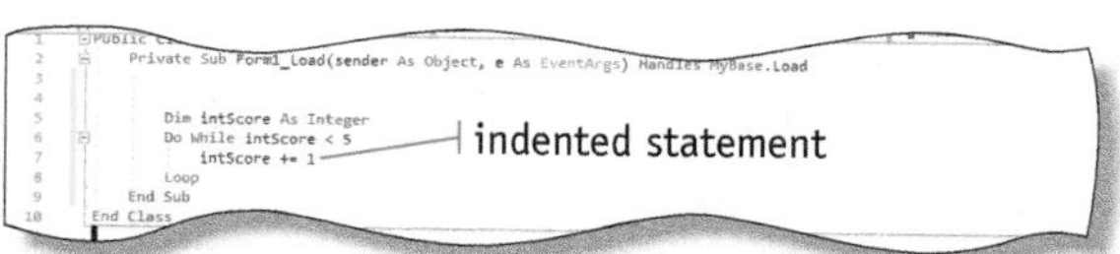

FIGURE 6-61

Bottom-Controlled Do While Loops

You can write a Do While loop in which the condition is tested at the bottom of the loop. A bottom-controlled loop works the same way as the top-controlled Do While loop except that the body of the loop is executed before the condition is checked the first time, guaranteeing that at least one iteration of a loop will be completed. The bottom-controlled Do While loop has the syntax shown in Figure 6-62.

General Format: Do While Loop (Bottom-controlled)

```
Do
            ' Loop Body
Loop While condition
```

FIGURE 6-62

In Figure 6-62, the word Do appears on its own line at the beginning of the loop. The loop body follows, and the Loop While statement is the last statement in the loop. The Loop While statement contains the condition that is tested to determine if the loop should be terminated. Because the While condition is in the last statement of the loop, the body of the loop is executed one time regardless of the status of the condition.

The code in Figure 6-63 is an example of a bottom-controlled Do While loop.

```
Dim intScore As Integer = 0
Do
    intScore = intScore + 1
Loop While intScore < 5
```

FIGURE 6-63

The body of the Do loop in Figure 6-63 is executed one time before the condition in the Loop While statement is checked. The variable intScore begins with the initial value of 0 and is incremented in the body of the loop, changing the value to 1. The condition is then tested and found to be true because 1 < 5. The loop repeats and the value of intScore increases, as shown in Figure 6-64.

Loop Iteration	Value of intScore at Start of the Loop	Value of intScore When Checked	Result of Condition Tested
1	intScore = 0	intScore = 1	True
2	intScore = 1	intScore = 2	True
3	intScore = 2	intScore = 3	True
4	intScore = 3	intScore = 4	True
5	intScore = 4	intScore = 5	False

FIGURE 6-64

The body of the loop in Figure 6-63 is executed four times because intScore is less than 5 during five iterations of the loop.

Use Do Until Loops

A loop similar to a Do While loop is called a Do Until loop. The Do Until loop allows you to specify that an action repeats until a condition becomes true. When the condition in a Do Until loop becomes true, the loop ends.

Top-Controlled Do Until Loops

A Do Until loop can be both top-controlled and bottom-controlled. The syntax of the top-controlled Do Until loop is shown in Figure 6-65.

General Format: Do Until Loop (Top-Controlled)

```
Do Until condition
            ' Loop Body
Loop
```

FIGURE 6-65

A top-controlled Do Until loop begins with the keywords Do Until. Next, as with the Do While top-controlled loop, the condition is specified. The condition is expressed using the same relational operators that are available with If statements. Any condition that can be specified in an If statement can be specified in a Do Until condition. The condition can compare numeric values or string values.

The Do Until loop example shown in Figure 6-66 displays a parking meter application that computes the number of minutes a user can purchase based on the cost of 25 cents for each 15 minutes of parking. If the user only has 88 cents in pocket change, for example, the application computes how many minutes of parking time 88 cents will purchase.

```
        Dim decAmount As Decimal = 0.88
        Dim intQuarters As Integer = 0
        Dim intTime As Integer = 15
        Dim intParkingTime As Integer

        Do Until decAmount < 0.25
            intQuarters += 1
            decAmount -= 0.25
        Loop
        intParkingTime = intQuarters * intTime
        lblParkingTime.Text = "Parking Time: " &
                               intParkingTime.ToString() & " minutes"
```

FIGURE 6-66

In the code example in Figure 6-66, the application checks the Do Until loop condition before executing the body of the loop. The first time the condition is tested, the expression decAmount < 0.25 is false because the decAmount variable contains 0.88. The body of the loop is executed because the Do Until statement specifies that the loop continues until the value in decAmount is less than 0.25. When the body of the loop is executed, it adds 1 to intQuarters to count the number of quarters the user has for the parking meter, and then subtracts 0.25 from decAmount because a quarter is worth 25 cents. Because decAmount is first assigned the value 0.88, the loop executes three times (decAmount = 0.88, decAmount = 0.63, and decAmount = 0.38) and stops when decAmount becomes less than 0.25. The lblParkingTime Label object displays the text "Parking Time: 45 minutes."

Bottom-Controlled Do Until Loops

The last of the four Do loops is the bottom-controlled Do Until loop. This Do Until loop checks the condition after the body of the loop is executed. The loop continues until the condition becomes true. The syntax of the bottom-controlled Do Until loop is shown in Figure 6-67.

General Format: Do Until Loop (Botttom-Controlled)

```
Do
            ' Loop Body
Loop Until condition
```

FIGURE 6-67

In Figure 6-67, the bottom-controlled Do Until loop begins with the word Do. The body of the loop is executed one time regardless of the condition being tested. The Loop Until statement checks the condition. The loop will be repeated until the condition is true.

CRITICAL THINKING

In a payroll program, should I use a For loop or Do While loop to repeat the process of entering the hours for each employee every two weeks?
Typically a Do While loop is the better option because the number of employees fluctuates. If you do not know the exact number of iterations, it is best to use the Do While loop structure.

Other Loop Considerations

Other considerations when using loops are creating user input loops, avoiding infinite loops, priming a loop, validating data with a loop, creating a nested loop, and selecting the best type of loop.

User Input Loops

Do loops often are written to end when the user enters a certain value or performs a certain action such as clicking the Cancel button in an input box. The developer determines the value or action. For example, a Do Until loop might accumulate the total of all the entered test scores until the user clicks the Cancel button in the input box. If the user clicks the Cancel button, the InputBox function returns a null string that is assigned to the strTestGrade variable. The Do Until statement tests the string. If it contains a null character, the loop is terminated.

Avoid Infinite Loops

Recall that an infinite loop is a loop that never ends. It happens when the condition specified to end the loop never occurs. If the loop does not end, it repeats until the program is interrupted. Figure 6-68 shows an example of an infinite loop.

```
Dim intProblem = 0
Do While intProblem <= 5
   Box.Show("This loop will not end", "Infinite Loop")
Loop
```

FIGURE 6-68

The Do While loop in Figure 6-68 never ends because the value in the variable intProblem is never changed from its initial value of zero. Because the value in intProblem never exceeds 5, the condition in the Do While loop (intProblem <= 5) never becomes false. The processing in a loop eventually must change the condition being tested in the Do While loop so the loop will terminate. When working in Visual Basic 2017, you can interrupt an infinite loop by clicking the Stop Debugging button on the Standard toolbar.

CONSIDER THIS

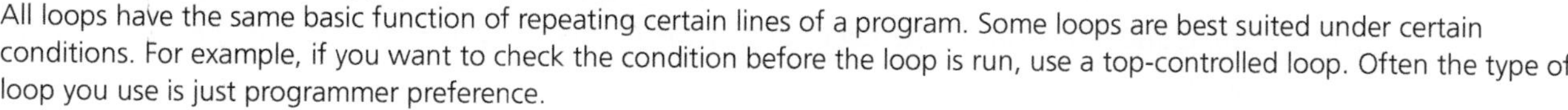

How do I know which type of loop to use?
All loops have the same basic function of repeating certain lines of a program. Some loops are best suited under certain conditions. For example, if you want to check the condition before the loop is run, use a top-controlled loop. Often the type of loop you use is just programmer preference.

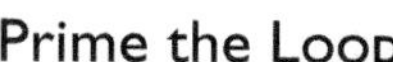

Prime the Loop

As you have learned, a top-controlled loop tests a condition prior to beginning the loop. In most cases, the value to test must be set before the condition is tested the first time in the Do While or Do Until statement. Starting a loop with a preset value in the variable(s) tested in the condition is called **priming the loop**. You have seen this in previous examples, such as in Figure 6-66 on page 306, where the value in decAmount is set before the condition is tested the first time.

In some applications, the loop is primed with a value the user enters or an action the user takes. For example, in the Fitness Challenge application, the user enters the weight loss value for each team member (up to eight values) or clicks the Cancel button in the input box. Prior to executing the Do Until statement the first time in the Do Until loop that processes the data the user enters, the InputBox function must be executed to obtain an initial value. Then, the Do Until statement can test the action taken by the user (enter a value and click the Cancel button). The coding to implement this processing is shown in Figure 6-69.

```
        Dim strCancelClicked As String = ""
        Dim intMaxNumberOfEntries As Integer = 8
        Dim intNumberOfEntries As Integer = 1
⋮
        strWeightLoss = InputBox(strInputMessage & intNumberOfEntries, strInputHeading, " ")

        Do Until intNumberOfEntries > intMaxNumberOfEntries Or strWeightLoss = strCancelClicked
⋮
                intNumberOfEntries += 1
⋮
            If intNumberOfEntries <= intMaxNumberOfEntries Then
                strWeightLoss = InputBox(strInputMessage & intNumberOfEntries, strInputHeading, " ")
            End If

        Loop
```

FIGURE 6-69

In the Do Until loop shown in Figure 6-69, the Do Until statement on line 40 tests two conditions: Is the value in the intNumberOfEntries variable greater than the value in the intMaxNumberOfEntries variable or is the value in the strWeightLoss variable equal to the value in the strCancelClicked variable, which is a null character (see line 30)? If either condition is true, the body of the loop is not executed.

The Do Until loop must have two primed variables: the intNumberOfEntries variable and the strWeightLoss variable. The intNumberOfEntries variable is initialized to 1 on line 32. The strWeightLoss variable is initialized by the InputBox function call on line 38. In this function call, the user either entered a value or clicked the Cancel button. If the user clicked the Cancel button, the body of the loop should not be entered.

To continue the loop, the processing within the body of the loop eventually must change one of the conditions being tested in the Do Until statement or the loop never terminates. In the sample program, the conditions being tested are whether the user entered eight weight loss values or clicked the Cancel button. Therefore, within the loop, the variable containing intNumberOfEntries must be incremented when the user enters a valid weight loss value. The user then must be able to enter more weight loss values or click the Cancel button. On line 47 in Figure 6-69, the value in intNumberOfEntries is incremented by 1 each time the user enters a valid weight loss value. In addition, the statement on line 57 displays an input box that allows the user to enter a new value or click the Cancel button as long as the number of valid entries is not greater than the maximum number of entries.

Validate Data

As you learned in Chapter 5, you must test the data a user enters to ensure it is accurate and that its use in other programming statements, such as converting string data to numeric data, will not cause a program exception. When using an input box, the data should be checked using the IsNumeric function and If statements, as discussed in Chapter 5. If the data is not valid, the user must be notified of the error and an input box displayed to allow the user to enter valid data.

For example, if the user enters nonnumeric data, the input box in Figure 6-70 should be displayed.

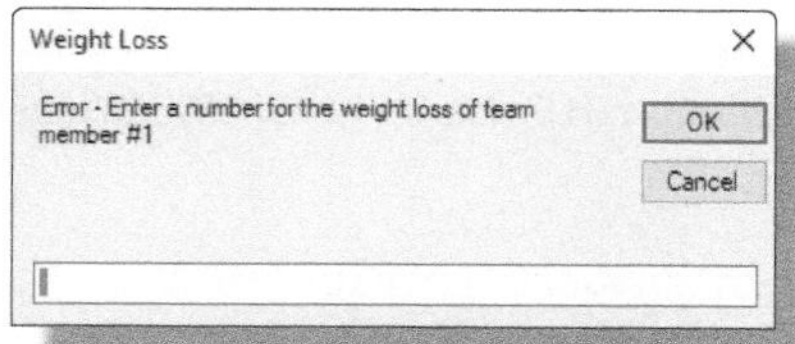

FIGURE 6-70

Similarly, if the user enters a negative number, the message in Figure 6-71 should be displayed in an input box.

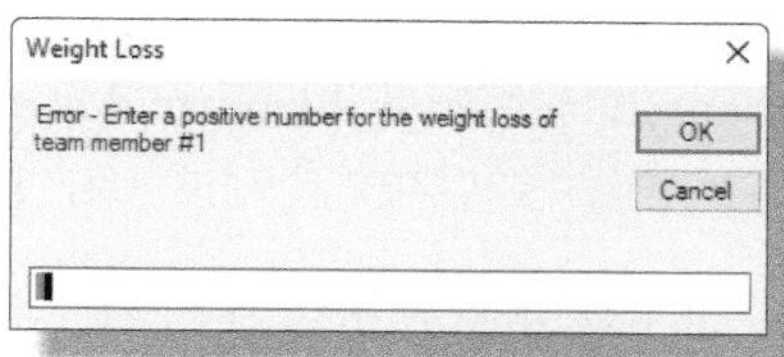

FIGURE 6-71

When error checking is performed within a loop and the user is asked to enter data in an input box, the body of the loop must be executed each time the user enters data, regardless of whether the data is valid or invalid. If the user enters valid data, then the data is processed according to the needs of the program.

If the user enters invalid data, an error message is displayed and the user is given the opportunity to enter valid data in the input box. The coding for the Fitness Challenge application that accomplishes these tasks is shown in Figure 6-72.

```
33          ' clicks the Cancel button or the Close button in the InputBox
34          strWeightLoss = InputBox(strInputMessage & intNumberOfEntries, strInputHeading, " ")
35
36          Do Until intNumberOfEntries > intMaxNumberOfEntries Or strWeightLoss = strCancelClicked
37              If IsNumeric(strWeightLoss) Then
38                  decWeightLoss = Convert.ToDecimal(strWeightLoss)
39                  If decWeightLoss > 0 Then
40                      lstWeightLoss.Items.Add(decWeightLoss)
41                      decTotalWeightLoss += decWeightLoss
42                      intNumberOfEntries += 1
43                      strInputMessage = strNormalMessage
44                  Else
45                      strInputMessage = strNegativeError
46                  End If
47              Else
48                  strInputMessage = strNonNumericError
49              End If
50              If intNumberOfEntries <= intMaxNumberOfEntries Then
51                  strWeightLoss = InputBox(strInputMessage & intNumberOfEntries, strInputHeading, " ")
52              End If
53          Loop
```

FIGURE 6-72

In Figure 6-72, the loop is primed by the InputBox function call on line 34. The Do Until statement on line 36 checks the two conditions—if the value in the intNumberOfEntries counter is greater than the maximum number of entries or if the user clicks the Cancel button. In either case, the body of the loop is not executed.

When the body of the loop is executed, the application checks the data the user entered to verify it is numeric. If it is numeric, the value is converted to a Decimal data type and then is checked to ensure it is greater than zero (line 39). If it is greater than zero, it is added to the lstWeightLoss ListBox object, the decTotalWeightLoss accumulator is incremented by the weight loss value the user entered, the intNumberOfEntries counter is incremented by 1, and the normal message is moved to the strInputMessage variable. This variable contains the message that is displayed in the input box (see line 34).

If the value the user entered is not greater than zero, the statement following the Else statement on line 45 moves the value in the strNegativeError variable to the strInputMessage variable so that the next time the InputBox function is called, the message will indicate an error, as shown in Figure 6-71.

If the value the user entered was not numeric (as tested by the statement on line 37), the statement on line 48 moves the value in the strNonNumericError variable to the strInputMessage variable so that the next time the InputBox function is called, the message will indicate a nonnumeric error, as shown in Figure 6-70.

On lines 50 and 51, as long as the number of entries is not greater than the maximum number of entries, the InputBox function is called. The message that is displayed in the input box depends on whether an error occurred. The Do Until statement on line 36 is executed and the process begins again.

Create a Nested Loop

In Chapter 5, you learned to nest If...Then...Else statements within each other. Loops can also be nested. You can place any type of loop within any other type of loop under the following conditions: Interior loops must be completely contained inside the outer loop and must have a different control variable. The example in Figure 6-73 uses a nested For loop to display a list of the weeks in the first quarter of the year (13 weeks) along with the days in each week. The outer For...Next loop counts from 1 to 13 for the 13 weeks, and the inner For...Next loop counts from 1 to 7 for the days in each of the 13 weeks.

The code in Figure 6-73 displays the output shown in Figure 6-74.

```
Dim intOuterCount As Integer ' Counts the first 13 weeks in a quarter
Dim intInnerCount As Integer ' Counts the 7 days in a week
For intOuterCount = 1 To 13 ' For weeks in the 1st quarter of the year
    For intInnerCount = 1 To 7 ' For the 7 days in a week
        lstDays.Items.Add("Week: " & intOuterCount.ToString() _
                          & " Day: " & intInnerCount.ToString())
    Next
Next
```

FIGURE 6-73

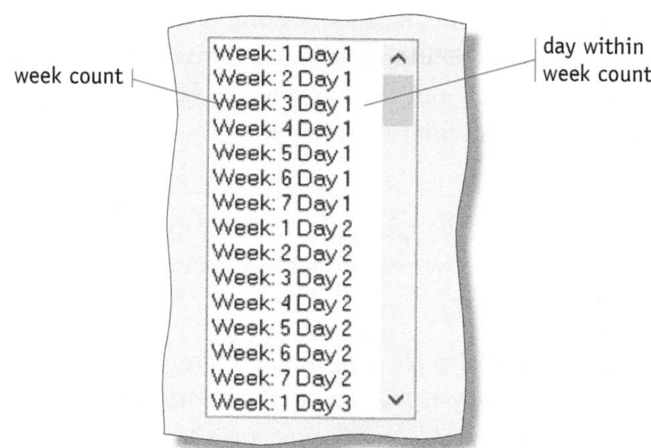

FIGURE 6-74

Select the Best Loop

When writing a program, you might have to make a decision regarding which loop structure to use. For...Next loops are best when the number of repetitions is fixed. Do loops are best when the condition to enter or exit the loop needs to be re-evaluated continually. When deciding which loop to use, keep the following considerations in mind:

1. Use a Do loop if the number of repetitions is unknown and is based on a condition changing; a For...Next loop is best if the exact number of repetitions is fixed.
2. If a loop condition must be tested before the body of the loop is executed, use a top-controlled Do While or Do Until loop. If the instructions within a loop must be executed one time regardless of the status of a condition, use a bottom-controlled Do While or Do Until loop.
3. Use the keyword While if you want to continue execution of the loop while the condition is true. Use the keyword Until if you want to continue execution until the condition is true.

Use a DataTip with Breakpoints

As programs become longer and more complex, the likelihood of errors increases, and you need to carefully find and remove these errors. Resolving defects in code is called **debugging**. When you debug a program, you collect information and find out what is wrong with the code in the program. You then fix that code.

A good way to collect information is to pause the execution of the code where a possible error could occur. One way to pause execution is to use breakpoints. **Breakpoints** are stop points placed in the code to tell the Visual Studio 2017 debugger where and when to pause the execution of the application. During this pause, the program is in break mode. While in break mode, you can examine the values in all variables that are within the scope of execution through the use of **DataTips**. In the Fitness Challenge application, you can insert a breakpoint in the assignment statement that increments the decTotalWeightLoss accumulator to view its value after each iteration of the loop as the user enters each weight loss value. To set a breakpoint in your code and then check the data at the breakpoint using DataTips, you can complete the following steps:

STEP 1 With the Fitness Challenge application open in the code window, click line 41, which contains the code where you want to set a breakpoint, and then click Debug on the menu bar.

The Debug menu opens that contains the Toggle Breakpoint command (Figure 6-75). Setting a breakpoint on line 41 means that the program will pause at that line during execution so that the values in variables within the scope of execution can be examined.

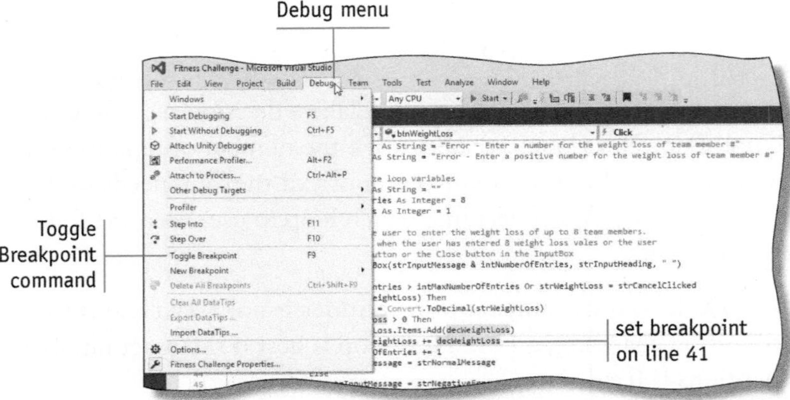

FIGURE 6-75

STEP 2 Click Toggle Breakpoint on the submenu.

A breakpoint is set on line 41, which is the line in the Do Until loop that adds the weight loss value the user entered to the weight loss accumulator — decTotalWeightLoss (Figure 6-76). The breakpoint is identified by the red bullet to the left of the line numbers and the highlight effect on the code.

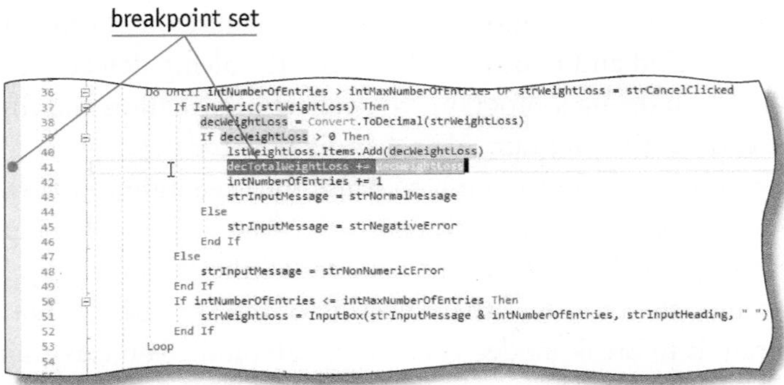

FIGURE 6-76

STEP 3 To run and test the program with the breakpoint, click the Start button on the Standard toolbar.

The program starts and the Fitness Challenge window opens (Figure 6-77).

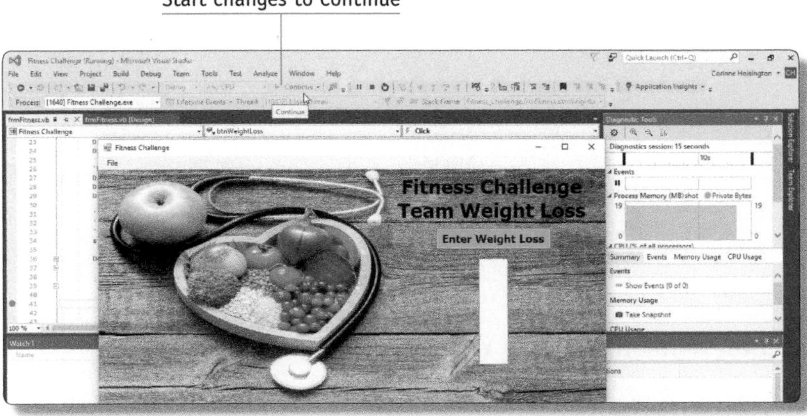

FIGURE 6-77

iStockphoto.com/udra

STEP 4 Click the Enter Weight Loss button. Type `3.4` as the weight loss amount of the first team member.

The Weight Loss input box contains 3.4 as the weight loss amount of the first team member (Figure 6-78).

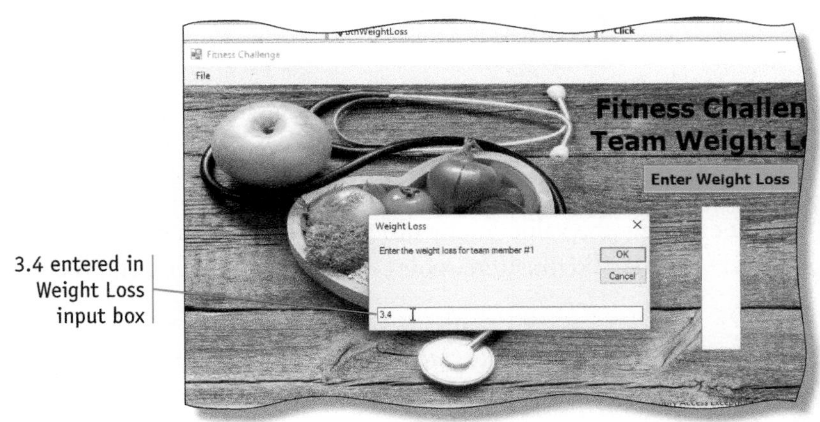

FIGURE 6-78

iStockphoto.com/udra

STEP 5 Click the OK button in the input box.

The program executes the lines of code in the event handler until reaching the breakpoint, where it pauses execution on the accumulator line (Figure 6-79). The application is now in break mode. Notice the breakpoint line is highlighted in yellow.

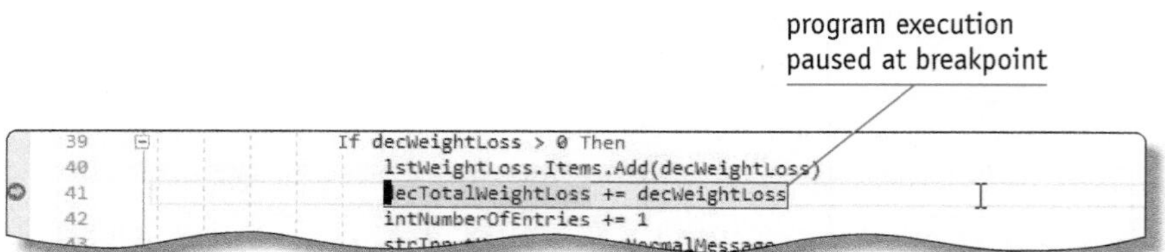

FIGURE 6-79

STEP 6 Point to the variable decWeightLoss on line 41.

A DataTip appears, displaying the value of the decWeightLoss variable when execution was paused (Figure 6-80). The value is 3.4 because the user entered this value in Step 4. It is a Decimal value (3.4D) because the statement in line 38 converted the value the user entered to a Decimal value.

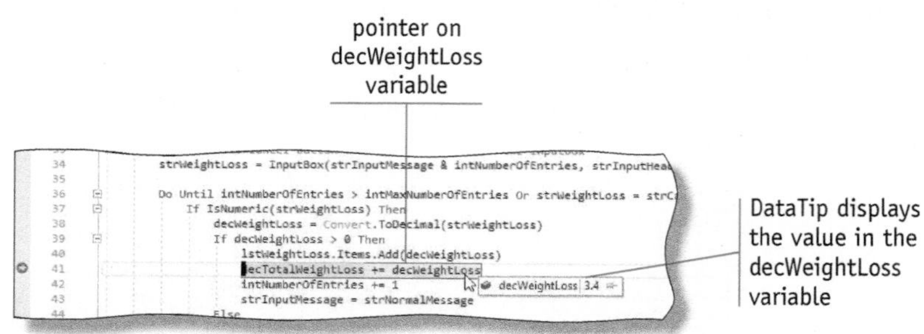

FIGURE 6-80

STEP 7 You can view the value in any other variable within execution scope by pointing to that variable. To illustrate, point to the variable decTotalWeightLoss on line 41.

The value in the decTotalWeightLoss variable is displayed (Figure 6-81). The value is zero, which means the assignment statement on line 41 has not yet been executed. When a breakpoint is set, the program pauses before executing the statement that contains the breakpoint.

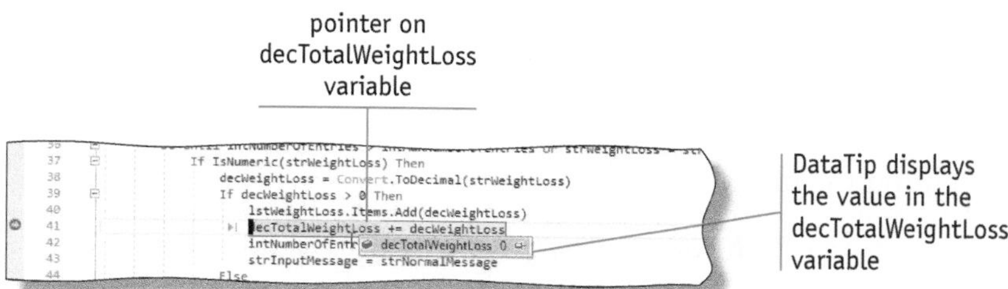

FIGURE 6-81

STEP 8 Continue the program by clicking the Continue button on the Standard toolbar. Notice that the Continue button is the same as the Start button.

The program continues by opening the next InputBox function, where the user can enter the weight loss value for the next team member. The program runs until it again reaches the breakpoint, where it pauses so you can point to any variable to view its present value in a DataTip (Figure 6-82).

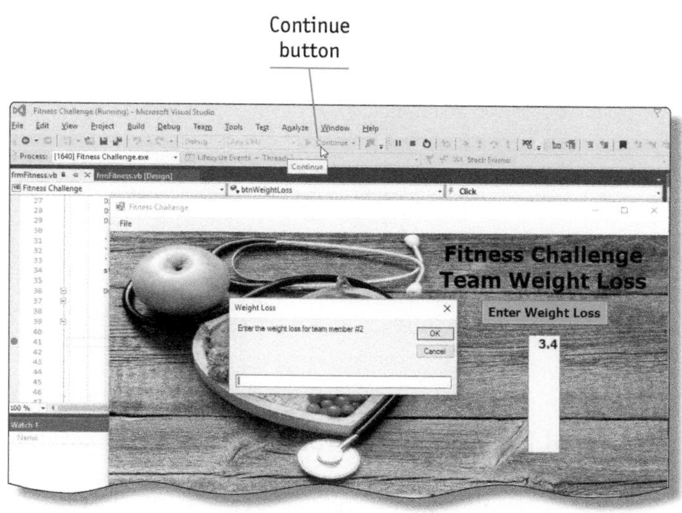

FIGURE 6-82

iStockphoto.com/udra

The preceding example illustrated the use of one breakpoint, but you can include multiple breakpoints in a program if they will be useful. Sometimes, breakpoints before and after an instruction that you suspect is in error can pinpoint the problem. Breakpoints can also be configured with conditions and actions to improve your debugging experience. For example, a breakpoint can be configured to stop after a coding situation has been reached a certain amount of times or a tracepoint can print a message to the output window to track a particular value.

To remove a breakpoint, you can complete the following steps:

STEP 1 Click the statement containing the breakpoint, and then point to the red bullet representing the breakpoint.

The pointer is located on the Breakpoint entry bullet (Figure 6-83).

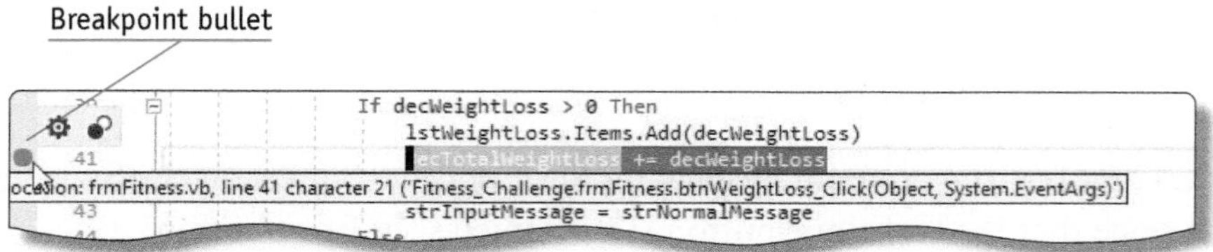

FIGURE 6-83

STEP 2 Click the red bullet breakpoint.

The breakpoint is removed when you click the red bullet (Figure 6-84).

breakpoint is removed, but variable is highlighted

```
Do Until intNumberOfEntries > intMaxNumberOfEntries Or strWeightLoss = strCancelClicked
    If IsNumeric(strWeightLoss) Then
        decWeightLoss = Convert.ToDecimal(strWeightLoss)
        If decWeightLoss > 0 Then
            lstWeightLoss.Items.Add(decWeightLoss)
            decTotalWeightLoss += decWeightLoss
            intNumberOfEntries += 1
            strInputMessage = strNormalMessage
        Else
            strInputMessage = strNegativeError
        End If
```

FIGURE 6-84

Using breakpoints and DataTips allows you to examine any variables during the execution of the program. By moving step by step through the program, normally you can identify any errors that might occur in the program.

Publish an Application with ClickOnce Deployment

After an application is completely debugged and working properly, you can deploy the project. Deploying a project means placing an executable version of the program on your hard disk (which then can be placed on CD, DVD, or in the cloud), on a web server, or on a network server.

You probably have purchased software on a CD or DVD or downloaded software from a cloud-based site. To install the application on your computer, you insert the CD or DVD into your computer and then follow the setup instructions. The version of the program you receive on the CD or DVD is the deployed version of the program.

When programming using Visual Basic 2017, you can create a deployed program by using **ClickOnce Deployment**. The deployed version of the program you create can be installed and executed on any computer that has the .NET framework installed. The computer does not need Visual Studio 2017 installed to run the program.

To publish the Fitness Challenge application using ClickOnce Deployment, you can complete the following steps:

STEP 1 With the Fitness Challenge application open, click Build on the menu bar.

The Build menu is displayed (Figure 6-85).

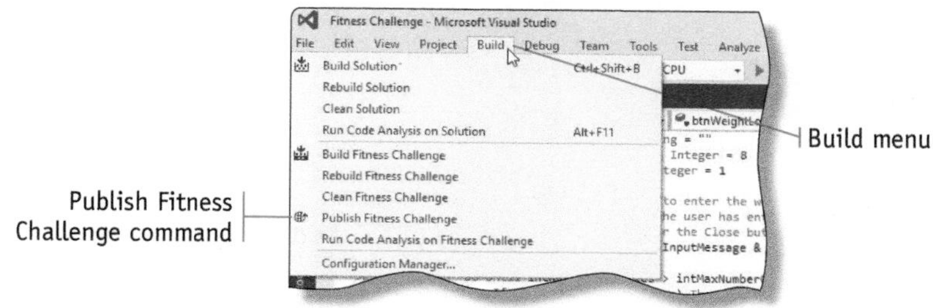

FIGURE 6-85

STEP 2 Click Publish Fitness Challenge on the Build menu.

The Publish Wizard starts (Figure 6-86). The first Publish Wizard dialog box asks where you want to publish the application. The application can be published to a web server, a network, or as a setup file on a hard disk or USB drive for burning on a CD or DVD. This dialog box includes publish\ as the default location, which you can change to a file location.

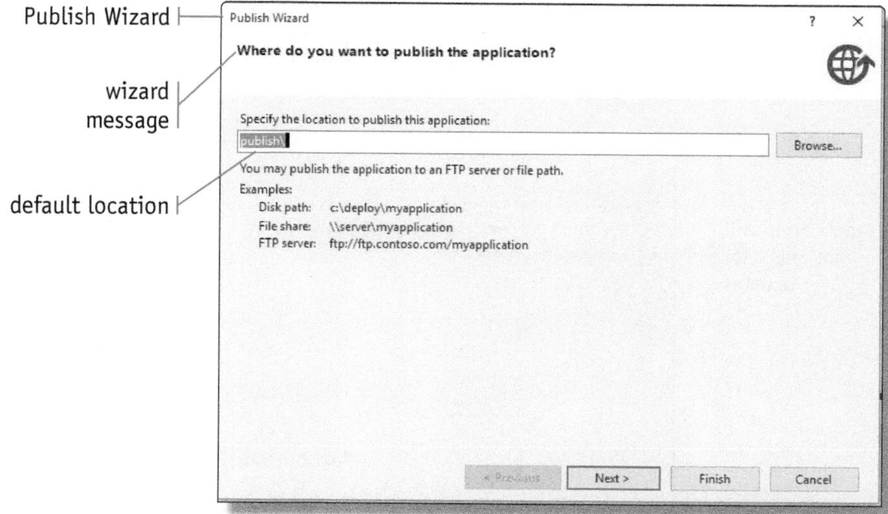

FIGURE 6-86

STEP 3 Change the default location from publish\ to a file location. To publish to a USB drive, type the drive letter. In this example, enter `D:` for a USB drive. Click the Next button.

The Publish Wizard dialog box requests where you want to publish the application. The Fitness Challenge application will be saved to the USB drive, which is drive D: in this example. The wizard next asks how users will install the application (Figure 6-87).

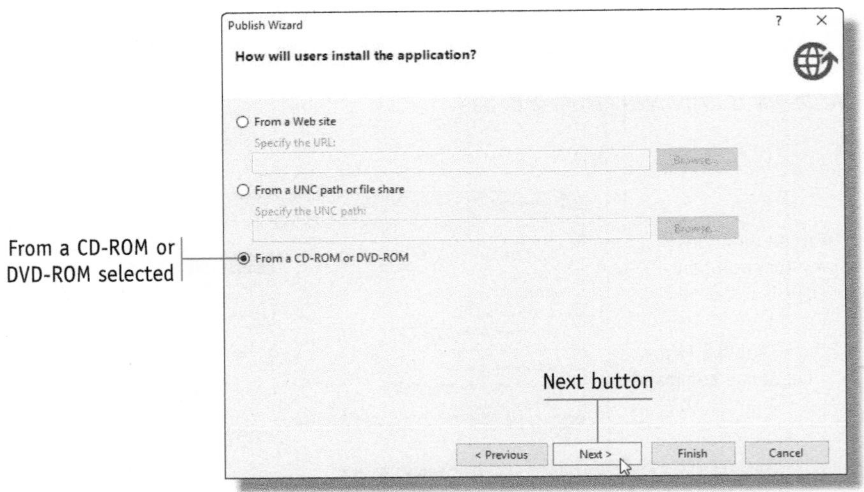

FIGURE 6-87

STEP 4 If necessary, click the From a CD-ROM or DVD-ROM radio button, and then click the Next button.

Visual Basic displays a Publish Wizard dialog box that asks, "Where will the application check for updates?" (Figure 6-88). You can select and enter a location or indicate that the application will not check for updates. Generally, when an application will be deployed to a CD, DVD, or USB drive, the application will not check for updates. If the application is deployed to a web server or network server, then it might check for updates before being executed on the user's computer.

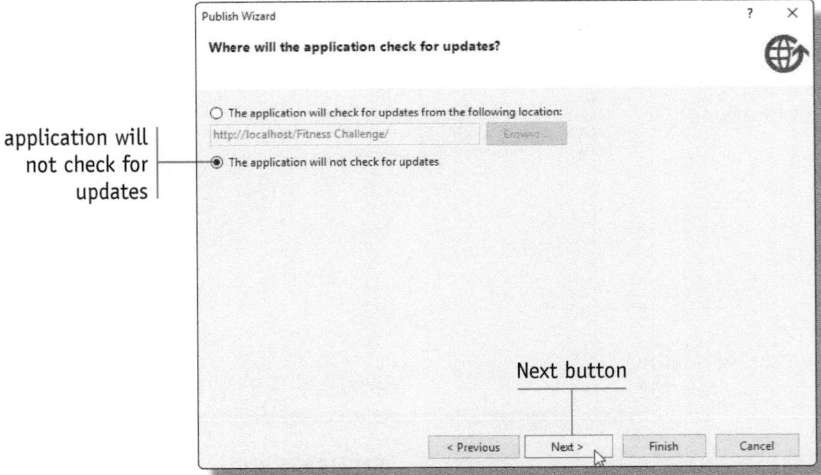

FIGURE 6-88

STEP 5 If necessary, click the "The application will not check for updates" option button, and then click the Next button.

The Ready to Publish! window is displayed (Figure 6-89). Notice the message in this window—when the program is installed on the user's machine, a shortcut for the program will be added to the user's computer, and the program can be deleted using the Add/Remove Programs function in the Control Panel.

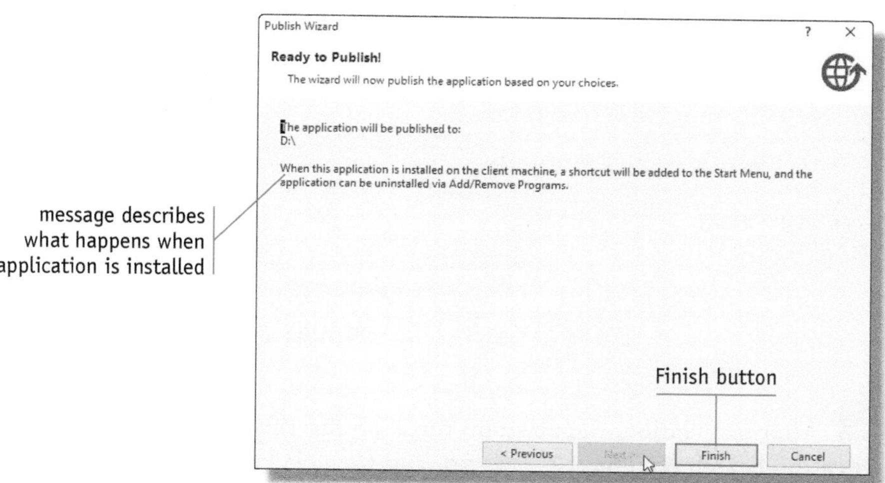

FIGURE 6-89

STEP 6 Click the Finish button.

The Visual Basic window displays several messages indicating that the application is being published. The last message is "Publish succeeded" and the USB drive dialog box opens. The installation files are placed on the USB drive, and the user can double-click the setup file to begin the installation (Figure 6-90).

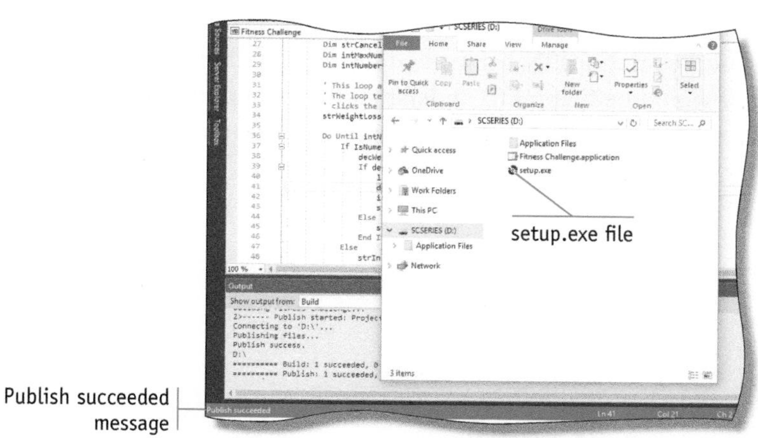

FIGURE 6-90

IN THE REAL WORLD

The installation files created by the ClickOnce Publishing Wizard can be burned to a CD or DVD and mass produced for a software release.

STEP 7 To install the application, double-click the setup file.

After the user double-clicks the setup file, the application is installed on the local computer. During installation, Windows might display the dialog box shown in Figure 6-91. This dialog box is intended to protect you from installing programs that might harm your computer. Because you know the source of this program, you can click the Install button to continue installing the program.

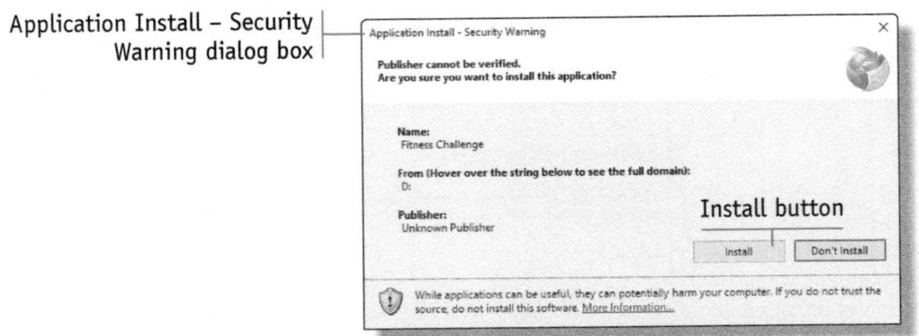

FIGURE 6-91

STEP 8 After installation, the program runs. To run the installed application again, click the Search box, type `Fitness`, and then click the Fitness Challenge icon.

Program Design

As you have learned, the requirements document identifies the purpose of the program being developed, the application title, the procedures to be followed when using the program, any required equations and calculations, any conditions that must be tested, notes and restrictions that must be followed by the program, and any other comments that would be helpful to understanding the problem. The requirements document for the Fitness Challenge application is shown in Figure 6-92.

REQUIREMENTS DOCUMENT

Date: September 30, 2019

Date Submitted:

Application Title: Fitness Challenge Application

Purpose: This application finds the average weight loss of a team of eight employees.

Program Procedures: In a Windows Classic Desktop application, the user enters the weight loss amounts of eight employees as positive numbers to compute the average weight loss for the entire team.

Algorithms, Processing, and Conditions:

1. The user must be able to enter each of eight weight loss values in pounds after clicking the Enter Weight Loss button.
2. Each weight loss value is validated to confirm it is numeric and greater than zero.
3. Each weight loss value is displayed in a ListBox object.
4. After the user enters eight weight loss values or clicks the Cancel button in an input box, the program calculates and displays the average weight loss for the team.
5. A menu bar includes the File menu, which contains Clear and Exit items. The Clear menu item clears the result and the weight loss values. The Exit menu item closes the application.

Notes and Restrictions:

1. If a nonnumeric or negative value is entered for the weight loss, the program should display an error message and ask the user to re-enter the value.
2. If the user clicks the Cancel button before entering any weight loss values, a message should indicate no weight loss values were entered. An average is not calculated when no weight loss values are entered.

Comments:

1. The picture shown in the window can be found on CengageBrain.com. The name of the picture is health.
2. The average weight loss should be formatted as a Decimal value with one decimal place.

FIGURE 6-92

The Use Case Definition shown in Figure 6-93 specifies the procedures the user will follow to use this application.

USE CASE DEFINITION

1. The Windows application opens, displaying the Fitness Challenge title, a ListBox object to hold the numeric entries, and a Button object that allows the user to begin entering up to eight weight loss values.
2. A menu bar displays the File menu, which has two menu items: Clear and Exit.
3. In an InputBox object, the user enters up to eight values representing the number of pounds lost, such as 3.2 pounds.
4. The program asks the user for the weight loss value again if a value is nonnumeric or negative.
5. The user ends data entry by entering eight values or by clicking the Cancel button in the InputBox object.
6. The program calculates the average weight loss for the values the user entered.
7. In a Label object, the program displays the average weight loss as a Decimal value with one decimal place.
8. The user can clear the input and the results by clicking the Clear menu item, and can then repeat Steps 3 through 7.
9. The user clicks Exit on the File menu to close the application.

FIGURE 6-93

Event Planning Document

You will recall that the event planning document is a table that specifies which objects in the user interface will cause events, the action taken by the user to trigger each event, and the event processing that must occur. The event planning document for the Fitness Challenge application is shown in Figure 6-94.

EVENT PLANNING DOCUMENT

Program Name: Fitness Challenge Application	**Developer:** Corinne Hoisington	**Object:** frmFitness	**Date:** September 30, 2019
OBJECT	**EVENT TRIGGER**	**EVENT PROCESSING**	
btnWeightLoss	Click	Display an InputBox object to obtain each team member's weight loss up to eight times or until the user clicks the Cancel button Check if strWeightLoss is numeric If the weight loss value is numeric, convert strWeightLoss to a Decimal value If strWeightLoss is numeric, check whether the value is positive If the weight loss value is positive: Display the value in lstWeightLoss Accumulate the total of the weight loss values in decTotalWeightLoss Update the number of entries Set the InputBox message to the normal message If the value entered is not numeric, display an error message in the input box If the value entered is not positive, display an error message in the input box After all weight loss values are entered, change the Visible property of lblAverageLoss to true If one or more weight loss values are entered: Calculate the average weight loss in decAverageLoss Display the average weight loss in lblAverageLoss If no values are entered: Display the text "No weight loss value entered" Disable the btnWeightLoss Button	
mnuClear	Click	Clear the lstWeightLoss ListBox Change the Visible property of lblAverageLoss to False Enable the btnWeightLoss Button	
mnuExit	Click	Exit the application	

FIGURE 6-94

Design and Code the Program

After identifying the events and tasks within the events, the developer is ready to create the program. As you have learned, creating the program means designing the user interface and then entering Visual Basic statements to accomplish the tasks specified in the event planning document. As the developer enters the code, she will also implement the logic to carry out the required processing.

Guided Program Development

To design the user interface for the Fitness Challenge application and enter the code required to process each event in the program, complete the steps on the following pages:

NOTE TO THE LEARNER

In the following activity, you should complete the tasks within the specified steps. Each of the tasks is accompanied by a Hint Screen. The purpose of the Hint Screen is to indicate where you should perform the activity in the Visual Studio window and to remind you which method to use. If you need further help completing a step, refer to the figure identified by *ref:*.

Guided Program Development

Phase I: Design the Form

1

- **Create a Windows Application** Open Visual Studio and then close the Start page. Create a new Visual Basic Windows Forms App project by clicking the New Project button on the Standard toolbar, selecting Windows Classic Desktop as the project type, selecting Windows Forms App in the center pane, naming the project `Fitness Challenge` in the Name text box, and then clicking the OK button in the New Project window.

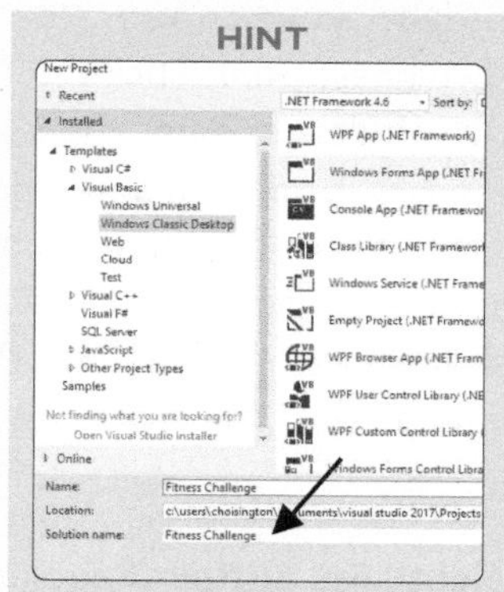

- **Display the Toolbox** Ensure that the Toolbox is displayed in the Visual Studio window and that the Common Controls are accessible.

- **Name the Windows Form Object** In the Solution Explorer window, right-click Form1.vb, click Rename, and then rename the form `frmFitness`.

- **Change the Text on the Title Bar for the Windows Form Object** Change the title bar text of the Windows Form object to `Fitness Challenge`.

- **Change the Size of the Form Object** Resize the Form object by changing the Size property to `883, 477`.

- **Add the MenuStrip Object** Drag a MenuStrip object from the Menus & Toolbars category of the Toolbox to the Windows Form object. The MenuStrip snaps into place below the title bar. Name the MenuStrip object `mnuFitness` in the Properties window. Click the Type Here box on the MenuStrip object, type `&File`, and then press the ENTER key. The ampersand creates a hot key for the letter F. Name the File menu item `mnuFile` (*ref: Figure 6-5*).

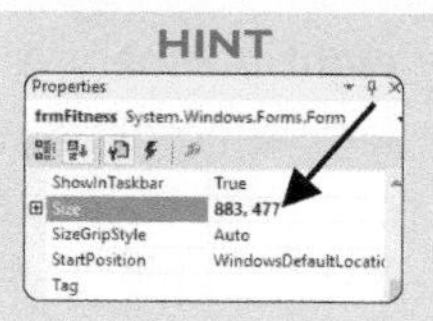

- **Add Menu Items** The next step is to add two menu items to the File menu. Click the Type Here box below the word File, and then enter `&Clear`. Name the Clear menu item `mnuClear`. Click the Type Here box below the Clear menu item, and then enter `E&xit` to make the "x" in Exit the hot key. Name the Exit menu item `mnuExit` (*ref: Figure 6-10*).

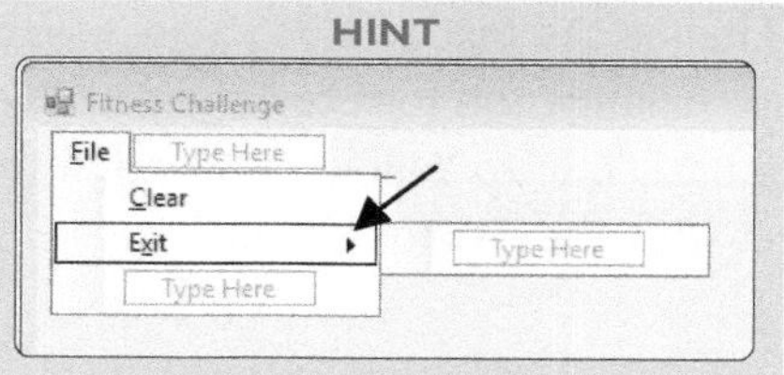

(continues)

Guided Program Development

- **Add the Title Label Object** Drag a Label .NET component onto the Windows Form object. Name the label `lblTitle`. Enter the text for this label as `Fitness Challenge Team Weight Loss` on two lines. (*Hint*: Click the Text property list arrow in the Properties window to enter a label with multiple lines. Press the ENTER key to move to a new line.) Choose Tahoma as the font, Bold as the font style, and 26 points as the size. Change the TextAlign property to MiddleCenter by clicking the TextAlign list arrow and then clicking the Center block. Change the Location property of the lblTitle Label object to `505, 33`.

HINT

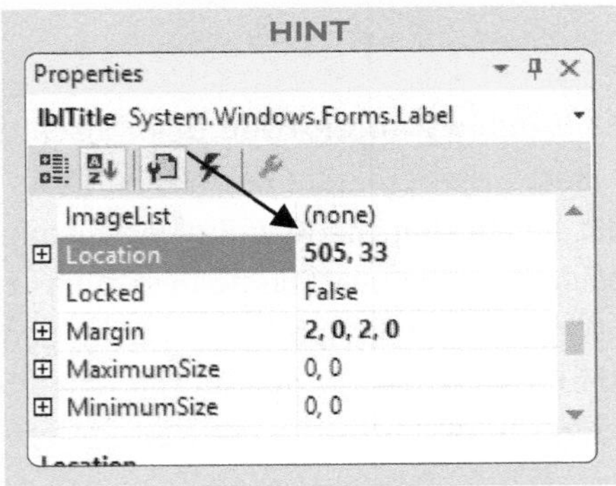

- **Add the Enter Weight Loss Button Object** Drag a Button object onto the Windows Form object below the title label. Name the Button `btnWeightLoss`. Change the text of the button to `Enter Weight Loss`. Change the font to 14-point, Bold, and Tahoma. Change the BackColor property to YellowGreen. Resize the Button object to view the complete text. Align the centers of the Button object with the title Label object.

- **Add the ListBox Object for the Team Members' Weight Loss** To add the ListBox object that displays the team members' weight loss, drag a ListBox object onto the Windows Form object below the Button object. Name the ListBox `lstWeightLoss`. Change the font of the text in the ListBox object to 14-point, Bold, and Tahoma. Resize the ListBox to the width of four characters because the top weight loss of a team member could reach an amount such as 46.3 pounds. Lengthen the ListBox object to display eight numbers. The Size property for the ListBox object in the sample program is 50, 188. Change the RightToLeft property to Yes to right-align the numeric values. Align the centers of the ListBox object with the Button object (*ref: Figure 6-22*).

HINT

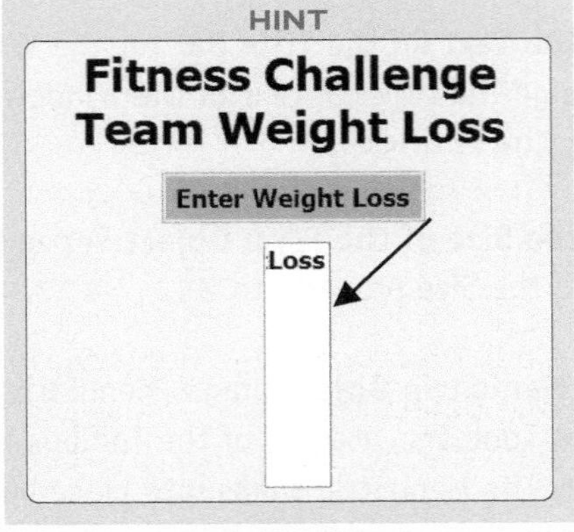

- **Add the Result Label** To add the label where the average weight loss message is displayed, drag a Label object onto the Windows Form object. Name the Label object `lblAverageLoss`. Change the text to `Average weight loss is XX.X lbs.` Change the font to Tahoma, Bold, and 18-point. Change the BackColor to YellowGreen. Align the centers of the Label object with the ListBox object.

Guided Program Development *continued*

The user interface mockup is complete (Figure 6-95).

RESULT OF STEP 1

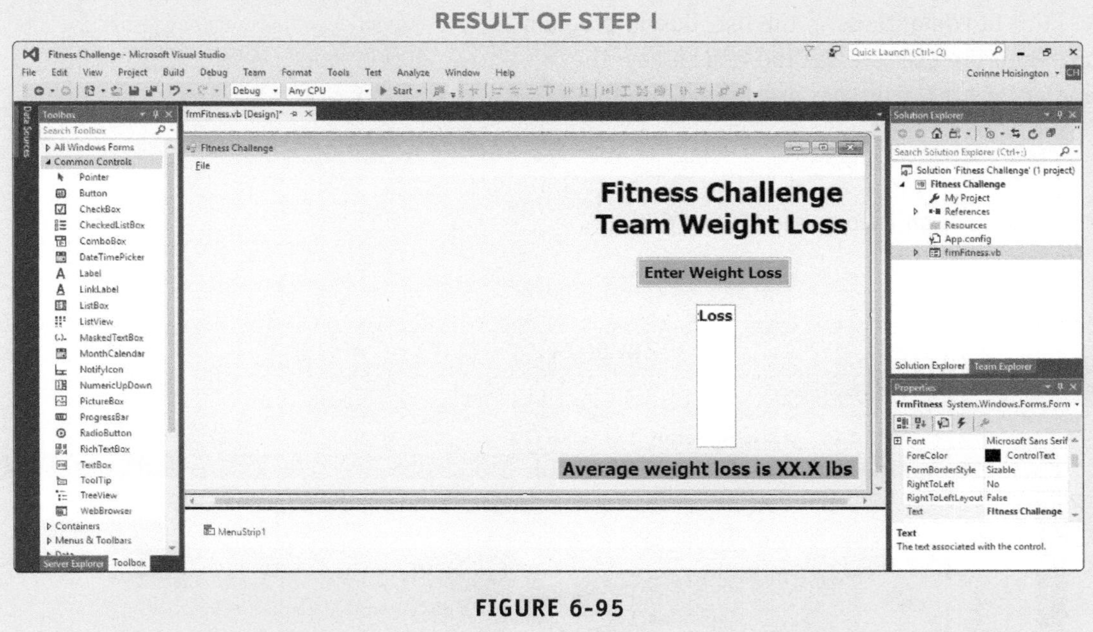

FIGURE 6-95

Phase 2: Fine-Tune the User Interface

2

- **Change the BackgroundImage Property of the Windows Form Object** Select the Windows Form object and then click the ellipsis button on the BackgroundImage property. Click the Import button and navigate to the health image. Click the OK button. Change the BackgroundImageLayout property to Stretch.

HINT

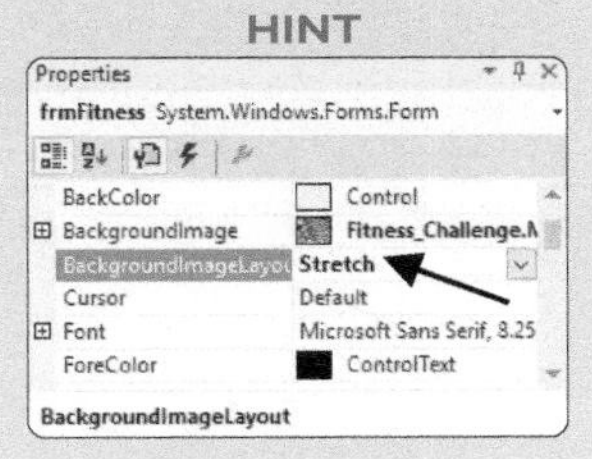

- **Change the Visible Property for the Average Weight Loss Label** Select the lblAverageLoss Label object and change its Visible property to False because the Label object is not displayed until the average weight loss is calculated.

(continues)

Guided Program Development *continued*

● **Make the Enter Weight Loss Button the Accept Button** Click the background of the Windows Form object to select it. In the Properties window, click the AcceptButton list arrow to display the buttons in the user interface. Click btnWeightLoss in the list. During program execution, when the user presses the ENTER key, the event handler for btnWeightLoss executes. Close the Toolbox pane.

HEADS UP

As you work on your program, do not forget to save it from time to time. You can save the work you have done by clicking the Save All button on the Standard toolbar.

The user interface design is complete (Figure 6-96).

RESULT OF STEP 2

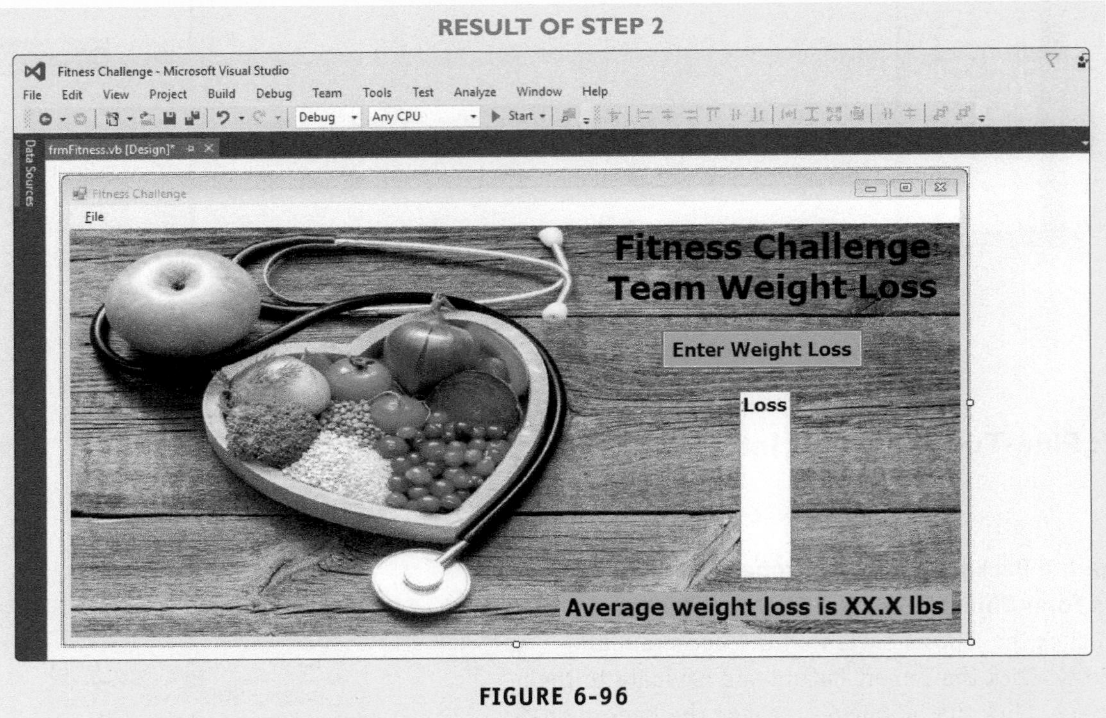

FIGURE 6-96

iStockphoto.com/udra

Guided Program Development *continued*

Phase 3: Code the Program

3

- **Enter the Comments for the Enter Weight Loss Button Event Handler** Double-click the btnWeightLoss Button object on the Windows Form object to open the button event handler. Insert the first four standard comments at the top of the code window. Insert the command `Option Strict On` at the beginning of the code to turn on strict type checking.

HINT

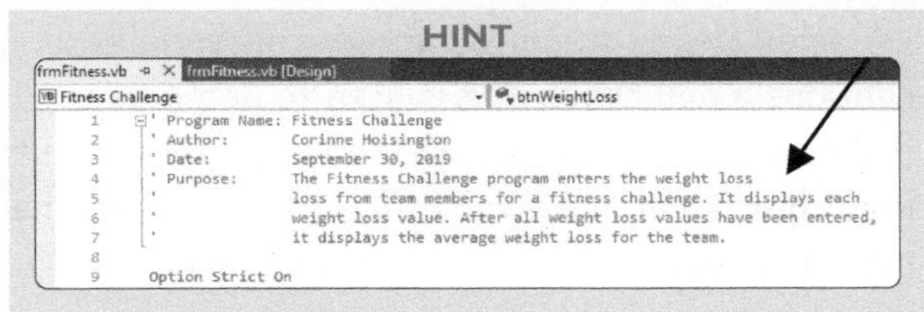

- **Comment on the btnWeightLoss_Click Event Handler** Enter a comment to describe the purpose of the btnWeightLoss_Click event handler.

HINT

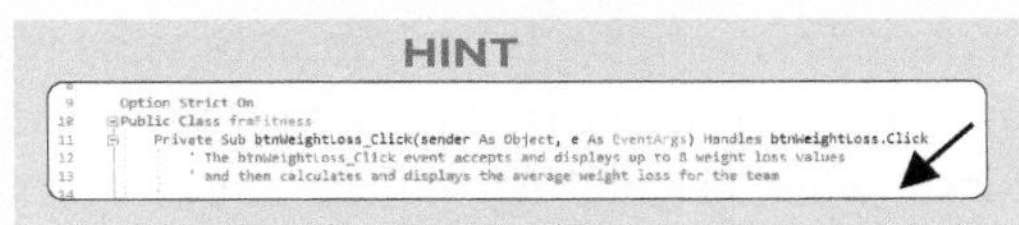

- **Declare and Initialize the Variables to Calculate the Average Weight Loss** Four variables are used to calculate the average weight loss (besides the team member count). These variables are: 1) strWeightLoss: Is assigned the value from the InputBox function call; 2) decWeightLoss: Is assigned the converted team member weight loss; 3) decAverageLoss: Contains the calculated average weight loss; 4) decTotalWeightLoss: The accumulator used to collect the total weight loss values entered by a user. Declare and initialize these four variables.

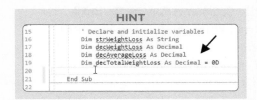

HINT

```
        ' Declare and initialize variables
        Dim strWeightLoss As String
        Dim decWeightLoss As Decimal
        Dim decAverageLoss As Decimal
        Dim decTotalWeightLoss As Decimal = 0D

    End Sub
```

- **Declare and Initialize the Variables Used with the InputBox Function Call** Five variables contain messages used in the input box to obtain the team members' weight loss. These variables are: 1) strInputMessage: Is used in the function call to contain the message displayed in the input box; 2) strInputHeading: Contains the message displayed in the title bar of the input box; 3) strNormalMessage: The normal message that appears in the input box when no error has occurred; 4) strNonNumericError: The message that appears in the input box when the user has entered a nonnumeric value; 5) strNegativeError: The message that appears in the input box when the user has entered zero or a negative number. Declare and initialize these five variables.

HINT

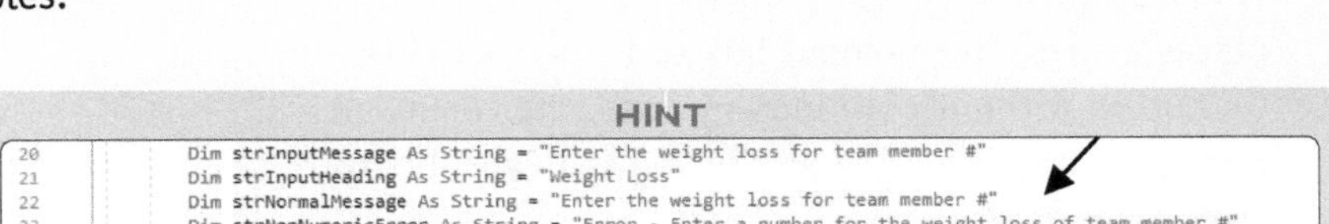

(continues)

Guided Program Development *continued*

HINT

```
'Declare and initialize loop variables

Dim strCancelClicked As String = ""
Dim intMaxNumberOfEntries As Integer = 8
Dim intNumberOfEntries As Integer = 1
```

- **Declare and Initialize Variables Used in the Loop Processing** Three variables are used for processing the loop in the program. These variables are: 1) strCancelClicked: This variable contains a null string and is used to determine if the user tapped or clicked the Cancel button in the input box; 2) intMaxNumberOfEntries: Contains the maximum number of entries for team member weight losses (program requirements state the maximum number is eight); 3) intNumberOfEntries: The counter for the valid number of team member weight loss values entered by the user. This variable is used to determine when the maximum number of entries has been made and to act as the divisor when calculating the average weight loss per team member.

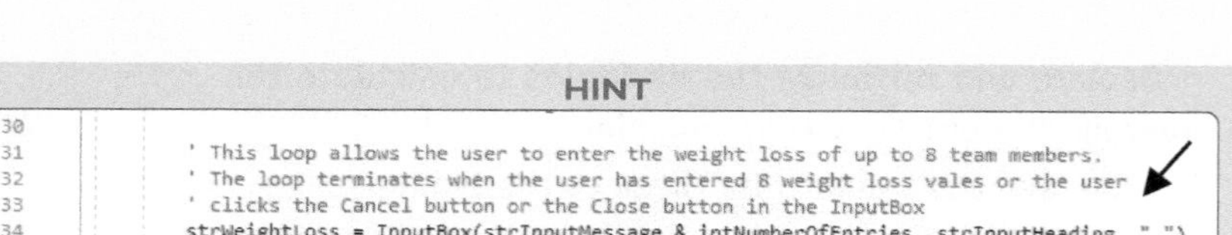

HINT
' This loop allows the user to enter the weight loss of up to 8 team members.
' The loop terminates when the user has entered 8 weight loss vales or the user
' clicks the Cancel button or the Close button in the InputBox
strWeightLoss = InputBox(strInputMessage & intNumberOfEntries, strInputHeading, " ")

- **Write Comments for the Do Until Loop and Write the Priming InputBox Function Call** You often can use comments to document a loop or other set of major processing statements. The comments here alert the reader to the role of the Do Until loop. The priming InputBox function call obtains the first team members' weight loss or allows the user to click the Cancel button. The normal message is displayed. The space at the end of the argument list places a space in the input box so if the user clicks the OK button without entering any data, the command will not be treated the same as clicking the Cancel button *(ref: Figure 6-70)*.

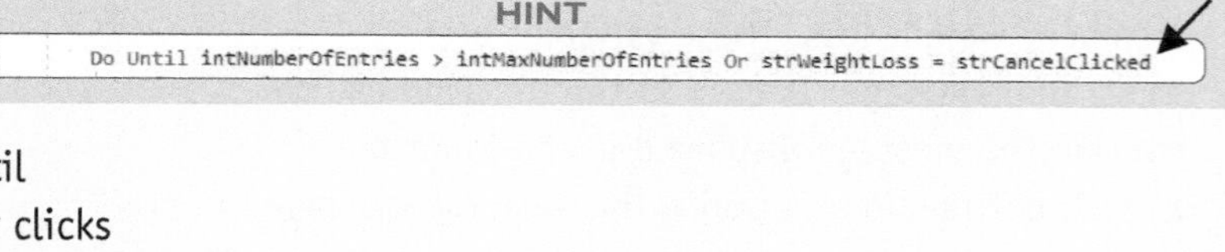

HINT
Do Until intNumberOfEntries > intMaxNumberOfEntries Or strWeightLoss = strCancelClicked

- **Code the Do Until Loop** Because the application requests the weight loss values of up to eight team members, the Do Until loop should continue until eight weight losses are entered or until the user clicks the Cancel or Close button in the input box. Enter the Do Until loop using IntelliSense *(ref: Figure 6-63, Figure 6-69)*.

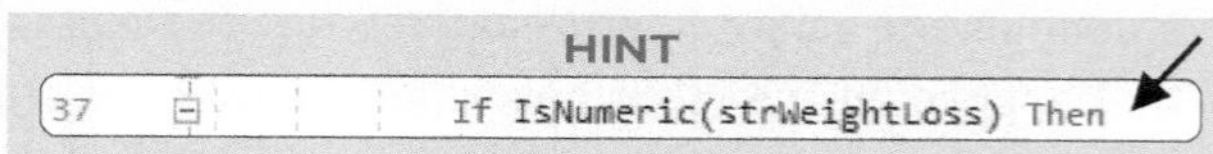

- **Validate That the Entry Is a Number** The first process in the Do Until loop is to validate that the team member weight loss entered by the user is a numeric value. Enter the If...Then statement to test if the value in the strWeightLoss variable is numeric.

Guided Program Development *continued*

- **Convert the Value Entered from a String to the Decimal Data Type** If the user entered a numeric value, the next step is to convert the string value the user entered to a Decimal data type. Using IntelliSense, enter the code to convert the value in the strWeightLoss variable from the String to the Decimal data type and place the result in the decWeightLoss variable.

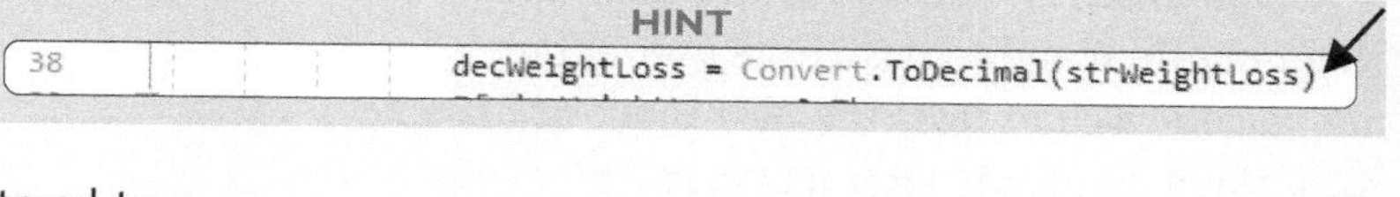
HINT
decWeightLoss = Convert.ToDecimal(strWeightLoss)

- **Validate That the Entered Value Is a Positive Number** After the value is converted, the program must validate that the number is positive. Write the If...Then statement to test whether the value in the decWeightLoss variable is greater than zero.

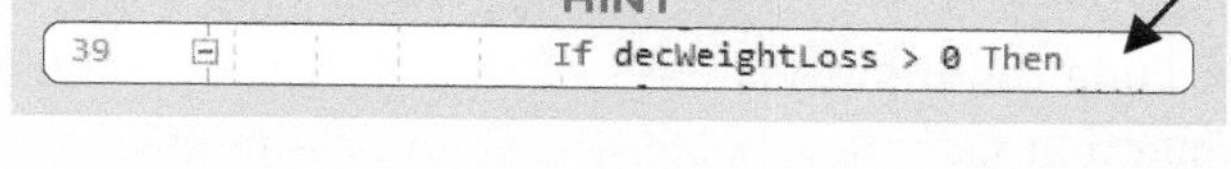
HINT
If decWeightLoss > 0 Then

- **Perform the Processing When the User Enters a Valid Weight Loss** After ensuring the weight loss entered by the user is valid, the next steps are to perform the processing for valid weight loss. Four steps are required: 1) Add the weight loss as an item to the lstWeightLoss ListBox object *(ref: Figure 6-26)*; 2) Add the weight loss the user entered to the decTotalWeightLoss accumulator *(ref: Figure 6-38)*. The accumulated weight loss is used to calculate the average weight loss; 3) Increment the intNumberOfEntries counter by 1 because the user entered a valid weight loss *(ref: Figure 6-38)*. This value is used as the divisor to determine the average weight loss, and as one of the indicators that the loop should be terminated; 4) Because the user entered a valid weight loss, the normal message should appear the next time the input box is displayed. Therefore, the normal message should be moved to the strInputMessage variable. Using IntelliSense, enter the code for these four activities.

HINT

```
lstWeightLoss.Items.Add(decWeightLoss)
decTotalWeightLoss += decWeightLoss
intNumberOfEntries += 1
strInputMessage = strNormalMessage
```

- **Assign an Error Message If the User Entered a Negative Weight Loss** If the user entered a negative weight loss, the next input box should display the negative number error message *(ref: Figure 6-71)*. Following the Else statement for the If statement that checks for a number greater than zero, enter the assignment statement that places the value in the strNegativeError variable in the strInputMessage variable.

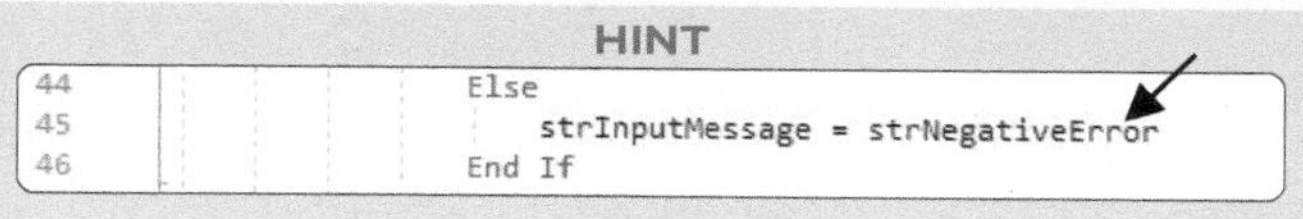
HINT
Else
strInputMessage = strNegativeError
End If

(continues)

Guided Program Development *continued*

- **Assign an Error Message If the User Enters a Nonnumeric Weight Loss** If the user enters a nonnumeric weight loss, the next input box should show the nonnumeric error message *(ref: Figure 6-70)*. Following the Else Statement for the If statement that checks for numeric data, enter the assignment statement that places the value in the strNonNumericError variable in the strInputMessage variable.

HINT

```
            Else
                strInputMessage = strNonNumericError
            End If
```

- **Code the InputBox Function Call** The first InputBox function call was placed before the Do Until loop to prime the loop. To continue the process after the first value is entered, another InputBox function is needed as the last statement inside the loop to request subsequent values. This statement should be executed only if the maximum number of entries has not been exceeded. So, an If structure is required to determine if the maximum number of entries has been reached. If not, the InputBox function call is executed *(ref: Figure 6-72)*.

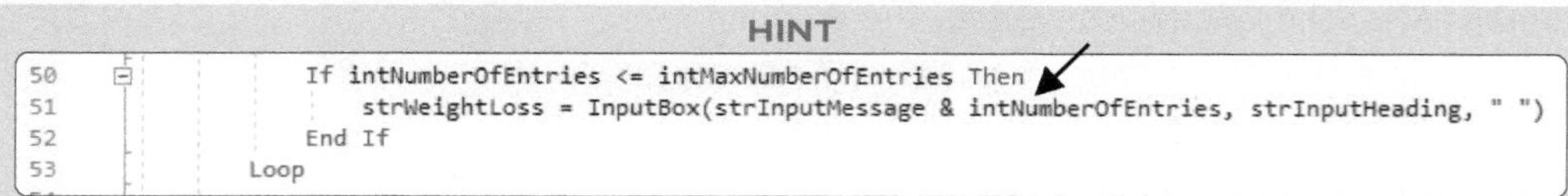
HINT
If intNumberOfEntries <= intMaxNumberOfEntries Then
strWeightLoss = InputBox(strInputMessage & intNumberOfEntries, strInputHeading, " ")
End If
Loop

The coding for the variables and Do Until loop that processes the data in the program is complete (Figure 6-97). Examine the code in Figure 6-97 to understand the loop processing. The priming of the loop, by both setting the value in the intNumberOfEntries variable (line 29) and calling the InputBox function (line 34), is critical for proper execution of the loop. Increasing the loop counter when a valid entry is made (line 42) also is fundamental in the loop processing because testing this counter is one way the Do Until loop can be terminated. Also, using variables for messages instead of literals in the actual code demonstrates how professional programs are coded. You should follow these examples in your programming.

Guided Program Development *continued*

RESULT OF STEP 6

```
' This loop allows the user to enter the weight loss of up to 8 team members.
' The loop terminates when the user has entered 8 weight loss vales or the user
' clicks the Cancel button or the Close button in the InputBox
strWeightLoss = InputBox(strInputMessage & intNumberOfEntries, strInputHeading, " ")

Do Until intNumberOfEntries > intMaxNumberOfEntries Or strWeightLoss = strCancelClicked
    If IsNumeric(strWeightLoss) Then
        decWeightLoss = Convert.ToDecimal(strWeightLoss)
        If decWeightLoss > 0 Then
            lstWeightLoss.Items.Add(decWeightLoss)
            decTotalWeightLoss += decWeightLoss
            intNumberOfEntries += 1
            strInputMessage = strNormalMessage
        Else
            strInputMessage = strNegativeError
        End If
    Else
        strInputMessage = strNonNumericError
    End If
    If intNumberOfEntries <= intMaxNumberOfEntries Then
        strWeightLoss = InputBox(strInputMessage & intNumberOfEntries, strInputHeading, " ")
    End If
Loop
```

FIGURE 6-97

4

- **Set the Result Label's Visible Property** When you finish the Do Until loop, you must complete three tasks to finish the Enter Weight Loss button click event handler: 1) Make the label that will contain the average weight loss visible; 2) Calculate and display the average weight loss; 3) Disable the Enter Weight Loss button. If at least one weight loss value has been entered using IntelliSense, write the code to create the If statement and make the lblAverageLoss label visible.

HINT

```
'Calculates and displays average team weight loss
If intNumberOfEntries > 1 Then
    lblAverageLoss.Visible = True
    decAverageLoss = decTotalWeightLoss / (intNumberOfEntries - 1)
    lblAverageLoss.Text = "Average weight loss is " &
        decAverageLoss.ToString("F1") & " lbs"
Else
    MsgBox("No weight loss value entered")
End If
```

(continues)

Guided Program Development *continued*

- **Calculate the Average Weight Loss** To calculate the average of the weight loss values the user entered, the value in the decTotalWeightLoss variable (accumulator) must be divided by the number of team members entered (counter). At the end of the loop shown in Figure 6-97, the value in the intNumberOfEntries variable always will be one greater than the actual number of team members entered, so the total weight loss must be divided by the value in intNumberOfEntries minus 1. This calculation should occur only if one or more team members weight loss values were entered, so an If statement must be used to check whether the value in the intNumberOfEntries variable is greater than 1. If so, the average weight loss is calculated; if not, the "No weight loss value entered" message should be displayed using a MsgBox. Using IntelliSense, write the code to perform this processing.

HINT

```
            decAverageLoss = decTotalWeightLoss / (intNumberOfEntries - 1)
            lblAverageLoss.Text = "Average weight loss is " &
                decAverageLoss.ToString("F1") & " lbs"
        Else
            MsgBox("No weight loss value entered")
        End If
```

- **Change the Enter Weight Loss Button Enabled Property to False** After the average weight loss is calculated and displayed, the Enabled property of the btnWeightLoss button is set to False to dim the button. Using IntelliSense, write the code to accomplish this processing.

The code for the btnWeightLoss button click event handler is completed (Figure 6-98).

RESULT OF STEP 6

```
        'Calculates and displays average team weight loss
        If intNumberOfEntries > 1 Then
            lblAverageLoss.Visible = True
            decAverageLoss = decTotalWeightLoss / (intNumberOfEntries - 1)
            lblAverageLoss.Text = "Average weight loss is " &
                decAverageLoss.ToString("F1") & " lbs"
        Else
            MsgBox("No weight loss value entered")
        End If

        ' Disables the Weight Loss button
        btnWeightLoss.Enabled = False
    End Sub
```

FIGURE 6-98

Guided Program Development *continued*

5

- **Run the Program** After coding a major section of the program, you should run the program to ensure it is working properly. Click the Start button on the Standard toolbar to run the Fitness Challenge application. Click the Enter Weight Loss button and then enter the weight loss of eight team members. Verify the weight losses are displayed properly and the average weight loss is correct. Close the program by clicking the Close button. Run the program again, click the Enter Weight Loss button, enter the weight loss for four team members, enter a nonnumeric weight loss, enter a weight loss that is less than zero, and then click the Cancel button in the input box. Ensure that the weight loss values are displayed properly, the average weight loss is correct, and the error messages are displayed properly in the input box. Close the program. Run the program again, click the Enter Weight Loss button, and then click the Cancel button in the input box. Ensure that the "No weight loss value entered" message is displayed. Close the program and then run it as many times as necessary to ensure the program is working properly. If the program does not run properly, consider setting a breakpoint and checking the values in the variables *(ref: Figure 6-76)*.

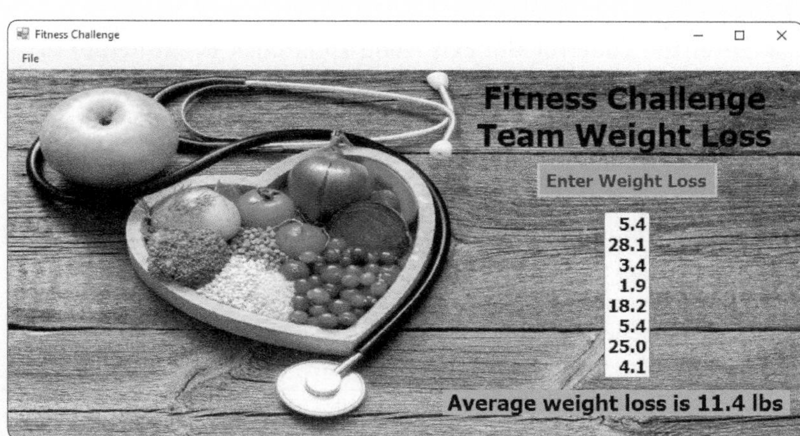

iStockphoto.com/udra

6

- **Enter the Code for the Clear Menu Item Click Event** Click the frmFitness.vb [Design] tab in the code window to display the design window. Click File on the MenuStrip object, and then double-click the Clear menu item to open the Clear click event handler in the code window. The Clear click event handler must perform three tasks: 1) Clear the lstWeightLoss list box; 2) Hide the average weight loss Label object; 3) Enable the Enter Weight Loss Button object. Using IntelliSense, write the code for these three tasks.

HINT

```
Private Sub mnuClear_Click(sender As Object, e As EventArgs) Handles mnuClear.Click
    ' The mnuClear click event clears the ListBox object and hides
    ' the average weight loss label. It also enables the Weight Loss button

    lstWeightLoss.Items.Clear()
    lblAverageLoss.Visible = False
    btnWeightLoss.Enabled = True
End Sub
```

(continues)

Guided Program Development *continued*

- **Enter the Code for the Exit Menu Item Click Event** Return to the design window. Double-click the Exit menu item. In the code window, enter a Close procedure call that will close the window and exit the program.

The code for the Clear menu item click event and the Exit menu item click event is completed (Figure 6-99). The code for the program is also completed.

RESULT OF STEP 6

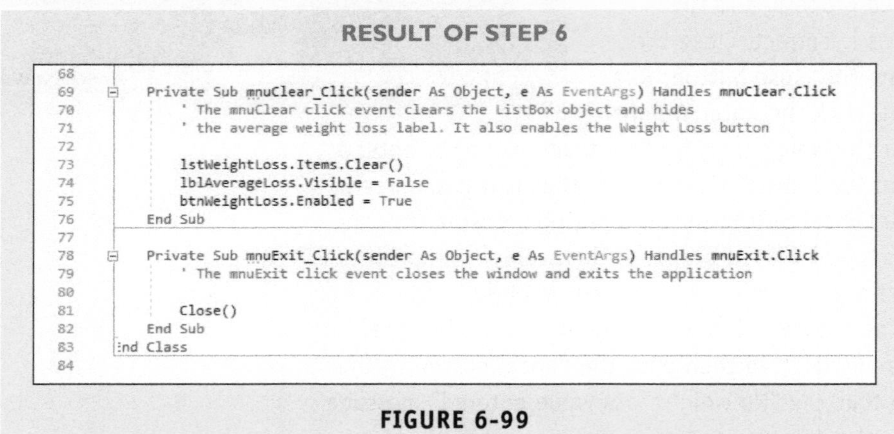

```
    Private Sub mnuClear_Click(sender As Object, e As EventArgs) Handles mnuClear.Click
        ' The mnuClear click event clears the ListBox object and hides
        ' the average weight loss label. It also enables the Weight Loss button

        lstWeightLoss.Items.Clear()
        lblAverageLoss.Visible = False
        btnWeightLoss.Enabled = True
    End Sub

    Private Sub mnuExit_Click(sender As Object, e As EventArgs) Handles mnuExit.Click
        ' The mnuExit click event closes the window and exits the application

        Close()
    End Sub
End Class
```

FIGURE 6-99

7

- **Publish the Fitness Challenge Application** After completing the program, you can publish it using ClickOnce deployment so it can be installed on multiple computers. To open the Publish Wizard and begin the deployment process, click Build on the menu bar and then click Publish Fitness Challenge on the Build menu *(ref: Figure 6-86)*.

HINT

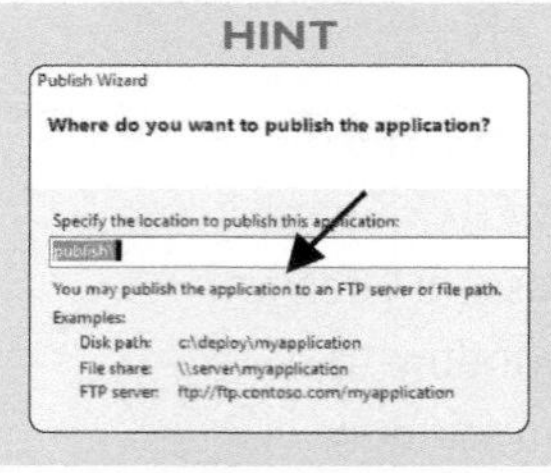

- **Select the Publish File Location** The Publish Wizard dialog box asks where you want to publish the application. Change the default location to the same file location that you used to save your Windows application by clicking the Browse button and then selecting the drive. For example, select the D: drive, a USB drive. After selecting the drive, click the Next button in the Publish Wizard dialog box *(ref: Figure 6-86)*.

Guided Program Development *continued*

- **Select How Users Will Install the Application** In the next Publish Wizard dialog box, select the option that lets users install the application from a CD-ROM or DVD-ROM. Then, click the Next button *(ref: Figure 6-87)*.
- **Indicate the Application Will Not Check for Updates** Click the "The application will not check for updates" radio button to indicate no updates will be checked. This is the normal selection when programs are placed on CDs or DVDs. Then, click the Next button in the Publish Wizard dialog box *(ref: Figure 6-88)*.
- **View the Summary Window** The Publish Wizard summary is displayed. Click the Finish button to publish the application *(ref: Figure 6-89)*.
- **View the Installation Files** After the publishing succeeds, a folder is created with the installation files that could be placed on a CD, DVD, or other computer (*ref: Figure 6-90*).

HINT

Code Listing

The complete code for the sample program is shown in Figure 6-100.

Fitness Challenge

frmFitness.vb

Fitness Challenge | frmFitness

```
' Program Name: Fitness Challenge
' Author:       Corinne Hoisington
' Date:         September 30, 2019
' Purpose:      The Fitness Challenge program enters the weight loss
'               loss from team members for a fitness challenge. It displays each
'               weight loss value. After all weight loss values have been entered,
'               it displays the average weight loss for the team.

Option Strict On
Public Class frmFitness
    Private Sub btnWeightLoss_Click(sender As Object, e As EventArgs) Handles btnWeightLoss.Click
        ' The btnWeightLoss_Click event accepts and displays up to 8 weight loss values
        ' and then calculates and displays the average weight loss for the team

        ' Declare and initialize variables
        Dim strWeightLoss As String
        Dim decWeightLoss As Decimal
        Dim decAverageLoss As Decimal
        Dim decTotalWeightLoss As Decimal = 0D
        Dim strInputMessage As String = "Enter the weight loss for team member #"
        Dim strInputHeading As String = "Weight Loss"
        Dim strNormalMessage As String = "Enter the weight loss for team member #"
        Dim strNonNumericError As String = "Error - Enter a number for the weight loss of team member #"
        Dim strNegativeError As String = "Error - Enter a positive number for the weight loss of team member #"

        'Declare and initialize loop variables
        Dim strCancelClicked As String = ""
        Dim intMaxNumberOfEntries As Integer = 8
        Dim intNumberOfEntries As Integer = 1

        ' This loop allows the user to enter the weight loss of up to 8 team members.
        ' The loop terminates when the user has entered 8 weight loss vales or the user
        ' clicks the Cancel button or the Close button in the InputBox
        strWeightLoss = InputBox(strInputMessage & intNumberOfEntries, strInputHeading, " ")

        Do Until intNumberOfEntries > intMaxNumberOfEntries Or strWeightLoss = strCancelClicked
            If IsNumeric(strWeightLoss) Then
                decWeightLoss = Convert.ToDecimal(strWeightLoss)
                If decWeightLoss > 0 Then
                    lstWeightLoss.Items.Add(decWeightLoss)
                    decTotalWeightLoss += decWeightLoss
                    intNumberOfEntries += 1
                    strInputMessage = strNormalMessage
                Else
                    strInputMessage = strNegativeError
                End If
            Else
                strInputMessage = strNonNumericError
            End If
            If intNumberOfEntries <= intMaxNumberOfEntries Then
                strWeightLoss = InputBox(strInputMessage & intNumberOfEntries, strInputHeading, " ")
            End If
        Loop
```

FIGURE 6-100 (continues)

```
    'Calculates and displays average team weight loss
    If intNumberOfEntries > 1 Then
        lblAverageLoss.Visible = True
        decAverageLoss = decTotalWeightLoss / (intNumberOfEntries - 1)
        lblAverageLoss.Text = "Average weight loss is " &
            decAverageLoss.ToString("F1") & " lbs"
    Else
        MsgBox("No weight loss value entered")
    End If

    ' Disables the Weight Loss button
    btnWeightLoss.Enabled = False
End Sub

Private Sub mnuClear_Click(sender As Object, e As EventArgs) Handles mnuClear.Click
    ' The mnuClear click event clears the ListBox object and hides
    ' the average weight loss label. It also enables the Weight Loss button

    lstWeightLoss.Items.Clear()
    lblAverageLoss.Visible = False
    btnWeightLoss.Enabled = True
End Sub

Private Sub mnuExit_Click(sender As Object, e As EventArgs) Handles mnuExit.Click
    ' The mnuExit click event closes the window and exits the application

    Close()
End Sub
End Class
```

FIGURE 6-100 (continued)

Summary

In this chapter you have learned to design and write code to implement loops and to create menus, list boxes, and an input box.

Knowledge Check

1. Write a statement that displays the default value of $5.49 in the input box shown in Figure 6-101 and assigns the return value from the InputBox function to a variable named decPizzaSlice with the message Cost of Pizza Slice with the title Giordano's Pizza.

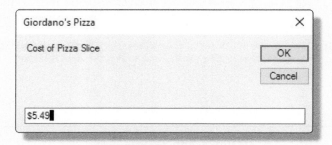

FIGURE 6-101

2. Write compound operators for the following equations:

   a. intStrike = intStrike+ 10

   b. dblCube = dblCube ^ 3

   c. strDog = strDog & "Treat"

   d. decOvertime = decOvertime *1.5

3. Write For...Next loops that calculate the sum of the following ranges and assign their sum to a variable named intSum:

   a. The first 50 numbers starting with 0

   b. The even numbers beginning at 10 and ending with 100

   c. The numbers 20, 30, 40, 50, 60, 70 and 80

4. Find the error(s) in the following For...Next header statements:

   a. For intCounter = "1" To "19"

   b. For strNumber = 98 To 71 Step 2

   c. For intValue = 12 To 52 Step –4

Knowledge Check *continued*

5. Explain the purpose of placing an ampersand before or within a MenuStrip item.
6. Write a command to add a list of precipitation types to a ListBox object named lstWater.
7. Write the command to clear a ListBox object named lstWinners.
8. What is the name of the property that displays an image as the background of a Form object?
9. What is the name of the property that can be used to stretch the background image of the Form object?
10. Using a compound operator, write an assignment statement to decrease the value in intCounter by 6.7.
11. Write a top-controlled Do Until loop with an empty body that would continue until intValue is less than 19.
12. Write a bottom-controlled Do While loop with an empty body that continues while the user enters "Yes" into the strContinue variable.
13. Write a Do While loop to validate that the user enters a nonzero integer into an input box for a variable named intDenominator.
14. Is the For...Next loop top-controlled or bottom-controlled?
15. Write the code for an infinite Do Until loop with the variable intForever.
16. Which loop should be used if you know the required number of times the loop will be executed?
17. What is the fewest number of times a top-controlled Do Until loop is executed?
18. Write a data validation Do loop to check that the variable intValidAge entered from an input box is between 1 and 118.
19. A loop inside another loop is called a __________ ________.
20. When you insert standard items in a MenuStrip object, what File menu items are automatically created by default?

Debugging Exercises

1. The loop shown in Figure 6-102 should repeat 10 times. If it will not repeat 10 times, change the code so it will.

```
For intRepeat = 20 To 10
    MsgBox("The value is " & intRepeat.ToString("C0"))
Next
```

FIGURE 6-102

(continues)

Debugging Exercises *continued*

2. What output does the code shown in Figure 6-103 produce? How would you change the code to produce a list box containing the values 12–22?

```
intRate = 12
Do While intRate <= 10
    lstDisplay.Items.Add(intRate)
    intRate += 1
Loop
```

FIGURE 6-103

3. What is the output of the code shown in Figure 6-104?

```
Dim intAdd As Integer
Dim intOuterLoop As Integer
Dim intInnerLoop As Integer

intAdd = 0
For intOuterLoop = 1 To 8
    For intInnerLoop = 3 To 7
        intAdd += 1
    Next
Next
MsgBox.Show("The final value is " & intAdd.ToString())
```

FIGURE 6-104

4. What is the output of the code shown in Figure 6-105?

```
Dim intValue As Integer

intValue = 2
Do While intValue <= 9
    lstDisplay.Items.Add(intValue & " " & intValue ^ 3)
    intValue += 2
Loop
```

FIGURE 6-105

5. Fix the errors in the loop shown in Figure 6-106.

```
Dim intStart As Integer = 8

Loop
intStart = +4
Do While intStart < 24
```

FIGURE 6-106

Debugging Exercises *continued*

6. What is the output of the code shown in Figure 6-107?

```
intCount = 40
Do Until intCount < 26
    intCount -= 2
    lstCount.Items.Add(intCount)
Loop
```

FIGURE 6-107

Program Analysis

1. What is the value of lblResult after the code shown in Figure 6-108 is executed?

```
Dim intCounter As Integer = -15

Do While intCount < 25
    intCount += 5
    lblResult.Text &= intCount.ToString() & " "
Loop
```

FIGURE 6-108

2. What is the value of lblResult after the code shown in Figure 6-109 is executed?

```
Dim intCountIt As Integer

intCountIt = 6
Do
    intCountIt += 3
    lblResult.Text &= intCountIt.ToString() & " "
Loop Until intCountIt = 21
```

FIGURE 6-109

3. Rewrite the top-controlled Do While loop shown in Figure 6-110 as a top-controlled Do Until loop.

```
Dim intQuantity As Integer

intQuantity = -5
Do While intQuantity < 30
    intQuantity += 5
Loop
```

FIGURE 6-110

(continues)

Program Analysis *continued*

4. Convert the Do loop shown in Figure 6-111 to a For...Next loop.

```
        Dim intIncrease As Integer

        intIncrease = 10
        Do While intIncrease < 40
            lstDisplay.Items.Add(intIncrease)
            intIncrease += 2
        Loop
```

FIGURE 6-111

5. How many times will the inner statement inside the nested loop in Figure 6-112 be executed?

```
        For intOuterLoop = 3 To 5
            For intInnerLoop = 6 To 10
                lstDays.Items.Add("Value: " & intOuterLoop.ToString() & _
                    " Count: " & intInnerLoop.ToString())
            Next
        Next
```

FIGURE 6-112

6. Write a For...Next loop that adds the odd numbers 1 through 49 and assigns their sum to the variable intSum. The program should start with the lines shown in Figure 6-113 (use the variables shown in lines 120–123 in your code).

```
120         Dim intLoopValue As Integer
121         Dim intStartvalue As Integer
122         Dim intEndvalue As Integer
123         Dim intSum As Integer
124
125         intStartvalue = 1
126         intEndvalue = 49
127         intSum = 0
```

FIGURE 6-113

Case Programming Assignments

Complete one or more of the following case programming assignments. Submit the program and materials you create to your instructor. The level of difficulty is indicated for each case programming assignment.

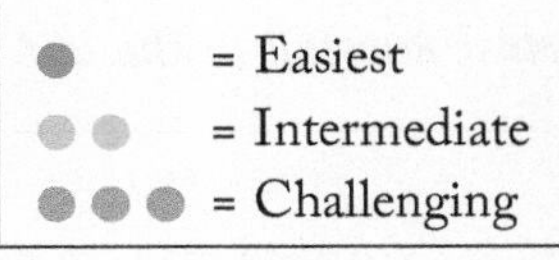

1 ● MOST RAINFALL IN THE USA

Design a Windows application and write the code that will execute according to the program requirements shown in Figure 6-114. Before writing the code, create an event planning document for each event in the program. The Use Case Definition document is shown in Figure 6-115 on the following page. The completed user interface is shown in Figure 6-116 on the following page.

REQUIREMENTS DOCUMENT

Date: March 17, 2019

Date Submitted:

Application Title: Most Rainfall in the USA

Purpose: This Windows Classic Desktop application is written for Kauai, Hawaii, the rainiest location in the United States, to compute the average monthly amount of rainfall per year.

Program Procedures: In a Windows application, the user enters up to 12 values representing the number of inches of rain each month to compute the average rainfall in a given number of months or a full year.

Algorithms, Processing, and Conditions:

1. In an InputBox object, the user enters up to 12 amounts of rainfall per month in inches.
2. Each amount of rainfall per month is displayed in the ListBox object.
3. After 12 entries of rainfall values are entered, the average rainfall is calculated and displayed.
4. A File menu contains a Clear and an Exit option. The Clear menu item clears the average rainfall and the 12 values representing the amount of rainfall per month in Kauai. The Exit menu item closes the application.
5. If the user clicks the Cancel button in the input box before entering 12 values, compute the average amount of rainfall entered.
6. If the user clicks the Cancel button before entering any rainfall values, display a message indicating the user did not enter a value.

Notes and Restrictions:

1. Nonnumeric values should not be accepted.
2. Negative values should not be accepted.
3. The average rainfall should be rounded to the nearest tenth of an inch.

Comments:

1. The application allows decimal entries.
2. Obtain a background image for this program from CengageBrain.com. The name of the image file is hawaii.

FIGURE 6-114

(continues)

Case Programming Assignments *continued*

Most Rainfall in the USA

USE CASE DEFINITION

1. The Windows application opens with the heading "Most Rainfall in US - Kauai," a ListBox object that displays the monthly rainfall amounts, an image, and a Button object that allows the user to begin entering their rainfall amounts in inches.
2. A menu bar displays the File menu, which has two menu items: Clear and Exit.
3. The user enters up to 12 monthly values in an InputBox object, with each value representing the number of inches of rainfall per month in Kauai.
4. The program asks the user for the rainfall amount again if the value is a negative number or the entry is a nonnumeric value.
5. The program displays the average inches of rainfall rounded to one decimal place.
6. The user can clear the input and the result by clicking the Clear menu item, and then can repeat Steps 3–5. If the user clicks the Cancel button in the input box, the average for the values entered is calculated. If the user did not enter any values, the program displays an appropriate message.
7. The user clicks the Exit menu item to close the application.

FIGURE 6-115

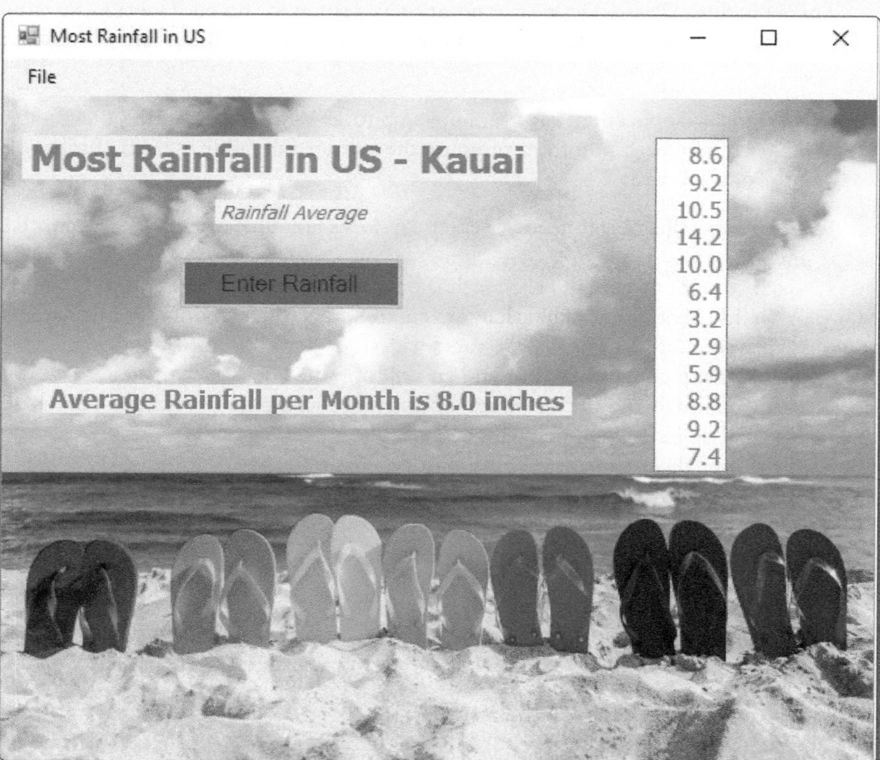

FIGURE 6-116

iStockphoto.com/EllenSmile

Case Programming Assignments

2 ● INTERNET SPEED TEST SURVEY

Design a Windows application and write the code that will execute according to the program requirements shown in Figure 6-117. Before writing the code, create an event planning document for each event in the program. The Use Case Definition document is shown in Figure 6-118 on the following page. The completed user interface is shown in Figure 6-119 on the following page.

REQUIREMENTS DOCUMENT

Date: July 31, 2019

Date Submitted:

Application Title: Internet Speed Test Survey

Purpose: This Windows Classic Desktop application finds the average speed of a home Internet connection (see speedtest.net to measure your own connection's download speed).

Program Procedures: To test the average speed of an Internet service provider with their local customers, a Windows application will compute the average Internet download speed. The application allows the user to enter up to 10 download speeds. The average speed is displayed in Mbps (Megabits per second).

Algorithms, Processing, and Conditions:

1. The user clicks the Enter Internet Speed button to enter their Internet speed in Mbps.
2. Each speed is displayed in a ListBox object with a scroll bar that appears when the number of values exceeds the given space.
3. After 10 values have been entered, the average is displayed.
4. If the user clicks the Cancel button before entering any time values, display an appropriate message.

Notes and Restrictions:

1. The result should include two places after the decimal point.
2. Nonnumeric values should not be accepted.
3. Negative numbers should not be accepted.

Comments:

1. The application allows decimal entries.
2. Obtain a background image for this program from CengageBrain.com. The name of the image file is speed.

FIGURE 6-117

(continues)

Case Programming Assignments *continued*

Internet Speed Test Survey

USE CASE DEFINITION

1. The Windows application opens, displaying Internet Speed Test Survey as the heading, a ListBox object with a scroll bar as needed that will display the Internet download speed of each home user tested at speedtest.net, and a Button object that allows the user to enter their download speed in Mbps.
2. In an InputBox object, the user enters up to 10 values representing the Internet speed of their home connection.
3. The program asks the user for the Internet speed again if the value is a negative or nonnumeric value.
4. The program displays the average time to two decimal places.
5. If the user clicks the Cancel button in the input box before entering 10 time values, the program uses the number of seconds entered for calculations. If the user enters no values, an appropriate message is displayed.

FIGURE 6-118

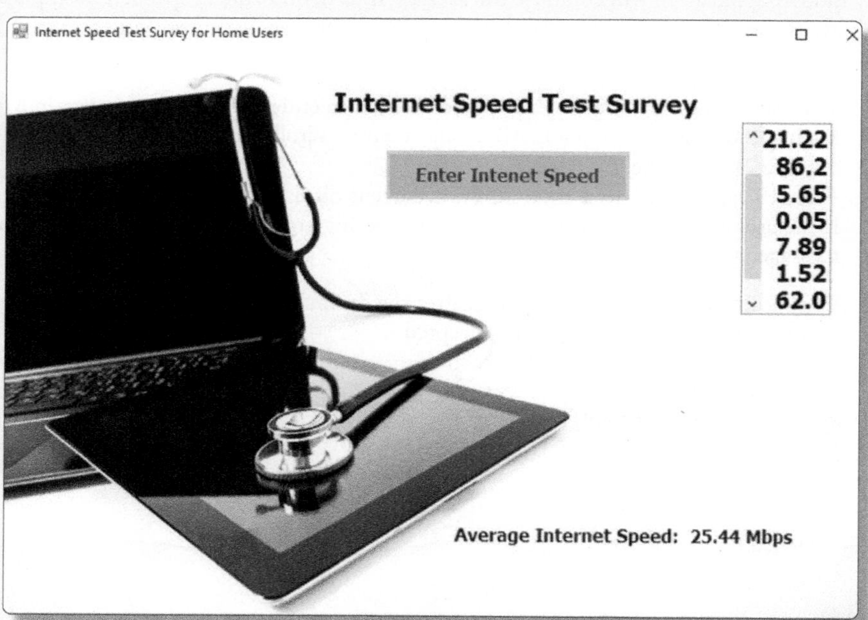

FIGURE 6-119

Case Programming Assignments

3 ●● SOFTBALL SCOREBOARD

Design a Windows application and write the code that will execute according to the program requirements shown in Figure 6-120. Before writing the code, create an event planning document for each event in the program.

REQUIREMENTS DOCUMENT

Date:	November 3, 2019
Date Submitted:	
Application Title:	Softball Scoreboard
Purpose:	This application calculates the score of each inning during a softball game for one team.
Program Procedures:	In a Windows Classic Desktop application, the user enters the score of each inning to display the total on the scoreboard after the seven innings in a regulation softball game.
Algorithms, Processing, and Conditions:	1. The user clicks the Enter Score button in an InputBox object to enter a score after each inning of the game. 2. The number of runs and the running score is displayed in a ListBox after each inning. 3. The total final score is displayed after the seventh inning. 4. A File menu contains a Clear and an Exit option. The Clear menu item clears the result and the number of runs. The Exit menu item closes the application.
Notes and Restrictions:	1. Nonnumeric values should not be accepted. 2. A negative value should not be accepted.
Comments:	Locate an appropriate image online. This image should be placed as a background image and stretched across the Form object.

FIGURE 6-120

Case Programming Assignments

4 ●● PENNY OR NICKEL CHALLENAGE

Design a Windows application and write the code that will execute according to the program requirements shown in Figure 6-121. Before writing the code, create an event planning document for each event in the program. Create a Use Case Definition document for the application.

REQUIREMENTS DOCUMENT

Date:	June 21, 2019
Date Submitted:	
Application Title:	Penny or Nickel Challenge
Purpose:	This Windows Classic Desktop application finds the amount of your monthly pay if you are paid a penny or nickel for the first workday and the pay is doubled each subsequent workday. New employees are paid a penny for the first workday and experienced employees are paid a nickel for the first day.
Program Procedures:	The user enters the number of workdays in a monthly pay period and the pay for the first day. The program calculates and displays the amount of pay for the pay period.
Algorithms, Processing, and Conditions:	1. The user enters the number of days in the pay period. 2. The user selects a RadioButton object to indicate the pay amount for the first day: a penny or a nickel. 3. After the user enters the number of days and pay for the first day, the total amount earned is calculated and displayed. 4. A File menu contains a Clear and an Exit option. The Clear menu item clears the result and the RadioButton object. The Exit menu item closes the application.
Notes and Restrictions:	1. Nonnumeric values should not be accepted. 2. Negative values should not be accepted. 3. The minimum number of workdays in the pay period is 10 days. The maximum number of workdays in a pay period is 22 days. 4. A background image should be located online and displayed on the form.
Comments:	n/a

FIGURE 6-121

Case Programming Assignments

5 ●●● FACTORIAL CALCULATOR

Create a requirements document and a Use Case Definition document and design a Windows application based on the case project shown in Figure 6-122:

Most calculators have an operation called a "factorial," which is shown on a calculator key as an exclamation point. For example, 5! (5 factorial) multiplies 5 * 4 * 3 * 2 * 1 to calculate the result of 120. Request that the user select a number from 1 to 12 and display all the factorials up to the value, including that value. Using loops to compute the factorial, display the following factorials in a ListBox object. The application should have a single background image and menus. Publish the application.

1! 1
2! 2
3! 6
4! 24
5! 120
...
12! 479001600

FIGURE 6-122

Case Programming Assignments

HOME DOWN PAYMENT

Create a requirements document and a Use Case Definition document and design a Windows application based on the case project shown in Figure 6-123:

> Write a Windows application that allows you to enter the amount of money you would like to place as a down payment on a home, the interest rate, and a number of years. For example, if you hope to buy a home in five years with a down payment, would the principal of $17,000 grow over five years at 4 percent interest to a down payment of $20,000? Display a ListBox object for each year and the amount of money in the account at the end of that year. Determine whether you have saved enough money for the home example. Nonnumeric and negative values should not be accepted. Publish the application. *Hint*: The formula for compound interest for one year is: Amount = Principal * (1 + Rate). For 5 years of compound interest, this formula should be executed 5 times with the principal increasing to the new amount each year. The application should have a single background image and menus.

FIGURE 6-123

APPENDIX A

Unicode

The 256 characters and symbols that are represented by ASCII and EBCDIC codes are sufficient for English and western European languages (see Figure A-1 on the next page), but do not provide enough characters for Asian and other languages that use different alphabets. Further compounding the problem is that many of these languages use symbols, called ideograms, to represent multiple words and ideas. One solution to the problem of accommodating universal alphabets is Unicode. Unicode is a 16-bit coding scheme that can represent all the world's current, classic, and historical languages in more than 65,000 characters and symbols. In Unicode, 30,000 codes are reserved for future use, such as ancient languages, and 6,000 codes are reserved for private use. Existing ASCII coded data is fully compatible with Unicode because the first 256 codes are the same. Unicode is implemented in several operating systems, including Windows 10, Windows 8, Windows 7, Mac OS X, and Linux. To view a complete Unicode chart, see www.unicode.org.

UNICODE KEYBOARD CHARACTERS				
Decimal	**Hexadecimal**	**Octal**	**Binary**	**Character**
32	20	040	00100000	
33	21	041	00100001	!
34	22	042	00100010	“
35	23	043	00100010	#
36	24	044	00100100	$
37	25	045	00100101	%
38	26	046	00100110	&
39	27	047	00100111	‘
40	28	050	00101000	(
41	29	051	00101001	)
42	2A	052	00101010	*
43	2B	053	00101011	+
44	2C	054	00101100	,
45	2D	055	00101101	-
46	2E	056	00101110	.
47	2F	057	00101111	/
48	30	060	00110000	0
49	31	061	00110001	1
50	32	062	00110010	2
51	33	063	00110011	3
52	34	064	00110100	4
53	35	065	00110101	5
54	36	066	00110110	6
55	37	067	00110111	7
56	38	070	00111000	8
57	39	071	00111001	9
58	3A	072	00111010	:
59	3B	073	00111011	;
60	3C	074	00111100	<

FIGURE A-1 (continued)

Decimal	Hexadecimal	Octal	Binary	Character
61	3D	075	00111101	=
62	3E	076	00111110	>
63	3F	077	00111111	?
64	40	100	01000000	@
65	41	101	01000001	A
66	42	102	01000010	B
67	43	103	01000011	C
68	44	104	01000100	D
69	45	105	01000101	E
70	46	106	01000110	F
71	47	107	01000111	G
72	48	110	01001000	H
73	49	111	01001001	I
74	4A	112	01001010	J
75	4B	113	01001011	K
76	4C	114	01001100	L
77	4D	115	01001101	M
78	4E	116	01001110	N
79	4F	117	01001111	O
80	50	120	01010000	P
81	51	121	01010001	Q
82	52	122	01010010	R
83	53	123	01010011	S
84	54	124	01010100	T
85	55	125	01010101	U
86	56	126	01010110	V
87	57	127	01010111	W
88	58	130	01011000	X
89	59	131	01011001	Y
90	5A	132	01011010	Z

FIGURE A-1 (continued)

Decimal	Hexadecimal	Octal	Binary	Character
91	5B	133	01011011	[
92	5C	134	01011100	\
93	5D	135	01011101	]
94	5E	136	01011110	^
95	5F	137	01011111	]
96	60	140	01100000	,
97	61	141	01100001	a
98	62	142	01100010	b
99	63	143	01100011	c
100	64	144	01100100	d
101	65	145	01100101	e
102	66	146	01100110	f
103	67	147	01100111	g
104	68	150	01101000	h
105	69	151	01101001	i
106	6A	152	01101010	j
107	6B	153	01101011	k
108	6C	154	01101100	l
109	6D	155	01101101	m
110	6E	156	01101110	n
111	6F	157	01101111	o
112	70	160	01110000	p
113	71	161	01110001	q
114	72	162	01110010	r
115	73	163	01110011	s
116	74	164	01110100	t
117	75	165	01110101	u
118	76	166	01110110	v
119	77	167	01110111	w
120	78	170	01111000	x

FIGURE A-1 (continued)

Decimal	Hexadecimal	Octal	Binary	Character
121	79	171	01111001	y
122	7A	172	01111010	z
123	7B	173	01111011	{
124	7C	174	01111100	|
125	7D	175	01111101	}
126	7E	176	01111110	~
127	7F	177	01111111	DEL

FIGURE A-1

APPENDIX B

Naming Conventions

The table in Figure B-1 displays the common data types used in Visual Basic 2017 with the recommended naming convention for the three-character prefix preceding variable names of the data type.

Data Type	Sample Value	Memory	Range of Values	Prefix
Integer	48	4 bytes	−2,147,483,648 to +2,147,483,647	int
Double	5.3452307	8 bytes	−1.79769313486232E308 to +1.79769313486232E308	dbl
Decimal	3.14519	16 bytes	Decimal values that may have up to 29 significant digits	dec
Char	'?' or 'C'	2 bytes	Single character	chr
String	"The Dow is up 0.03%"	Depends on number of characters	Letters, numbers, symbols	str
Boolean	True or False	Typically 2 bytes; depends on implementing platform	True or False	bln

FIGURE B-1

The table in Figure B-2 displays the less common data types used in Visual Basic 2017 with the recommended naming convention for the three-character prefix preceding variable names of the data type.

Data Type	Sample Value	Memory	Range of Values	Prefix
Byte	7	1 byte	0 to 255	byt
Date	April 22, 2019	8 bytes	0:00:00 (midnight) on January 1, 0001 through 11:59:59 PM on December 31, 9999	dtm
Long	345,234,567	8 bytes	−9,223,372,036,854,775,808 to +9,223,372,036,854,775,807	lng
Object	Holds a reference	4 bytes (32-bit) 8 bytes (64-bit)	A memory address	obj
Short	16,567	2 bytes	−32,768 to 32,767	shr
Single	234,654.1246	4 bytes	−3.4028235E+38 to −1.401298E−45 for negative values and 1.401298E−45 to 3.4028235E+38 for positive values	sng

FIGURE B-2

Form Object Naming Conventions

The table in Figure B-3 displays the prefix naming conventions for Form objects. The three-letter prefixes used before variables names especially are helpful when you use IntelliSense.

Object Type	Prefix	Object Type	Prefix
Button	btn	ListBox	lst
Calendar	cld	MenuStrip	mnu
CheckBox	chk	NumericUpDown	nud
ComboBox	cbo	PictureBox	pic
CompareValidator	cmv	RadioButton	rad
DataGrid	dgd	RangeValidator	rgv
DateTimePicker	dtp	RegularExpressionValidator	rev
DropDownList	ddl	RequiredFieldValidator	rfv
Form	frm	TextBox	txt
GroupBox	grp	ValidationSummary	vsm
Label	lbl		

FIGURE B-3

INDEX

Note: **Boldface** page numbers indicate key terms.

C

E

M

U

V

X

Z